Y0-ABH-208

Understanding Computers and Data Processing: Today and Tomorrow

with BASIC

Understanding Computers and Data Processing: Today and Tomorrow with BASIC

Charles S. Parker

Northern Arizona University
Flagstaff, Arizona

Holt, Rinehart and Winston
New York   Chicago   San Francisco   Philadelphia
Montreal   Toronto   London   Sydney   Tokyo
Mexico City   Rio de Janeiro   Madrid

To Mom and Dad

Publisher: Paul Becker
Senior Editor: Brete Harrison
Development Editor: David Chodoff
Production Manager: Pat Sarcuni
Production Coordination: Lila M. Gardner, Cobb/Dunlop Publisher Services, Inc.
Interior Design and Color Sections: Marsha Cohen
Cover Design: Jerry Wilke
Photoresearch: Freda Leinwand
Illustrations: Vantage Art, Inc.
Composition: Science Press
Printing and Binding: Von Hoffman Press

Copyright © 1984 by CBS College Publishing
All rights reserved.
Address correspondence to
383 Madison Avenue, New York, NY 10017

Library of Congress Cataloging in Publication Data

Parker, Charles S.
   Understanding computers and data processing.

   Includes bibliographies and index.
   1. Electronic digital computers.   I. Title.
QA76.5.P318 1984   001.64   83-22724
ISBN 0-03-063427-X

Printed in the United State of America
Published simultaneously in Canada

4 5 6 7   032   9 8 7 6 5 4 3 2 1

CBS COLLEGE PUBLISHING
Holt, Rinehart and Winston
The Dryden Press
Saunders College Publishing

Brief Contents

For detailed contents see page vii

The Windows

vi

Detailed Contents

Module B   *Hardware*   *87*

Module C Software 233

Module D *Computer Systems* *369*

Preface

Modern society has become an information society, and the key to information is computers. You know it and your students know it. In fact, it's hard to think of any profession unaffected by computers. The explosive demand for personal computers, desk-top work stations, and computer-driven gadgets of all sorts has placed "computer power" virtually everywhere—the home, office, laboratory, factory floor, check-out counter, artist's studio, local fitness center—and so on. Just to get along these days requires some knowledge of computer systems—how they can help people do their work better, what information resources they can unlock, what effects they have on our world and on our lives, and what to expect from them tomorrow.

I have been teaching an introductory computer data processing course in one form or another for 14 years. In that time the number of students taking the course has risen dramatically. College administrators, knowing they have a responsibility to prepare students for a rapidly changing workplace, have made this course a requirement for a variety of curricula. But many students today don't need administrative prodding. No matter what their major field of study, they see familiarity with computers as a basic marketable skill.

That leaves you and me as instructors standing before students with diverse backgrounds and a variety of expectations. We need tools that can help us communicate the excitement we feel about computers and give our students the preparation they need for today's world and tomorrow's. *Understanding Computers and Data Processing: Today and Tomorrow* fills that need with a complete teaching package. This package includes the textbook itself, available in two versions—one with an appendix on BASIC programming and one without—and a comprehensive set of student and teacher support materials.

THE TEXTBOOK

Understanding Computers and Data Processing: Today and Tomorrow is designed for students taking a first course in computers and data processing. It provides a comprehensive introduction to the world of computers, but it is not overly technical. It emphasizes both commercial and personal applications of computers. In writing it I kept in mind the fact that the scope of computing is changing. It now includes applications unheard of ten years ago, and the number of people who need some background in the subject has grown accordingly. Thus one of the primary goals of this book is to give students a readable introduction to important computer principles and a clear perspective on the present and future uses of computers.

Key Features

This book is both current and comprehensive. It offers you a flexible teaching organization and your students a readable and engaging presentation. Learning aids in each chapter help students master important concepts. Tomorrow boxes and other boxed features provide extra insight on major issues. The 80 pages of full-color photographs, organized into nine thematic "Windows" bring the world of computers to life. A glossary at the end of the book gives concise definitions of important terms. And the appendix on BASIC, for those who adopt the version of the text that contains it, provides a comprehensive introduction to BASIC in a style students will find easy to read.

Currency. Almost daily an existing computer product becomes obsolete and a new one takes its place. In some cases, entire technologies fall by the wayside. We are rapidly evolving into a society in which powerful, easy-to-use computer systems will be available to almost everyone. The state-of-the-art content of this book reflects these and other trends. Take a look, for example, at the chapters on teleprocessing (7) and personal computers (13). In the chapter on input and output devices (6), note the emphasis on modern display terminals and source-data-automation techniques. Glance at the Tomorrow boxes in each chapter, which give students a sense of the direction of change in the world of computers. And look at the array of state-of-the-art applications and technologies illustrated in the nine full-color "Windows" that appear throughout the book.

Comprehensiveness and Depth. Before work began on this book the publisher conducted several extensive research studies to determine the selection of topics, degree of depth, and other features that instructors of introductory data-processing courses most want to see in a textbook of this type. As the project took shape, instructors at a variety of institutions around the country were asked to review the manuscript. The resulting textbook accommodates a wide range of teaching preferences. It not only covers traditional topics thoroughly, but it also includes the facts your students should know about today's "hot" topics, such as teleprocessing, user-friendly software products, interactive terminal use, personal computers, office systems, database management systems, computer graphics, and systems development.

Flexible Organization. A textbook locked into a rigid organization, no matter how thorough, will inevitably find its uses limited. In order to appeal to a wide audience, I have designed this book to be flexible. Its eighteen chapters are grouped into five modules: Introduction (Chapters 1–3), Hardware (Chapters 4–7), Software (Chapters 8–12), Computer Systems (Chapters 13–16), and Computers in Society (Chapters 17 and 18). Every effort was made to have each chapter as self-contained as possible, making it easy for you to skip chapters or teach them in a sequence other than the one followed in the book. And each chapter is organized into well-defined sections, so you can assign only parts of a chapter if the whole provides more depth than you need.

Readability. Students remember more about a subject if it is presented in a straightforward way and made interesting and exciting. This book is written in a conversational, down-to-earth style to make students comfortable with the material. Concepts are explained clearly and simply without use of confusing terminology. And technical points are made vivid with realistic examples from everyday life.

Chapter Learning Aids. Each chapter contains a number of learning aids to help students master the materials.

- Chapter Outline   An outline of the headings in the chapter shows the major topics to be covered.
- Overview   Each chapter starts with an overview that puts the subject matter of the chapter in perspective and lets students know what they will be reading about.

- **Boldfaced Key Terms** Important terms appear in boldface type as they are introduced in the chapter. These terms are also defined in the glossary.
- **Tomorrow Boxes** These special features (there's one in each chapter and two in chapter 18) provide students with a look at possible future developments in the world of computers and serve as a focus for class discussion.
- **Other Boxed Features** Each chapter has one or more additional features with supplementary information designed to stimulate class discussion.
- **Photographs and Diagrams** Instructive photographs and two-color diagrams appear throughout the book to help illustrate important concepts. The use of color in the diagrams is a functional part of the book. To give one example, operator input and computer output on a display terminal always appear in different colors.
- **Summary and Key Terms** This is a concise summary of the main points in the chapter. Every boldfaced key term in the chapter also appears in boldface type in the summary. Students will find this summary a valuable tool for study and review.
- **Review Questions** These short-answer questions allow students to test themselves on what they have just read. You may also find many of them useful for class discussion.
- **Suggested Readings** Most chapters end with a list of sources for further study.

Windows. The book contains nine full-color photo essays. Each of these "Windows" on the world of computers is organized around a major text theme (see page vi for details).

Glossary. The glossary at the end of the book defines approximately 470 important computer terms mentioned in the text, including all the boldfaced key terms. Each glossary item has a page reference indicating where it is boldfaced or where it first appears in the text.

A Beginner's Guide to BASIC. The version of this book that contains an appendix on BASIC provides a comprehensive, 96-page introduction to that language. It is not just a list of rules and procedures, but an engaging, easy-to-read tutorial that encourages students to begin creating programs immediately.

STUDENT AND TEACHER SUPPORT MATERIAL

Understanding Computers and Data Processing: Today and Tomorrow comes with a complete package of support materials for you and your students. These include a student *Study Guide,* an *Instructor's Manual, Transparency Acetates,* a *Test Bank,* and instructional software to accompany the appendix on BASIC.

Study Guide

The *Study Guide* is designed to help students master the material in the text through self-testing. For each of the eighteen chapters in the text the *Study Guide* provides:

- A list of *Chapter Objectives.*
- A *Pretest* that lets students test their knowledge of the chapter before they begin to study it intensively.
- An *Overview* that puts the subject matter of the chapter in perspective.
- A *Summary* of the chapter, written in narrative form. This summary is more detailed than the end-of-chapter summary in the text.
- A list of the *Key Terms* in the chapter, with page references indicating where each is boldfaced.
- Five types of *self-testing questions:* matching, true/false, multiple-choice, fill-in, and short answer.
- An *Answer Key.*

The *Study Guide* also covers the appendix on BASIC programming. For each section of the appendix the *Study Guide* provides a brief summary, a review of BASIC commands, multiple-choice questions, and new programming problems.

Instructor's Manual

In the *Instructor's Manual* I draw on my own teaching experience to provide you with practical suggestions for enhancing your classroom presentation. The *Instructor's Manual* also contains suggestions for adapting this textbook to various course schedules, including one-quarter, two-quarter, one-semester, two-semester and night courses. For each of the eighteen chapters of the text the *Instructor's Manual* provides:

- A list of *Chapter Objectives.*
- A *Summary,* oriented to the instructor, with teaching suggestions.
- A list of the *Key Terms* in the chapter, with a page reference indicating where each is boldfaced.
- A *Teaching Outline* that gives a detailed breakdown of the chapter, with all headings and subheadings as well as points to cover under each. References to the *Transparency Acetates* are keyed to this outline.
- *Activity Notes,* with recommended topics for class discussion, suggestions for using the windows and boxes, important points to cover on the transparency acetates, and mention of additional instructor resources.
- *Answers* to the end-of-chapter Review Questions.

The *Instructor's Manual* also covers the appendix on BASIC programming. For each section of the appendix it includes a brief teaching summary and suggested solutions to the Programming Exercises.

Transparency Acetates

A complete set of two-color, ready-to-show *Transparency Acetates* for use with an overhead projector is available to help you explain key points. The figures are derived from the text diagrams. The *Teaching Outlines* of the *Instructor's Manual* indicate when to show the acetates, and the *Activity Notes* lists points to make about each.

Test Bank

The *Test Bank* contains approximately 3000 test items in various formats, including true/false, multiple-choice, matching, fill-in, and short-answer questions. Answers are provided for all but the short-answer questions. The *Test Bank* is also available on disks for the IBM PC, the Apple II, and the TRS-80 Model III.

Software for the BASIC Appendix

Instructor's who adopt the version of this book that contains *A Beginner's Guide to BASIC* will receive self-documenting, interactive instructional software to accompany it. The software is available on disks for the IBM PC, the Apple II, and the TRS-80 Model III.

ACKNOWLEDGMENTS

I could never have completed a project of this scope alone, and I would like to thank all those who helped make it a reality. Especially important were the many people who reviewed and participated in the project at various stages in its development. I am particularly grateful to the following people: James Ambroise, Jr., Southern University, Louisiana; Richard Batt, St. Louis Community College; James Bradley, University of Calgary; Laura Cooper, College of the Mainland, Texas; John DiElsi, Mercy College, New York; William Hightower, Elon College, North Carolina; Peter L. Irwin, Richland College, Texas; Richard Kerns, East Carolina University, North Carolina; Glenn Kersnick, Sinclair Community College, Ohio; Wayne Madison, Clemson University, South Carolina; Gary Marks, Austin Community College, Texas; Robert Ralph, Fayetteville Technical Institute, North Carolina; Alfred C. St. Onge, Springfield Technical Community College, Massachusetts; John J. Shuler, San Antonio College, Texas; Michael L. Stratford, Charles County Community College, Maryland; Joseph Waters, Santa Rosa Junior College, California; Charles M. Williams, Georgia State University; A. James Wynne, Virginia Commonwealth University.

My colleagues at Northern Arizona University—John Durham, Alden Lorents, and Mac Bosse—also deserve a great deal of credit for their helpful suggestions and emotional support. I am especially indebted to Dean Norval Pohl, who graciously approved two leaves of absence to enable me to research and write the book.

A special word of thanks must go to Lila Gardner of Cobb/Dunlop Publisher Services, who oversaw the design and production of the project. I would also like to thank David Crook for his editorial skills, Marsha Cohen for an inviting design, Jerry Wilke for an intriguing and unusual cover, and Freda Leinwand for her photoresearch.

The modesty of my publisher has forced me to tone down the praise I would like to give the two people most instrumental in the development of this project—Brete Harrison and David Chodoff of Holt, Rinehart and Winston. Brete contributed many key ideas, and his initial faith and perseverance got me started on the project to begin with. David shaped my sometimes cryptic prose into the textbook you now hold. Also to be thanked at Holt are Paul Becker, Tom Gornick, Susan Katz, Bob Woodbury, and David Scott.

I sincerely hope that you and your students find *Understanding Computers and Data Processing: Today and Tomorrow* a useful and interesting textbook.

C. S. Parker

B:DAILY   PAGE 1 LINE 16 COL 20

GOOD MORNING!

CAN I HELP YOU?

ENTER YOUR NEXT COMMAND:_

Module A

INTRODUCTION

We are living today in an age of computers. Businesses, government agencies, and other organizations use computers extensively to handle tedious paperwork, to provide better service, and to assist in decision making. As the cost of these machines continues to decrease relative to the price of everything else, computers will become even more widespread in our society. It is therefore essential to know something about them.

The chapters that follow are an introduction to the computer and some of its uses. Chapters 1 and 2 orient you to what computer systems are, how they work, and how they're used. Also, these chapters present some key terminology that you will see repeatedly throughout the text. Chapter 3 describes how the fast-paced world of computers has evolved.

Chapter 1

Introduction to the World of Computers

Chapter Outline

OVERVIEW

WHAT'S A COMPUTER AND WHAT DOES IT DO?

Computer Systems
Data and Programs
A Look at Computer Memory
Hardware and Software
Users and the Experts

USING COMPUTERS: A SIMPLE EXAMPLE

COMPUTERS AND SOCIETY

COMPUTER SYSTEMS TO FIT EVERY NEED AND POCKETBOOK

Microcomputers
Minicomputers
Mainframes

COMPUTERS IN ACTION

OVERVIEW

Unless you plan to spend your life raising sled dogs in the upper reaches of the Yukon, computers will probably have an impact on your life. Whether that makes you glad, sad, or mad really doesn't matter. Computers are here to stay, and it's getting ever more difficult to get along, much less get ahead, without some knowledge of what they are and what they do.

Computer systems keep track of our bank accounts and credit card purchases. They control the massive reservations systems of the airlines. They perform the millions on millions of computations needed to send astronauts into outer space and bring them back safely. They also direct production at our factories and provide executives with the up-to-date information they need to make decisions. Additionally, they are embedded in cheap watches and expensive satellites. The applications seem almost endless. Fifty short years ago, these machines were part of an obscure technology of interest to only a handful of scientists. Today they are part of daily life for millions of people.

Many people are intimidated by computers and think they need an advanced degree to understand them. In fact, computers are very much like cars—you don't need to know everything about them to use them intelligently. You can learn to drive a car without knowing about internal combustion engines, and you can learn to use a computer without knowing about technical details such as logic circuits.

Still, with both cars and computers, a little knowledge can give you a big advantage. Knowing something about cars can help you make wise purchases and save money on repairs. Likewise, knowing something about computers can help you better use these machines to your advantage.

This book is about computers—what they are, how they work, and what they do. Its purpose is to give you the knowledge you need to use them to your advantage today, and through the special chapter boxes labeled "Tomorrow," to give you a look into the future. Other boxed features throughout the text give added insights into the dynamic world of computers.

This book is not designed to make you a computer expert. It's a beginner's guide. If you're considering a career in computers, it will give you a comprehensive introduction to the field. If you're not, it will give you the basic knowledge you need to understand and use computers in school and on the job. Who knows, even if you do plan to breed sled dogs in the upper reaches of the Yukon, you may find yourself using a computer.

In the rest of this chapter we'll first take a look at what computers are and how they work. Then we'll examine an example of a computer system in action. Finally, we'll look at the various sizes in which computers come. The full-color Window that follows page 12 gives you a glimpse at the myriad applications of computers in today's world.

WHAT'S A COMPUTER AND WHAT DOES IT DO?

Three words sum up the operation of a computer system: **input, processing,** and **output.** To see what these words mean, let's look at something many of you probably have in your own homes—a stereo system.

A simple stereo system consists of a turntable, an amplifier, and a pair of speakers. To use the system you place a record on the turntable, turn the system on, and place the tone arm on the record. The needle in the tone arm converts the patterns in the grooves of the record into vibrations and transmits them to the amplifier as electronic signals. The amplifier takes the signals, makes them stronger, and transmits them to the speakers, producing music. In computer terms, the turntable sends signals as *input* to the amplifier. The amplifier *processes* them and sends them to the speakers, which produce a musical *output.* The turntable is an **input device,** the amplifier is a *processing unit,* and the speakers are **output devices.** The amplifier is the heart of the system, and the turntable and speakers are **support equipment.**

Most stereo systems have a variety of support equipment. A stereo FM tuner, for example, is another kind of input device. Headphones are another kind of output device. A tape recorder is both an input and an output device—you can use it to play music into the system or to record music from it. The tapes and records you have in your collection are—in computer terms— **input and output (I/O) media.** They store music in a **machine-readable** form—a form that the associated input device (a tape recorder or turntable) can recognize (that is, "read") and convert into signals for the amplifier to process.

Computer Systems

All the elements in a stereo system have their counterparts in a computer system. A **computer system** consists of the computer itself, all the support equipment, the machine-readable instructions and facts it processes, as well as operating manuals, procedures, and the people who use the system. In other words, all the components that contribute to making the computer a useful tool can be said to be part of a computer system.

At the heart of any computer system—equivalent to the stereo amplifier—is the **computer** itself, or **central processing unit (CPU).** Like a stereo amplifier, the computer can't do anything useful without support equipment for input and output and I/O media for storage. Computer input and output devices include, to name just a few, display terminals, disk units, tape units, and printers. I/O media include disks, tapes, and paper. We will discuss these and many other items in Chapters 2, 5 and 6.

A computer system, of course, is not a stereo system, and a computer is much more powerful than a stereo amplifier.

tomorrow

IS THERE A COMPUTER IN YOUR FUTURE?

Over the past several decades, computers and computer technology have become ever more deeply embedded in the workplace, often greatly changing the kinds of jobs people do and the way they do them. Some people responded to these changes with enthusiasm, welcoming the chance to learn new skills and being excited by the efficiencies the new technologies made possible. Others responded differently. They were comfortable with their jobs as they were, they resented the need to retrain, and they feared, often with reason, that the new technologies might eliminate their jobs altogether.

Some people, reluctant to come to grips with the computer revolution, have paid a heavy toll. Take, for example, Bob Gant (a fictitious name). He had been a travel agent almost since the beginning of the commercial airline business. Capable and energetic, he rose through the ranks of an agency to become an office supervisor after several years of service. When the airlines first started to use computers to help cope with the growing paperwork involved in reservations, Bob ignored the event. He could still afford to then, since almost all agents continued to rely on weighty paperback flight schedules and telephone calls to a central reservations desk to work out itineraries and make reservations.

Then, suddenly, Bob's world changed. Many competing agencies began to order display terminals linked directly to reservations-oriented computers. With these display terminals, which look much like television sets with keyboards attached, agents could bypass both the paperback schedules and the busy reservations desks. Reservations could be made more quickly than before, and customers received speedier, more efficient services. But to use the new system, agents had to learn highly specialized programming languages (which some have jokingly called "airlinese"). Bob resisted the change. He liked the old system and mistrusted the new one. After his agency began to lose business to competitors, however, he was forced quietly to resign. He was able for a while to find jobs as a manager at a couple of other agencies.

- A computer can perform an enormous variety of processing tasks; a stereo amplifier only a few.
- A computer can support a much greater variety of input and output devices than can a stereo amplifier.
- A computer operates at fantastically higher speeds than a stereo amplifier would ever need to operate.

What gives a computer its flexibility? In a word, *memory*. A computer has a memory, or "workspace," that allows it to store whatever input it receives and whatever results it produces from these inputs. A stereo amplifier has no memory—what's playing on the turntable or tape recorder passes directly through the amplifier to the speakers. Because a computer can store materials in its memory, it can be directed to rearrange or recombine that material in an amazing variety of ways before it sends it

But at each one he either resisted computerization, or if the agency was already computerized, complained persistently that the system was unworkable and full of errors. As a result, Bob found himself either being fired or quitting. Finally, he left the travel business altogether and took a lower-level job in another profession.

Bob's story is not an isolated one. Like many people, he began his career when the computer was little more than a science fiction writer's fantasy. When the computer revolution began to edge its way into his life he ignored it. He had little understanding of what computer systems could do, and he thought, mistakenly, that he could not learn to work with them.

You are in a better position than Bob. Today computer systems are easier to use than they were when he first encountered them, and their importance in the workplace is now clear. But computer technology is still developing at an incredibly rapid pace, and it's not possible to know for sure all the applications of this technology for tomorrow. Unlike Bob, you know you may encounter a computer in your future. But if you don't want to be taken by surprise by what you find, it's a good idea to keep current with new developments.

Keeping current.

along as output. Thus, if you could hook up a computer to your home stereo, you'd be able to do things like play the selections on a record in any order you wished, create your own music, or combine and manipulate music from many different sources in any way that struck your fancy.

Data and Programs

The material that a computer receives as input is of two kinds: data and programs. **Data** are, essentially, facts. **Programs** are instructions that tell the computer how to process those facts to produce the results that you, the person using the computer system, want. Turning back to our example of a computer-driven stereo system, we could say that the tunes input to the system by the turntable or tape deck are data (facts), and the instructions that tell the computer system the order in which to play those tunes are a program. Now let's discuss these important terms in a little more detail.

Data. Almost any kind of fact can become computer data—facts about a company's employees, facts about airline flight schedules, or facts about the orbit of a satellite. When we input data into a computer system we aren't usually interested in getting them back just as we entered them. We want the system to process the data and give us useful, new **information.** (*Information,* in the language of computers, usually means data that have been processed.) We might want to know, for example, how many employees make over $15,000, how many seats are available on flight 495 from Los Angeles to San Francisco, or when a damaged satellite might plunge back into the earth's atmosphere.

Of course you don't necessarily need a computer system to get this kind of information from a set of facts. For example, anyone can go through an employee file and make a list of people earning a certain salary. But to do so would take a lot of time, especially for a company with thousands of employees. Computers, because they work at electronically fast speeds, can do such jobs almost instantly. The processing of data on computers is called *electronic data processing* (EDP), which, as the title of this book attests, is commonly shortened to **data processing.** For an example of the way one large company uses a computer to process enormous amounts of data, see the box on page 9.

Programs. The amplifier in your home stereo system, like most machines, is a special-purpose device. It is designed to do only a few specific jobs—play a record, make a recording on tape, play music into speakers or headphones, and so forth. These jobs are built into its circuitry. To put it another way, it is "hardwired" to perform certain specific tasks.

Most computers, in contrast, are general-purpose devices. They must perform an enormous variety of tasks, any one of which might involve extremely complex processing. In a small company, for example, one person may want the computer system to scan a list of customer accounts and print a report of all customers who owe more than $300. Another person may want a report, in a different format, of all customers with good credit references. After hours, an employee might use the computer to balance his personal checkbook. And on a rainy Saturday afternoon the same computer might keep an executive's ten-year-old son amused with video games while she puts in a little extra work on an important account.

Because most computers must be flexible, they can't be hardwired to do all the jobs they need to do. Instead, they rely on programs to tell them what to do. As we said before, a program is a list of instructions. A program is read into the computer system with the data it is supposed to process. The program then directs the circuits in the computer to open and close in the manner needed to do whatever job needs doing.

Hertz Corporation

There are seven million Hertz credit cards in the hands of people throughout the world. How do you approve new applications for credit in a system this large? Naturally, by using the computer. When a potential customer fills out an application for a credit card, the information is keyed into the computer system by a clerk. A computer program on the system then "scores" the application on factors such as credit references, income, and current employment. If the score is high enough, a credit card is issued; otherwise, the computer system automatically types up a letter of denial or indicates that more information is required.

Credit approval: A headache in paper work.

Programs cannot be written in ordinary English. They must be written in a **programming language**—a language the computer system can read and translate into the electronic pulses that make it work. Programming languages come in many varieties. In the early days of computers they consisted of strings of numbers that only experts could understand. Over the years they have become more and more "friendly"—that is, easier for ordinary mortals to understand and use. Programming languages are not universal—any given computer system will understand some languages but not others. Most computer systems, however, can understand several different languages. We will discuss programs and programming languages in detail in Module C.

A Look at Computer Memory

So far we've seen that if you want to get something done on a computer system you must supply it with both facts (data) *and* instructions (a program) specifying how to process those facts. For example, if you want the system to write payroll checks, you need to supply such data as employees' names, social security numbers, and salaries. The program instructions must "tell" the system how taxes are computed, how deductions are taken, where and how the checks are to be printed, and so forth. Also, the computer relies on a memory (storage) to remember all these details as it is doing the work.

Actually, computer systems contain two types of memory. A **primary (internal) memory,** which is built into the computer itself, is used to hold the data and programs the computer is *currently* processing. When data is "captured" in the computer's primary memory, it can be rearranged or recombined following the instructions in the program.

Data and programs the computer doesn't need for the job at hand are stored in **secondary (external) memory.** In many computer systems, secondary memory is located in a separate device, apart from the computer itself. This piece of equipment is called a *secondary storage device.* A computer system may have a secondary storage device hooked up to its CPU that can store thousands of programs and millions of pieces of data. This enables us to conveniently store large quantities of data and programs in machine-readable form, so we don't have to rekey them into the system every time we want to use them.

When the CPU needs a certain program and set of data it requests them from the secondary memory device—much as you might request a particular song from a jukebox—and reads them into its internal memory for processing. In other words, secondary memory is like a large library of programs and data resources on full-time call to the CPU.

Figure 1-1 illustrates the relationships among input, processing, output, internal memory, and secondary memory. We will discuss secondary memory devices and their associated media in Chapter 5.

Hardware and Software

In the world of computers it is common to distinguish between hardware and software. The word **hardware** refers to the actual machinery that makes up a computer system, for example, the CPU, I/O devices, and storage devices. The word

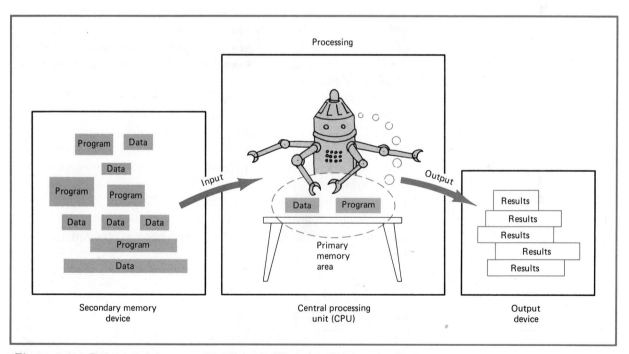

Figure 1-1.   Doing work in a computer system. The computer system obtains the programs and data it needs from secondary storage, puts them in its internal memory, and processes them according to the instructions in the program. The results are then delivered to an output device.

software refers to computer programs. It can also refer to the manuals that help people work with the computer system, such as programming language guides and technical manuals for computer operators.

Users and the Experts

In the early days of computers and computing there was a clear distinction between the people who made the machines work and the people who used the results the machines produced. This distinction still exists, but as computers become more available and easier to use, it is breaking down.

Users are the people who need the output that computer systems produce. They include the accountant who needs a report on a client's taxes, the engineer who needs to know whether a bridge will be structurally sound, the shop-floor supervisor who needs to know whether the day's quotas were met, and the company president who needs a report on the company's profitability over the last ten years. **Programmers** are the people who write the programs to produce this information. There are also *systems analysts* present in a computing environment to determine the company's processing needs, as well as other specialists to run, repair, and maintain the machines themselves.

Most large companies have a library of thousands of programs to carry out well-defined tasks—do the payroll, write checks, prepare accounting reports, and so forth. Such companies usually employ a staff of programmers and other experts to make changes in existing programs, write new programs as they are needed, and keep the system running. Often, however, a user—say an important executive—will have a desk-top computer terminal and the knowledge to independently create and run certain kinds of programs to get hold of needed information.

USING COMPUTERS: A SIMPLE EXAMPLE

Now that we've covered in a very basic way how a computer system works, let's "walk through" an application to put many of the concepts you've just read about into better focus (see Figure 1-2).

COMPUTER APPLICATIONS

A visual demonstration of the widespread use of computers

1

Computers have rapidly become an important force in almost every segment of our society. This first "window to the world of computers" presents a small sample of the many tasks to which these machines may be applied. Included are examples from the fields of education, business and finance, advertising, manufacturing, engineering, art, environmental control, retailing, toys and games, travel and transportation, medicine, sports, and research.

EDUCATION Computers are used today in thousands of educational institutions throughout the world for instruction, faculty research, and adminstrative support.

1. A Harris computer system is used to teach students at the American College in Paris, France.

BUSINESS AND FINANCE   Business and financial institutions first used computer systems to tackle mounting paperwork problems. Today they also use them to provide better customer service and to aid in decision making.

2.   Terminals allow travel and insurance agents, bankers, accountants, and salespeople to have desk-top computing power within an arm's reach to serve the needs of clients.

3.   Managers using Apple's Lisa computer to find information they need to make a decision.

4.   Banks doing international business, such as France's Societé Générale Alsacienne de Banque, use local terminals to access world-wide information sources.

5. Presenting a card with a machine-readable account identification to an automatic teller terminal.

6. A large Pacific coast aircraft manufacturer uses a variety of IBM terminals to make its personnel more productive.

7. Computers are used extensively to process securities transfers and supply floor brokers with the latest trading information.

ADVERTISING Advertisers are increasingly relying on computer graphics to create visually stunning images that have an impact on buyers. Today, television advertising can easily cost $1000 per second, or $30,000 for a 30-second spot. Technological and cost improvements in computer-generated imagery have thus made computerized animation an attractive alternative to conventional production methods. The images on this two-page spread, all courtesy of Digital Effects, Inc., represent the state of the art.

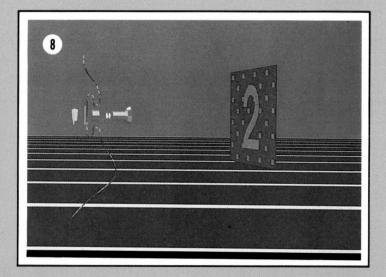

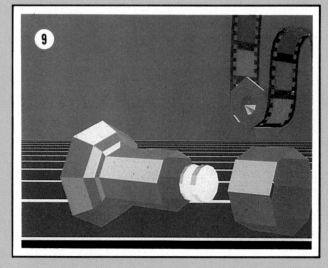

8, 9, 10. To create these three surrealistic scenes for *Scientific American* advertisements, animators started with film sequences. Later, the selected shots were digitized and mixed with computer-generated images to produce dazzling effects.

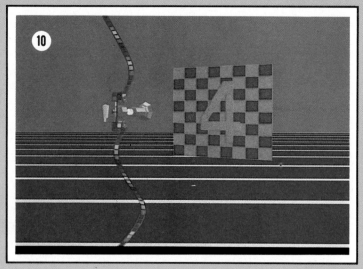

11. A computer-generated ad for Pirelli tires. The systems used to make such ads enable hundreds of different colors to be created for a single display image, making possible realistic effects such as shading.

12, 13. Television advertisements produced for the NBC Nightly News. To create the globe image, photographs were first digitized and, later, "mapped" by the computer system onto a sphere.

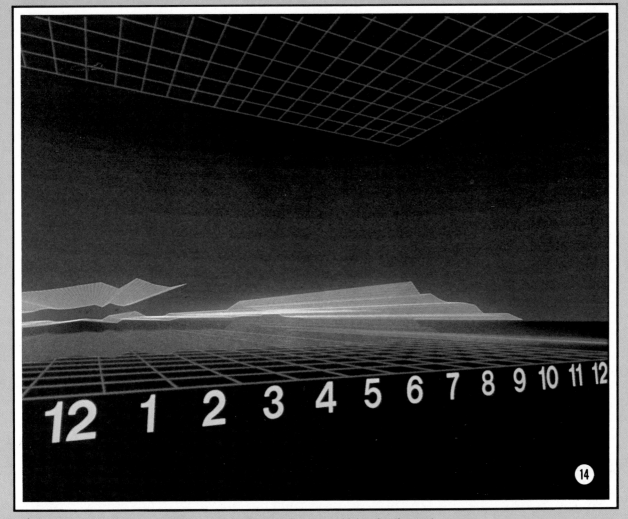

14. A computer-generated image produced for a Carolina Power and Light advertisement.

MANUFACTURING   Computers are used extensively in production environments to do a variety of tasks. Here is a small sampling of a few applications.

15. Inventory control. Thomas and Howard, Inc., of Charlotte, North Carolina uses six Univac computers to manage more than 10,000 grocery, meat, and produce items.

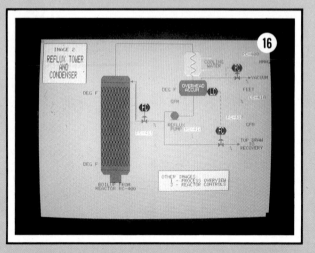

16. Plant control. A computer-generated schematic of a reactor. The status of the reactor may be automatically monitored by computer and displayed in visually understandable ways to supervisory personnel.

17. A control-room operator in a Foxboro Spectrum workstation directs a plant computer system to do a task. The system can be used to open and shut valves, start or stop a process, or supply valuable operational data.

COMPUTER-AIDED DESIGN/COMPUTER-AIDED MANUFACTURING
(CAD/CAM) These three photographs show how a part can be designed and
manufactured by computer.

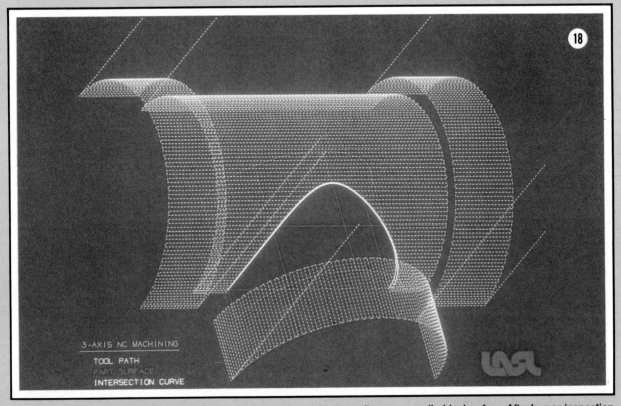

18. Computer-aided design. An image of the path of a machine tool cutter as it crosses a cylindrical surface. After human inspection of this computer-simulated manufacturing operation, the actual precision part can be manufactured using a computer-controlled machine. The part can also be stress-tested by computer before it is made.

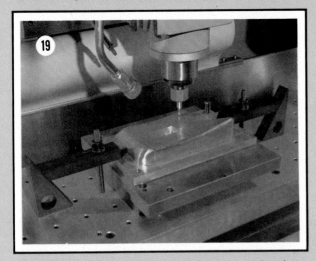

19. Computer-aided manufacturing. Once a part has been designed and tested, it is manufactured by a computer-controlled machine.

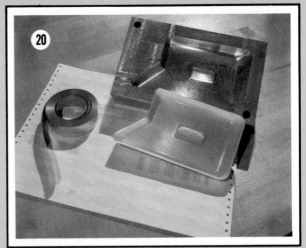

20. The finished part.

AUTOMOBILE PRODUCTION

21. Porsch-Sonauto, Paris, imports and markets Porsche and Mercedes cars, and Yamaha motorcycles, throughout France. They use Univac computers for management information and inventory control purposes.

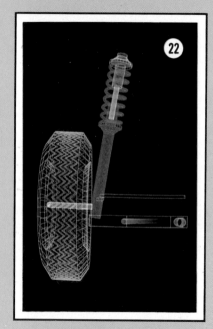

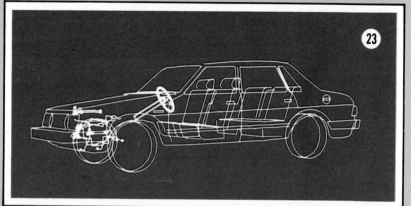

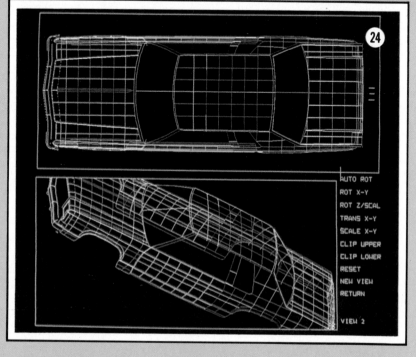

22, 23, 24. Computer-aided automobile design. Engineering data can be stored in computer data banks and used to create frame drawings. The drawings may be rotated in three-dimensional space to highlight important views, "blown up" to let engineers check specific subassemblies and, later, "painted" different colors on the screen to permit designers to quickly examine the aesthetic appeal of various exteriors.

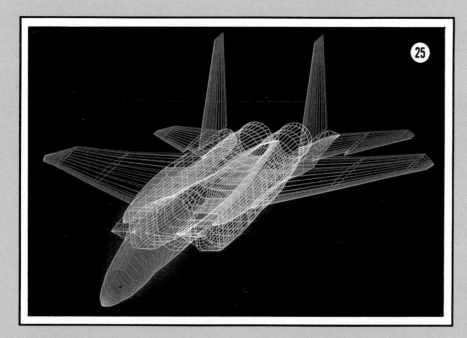

PLANE DESIGN AND TESTING

25. As with automobiles, frame drawings of planes may be created, rotated, and colored on a display screen.

26, 27, 28. Once the image of the plane is stored in the computer, its actual operation can be realistically simulated using computer graphics techniques. The use of simulation test equipment greatly reduces manufacturing development time and ensures airworthiness, safety, and reliability well in advance of the actual building of the plane. When these techniques can be used in lieu of a flight test, they can lead to a 100-fold cost savings. When the images produced are three-dimensional, a "sun" can be created, assigned to graphical coordinates in computer memory, and used to generate shadows as in (28).

ART   The use of computer systems to produce artistic images is one of the wonders of the last few years. The best computer artwork is generally made by individuals working in laboratories that use highly specialized graphics systems.

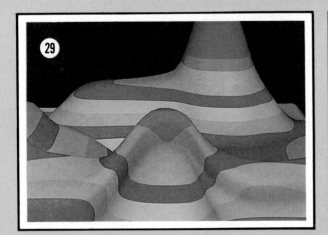

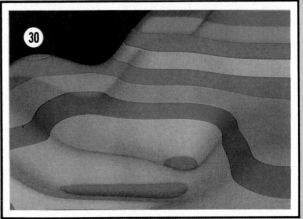

29, 30, 31.   A few creative outputs produced by Melvin Prueitt at Los Alamos National Laboratories.

32, 33, 34.   These spectacular mountain scenes were computer-drawn by Loren Carpenter and photographed from a graphics terminal display screen using a Matrix Instruments color camera. The images were developed using "fractals" procedures. The theory of fractals recognizes that the world is not made up of uniform shapes but, rather, that the earth and its features are eroded by countless randomlike variations. Thus, by randomly subjecting otherwise-smooth surfaces to thousands of such deformations, startlingly realistic scenes can be generated by computer.

ENVIRONMENTAL CON-
TROL Computer systems en-
able us to better control the
environment in which we live, as
illustrated by the applications
below developed at Los Alamos
National Laboratory in New
Mexico.

35, 36. A digitized photograph of a landscape (35) is integrated with computer-simulated atmospheric pollution to demonstrate the visual effects of air pollution (36).

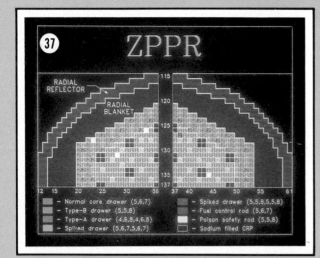

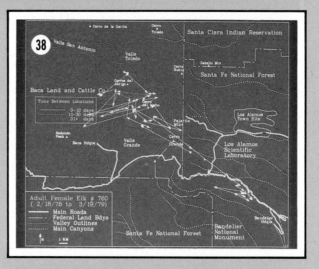

37. Used in nuclear safeguard studies, this computer image represents a cross section of the fuel distribution in the core of a research reactor. The small squares, which are colored and numbered, indicate the type and amount of nuclear fuel present in the core.

38. A computer-generated display showing elk movement in the eastern Jemez mountains of New Mexico. The yellow lines trace the migration of a radio-collared elk tracked by Los Alamos National Environmental Research Park personnel.

RETAILING Retail businesses, such as department and food stores, use computers to provide rapid customer checkout service, manage inventories of goods, and perform general accounting functions.

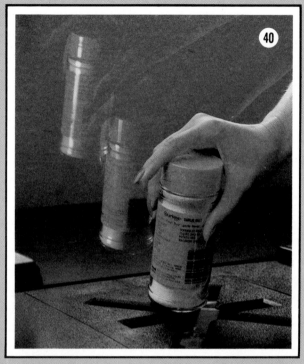

39, 40. As products are checked out at many supermarkets, they are passed over scanning stations that read the bar codes on the packaging. Once the computer system interprets the unique codes on the packages, it can automatically determine the descriptions and prices of the products, print out a detailed register receipt for the customer, and record and monitor inventory outflow.

41. A hand-held wand is used to input optically the machine-readable characters encoded in a price tag when a purchase is made. The information on the tag is sent to an electronic cash register that both bills the customer and records the sale information for subsequent sales and inventory status reports.

ENTERTAINMENT The number of computer-driven toys and games introduced over the last several years has been phenomenal. The video-game industry is featured in these photographs.

42. The ColecoVision™ video game system. The attached game controllers facilitate fast-paced screen action.

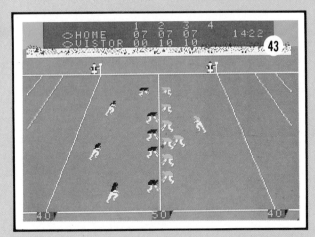

43. A display from Coleco Industries' Head to Head™ Football. When you're on offense, you can go for the bomb, run a draw play, call for a sweep right, or something else. Similarly, the defense can blitz, tackle, or intercept passes.

44. Blackjack or poker anyone? In this game, by Coleco Industries, you let the "dealer" know whatever option suits your fancy.

45. Go for it! Although a trip to Aspen or Snowbird may excite you more than "skiing" in your living room, you can practice for the slopes with this skiing game. You get to see the course from the skier's perspective, and must negotiate sharp curves, moguls, trees, and other obstacles to reach the bottom in record time.

46. In Peyo's SMURF™, you control the actions of the Smurf, who must save the Smurfette from Garmagel. During your odyssey, you must jump over and duck natural obstacles, avoid dangerous animals, and maintain your strength by snacking on hard-to-find berries.

TRAVEL AND TRANSPORTATION   Computer systems are used in a variety of ways to manage travel and transportation systems, as shown in the photographs on this page.

47.   The NCR 2251 Guest Accounting Control System lets hotels and motels keep accurate records on guests and provides useful accounting information. The system lets management personnel monitor every transaction from the time the guest checks in to the time of payment.

48.   Airline reservations systems are used by agents to rapidly check up-to-date flight schedules, confirm seat availability, and place bookings. The airline industry maintains its own extensive network of computer systems, which are also accessed by authorized independent agents.

49.   With over a third of America's freight being shipped by rail, it's not unusual for a switching yard to handle over 2500 railroad cars simultaneously. Computer systems are commonly used to keep track of the mind-boggling variety of information needed to effectively manage the yards.

OTHER APPLICATIONS Window 1 closes with a look at three other applications areas. There are, of course, many more, but the space is not available to show them all.

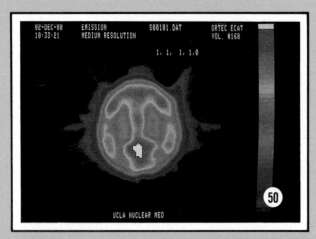

50. Medicine. Research scientists at UCLA School of Medicine's Biophysics and Nuclear Medicine Divisions use an ECAT scanner, an image processing system, and a method called computer tomography to create images of metabolic states in the body on a display screen. Here, as a human brain interprets sensory data, such as music or language, the metabolic changes taking place in the brain are visible on the screen.

51. Sports. Tampa Bay Buccaneer football players and coaches use game analysis reports and statistics generated by Mohawk Data Sciences' Sports-Pac software to improve playing strategies. Off the field, the team's front office uses the software package as a defensive weapon to defray escalating administrative costs.

52. Research. A computer image, by Nelson Max of Lawrence Livermore National Laboratory, showing several different amino acid chains in a tomato bushy stunt virus. The three-dimensional photo image was created by the computer system from data on the virus that was input to the system and analyzed.

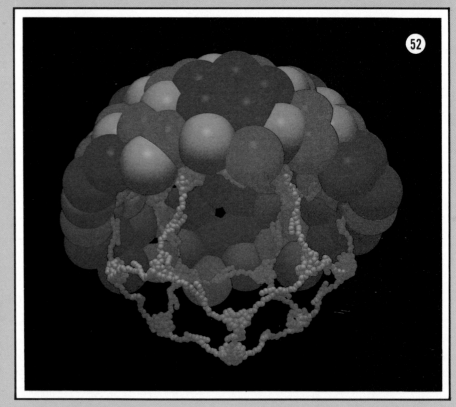

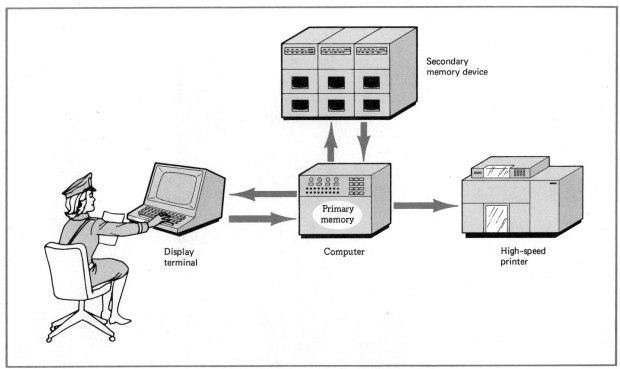

Figure 1-2. *Example application.* A detective interacts with a computer system.

The setting is a state police headquarters. The computer system involved is operated and managed by the state police. Many of the hardware devices, including the CPU and the secondary storage device, are located in the "computer center" in the basement of the police headquarters building.

The secondary storage device contains massive amounts of data on stolen cars, outstanding arrest warrants, and so forth. It also contains hundreds of programs that make it possible for users—various police personnel—to extract useful information from the data. In other words, the secondary storage device has available all the resources the computer needs to process a request from a user for information.

Now let's imagine that a user of this system—a detective trying to solve a rash of car thefts—gets a call from an officer on patrol who has spotted what he thinks may be one of the stolen cars. The license plate number on the car is APLF65 (Arizona). In her office the detective has a hardware device called a *display terminal* (see Figure 1-3) that is connected to the computer system by ordinary phone wires. The display terminal looks like a television screen hooked up to a typewriter keyboard. The

Figure 1-3. The display terminal. A device with a keyboard and a televisionlike display screen is used for both input and output to the computer. As the operator types on the keyboard, the keyed text is input to the computer system. After the system processes the operator input, it outputs the results on the terminal's screen.

detective sits down at the terminal and types in

```
FIND STOLEN-CAR
```

This message informs the computer system that she wishes to use a program named STOLEN-CAR. The program was created previously by a programmer to process stolen car data. The computer system looks for the program on its secondary storage device, finds it, and temporarily copies it into the CPU's, internal memory to make it available to the detective. It then sends the message

```
READY
```

to the detective's display screen. This message informs her that the computer system has found the program and wants to know what to do with it. The detective then types in

```
RUN
```

an instruction that commands the computer system to run the program. STOLEN-CAR can provide all sorts of interesting information about stolen cars. First, however, it has to know just what kind of information each user wants, so it sends the message

```
REQUEST?
```

to the user's terminal. In this case, the detective wants to know whether the license plate number is from a stolen car. She responds with her special request

```
SEARCH STOLEN-LIST APLF65, ARIZ
```

which STOLEN-CAR interprets to mean, "Inspect the collection of data residing on the secondary storage device that is entitled STOLEN-LIST. Report to the user on whether or not Arizona plate APLF65 is there."

The computer system then processes the request by comparing each license plate number in its list of stolen cars against the number APLF65 to see if one matches it. If it fails to find that number in its list, it sends the message

```
SORRY, NO MATCH
```

to the detective's terminal. If the number is in its list, it would tell the detective that it had found a match. The detective might then ask for additional information: Who owns the car? What kind of car is it? When was it stolen? All this information would be sent directly to her terminal.

Tomorrow, the detective might decide she needs a report of all cars stolen in the last month. This list is too long to appear all at once on her terminal's display screen. And besides, she needs a printed list she can make notes on and take with her to a meeting. As before, she calls up STOLEN-CAR and asks it to search for the information she needs, but this time she adds a command directing it to send the output to a *high-speed printer* (Figure 1-4) rather than to her screen. Within a few seconds the computer system sends a message to her terminal that her request has been processed. She then walks to the computer center, goes over to the printer, and picks up her report.

While our detective is using the computer system to track down stolen cars, dozens of her co-workers may be using it at the same time for other jobs. Another detective may be using a different program to run a check of drivers' licenses. A county chief may have asked for a report on crime statistics in the county over the last five years. The payroll department may be using the system to calculate the detective's pay and print her paycheck. The list of potential applications goes on and on.

Figure 1-4.   The high-speed printer. This is an output device that prints information on paper. It is used when volumes of material are needed in printed form.

COMPUTERS AND SOCIETY

The example we just presented gives you some idea of why computer systems have become such an important part of modern life. Their ability to sort through massive amounts of data and quickly produce useful information for any kind of user—from payroll clerk to president—makes them indispensable in a society like ours. Without computers, for instance, the government couldn't possibly tabulate all the data it collects for the census every ten years. Banks would be overwhelmed by the job of keeping track of all the transactions they must process. The efficient telephone service we are used to would be impossible. Moon exploration and the space shuttle would still be science fiction fantasies. The list is virtually endless.

But along with the benefits computers bring to society have come some troubling problems, ranging from health to personal security and privacy. The detective in our example, for instance, spends many hours in front of a computer terminal. Does this have any effect on her health? She has a clear need for the information on stolen cars she has requested, but what keeps anyone else with a computer terminal, a knowledge of computers, and access to the telephone system from getting hold of the same information? Banks keep data about customers' accounts on external storage devices. Can they prevent clever "computer criminals" from using the computer system to steal from those accounts? The Internal Revenue Service has confidential information about every American taxpayer. Can that information be protected from unauthorized use?

These are serious issues, but we can only mention them in this chapter. In Chapter 18, "Problems and Opportunities," we will discuss them at length.

COMPUTER SYSTEMS TO FIT EVERY NEED AND POCKETBOOK

A great variety of computer systems are available commercially to serve the needs of computer users. In Module D you will learn how computers fit into settings that range from the living room to the offices of giant corporations. Here we'll consider one important way in which computers differ from one another: size.

Computers are generally classified in one of three categories: small, or "microcomputers"; medium-sized, or "minicomputers"; and large, or "mainframe computers." In practice, the distinction among these different sizes is not always clear-cut. Large minicomputers, for example, are often bigger than small mainframes.

In general, the larger the computer, the greater its processing power. For example, big computers can process data at faster speeds and can perform more complicated types of processing than small computers. Big computers can also accommodate larger, more powerful support devices. Naturally, the larger the computer and its support equipment, the greater the price. A computer system can set you back anywhere from a few hundred dollars to many millions.

Microcomputers

A technological breakthrough in the early 1970s made it possible to produce an entire CPU on a single silicon chip smaller than a dime. These "computers-on-a-chip," or microprocessors, can be mass-produced at very low cost. They were quickly integrated into all types of products, making possible powerful hand-held calculators, digital watches, a spate of electronic toys, and sophisticated controls for household appliances such as microwave ovens and automatic coffee makers. Microprocessors also made it possible to build inexpensive computer systems small enough to fit on a desk top (see Figure 1-5).

Figure 1-5.   A microcomputer system.

Microcomputers and Computer Literacy

These days, it seems that anyone who can understand how to follow a few simple instructions is learning how to use the computer. "Computer literacy," the term coined to describe a general knowledge of computer systems and their uses, is gaining momentum in many segments of society, touching young and old alike.

One of the biggest single developments contributing to the recent surge of interest in computers has been the microprocessor. Microprocessors, which are used to make the personal computers one often sees in homes, have made computing relatively cheap and easy to learn. This, in turn, has made the computer so widely available that an increasing number of jobs are becoming dependent on its use.

Microcomputers were initially purchased for the home, usually so that the younger members of the family could do homework assignments and play electronic games. The younger generation quickly embraced the new technology and became eager to do more computing. Parents, seeing the rapid encroachment of computer systems into virtually every niche of society, pressed school boards for more computer education. In turn, schools that could afford to do so—seeing a willingness to learn as well as the growing emergence of the computer as a social force—began to provide this education. And so it goes. Several school districts, such as Saddleback Valley Unified School District in southern California, have made computer literacy a mandatory graduation requirement.

Colleges and universities have for years had computer curricula, stressing the importance of computers as an effective tool for all types of work, whether students major in them or not. In many cases, graduation requirements for certain majors include one or several computer courses. Some schools have recently imposed requirements that *all* degree-seeking students must successfully pass a course in computers. Institu-

tions such as Carnegie-Mellon University, Clarkson College, Drexel University, and Stevens Institute of Technology are providing educational environments in which every student has his or her own microcomputer.

Beyond the educational institutions, microcomputers (or terminal stations which are hooked up to larger computers) are rapidly finding their way onto office desk tops for a variety of reasons. Small businesses and individuals find that they have too much paperwork to handle manually—a computer system is just much faster. Salespeople need to interact on a timely basis with their customers, who often place orders by computer. It is estimated that close to 60 percent of all microcomputers sold in stores today are purchased for business use.

Even for those who don't interact with computers directly, the presence of these machines in society is so pervasive that people feel they will be left behind if they remain ignorant of them. As a result, in many cities, schools, corporations, special-interest groups, and individuals are offering courses and seminars on computers to meet a variety of learning needs. As one person, whose business has been dramatically reshaped by the use of computers, aptly stated in a computer literacy course, ". . . if you don't have a computer today, you're sunk!"

Computer education: Starting 'em early.

These small computers have come to be called **microcomputers.** Because they are inexpensive and small enough for individuals to use at home for personal needs, they are also commonly called **personal computers.** The two terms—*microcomputer* and *personal computer*—have become almost interchangeable.

Microcomputers (or micros) appear in homes, offices, and classrooms. At home they help families keep track of their finances, help students write term papers, regulate heating systems to lower fuel bills, and challenge all comers at PAC-MAN™, DONKEY KONG™, and chess. They help businesses keep track of merchandise, prepare correspondence, bill customers, and do routine accounting. Universities, high schools, and even elementary schools—attracted by the low cost of these machines and the fact that they are "friendlier" than larger computers—are purchasing micros for courses in computing. In fact, several universities now require entering students to buy or rent their own microcomputers.

Minicomputers

Minicomputers (or minis) are generally regarded as "medium-sized" computers (see Figure 1-6). Most of them fall between microcomputers and mainframes in their processing power. The very smallest minicomputers, however, are virtually indistinguishable from some microcomputers, and the largest (sometimes called *super-minis*) closely resemble mainframes. Minicomputers are generally far more expensive than microcomputers and not affordable for most individuals.

Any of several factors might lead an organization to choose a minicomputer over a micro or mainframe. A small or medium-sized company, for example, may find microcomputer systems just too small or too slow to handle its current volume of paperwork. Or the company may need a computer system that can do several jobs at once and interact with several users at the same time. Few microcomputer systems have enough power for such applications. Mainframes, of course, have these capabilities, but they are far larger and more expensive than minis.

Mainframes

The **mainframe** (see Figure 1-7) is the mainstay of almost all large organizations. It often operates twenty-four hours a day—

Figure 1-6. A minicomputer system.

serving hundreds of users on terminals during regular business hours, and processing large jobs such as payroll and billing late at night. Many large organizations need several mainframes to complete their computing workloads. Typically, these organizations own or lease a variety of computers—mainframes, minis, and micros—to meet all their processing needs.

Some organizations—such as large scientific and research laboratories—have extraordinary demands for processing data. Applications such as sending an astronaut into outer space and weather forecasting, for example, require extreme degrees of accuracy and a wealth of computations. To meet these needs, a few vendors offer very large, sophisticated mainframes called **supercomputers.** These machines are very expensive, often costing in the range of $10 to $20 million.

Figure 1-7. A mainframe system.

COMPUTERS IN ACTION

Where would you expect to find computers? In our discussion so far we've given some indication of the amazing variety of ways in which computers have become embedded in our lives. As you read through this book you should get a good idea of what computer systems can and cannot do, and where they do and do not belong. Window 1, which follows page 12, presents an extensive picture essay of computers in action in just a few of the many settings in which you are likely to encounter them.

Summary and Key Terms

Computers are seen almost everywhere in the world today. They're embedded in consumer products, used to run businesses, and employed to direct production in our factories, to name just a few applications.

Three words summarize the operation of a **computer system: input, processing,** and **output.** The processing function is performed by the **computer** itself, which is sometimes called the **Central Processing Unit,** or **CPU.**

The input and output functions are performed by **support equipment,** such as **input devices** and **output devices.** Just as your stereo amplifier would be useless if it didn't have speakers, headphones, or a turntable to supplement it, the computer would be helpless without this support equipment.

On most of the support equipment are mounted **input/output media (I/O media).** Many of these media store materials in **machine-readable** form, a form that the computer system can recognize and process.

The materials that a computer receives as input is of two kinds: data and programs. **Data** are "facts" the computer has at its disposal, and **programs** are "instructions" that explain to the computer what to do with these facts. Programs must be written in a **programming language** which the computer can understand.

The processing of data on a computer system is commonly referred to as **data processing.** The results produced through data processing are called **information.**

Computer systems have two types of memory, or storage. **Primary (internal) memory,** which is part of the computer itself, holds programs and data the system is currently processing. **Secondary (external) memory** stores other programs and data. In many systems, secondary memory is located in a separate hardware device.

In the world of computers it is common to distinguish between hardware and software. **Hardware** refers to the actual machinery that makes up the computer system, such as the CPU, input and output devices, and secondary memory device. **Software** refers to computer programs. It can also refer to the manuals that help people work with computer systems.

Users are people who need the output computer systems produce. There are many types of "experts" in a computing environment who help users meet their computing needs, for example, **programmers,** whose job it is to write programs.

Although computer systems have become an indispensable part of modern life, their growing use often creates troubling problems, ranging from health to personal security and privacy.

Small-sized computers are often called **microcomputers** (or **personal computers**); medium-sized computers, **minicomputers;** and large-sized computers, **mainframes.** The very largest of the mainframes are called **supercomputers.** Although classifying computers by size can be helpful in practice, it is sometimes difficult to classify computers that fall on the borders of these categories.

Review Questions

1. What do you believe will be the greatest impact computers will have on your life? On society at large?
2. What is the difference between a computer and a computer system?
3. Name as many computer support devices as you can. What is the purpose of each?
4. What are the major differences between primary and secondary memory?
5. What is the difference between programs and data?
6. Define and give some examples of a computer user.
7. Identify some social problems created by the existence of computer systems.

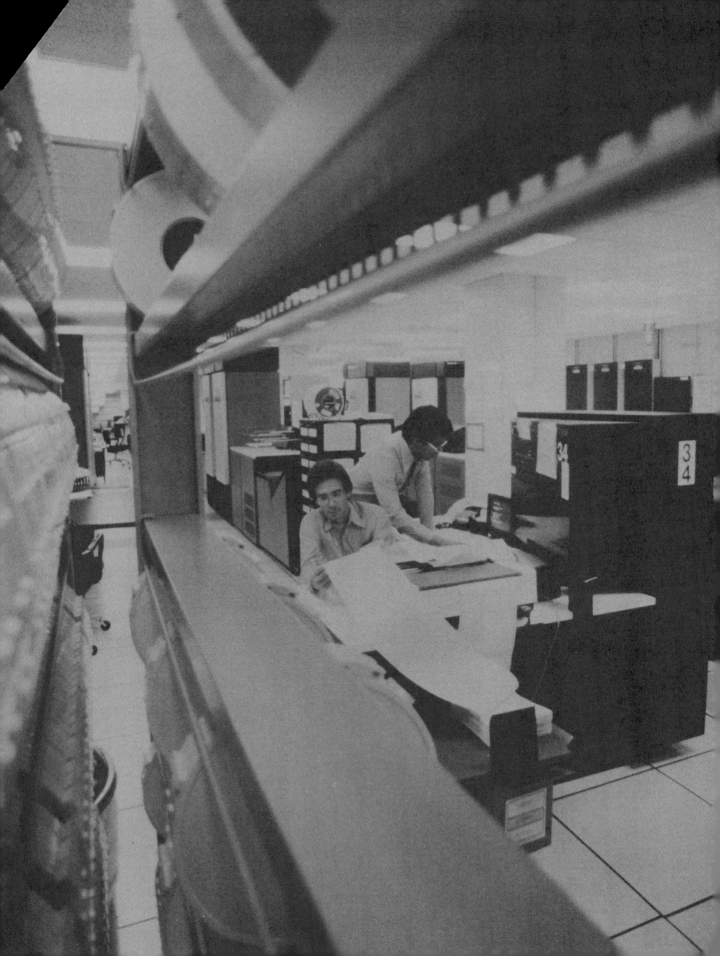

Chapter 2

How Computer Systems Process Data

Chapter Outline

OVERVIEW

As you learned in Chapter 1, input, processing, and output, together with storage, are the major aspects of any computer system. In this chapter you will learn in more detail how these four aspects work together.

First we'll take a look at computer hardware. We'll cover some basic hardware concepts and discuss some of the most important kinds of input, output, and storage equipment. Then, we'll see how these can be linked together in a typical small computer system and a typical large computer system. This section will give you an introduction to the detailed discussion of hardware in Module B.

Next we'll take up the subject of data, specifically how data must be organized for processing on a computer system. Study the terms introduced in this section carefully, because you will encounter them frequently throughout the rest of the book.

From data we'll go on to a discussion of program software to give you an introduction to a subject we cover extensively in Module C.

The chapter ends with a discussion of data processing on computer systems. We'll discuss representative examples of some of the most common types of processing to see how hardware, data, software, and users interact to do useful work.

COMPUTER HARDWARE

All computer systems consist of some combination of computers and support equipment. The **computer** (which is often called the Central Processing Unit, or CPU) is the heart of the system—it's the machine that does the actual processing of data and programs. **Support equipment** consists of all the machines that make it possible to get data and programs into the CPU, get processed information out, and store data and programs for ready access to the CPU. Figure 2-1 summarizes the relationship of these hardware elements and lists some of the most important examples of each.

Support Equipment

There are a number of ways to classify support equipment for computer systems. One of the most basic is by function: Is the

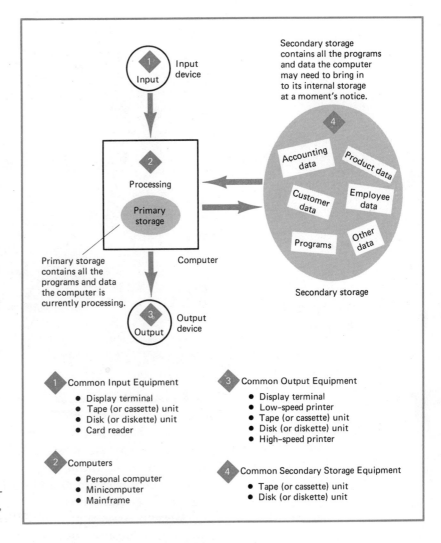

Figure 2-1. The four major aspects to computing: input, output, processing, and storage.

device predominantly for input, output, or storage? Another is by medium: Does it use cards, tape, or disks? A third is by relation to the CPU: Is it peripheral or auxiliary? Online or offline? Let's consider each of these in turn.

Is It for Input, Output, or Storage?

Input devices are machines that convert data and programs into a form that the CPU can understand and process. **Output devices** are machines that convert processed data into a form that users can understand. **Secondary storage devices** are

Figure 2-2.   CRT terminal.

machines that can make frequently used data and programs readily available to the CPU. These functions often overlap in a single machine. Many machines, for example, work as both input and output devices. And all secondary storage devices also function as both input and output devices. Now let's discuss some of the most common kinds of support equipment in terms of these three functions.

Display terminals, or CRTs (see Figure 2-2), figure in almost all computer systems. These consist of a typewriterlike keyboard and a televisionlike screen (usually a cathode ray tube, hence CRT). They are used for both input and output. The CRT operator enters commands to the computer system through the keyboard. Both the input the operator enters and the output the CPU produces appear on the screen.

Card readers (see Figure 2-3) convert data and programs on punched cards into input for the computer system. These devices are just for input and are usually associated with large and medium-sized computer systems.

Printers are used to produce output. *Low-speed printers* (Figure 2-4) are designed to output small amounts of printed information. Because of their low cost, they are very popular devices for personal computer systems. Many low-speed printers also contain keyboards, which enable operators to send data to the computer system. *High-speed printers* (Figure 2-5) are

Input hopper

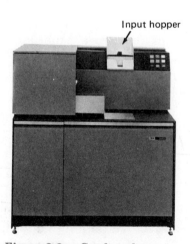

Figure 2-3.   Card reader.

Figure 2-4.   Low-speed printer.

used to produce extensive printed reports. They may operate at speeds ten to thirty times faster than low-speed devices.

Secondary storage devices hold frequently used data and programs for ready access to the CPU. They also function as both input and output devices; they contain stored data and programs which are sent to the CPU as input, and the CPU can transmit new data and programs to them as output. The most common types of secondary storage devices are *magnetic tape units* and *magnetic disk units.*

Large tape units (Figure 2-6), which use detachable tape reels as input/output media, are usually associated with large computer systems. *Cassette tape units* (Figure 2-7), which use small tapes encased in a plastic cartridge, are usually associated with small computer systems. Disk units store data and programs on magnetized platters called *disks. Hard disk units* (Figure 2-8), which work with rigid disks, are faster than tape units and can make larger volumes of material immediately available to the CPU. *Floppy disk (diskette) units* (Figure 2-9), which work with flexible disks, are slower than hard-disk units and have much less data-carrying capacity. However, they are far cheaper. Hard-disk units are usually found with larger systems, and diskette units with smaller systems.

Input/Output Media

Input and output devices are machines for, respectively, getting data and programs into a computer and getting the results out

Figure 2-5.   High-speed printer.

Figure 2-6.   Large tape unit.

Figure 2-7.   Cassette tape unit.

Figure 2-8.   Hard-disk unit.

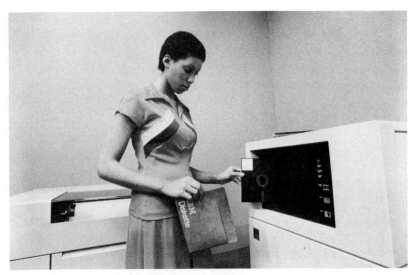

Figure 2-9.   Floppy disk unit.

in a usable form. Data and programs, however, are often not permanently stored *in* a particular device. Usually, they are recorded *on* **input/output (I/O) media,** in a form the associated device can read and transmit to the CPU. In other words, just as the record player on your stereo system at home works together with vinyl records, input/output devices work together with specific input/output media. Five of the most common input/output media in use today are *punched cards, magnetic tape* (both on *detachable reels* and in *cassettes*), *hard magnetic disks,* and *floppy disks*. These are illustrated in Figure 2-10 and will be discussed in detail in Chapters 5 and 6.

Peripheral and Auxiliary; Online and Offline

Support equipment is either peripheral or auxiliary, online or offline. **Peripheral equipment** consists of machines that can be "plugged into" the CPU so that they can communicate with it directly. All the machines we have discussed so far—display terminals, card readers, printers, and secondary storage devices—fall into the peripheral category.

Auxiliary equipment consists of machines that always work independently of the CPU in what is called the *standalone mode.* Examples are *keypunch machines* (Figure 2-11), *key-to-tape units* (Figure 2-12), and *key-to-disk units* (Figure 2-13).

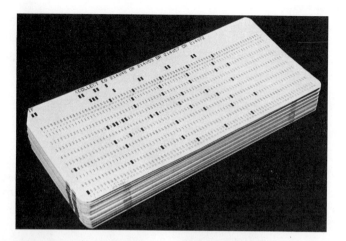

Figure 2-10. **Common types of input/output media.** At the top, punched cards, left to right: magnetic tape on reels, cassette tape, hard magnetic disks, and floppy disks.

Figure 2-11.   Keypunch machine.

These three machines are also examples of **data preparation devices,** because their purpose is to get input materials onto a particular input/output medium—punched cards for a keypunch machine, tape for a key-to-tape machine, and disk for a key-to-disk machine. After the data have been entered onto an input/output medium with one of these machines, the medium must be loaded onto the appropriate peripheral device—a card reader, tape unit, or disk unit—for the data to be processed by the CPU.

Figure 2-12.   Key-to-tape unit.

Any device that is under the automatic control of the computer at a given time is said to be **online** at that time. If a device isn't online, it's **offline.** When peripheral equipment is plugged into the computer, it's considered online. Some peripherals also have standalone capability. Thus, when we "pull the plug," taking them away from the computer, they're offline. Auxiliary equipment, since it functions independently of the CPU, is always offline.

Getting It Together: Combining Hardware Into a System

Now that we've covered some basic hardware concepts and discussed some particular machines in terms of these concepts, let's see how hardware is linked together in a computer system. We'll consider two examples: a large computer system and a small computer system.

Figure 2-14 illustrates a large computer system. Such a system might be run by a mainframe computer or a large minicomputer capable of running the most powerful types of support equipment. The simple system shown here includes a

Figure 2-13. Key-to-disk unit.

- Large CPU
- Display terminal
- Low-speed printer
- Keypunch machine
- Card reader

- Key-to-tape unit
- Tape unit
- Key-to-disk unit
- Disk unit
- High-speed printer

It is not unusual for a system run by a large computer to contain hundreds of terminals, several tape and disk units, several printers, and so forth. Also, a number of large computer systems contain several computers that are hooked up to each other.

Figure 2-15 illustrates a system run by a small computer—a microcomputer or a small minicomputer. The system includes a

- Small CPU
- Cassette tape unit
- Floppy disk unit

- Display terminal
- Low-speed printer

Window 2, which follows page 44, shows several types of equipment and media you've read about in this chapter in real situations.

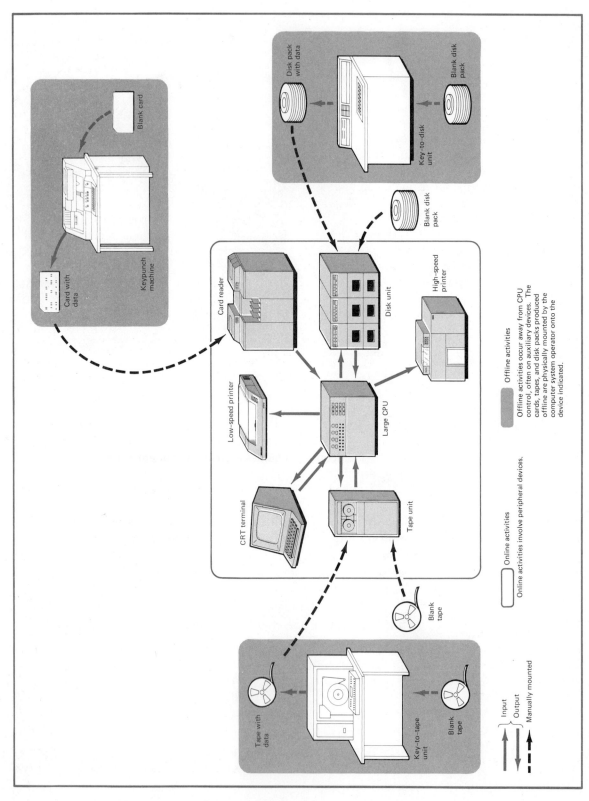

Figure 2-14. Components of a large computer system run by a mainframe or large minicomputer. Note the relationship of input/output media to online and offline activities and peripheral and auxiliary devices.

Texas School System Charts Students' Courses

TARRANT COUNTY, Texas—A computer application for student degree planning at Tarrant County Junior College is getting an A+ from school officials here.

An IBM computer and several online terminals scattered across the school's three campuses have simplified life for Tarrant counselors and students alike, according to a spokesman.

Working at a terminal, a counselor calls up a report that shows the student precisely what courses he must complete to earn his two-year degree, and the student gets a hard copy of his requirements from a nearby printer.

"We were spending an hour or more on each student," said Joseph W. Rode, director of counseling, placement and testing at the school's northwest campus. This was creating big problems, according to Rode, with enrollment at the college bulging at 25,085 in 1981.

"It took at least 15 minutes to handcopy facts from the student's permanent records onto the degree planning sheet. Then a secretary would type the whole thing on a three-part form . . . even if a secretary was available on the spot, the student had to wait half an hour or more. Usually we'd have to make another appointment to finish the counseling and get a degree plan squared away," Rode commented.

Now the student's transcript, permanent record and degree program are all generated from the data banks of the school's IBM 370 Model 138 mainframe. An IBM 3287 printer then produces for the counselor the entire academic story: courses completed, courses pending, additional requirements and their sequence and hours needed toward degree completion.

"The counselor really has no excuse for making a mistake in advising a student," Rode continued, "and the same is true for the student."

The document is complete and concise, Rode said. It succinctly spells out grade point average, transferred credit hours, upper-level hours completed and more. The instant tapping into the student's college history provides a useful tool in making other academic plans as well, Rode explained.

Major Changes

"Students frequently want to change their majors and no counselor can possibly remember the different requirements." Rode said that before they installed the computer, counselors were forever thumbing through the college catalog to figure out, for example, what completed courses a business student could apply toward a new major in agriculture. "It took a lot of time, and with 140 courses there was plenty of room for error," he claimed.

"Now we just instruct the system to adjust that old degree plan to the new requirements, and we have the whole story in a few seconds—no mistakes," Rode remarked.

While some advisors were originally worried about the impersonality of the new system, they soon found that the IBM printout did not replace or undermine academic advisement, but instead enhanced it, enabling them to be more useful and accountable to the student body.

"Today, really for the first time," Rode concluded, "I'm a full-time counselor, not a part-time clerk."

Source: Computerworld, June 7, 1983, p. 41. © 1983 by CW Communications, Inc. Framingham, MA 01701. Reprinted from COMPUTERWORLD.

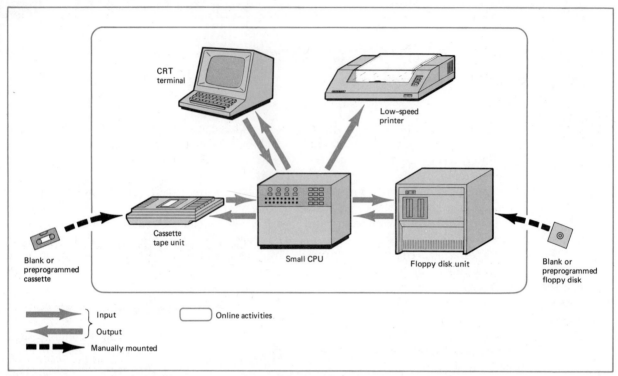

Figure 2-15.   Components of a small computer system run by a microcomputer or a small minicomputer. In microcomputer systems, the display, keyboard, CPU, and floppy disk device are often all housed in the same physical unit.

ORGANIZING DATA FOR COMPUTER SYSTEMS

Data, as we said before, are essentially facts. But you can't just randomly input a collection of facts into a computer system and expect to get results. Data to be processed in a computer system must be organized in a systematic way. A common procedure is to organize data into files, records, and fields. These words have a precise meaning in a computing environment and you should use them with care.

A **field** is a collection of characters (a character is a single number, letter of the alphabet, or special symbol such as the decimal point) that represents a single type of data. A **record** is a collection of related fields, and a **file** is a collection of related records. Files, records, and fields are normally stored on an input/output medium such as punched cards, tapes, or disks. Your school, for example, probably has a *file,* perhaps stored on tape, of all students currently enrolled (see Figure 2-16). The file would contain a *record* for each student. Each record would have a *field* for various types of information about each student:

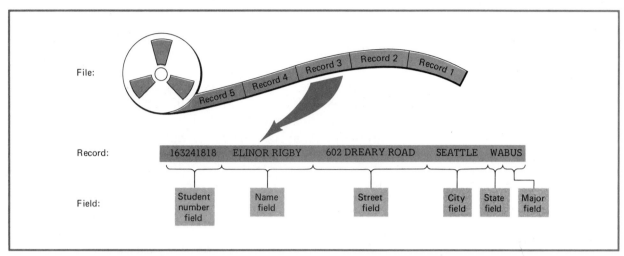

Figure 2-16. **Difference between a file, record, and field.** The file shown above contains name and address data on students enrolled at a college. If there are 2000 active students at the college, this file would contain 2000 records. Each record in the file has six data fields—student's number, name, street, city, state, and major.

the student's ID number, name, street, city, state, major subject area, and so forth.

Files, records, and fields vary in size. Some files are bigger than others in that they contain more records. And some files have greater data content than others in that their records contain more fields. And, of course, fields can vary in length from one to many characters.

Programs are also technically considered to be files. However, it is often not useful to talk about records and fields in connection with program files.

In most large computer systems many data files are kept on disk storage for immediate access to the system. These files often contain operational data. For example, most businesses (such as your local department store) will have data files such as the following:

- Daily customer transactions (called a customer *transaction* file)
- Key customer data, such as names, addresses, and credit standings (called a customer *master* file)
- Amounts owed by customers buying on credit (called a *receivables* file)
- Outstanding debts the organization itself must pay (called a *payables* file)

Whatever the medium on which they are stored, files always have a name. The computer system uses this name to identify the file when it needs to access it. For example, "AR-D200" may be the name of a receivables data file and "AR-P201" may be the name of a program that produces from this file a list of customers with overdue balances. Each organization will have its own convention for naming files. In the preceding example, "AR" stands for accounts receivable, "P" for program file, and "D" for data file. All 100-numbered program files may be related to billing, 200-level to overdue balances, and so forth.

A BRIEF INTRODUCTION TO SOFTWARE

As mentioned earlier, the word software refers to programs. Programs direct the computer system to do specific tasks, just as your thoughts direct your body to speak or move in certain ways. There are two classes of software: applications software and systems software.

Applications software is written by users or programmers to perform tasks such as computing the interest or balance in banking accounts, preparing bills, playing games, scheduling passengers on airlines, diagnosing the illnesses of hospital patients, and so forth. In other words, applications software is what makes possible the "computer work" people have in mind when they acquire computer systems.

You can buy applications software prepackaged (video games are an example) or write it yourself. If you write it yourself, you must know a specific programming language. The tradeoffs involved with buying or creating software are covered in Chapters 9 and 10. Some of the more popular programming languages are discussed in Chapter 11.

Systems software consists of "background" programs that enable applications software to run smoothly. One of the most important pieces of systems software is the *operating system,* a set of control programs that supervise the work of the computer system. Viewed another way, the operating system enables applications software to interface with a specific set of hardware. In the 1982 movie *TRON,* the villainous Master Control Program is the fictionalized counterpart to this perfectly harmless piece of software. Hollywood aside, operating systems don't control people, but rather, people control operating systems. These and other types of systems software are addressed in more depth in Chapter 8.

Dinner for 51, Please, James

How do you quickly convert a beef bourguignonne recipe for 6 to one that will meet the gastronomical needs of 51 people? With a computer program, of course.

Writing such a program is not difficult. For example, one palate-titillating version of beef bourguignonne calls for the following ingredients:

    7-ounce chunk of bacon
    1 tablespoon of olive oil
    4 pounds of lean stewing beef
    1 sliced carrot
    1 sliced onion
    ½ teaspoon of pepper
    2 tablespoons of flour
    3 cups of Chianti wine
    2 cups of beef stock
    1 tablespoon of tomato paste
    2 cloves of garlic
    ½ teaspoon of thyme
    1 bay leaf
    20 small white onions
    1 pound of mushrooms

To convert this recipe for 6 to a recipe for 51 (or any other number of people), you must first store the ingredients and their associated amounts in a data file on the computer system's storage device. Then, a computer program can be written to use this file.

Each ingredient in the recipe would constitute a record in the data file. The records would have at least three fields—one for the name of the ingredient, one for the type of measurement (cups, tablespoons, ounces, pounds), and one for the amount. The program would examine each ingredient (or record) in the file in turn, multiplying the associated amount field by a factor determined by both the number of people to be fed and the size of the recipe. In the present example, the factor would be 51/6, or 8.5. This means that all of the recipe-for-six amounts have to be multiplied by 8.5 in order to feed 51 people. Each ingredient can then be printed out with its new, adjusted amount.

The computer program could also have enough "intelligence" (through additional instructions) to automatically convert ounces to pounds, pints to quarts, and so forth, to simplify buying. And, since the computer can recalculate the requirements of a meal at electronically fast speeds, if there's a sudden change in the number of people coming to dinner, a new recipe can be recomputed in seconds.

The chef may need to temper the results determined by the computer program with a little common sense from time to time. For example, if foods such as eggs are involved, and the computer program shows that a recipe needs 2.3 of them, the chef would obviously need to round up or down, depending on personal taste and judgment. Also, whereas 1 bay leaf might be suitable for a recipe for 6 people, 8.5 bay leaves might be too flavorful in a recipe for 51.

Computer programs can also be written to calculate how much a meal of any size will cost to prepare and to keep track of which meals were fed to which people. This last ability is especially important if you want to avoid serving the same dish twice to certain dinner guests. An added benefit to computerization is that a recipe can be painlessly printed out by the system for easy reference in the kitchen. If soiled, it can be thrown away.

Bringing the computer into the kitchen.

PROCESSING DATA

Computer systems process data. When we talk about data processing, however, what kinds of processing do we have in mind? Many of the common types of data processing fall into the following seven categories:

- Selection
- Summarizing
- Computation
- Sorting
- Updating
- Query processing
- Word processing

We will discuss each of these in turn and illustrate each with an example.

Selection.   **Selection** involves going through a set of data and picking out only those items that meet certain criteria. Figure 2-17 illustrates a selection problem and how it could be processed on a computer system. The problem illustrated is to select from a data file—in this case one that contains data on a company's unpaid invoices—a specific group of records (unpaid invoices over $5000), and to print a report of the results. The user works at a CRT terminal, the data file and program are stored on a disk unit, and the report is printed on a high-speed printer.

Summarizing.   **Summarizing** involves reducing a mass of data to a manageable form. A building supply company, for example, might have a file of weekly sales on disk whose records contain fields for product sold, sales region, and number of units sold. If a sales manager wanted to know the total sales of each item in each region, the data would have to be *summarized* by product and region. Figure 2-18 shows how such a summarization problem might be processed on a computer system.

Computation.   Computer systems can perform all the basic mathematical operations such as addition, subtraction, multiplication, division, and roots. Also, they can execute these operations and various combinations of them at tremendous speeds. A common business application involving **computations** is payroll processing, illustrated in Figure 2-19.

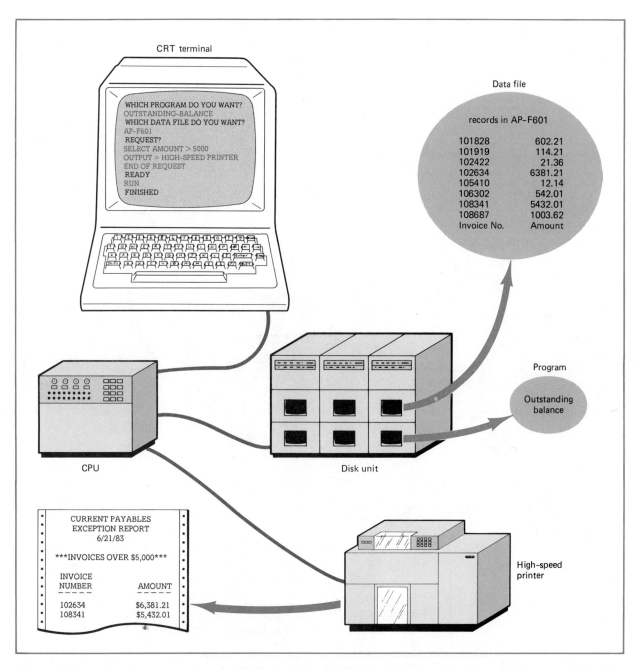

Figure 2-17.   Selecting records from a file. A company treasurer has asked for a list of unpaid bills over $5000. Data on all unpaid bills (current payables) are stored on disk in a file named AP-F601. A program called OUTSTANDING-BALANCE, created to process the payables file, is also stored on disk. Using the CRT, the treasurer runs the program with the data file, specifying the records needed and requesting that a printed report be sent to the high-speed printer.

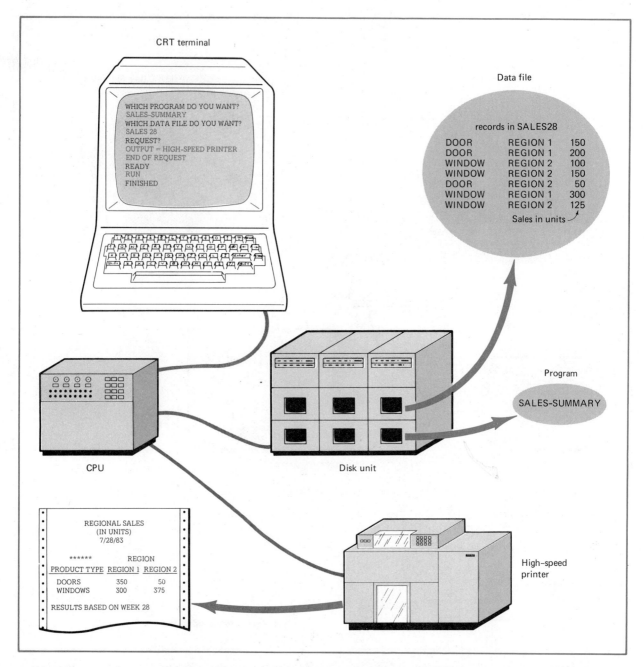

Figure 2-18. *Summarizing information.* A sales manager at a CRT uses a program, SALES-SUMMARY, which contains instructions to total sales data by geographical region and product type. One of the data files which can be used with this program, SALES28, contains data recorded during the twenty-eighth week of the year. SALES-SUMMARY instructs the computer system to total data from this file by region and product type. The manager directs the system to print the results on the high-speed printer.

COMPUTER SYSTEMS

**A glimpse at a variety of computers and
their support equipment**

No matter what size or type, all computer systems perform four basic tasks: input, processing, output, and storage. This Window illustrates the way these tasks are performed on different computer systems.

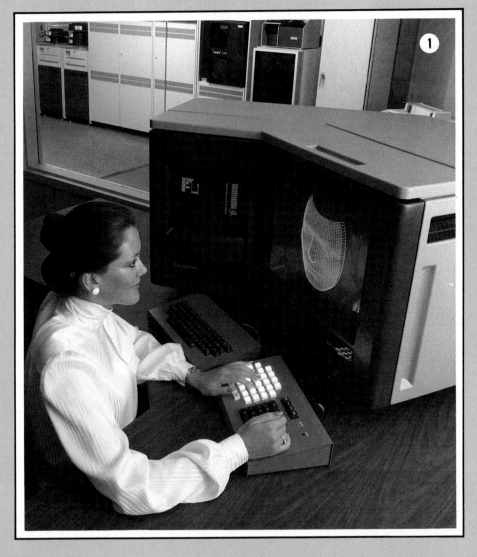

COMPUTERS Computers are the machines that do the processing. The following photographs highlight computers of various sizes—microcomputers, minicomputers, and mainframes—as well as the special applications they serve.

1. A contoured face is created and displayed at a graphics workstation linked to a minicomputer system. Many commercial graphics applications are performed on dedicated minicomputers.

2. An operator sits at the console panel of a Univac 1100/90 mainframe. Using the keyboard, the operator enters commands, such as "load a tape" or "change a user password," directly to the system. Output messages sent by the system to the operator are flashed onto the display screens on the panel.

3. Row upon row of mainframes are shown in a building, longer than a football field, that houses more than $100 million worth of computers at the McDonnell Douglas Automation (McAUTO) Company's St. Louis center. McAUTO claims this is the largest known concentration of computing power under a single roof. The mainframes shown here handle McAUTO's business and manufacturing operations. An entirely different set of mainframes (not shown) is used to process other applications.

4. The very largest mainframes are called "supercomputers." Generally, these machines are used for scientific applications that require enormous amounts of computation, such as weather forecasting, defense planning, and research activities. The CRAY-1 supercomputer shown here is the property of Los Alamos National Laboratory, which owns five of them (along with seven other mainframes). The CRAY-1 is capable of executing over 100 million instructions a second.

5. The IBM System/38 is a minicomputer system used primarily for small-business applications. Like most small-business computers, it can support several terminals operated at the same time.

6. The DEC Rainbow personal computer, with a small, lightweight keyboard, is designed especially for managers and serious home users.

DISK PROCESSING Of the two major types of secondary storage—disk and tape—disk permits the fastest and most sophisticated types of processing. On these two pages are a number of photographs depicting disk operations.

7. Disk packs. These BASF 12-platter-high disk packs have storage capacities ranging from 100 to 300 million characters of data. Each pack is mounted on a device called a disk drive (several of which are shown in photograph 8), enabling the computer to access the data on the packs.

9. Many smaller minicomputer systems use "floppies" rather than conventional hard-disk packs for data storage.

10. Data entry. Organizations with large computer systems often have data-entry departments, such as the one shown, to key data directly onto disk or tape. Programmers and users can then access the data from terminals hooked up to the computer.

8. Disk drives. A "few" disk drives supporting the mainframes at McAUTO's St. Louis center (few in the sense that McAUTO owns over 600 such drives). For some perspective on this awesome storage power, consider that most universities and colleges could meet all of their processing needs with fewer than 10 such devices.

TAPE PROCESSING   Tape is often used as a back-up to disks for important computer files and to save information that is too costly to store on disk (perhaps because of infrequent use). The photographs on these two pages illustrate tape processing.

11. "Memory Lane." Approximately 20,000 tapes are currently on file in the tape library at the Computing Division of Los Alamos National Laboratory. The lab, which is perched atop a jagged string of 7000-foot mesas in New Mexico's scenic Jemez Mountains, also has a "mass storage device" (see Chapter 5) to hold an additional 600,000 files. Before the installation of the mass storage device, the tape library consisted of 55,000 reels. Computer files at Los Alamos are growing at a rate of 200,000 annually.

12. A row of Storage Technology 3670 tape drives. Each drive can handle a single reel of tape, and an accompanying takeup reel, at any one time. A single tape can store thousands of data records.

13. These small IBM 4969 magnetic tape units can fit on a desk top.

14. Readying a tape unit for processing. The mounted tape may contain data to be input to the computer or, alternatively, may receive output from it.

OUTPUT

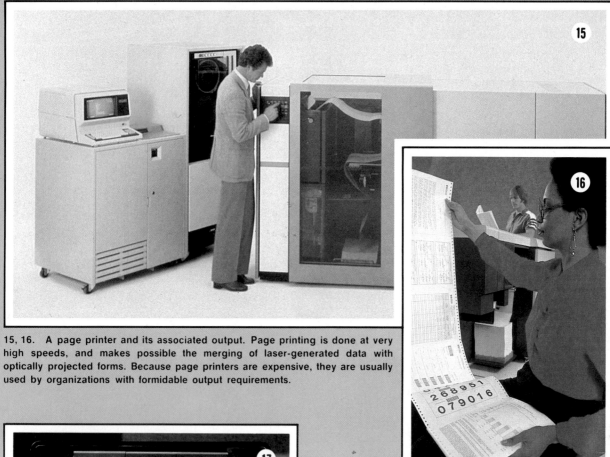

15, 16. A page printer and its associated output. Page printing is done at very high speeds, and makes possible the merging of laser-generated data with optically projected forms. Because page printers are expensive, they are usually used by organizations with formidable output requirements.

17. Display terminals are a popular means of both input (by keyboard) and output (by screen). This new IBM display device is currently being evaluated for a variety of applications that require attractive outputs.

18. Even small printers used with microcomputer-based systems can easily be set up to process payroll checks, business reports, and correspondence.

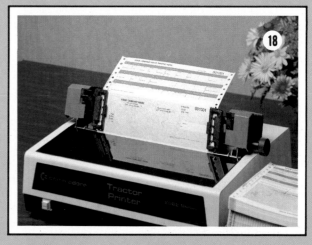

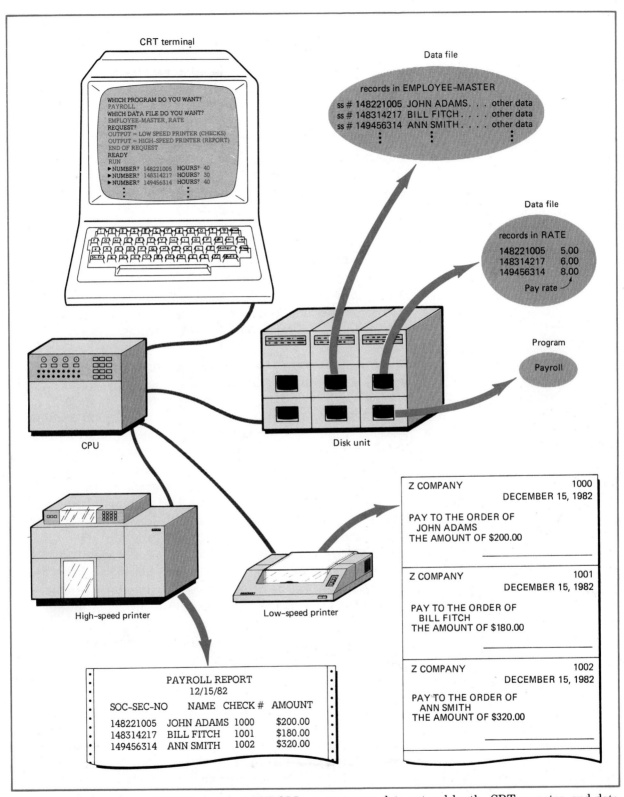

Figure 2-19. *Computing a payroll.* The PAYROLL program uses data entered by the CRT operator, and data stored on disk in the EMPLOYEE-MASTER and RATE files, to calculate each employee's pay. The operator commands the program to print checks on the low-speed printer and to output a payroll report on the high-speed printer.

As this example shows, computer systems can process data from several sources at once. In this example, data comes from three sources. The CRT operator enters each employee's social security number and hours worked that pay period. The EMPLOYEE-MASTER file contains a record for each employee with the employee's social security number, name, and other data. The RATE file contains records with each employee's social security number and pay rate. The PAYROLL program processes these three sources of data and, following the operator's commands, directs the computer system to print checks on a low-speed printer and a payroll report on a high-speed printer.

Normally, payroll processing is much more complicated than Figure 2-19 suggests. Payroll programs must also compute and deduct federal and local taxes and save this information in storage for reporting to the Internal Revenue Service.

Sorting. **Sorting** involves arranging data in a specific order—a list of names in alphabetic order, for example, or a list of numbers in ascending or descending order. Figure 2-20 shows how a typical sorting problem might be handled on a computer system. A manager wants a report of the company's products listed in order of the amount of sales revenue each generates. Data on the sales revenue for each product are in a file called PRODUCT-SALES. The sorting program is called SORT-CUM. The CRT operator directs the system to produce the report on a high-speed printer. In addition to showing the rank order of each product by sales, this program also generates information (by computation) on the percentage of total sales each product represents and the cumulative percentage of sales. Reports like these help managers decide which products are making the most money and which need special attention.

Updating. **Updating** involves changing the data in a file to reflect new information. Credit card companies, for example, update their customer files monthly to reflect payments and purchases their customers have made. Updating is done on either a batch or online basis.

Batch processing involves accumulating (batching) transactions over time in a separate file and processing them all at once against a master file. For example, when you update your checkbook at the end of a month, using data from the checking transactions made throughout that month, you are updating on a batch basis.

The airline industry updates flight reservations on an online basis. Every time a seat is sold by an agent, everyone else using the system needs to know the most up-to-date informa-

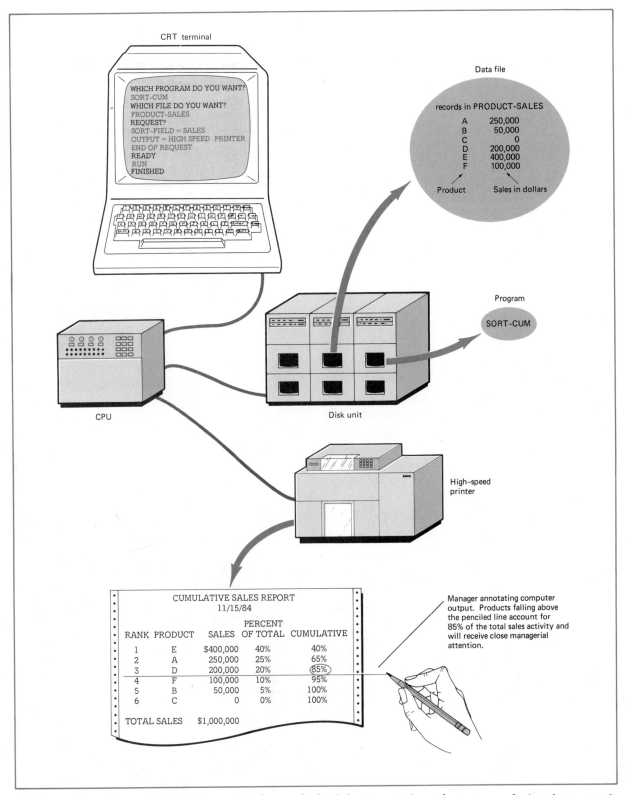

Figure 2-20. Sorting. A manager wants to know which of the company's products are producing the most sales revenue. The SORT-CUM program instructs the computer system to sort the data in the PRODUCT-SALES file in rank order by sales. The program also contains instructions directing the computer to calculate useful information on the percent of sales each product generates.

tion on seat availability. *Online processing* means updating the file immediately after each individual transaction.

Figure 2-21 illustrates online processing in a bank. A customer makes a withdrawal from her savings account. The teller enters the transaction on the CRT terminal, and the record for that customer is immediately updated.

Query Processing. Programs created for **query processing** enable users to extract information from many different data files with a series of questions entered on a terminal. For example, a bank manager may want to check a customer's credit

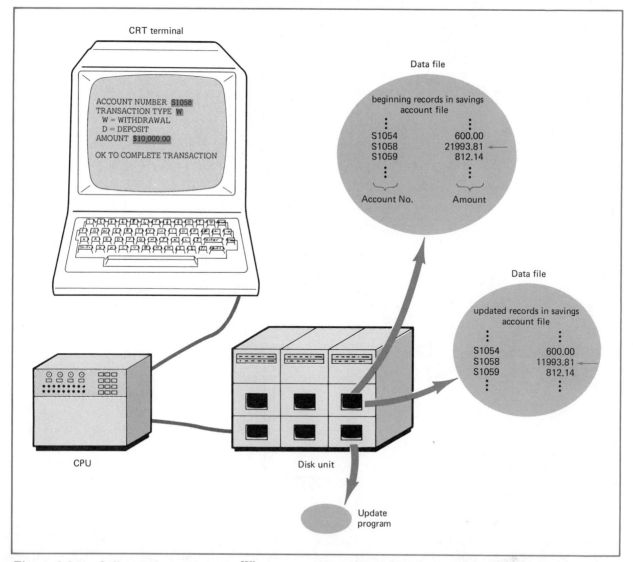

Figure 2-21. Online update at a bank. When a customer makes a deposit or withdrawal, the teller enters the transaction on a CRT. If the transaction is valid, the computer system immediately updates the customer's account.

rating. The data needed to determine credit ratings are contained in several different files—checking, savings, trusts, loans. A query program responding to the manager's request for a credit check could extract all the needed information from each of these files and calculate the customer's credit rating automatically. Figure 2-22 illustrates this kind of processing in an inventory environment.

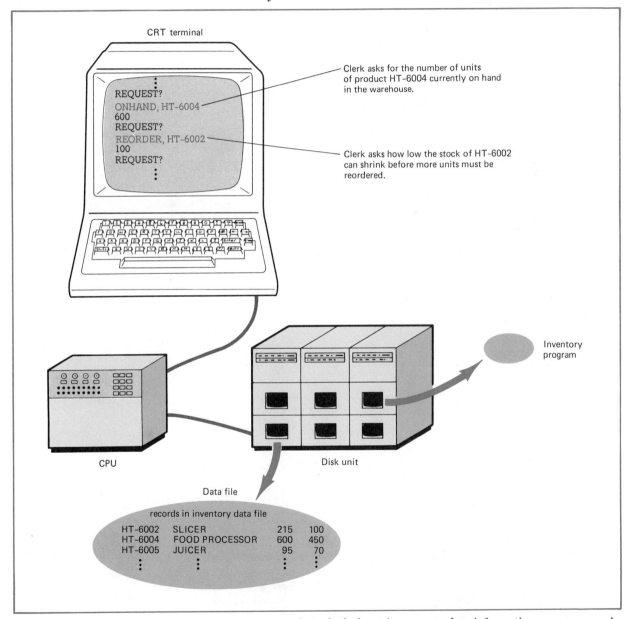

CRT terminal

REQUEST?
ONHAND, HT-6004
600
REQUEST?
REORDER, HT-6002
100
REQUEST?

Clerk asks for the number of units of product HT-6004 currently on hand in the warehouse.

Clerk asks how low the stock of HT-6002 can shrink before more units must be reordered.

Inventory program

CPU

Disk unit

Data file

records in inventory data file

HT-6002	SLICER	215	100
HT-6004	FOOD PROCESSOR	600	450
HT-6005	JUICER	95	70

Figure 2-22. *Query in an inventory environment.* A stock clerk retrieves up-to-date information on a company's products at a CRT terminal. If the computer program driving this application is well designed, the user need only learn a few simple commands, like those shown, to query the computer system about the current status of any filed facts.

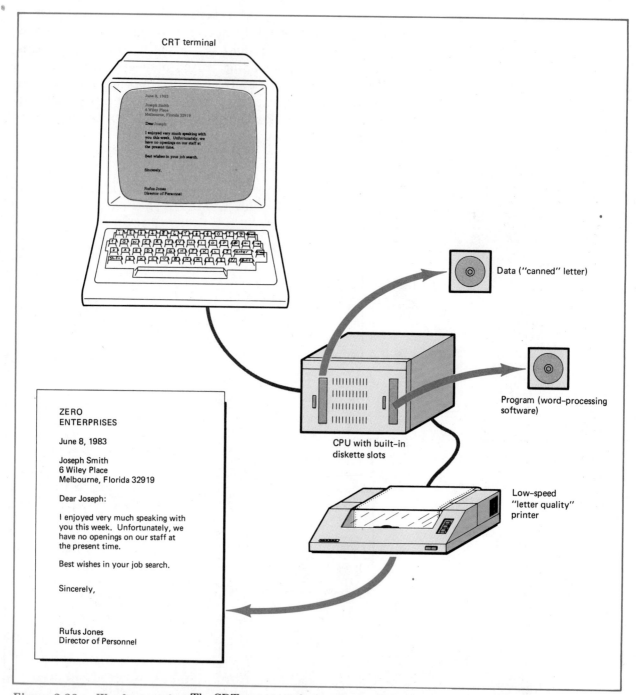

Figure 2-23. Word processing. The CRT operator asks for a "canned" letter from disk storage. All the information that remains the same from letter to letter is contained in the diskette file. All the information that is personalized for each letter is typed in by the operator at the CRT. The word-processing system then produces the letter on a special printer that yields results comparable to those of a standard electronic typewriter.

Word Processing. The term **word processing** refers to the preparation of documents with computer assistance. A common example is the composition of form ("canned") letters. This task may be done on special word-processing equipment or on general-purpose computer systems with word-processing software. An example of an application is given in Figure 2-23.

Summary and Key Terms

All computer systems consist of some combination of **computers** and **support equipment.** The most common types of support equipment are **input devices, output devices,** and **secondary storage devices.**

Input and output devices include *display terminals* (or CRTs), *card readers, low-speed printers,* and *high-speed printers.*

Secondary storage devices include *hard-disk units, diskette units, large tape units,* and *cassette tape units.* These devices use, respectively, *hard disks, floppy disks (diskettes), detachable tape reels,* and *cassette tapes* as their **input/output (I/O) media.**

If support equipment is capable of being plugged into the computer it is considered **peripheral equipment.** Otherwise, it's **auxiliary equipment.** Peripheral devices may be either **online** or **offline** to the CPU at any particular point in time. Auxiliary equipment, such as **data preparation devices,** is always offline.

Data is commonly organized into files, records, and fields. A **file** is a collection of records; a **record,** a collection of fields; and a **field,** a collection of individual characters (such as digits and letters of the alphabet).

Software falls into one of two categories: applications software and systems software. **Applications software** is the "computer work" most people have in mind when they buy a computer system. **Systems software** consists of support programs that keep the applications software running smoothly.

Seven common types of data processing are selection, summarizing, computation, sorting, updating, query processing, and word processing. **Selection** involves extracting from files only those fields or records which meet certain criteria. **Summarizing** involves reducing a mass of data to a manageable form. **Computation,** or performing arithmetic on data, is one of the most common data-processing operations. **Sorting** involves arranging data in some specified sequence, such as alphabetical order. **Updating,** which involves changing data in a file to reflect new information, can be done on a *batch* (periodic) or *online* (immediate) basis. **Query processing** enables users to extract information from data files. **Word processing** refers to the preparation of documents with computer assistance.

tomorrow

PLANNING FOR TOMORROW WITH COMPUTER SIMULATION

One very important way computers help us to plan for tomorrow is by simulation. Simulation involves modeling a process as a series of mathematical relationships, and testing the process under a variety of conditions before it is actually implemented. Since the computer can rapidly generate the thousands (or perhaps millions) of different conditions the process might encounter in the future when implemented, as well as record and summarize all of the important events that occur as a result of these conditions, it is a natural tool for conducting simulation studies. Processes such as operating nuclear reactors, using a new highway, or making a price change on a product can all be simulated on a computer today to help determine what their individual effects would be tomorrow. Because the computer modeling takes place *before* any actual building or decision making is done, computer simulations can help to avoid expensive mistakes or to identify new opportunities.

Oil companies often simulate the loading and unloading of ships at port areas to determine the best possible number of berths to build.

For example, suppose an oil company has room for anywhere between two and five berths on the waterfront of a certain refinery. Five berths, for example, cost more than two to build and maintain, but ships can be serviced much faster from five berths than from two. A ship that is rapidly serviced and turned out to sea will generate more revenue than one kept tied up waiting. Thus, there's a classic trade-off involved here, and a computer system can be used to test out each strategy to see which one is superior.

For example, you could command the computer system to first test out the strategy "build two berths." It might then simulate millions of days of operation of a two-berth facility, where ships are loaded and unloaded daily according to some mathematical relationships. For example, 30 percent of the time it might take 20 hours to load a ship, but only 15 hours 70 percent of the time. The computer system can be used to select a loading time for each ship serviced based on these frequencies. In a sense, it is almost as if the computer system flips a coin to determine which loading time to use, but the probabilities involved are 30–70 instead of 50–50. A similar procedure can be used for unloading. Also, the computer system can generate ships into the

Review Questions

1. Name some common types of computer support equipment and say whether each is used for input, output, storage, or some combination of these functions.

2. Name some common types of secondary storage devices and the I/O media each uses.

3. Create a small file of data. Can you identify the records and fields?

4. What is the difference between applications software and systems software?

5. Identify and define the seven types of data processing discussed in this chapter. Can you think of any other examples of data processing?

berthing facility at any frequencies requested by the researcher.

The computer program driving the simulation can also be used to keep an accounting of how long ships were in the berthing areas, what the berthing cost was for a ship, and other useful statistics. Since the computer can generate different patterns of ship arrivals and servicings at electronically fast speeds, the average daily cost of the strategy "build two berths" can be quickly determined.

The economics of other strategies are found in the same way. Thus the managers of the

The oil companies: Finding simulation a popular tool.

refinery can compare the costs and benefits of all the possible berthing strategies and use this information to help reach a final decision on the number of berths to build. The information the computer simulation provides is not, of course, the only information used to make a decision. The managers must also consider such information as what funds are available and the environmental impact of any of the strategies.

Simulation is also a very useful tool to scientists. For example, an ambitious project undertaken by MIT Professor Jay Forrester and several colleagues over the last twenty years has been to simulate what the world environment might look like in a number of years. Future scenarios are simulated from present trends and the possible consequences of policy decisions that affect the environment. Although the results of these studies have been controversial, they have shown that simulation can help avoid both global and local disasters. Scientists in fields as diverse as medicine, sociology, biology, chemistry, genetics, education, psychology, and engineering have turned to computer simulation as a tool to discover more about what their worlds may look like tomorrow based on certain events happening today.

Chapter 3

Computers Past and Present

OVERVIEW

It's natural for many of us to want to dismiss learning about our technological heritage. After all, it seems that many of the synthetic objects we see and use regularly—the television, automobile, airplane, and computer—have been around since time immemorial. But the history of a subject gives us insight into the way things are now. And the history of computers is especially significant because we're only in its earliest stages. Thus, as with any good book, reading the beginning whets our appetite for what comes next.

Electronic computers as we know them were invented fewer than fifty years ago. Since then, because the need for processing rapidly large volumes of paperwork has been so great, their rise to prominence has been spectacular. But the history of computers goes back much further than fifty years. Since the beginning of civilization, merchants and government officials have used computing devices to help them with calculations and record keeping. The abacus, invented thousands of years ago, is an example of such a device. We will begin our story, however, in the 1600s, with the invention of the first mechanical calculating machines.

In the first part of this chapter we will discuss the early advances that made possible today's electronic computer. In the rest of the chapter we will cover the development of commercial computer systems from the 1950s to the present.

FROM GEARS AND LEVERS TO WIRES AND TUBES

Pascal and Leibniz

Blaise Pascal, the French mathematician, is credited with the invention of the first **mechanical calculating machine** around 1642. Pascal got the inspiration for his invention when he was nineteen, after helping his father, a tax official, prepare reports for his superiors in Paris. Pascal and his father had to spend many hours poring over columns of figures and tediously adding them up. Pascal realized that this thankless chore could be done faster and more accurately by a machine. After much effort, he built one. This device—called the **pascaline** for its inventor—was run by levers and gears and could add and subtract automatically (see Figure 3-1).

Curiously, the pascaline never caught on. Clerks and book-keepers, fearing for their jobs, refused to use it.

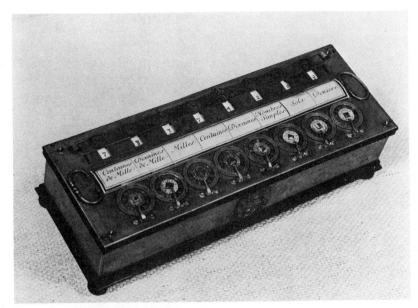

Figure 3-1.   Pascal's adding machine.

Later in the 1600s, Gottfried van Leibniz, the German philosopher and mathematician, went one step beyond Pascal and devised a machine that could multiply and divide as well as add and subtract. This device, like Pascal's, was also run by levers and gears.

Jacquard's Loom

One important event in the development of the computer might at first glance seem unrelated. In the early 1800s a weaver named Joseph Jacquard invented a loom that produced patterned cloth automatically. The remarkable thing about this loom was that it used punched cardboard cards to control the pattern in the cloth. A string of cards passed one by one over a group of rods. The rods were attached to the various colored threads used in the pattern. The holes in the cards determined which rods were engaged at any given time.

Jacquard's loom introduced two concepts important to the future development of the computer. One was that information could be coded on punched cards. Punched cards, as we'll see, were to become the main input/output medium for the first computers and are still used today. The second important concept was that the information stored in the cards could act as a series of instructions—in effect, a program—when the cards were strung together.

Babbage and His Engines

One of the most remarkable figures in the history of computers was the nineteenth-century English mathematician Charles Babbage. Babbage was a man ahead of his time. About 150 years ago he designed a machine that was amazing in its similarity to the first modern computers.

Babbage first became interested in mechanical computing devices while studying mathematical tables. He found that these tables had many errors in them, mistakes made by the clerks who calculated the numbers in the tables and mistakes made by the print-shop personnel who hand-set them into print. Babbage realized that a machine that could automatically calculate the numbers *and* print the results would produce much more reliable tables.

Babbage was able to get funds from the British government to build such a machine, which he called the **difference engine.** He succeeded in building a small prototype (Figure 3-2). His

Figure 3-2. Babbage's difference engine.

The First Programmer

Much of what we know about Charles Babbage's Analytical Engine comes not from Babbage himself, but from the work of his close friend and associate Ada Augusta, Countess of Lovelace, the daughter of the poet Byron. Ada showed remarkable intellectual abilities from an early age, and was especially talented in mathematics. She first met Babbage when she was still a child. On one early visit, she and a group of friends were shown Babbage's first creation, the Difference Engine. According to one observer, Ada was the only member of the group who "understood its workings and saw the great beauty of its invention."

In 1842, an Italian military engineer, L. F. Menabrea, published an article in French on the Analytical Engine. Lady Lovelace, then 27, translated this article into English. She supplemented the translation with notes of her own that ran twice the length of the article itself. These notes provide one of the best available explanations of the principles behind the Analytical Engine.

Ada Lovelace.

Charles Babbage.

Many of Lady Lovelace's insights into Babbage's work are relevant to modern computers. She has been called "the first programmer" because of her work on the kinds of instructions that would have to be fed into the Analytical Engine to make it work. And she was one of the first people to speculate on whether or not machines might in some sense be able to think. Commenting on just what the Analytical Engine could or could not do, for example, she observed

> The Analytical Engine has no pretensions whatever to *originate* anything. It can do whatever we *know how to order it* to perform. It can *follow* analysis; but it has no power of *anticipating* any analytical relations or truths. Its province is to assist us in making *available* what we are already acquainted with.

In other words, computers can only do what they're programmed to do.

attempts to build a larger version ended in failure, however, because the technology did not then exist to create the parts he needed.

While working on the difference engine, Babbage conceived of another, much more powerful machine, which he called the **analytical engine.** Like the difference engine, it was to consist of gears and shafts run by a steam engine. It is this machine that is so similar in concept to the modern computer. It was to be a general-purpose machine—capable of many kinds of computing work. It was to be directed by instructions on punched cards. It was to have an internal memory to store instructions and the intermediate results of calculations. And it would automatically print results.

Babbage became obsessed with the analytical engine and devoted all his energy and resources to creating it. People came to think of him as a misguided eccentric. He was never able to complete a working model, and he died without knowing how his vision was to shape the future.

Hollerith, the Census, and Punched Cards

Another milestone on the way to the modern computer was passed during the tabulation of the U.S. census of 1890. Until 1890, census figures had been tabulated manually. As the population of the United States expanded, however, and as the kind of information Congress wanted the census to provide grew more complex, it became clear that manual tabulation was too time-consuming. The census of 1880 took seven years to complete, and officials worried that if something weren't done, the results of the 1890 census would not be completed before it was time to begin the census of 1900.

The government commissioned a man named Herman Hollerith to build a machine to aid in the tabulation of the 1890 census. The machine Hollerith built (Figure 3-3) used punched cards and was powered by electricity. With its help, the results of the census were finished in three years.

Hollerith did not rest on his laurels. He founded the Tabulating Machine Company to develop punched-card equipment to sell to business and government. Hollerith's company merged with several others in 1911 to become the Computer-Tabulating-Recording Company. In 1924 this company changed its name to International Business Machines Corporation (IBM).

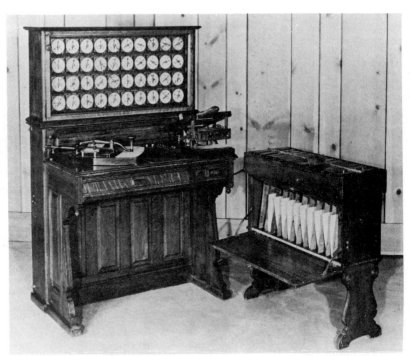

Figure 3-3. *Hollerith's census tabulator*

IBM rapidly became the leader in the manufacture of punched-card equipment, with an 80 percent market share by the mid-1930s. By this time, the mechanical machines of the nineteenth century had been replaced by *electro*mechanical devices such as the one pioneered by Hollerith. **Electromechanical machines** are, simply, mechanical machines driven by electricity. Although these devices were a vast improvement over their hand-cranked ancestors, they did have some serious drawbacks. Their moving parts took time to align themselves, for example, limiting their speed. Also, the repeated movement of those parts caused wear, making the machines prone to failure.

Aiken, IBM, and the Mark I

The age of electromechanical computing devices reached its zenith in the early 1940s with the work of Howard Aiken of Harvard University. Aiken had long been interested in developing ways to use electromechanical punched-card machines for scientific calculations. IBM and other manufacturers designed these machines with business users in mind, but during the late

Figure 3-4. *The Mark I computer.* The Mark I was built in IBM's Endicott, New York, plant and was subsequently donated to Harvard.

1920s and early 1930s, many scientists began to use them for their work also. Aiken had the important insight that the technology of these machines could be adapted to create a *general-purpose computer*—one that could be programmed to do a variety of computing tasks.

With the support of a $500,000 grant from IBM and the help of four of IBM's top engineers, Aiken started work on his machine in 1939. Its official name was "The Automatic Controlled Sequence Calculator," but it came to be called simply the **Mark I.** It was completed in 1944 and was gargantuan, as Figure 3-4 shows. It contained 500 miles of wire and 3 million electrical connections. It could do a multiplication in about six seconds and a division in about twelve seconds. When it was in operation its thousands of electromechanical relays made clicking sounds as they opened and closed.

After Aiken had already begun work on the Mark I he came across the writings of Babbage. He was astonished to see how many of his ideas Babbage had anticipated. The Mark I was, in a sense, the realization of the analytical engine.

Despite the success of the Mark I, Aiken and IBM never collaborated on another project. During the dedication ceremony for the machine at Harvard, Aiken apparently neglected to acknowledge the contribution of IBM and its supportive chairman, the venerable Thomas Watson. After the incident, Watson reportedly said, "I'm just sick about the whole thing."

The ABC

While Aiken and IBM were still at work on the Mark I, others were exploring the use of a new technology in computer design—electronics—that was to make the Mark I obsolete almost as soon as it was turned on. Computers with electronic components, unlike electromechanical machines, have no moving parts. The relays of a machine like the Mark I have to open and close physically. In **electronic machines** the main elements change from one state to another, depending on, for example, the presence or absence of current flowing through them. Because they have no moving parts, electronic machines are much faster than electromechanical machines.

The first person to design and build an electronic computing machine was John Atanasoff at Iowa State University. Atanasoff, in the late 1930s, wanted a machine that could help his graduate students with the tedious job of solving simultaneous linear equations. None of the machines available at the time met his needs, so he began to design his own.

In early 1939, Atanasoff received a $650 grant from Iowa State University. This sum was enough to buy the part-time services of a graduate student, Clifford Berry, and some materials. He and Berry built a machine they called the **ABC,** for **Atanasoff-Berry Computer** (Figure 3-5). The main electronic components in the ABC were 300 vacuum tubes. The machine could solve a set of twenty-nine simultaneous equations with twenty-nine variables.

The ABC was the first electronic digital computer. It was not, however, a large-scale general-purpose computer. It could

Figure 3-5. **The ABC.**

only do one job—solve limited types of mathematical problems. Nonetheless, it embodied many of the basic design features of the more powerful machines that followed it.

ENIAC

World War II created a sudden demand for computing power. The army, for example, had a pressing need for accurate tables that would tell gunners how to aim their weapons. These tables required vast numbers of arduous calculations. As a result, when J. Presper Eckert, an electrical engineer, and John Mauchly, a physicist, presented a proposal to the army for an electronic computer that could do these calculations in seconds, they received enthusiastic backing.

Eckert and Mauchly's computer, called **ENIAC** (*Elec*tronic *N*umerical *I*ntegrator *a*nd *C*alculator), was unveiled in 1946. It was the world's first large-scale, general-purpose electronic digital computer. As you can see in Figure 3-6, compared

Figure 3-6.   ENIAC.

Who Invented the Electronic Computer?

Who should get the credit for inventing the electronic digital computer, Dr. John Atanasoff, with the Atanasoff-Berry Computer, or Dr. J. Presper Eckert and Dr. John W. Mauchly with ENIAC? Until 1973, Eckert and Mauchly garnered most of the credit. In 1973, however, a federal judge ruled that Atanasoff was the principle inventor.

The issue came to the courts as a dispute over patents. In 1964, Sperry Rand, which had purchased the rights to Eckert and Mauchly's design, was granted a patent the two had applied for many years before. The patent was potentially worth a great deal of money in royalties from other companies. Another computer manufacturer, Honeywell, challenged the patent, claiming that Eckert and Mauchly had taken some of their most important ideas from Atanasoff.

Eckert had, in fact, travelled to Iowa in the early 1940s to see Atanasoff and the ABC. And he later wrote to Atanasoff to ask if he had any objections "to my building some sort of computer which incorporates some of the features of your machine?" These items, among others, con-

Dr. John Atanasoff.

vinced the judge presiding over the case to rule in favor of Atanasoff.

In spite of the ruling, many people still feel that Eckert and Mauchly deserve the credit they received. ENIAC, these people point out, was the first true large-scale *general-purpose* computer. It was a powerful machine that could be programmed to do a variety of complex computations. The ABC, in contrast, was little more than an experimental device that was limited to a single application.

Atansoff concedes that his machine was small and limited, but, he says, "That's not the point. I introduced seven or eight fundamental things for which other people have taken credit."

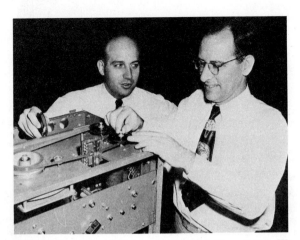

Dr. J. Presper Eckert (left) and Dr. John W. Mauchly.

to today's computers, it was enormous. It was 100 feet long, 10 feet high, and 3 feet deep. It contained 18,000 vacuum tubes and consumed 140 kilowatts of electricity when in operation.

Von Neumann and the Stored-Program Concept

ENIAC, though a major breakthrough, was still one step short of the computer as we know it today. Every time its operators wanted to do a new series of computations, they had to rewire it and reset switches, a process that could take several hours. John Von Neumann, a mathematician, conceived of a way around this shortcoming. He pointed out that a computer could be designed in which processing instructions could be fed in together with the data to be processed. Both the program and the data could be stored in the computer's memory. In such a **stored-program** computer, operators would only have to feed in a new set of instructions when they wanted the computer to execute a new program. They would not have to rewire the machine. With this stored-program concept, the idea of software and written programs was born.

The first stored-program computer, called **EDSAC** (*Electronic Delay Storage Automatic Calculator*) was completed in England in 1949. The second, **EDVAC** (*Electronic Discrete Variable Automatic Computer*), was completed in the United States in 1950. With these machines, the stage was set for the computer revolution and the explosive growth of the commercial computer industry.

THE COMPUTER AGE

Up until the early 1950s, electronic computers were exclusively the tool of scientists, engineers, and the military. The early machines had been built in military and academic settings with massive support from the government. None had yet served a role in commerce. With the success of the first machines, however, big business was ready to enter the field, both as a producer and user of computers.

The history of commercial computing is often separated into four distinct *generations*. What distinguishes each generation is the main electronic logic element in use at the time. The term *logic elements* refers to the electronic components used to facilitate the circuit functions within the computer. The four generations and their logic elements are as follows:

- First generation (1951–1958): vacuum tube
- Second generation (1959–1964): transistor
- Third generation (1965–1970): integrated circuit
- Fourth generation (1971–?): microminiaturized integrated circuit

Each new logic element led to improvements that made computers significantly faster, smaller, cheaper, more flexible, and capable of more storage than those of past generations. Computer people often refer to this trend as the "decreasing price/performance ratio." If the cost of other things had decreased as fast as that of computers has, you'd be able to pay for both an around-the-world trip and a Rolls Royce with a $5 bill . . . and receive change!

UNIVAC I: THE FIRST GENERATION BEGINS

The **first generation** and the era of commercial computing began in earnest in June 1951, when the U.S. Census Bureau purchased a computer called **UNIVAC I.** This machine was the brainchild of the pioneers of ENIAC, J. Presper Eckert and John Mauchly. Seeing the great commercial potential of computers, they had formed their own company. In order to secure operating capital, they became a subsidiary of Remington-Rand (currently known as the Sperry Corporation), which marketed the computer under its own name. The venture was a success, and the Computer Systems Division of Sperry Corporation is still alive and well.

The UNIVAC I differed from its predecessors in a very important respect. It was the first electronic computer manufactured by a business-machine company, specifically for commercial data-processing applications. A general-purpose machine was now available for payroll processing and other routine, labor-intensive accounting work. Figure 3-7 shows an early UNIVAC I.

Attributes of the First Generation

Vacuum Tubes.   The most important attribute of first-generation computers was the use of **vacuum tubes,** like those you

Figure 3-7.   UNIVAC I. This was the first machine used to tabulate returns in a U.S. presidential election. In 1952, it declared Dwight Eisenhower to be the victor over Adlai Stevenson only forty-five minutes after the polls closed. In this picture, Walter Cronkite, right, confers with J. Presper Eckert, one of the inventors of the UNIVAC. An unidentified operator sits at the console.

find in old radios and televisions, as the main logic element. Though tubes were a vast improvement over electromechanical parts, like those in the Mark I, they had many problems. They generated excessive heat; they were large; and they were prone to frequent failure. Because of the heat the tubes generated, first-generation computers had to be cooled by extensive air-conditioning units. And because the tubes were large, first-generation computers were colossal.

Punched-Card Orientation.   The punched card, used to process data since the 1800s, continued as the primary input/output medium for computer systems. Processing speeds for punched cards are atrociously slow compared with those of disk and tape, but these latter technologies did not mature until subsequent generations.

Magnetic Drum Internal Storage.   Many computers of the first generation used rotating magnetic drums for internal storage. Programs and data could be read from punched cards and stored on the drum, along with intermediate computations and final results. Because the drum contained moving parts, first-generation internal memories were much slower than those of later generations.

Limited Applications.   The typical commercial applications of the first generation were payroll, billing, and accounting. These applications were very easy to "cost justify." For example, if a computer system could do the work of twenty clerks, who each earned $5000 annually, a cost of $100,000 was a bargain. The system could pay back its purchase price in one year.

Programming in Machine and Assembly Languages.   The first programmers had to work in something called machine language. **Machine-language** instructions consist entirely of strings of 0s and 1s (called *bits*). Each 0 or 1 in an instruction activates or deactivates a circuit in the computer. A machine-language statement might look like this:

Binary → 0101100001110000000000001000000

Since a program might consist of hundreds of lines like this one, you can imagine that programming in machine language was difficult and that errors were frequent.

Fortunately, other languages have since become available to spare people the awesome task of machine-language programming. Dr. Grace Hopper at the University of Pennsylvania made the first breakthrough in 1952 when she produced an assembly language. **Assembly languages** made it possible to write instructions in a shorthand way. The assembly-language equivalent of the machine-language instruction you just read might be

```
L  REG7,A
```

"L," meaning "load," replaces "01011000" (the first eight bits); "REG7," meaning "storage register 7," replaces "0111" (the next four bits); and so forth. Assembly languages, by replacing numbers with understandable symbols, made it much easier for experienced programmers to code instructions. Assembly-language programming, however, is still tedious and is usually only done by programming experts.

THE SECOND GENERATION (1959–1964): THE TRANSISTOR

In **second-generation** computers, **transistors** replaced vacuum tubes as the main logic element. Transistors perform the same function as tubes, but they are faster, smaller, and more reliable. They also generate less heat and require less power

Figure 3-8. *A second-generation computer system.* Note the size difference between this machine and earlier computers, such as the Mark I, ENIAC, and UNIVAC I.

than tubes. As a result, second-generation computers were faster, smaller, more reliable, and cheaper to operate than first-generation computers. A second-generation computer system is shown in Figure 3-8.

Attributes of the Second Generation

The transistor was only one of several improvements in the second generation. Other noteworthy developments included the rise of magnetic tape and disk, magnetic-core internal storage, modular hardware design, and high-level programming languages.

Tape and Disk Secondary Storage. Although the potential of magnetic tape as a storage medium had been known in the first generation, it was not until the second generation that tape technology developed enough to make it competitive with punched cards. Not only is magnetic tape a fast input/output medium (over fifty times the speed of punched cards), but it also packs a lot of data into very little space. For example, a single reel of magnetic tape small enough to hold in your hand can store the contents of an 80-foot stack of punched cards.

Disk storage was also introduced during the second generation, although its full potential was not realized until a generation later. The advantage of disk over tape is that it allows direct access to data, making input and output much faster for many applications. There are some commercial applications that couldn't exist today, in the form we've grown used to, if disk processing weren't available. Making airline reservations, which involves millions of transactions daily, is one of them. Processing speeds are critical in such high-volume applications in which people need information quickly.

Magnetic-Core Internal Storage. Small, doughnut-shaped **magnetic cores,** which were strung on racks within the computer, began to replace magnetic drums as internal memory devices on many second-generation machines. Core planes (see Figure 3-9) offered much faster storage access speeds than first-generation drums. They have no moving parts, so they are not subject to the time-consuming rotation required of mechanically driven drums.

Figure 3-9. Magnetic core internal memory. Notice how the cores are wired into planes. The planes are tiered on top of each other to form the internal memory unit. The inset shows magnetic cores compared to a paper clip.

Modular Hardware Elements.   A big headache with early computers was maintenance. When components failed, they had to be replaced individually, which was very time-consuming. Manufacturers countered this problem in the second generation by introducing modular design. In *modular* design, related components are grouped together onto portable boards. If a component on a board fails, the entire board is replaced. Although this might seem wasteful, modular design makes it easier to diagnose and correct malfunctions. It also saves costs by reducing maintenance time.

High-Level Languages for Programming.   Software and programming took an important step forward during the second generation with the emergence of **high-level programming languages.** In machine and assembly languages, the programmer has to spell out every step the computer must take in an operation. Getting the computer to add two numbers, for example, might take three separate instructions. In high-level languages, a single simple statement like

$$A = B + C$$

might accomplish the same result.

Another important feature of high-level languages is that they use simple words and mathematical expressions. As a result, they are less intimidating and easier to learn and use than machine and assembly languages.

Among the first high-level languages were *FORTRAN* (*FOR*mula *TRAN*slation) and *COBOL* (*CO*mmon *B*usiness *O*riented *L*anguage). FORTRAN, developed at IBM, was designed for scientific applications. COBOL, developed with support from the government, was designed for business use. Both of these languages are still widely used today.

As high-level languages gained in popularity, users often found that programs they had written for one computer system wouldn't work on equipment made by another manufacturer. This was because manufacturers developed radically different versions of the same language. Often, when a company changed from one kind of equipment to another, it had to completely rewrite all its programs. As a result, the American National Standards Institute (ANSI) began to establish rules to standardize the more popular languages. This made it possible to write programs on one machine, which with a few minor alterations, could run on another.

THE THIRD GENERATION (1965–1970): THE FAMILY CONCEPT AND THE INTEGRATED CIRCUIT

In mid-1964, IBM made one of the most important product announcements in the history of computers. It had designed a *family* of six upward-compatible computers, the System/360 line. A machine at the "high end" of the line (such as the 360/Model 195) would be bigger and more powerful than one at the "low end" of the line (such as the 360/Model 44). *Upward compatibility* meant that programs written for a low-end machine would work on a larger machine in the series. A company that found itself with growing processing needs and a low-end machine could buy a larger machine in the series without having to redo its applications software. Up until the time of the System/360, conversion from one computer to another normally was quite a headache, requiring massive amounts of reprogramming and staff retraining. A member of the 360 family is shown in Figure 3-10.

Figure 3-10. The IBM System/360.

The System/360 featured, as its main logic element, a device called an **integrated circuit (IC)**. The IC, which replaced the second-generation transistor, consists of thousands of small circuits etched onto a small silicon chip. These chips are so tiny that several of them can fit into a thimble. An IC is compared with the logic devices of earlier generations in figure 3-11.

The 360 family was also accompanied by an array of approximately forty new peripheral devices, which enhanced the strength of the family concept. Having six computers and forty peripherals to choose from, customers could tailor systems exactly to their needs.

Ever since IBM introduced the System/360, the family concept has become widespread in the computer industry. Sperry followed IBM's lead with the Univac 1100 series. Digital Equipment Corporation introduced the DECsystem 10 series. And all other major manufacturers eventually followed suit. IBM itself followed up on the System/360 with the System/370,

Rich and Famous: How IBM Made the Grade

An interesting tale from the computer past is the IBM success story. Since 1956, IBM (the International Business Machines Corporation) has been the world sales leader in the computer industry, with a market share recently of 60 to 70 percent. This position of competitive strength is unparalleled in modern business history. It is especially remarkable when you consider that IBM was a late starter in the computer business, following the lead of Remington Rand.

In the early 1950s, IBM was the leader in the sale of electromechanical punched-card office machines. The company's managers had realized for some time, however, that electronic computers would soon make many of their existing products obsolete. It was either "go computers" or "go out of business."

Two things helped IBM come from behind and grab the lead. First, the company had built a large, loyal customer base with its punched-card equipment. It thus had firmly established distribution channels that it could use for selling computer products.

Second, and probably most important, IBM stressed the marketing of its products from the outset. The competition simply sold hardware. IBM's philosophy, in contrast, was to "sell solutions, not just machines." This strategy proved enormously successful. Most potential computer buyers in the 1950s were intimidated by these weird new electronic "brains," and for good reason. The machines were very temperamental. Storms frequently knocked out power. Tubes were always blowing, and circuits would become disconnected. Without good service, most user organizations couldn't possibly keep the machines running. What's more, most people hadn't the foggiest notion how to use the machines for the solution of their business problems.

To sell computers to organizations that weren't sure what to do with them, IBM developed a user-oriented approach. The IBM sales force was extremely successful in placing computers where they were really needed. And once a machine was in place, IBM provided strong,

Figure 3-11.   *Main logic components of the first three generations.*

continuing support. An IBM contact was always available to help if a problem arose. And IBM made sure that the people who dealt with customers understood their needs. The competition, in contrast, was technically oriented, and often sent engineers to try to deal with customers who had business and accounting backgrounds. The result was often poor communication between the customer and the engineer. Although the competition had products that might have been technologically better, IBM moved quickly into first place.

Although IBM was the sales leader in computers by the mid-1950s, it was not then regarded as a pacesetter in scientific research. Its strengths were primarily in the marketing and assembling of computers rather than in advanced computer design. IBM's management realized this deficiency early, and began a series of research programs that gained the company recognition as a leader in electronics, mathematics, and physics. The result of this initial thrust into research was the fantastically expensive System/360 project, an enormously risky venture that might have resulted in IBM's bankruptcy had it failed. Fortunately for IBM, this new computer system was highly successful, thrusting the company into the commanding industry lead it has yet to relinquish, and establishing its reputation for innovations.

IBM equipment delivery, circa 1930.

a family of over twenty computers that were upward-compatible with the System/360. The buzzword in the computer industry was quickly becoming "migration path," which meant designing computers so that customers could (and would) "migrate" naturally to a more powerful and more expensive computer in one's product line as their processing needs expanded. With the family concept, users began to feel that they had a solution to the massive conversion problems they had encountered in the transition from the first to the second generation and, later, from the second to the third.

The System/360 was immensely successful for IBM. Over 30,000 systems were sold. But the decision to produce it was a tremendous financial risk. IBM spent $5 billion in development costs, an unheard-of amount in that day. If sales had been poor, IBM probably would have failed. However, not only did it catapult IBM into the commanding industry lead it has yet to relinquish, it also upped the stakes of being in the business of making mainframes. A company could no longer hope to be a factor in the industry with only a single, inflexible machine. Customers now expected multiple equipment options and a migration path. In the following years, industrial giants like GE, RCA, and Xerox, which had made computers a sideline business, bowed out of the mainframe manufacturing side of the industry. It had simply become too expensive.

Attributes of the Third Generation

Besides the integrated circuit and family concept, there are several other noteworthy developments that characterize the **third generation.** Perhaps the most important of these are the operating system, continued improvements in software, and the minicomputer.

Operating Systems.   An **operating system,** which Chapter 8 covers in detail, is a set of control programs that supervise the work of the computer system. First- and second-generation computers did not use operating systems. Programs were entered one by one and monitored individually by the computer operator. Also, automatic communication between the CPU and devices such as the printer was not then possible. They had to be coordinated manually. With operating systems, these tasks are accomplished automatically under program control.

Also, computers in the first and second generations were serial processors. That is, a computer would do all its work in a one-program-at-a-time fashion. For example, job 1 would be started and completed, then job 2 would be processed, and so forth. Sophisticated operating systems enable computer systems to work on several programs at the same time and to divide the work on each program into small, manageable pieces. The operating system, for example, might instruct the computer to do computations on one program while awaiting disk input from another. Because the work on programs is divided into pieces, the computer can work in a round-robin fashion on several programs. As a result, a user with a long program can't tie up the entire system.

Improvements in Software. The development of new high-level languages flourished in the third generation. Each new language was created in response to the needs of an important market of users. *BASIC* (*B*eginners *A*ll-purpose *S*ymbolic *I*nstruction *C*ode), for example, was developed in response to the need for a language that was easy to learn and use. It is still one of the most popular languages. Not only is it used extensively to introduce people to computer programming, but it has also evolved as the most popular language for microcomputers.

The development of *RPG* (*R*eport *P*rogram *G*enerator) in the mid-1960s signaled a new trend in programming languages. With RPG, a user or programmer merely declares to the computer system what a report is to look like, not how to produce it. Once given the output format, the computer system automatically generates its own computer program to produce the report. These "program generator" languages have proven to be incredibly time-saving, and companies have made extensive use of them.

An additional boost to the quality of software came in 1969, when IBM decided to "unbundle" pricing on software and hardware. Roughly translated, this meant that an organization would be billed separately for hardware and software. Purchasers of IBM equipment were no longer locked into buying their programs from IBM. Almost immediately, dozens of companies went into the business of designing better and cheaper software for IBM machines, which dominated the marketplace. Many succeeded, and the software industry soon became a big business. Over the years this industry has expanded so that it now provides software for many other computer products, not just IBM equipment.

Time-Sharing and Minicomputers. In the mid-1960s many industry experts, looking at the growing demand for computing

Figure 3-12.   DEC PDP-8 mini-computer.

services from organizations that could not afford a mainframe, predicted that time-sharing would be the wave of the future. In *time-sharing* several users simultaneously share the resources of a single, large, centralized computer. The users have their own terminals that are connected to the central computer. The experts expected that soon there would be many large time-shared computers in every major city and that small businesses and individuals by the boatload would hook up to them. A company owning a time-shared computer would be a "utility," just like the phone company. Clients would be billed for the resources they used.

Companies providing time-sharing services did, in fact, flourish in the late 1960s, and many are still in existence, but by the early 1970s they were on the wane. The cause of the reversal was a relatively new "kid on the block" named Digital Equipment Corporation (DEC). In the late 1960s, DEC had introduced a machine called a *minicomputer,* a scaled-down version of the larger computers of the day (see Figure 3-12). Miniaturization in logic and storage technology had made this innovation possible. Minicomputers are less powerful than mainframes, but they are also much less expensive. After DEC's success, other companies soon started to manufacture minis.

The early minicomputers were short on software and vendor service. Also, they were designed mostly for scientific and engineering uses. It wasn't long, however, before minicomputer makers saw that the small business market was a gold mine and packaged their machines accordingly.

By the early 1970s, many small businesses started buying minicomputers and turning away from time-sharing services. The reasons were clear. A company with its own computer no longer had to put up with the uncertainties, delays, and loss of control it experienced with someone else's computer. Even big companies were snapping up these new machines. They realized they could distribute some of the work previously done by a central computer at headquarters to minicomputers located at the divisional level.

THE FOURTH GENERATION (1971–?): THE ERA OF THE USER

The transition from the third to the **fourth generation** is either subtle or great, depending on your frame of reference. It's subtle in that the main logic element of the third generation, the integrated circuit, is still the main logic element of the fourth.

Although integrated circuits are much smaller, faster, and cheaper now, improvements in price and performance from the third to the fourth generation are not anywhere near as dramatic as those experienced earlier. The great difference between the fourth and the third generation, however, is that the fourth generation has seen an unprecedented growth in computer use. Indeed, the fourth generation has emerged as the era of the user.

Attributes of the Fourth Generation

Many developments characterize the fourth generation, which is still very much in progress. These include microminiaturization, semiconductor internal memory, database management systems, and user-friendly languages.

Microminiaturization. The technological hallmark of the fourth generation is **microminiaturization.** Over the years, more and more circuits have been packed into less and less space, and integrated circuits have become ever smaller. The terms *large-scale integration (LSI)* and *very large-scale integration (VLSI)* refer to this process. A single silicon chip can now contain tens of thousands of circuits. The result is computer systems that are both smaller and more powerful than their predecessors.

Microminiaturization has made possible one of the most important innovations of the fourth generation—the microprocessor. A *microprocessor* is a single silicon chip upon whose surface is etched the circuitry of an entire computer. These "computers-on-a-chip" have put processing power into watches, toys, delicatessen scales, and automobiles. Microprocessors have also made possible a new breed of computers—*microcomputers* (also called *personal computers* and *home computers*)—which are now placing computing power at the fingertips of almost everyone. Today you can walk into a store and buy a hand-held computer (Figure 3-13) for less than $200 or a complete system for a few thousand.

The microprocessor was developed by Intel Corporation in 1971, at the request of a Japanese company. Today, Japan is a leading producer of microcomponents. The microprocessor industry is currently estimated to be worth almost $10 billion, with about 250,000 employees worldwide.

Some of the marvels of the age of microminiaturization are observable in Window 3, which follows page 108.

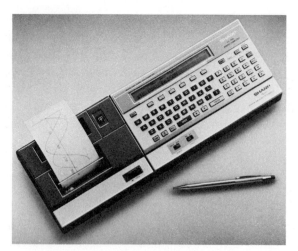

Figure 3-13.   A pocket computer.

Figure 3-14.   Semiconductor memory chip.

Semiconductor Internal Memory.   Core memory gave way to MOS (metal oxide semiconductor) memory slowly over the course of the third generation. This newer memory proved to be faster and smaller, but the cost was initially higher. As more and more semiconductor memories were produced, however, the cost dropped. Today, core storage is rapidly becoming a ghost of the past.

Semiconductor memories are similar to integrated circuits in that the memory is etched onto a small silicon chip. A semiconductor memory chip is shown in Figure 3-14.

One disadvantage of semiconductor memory is that it's *volatile*—that is, when the power is shut off, the semiconductor chips lose their stored contents. Core memory (as well as magnetic tape and disk), on the other hand, is *nonvolatile.*

Database Management Systems.   A *database* is an integrated collection of related data—airline flight schedules and fares, for example. Often, related data exist in scores of different computer files, making it difficult for users to pull together the information they need. A *database management system (DBMS)* is a collection of software and hardware that helps systematize such data, making processing easier.

DBMSs have evolved largely because of the mushrooming, unanticipated growth of computers in large organizations. Some companies, which may have had ten programs and a few files in 1955, have found themselves with perhaps a quarter of a million programs and billions of computerized facts today. This kind of

tomorrow

THE FIFTH GENERATION: WILL THE UNITED STATES KEEP ITS LEAD IN COMPUTER TECHNOLOGY?

Since World War II, the United States has been the world leader in computer technology and in the manufacture and sale of computer hardware and software. According to some industry observers, however, Japan may overtake the United States in the 1990s. Other observers disagree, pointing out that Japanese products at the moment account for less than 5 percent of the computer market outside of Japan. Until recently, the Japanese have not attempted to break new technological ground.

Most observers do agree that Japan is an emerging force in computers. It is already the leading producer of industrial robots, and is highly competitive with the United States in the sale of computer chips, semiconductor memories, and certain types of peripheral equipment. If it does take the lead, two factors will play an important role—efficient manufacturing and government-backed research.

The Japanese excel at manufacturing. Their factories are among the most automated in the world. And a number of unusual labor practices—including lifetime employment and efforts to involve workers actively in the production process—have created an efficient and highly motivated workforce. The results so far, as U.S. automakers have found to their chagrin, are extremely competitive products.

In late 1981, the Japanese government and the computer industry conducted a widely publicized and well-attended conference on "Fifth-Generation Computing." The key to the fifth generation, as the Japanese see it, is artificial intelligence (AI), and Japan has announced its firm commitment to be a leader in AI technologies. Artificial intelligence research involves the development of machines that can deduce, infer, and learn—in other words, machines that can figure out how to solve problems on their own. A computer system with AI, for example, might be able to communicate verbally with a person about a problem until the system came up with a solution. All this would take place in the person's native language. The computer's "intelligence," of course, would be in the form of a program for making deductions about a problem the way people do. If AI were combined with robot technology, it might be possible to create a robot that looked and acted like a human being.

The practical barriers to these developments are great, and many have been quick to scoff at the Japanese fifth-generation project. The British and French, however, have expressed an interest in collaborating with the Japanese on their efforts. Even if they only partially fulfill their dream of producing human-like computers, the results could have an enormous effect on the industry. A computer that could just understand natural language commands spoken by a user, for example, would be a giant step forward. Such a development would make almost all existing "user-friendly" software obsolete.

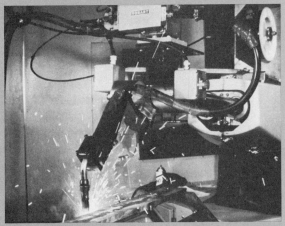

Robots: How smart will they get in the fifth generation?

growth has made necessary the kind of systematic organization a DBMS offers.

User-Friendly Languages. Many people are intimidated by computers, and especially by programming languages. Yet computers are here to stay, and people who never expected to use these machines are coming face to face with them. To cushion the shock, software producers are constantly attempting to make programming languages easier to use.

A number of software vendors, over the last several years, have developed so-called *user-friendly languages*. These languages are much more powerful and easier (i.e., "friendlier") to use than BASIC, FORTRAN, COBOL, and other high-level languages. However, they are generally tied into specific applications and are not very flexible. For example, an airline clerk might type in a command as simple as

```
LIST/LAX-SFO/010884
```

to get a listing of all flights from Los Angeles to San Francisco on January 8, 1984. However, a language supporting "airlinese" commands would probably not allow a clerk to calculate the rate of return on a bank account. Despite its inherent specificity, user-friendly software is expected to increase the base of computer users substantially by the turn of the next century. Perhaps, after that, we will have created computer systems to understand even the most garbled human voice, thereby laying programming language syntax to rest with the vacuum tube, electromechanical relay, and Babbage's difference engine.

Summary and Key Terms

The world's oldest computing device, the abacus, dates back thousands of years. The first **mechanical calculating machine,** the **pascaline,** was developed by Blaise Pascal in the early 1600s. This device could only add and subtract. Later in the 1600s, Gottfried van Leibniz devised a calculator that could also multiply and divide.

The weaver Joseph Jacquard invented an automated loom in the early 1800s that introduced two concepts important to the development of the computer—data could be recorded on punched cards, and a sequence of cards could act as a program.

The first computing device bearing a resemblance to today's computers was proposed by Charles Babbage in the 1800s. He initially conceived a machine called the **difference engine,** which would both compute and print results. Later, he developed a more ambitious machine called the **analytical engine,** which embodied the principles of input, processing, output, and storage found in today's modern computers. Unfortunately, Babbage died without seeing either machine completed.

The first **electromechanical machine** to perform computing was built by Herman Hollerith to aid in the tabulation of the 1890s census. Hollerith went on to become a pioneer in the development of business-oriented electromechanical tabulating machines.

Howard Aiken, with the help of IBM, designed and built the first large-scale, general-purpose electromechanical computer. It was completed in 1944 and called the **Mark I.**

While Aiken was constructing his machine, John Atanasoff was at work in the Midwest with a technology that would make the Mark I obsolete almost as soon as it was completed. With the assistance of Clifford Berry, Atanasoff created the **Atanasoff-Berry Computer (ABC),** the first **electronic machine** to do computing. A few years later, in 1946, J. Presper Eckert and John Mauchly created the world's first large-scale, general-purpose electronic digital computer, the **ENIAC.** Later in the 1940s, mathematician John Von Neumann developed the concept of **stored programs.** This concept was originally implemented on two computers, the **EDSAC** and **EDVAC.**

The era of commercial computing, which began when the **UNIVAC I** computer was completed and delivered to the U.S. Census Bureau in 1951, is commonly divided into four distinct generations.

First-generation (1951–1958) computers used **vacuum tubes** as the main logic element. They also relied heavily on the use of punched cards and magnetic-drum internal storage. Programs were written in either **machine language** or (later) **assembly language.** Most first-generation commercial computers were limited to accounting-type applications, because these were relatively easy to "justify" in terms of costs.

In **second-generation** (1959–1964) computers **transistors** replaced vacuum tubes as the main logic element. Other noteworthy developments included the rise of magnetic tapes and disks for secondary storage, **magnetic-core** internal storage, modular hardware design, and **high-level programming languages** (such as FORTRAN and COBOL).

In **third-generation** (1965–1970) computers, **integrated circuits (ICs)** replaced transistors as the main logic element. Other major developments were the family concept of computers, **operating systems,** improvements in application language software (such as BASIC and RPG), and minicomputers.

Three terms sum up the **fourth generation** (1971 to present): "small," "smaller," and "even smaller." It is a period of **microminiaturization,** characterized by microprocessors (computers-on-a-chip) and **semiconductor memories** (memories-on-a-chip). Microminiaturization has lowered the cost of computing to a level that has made computers widely available. Thus, the fourth generation has emerged as the era of the user. *Database management systems (DBMSs)* have evolved that make it easy for users to pull together related information that before may have been kept in scores of different computer files. *User-friendly languages* are being developed to meet the needs of the growing body of users who are not programming experts.

Review Questions

1. Discuss the contribution of the following people to the early development of computers: Blaise Pascal, Gottfried van Leibniz, Joseph Jacquard, Charles Babbage, and Herman Hollerith.
2. Explain the major differences among the following early computers: Mark I, ABC, ENIAC, EDSAC, and UNIVAC I.
3. Identify the major technological development associated with each of the four generations of commercial computing.
4. Every important technological development in computers has occurred in response to some critical problem. Identify what problem each of the following developments attempted to solve: assembly languages, operating systems, high-level programming languages, tape and disk secondary storage, and database management systems.
5. What was the significance of the "family concept" of computers?

6. Why did minicomputers become so popular in the early 1970s? Why are microcomputers becoming so popular today?

7. Name three major trends that have existed throughout the evolution of computers.

Suggested Readings

Bernstein, Jeremy. *The Analytical Engine: Computers—Past, Present, and Future.* New York: Morrow, 1981.

Evans, Christopher. *The Micro Millenium.* New York: Viking, 1980.

Goldstine, H. H. *The Computer from Pascal to von Neumann.* Princeton, N.J.: Princeton University Press, 1980.

Metropolis, N., et al. (eds.). *A History of Computing in the 20th Century.* New York: Academic, 1980.

Module B

HARDWARE

When most people think of computers or computer systems today it is the hardware that readily comes to mind. These are the exciting pieces of equipment that are delivered in crates or boxes when you buy a computer system. As you'll find out in this module, there's a rich variety of computer hardware available in today's marketplace. But as you'll learn later in this book, the hardware needs a guiding force—software—to be of any use. Hardware without software is like a human being without the ability to reason and manipulate thoughts.

The hardware in this module is divided into four areas. Chapter 4 describes the role of the CPU—the computer itself. Chapter 5 discusses the hardware that provides an indispensible library of resources for the CPU—secondary storage devices. Chapter 6 delves into input and output devices. Module B closes, in Chapter 7, with a discussion of telecommunications hardware, which makes it possible to transmit data and programs between the hardware devices covered in Chapters 4, 5, and 6.

Chapter 4

The Central Processing Unit (CPU)

OVERVIEW

So far, we've considered the central processing unit to be a mysterious "black box," a machine that somehow processes programs with their data and, following the instructions laid out in the program, produces results. In this chapter, we'll take a look inside the CPU. First we'll see how it is organized and how it carries out its tasks. Then we'll discuss the way data and programs are represented inside it. We'll talk about the codes that have been developed for translating back and forth from symbols the CPU understands to symbols people understand. Finally, we'll discuss certain kinds of devices that make it possible to build some software functions directly into hardware.

HOW THE CPU WORKS

Every CPU is, basically, a collection of electronic circuits. Electronic impulses come into the CPU from an input device. Within the CPU, these impulses are sent under program control through circuits to create a series of new impulses. Eventually, a set of impulses leaves the CPU, headed for an output device. What happens in those circuits? To begin to understand this process, we need to know first how the CPU is organized—what its parts are—and then how electronic impulses move from one part to another to process data.

The Three Sections of the CPU

The CPU has three major sections: primary memory, an arithmetic/logic unit (ALU), and a control unit.

Primary memory (also called **main memory** and **internal storage**) is the section of the CPU that holds

- The programs and data that have been entered into the computer
- Intermediate processing results
- Output that is ready to be transmitted to secondary storage or to an output device

Once programs, data, intermediate results, and output are stored in primary memory, the CPU has to be able to find them again. Thus each location in primary memory has an address. In many computers, a single address will store a single character of data. The size of primary memory varies from computer to computer. The smallest computers have a memory capacity of only a few thousand characters. The largest have a capacity of many million. Whenever an item of data, an instruction, or the result of a calculation is stored in memory, it is assigned an address so the CPU can locate it again when it is needed.

Primary memory is relatively expensive and limited in size. For this reason it can only be used temporarily. Once the computer has finished processing one program and set of data, another is written over them in the storage space they occupy. Thus the contents of each storage location are constantly changing. The address of each location, however, never changes. This process can be compared to what happens to the mailboxes

Digital and Analog Computers

When most of us chat about computers today, we are referring to *digital computers*. Digital computers are the ones that help run businesses, sit on desk tops in homes, and perform most of the tasks we generally think of as "computer work." In fact, digital computers are really what this book is about. There is, however, another relatively common type of computer—the *analog computer*.

These two types of computers can be distinguished rather easily: digital devices *count,* and analog devices *measure.* Counting and measuring, which are the most basic types of computation, were with us long before computers existed. When we observe that there are fifteen people in a room, for example, we are counting. Entities that exist as *discrete* phenomena—such as people, books, and dollars—are capable of being counted. When we estimate that there are 10 gallons of fuel in a gas tank, on the other hand, we are measuring. There may actually be 10.0001, 9.872, or some other quantity of fuel. Entities that exist as *continuous* phenomena—such as speed, height, and length—are capable

only of being measured, because they don't exist naturally as indivisible units.

The modern digital computers in use today do all their processing by representing programs and data as strings of 0s and 1s. This two-state, or binary, representation is natural for electronic machines, since electronic components are generally designed to operate in two discrete states. For example, current along a wire runs in one of two directions, an electronic circuit is either "open" or "closed," a magnetic field is either "present" or "not present." Digital computers perform computations at very rapid rates when data are represented in this two-state form.

Analog computers, by contrast, measure continuous phenomena and convert them into numbers. For example, a gasoline pump contains an analog computer to measure the amount of gas pumped and to convert it into gallon and price amounts that appear on the pump's register. A car has an analog computer to measure drive shaft rotation and to convert it into a speedometer reading. Oil refineries use analog computers to measure pressure and temperature.

in a post office. The number on each box remains the same, but the contents change as patrons remove their mail and as new mail arrives.

The **arithmetic/logic unit (ALU)** is the section of the CPU that does arithmetic and logical operations on data. *Arithmetic* operations include tasks like addition, subtraction, multiplication, and division. *Logical* operations involve the comparison of two items of data to determine if they are equal, and if not, which is larger. As we'll see, all data coming into the CPU—including nonnumeric data like letters of the alphabet— are coded in digital (numeric) form. As a result, the ALU can perform logical operations on letters and words as well as on numbers.

Such basic arithmetic and logical operations are the only ones the computer can perform. That might not seem very impressive. Yet when combined in various ways at great speeds, these operations enable computers to perform immensely complex tasks.

The **control unit** is the section of the CPU that directs the flow of electronic traffic between primary memory and the ALU and between the CPU and input and output devices. In other words, it is the mechanism that coordinates the operation of the computer. Figure 4-1 shows the three parts of the CPU.

Registers

To enhance the effectiveness of the control unit and ALU, the CPU also contains special storage locations that act as high-speed staging areas. These areas are called **registers,** and they're not considered part of primary storage. The contents of the registers can be located and retrieved much more rapidly than can the contents of primary memory, so program instructions and data are normally loaded into the registers from primary memory just before processing. These devices, which are supervised by the control unit, play a crucial role in making computer speeds extremely fast.

There are several types of registers, including those listed here:

- **Instruction register and address register** Before each instruction in a program is processed, the control unit breaks it into two parts. The part that indicates what the ALU is to do next (for example, add, multiply, compare), is placed in the **instruction register.** The part that gives the

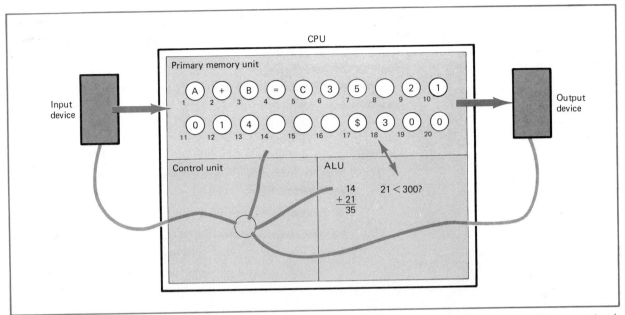

Figure 4-1. *The three sections of the CPU.* Primary memory temporarily stores any program the computer is currently working on as well as its input data, intermediate computations, and output. Each location in the memory has an address, and often, a single address can store a single character. Although only twenty locations are shown, primary memories typically contain from a few thousand addresses to several million. All "figuring" done by the computer is accomplished in the arithmetic/logic unit (ALU). Data are transferred between primary memory and the ALU under supervision of the control unit.

address of the data to be used in the operation is placed in the **address register.**

- **Storage register** The **storage register** temporarily stores data that have been retrieved from primary memory prior to processing.
- **Accumulator** The **accumulator** temporarily stores the results of ongoing arithmetic operations. As each operation takes place, results such as totals are "accumulated" into this register.

The instruction and address registers are often located in the control unit, and the storage register and accumulator are often in the ALU.

Machine Cycles

Now that we've discussed the three parts of the CPU and the function of registers, let's see how these elements work together to process an instruction. The processing of a single instruction is called a **machine cycle.** A machine cycle has two parts: an instruction cycle (I-cycle) and an execution cycle (E-cycle). During the **I-cycle,** the control unit fetches an instruction from main memory and prepares for subsequent processing. During the **E-cycle,** the data are located, the instruction is executed, and the results are stored in the accumulator. Let's see how this works in a little more detail.

I-cycle:

1. The control unit fetches from main memory the next instruction to be executed.
2. The control unit decodes the instruction.
3. The control unit puts the part of the instruction showing what to do into the instruction register.

tomorrow

TOMORROW'S CHIPS

Will computing speeds ever approximate the speed of light? Today's scientists are exploring ways to make such a possibility a reality for tomorrow. Although many of us think computers are fast enough in their present form, a great demand exists for speedier machines. If we are ever to have computer systems that think and act like humans, the computer must be able to process data several orders of magnitude faster than currently possible. One of the many solutions that have been proposed to making computers faster is faster chips.

Today, the majority of computers employ silicon-based chips. Thousands of tiny circuits are packed on a chip that is about a quarter of an inch square. The average number of components placed on a chip has doubled every year since the mid1960s. But the smaller and faster chips become, the greater the heat and electrical interference they generate. Many scientists and researchers think these factors may limit further advances in silicon-based chips. Although most knowledgeable observers feel that silicon will remain a strong force in the production of chips for many years to come, there are some newer technologies on the horizon that may offer greater promise.

One of the most widely discussed alternatives to silicon involves *cryogenics,* the field of study that deals with extremely low temperatures. When circuits are cooled to temperatures near absolute zero, they lose much of their resistance, enabling a faster flow of electricity. The cooling process is accomplished by immersing the circuits in a very cold liquid bath. The *Josephson junction,* a device introduced in 1962 by British Nobel Prize winner Brian Josephson, uses liquid helium as the coolant. The "junction" is actually a superconducting switch that enables computers to change from a 0-state to a 1-state many times faster than silicon-based devices currently available in the marketplace. Some industry observers predict that when this technology becomes commercially feasible, possibly sometime in the early 1990s, it may make possible computers that have internal switching speeds 100 times faster than today's most powerful mainframes.

A second possible technology for tomor-

4. The control unit puts the part of the instruction showing where the associated data are located into the address register.

E-cycle:

5. The control unit, using the information in the address register, retrieves data from main memory and places them into the storage register within the ALU.
6. The control unit, using the information in the instruction register, commands the ALU to perform the required operation.
7. The ALU performs the required operation.
8. The control unit transfers the result of the operation from the ALU to the accumulator.

row's chips is *optoelectronics*. Scientists at the University of Illinois are currently experimenting with a photon chip, which uses light rather than electrical impulses to transmit data through circuits. Although the photon chip is still in the early research stage and may not be fully developed for about twenty years, it promises to be very small and fast, and to give off little heat.

Biotechnology offers yet another possible alternative to today's silicon chip. Many scientists feel that tiny molecules can be grown and shaped to act as circuits. With such a technology, electrons are passed from molecule to molecule. Some scientists believe that, if such a technology is ever perfected, it could result in circuits that are possibly 500 times smaller than today's silicon devices.

Fully developing these new technologies to the point where they are commercially viable is not a simple process. After an experimental version of a device is created, and thoroughly tested, it must be incorporated—on a larger scale—into a working machine. It often takes years to build such a machine and to work all the "bugs" out of it. Even if a laboratory version of a machine is successful, there is no guarantee that the new technology can be mass produced at an affordable price. And there's always the problem of getting both the computer manufacturers and potential consumers to accept the product. Thus, it is really only a handful of today's exciting ideas that will emerge as the technology of tomorrow.

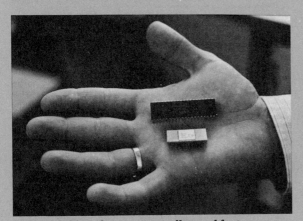

Chips: Making them ever smaller and faster.

Note in this example that the control unit initiates all the activity. Main memory, the registers, and the ALU perform specialized roles and must be summoned by the control unit. Figure 4-2 summarizes pictorially how the machine cycle works.

All this may seem like an extremely tedious process, especially when you consider that a computer may need to go through thousands, millions, or perhaps billions of machine cycles to process fully a single program. But of course computers are fast—very fast. In the slowest of them, cycle times are measured in **milliseconds** (thousandths of a second). In others, they are measured in **microseconds** (millionths of a second). In the fastest, they are measured in **nanoseconds** (billionths of a second). One of the fastest computers in the world has a cycle time of 12.5 nanoseconds, which means it can complete 80 million cycles every second.

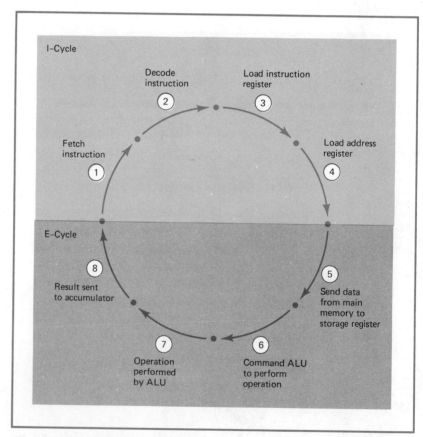

Figure 4-2.   The machine cycle.

BINARY-BASED DATA AND PROGRAM REPRESENTATION

The electronic components of digital computer systems work in two states. A circuit, for example, is either open or closed. A magnetic core is polarized either clockwise or counterclockwise. A magnetic spot is either present or absent, and so forth. This two-state, or **binary,** nature of electronics is illustrated in Figure 4-3. It is convenient to think of these binary states as the *0-state* and the *1-state.* Computer people refer to such zeros and ones as **bits,** which is a contraction of the two words "*bi*nary dig*its*." Computers, being primarily electronic, do all their

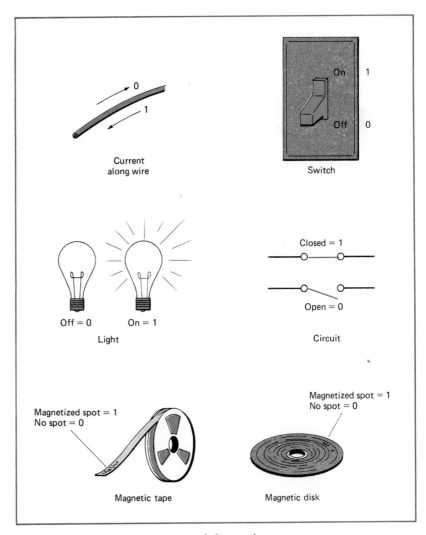

Figure 4-3.   The binary nature of electronics.

processing and communicating by representing programs and data in bit form. Binary is the "native tongue" of the computer.

People, of course, don't talk binary. You're not likely to go up to a friend on the street and say

```
1100100011001001
```

which, in one binary-based coding system, translates as "HI." People communicate with each other in *natural languages* like English, Chinese, and Spanish. In the United States, we speak English. Also, we write with a twenty-six-character alphabet, and we use a number system with ten digits, not just two.

Computers, however, only understand 0 and 1. So for us to interact with a computer, our messages to it must be translated into binary form, and its messages to us must be translated from binary into a natural language.

The programming languages most people use to interact with computer systems consist of a wide variety of natural language symbols. When we type a message such as

```
RUN FA-287
```

on a CRT screen, the computer system must translate all the natural language symbols in the message into 0s and 1s. After processing is finished, the computer system must translate the 0s and 1s it has used to represent the program's results into natural language. This conversion process is illustrated in Figure 4-4.

Number Systems

How do computers (and people) translate data back and forth from a binary form to a natural language? Before we answer this question, we have to discuss the concept of number systems.

A number system is a way of representing numbers. The system we most commonly use is called the *decimal*, or base 10, system (the word decimal comes from the Latin word for ten). It is called base 10 because it uses ten digits—0, 1, 2, 3, 4, 5, 6, 7, 8, 9—to represent all possible numbers. Numbers greater than nine are represented by a combination of these digits.

The *position* of each digit in any decimal number represents the number 10 (the base number) raised to a power, or

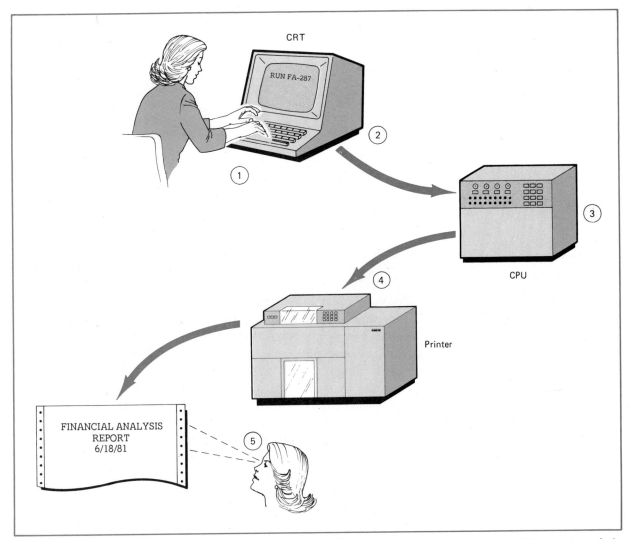

Figure 4-4. *Conversion to and from binary-based form.* 1. The user types in a message in natural-language symbols. 2. The computer system translates the message into binary-based form (this conversion often takes place in the input device). 3. The CPU does all the required processing in binary-based form. 4. The computer system translates the output back into natural-language symbols (this conversion usually takes place in the output device). 5. The user is able to read the output.

exponent, which is based on that position. Going from right to left, the first position represents 10^0, or 1; the second position represents 10^1, or 10; the third position represents 10^2, or 100; and so forth. Thus, as Figure 4-5 shows, a decimal number like 7216 can be understood as $7 \times 10^3 + 2 \times 10^2 + 1 \times 10^1 + 6 \times 10^0$.

Because we are so familiar with the decimal system, it never

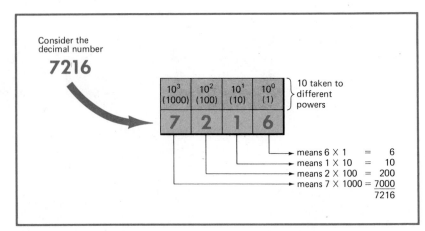

Figure 4-5. *How the decimal (base 10) system works. Note:*

$$7216 = 7 \times 10^3 + 2 \times 10^2 + 1 \times 10^1 + 6 \times 10^0.$$

occurs to most of us that we could represent numbers in any other way. In fact, however, there is nothing that says a number system has to have ten possible digits. Any other number would do as a base. We could, for example, use an *octal,* or base 8 system, which has only eight digits—0, 1, 2, 3, 4, 5, 6, 7. The position of each digit in an octal number represents the number 8 (the base number) raised to an exponent based on that position. Thus a number in base 8 would look like a decimal number, but it would have a different meaning than the same pattern of digits in base 10. The base 8 number 725, for example, means

$$7 \times 8^2 + 2 \times 8^1 + 5 \times 8^0$$

which, translated into base 10, is 469.

The *binary,* or base 2 system, works the same way, but it has only two digits—0 and 1. The position of each digit in any binary number represents the number 2 (the base number) raised to an exponent based on that position. Thus the binary number 11100 represents

$$1 \times 2^4 + 1 \times 2^3 + 1 \times 2^2 + 0 \times 2^1 + 0 \times 2^0$$

which, translated into the decimal system, is 28. Figure 4-6 shows how to convert a decimal number into a binary one.

Another number system important for computers is the *hexadecimal,* or base 16 system. We will discuss this system later in the chapter.

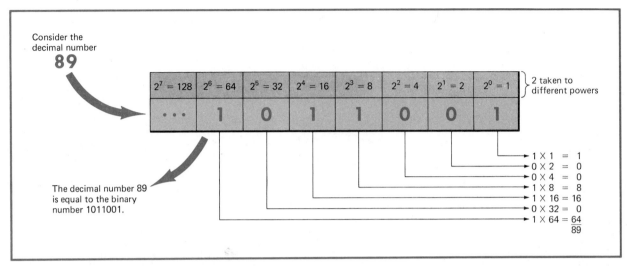

Figure 4-6.   Decimal-to-binary conversion. If you understand Figure 4-5, this one should be easy as it's set up in the same way. In this figure, however, each of the boxes represents the base number 2 systematically taken to a different power (0, 1, 2, . . .). To compute a binary number from a decimal number, construct a line of these boxes in the manner shown until you reach a box having a value greater than the decimal number. Place a 1 in the box immediately to its right. If the value of the next box to the right added to the value of the box with the 1 is greater than the decimal number, put a 0 in it. If it is less, put a 1 in it. Continue this process with the rest of the boxes, moving one box at a time to the right, until the value represented by the sum of all the boxes with 1s equals the decimal number.

Actually, the computer uses a faster process for this conversion, but the one shown here is easier to understand for demonstration purposes.

Binary-Based Data Codes

True Binary Representation.   Any decimal number can be translated to a binary one, and vice versa. Using the binary number system to represent numbers, in the manner shown in the previous section, is called **true binary representation.** The number of bits needed to form a true binary number varies. For example, the number 19 requires 5 bits (10011), whereas 4649 requires 13 (1001000101001). Regardless of the number of bits required, true binary representation can only represent numeric data.

The computer often uses numbers in true binary form when it is doing computations, for example, counting. But true binary representation has two major shortcomings. First, as hinted earlier, it can't handle either letters of the alphabet or special characters such as punctuation marks, dollar signs, and commas. Second, it's not a very convenient code for sending data over communications lines. Because the length of the true binary representation of a number depends on the magnitude of the number (for example, 19 versus 4649), and data files usually contain numbers of different magnitudes, a device transmitting or receiving data in pure binary form would have some difficulty keeping track of the start of one string of bits and the end of another.

EBCDIC and ASCII. To overcome the shortcomings of true binary representation, several fixed-length binary-based codes have been developed. These codes make letters and other kinds of characters, as well as numbers, available to the computer in a binary form. Because they are fixed-length codes, the computer can easily tell when one character ends and another begins. Probably the two most popular of these are **EBCDIC** (*Ex*-tended *B*inary-*C*oded *D*ecimal *I*nterchange *C*ode) and **ASCII** (*A*merican *S*tandard *C*ode for *I*nformation *I*nterchange). IBM developed EBCDIC and it is used heavily on IBM computers. ASCII, developed by the American Standards Institute and a number of other computer vendors, is used on many other CPUs. Also, ASCII has evolved as the de facto standard for data transmission between distant machines.

Both EBCDIC and ASCII represent each printable character as a unique combination of a fixed number of bits (see Figure 4-7). EBCDIC uses 8 bits to represent a character. A group of 8 bits has 256 (2^8) different combinations, so EBCDIC can represent up to 256 characters. This is more than enough to account for the twenty-six upper-case and twenty-six lower-case characters, the ten decimal digits, and several special characters.

ASCII was originally designed as a 7-bit code that could represent 128 (2^7) characters. An 8-bit version of ASCII (called *ASCII-8*) that makes it more compatible with EBCDIC has also been developed. Many computer systems can accept data in either coding system and perform the conversion to its native code. The eight (or seven) bits used to represent a character in EBCDIC (or ASCII) are referred to as a **byte.** The concept of a byte is an extremely important one and we will be referring to it repeatedly throughout the remainder of the text.

The conversion from natural-language words and numbers to their EBCDIC or ASCII equivalents and back again usually takes place on an input/output device. For example, when a user types in a message such as

RUN

on a CRT terminal, the terminal translates it into EBCDIC (or ASCII) and sends it as a series of bytes to the CPU. The output the CPU sends back to the terminal or some other output device

Character	EBCDIC Bit Representation	ASCII Bit Representation	Character	EBCDIC Bit Representation	ASCII Bit Representation
0	11110000	0110000	I	11001001	1001001
1	11110001	0110001	J	11010001	1001010
2	11110010	0110010	K	11010010	1001011
3	11110011	0110011	L	11010011	1001100
4	11110100	0110100	M	11010100	1001101
5	11110101	0110101	N	11010101	1001110
6	11110110	0110110	O	11010110	1001111
7	11110111	0110111	P	11010111	1010000
8	11111000	0111000	Q	11011000	1010001
9	11111001	0111001	R	11011001	1010010
A	11000001	1000001	S	11100010	1010011
B	11000010	1000010	T	11100011	1010100
C	11000011	1000011	U	11100100	1010101
D	11000100	1000100	V	11100101	1010110
E	11000101	1000101	W	11100110	1010111
F	11000110	1000110	X	11100111	1011000
G	11000111	1000111	Y	11101000	1011001
H	11001000	1001000	Z	11101001	1011010

Figure 4-7. *EBCDIC and ASCII.*

is also in EBCDIC (or ASCII), which the output device translates into understandable words and numbers. If the CPU sent the EBCDIC message

1100100011001001

to your terminal, the word "HI" would appear on your screen.

Parity Bit. Suppose you are at a terminal keyboard and press the *B* key. If the terminal supports EBCDIC coding, it will transmit the byte "11000010" to the CPU. Sometimes, however, something happens during transmission, and the CPU receives a garbled message. Interference on the line, for example, might cause the third bit to change from 0 to 1, and the CPU would receive the message "11100010." Unless it had some way of knowing that a mistake had been made, it would wrongly interpret this byte as the letter *S*.

To enable the CPU to detect such transmission errors, EBCDIC and ASCII have an additional bit position. This bit, called the **parity bit,** is automatically set to either 0 or 1 in order to make all the bits in a byte add up to either an even or an odd number. Computer systems support either an even or an odd parity. In odd-parity systems, the parity bit makes all the 1 bits in a byte add up to an odd number. In even-parity systems, it makes them add up to an even number. Figure 4-8 shows how the parity bit works for the EBCDIC representation of the word "HELLO" on an even-parity system.

The parity bit is automatically generated by the terminal you use, so if you typed the *B* character on an even-parity terminal, "110000101" would be sent up the line to the CPU. If the message were garbled, so that the even-parity computer received "111000101" (an odd number of 1-bits), it would sense the error immediately.

The parity check is not foolproof. For example, if two bits are mistransmitted in a byte, they are self-canceling. A two-bit error, however, has an extremely small chance of occurring.

Computer Power

In many computer systems one byte represents a single address-able storage location. For this reason, computer manufacturers use the byte measure to define the storage capacity of their

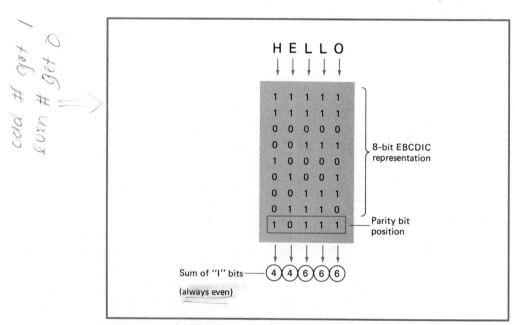

Figure 4-8. ***The parity bit.*** If the system used supports even parity, as shown here, the 1-bits in every byte must always add up to an even number. The parity bit is set to either 0 or 1 in each byte to force an even number of 1-bits in the byte.

machines. As you may have noticed, computer advertisements are filled with references to KB (kilobytes) and MB (mega-bytes). One **kilobyte (KB)** is equal to a little more than 1000 bytes (1024 to be precise) and one **megabyte (MB)** equals about 1 million bytes. When you read of a system with a 512KB computer and a 100MB disk storage unit, it means the primary memory of the computer can store about 512,000 characters of data and the disk unit can store an additional 100 million.

In Chapter 1 we mentioned that a common way of classify-ing computers is by size: microcomputers are small, minicom-puters are medium-sized, and mainframes are large. Storage capacity is one of the things computer people have in mind when they talk about computer size. Most microcomputers have a primary memory of about 16KB to 256KB. Minicomputers have a primary memory of about 512KB to a few megabytes. The capacity of primary memory in mainframes ranges from a few to many megabytes. These are not hard and fast boundaries, however, and as computer components get ever smaller and more complex, the boundaries tend to shift upward. Some micros today have a primary memory in the 1MB range, and many so-called superminis have a greater storage capacity than some smaller mainframes.

Computer Word Sizes

Another important way in which computers differ from one another is in word size. A computer **word** is a group of bits or bytes that may be manipulated and stored as a unit. It is a critical concept because the internal circuitry of every computer is designed around word size. Many mainframes and large minicomputers are, for example, 32-bit word machines, and smaller minis and large micros are 16-bit word devices. Small micros can usually only accommodate 8-bit words. Why is word size so important? There are several reasons.

First, consider speed. Just as a four-lane highway can accommodate more cars per period of time than a two-lane road, so a 32-bit machine can work much faster than a 16-bit one. Words are the units that move from one part of the CPU to another during the machine cycle. Thus the longer the word, the more bits of information that can be transferred between the ALU and main memory on each machine cycle and the more work that is done with each action of the machine.

Second, the greater the size of the word used, the greater the number of bits available to represent machine-level instructions. For example, most 32-bit machines are designed so that the first 8 bits are reserved for instructions. This permits a total of 2^8, or 256 different instructions. Sixteen-bit machines, on the other hand, have a smaller number of bits available for this purpose. Typically, these computers reserve 6 bits for instructions, which permits only 2^6, or 64, different instructions. So the bigger the word size, the larger the set of instructions available to the computer.

Third, the longer the word size, the greater the capacity of addressable primary memory. A 32-bit machine can have over a billion addressable memory locations. A 16-bit machine, in contrast, is often limited to several thousand.

Fourth, longer word sizes generally make for greater precision. A big number that occupies one word in a large computer may occupy two words in a smaller computer, which results in some loss in accuracy. On very large scientific computers, where speed and accuracy are extremely important, word sizes as great as 60 or more bits are not unusual.

As mentioned earlier, some computers are designed to assign each character (byte) of data to a single memory address. These machines use what is called a **variable-length word approach,** because they may need to manipulate a *different* number of characters every time an input or output operation takes place. Such computers are targeted for business applications, which are characterized by a high percentage of alphabetic text (which is easy to manipulate in units of single characters).

In a **fixed-length word approach,** on the other hand, more than a single character of data can occupy a single address. Each address holds a word of a fixed number of characters. Computers using this approach are often used for scientific and engineering purposes, because packaging data in this way makes it possible to store long, highly precise numbers in a single location, resulting in faster computation and greater accuracy.

Many computers made today utilize both variable-length and fixed-length word approaches to store data.

Binary-Based Programming Language: Machine Languages

Binary-based codes such as true binary, EBCDIC, and ASCII are used to represent *data*. **Machine language,** in contrast, is the binary-based code used to represent *programs*. An example of a typical machine-language instruction is shown in Figure

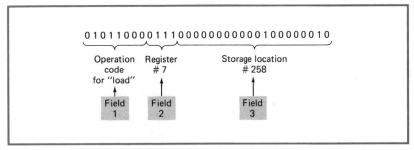

Figure 4-9. A 32-bit machine-language instruction. The instruction commands the computer to load the contents of main memory location 258 into register 7. In the example, the numbers 7 and 258 are represented in the instruction by their true binary counterparts.

4-9. As you can see, what looks like a meaningless string of 0s and 1s actually consists of groups of bits that represent specific locations, operations, and characters. Each computer has its own machine language. A code that works on an IBM computer will be totally foreign to a Honeywell computer.

Machine-language instructions are what the CPU works on during the machine cycles we talked about earlier in the chapter. Because it is patterned after the actual behavior of the computer, machine language is often called a *low-level language. Assembly languages,* developed in the 1950s, are symbolic counterparts of machine languages—they replace binary code with understandable symbols composed of numbers and letters. But because they are so closely tied to machine language, and tedious for the average programmer to work with, assembly languages are also considered to be low-level languages.

With the first computers, all programs were written in machine language. Today, although it is still possible to write in machine language, hardly anybody does. As we mentioned in Chapter 3, programmers can now work in high-level languages that are much easier to read. Programs written in *high-level languages* (such as BASIC or Pascal) or in an assembly language must, however, be translated into machine language before they can be executed. This takes place automatically under the control of a special program called a *language translator* (discussed in Chapter 8).

Hexadecimal Representation

New programs almost always contain errors. When the computer encounters an error in a program it usually immediately stops processing the program and sends an error message to the programmer. Sometimes the programmer can find and correct the problem easily. But when an error is hard to track down, the programmer may ask the computer for a memory "dump" when the program aborts. A *dump* is a printout of the contents of primary memory, and it lets the programmer see exactly what the program was doing when execution stopped. Dumps are printed in **hexadecimal** notation, which is a shorthand method for representing the 8-bit bytes that are actually in the computer.

Hexadecimal means base 16. As you may remember from our discussion of number systems, base 16 has sixteen digits. Since we have only ten digits in our base 10 notation, letters are used instead of numbers for the extra six digits. Hexadecimal notation is illustrated in Figure 4-10.

Hexadecimal (called *hex,* for short) is not itself a code the computer uses to perform computations or to communicate with other machines. It does, however, have a special relationship to the 8-bit bytes of EBCDIC and ASCII-8 that makes it ideal for displaying a dump. As you can see in Figure 4-10, each hex character has a 4-binary-bit counterpart, so any combination of 8 bits can be represented by exactly two hexadecimal characters. Thus the letter *A* (represented in EBCDIC by 11000001)

Hexadecimal Character	Decimal Equivalent	Binary Equivalent
0	0	0000
1	1	0001
2	2	0010
3	3	0011
4	4	0100
5	5	0101
6	6	0110
7	7	0111
8	8	1000
9	9	1001
A	10	1010
B	11	1011
C	12	1100
D	13	1101
E	14	1110
F	15	1111

Figure 4-10. *Hexadecimal characters and their decimal and binary equivalents.*

HOW COMPUTER CHIPS ARE MADE

From the drawing board to final product assembly

The microprocessor, or computer-on-a-chip, is found in a multitude of products, including toys, phones, digital watches, delicatessen scales, and personal computers. The story of how microprocessor chips are produced is a fascinating one. An engineer first makes a composite drawing of the circuits on the chip. The drawing is then digitized into computer memory and tested by a series of computer programs. The final circuit design is later converted back into physical form, some 500 times smaller than the engineer's original drawing. The chip design is then replicated many times on a 3-inch-diameter silicon wafer, producing a pattern similar to a sheet of postage stamps. Finally, the individual chips are cut off the wafer, mounted in carrier packages, and sold for a few dollars. Look through this Window to see more clearly how this process takes place.

1.   A microchip on the petals of a daisy.

2.   A microchip mounted in its carrier package. The carrier has prongs that plug into a circuit board socket.

How small is a microchip?

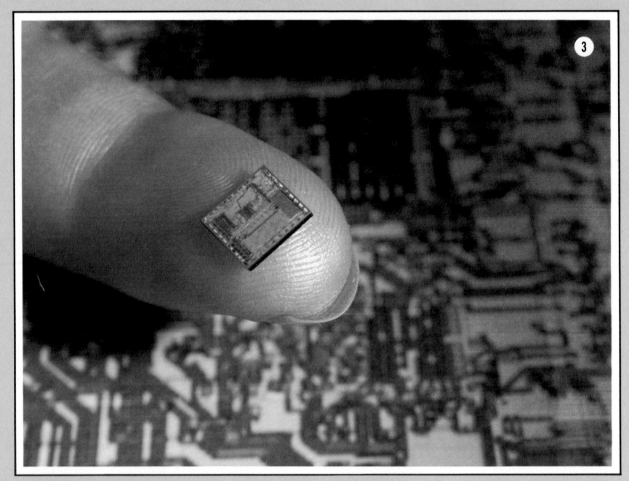

3. Small enough to fit on a finger, this Intel 8748H microprocessor is a totally self-sufficient computer, with 27 input/output lines for support functions.

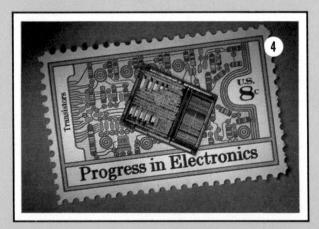

4. The "stamp of progress." This BELLMAC™ microprocessor, etched on a chip that is only 1.5 centimeters square, packs as much processing power as some minicomputers.

5. Mounted in its carrier package, this dime-sized microprocessor contains the power of almost 150,000 transistors.

ANATOMY OF INTEL'S 80186

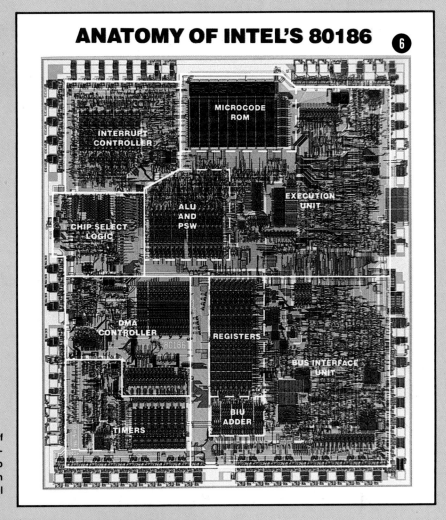

6. A blow-up showing the anatomy of Intel's 80186 processor, with important functional areas of the chip labeled. This "16-bit" CPU is used on some of the newer, more powerful microcomputers.

7. Microprocessors are packaged in many different ways for a wide variety of purposes.

INITIAL DESIGN AND TEST-
ING The early stages of microchip production involve creating a
circuit design on paper, digitizing
the drawing into computer memory, and thoroughly testing the
design for potential voltage, speed,
temperature, and timing problems. The following photographs
illustrate some of the steps in this
process.

8, 9. Composite drawings of chips are
created by circuit designers and placed on
flatbed digitizing devices. A cursor mechanism on the bed can be slid up and down a
vertical guide bar by the operator, who traces
over the drawing and presses buttons on the
cursor device to enter information about
circuit elements and their coordinates. The
information gathered during the digitizing
process is placed in computer storage. Later,
the entire circuit can be recalled to a CRT
screen, modified, and tested (see photograph
10).

10. Designer modifying microchip circuitry
on a CRT screen. By redrawing a circuit with a
light pen, or typing in update commands,
circuit elements can be added, deleted, or
moved.

11. A photomask image 500 times larger than the actual circuit is carefully examined in a final inspection just prior to manufacturing. Later, this image will be scaled down photographically to the size of a finished chip and replicated several hundred times, like a large sheet of postage stamps, on a three-inch-diameter silicon wafer.

12. A wafer of microchips sits under a single microchip that has been cut from the wafer and mounted in its carrier package.

MANUFACTURING The raw material most often used in the fabrication of microchips is silicon, one of the earth's most abundant substances. It is an ideal backing for the circuits because it is electrically inert and can be processed into an exceptionally pure form. In fact, it can be purified to less than one flaw per billion parts, which is roughly equivalent to one tennis ball in a chain of golf balls extending from the earth to the moon.

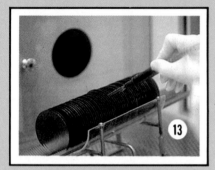

13. Molten silicon is formed into cylindrical ingots, which are then sliced into wafers, like rolls of sausage.

14. Dipping and washing. The wafers are then immersed in photoresist, a honey-like emulsion that hardens with exposure to ultraviolet light.

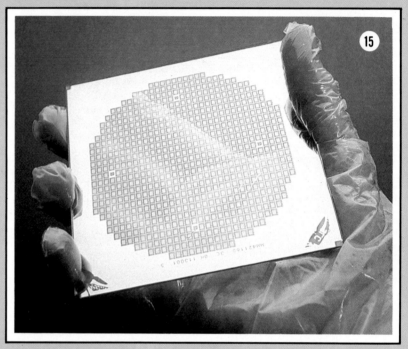

15. A mask, representing a circuit pattern is then placed over each wafer, and ultraviolet light is projected through the mask. Where the light penetrates the mask, the photoresist hardens to form an outline of the circuit. Later, the wafer is washed again to remove the unhardened photoresist. Separate masks are made for each circuit layer of the chip. Depending on the technology used, a chip may require anywhere from 5 to 20 circuit layers.

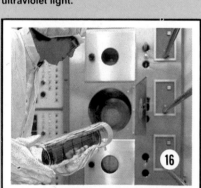

16. After a single circuit layer is placed on each chip, the wafers are baked in a diffusion furnace. The oxygen in the furnace reacts with the exposed silicon areas to produce an insulating glass layer on the circuits.

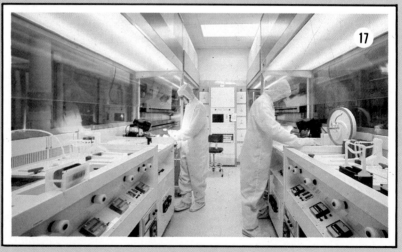

17. Because microscopic impurities in the air could easily cause a microprocessor to malfunction, chip manufacturing is performed in highly controlled, sterile rooms.

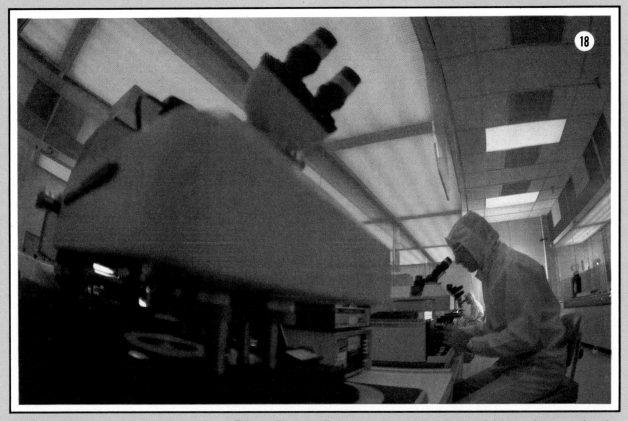

18.   A technician inspects a wafer for flaws. This "yellow room" prevents any extraneous ultraviolet rays from entering the environment.

19.   A die-cutting machine cuts the individual chips out of the wafer.

20.   Minute wires are connected between the chip and the metal leads in the carrier. These wires permit electrical current to run into and out of the chip.

21.   The finished product: a chip in its carrier package.

ASSEMBLY INTO PRODUCTS

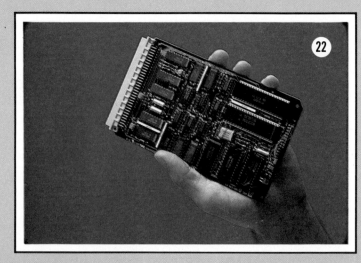

22. Circuit boards in many computer products are comprised of several chip/carrier assemblies that are plugged into the board.

23. Computer products, such as these terminals, are often composed of several microcomponent-bearing circuit boards mounted into parallel tracks similar to those found with sliding doors.

```
41000000   0A9C4110   01509101   10A04710
00369610   10744100   008045E0   10309240
010E00B2   D2130117   00854110   03F44100
FFFFFFFF   FFFFFFFF   FF00FFFF   FFFFFFFF
00000150   40000000   41100150   41000003
F1F0F9F6   F0E6C9D5   C7D3C1D5   C4634002
F0F0F3F5   F0F0F0F1   F0F0F2F0   F0F0F0F0
40404040   40404040   40404040   40404040
F0404040   404040E6   C9D5C7D3   C1D5C468
40404040   40404040   40404040   40404040
0011A000   0011A800   0000006A   80000000
```

Figure 4-11.   A sample from a dump. Each pair of hexadecimal digits represents a byte in memory.

has a hex representation of C1. Clearly, a dump printed in hex is a lot more compact and easier to read than would be the equivalent string of 0s and 1s. Figure 4-11 shows a sample dump.

Another place you might encounter hexadecimal numbers is in working with microcomputers. You might, for example, receive a message on a microcomputer display screen like

PROGRAM LOADED AT LOCATION 4F6A.

This message tells you the location in primary memory of the first byte in your program. To determine the decimal equivalent of a hexadecimal number such as 4F6A, you go through a process like the binary-to-decimal conversion shown in Figure 4-5. Figure 4-12 shows how to convert from hexadecimal to decimal.

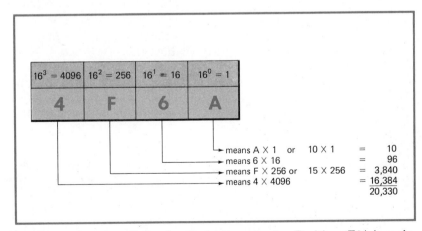

Figure 4-12.   Hexadecimal-to-decimal conversion. Position 4F6A in main memory corresponds to the 20,330th byte position.

PRIMARY MEMORY AND FIRMWARE

Primary storage is commonly referred to by the acronym **RAM,** which stands for **Random Access Memory.** *Random access* means that, since the memory has addresses, the computer can go to the programs and data it wants directly, as opposed to *serial access,* where the computer must check each memory location in turn. Thus, when you see a personal computer advertised with 64KB RAM, it usually means that the machine has 64 kilobytes of primary storage built into it. The term RAM can be slightly misleading in studying computers, because as

Can Computers Really Think Like Humans?

To some extent, yes. A computer is a device that given some instructions, can perform work at extremely fast speeds, drawing on a large memory. It can also be programmed to draw certain types of conclusions based on the input it receives or the results of computations it performs. A good deal of human mental activity involves these very processes. But computers aren't human and will probably never be capable of the self-awareness that all humans have. For this reason, the mental acuity attributed to computers is commonly referred to as *artificial intelligence (AI).*

The field of AI evolved from attempts to write programs that would enable computers to rival skilled humans at games such as chess and checkers, to prove difficult mathematical theorems, and so forth. Since these tasks normally require a high degree of human intelligence, the assumption has been that the computers that can do them must in some way be mimicking human intelligence.

Early attempts at using computers to do humanlike thinking primarily exploited the awesome speed of these machines. For example, the first chess programs instructed computer systems to make decisions by looking several plays ahead and calculating the effects of all possible moves and countermoves. Unfortunately, even planning ten moves ahead is a computationally burdensome chore, even for a computer. It is also not the way skilled chess players think. Most chess masters rely on intuitive rules of thumb, called *heuristics.* One highly successful heuristic for playing chess is to control the center of the board. As programmers began supplying computers with the logic for using such heuristics, the quality of chess-playing programs improved dramatically.

A stunning example of the use of computer programs to employ heuristics was recently demonstrated by Douglas Lenat, a faculty member of Stanford University who also works at Xerox's Palo Alto Research Center (PARC). Lenat had created an AI program, called *Eurisko,* which both discovers and applies heuristics based on its analysis of certain environments. Lenat had already used Eurisko to develop useful heuristics in the fields of mathematics, computer design, and evolution when he decided to match his program against human opponents in an intergalactic game called *Traveller.* The game is not a simple one like those found in your local neighborhood arcade. Players must master approximately 100 pages of rules just to design a suitable space fleet. Lenat supplied Eurisko with the

we'll see in the next chapter, some kinds of secondary storage devices also have random access capabilities.

One of the most important traits of primary memory is that it is temporary. When the CPU is finished with one set of data and programs in memory, it writes another set in its place. To be used again, programs and data must be kept in secondary storage. In recent years, however, there has been a trend to build some software functions directly into computer hardware. There, programs can be accessed very rapidly. On many microcomputers, for example, the program for translating a language like BASIC into machine language is built into a compact

rules of the game and a few intuitively appealing heuristics to begin play. Eurisko was also able to develop some valuable heuristics on its own, as it simulated thousands of battles based on the same rules lodged in its memory. Eventually, the program discovered that the rules favored a fleet consisting primarily of inexpensive, heavily armored vessels with light offensive arsenals. Such a fleet could sustain heavy losses but still outnumber the enemy. Eurisko's militia also

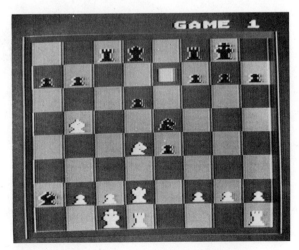

Computers and chess: An early AI application.

included a fast, powerfully armed warship, whose objective was to outlast all other vessels. In the championship tournament held in July 1981, Eurisko breezed to a win. In many instances, opponents were forced to resign without firing a single shot.

Gaming aside, one of the greatest challenges currently facing scientists in the field of AI is to equip computers with the ability to master natural languages. This would make the programming languages of today—such as BASIC, COBOL, and FORTRAN—obsolete. Unfortunately, this is not easy to do. People have personalized ways of communicating, and the meaning of words varies with the context in which they are used. Also, the heuristics people employ to reach an understanding of what others are saying are highly complex and still not well understood by language researchers. So if you think you don't need to learn today's programming languages because highly powerful, natural-language-speaking computer systems are right around the corner, you're in for a disappointment. Although AI research will continue to supply remarkable demonstrations of intelligence on highly structured problems, breakthroughs in areas like the use of natural language will probably remain slow.

hardware module. These modules either come with the machine or can be purchased separately and plugged into a board inside the computer.

This kind of software-in-hardware is called **firmware.** Several kinds of firmware are available.

- **Read-only memory (ROM)** is probably the most common form of firmware (see Figure 4-13). A ROM module contains a program supplied by the manufacturer. The program can be read from the module, but it is impossible for a user to destroy the contents of the module by accidentally writing over them (hence "read-only"). Many microcomputer manufacturers make some of their systems software available in ROM modules.

- **Programmable read-only memory (PROM)** is identical to ROM, except that the buyer writes the program. In other words, a PROM module is like a blank ROM module. Special equipment is needed to write a program onto a PROM module, and once the program is on, it can't be erased.

- **Erasable programmable read-only memory (EPROM)** is like PROM, except that its contents can be erased and a new program written on. The newest type of EPROM, which is *electrically* erasable, is called EEPROM.

Figure 4-13. A ROM module. Piggybacked on a microcomputer module this ROM provides instructions for the microcomputer.

Summary and Key Terms

The CPU has three major sections: primary memory, an arithmetic/logic unit (ALU), and a control unit.

Primary memory (also called **main memory** and **internal storage**) is the section of the CPU that holds the programs and data that have been entered into the computer, intermediate processing results, and output that is ready to be transmitted to secondary storage or an output device.

The **arithmetic/logic unit (ALU)** is the section of the CPU that does arithmetic and logical operations on data.

The **control unit** is the section of the CPU that directs the flow of electronic traffic between primary memory and the ALU and between the CPU and input and output devices.

Registers are high-speed staging areas within the CPU that hold program instructions and data immediately before they're processed. The part of a program instruction that indicates what the ALU is to do next is placed in the **instruction register,** and the part showing the address of the data to be used in the operation is placed in the **address register.** Before data are processed they are taken from primary memory and placed in the **storage register.** The **accumulator** is a register that temporarily stores the results of ongoing operations.

The processing of a single instruction is called a **machine cycle.** A machine cycle has two parts: an **I-cycle** (instruction cycle), in which the control unit fetches and examines an instruction, and an **E-cycle** (execution cycle), in which the instruction is actually executed by the ALU under control unit supervision. A computer may need to go through thousands, millions, or perhaps billions of machine cycles to fully process a single program. Computer cycle times are generally measured in **milliseconds** (thousandths of a second), **microseconds** (millionths of a second), or **nanoseconds** (billionths of a second).

The electronic components of digital computers work in a two-state, or **binary,** fashion. It is convenient to think of these binary states as the 0-state and the 1-state. Computer people refer to such 0s and 1s as **bits.**

The computer uses several binary-based codes to process data. **True binary representation** is a form that uses the binary number system, exclusively, to represent numbers of any size as continuous strings of 0- and 1-bits. It is a code that can represent numeric data only. **EBCDIC** and **ASCII,** in contrast, are fixed-length codes that can represent any single character of data—a digit, alphabetic character, or special symbol—as a string of seven or eight bits. This string of bits is called a **byte.** EBCDIC and ASCII allow for an additional bit position, called a **parity bit,** to enable computer systems to check for transmission errors.

The storage capacity of computers is often expressed in **kilobytes (KB),** or thousands of bytes, and **megabytes (MB),** or millions of bytes.

A computer **word** is a group of bits or bytes that may be manipulated and stored as a unit. Machines using a **variable-length word approach** can store each character of data in one address, whereas with a **fixed-length word approach,** more than a single character of data can occupy one address.

Machine language is the binary-based code used to represent programs. A program must be translated into machine language before it can be executed on the computer.

Hexadecimal representation is a binary-based code that is useful to programmers for debugging programs, but it is not itself a code the computer uses to perform computations or to communicate with other machines.

Primary storage is commonly referred to by the acronym **RAM,** which stands for **Random Access Memory.** This memory is used to store temporarily programs and data that the computer is currently working with.

Permanent storage of important programs is commonly provided through **firmware,** which are software-in-hardware modules. There are several types of firmware, including **ROM (read-only memory), PROM (programmable read-only memory),** and **EPROM (erasable programmable read-only memory).**

Review Questions

1. Describe the three main parts of the CPU and their roles.
2. Identify some of the registers within the CPU and their functions.
3. Describe how a program instruction is executed.
4. Describe how the binary system is used to represent data and programs.
5. Demonstrate how to convert a decimal number to a binary one.
6. What is the purpose of the parity bit and how does it work?
7. What are the differences among a bit, byte, kilobyte, megabyte, and word?
8. What is the purpose of the hexadecimal numbering system?
9. Distinguish among RAM, ROM, PROM, and EPROM.

Chapter 5

Secondary Storage

Chapter Outline

OVERVIEW

MAGNETIC TAPE

Processing Tapes
Storing Data on Tape
Blocking Records
How Are Tapes Prepared?
Protecting Tapes

MAGNETIC DISKS

Hard Disks
Floppy Disks
Winchester Disks

TAPE VERSUS DISK: ADVANTAGES AND DISADVANTAGES

DATA ACCESS AND DATA ORGANIZATION

Access Methods
Data Organization

OTHER SECONDARY STORAGE MEDIA AND EQUIPMENT

Mass Storage Unit
Magnetic Bubble Storage
Optical Disks

OVERVIEW

In Chapter 4, we highlighted the role of primary (internal) memory in the CPU. Primary memory is designed to provide rapid access to information. It is here that programs, data, intermediate results, and output are temporarily stored. As soon as a program has been executed, however, new data and programs are written over the existing ones. Thus, if data, programs, and the results of processing are to be preserved for repeated use, additional storage capacity outside the CPU must be made available. Secondary (external) storage serves this purpose. Although it is slower than primary memory, secondary storage is far less expensive.

Any secondary storage system involves two physical parts: a *device* and a *medium*. Data and programs are written onto and read from the medium. The device is online to the CPU, but the medium—in many cases—must be loaded onto the device before the CPU can read data and programs from it or write new data and programs onto it. While not in use, these storage media are often kept offline, in racks and cabinets.

We will begin this chapter with a discussion of the two most important kinds of secondary storage systems today—those using magnetic tape and those using magnetic disk. We will then cover two related subjects—data access and data organization. *Data access* refers to the ways computer systems retrieve data from a storage medium. *Data organization* refers to ways of storing data on a medium for efficient access. Finally, we will look at some less common secondary storage systems.

MAGNETIC TAPE

Figure 5-1.   Magnetic tape reels.

Detachable **magnetic tape** reels, which are mounted on large tape units, have long been popular and are still widely used (see Figure 5-1). Normally ½-inch wide, the tape is typically made of plastic Mylar and coated with a magnetizable substance. A standard diameter for the tape reels is 10½ inches, although smaller "mini reels" are also quite common. A typical reel of 2400 feet can pack data at a density of about 1600 bytes per inch. This is the storage equivalent of about 400,000 punched cards.

Magnetic tape is also available in cassette form (see Figure 5-2), where the tape is housed in a small plastic cartridge. **Cassette tapes** used for storing data look similar to the ones

Figure 5-2.   Cassette tape.

you see around the home for recording music but are of higher quality. A typical cassette tape, which is ⅛ inch wide and 200 feet long, can store about 200 bytes per inch. Cassettes are commonly used with microcomputer systems, but because they are extremely slow, their value is limited. Cassettes are rapidly losing their purely economic advantage to small disks as technological advancements and costs on small disk systems continue to become more favorable.

The discussion that follows in this section applies principally to the larger tapes, as they are by far the most common tape media used in commercial data-processing applications.

Processing Tapes

A tape must be mounted onto an online **tape unit** (see Figure 5-3) if it is to be processed by the computer. These units are about the size of a common household refrigerator. The *supply reel* on the unit contains the tape that is to be read from or written on by the computer system. The *take-up reel* collects the tape as it is unwound from the supply reel. As it is processed, the tape passes by a mechanism called a **read/write head,** which reads data from the tape or records data on it. The tape is allowed to droop in a vacuum chamber so that it will not break if the two reels should move at different speeds. When processing is finished, the tape is rewound onto the supply reel and removed from the unit. The take-up reel never leaves the unit.

Storing Data on Tape

Figure 5-4 shows how data is stored on magnetic tape. Data may be coded using the eight-bit byte of either EBCDIC or ASCII-8, depending on the equipment used. Magnetized spots of iron oxide represent 1s; nonmagnetized spots represent 0s. The tape contains a **track** for each bit of information in a character, plus an additional parity track so that the computer system can check for transmission errors. The tape unit reads across the nine tracks to identify the character represented in each column. You'll recall from Chapter 4 that in *odd* parity machines, all 1-bits add up to an odd number; in *even* parity machines, an even number. An incorrect sum indicates an error. The parity bit is included with the byte representation of each character when it is placed onto tape.

A magnetic tape is, basically, a long narrow strip, so when the records in a data file are stored on tape, they must be placed

Figure 5-3.   Magnetic tape unit.

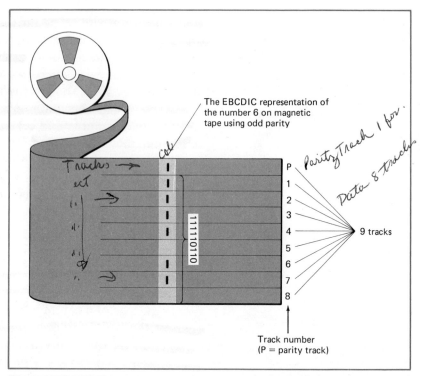

Figure 5-4.   **Storing data on nine-track magnetic tape.** Shown is the number 6 represented in EBCDIC (11110110, or 111110110 with the odd-parity track). In the shaded cross-section of the tape the magnetized spot representing the 1-bit is shown by a vertical mark in the appropriate track. The 0-bit is characterized by the absence of a mark.

one right after another in sequence. The sequence is often determined by a **key field**—customer ID number, for example—which can be ordered numerically. The key field generally has a different value for every record.

If you want to read a particular record from a tape, you can't go directly to it. Instead, you have to pass through all the records that come before it. In a sense, this is similar to the "fast forwarding" you need to do on a music tape when the tune you want to hear is in the middle of it. Retrieving records this way—in the order in which they are stored—is called *sequential access,* and organizing data in sequence by a key field is called *sequential organization.* We will talk more about data access and organization later in the chapter.

Blocking Records

Tape units are not purely electronic like the CPU. They have moving parts that have to stop and start. Because all records read from tape must pass by the read/write heads at the same speed, some "dead space" must exist before and after each record, to allow the tape to speed up and slow down between starts and stops. These spaces are called **interblock gaps** (or **interrecord gaps**). Unfortunately, each interblock gap occupies about ½ inch of tape, whereas a single record may use only ¹⁄₂₀ of an inch. This means that a tape could conceivably consist of about 10 percent data and 90 percent dead space.

To correct this problem, a solution called **blocking** is often employed. Individual records, called **logical records,** are grouped into larger units of fixed size, called **physical records.** The number of logical records in each physical record is the **blocking factor.** If each physical record contains ten logical records, the blocking factor is ten. An interblock gap is then placed between each of the physical records. This technique is illustrated in Figure 5-5.

Besides the great saving of space, a second reason for blocking is faster processing. Computer systems that permit blocking contain special high-speed memory areas within the computer unit called **buffers.** Buffers used for blocking work much like the registers in the CPU: they stage data in a

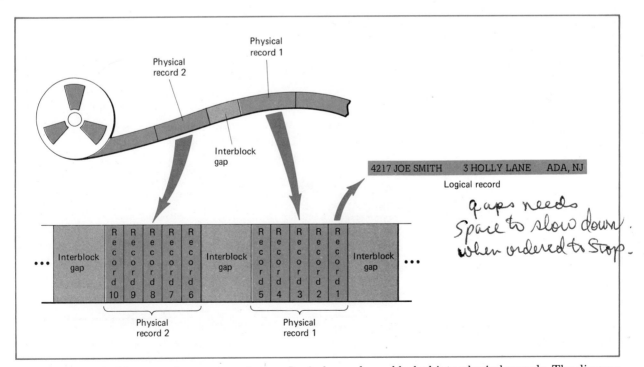

Figure 5-5.   Blocking records on magnetic tape. Logical records are blocked into physical records. The diagram illustrates a blocking factor of 5. In other words, five logical records form a single physical record. Usually, much larger blocking factors are employed to save space.

fast-access area just before processing. As the tape is being processed, physical records are placed into the buffers, as shown in Figure 5-6. Often, there are two of these buffers. Whenever a program issues a READ instruction, the logical record can be retrieved directly from the buffer rather than from the remote tape unit, which must spin and read the tape in response to each request. Because the buffers are entirely electronic, like the rest of the computer unit, data can be retrieved much more rapidly than it can from the mechanical tape unit. When all the logical records in one of the buffers have been processed, reading continues in the other buffer. In the meantime, the next physical record on the tape is loaded into the first buffer, writing over the physical record that was stored there before. This process continues until the file is exhausted.

Buffering normally makes sense only when records are processed sequentially, as is always the case with tape (and sometimes disk). This is because, in order to fill the buffers, the computer system must be able to anticipate which records will

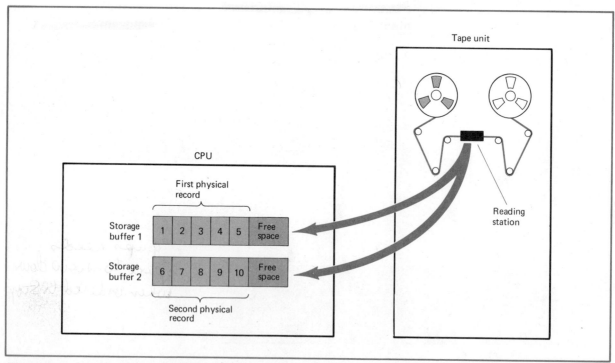

Figure 5-6. Buffering of physical records in storage. Suppose records are blocked in the manner suggested by Figure 5-5. The computer's systems software will initially place the first physical record in buffer 1 and the second in buffer 2. All READ instructions in an applications program retrieve data from these buffers, where the computer can retrieve logical records at faster speeds than if they were in secondary storage. When the first buffer has been exhausted, reading shifts to the physical record in the second buffer. Meanwhile, the third physical record is loaded into the first buffer.

come next, something it can't do as effectively if the records are not processed in a fixed sequence.

How Are Tapes Prepared?

Tapes may be prepared for computer processing in several ways. If the data to be loaded onto tape is not already on the computer system, it can be entered by using an offline device called a **key-to-tape unit** (see Figure 5-7). This unit typically consists of a keyboard, used to type in the data, as well as a small memory and televisionlike screen. The memory stores the newly entered data so that the data-entry operator can check it for accuracy on the screen before it is inscribed onto tape.

If the data to be loaded onto tape is on another storage medium, such as a disk, an operator need only call up a system program on a CRT terminal and instruct the computer system to transfer the data. In the same way, data and programs can also be transferred from one tape to another.

Figure 5-7.   A key-to-tape unit. With such a unit an operator can place input data directly onto tape with a keyboard. Once tapes are prepared, they are mounted on a tape unit (see Figure 5-3) for processing.

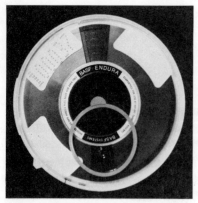

Figure 5-8. A magnetic tape with a rubber file-protection ring. When the ring is off the reel, you can read from the tape but you can't write onto it. When the ring is on, you can both read from and write onto the tape.

Protecting Tapes

Tape reels are equipped with safety features that prevent operators from destroying the contents of the tape accidentally. One such device is the **file-protection ring** (see Figure 5-8). When tapes are stored offline, these rings are not mounted on the reel. In order to write onto any part of the tape, thereby destroying any data which may already be stored on that part of it, the operator must insert this ring into the center of the reel. The tapes can be read, however, whether or not the ring is present.

Another device designed to protect tapes is the **internal header label.** This label appears at the beginning of the tape and identifies it. The identifying information in the label is usually generated automatically by the computer system or key-to-tape unit. Thus, if you were to command the computer system to process tape AP-601, and the operator accidentally mounted tape AR-601 instead, no processing would take place. Also, a warning message would be sent to the operator.

MAGNETIC DISK

Magnetic disk is without doubt the most important secondary storage medium in data processing today. Disks permit much faster retrieval of information than do tapes because disks allow *direct access* to records. The computer system can go directly to the location of a particular record on the disk. It does not have to read through a series of records before reaching the desired one, as is the case with tapes. In addition, disk systems are capable of storing more data online to the CPU than tape systems. Without disk storage, many of the computer applications that we see around us would not be possible. Banking with automatic tellers and airlines reservations systems are just a few of the many activities that depend on the rapid access to data that magnetic disks make possible.

Two popular types of magnetic disk are hard disks and floppy disks. **Hard disks** are used primarily on mainframes and large minicomputers. Some smaller hard-disk units have also recently become available for smaller computers. **Floppy disks,** on the other hand, are more common on microcomputers and small minicomputers. They are also becoming increasingly popular for limited use on some larger computers. Floppy disks provide small quantities of offline storage and facilitate communication with the larger machines by microcomputer users.

Hard Disks

A hard disk is a metal platter commonly 14 inches in diameter and coated on both sides with a magnetizable substance such as ferrous oxide (see Figure 5-9). Records are stored in concentric rings, or tracks. Characters are represented by binary bits, which appear as magnetic spots in the tracks. Each track may consist of several logical records, which are often blocked into physical records in a manner similar to blocking on tape. Although it may seem wasteful, each track on a disk surface is designed to carry the same total amount of data, even though the tracks near the outer edge are much longer than those nearer the center and move past the read/write head faster. This design constraint keeps the data transfer rate constant throughout the

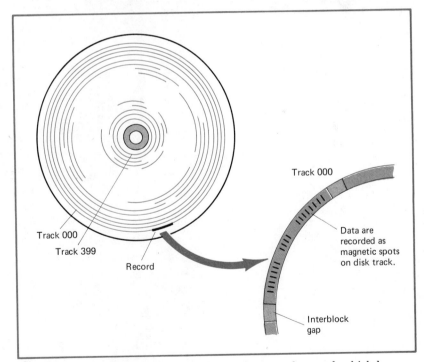

Figure 5-9. *Surface of a disk.* Unlike a phonograph record, which bears a single spiral groove, a disk is composed of concentric tracks. Each track has the same data-carrying capacity. The number of tracks per surface varies from manufacturer to manufacturer. The disk shown here has 400 tracks.

Figure 5-10.   A disk pack.

system, independent of the location of the track being accessed. The number of tracks per disk varies with the manufacturer, but many disks contain several hundred. Data are read or written by a read/write head, which moves above or below the spinning disk to access the disk tracks.

Disk platters are often assembled into groups of six, eight, ten, or twelve, depending on the manufacturer, and mounted on a shaft that spins all the disks at the same rate of speed. The disks are spaced far enough apart to permit the read/write heads to move in and out between the disks. Such an assembly is called a **disk pack** (see Figure 5-10). The disk pack is encased in a plastic shell, similar to a cake cover, to protect the recording surfaces from foreign objects. Usually the top and bottom surfaces of the pack aren't used, because they are the ones most exposed to dust.

Disk packs are mounted on a device called a **disk storage unit,** or **disk unit** (see Figure 5-11). These units are plugged into the CPU, enabling it to access any of the data recorded on

Figure 5-11.   A disk storage unit.

the disks. A disk pack stands in the same relation to a disk unit as a row of phonograph records does to a jukebox. The relationship among a disk, disk pack, and disk unit is illustrated in Figure 5-12.

Some disk packs can be removed from the storage unit, whereas others cannot. Systems with *nonremovable* disk packs are normally faster and have greater online capacity than systems with *removable* packs. However, because the packs cannot be dismounted, it is frequently necessary to transfer some disk data to tape or floppy disk in order to free up online disk space.

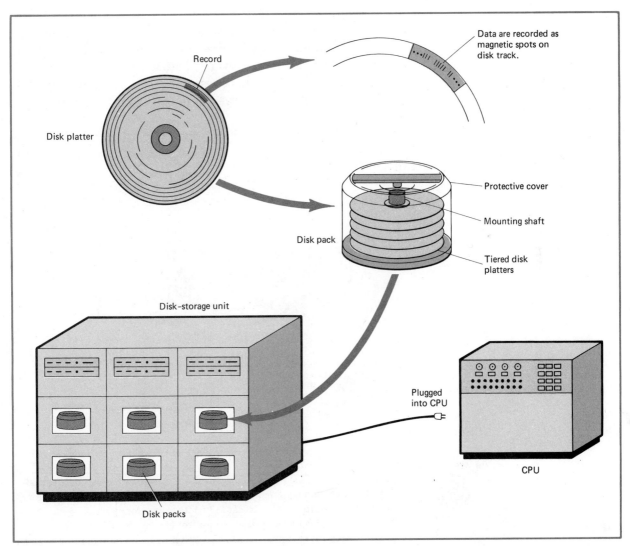

Figure 5-12. **Hard-disk storage.** Disks are assembled into disk packs. Here, each pack contains five disk platters. Disk packs, in turn, are mounted in the disk storage unit, which is plugged into the computer.

Reading and Writing Data.   Data on disk, as on tape, are read or written by a read/write head. In disk systems, there is at least one read/write head for each recording surface. These heads are mounted on a device called an **access mechanism.** Figure 5-13 shows how access is accomplished on a disk unit that uses movable read/write heads. Such a device is called a *movable-head disk unit*. It is by far the most popular type of hard-disk system. The rotating shaft spins at high speeds (3600 revolutions per minute is common), and the heads move in and out together, between the disk surfaces, to access the required data.

A head never touches the surface of a disk at any time, even during reading and writing. Head and disk are very close, however. The IBM 3350 disk heads, for example, glide 17-millionths of an inch above the recording surfaces. If present on a surface, a human hair or even a smoke particle (about 2500 and 100 millionths of an inch, respectively), would damage the disks and heads. As you can see in Figure 5-14, the results would

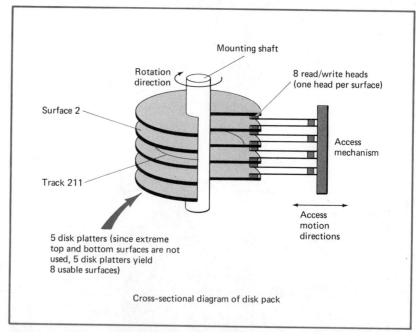

Cross-sectional diagram of disk pack

Figure 5-13.   A movable-head disk system. Each read/write head is assigned to a particular disk surface. As the mounting shaft spins the disks, the comblike access mechanism moves the heads in or out between the disks to read or write data on the tracks. On most systems, all the heads move together. So if you needed to retrieve data from track 211 on surface 2, all the read/write heads must move together to track 211. At that point, the head assigned to surface 2 would read the data. Only one head may be actively reading or writing at any one time.

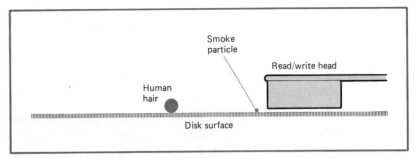

Figure 5-14.   The space between a disk and a read/write head compared to a smoke particle and a human hair. A human hair or even a smoke particle, if present on a disk surface, can damage both the surface and the read/write head.

be like placing a pebble on your favorite phonograph album while playing it.

Disk Cylinders.   An important principle for understanding disk storage and access strategies is the concept of **disk cylinders.** Again, consider the disk system of Figure 5-12. In the disk pack shown, there are eight possible recording surfaces, with 400 tracks per surface. One might envision the disk pack to be composed of 400 imaginary, concentric cylinders, each consisting of eight tracks, as illustrated in Figure 5-15. Outer cylinders fit over the inner ones like sleeves. Each cylinder is equivalent to

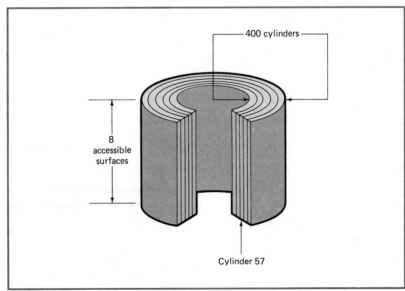

Figure 5-15.   The cylinder concept. To imagine any particular cylinder, think of pushing an actual cylinder such as a tin can downward through the same track in each disk in the pack. In this example, cylinder 57 is made up of track 57 on surfaces 1 through 8.

a track position to which the heads on the access mechanism can move. In a movable-head disk system, all the read/write heads are positioned on the same cylinder when data is read from or written to one of the tracks on that cylinder.

Disk Access Time. In movable-head disk systems, there are three tasks that must be accomplished in order to access data. First, the read/write head must move to the cylinder on which the data are stored. Suppose, for example, the read/write head is on cylinder 5, and we wish to retrieve data from cylinder 36. To do this, the mechanism must move inward to cylinder 36. The time required to do this is referred to as **access motion time.**

Second, when a read or write order is issued, the heads are not usually aligned over the position on the track where the required data are stored. So, there is some delay involved while the mounting shaft rotates the disks into the proper position. (The disks are always spinning, whether or not reading or writing is taking place.) The time needed to complete this alignment is called **rotational delay.**

Third, once the read/write head is positioned over the correct data, the data must be read from disk and transferred *to* the CPU (or transferred *from* the CPU and written onto disk). This last step is known as **data movement time.** The sum of these three components is known as **disk access time.**

In reading from and writing to disk storage, two strategies can be used to reduce disk access time. An inexpensive strategy, which is almost universal in data-processing shops, is to store related data on the same cylinder—which sharply reduces access motion time. For example, if we need to store 500 records, and it is possible to place 100 records on a track (requiring five tracks), it is better to select five tracks on the same cylinder rather than on different ones. Thus, if we store the 500 records on cylinder 235, we need only one movement of the access mechanism to reach all 500 records.

A second solution is to acquire a *fixed-head disk unit.* These systems have a read/write head for *each* track on *every* surface, eliminating access motion time entirely. For example, eight accessible surfaces and 400 tracks per surface would require a total of 3200 read/write heads mounted onto the eight access-mechanism arms. Fixed-head systems are much faster than movable-head ones, but because they are much more expensive, they aren't as widely used.

Disk Addressing. Disk systems are addressable. This means that each record is located at a unique **disk address,** which can be automatically determined by the computer system. A single disk address may store a single record of a data file, and several such addresses may store a complete program or data file. Figure 5-16 shows one method of accessing disk records by address. In the system illustrated, the address for each record is a combination of the cylinder number, the surface number, and finally, the record number. In the figure, a program called "FINANCE-FORECAST" is stored on cylinder 57, on surface 4, in record position 2. Thus the address of the beginning of this program is 0570402.

Key-to-Disk Unit.   Earlier, we mentioned that a key-to-tape unit is used to transcribe data onto tape. A similar device, called a **key-to-disk unit,** is used for entering data onto disk. To lower the cost of the data-entry operation, several keyboards may be clustered around a single key-to-disk unit. This arrangement permits two or more operators to enter data onto different parts of the disk at the same time. A key-to-disk device is shown in Figure 5-17.

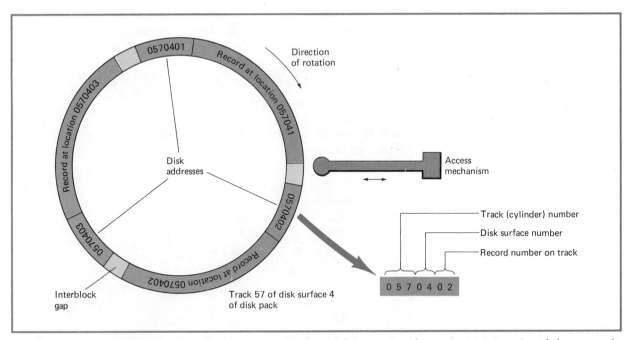

Figure 5-16.   Addressing on disk. Suppose all programs and data are stored on a single disk pack and three records can be stored per track. Also assume that all disk addresses are seven digits long and are composed of track number, disk surface number, and record number, as shown. The computer system uses a directory (similar to a telephone book), which can be searched to find the disk addresses at which any program or block of data begins.

For example, if a user wants a program named "FINANCE-FORECAST," the system would look up FINANCE-FORECAST in the directory. Here it would find the address at which this program begins, say 0570402. This number tells the disk unit that the program starts on the 57th cylinder, on surface 4, at the second record position. The read/write head then moves to this position to fetch the program.

Figure 5-17. A key-to-disk unit.

Floppy Disks

Floppy disks (sometimes called *floppies* or *diskettes*) are made of a tough, flexible plastic and coated with a substance that can be magnetized. They are generally available in two sizes (diameters), 5¼ inch and 8 inch, as shown in Figure 5-18. Recently, floppies with diameters of less than 4 inches have also become commercially available.

Floppy disks function in much the same way as hard disks. Data are recorded as magnetized spots on concentric tracks, and

Figure 5-18. Floppy disks. These small diskettes are popular for microcomputer systems.

The "Inside Track" on Floppy Disks

Today, floppy disks, or diskettes, are the most popular storage medium for home computer systems. These disks are round plastic platters coated with a layer of material that can be magnetized. The concentric tracks are polarized so as to represent data and programs in terms of 0- and 1-bits.

A floppy disk is encased in a jacket lined with soft material that wipes the disk clean as it turns. The openings in the cover enable the disk drive to clasp the hub in the center of the disk. They also permit the read/write heads to retrieve data from the recording surfaces. The small write-protect notch at the periphery of the jacket prevents the user from writing on the disk. With 5¼-inch diameter diskettes, covering the notch makes it impossible to write on the surface. The convention on 8-inch diameter diskettes is completely the opposite: exposing the notch makes writing impossible.

Diskettes can function only when they are inserted into a disk drive. The drive spins the disk at a speed of about 300 to 400 revolutions per minute. The read/write heads, which are in the drive mechanism, are controlled by commands issued by the computer system. Some disk units contain only one drive; others contain several. Most computer systems allow the user to increase the number of disk drives to meet growing processing needs. An additional feature of the drives is that they may be either single- or double-sided. Single-sided drives permit access to only one side of a floppy disk, whereas double-sided drives allow access to both sides.

Diskettes are recorded at one of two bit densities. Single-density diskettes are written to pack data at 3200 bits per inch (bpi), as measured along the innermost track of the disk, and double-density diskettes employ a density of 6400 bpi. Drives that support double-density recording usually support single-density recording as well. Floppy disks range in storage capacity from 125,000 to 500,000 bytes of data.

Diskettes usually cannot be read by an operating system other than the one that recorded them, even though they could be mounted on the drive of another system. Thus, unless you and a friend use the same operating system, you will not be able to trade diskettes.

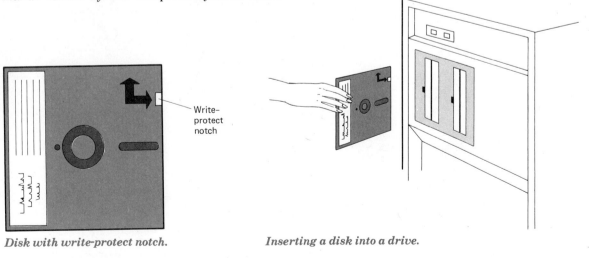

Write-protect notch

Disk with write-protect notch.

Inserting a disk into a drive.

records can be retrieved directly. There are, however, some important differences between floppies and hard disks:

- Floppy disks are not grouped in tiered packs, as hard disks are. They are available as single platters stored in a paper or plastic envelope. As a result, they are as portable as magnetic tape.
- Retrieval of data from floppies takes place between ten and 100 times more slowly than from hard disks.
- Floppy disks can store far fewer data than hard disks. For example, a single floppy disk for the IBM Personal Computer has a storage capacity of approximately 160,000 bytes, about enough to store thirty-five typewritten pages. The IBM 3350 disk storage unit, on the other hand, has a capacity of more than 317 million bytes, nearly the equivalent of 2000 floppy disks.
- As you might imagine, floppy disk systems are much less expensive. A hard-disk pack may cost several hundred dollars, whereas a floppy disk costs about $5. Also, whereas users may have to pay several thousand dollars for a hard-disk unit, they can purchase a floppy disk unit for under $500.

Figure 5-19 shows two floppy disk units.

Figure 5-19.   Two floppy disk units.

Figure 5-20.   Winchester disk unit. The outer plastic case contains both the disk pack and the access mechanism.

1. Sealed in plastic container
2. Sealed with pericght heads

Winchester Disks

Although most microcomputer systems use floppy disks today, small sealed units called **Winchester disks** (see Figure 5-20) are threatening to become the major secondary storage devices on these computer systems in the future. Winchesters, which are a special type of hard disk, have far greater data-carrying capacity than floppies. Floppy disk systems (which typically have drives for several floppy disks) usually have a maximum capacity of about 2 million bytes, whereas comparable Winchester systems may have a capacity of 50 million or more. Because the Winchesters can store so much more data, the operator is not burdened with shuffling disks in and out of disk drives, as is the case with floppies. Winchesters are also much faster than floppy disks. Because of their sealed design, some Winchesters can even achieve speeds greater than those of conventional hard-disk drives.

Winchesters do have some disadvantages, however. They are more expensive and less portable than floppies. Chances are that small computers in the future will use both Winchester and floppy technologies—Winchesters for their speed and large storage capacity and floppies for their portability and backup capability.

TAPE VERSUS DISK: ADVANTAGES AND DISADVANTAGES

Although tape was developed earlier than disk, it retains some key advantages in large-scale commercial applications. For example,

- Most organizations keep *backup files* of important programs and data, in case the originals are lost or destroyed. It is much cheaper to store such material offline on tape than on disk. A disk pack may cost fifty times more than the tapes required to store the same amount of data.

- Many program and data files are not processed on a day-to-day basis. Organizations often store such files offline. Again, tape is more economical for this purpose.

- It is easier to transport tape because of the size and portability of reels. Disk packs are more awkward, fragile, and costly to ship than reels of tape.

These advantages must be weighed against the problems of working with tape. Chief among the difficulties is the sequential nature of tape. Data on tape must be processed in a fixed order. To find a specific record, the read/write head must first pass over all intervening records, a process that wastes time.

Disks represent a significant improvement over tapes in several ways. For example,

- Files can be organized so that records can be processed not only in a fixed order but also in a random order. Airline reservations data, for example, are stored on disk because it is impossible to anticipate the order in which customers will request flight information.
- Access to disk is much faster than to tape, because read/write heads can move directly to the desired record. In large systems, where there may be millions of independent accesses to a file daily, tape processing is impossible.
- More data can be stored online with disk units than with tape units.

Because of these key advantages, disk has evolved as the most important secondary storage medium, with tape clearly taking a back seat. The advantages notwithstanding, however, disk storage is relatively expensive and requires more sophisticated hardware and software than does tape.

DATA ACCESS AND DATA ORGANIZATION

When the computer system is instructed to use data or programs residing in secondary storage, it must be able to find the materials first. The process of retrieving data and programs in storage is called **data access.** Arranging data so they can be retrieved efficiently is called **data organization.**

Of course, the way in which information is organized affects how we gain access to it as well as how quickly we can do so. Because encyclopedias have an index and are alphabetically arranged, we can find a description of, say, the Oracle at Delphi much more quickly than if we simply thumbed through one volume after another, looking for the appropriate passages. Conversely, the kind of access we want strongly influences the way in which we organize our data. The encyclopedia has been set up deliberately to promote rapid access to information. In the following pages, we will see how access and organization are related to each other in the context of secondary storage.

Access Methods

As we have seen, a major difference between tape and disk is that data on tape can only be retrieved sequentially, whereas data on disk can be retrieved both sequentially and in a direct (random) fashion. With **sequential access** the records in a file can only be retrieved in the same sequence in which they are physically stored. For example, if we have an employee file containing 700 records and we want the 605th record, we would have to "thumb through" the first 604 records to get to it. As you might imagine, this procedure wastes a lot of time. With **direct access** (also known as **random access**), on the other hand, a record can be retrieved immediately. Thus, if direct access is possible on the employee file, we would not have to pass through 604 records to obtain the 605th one. We could get to it right away. This can make a big difference if the file contains thousands of records and if data from them must be retrieved thousands (or millions) of times in a short period of time.

The distinction between sequential and direct access can be observed on a typical home stereo system. Suppose you have both a cassette tape and a phonograph record of the same album of music. Say, for example, you want to hear the fifth song on side 1 of the record. Suppose also that this song is the fifth selection on the tape. On the tape, you must pass sequentially through the first four songs to hear the fifth one. With the phonograph record, however, you can place the needle directly on the fifth song and listen to it immediately.

The phonograph record is also effective as a sequential-access device. If you want to listen to the entire first side of the album, you simply place the needle at the beginning of the record and play the tunes in sequence. Thus, the phonograph record is really both a sequential- and a direct-access medium, in that we can play a series of songs sequentially or pick individual ones in random order.

Now, let's apply this distinction to computer systems. Machine-readable magnetic tape has the sequential properties of music tape, and magnetic disk has both the sequential and direct properties of the phonograph record. Magnetic disk, however, has properties that a phonograph record does not have:

- It is erasable.

- It can store far more information than a phonograph record. Thus, magnetic disks do not have to be mounted and dismounted frequently like phonograph records. In fact, many magnetic disks aren't ever removed from their disk units.

- It has tracks that are concentric rather than spiral (see Figure 5-21).

Additionally, computer disks and tapes operate at far greater speeds than the records and tapes of the stereo system.

Some data-processing applications are esssentially sequential in nature, and others are direct. For example, the preparation of mailing labels is often a sequential operation. If we want to send Christmas cards to all employees in a company, we can process the computerized employee file sequentially, from the beginning of the list to the end. As names and addresses are extracted from the file, they are printed on the mailing labels. Obtaining the latest inventory information about products, on the other hand, often involves direct processing, because requests are made to the inventory file in random order. For example, a salesperson for a book publisher might query a computerized product file on a CRT terminal to find out how many units of item 6042, *How to Raise and Train a Labrador Retriever,* are on hand. A minute later, a customer may call to find out the price of item 36, *Cooking Chinese Style.* Then a question comes up regarding deliveries of item 988, *Paris on $25*

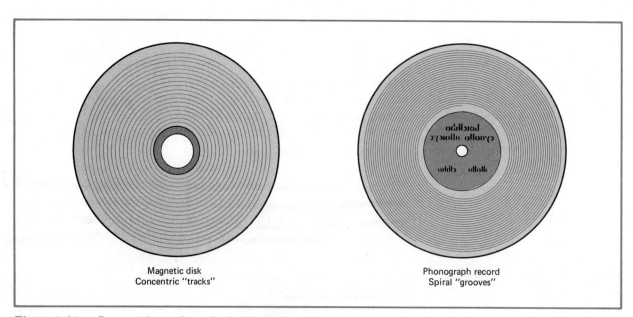

Magnetic disk
Concentric "tracks"

Phonograph record
Spiral "grooves"

Figure 5-21.   Concentric tracks and spiral grooves.

a Day or More. We move randomly back and forth through the records to obtain information from this file.

We could process mailing labels easily by using either tape or disk, but the inventory application is possible only on disk. We can't move the tape forward and backward to access information on today's tape units. Even if we could, the delay caused by fast-forwarding and fast-reversing the tape would be enormous. Disks are much better suited to this kind of operation.

We can categorize all secondary storage media and their devices in terms of whether they permit sequential or direct access. Those that are classified as direct, such as disk, generally allow both sequential and direct access.

Data Organization

Our need for certain access methods necessarily dictates our choice of ways to organize data files. Only if data are organized in certain ways can they be retrieved in others. Let's consider a practical example. Most book libraries are organized with card indexes ordered by title, author, and subject, so you can retrieve books directly. If you want James Martin's *Computer Networks and Distributed Processing,* you simply look under the title of the book in the index, find its call number (QA 76.9 D5), and go directly to the QA shelves to find the book. This type of organization is referred to as an *indexed organization.* Indexed organization schemes facilitate direct access.

Suppose, however, there are no card indexes and books were organized alphabetically by title on a single continuous shelf. With such a *sequential organization* of books, it would take much longer to retrieve the title you want. You might go to the middle of the shelf and find the titles starting with the letter *F*. Then, you would backtrack several yards until you saw titles beginning with *C*. Finally, you would find *Computer Networks and Distributed Processing.* As you can see, sequential organization does not permit easy access to a specific book.

Data organization on computers works in a similar fashion. *First* we decide the type of access we need—direct, sequential, or both. *Then* we organize the data in a way that minimizes the time needed to retrieve data with these types of access.

There are many ways to organize data. Here we will describe three—sequential, indexed-sequential, and relative organization.

Sequential Organization. In a file having a **sequential organization,** records follow one another in a fixed sequence. Sequentially organized files are generally ordered by a key field or fields, such as an ID number. Thus, if a four-digit ID number were the key field being used to order the file, the record belonging to ID number 0612, say, would be stored after number 0611 but before number 0613, as shown in Figure 5-22. When tape is the medium, records can only be organized sequentially. Any other organization is physically impossible. On disks, however, records may be organized sequentially or otherwise.

tomorrow

DIRECT-ACCESS SECONDARY STORAGE: A LOOK AT THE FUTURE

If you think that direct-access secondary storage is fast approaching its limits, you're in for a surprise. About twenty-five years ago, storing a million bytes of data required a surface area about the size of a double bed. Today, the same amount of memory can fit on a silicon chip the size of a fingernail. If current trends continue, and many knowledgeable people believe they will, a million bytes of memory will fit on a surface smaller than the head of a pin in another twenty-five years.

To date, the storage density of disks has doubled about every 2½ years. This means that there has been about a 5000-fold improvement in storage efficiency since the first commercial magnetic disk was produced in the mid-1950s. How will secondary storage technologies change in the future in order to maintain this trend toward more efficient memory? There are several possibilities.

Most experts agree that magnetic disk storage will not be the secondary storage technology of tomorrow for two reasons: speed and density. Because disk drives rely heavily on moving parts, there is a limit to the speed at which they can operate. And because magnetic recording techniques enable bit data to be packed only so close before interference occurs, there is a forsee-able limit to the amount of data that can be packed onto a conventional disk. The two most promising technologies that offer a way past the limitations of conventional disk storage are optical disk devices and semiconductor mass memories.

Optical Disk Devices. Storage devices based on this technology use laser beams of high intensity to burn tiny holes in the surface of a disk platter, thereby storing data in digital form. The data can then be read from the disk by means of a laser beam of lower intensity. Since it is possible to pack data closer together by using light than by current magnetic technologies, much more data can be placed onto a disk. Densities on the optical disk can be as high as hundreds of millions of bits per square inch. A single surface of an optical disk may contain up to 50 billion bytes, whereas the best magnetic disk packs are limited to a storage capacity of a few hundred million bytes. According to one estimate, the entire contents of the National Archives could be stored on about 1000 optical disks.

In optical disk devices, moving mirrors project the beam from a stationary laser through a lens system to any point on the disk. This technology makes the optical disk much faster than conventional disk drives, which have more moving parts.

One problem with the optical disk systems

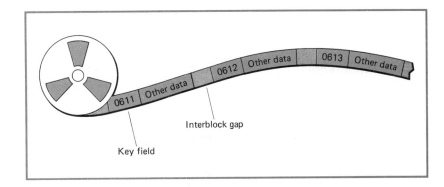

Figure 5-22. Sequential organization of records on tape.

of today is that data, once recorded, cannot be erased. Recently, however, researchers have found ways to overcome this limitation, and erasable optical disks are expected to reach the market by the 1990s. Even though today's disks cannot be erased, optical disk systems are still a viable alternative for storing archival data and other information that does not need to be updated or changed in other ways. Optical disks are expected to compete strongly with microfilm systems, which are discussed in Chapter 6.

Semiconductor Mass Storage. The dominant technology today for fast *primary* computer memory is the semiconductor. Semiconductor technology could also be used for secondary storage, and would have many advantages if it were. Semiconductor devices, for example, are all electronic—they have no mechanical parts—which makes them much faster than conventional disk drives.

Any secondary storage devices based on semiconductors must be designed so that data and programs stored on them would not be erased if the power were turned off. Even though today's semiconductor *primary* memories are volatile, meaning they lose their contents in the absence of power, nonvolatile semiconductor (EEPROM) memories are beginning to become available. But the main problem today with using semiconductor devices for secondary stor-

age is economic, not technical. They cost too much to be practical. Prices, however, have fallen dramatically over the past several years. And because semiconductors are so important for primary memory, many experts feel that continuing demand will lead to new technological improvements. These improvements, coupled with high production volumes, could drive prices down even further. Whether the cost of semiconductor storage devices will fall low enough in the next several years to make them a feasible replacement for conventional disk storage is an issue of heated debate.

An optical disk.

Now that you have an idea of what sequential organization is, let's see how it is used in data processing. Many companies update customer balances and prepare bills at the end of the month. Such an operation is known as a *sequential update.* Two data files are used. The *master file* normally contains the ID number of the customer, the amount owed at the beginning of the month, and additional information about the customer. This file is sorted by the key field, customer ID number, and records are arranged from low ID numbers to high. The *transaction file* contains all the transactions carried out during the month by the old customers, who appear in the master file, and by new customers, who do not. Transactions might include purchases and payments. Like the master file, the transaction file is ordered by customer ID number and arranged from low to high.

In a sequential update, the two files are processed together, in the manner shown in Figure 5-23. The sequential-update program reads a record from each file. If the key fields match, the operation specified in the transaction file is made. You'll note, in the figure, that the key fields of the first records in each file match. Thus, record 101 is updated in the updated customer master file. For example, if the transaction file shows that customer 101 bought a toaster, data on this purchase are added to the master file. Next, both files are "rolled forward" to the next records. Here the program observes that customer 102 is not in the master file, since the next master file record after 101 is 103. Therefore, this must be a new customer, and the program will create a new record for customer 102 in the updated master file. At this point, only the transaction file will be rolled forward, to customer 103. The program now observes that this record matches the one it is currently pointing to in the master file. However, the transaction file indicates that 103 is a new customer. Hence, there appears to be an inconsistency, since the master file contains only old customers. The program makes no entry in the updated master file but sends information about this transaction to the error report.

The processing continues in this manner until both files are exhausted. The processing is sequential in nature because the computer processes the records in both files in the order in which they physically appear.

Indexed-Sequential Organization. **Indexed-sequential organization** (often called *ISAM,* for *Indexed-Sequential Access Method*) is a way of organizing data for both sequential and direct access. This type of organization requires a disk medium, since tapes can't provide direct access. Records are stored sequentially on the disk. In addition, each record is listed under its key field in an index much like the indexes in a book library. This index permits direct access to records.

The first step in locating a specified record is finding its key in the index. Opposite the key field of the record in the index is its disk address. The CPU then directs the read/write heads to

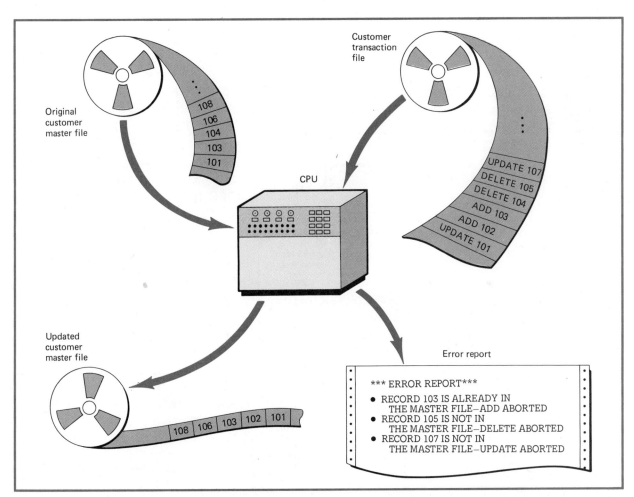

Figure 5-23. *A sequential update of a master file.* Each customer record in the original master file might contain the customer's ID number (the key field), name, address, amount owed, and credit limit. For simplicity, only the key field is shown in the illustration.

The transaction file contains a record of each customer transaction. Each record in this file might contain the customer's ID number (the key field), the amount of the purchase or payment, and the type of transaction involved (update, add, or delete). Only the key field and type of transaction are shown in the illustration, again for simplicity.

As both files are processed together, an updated master file is produced as well as a printed listing of records, which for one reason or another couldn't be processed because of some discrepancy.

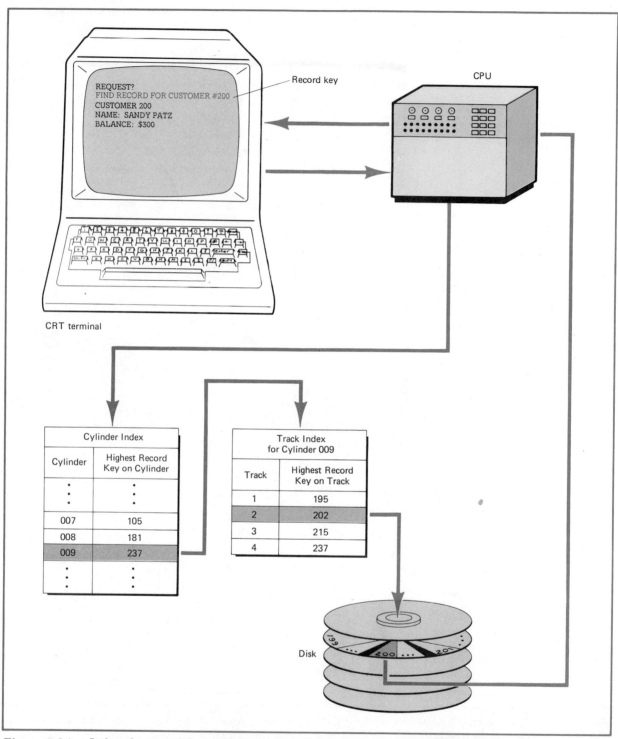

Figure 5-24. *Indexed-sequential organization.* Records are ordered sequentially by key on disk, and all disk addresses are entered in an index. To access any record, say number 200, the computer system proceeds as follows. After the request has been relayed from the terminal to the CPU, the computer system first searches a cylinder index and then a track index for the address of the record. In the cylinder index, it learns that the record is on cylinder 009. The computer system then consults the track index for cylinder 009, where it observes that the record is on track 2 of that cylinder. The access mechanism then proceeds to this track to locate the record.

proceed directly to this disk address. This procedure is illustrated in Figure 5-24.

Many computer systems have systems programs that help programmers set up indexes and indexed-sequential-organized files painlessly. As records are added to or deleted from a file, the computer's systems software automatically adds them to or deletes them from the disk and updates the index.

Since the records remain organized sequentially on the disk, the file can be processed sequentially at any time. Sequential processing may begin either with the first record of the file or with some record further along.

Relative Organization. Although indexed files are suitable for many applications, the process of finding disk addresses in one or more indexes can be time-consuming. Schemes of relative organization have been developed to overcome this disadvantage by permitting direct access in the shortest possible time.

Relative organization eliminates the need for an index by translating the key field of the record directly into a disk address. In the simplest possible case, the key is itself the disk address of the record. For example, if there were only ten possible addresses on a disk, and if we had ten records, then a single-digit key, ranging from 0 to 9, could be used to place each record in a relative location with a unique disk address. Thus, record 0 would be placed in the disk location with the address 0. Once the computer system knows the key of the record, it also knows the address of the record, and it can retrieve the record directly, without reading other records.

In the real world, the process of transforming the key field of a record in any file into a relative disk location is more complicated. Generally, the number of possible keys is larger than the number of actual records. Suppose, for example, a company has 1000 employees and, therefore, 1000 active employee numbers. Also suppose that all employee identification numbers (the key field) are four digits long. Therefore, the possible range of ID numbers is from 0000 to 9999. It would be a waste of space to use ID numbers for the disk addresses, since there are 10,000 possible ID numbers but only 1000 employees.

A solution to this problem is to use a mathematical formula to transform key fields into disk addresses, a process called **hashing.** A number of hashing procedures have been developed. One of the simplest involves dividing the key field by the prime number closest to, but not greater than, the number of records to be stored. A prime number can be divided evenly by itself and 1, but not by any other number. The remainder of the division by the prime number (not the quotient) becomes the address of the relative location in which the record will be stored.

Suppose that the company in our example wants to place the record of employee number 8742 onto disk. The hashing procedure would take place as follows. The prime number closest to 1000, the number of records to be stored, is 997. Figure 5-25 shows that the address of the relative disk location is 766. (Note that records organized according to a relative scheme are not stored sequentially by key field, as they are in indexed-sequential organization.) After the record has been placed at the designated address, the computer can retrieve it as needed by applying the hashing procedure to the key field of the record again. Calculation of an address in this manner usually consumes much less time than would a search through one or more indexes.

Procedures for hashing are difficult to develop and are certainly not without problems. For example, it is possible for two or more records to be hashed to the same relative disk location. This, of course, means they will "collide" at the same disk address. When this happens, one record is placed in the computed location and assigned a "pointer" chaining it to the other, which is often placed in the available location closest to

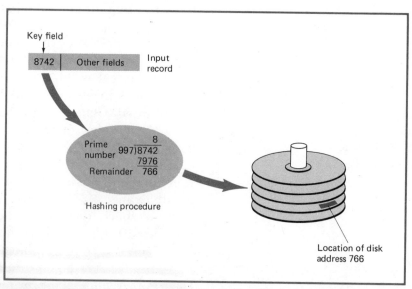

Figure 5-25. Hashing illustrated. The CPU follows a hashing procedure to assign a record to a disk address. In this case the hashing procedure involves dividing the key field by the prime number closest to 1000—997. The remainder becomes the disk address.

the hashed address. Good hashing procedures result in few collisions. A detailed discussion of them is well beyond the scope of this book.

OTHER SECONDARY STORAGE MEDIA AND EQUIPMENT

Although tape and disk systems are by far the most common form of secondary storage, a number of other systems are in use today. Among these are the mass storage unit, magnetic bubble memory, and optical disk storage.

Mass Storage Unit

Disk storage units can make large amounts of data available online, but they have limitations. In many systems, disk packs must be manually loaded onto the disk unit, which takes time. Disk systems with nonremovable packs avoid this problem but are limited in the amount of data they can store. For most applications, these are not serious drawbacks. But because the capacity of the largest disk units is only a few billion characters, organizations that must keep massive amounts of data online to the CPU have found **mass storage units** extremely useful. A device such as the IBM 3850 mass storage unit can store 472 billion bytes of data, the equivalent of almost 50,000 reels of magnetic tape.

The IBM 3850 consists of 9440 cylindrical data cells, each capable of storing 50 million bytes of data. Each cell contains a spool of 3-inch magnetic tape, 770 feet long. The cells reside in a honeycombed shaped rack, as you can see in Figure 5-26. When the data in a cell must be retrieved, a mechanical arm pulls the correct cell from its container. Next, the tape is unwound, the data are transferred to disk, and processing is performed. All this takes place automatically, without the aid of human operators.

With mass storage, the user sacrifices speed to gain storage capacity. Retrieval of the data cell and transfer of the data to disk may take as long as fifteen seconds. Compared to the fraction of a second that elapses during access to disk, fifteen seconds is a long time. Therefore, mass storage is only feasible for applications with enormous online storage requirements.

Magnetic Bubble Storage

Magnetic bubble storage is a secondary memory technology in which thousands of magnetized bubbles, each a fraction of the diameter of a human hair, are arranged on a thin film of magnetic material. The presence of a bubble in a location represents a 1-bit, and its absence, a 0-bit. Bubble storage is often packaged in chip form, as shown in Figure 5-27.

During the late 1970s, many experts thought that magnetic bubble devices would replace disks as the major secondary storage medium in computer systems. This optimism was grounded in the fact that magnetic bubble units are static, requiring no moving parts. By contrast, disk units generally employ spinning platters and movable access heads. Besides being faster, static assemblies are generally much more reliable

Figure 5-26.   The IBM 3850 mass storage unit. The unit pictured here has enough memory capacity to store a 100-character record for every person in the world or, alternatively, the capacity to hold as many words as there are in 27 million pages of a typical daily newspaper.

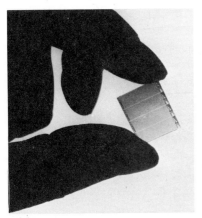

Figure 5-27. *A magnetic bubble memory chip.*

than nonstatic ones, resulting in fewer errors and maintenance problems. So far, bubble devices have failed to live up to expectations, largely because their cost is still relatively high when compared to that of disks.

Despite their apparent failure to capture the market for storage devices, magnetic bubbles are popular components in many electronic machines. They are often used as memory units in terminals, desk-top computers, robots, and communications devices.

Optical Disks

An emerging technology that many expect to have profound effects on the capacity and techniques of secondary storage is the **optical disk.** With this technology, laser beams write and read data at incredible densities, thousands of times greater than the density of a typical disk. Data are placed onto optical disks with high-intensity laser beams that burn tiny holes into the surface of the disk. A laser beam of lower intensity then reads the data that have been inscribed.

Optical disks are similar to, but not the same as, the "video disks" marketed for home use by companies in the entertainment industry. For one thing, not all video disks use optical laser technology. Also, today's video disk systems involve a disk that can only be read, not written upon. Moreover, this technology is designed to work with a television set. By contrast, optical disk is evolving as a read/write technology available for a wider number of applications.

Summary and Key Terms

Secondary storage technologies make it economically feasible to keep large quantities of programs and data online to the CPU. The most common types of secondary storage media are magnetic tape and magnetic disk.

Magnetic tape normally consists of ½-inch-wide plastic Mylar, coated with a magnetizable substance, and wound on a 10½-inch-diameter reel. Each character of data is represented in byte form across **tracks** in the tape. Many tapes contain nine tracks—eight corresponding to the eight bits in a byte, and an additional parity track to check for transmission errors.

Magnetic tape is also available in cassette form. Although **cassette tape** is popular on microcomputer systems, it is rapidly losing its purely economic advantage to small disks as technological advancements and costs on small disk systems continue to become more favorable.

In order for the tape to be processed by the CPU it must be mounted on a hardware device called a **tape unit.** The drives on the tape unit spin the tape past a **read/write head,** which either reads from or writes to the tape. Records are often systematically organized on a tape with respect to a **key field,** such as a customer ID number.

Because the tape unit requires records to pass by the read/write head at a constant speed, **interblock (interrecord) gaps** must be provided on the tape for acceleration and deceleration between records. To minimize the number of these gaps on the tape, a technique called **blocking** is frequently used. With this technique, conventional data records (called **logical records**) are grouped, or *blocked,* into **physical records.** The number of logical records blocked into a physical record is called the **blocking factor.**

The size of a physical record depends, to a large extent, on the size of input-record **buffers** within the computer unit. Often, there are two of these buffers. Each buffer can contain a complete physical record. Because the buffers are within the all-electronic computer unit, records in them can be fetched quickly by active programs.

Tapes are often prepared offline for computer processing on a device known as a **key-to-tape unit.** If data to be recorded onto tape are already somewhere in the computer system in machine-readable form, *systems programs* are normally available to transfer the data from their present medium onto tape.

Tapes have many features designed to prevent careless processing errors. A **file-protection ring,** for example, must be inserted at the center of a tape reel in order to write onto the tape. Also, an **internal header label** is used to carry identifying information about the tape, so this information can be carefully verified by the computer system before any processing takes place.

Magnetic disk is commonly available in the form of hard disks and floppy disks.

A **hard disk** is a magnetized metal platter which is frequently 14 inches in diameter. Data are represented in byte form on concentric tracks on the disk surface. The same amount of data is stored on each track of the disk to keep the data-transfer rate constant throughout the disk system.

Usually, several disks are assembled into a **disk pack.** The disk pack, in turn, is mounted onto a **disk storage unit** (**disk unit**), which enables the data on the disk to be online to the CPU. In a *movable-head disk unit,* which is the most common type of disk system, a read/write head is assigned to each recordable disk surface. The heads are mounted onto an **access mechanism,** which can move them in and out among the concentric tracks to fetch data.

All tracks in the same position on the tiered platters of a disk pack form what is known as a **disk cylinder.**

Three primary factors determine the time needed to read from or write to disk. **Access motion time** is the time required for the access mechanism to reach a particular track. The time needed for the disk to spin to a specific area of a track is known as **rotational delay.** Once located, data must be transferred to or from the disk, a process known as **data movement time.** The sum of these three time components is collectively called **disk access time.** If related data are placed on tracks belonging to the same disk cylinder, access motion time can be reduced considerably. Disk units that have a read/write head for every track eliminate access motion time entirely.

Each location on disk has a unique **disk address,** so that the computer system can easily keep track of programs and data on the disk unit.

Data are often placed onto disk offline, using a device called a **key-to-disk unit.**

Floppy disks (sometimes called *floppies* or *diskettes*) are small disk platters that are commonly used with personal computers and small minicomputers. Small, sealed hard-disk units called **Winchester disks** are also becoming very popular on these computer systems. Winchesters are faster and have greater data-carrying capacity than floppies. However, they are less portable and more expensive than floppies.

In large-scale commercial applications, disk has several advantages over tape. For example, disk is faster, directly accessible, and capable of greater amounts of online storage. The key advantages of tape over disk are economy for offline storage and portability.

The process of retrieving data and programs in storage is called **data access.** Systematically arranging data so they can be retrieved efficiently is called **data organization.**

There are two general classes of access: sequential and direct. In **sequential access** the records in a file are retrieved in the same relative sequence in which they are stored. In **direct (random) access** the records in a file are retrieved in any order. Tape is strictly a sequential access medium. Disk is capable of both sequential and direct access to data.

There are three major methods of storing files in secondary memory: sequential organization, indexed-sequential organization, and relative organization. In **sequential organization** records are generally arranged with respect to a key field. With **indexed-sequential organization,** records are arranged sequentially by key field on the disk to facilitate sequential access. In addition, one or several indexes are available to permit direct access to the records. **Relative organization** facilitates even further direct access to data. It uses a process called **hashing** to transform the key field of each record into a relative disk address.

Besides tape and disk, several other devices may be used for secondary storage. The **mass storage unit** is particularly suitable for storing enormous quantities of data online. Although slower than disk, it is more cost effective when the CPU must have large quantities of data readily accessible. **Magnetic bubble storage** is frequently used for small amounts of local memory in devices such as terminals, desk-top computers, robots, and communications devices. **Optical disks,** which work with laser read/write devices, are a relatively recent secondary storage technology. Their potential is yet to be realized.

Review Questions

1. How does secondary storage differ from primary storage?
2. Explain how data are stored on magnetic tape.
3. How and why are records blocked on tape?
4. How does buffering work in sequential processing?
5. Compare tape and disk storage in terms of their comparative advantages and possible applications.
6. Identify three types of magnetic disk, and for each type describe a possible situation in which each may be useful.
7. Explain what a disk cylinder is and why it is an important concept.
8. Identify the three components of disk access time and explain how each one works.
9. Why are disk systems addressable?
10. Explain the difference between data access and data organization.
11. Provide an example of both sequential access and direct access to data.
12. How does sequential organization differ from indexed-sequential organization?
13. What is the purpose of hashing a key field in a record?
14. In what type of situation would a mass storage device be useful?

Chapter 6

Input and Output Equipment

Chapter Outline

OVERVIEW

In Chapter 5, we talked about secondary storage devices, which perform both input and output operations for the computer, although storage is their main role. In this chapter, we turn to equipment that is designed primarily for input of programs and data into the computer, for output, or for both. Many of these devices possess a limited amount of storage capacity as well.

We'll begin the chapter with a look at display terminals, which are capable of both input and output. For this reason, they are ideally suited for applications that require considerable interaction between the operator and the computer. We'll also highlight some of the qualities that distinguish one display terminal from another.

After display terminals, we'll discuss printers, which specialize in output. Printers place the results of data processing onto paper, sometimes at incredible speeds. We'll then turn to punched-card equipment, which represents the oldest technology for translating data into a form that the computer can understand.

Next, we'll cover hardware designed for source-data automation. This equipment provides fast and efficient input for certain kinds of applications.

Finally, we'll describe some special-purpose input/output equipment. Included among these devices are machines that can record output on microfilm, equipment created for graphics-oriented applications, and machines that can talk.

Keep in mind that the hardware we describe in this chapter is only a small sample of the kinds of input/output equipment available today. There are, in fact, thousands of products available, and these can be put together in so many ways that it is possible to create a computer system to fit almost any conceivable need.

INPUT AND OUTPUT

Input and output equipment makes it possible for people and computers to communicate. **Input devices** convert data and programs that humans can understand into a form that is comprehensible to the CPU. These devices translate the letters, numbers, and other natural-language symbols that humans conventionally use in reading and writing into the configurations of 0- and 1-bits that the computer uses to process data. **Output devices,** on the other hand, convert the strings of bits used by the computer back into natural-language form to make them understandable to humans. These devices produce output on display terminal screens, paper, or some other medium.

The equipment that we are about to discuss can be classified in a number of ways. Some of it is *peripheral equipment.* These are input or output devices that are under the direct control of the computer. Card readers, display terminals, and printers are examples. Other input or output equipment, such as keypunch machines and verifiers, are *auxiliary equipment.* These devices work independently of the CPU. Some auxiliary devices prepare input data so that these data can later be mounted onto a peripheral device. Others take output that has been produced on a peripheral device and make it more useful to humans.

The equipment, of course, can also be discussed in terms of its input or output functions. Display terminals and teleprinters, for example, are capable of both input and output. Optical character devices are designed primarily for input. Printers and most computer microfilm devices, on the other hand, specialize in output.

DISPLAY TERMINALS

Display terminals are peripheral devices that contain a televisionlike screen for output and, often, a keyboard for input. This type of terminal is commonly called a **CRT (Cathode-Ray Tube).** Although some display terminals use other technologies to produce the image on the screen, CRTs are by far the most common. Thus, we'll use the terms *CRT* and *display terminal* synonymously throughout this text.

CRTs are used when only small amounts of input or output are required. A student writing a program for a class, an airline clerk making inquiries to a flight information file, a stockbroker analyzing a security, or a bank teller checking the status of a customer—each of these people would employ a CRT. The CRT is not suitable for all types of applications. If, for example, the student writing the program expected 100 pages of results, it would be more appropriate to direct output to a high-speed printer. Such a request could easily be initiated, however, from the CRT. After typing in the program, the student need only type in a command like

```
RUN,OUTPUT = PRINTER
```

and then walk over to the printer to pick up the results.

There are many ways to classify the myriad CRTs that are currently available in the marketplace (see Figure 6-1). In this section, we'll differentiate CRTs in terms of the following features:

- Degree of intelligence
- Display-screen characteristics
- Alphanumeric versus graphic capability
- General-purpose versus special-purpose orientation

Degree of Intelligence

The *intelligence* of a CRT is the degree of ability it has to perform certain types of work. With respect to intelligence, CRTs can be classified into three groups: dumb, smart, and user-programmable.

Dumb terminals can handle only the most unsophisticated types of input and output. Often, such CRTs contain no storage facilities. As a result, when the operator types in characters at the keyboard, they are sent directly "down the line" to the computer. If the operator makes a mistake, it is often necessary to backspace to the error and retype the rest of the line. Although dumb terminals may be purchased cheaply, they contain very few features that make the work of the operator easy.

Smart terminals, in contrast, offer sophisticated editing and formatting features designed to expedite typing. These features are implemented with firmware—in other words, the features are available through preprogrammed plug-in modules. A major attraction of smart terminals is cursor flexibility. The **cursor** is a highlighted position on the screen indicating where the next character to be typed in by the operator will be placed. Whereas the cursor in dumb terminals can move only to the right or left, in smart terminals, it can move in many directions. Flexible cursor movement, together with storage capacity in the terminal, enables operators to transmit a block of several lines to the computer system at one time, thereby speeding data entry.

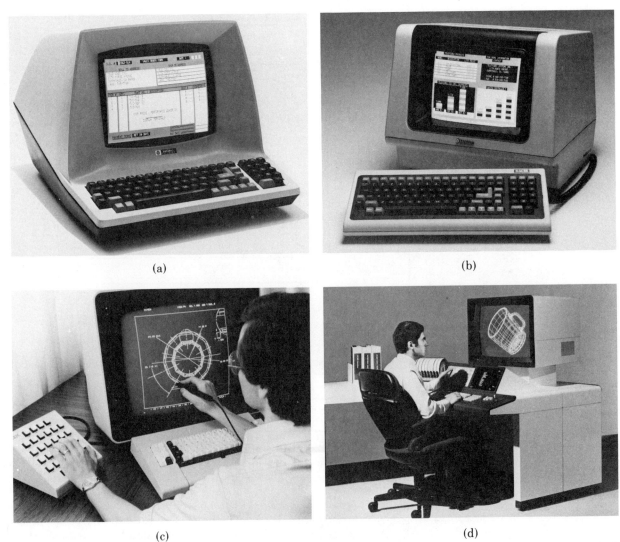

Figure 6-1. *A variety of CRT terminals.* (a) A terminal permitting a formatted screen. (b) A split-screen terminal. (c) A terminal with a touch-sensitive screen. (d) A graphics display terminal.

Another firmware feature that many smart terminals utilize is **softkeys,** also known as **function keys.** When the operator depresses one of these keys, it activates a program that is ROM- or PROM-based. Softkeys may make it easier to fill out forms, such as the one shown in Figure 6-2. These softkeys are often located on the top row of the terminal keyboard and are labeled F1 F2 F3 etc. Pressing the F1 key might erase the current record typed into the form and present a fresh, blank form to the operator. Pressing key F2 might send a

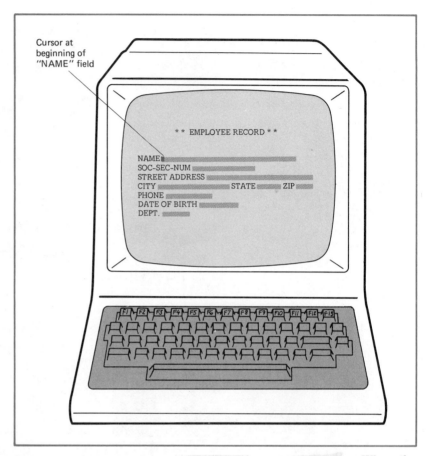

Figure 6-2. Completing a form with a smart terminal. When the operator hits the appropriate softkey, a blank form is presented at the terminal, and the cursor automatically moves to the beginning of the first field. The operator then types data into the shaded areas of the form. Smart terminals often permit automatic tabbing. When the operator types into the last character position in a field, the cursor automatically jumps to the beginning of the next field. Also, many terminals alert the operator to certain kinds of errors, such as the entry of a letter where a number belongs.

completed form to an attached printer for printing. Since the ROM and PROM chips are removable, users of this kind of terminal can assign new functions to softkeys simply by replacing old chips with new ones.

User-programmable terminals are essentially computers. They contain an operating system, language translators, and a local primary memory. In many cases, these terminals also support their own secondary storage devices, such as diskette drives or cassette tape units. They also typically contain all the sophisticated editing, formatting, and softkey features of smart

CRTs. A user-programmable CRT can usually operate both by itself, in a standalone mode, or online to a larger computer. Except for the fact that these terminals have special communications features to facilitate transmission with large computers, many of them are almost identical to microcomputers in many respects.

Characteristics of Display Screens

CRTs differ widely in the display features available on their screens. Some of these differences are described as follows.

Color.   Most CRTs sold today have two-color displays—white on black, green on black, amber on black, and so forth. Some machines also have a *reverse video* feature for two-color output so that, for example, a white-on-black image can be changed to a black-on-white one. Multicolor displays offering a variety of colors are also commonly available.

Highlighting.   Some terminals permit operators to vary the brightness of selected characters on the screen. Thus, certain key words or fields can be highlighted (see Figure 6-1*a*). Additionally, some CRTs can make selected characters blink.

Paging and/or Scrolling.   A *paging* facility enables operators to flip through a long program or data file page by page on the terminal screen. Since a screen often consists of twenty-four lines, each page will be this length. The operator can generally display any page of a file simply by issuing the appropriate command at the terminal.

In *scrolling,* a program or data file is displayed on the screen similarly to the way the roll on a player piano is unwound. As lines successively disappear from the top of the screen, new ones appear from the bottom. Almost all CRTs with this feature allow the operator to halt the scrolling at any time, and some even permit manipulation of the scrolling speed. Most terminals enable operators to work in either the page or scroll mode.

Split-Screen Display.   As illustrated in Figure 6-1*b*, on some CRTs it is possible for operators to display two page images on one physical screen. This is very similar to the split-screen effect one often sees in sporting events on television.

Touch-Sensitivity. Some terminals respond when the operator touches a finger or light pen to a position on the display screen. Machines with such a feature are called *touch-sensitive CRTs*. They are especially effective in graphics applications or in applications in which the input procedures followed by the CRT operator must be simple. A touch-sensitive CRT is shown in Figure 6-1c. The *light pen* contains a light-sensitive cell at its tip. When the tip of the pen is placed against the screen, the terminal can identify its position. Additionally, many pens are equipped with a press-button feature, which flips through pages on the display screen. This process is shown in Figure 6-3.

Windowing. Computer systems can create displays in memory that are far larger than can be shown on a CRT screen at any one time. For this reason, many display terminals have a feature called *windowing,* which makes it possible for users to call up any portion of a large display that will fit on the screen. For example, a system might allow an accountant to create a spreadsheet with 256 columns and 256 rows of data. The terminal the accountant is working at, however, may only be able to display 8 columns and 24 rows at a time. But because the terminal permits windowing, the accountant can use the screen as a *window* on any 8 by 24 block of data from the spreadsheet. By pressing the appropriate cursor movement keys, the accountant can move the window around the spreadsheet at will to see other data.

Other Features. CRTs also vary in many other characteristics. Some examples are screen size, the number of characters that can fit on the screen, the clarity (or *resolution*) of the characters, and the ability to display lowercase as well as uppercase letters.

Alphanumeric and Graphic Capability

Alphanumeric display terminals are CRTs that are designed primarily to display character data, that is letters, digits, and other symbols. **Graphic display terminals,** as shown in Figure 6-1d, go a step further. They can display both characters and high-quality graphic material such as graphs, charts, diagrams, maps, and pictures. As you might expect, graphic display terminals are considerably more expensive than alphanumeric ones.

The largest market for graphics CRTs today is in the engineering and scientific fields. The terminals are used for

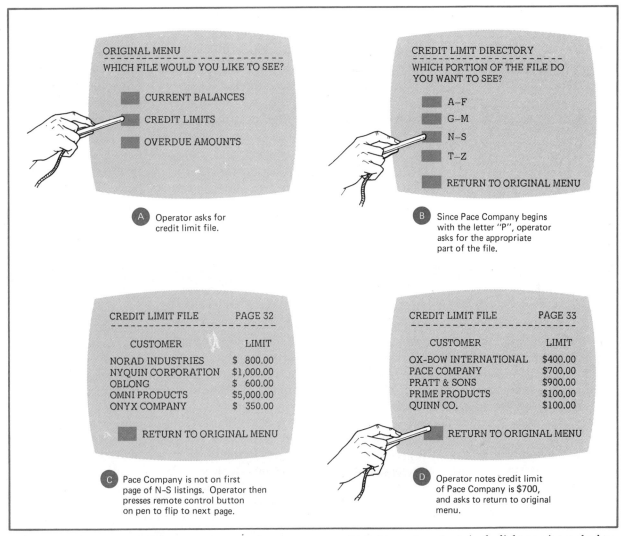

Figure 6-3. *Simple series of screens presented to an operator of a light-pen terminal.* As the light pen is touched to the desired option, the terminal automatically flips to the appropriate display. In the panel of screens shown, the operator is attempting to locate the credit limit of Pace Company.

mapping, circuit design, mechanical design, drafting, and other tasks. Such applications collectively fall under the heading of *computer-aided design/computer-aided manufacturing (CAD/ CAM)*. Many graphics terminals that are operated in a CAD/ CAM environment use a light-pen to facilitate drawing directly on the display screen. A few CAD/CAM applications are illustrated in Windows 1 and 4.

Most industry observers expect the greatest future demand for graphics terminals to come from the business sector. Managers can easily become overwhelmed as they try to make decisions from piles of raw data. A possible solution is suggested by the old adage, "One picture is worth a thousand words." From a multicolored graphics screen, a decision maker can easily spot problems, opportunities, trends, and so on.

One automobile manufacturer, for example, uses computer graphics to identify promising locations for new dealerships. All the company's current dealerships and registered automobile owners are represented by tiny dots on a computer-drawn map. This information is combined with data on population, land values, profiles of competitors, and the like to calculate sales potential in various regions of interest. Computer-aided graphics can also increase the effectiveness of managerial and sales presentations, as suggested by Figure 6-4.

The Emergence of Computer Graphics

A technology that is rapidly on the rise is computer graphics, which concerns the creation, storage, and manipulation of images such as maps, charts, cartoons, and three-dimensional drawings. All these operations involve the translation of images into digital form.

One of the most important pieces of hardware in a graphics system is the graphics terminal. This is usually the device the operator uses most heavily to communicate with the computer system. Images are often developed at the terminal with the aid of a small computer system that is specially designed for graphics work. The software available on such a system allows terminal operators to create images, color and rotate

them, modify or enlarge them, test them, and so forth. Graphics systems are used by engineers, business people, artists, product designers, and a number of other workers (see the accompanying panel of photos).

A key characteristic of any graphics terminal is *resolution,* or sharpness of the screen image. Resolution is measured by the number of dots on the screen. In the world of computer graphics, these dots are called *pixels,* which is a contraction of the phrase "picture elements." The more pixels on the screen, the higher the resolution (i.e., the clearer the picture). Your home television set is a low-resolution display device. You may have noticed that when a televi-

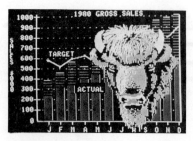 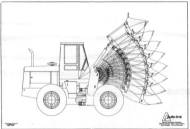 

A sample of graphics applications: business (left), engineering (center), art (right).

General- and Special-Purpose Terminals

Most display terminals sold today are *general-purpose,* meaning they can be used to perform a wide variety of tasks. Some tasks, however, are so specialized that they can be performed effectively only on a "highly dedicated" machine with a special keyboard. You've undoubtedly seen many terminals of this type—the fast-food cash registers with the "Cheeseburger Deluxe" and "Chicken Sandwich" keys, the grocery-store register with the "Produce" and "Meat" keys, and so forth. Such *special-purpose* terminals are also used heavily in banking, retailing, airlines, and securities environments. Figure 6-5

sion set is hooked up to a personal computer, the screen image leaves something to be desired. Almost all graphics terminals, on the other hand, are high-resolution units. Because a large amount of storage is needed to address (locate on the screen) and color all the pixels found in a typical graphics terminal, these devices tend to be much more expensive than the alphanumeric CRTs used for text data. Two-color alphanumeric CRTs generally possess a resolution that is better than that of the standard television set but still well below that of a graphics terminal. Alphanumeric CRTs may cost as little as $100, whereas graphics terminals of reasonable quality are often priced at about $10,000 and up.

Graphics terminals are often supplemented with a variety of input devices not found with other types of terminals. For example, some graphics terminals utilize a *crosshair cursor,* such as the one shown in the accompanying photo. The operator moves this cursor over hard-copy images of maps, survey photos, and even large drawings of microchips. The image is digitized into the computer system's memory as the cursor passes over it. Using a keypad on the cursor, the operator can enter supplementary

information into the memory. With maps, for example, features such as rivers, roads, and buildings may be scanned with the crosshair, and any identifying labels can be keyed in from the pad. Once the maps are in digital form, the operator can call them up for display on the screen and modify them at will. Normally, the graphics system contains a number of other special digitizing devices to assist in this chore. For example, if the modification is to take place on the screen, screen cursor movement devices such as a *light pen, mouse, thumb wheel,* or *track ball* might be used. On the other hand, if modifications are made on a *digitizing tablet,* a special stylus is generally available to enter strokes directly onto the tablet for digitizing.

A crosshair cursor.

Figure 6-4. Computer-aided graphics can facilitate managerial presentations.

shows a display terminal designed for use in a fast-food business.

Special-purpose terminals speed up transactions and place few demands on relatively unskilled operators. Despite these advantages, they suffer from the limitation of being locked into a specific application. As the needs of a business change, its terminals may become obsolete. Thus, if a fast-food chain were to add a very large number of new items to its menu, it might have to scrap the old terminals.

Figure 6-5. Display terminal used with Scan-Data's POSI-TRAN fast-food system. The terminal is equipped with special keys to enable easy and quick data entry, and the keyboard is sealed to be spill-proof. A special-purpose terminal is highly desirable in an environment where the user is not a touch typist or is either too busy or not sophisticated enough to learn how to manipulate a complicated set of commands.

PRINTERS

Display terminals have two major limitations as output devices: (1) only a small amount of data can be shown on the screen at one time, and (2) output is not portable. Also, you must have "hands-on" access to an online terminal to get any results of data processing. And to preserve the results in portable form, you virtually have to take notes.

Printers overcome these limitations by producing **hard copy,** a permanent record of output. Hard copy is created when digital electronic signals from the CPU are converted into printed material in a natural language that people can easily read and understand. A great deal of output can be placed onto such computer printouts, although as hard copy accumulates, it can become difficult to handle and store. In fact, many executives complain today that they are literally drowning in a sea of computer-generated paperwork.

Printers differ in a number of important respects. One involves the printing technology used—whether it is *impact* or *nonimpact*. Another involves speed of operation. *Low-speed (serial) printers* are capable of outputting only a character at a time, whereas *high-speed printers* can output either a full line or a full page at a time.

Impact Printing

Impact printing is the method used by conventional typewriters. A metal "hammer" embossed with a character strikes a print ribbon, which presses the image of the character onto paper. In other cases of impact printing, the hammer strikes the paper instead and presses it into the ribbon. Characters created through impact printing can be formed by either a solid-font or dot-matrix printing mechanism.

Solid-Font Mechanisms. A **solid-font mechanism** produces fully formed characters similar to ones made on conventional typewriters. One of the most popular devices for producing fully formed characters on low-speed printers is the *daisywheel* print element, shown in Figure 6-6. Daisywheel printers operate at very slow speeds—somewhere in the neighborhood of 30 to 60 characters per second—but the output quality is very high. Thus, daisywheel printers are sometimes called *letter-quality printers* because they are often used to produce attractive correspondence that is sent outside the user's organization.

Many high-speed printers also employ a solid-font mechanism to produce fully formed characters. In chain printers, for example, all characters are mounted on a *print chain* that revolves rapidly past the print positions, as you can see from Figure 6-7. Hammers are lined up opposite each of as many as 132 print positions. These hammers press the paper against a ribbon that, in turn, presses against the appropriate embossed character on the chain.

Preparing Newspapers Electronically

Few businesses today encounter deadline pressures so regularly as the daily newspaper. Not only must these enterprises handle prodigious volumes of text in a relatively short period of time, but also the information must be accurate, interesting, and attractive. As shown by the recent closing of several long-standing dailies, producing a newspaper is an extremely competitive business.

Newspapers are among the most sophisticated users of computing equipment. Because their needs are so diverse, and very different from those of other organizations, a number of highly specialized devices have been developed to streamline various phases of their operations. One such device, which many newspaper offices around the country have been installing, is the electronic page makeup station.

In the not-too-distant past, assembling the elements of a page was an extremely labor-intensive operation: workers had to cut columns of type and paste them on a form. Today, with the help of page makeup stations such as the Information International 2020 in the accompanying photo, editors can create newspaper pages electronically. All the elements of the page, which include text, headlines, rules, borders, line art, and photos, can be digitized on a variety of other peripheral devices and stored in a computer. Later, these elements can be assembled and viewed at the makeup station by the editor composing the page. The editor can interact with the host computer to acquire whatever resources are needed to put the page together. Once the page is fully composed, the editor can route it automatically to a typesetting machine attached to the computer system. After the page has been set into type, it is ready to be printed in quantity.

Automatic page makeup not only cuts production costs but also enables news to be published in a more timely and attractive fashion. For example, if a baseball game played at night goes into extra innings, and the contest isn't decided until the wee hours of the morning, the newspaper staff can quickly assemble the page electronically to have it ready for the morning edition. Also, since editors have access to an electronic image of the completed page, including artwork, they can quickly refine it in a number of ways to make it more visually attractive to readers before it reaches the final stages of preparation for printing.

Automated page makeup: providing timely and interesting news.

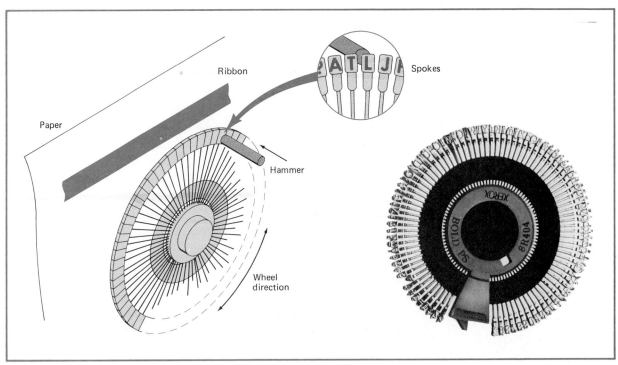

Figure 6-6. *The daisywheel.* Each spoke has an embossed character which strikes the ribbon when struck by a hammer.

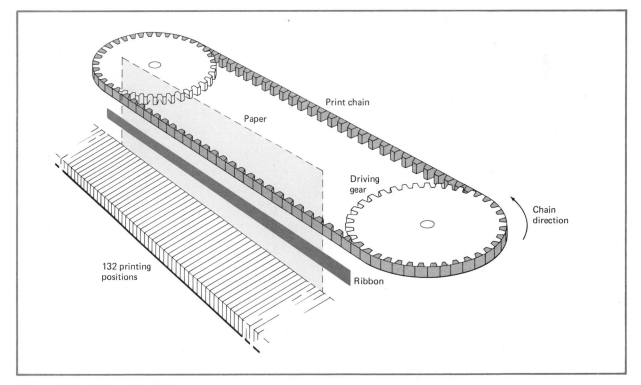

Figure 6-7. *The print chain.*

Dot-Matrix Mechanisms. A **dot-matrix mechanism** constructs printed characters by repeatedly activating a vertical row of pins, as illustrated in Figure 6-8. Dot-matrix printers are much faster than solid-font printers. For example, a speed of 200 to 300 characters per second is not unusual for a low-speed dot-matrix impact printer. Unfortunately, the quality of output is low when compared to solid-font devices. Recently, however, some manufacturers have increased the number of dots on the matrix-printing mechanism to produce an output density of 10,000 dots per square inch, thereby improving the quality of the output immensely. Some dot-matrix printers can now create characters that are virtually indistinguishable from those produced by solid-font printers, and do so at much faster speeds.

Nonimpact Printing

Nonimpact printing, which also can yield solid or dot-matrix characters, does not depend on the impact of metal on paper. In

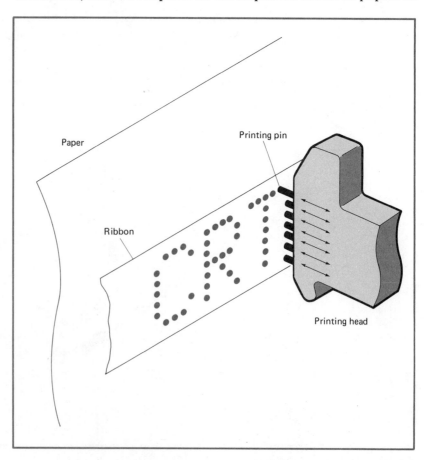

Figure 6-8. Dot-matrix printing. This technique is similar to the one used to light up electronic scoreboards at sports stadiums. The printing mechanism contains a vertical line of pins that form the characters on the paper. Depending on the character to be represented, different pins in the mechanism are activated. The characters shown are formed from a 5 by 7 dot matrix. The more dots in the matrix, naturally, the higher the quality of the printed character.

Paper

Ribbon

Printing pin

Printing head

fact, no physical contact at all is made between the printing mechanism and the paper. The most popular nonimpact methods utilize electrothermal, electrostatic, and electrophotographic technologies.

In *electrothermal* printing, characters are burned onto the page by heated rods arranged in a matrix. *Electrostatic* devices employ a matrix of wire pins that transfer to special paper electrically charged patterns in the shape of characters. When the paper later passes through an ink solution, particles of ink, which possess a charge opposite to that of the pattern, cling to the paper, forming each character. *Electrophotographic* printers first create an image of a character from a light source on a photoconductive surface. Then the image is transferred electrostatically onto paper.

There are many important practical differences between impact and nonimpact printers. For example, because nonimpact printers contain fewer moving parts, they are generally much faster and subject to fewer breakdowns. Additionally, because hammers aren't busily striking ribbons, nonimpact printers are less noisy. They are often cheaper, as well. However, because most nonimpact printers are dot-matrix devices, they generally can't match the output quality produced by impact, solid-font printers. Some common differences between impact and nonimpact printing are highlighted in Figure 6-9.

Criterion	Impact Printing	Nonimpact Printing
Noise	Most noisy	Least noisy
Speed	Slowest	Fastest
Print quality	High to medium	Low to medium
Paper used	Ordinary	Usually special
Reliability	Low to medium	High
Cost	Highest	Lowest
Graphics capabilities	Lowest	Highest

Figure 6-9. Comparison between impact and nonimpact printers.

Low-Speed (Serial) Printers

Low-speed printers are almost always serial printers. **Serial printers** output a single character at a time. They come in both impact and nonimpact varieties. Speeds are typically in the range of 10 to 300 characters per second. The slower units print in a single direction, like a conventional typewriter. The faster ones print in two directions (i.e., bidirectionally). Some serial printers can even print subscripts, superscripts, colors, graphic material, or multilingual and scientific text. Four of the approximately 500 now commercially available are shown in Figure 6-10.

(a)

(b)

(c)

(d)

Figure 6-10. *A variety of serial printers.* (a) A portable teleprinter. (b) A desk-top teleprinter. (c) A bidirectional daisywheel printer. (d) A small color graphics printer.

CREATIVE COMPUTER OUTPUT

A peek at the state of the art

Output is the "bottom line" of any computer processing and is a primary concern in the selection of a computer system. Over the last few years, a number of remarkable developments have greatly increased the quality and range of outputs possible. As a result, in the near future, various conventional computer products will be capable of generating outputs at one time thought impossible. This Window gives you a glimpse into this new world.

MOVIES AND ART

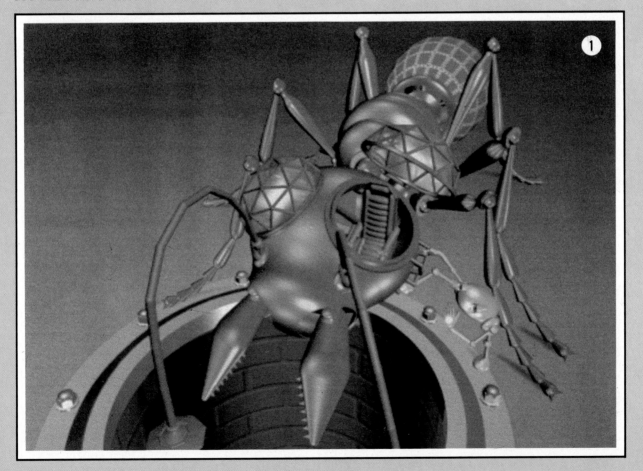

1.   A giant mechanical ant and its robot driver in a scene from "The Works," a 90-minute science-fiction film about an earth controlled by computer-directed robots. Every frame of the film, currently in production at the New York Institute of Technology (NYIT), is computer-generated. The picture's animators use sophisticated graphics techniques that enable them to "fine tune" the shadings at the edges of each figure, turning jagged surfaces into smoothly contoured ones. This unusual scene was created by Dick Lundin of the Computer Graphics Laboratory at NYIT.

2. A computer-generated image produced by OSU Custom Systems and photographed on an Image Resource color camera. This artwork demonstrates the ability of computer systems to create transparent surfaces.

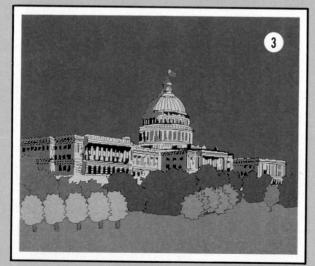

3. A computer-produced picture of the nation's capitol, created on a Tektronix 4027 graphics display.

4. A kaleidoscopic art pattern produced on Ramtek's RM-9300 terminal.

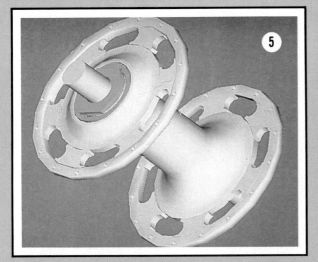

5. A bicycle hub mapped into three-dimensional space on a Lexidata graphics terminal.

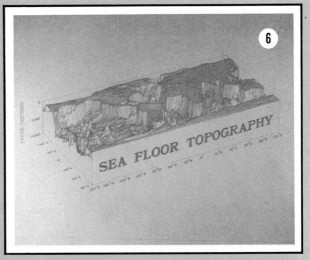

6. A computer mapping of the contour of a portion of the sea floor, produced on a Nicolet Zeta plotter.

ENGINEERING
AND RESEARCH

7. A computer-created test surface that represents the tracking of random neutrons and photons through cells that can cause the splitting of atomic particles.

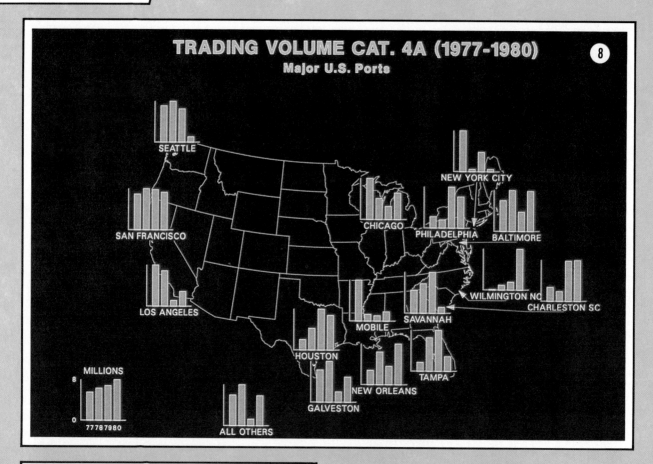

TRADING VOLUME CAT. 4A (1977-1980)
Major U.S. Ports

MANAGERIAL GRAPHICS

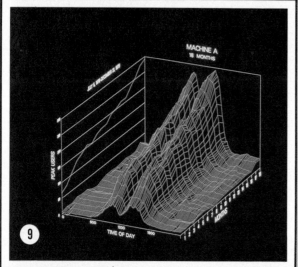

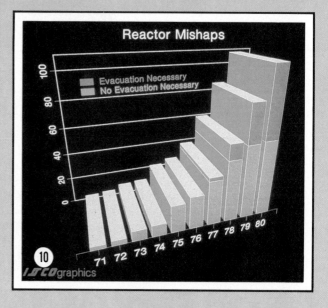

8, 9, 10. Computer-generated charts and graphs are powerful decision-making tools for managers. As these pictures show, graphics-oriented business software is not limited to simple bar and pie charts. Sophisticated systems can now display statistical information using three-dimensional shapes and other creative forms.

11, 12, 13, 14. Once an image has been produced by the computer system, it can be output on a variety of media. These four photographs show the same bar graph as displayed on a CRT terminal, as an overhead transparency, as hard copy in a bound booklet, and as a 35-mm slide.

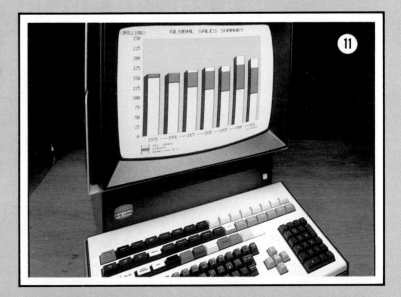

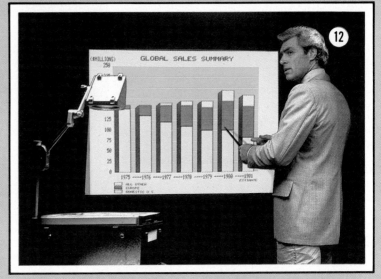

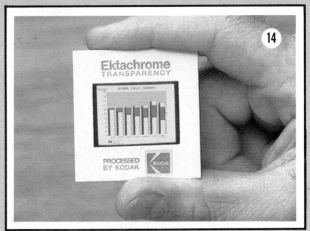

HOW COMPUTER SYSTEMS
CREATE IMAGES

15.   Some computer systems are intended specifi-cally for image-creation applications. Single work-stations, such as this **CALCOMP** Vistagraphic Display System, can cost several thousand dollars.

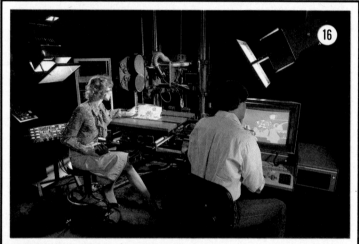

16.   Complex computer-generated animated scenes for movies and commercials are generally produced in special labs like the one shown here. Three-dimensional objects such as rectangular boxes, spheres, cubes, and cones can be stored in the computer system's memory and combined to form real-life objects. For example, approximately 2000 polygons were used to make a vehicle called the "solar sailer" in the movie *TRON*. Images can be varied in intensity for shading, and given random irregularities to make them more realistic.

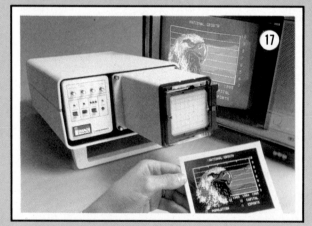

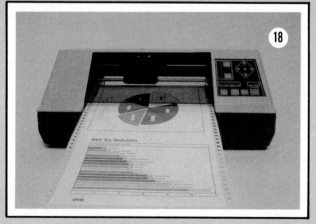

17.   Computer-generated images can be photographed directly from a graphics terminal using special camera equipment such as the Image Resource Videoprint system.

18.   A variety of plotters can produce hard copy from computer-generated images. These devices range from small units you can hold in your hand to devices with drawing platforms larger than a king-sized bed. Shown here is a desk-top plotter.

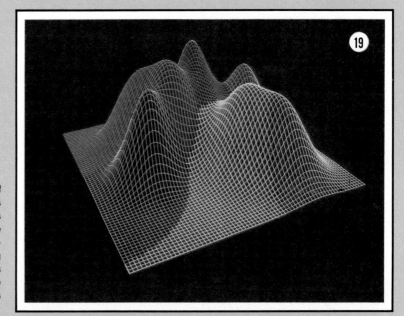

19. This image of a mountain is composed of intersecting, mathematically defined curves generated by a computer system. The graphics researcher can also use the system to color the surfaces to give the impression of solid contours. As this photograph suggests, using mathematical relationships to produce outputs like these is a complex process, and the people who do it are often competent mathematicians as well as skilled animators.

20. A series of spiral relationships combine to create an image of a telephone cord for an AT&T advertisement.

21, 22. These scenes, from a gallery of digital images entitled *Carla's Island,* were computer-painted by Nelson Max of Lawrence Livermore National Laboratory. The artist uses special techniques to place a sun or a moon in the picture to create striking shadow effects.

```
ABCDEFGHIJKLMNOPQRSTUVWXYZABCDEFGHIJKLMNOPQRSTUVWXYZ
abcdefghijklmnopqrstuvwxyzabcdefghijklmnopqrstuvwxyz
1234567890!#$%&'()*=+<>?'#$%&'()*=+<>?
EPSON MAKES MORE PRINT MECHANISMS THAN ANYONE ELSE IN THE WORLD.
Epson makes more print mechanisms than anyone else in the world.


ABCDEFGHIJKLMNOPQRSTUVWXYZ
abcdefghijklmnopqrstuvwxyz
1234567890:-!#$%&'()*=+<>?
EPSON MAKES MORE PRINT MECHANISMS
Epson makes more print mechanisms


ABCDEFGHIJKLMNOPQRSTUVWXYZ
abcdefghijklmnopqrstuvwxyz
1234567890:-!#$%&'()*=+<>?
EPSON MAKES MORE PRINT MECHANISMS
Epson makes more print mechanisms

ABCDEFGHIJKLMNOPQRSTUVWXYZABCDEFGHIJKLMNOPQRSTUVWXYZ
abcdefghijklmnopqrstuvwxyzabcdefghijklmnopqrstuvwxyz
1234567890!234567890!#$%&'()*=+<>?'#$%&'()*=+<>?
EPSON MAKES MORE PRINT MECHANISMS THAN ANYONE ELSE IN THE WORLD.
Epson makes more print mechanisms than anyone else in the world.
```

Figure 6-11. *Samples of characters produced on a single serial printer.* The high clarity of some of the characters is made possible by double-striking and moving the paper in small increments.

On many serial printers, character widths are adjustable, so that the operator can change the number of characters per line or lines per inch (see Figure 6-11). With dot-matrix units, these adjustments can be made by setting a switch or by the use of software. With solid-font devices, however, the operator must change the printing element by hand.

Serial printers utilize either a friction feed or an adjustable tractor feed, as illustrated in Figure 6-12. Friction feeding holds the paper as a conventional typewriter does. It is the cheapest type of paper-feed mechanism, but the paper often gets out of alignment and must be readjusted. Tractor feeding works with a sprocket mechanism, which passes through holes on the left and right sides of the paper to keep it in alignment. The sprocket

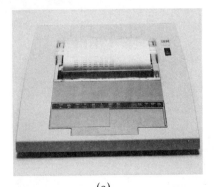
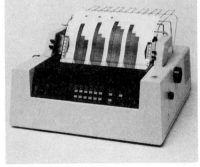

(a)   (b)

Figure 6-12. *Friction feed versus tractor feed.* (a) Friction feed. (b) Tractor feed.

mechanism can be adjusted by the operator to fit a wide range of paper widths.

Several different types of paper can be used for serial-printer output, as shown in Figure 6-13. Some of these same types of paper can also be used on the faster printers.

Teleprinters. **Teleprinters** are serial printers that include a keyboard for input by an operator. Since CRTs and teleprinters are both appropriate for small amounts of input and output, they are often compared. The biggest advantage of the tele-printer is that it creates hard-copy output. Teleprinters also tend to be more portable than CRTs. In almost every other category, however, including speed, silence, and reliability, the CRT is superior. Also, CRTs are often less expensive than teleprinters, but because so many CRT and teleprinter models are available, it is difficult to make a blanket statement about cost. For a summary comparison between CRTs and teleprint-ers, see Figure 6-14.

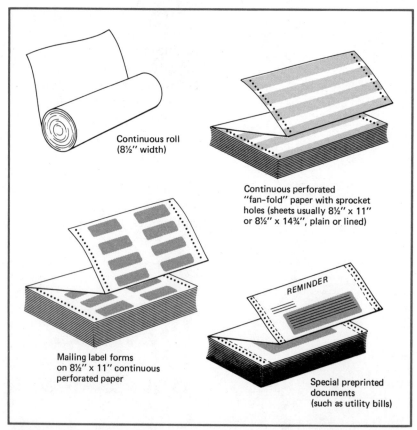

Continuous roll
(8½" width)

Continuous perforated
"fan-fold" paper with sprocket
holes (sheets usually 8½" x 11"
or 8½" x 14¾", plain or lined)

REMINDER

Mailing label forms
on 8½" x 11" continuous
perforated paper

Special preprinted
documents
(such as utility bills)

Figure 6-13. Paper choices for serial printers. Depending on the job, standard types of paper can be ordered from vendors or special stock can be made.

Advantages a Teleprinter Has Over a CRT

- Possibility of printed output
- Availability of highly portable units

Advantages a CRT Has Over a Teleprinter

- Speed
- Silence
- Reliability
- Cursor-controlled editing
- No paper cost

Figure 6-14. *Comparison between teleprinters and CRT terminals.*

High-Speed Printers

High-speed printers differ from serial printers in two important respects. First, as the name suggests, they are much faster. Whereas serial printers top out at speeds of around 300 *characters per second,* the slowest high-speed printers operate at about 300 *lines per minute* (roughly twice the speed of the fastest serial printer). In many commercial settings with both kinds of printers, you will often find the high-speed printers operating at speeds from ten to thirty times faster than the serial printers.

Second, high-speed printers are always *receive-only (RO) devices:* they can only accept computer output. There is no facility for operator input as with teleprinters.

High-speed printers fall into two major categories: line printers and page printers.

Line Printers. **Line printers** (Figure 6-15) are so named because they print a whole line at a time rather than just a character. One of the most common line printers uses the solid-font, impact print-chain mechanism, which was introduced by IBM in 1959 on its 1403 printer. This device has proven to be the most popular printer of all time and is still widely used today. Many other types of impact printers use mechanical devices such as print trains, drums, wheels, and belts. Impact line printing is typically done at speeds ranging from 300 to 3000 lines per minute.

Although most line printers are of the impact type, nonimpact devices are also quite common. Some are electrothermal or electrostatic, whereas a few others employ ink-jet technology.

Figure 6-15. *The IMPACT 2250 line printer.*

Figure 6-16. Decollator. This device removes carbon interleaves from continuous-form paper that has been impact printed.

Figure 6-17. Burster. The burster separates continuous-form pages along perforations.

Ink-jet printers use a dot-matrix mechanism. Electrically charged ink is sprayed toward the paper, but between the jet and the paper, an electronic field deflects the charged ink particles to form a dot-matrix character. These devices may use as many as 500 dots to represent a single character, so print quality is very high. Unfortunately, these machines are also very expensive.

Because line printers typically produce high volumes of output on perforated, continuous-form paper, a piece of special auxiliary equipment called a **burster** is often needed to separate the printed pages. Also, if forms with carbon-paper interleaves are used on an impact printer (nonimpact line printers can't produce multiple copies), another auxiliary machine called a **decollator** automatically removes the carbons. This operation can also be done by hand. If both operations must be performed on the same output, decollating is done before bursting. Figures 6-16 and 6-17 show a decollator and a burster, respectively.

Page Printers.   As its name suggests, the **page printer** (illustrated in Figure 6-18) can produce a page of output at a time. These devices, which can print up to 20,000 lines per minute, all employ nonimpact technology. Many of them utilize an electro-photographic process, similar to that used by the copying machines found in many offices.

The printing commonly takes place on 8 by 11 inch paper, which is cheaper than the larger, sprocket-fed paper usually used by line printers. The smaller paper is cheaper to file and mail as well. Also, since page printers do not use carbon paper, the decollating operation that accompanies impact printing is eliminated. Some page printers can print in color or on both sides of the page.

Figure 6-18.   An IBM 3800 laser printer.

An interesting feature of some of the newer page printers is their ability to store forms digitally. In fact, users of such systems can even design their own forms, with the aid of a digitizing device (described later in this chapter). Thus, a considerable savings can be realized over the line printer, in which paper and printing elements need to be changed when output requires a new form or format.

Page printers cost considerably more than line printers, whose cost ranges from $3,000 to $100,000. Page printers may cost between $150,000 and $300,000. In general, an organization that produces over a million lines of output per month should investigate the feasibility of acquiring one of these machines.

PUNCHED CARDS AND EQUIPMENT

One of the earliest media employed for entering data into computers was the *punched card*. Developed extensively in the 1880s for use with tabulating machines, punched cards have persisted as a data input medium. Even today they are quite common, although they are fading in importance because of their bulkiness and slow speed.

A punched card is a rectangular piece of thin cardboard, cut to a standard size. Characters are represented by columns of holes punched into fixed positions on the card in varying configurations. A *keypunch machine* is used to punch these holes. When enough cards have been generated to form a complete computer program or data file, they are manually inserted into the hopper of a *card reader,* which communicates their contents to the CPU.

The Standard Punched Card

A standard general-purpose **punched card** appears in Figure 6-19. The 3¼ by 7⅜ inch card contains 80 columns and 12 rows. An advantage to using standard punched cards is that they can be processed by standard punched-card equipment, which is still widely available.

The Keypunch Machine

The **keypunch machine** (Figure 6-20) is used to punch holes on cards to represent data. To enter data on cards, a stack of

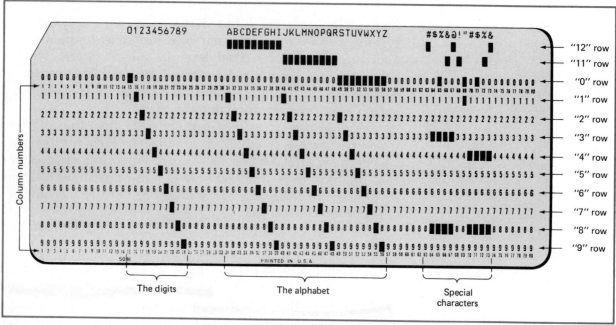

Figure 6-19. *The standard punched card.* Each column on the card can contain a single number, letter, or special character of data. As the card is punched, each character is represented by its own unique pattern of holes. For example, the letter "A" is always represented by a hole in the "12" row and a hole in the "1" row.

blank cards is first placed in the input hopper of the machine. The cards are then fed one by one into a punching station, where the operator fills each one with data.

Most keypunches today punch a hole in the card whenever the operator depresses a key. When processing speed is critical, however, a special *buffered keypunch* is sometimes used. This machine has a memory to store the contents of a whole card before it is punched. When the operator is satisfied that the data have been typed correctly, a special key is depressed, and the entire card is punched at once. A major advantage of the buffered keypunch is that the operator can make corrections before the card is punched. On nonbuffered machines, when the operator makes a mistake, the incorrect card must be discarded and a new one prepared. Many keypunches can also be programmed to handle certain functions automatically, such as skipping over unused columns at the end of a field and punching repetitive data.

Card Readers

A **card reader,** shown in Figure 6-21, is used to communicate the data on punched cards to the CPU. The operator places the

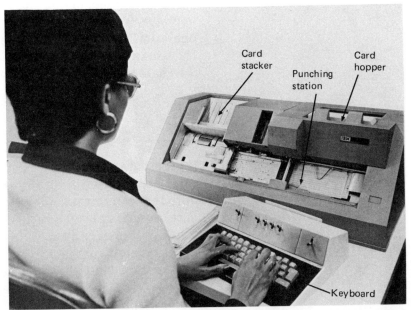

Figure 6-20. Keypunch machine. The operator places a stack of blank cards in the hopper on the right side of the machine. The cards are then fed to a punching station, which places holes on the card when the operator strikes the keyboard. After it punches in one column, the machine advances automatically to the next.

Figure 6-21. Card reader. The operator places a stack of punched cards in the input hopper and presses a button, prompting the machine to read the cards and send their contents to the computer system's memory for storage.

cards in an input hopper, where they are read sequentially. The contents of each card are scanned as it passes through a reading station. Stations designed to read standard cards contain twelve wire brushes or photoelectric sensors, corresponding to the twelve rows on the card. As each column passes through the station, the brushes or photoelectric sensors make electrical contact where the holes appear, thus identifying the character coded in the column.

Other Punched-Card Equipment

Numerous other types of equipment exist to process punched cards. Probably the most widely used of these today is the **verifier,** which checks to see if data punched onto a card are correct. The verification operation takes place after the cards have been keypunched but before they are sent to the card reader for processing.

To operate a verifier, which looks very much like a keypunch machine, the operator places the punched cards in an input hopper and retypes the contents of each card. If the newly typed characters do not match the characters on the card, the operator is notified. Verification is an extremely important operation for some applications. Imagine what could happen, for example, if a sale were mistakenly recorded as a $100 purchase instead of a $10,000 one.

SOURCE-DATA AUTOMATION

Before data can be processed, they must often be translated from handwritten form into machine-readable form, a procedure that can consume thousands of hours in some cases. When data input involves punched cards, the process can become time-consuming indeed. Data must be entered on coding forms, punched onto cards and verified, sorted and merged if necessary, and read into the computer. Entering data onto tape with a key-to-tape machine or onto disk with a key-to-disk machine is similarly time-consuming.

Source-data automation eliminates the need for keyboard work by making data available in machine-readable form at the time they are collected. Because data about transactions are collected on the spot in machine-readable form, source-data automation is both fast and accurate.

Source-data automation has been applied to a number of tasks. Students record the answers to exams on mark-readable forms, which can be processed by a document reader. Authors can type their manuscripts in a special machine-readable typeface. Later, a machine scans the manuscript and enters the contents onto tape or disk, where it can be retrieved for editing and typesetting. Source-data automation has also been used to speed check-out lines and inventory at supermarkets, quality-control operations in factories, and the processing of checks by banks.

In the next few pages, we will discuss several technologies that can be used to accomplish source-data automation: Optical Character Recognition (OCR), Magnetic Ink Character Recognition (MICR), and voice input.

Optical Character Recognition (OCR)

Optical Character Recognition (OCR) refers to a wide range of optical-scanning procedures and equipment designed for machine recognition of *marks,* *characters,* and *codes.* These symbols are transformed into digital form for storage in the computer. Most symbols designed for OCR can be read by humans as well as by machines. Optical scanning of hand-printed characters in addition to machine-printed material is also technically possible but not commercially practical at this time. OCR equipment is some of the most varied and highly specialized in the data-processing industry. A scanner that can read one type of document may be totally unable to read another.

Optical Marks. One of the oldest applications of OCR is the processing of tests and questionnaires completed on special forms (see Figure 6-22). Take the case of grading a test. Once respondents have darkened the bubbles on the answer sheet to

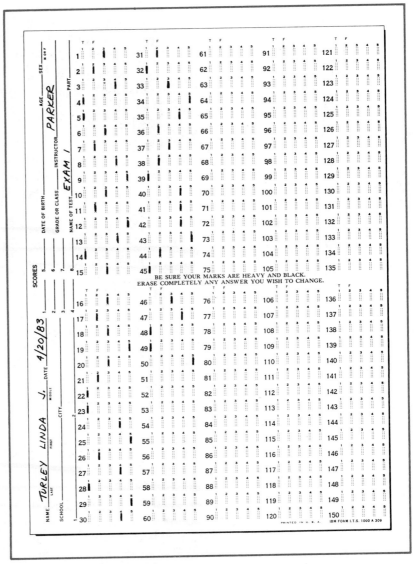

Figure 6-22.   Exam taken on an OCR form.

Figure 6-23.   A selection of characters from an optical character set.

indicate the answers to multiple-choice questions, an optical document reader scans the answer sheets offline. This machine passes a light beam across the spaces corresponding to the set of possible responses to each question. The light does not penetrate where a response is penciled in, and that choice is tallied by the machine. Some document readers can automatically score the tests from a key of correct responses. Others produce a magnetic tape of all the data gathered from the test forms for subsequent grading and analysis by a computer system. Few document readers can do extensive computations, so if the collected data must be processed in complex ways, a computer system usually must perform this task.

Optical Characters.   Optical characters are characters that are specially designed so as to be identifiable by humans as well as some type of OCR reader. Optical characters conform to a certain *font*, such as the one shown in Figure 6-23. The optical reader passes light through the character and converts it into a digital pattern for recognition. Only if the reader is familiar with the font used can it identify the character.

In the early days of optical character reading, fonts differed widely from one OCR manufacturer to another. As years passed, however, a few fonts became industry standards, making it easier for organizations to buy their equipment from several suppliers rather than from just one or two. Today, many machines are designed to read a number of fonts, even when these fonts are mixed on a single document.

Probably the best known use of optical characters is **Point-of-Sale (POS) systems**, employed widely in stores. POS systems allow a store to record a purchase at the time and place it occurs. A sale is automatically recorded from machine-readable information attached to the product. Figure 6-24 illustrates an OCR-character-coded price tag being read with a wand reader. The information on the tag is input to a special cash register.

Figure 6-24.   A wand reader. The wand scans the information on a price tag printed with OCR characters and sends it to a cash register.

```
        DATACHECKER
SANTA CLARA, CALIFORNIA
 06/11 18:53 1    201  48

KETCHUP                .89*
SHAMPOO               2.19 TX
COOKING OIL 48OZ      2.39*
MAGAZINE              2.50 TX
   2.35LB @ .98/LB
POTATO SALAD          2.30*
QT NONFAT MILK         .79*
DOZ. LARGE EGGS        .98*
RAISIN BRAN           1.09*
   2.34LB @ 39/LB
PEACHES                .91*
ASPARAGUS             1.59*
MAGAZINE             -2.50 TX
      GROCERY         1.29 TX
   2.34LB @ 6.10/LB
SLICED RST BEEF      14.27*
      GROCERY VCP      .10*CR
      TOTAL          28.75
      CASH TEND      50.00

      SUBTOTAL       28.59
      TAX PAID         .16

   113 TRADING STAMPS
  21.23 CHANGE

  WELCOME TO THIS STORE
```

Figure 6-25.   An informative cash register receipt made possible by a local memory.

Such a register often contains a magnetic journal tape to record all sales offline. Later, the tape can be read into a computer system, which will use it to generate inventory reports, sales analyses, and various other decision-making information. Many registers today are equipped with memories containing descriptions of stocked items, so they can print what each item is along with its price on the customer receipt (see Figure 6-25). In some systems, the registers function as online terminals to a CPU.

Another common application of optical characters is in billing operations, such as the processing of insurance and utility bills (see Figure 6-26).

Optical Codes.   The optical code with which you are probably most familiar is a **bar code** called the **Universal Product Code (UPC),** commonly found on packaged goods in supermarkets (see Figure 6-27). The UPC consists of several vertical bars of varying widths. Information in the code describes the product and identifies the manufacturer. This code has been in use since

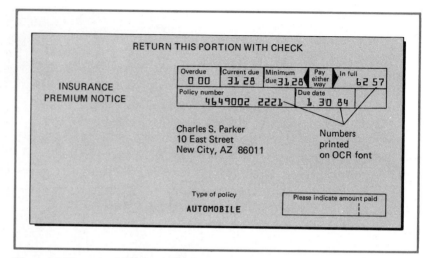

Figure 6-26.   An OCR-readable insurance bill.

1973, and currently over 80 percent of the products sold in supermarkets carry it. There are many other bar codes in existence besides the UPC. These other codes are used for applications such as credit card verification and warehouse freight identification.

The UPC can be read either by passing a wand containing a scanning device over the coded label or by sending the item past a fixed scanning station (see Figure 6-28). Using the data from the code, the computer system can identify the item, look up its latest price, and send this information back to the terminal/cash register, which prints the information on a receipt. Because the sale is automatically recorded from machine-readable data contained on the product, UPC codes are another example of a POS application.

Another example of source-data automation in a UPC environment is shown in Figure 6-29. Here, a store employee uses a hand-held data-entry device with a wand reader to record inventory data. The device contains a memory to store the data until they can be transmitted to a computer system.

Magnetic Ink Character Recognition (MICR)

Magnetic Ink Character Recognition (MICR) is a technology confined almost exclusively to the banking industry, where it is used for processing checks in high volume. Figure 6-30 shows the fourteen-character font adopted by the industry, and Figure 6-31 illustrates a check that has been encoded with

Figure 6-27.   A UPC code used on supermarket goods.

Figure 6-28. A UPC scanning station.

Figure 6-29. A clerk uses a wand scanner attached to a portable data-entry device to read Universal Product Codes (UPC). Using the keyboard of the device, the clerk types in supplementary data such as the number of units in stock.

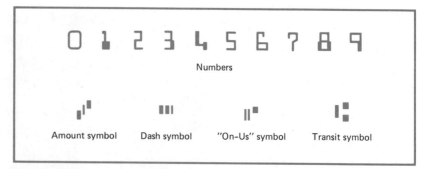

Figure 6-30. The fourteen-character E-13B font. This font has been adopted as the standard for Magnetic Ink Character Recognition (MICR) by the banking industry.

MICR characters. As with OCR readers, a machine called a MICR reader/sorter senses the identity of a MICR-encoded character on the check by recognizing the font. With MICR, checks can be quickly sorted, processed, and routed to the proper banks.

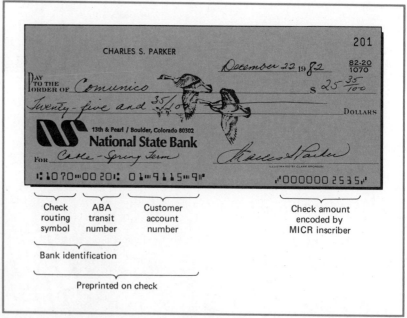

Figure 6-31. Check encoded with MICR characters. The characters at the bottom left of the check are preprinted and contain identifying information, including the customer's account number. The characters at the bottom right show the amount of the check and are imprinted by an operator after the check has been cashed. If there is a discrepancy in your account, you should see if the amount recorded by the operator is the same as the one you wrote on the check.

Voice-Input Devices

Machines that can convert spoken words into digital form for storage and processing by the CPU are known as **voice-input devices.** If you stop to think about how complicated the interpretation of spoken words can be for humans, you can begin to realize how tricky it is to design a voice-input device to do much the same thing. Two people may pronounce the same word differently because of accents, personal styles of speech, and the unique sound of each person's voice. Moreover, in listening to others, we not only ignore irrelevant background noises but also decode complex grammatical constructions as well as sentence fragments.

Engineers have tried to overcome these obstacles in a number of ways. Voice-input devices are designed to be "trained" by users, who repeat words until the machine knows their voices. These devices can also screen out background noise. Unfortunately, voice-input devices can recognize only a limited number of isolated words, generally not whole sentences. Thus, the complexity of the messages to which they can respond is quite limited.

Still, the possible applications of this technology are quite exciting. In fact, its potential is probably far greater than that of voice output (to be discussed later in this chapter), a more mature technology at this time. Imagine yourself speaking into a microphone and having your words typed automatically by a printer. Actually, such a system is commercially available today; however, the number of words the computer can "understand" is extremely limited, typically under 1000.

One of the few existing commercial applications of voice input is a system installed by a chemical company to sort roughly 25,000 pieces of mail that it receives each day. An operator speaks the recipient's first initial and the first four letters of the last name into a microphone headset. The corporate mail zone of the employee then appears on a CRT, and the package can be routed to the right place. The company claims that this procedure has doubled the operator's productivity.

SPECIAL-PURPOSE INPUT/OUTPUT EQUIPMENT

In this section, we consider input/output devices that are appropriate for specialized uses. The technologies we describe are Computer Output Microfilm (COM), plotters and digitizers, and voice-output devices.

(a)

(b)

Figure 6-32. Microfilm and microfiche. (a) Microfilm. (b) Microfiche.

Computer Output Microfilm (COM)

Computer Output Microfilm (COM) is a way of placing computer output on microfilm media, typically either a *microfilm reel* or *microfiche card,* both of which are pictured in Figure 6-32. Microfilming can result in tremendous savings in paper cost, storage space, and handling. For example, a 4 by 6 inch microfiche card can contain the equivalent of 270 printed pages. COM is particularly useful to organizations that must keep massive files of information that do not need to be updated. It's also useful to those organizations that need to manipulate large amounts of data but find fast methods of online access too costly.

The process of producing microfilm or microfiche output generally takes place offline on a special COM unit. If a report is to be generated and placed on microfilm, the computer system first dumps it onto magnetic tape. Then the tape is mounted offline on the COM unit, which typically can produce both microfilm and microfiche. This device displays an image of each page on a screen and produces microfilmed photographs from these images. In online processes, output passes directly from the computer to the COM unit. Most COM units can work both online and offline, depending on the needs of the organization.

Figure 6-33. The Kodak IMT-150 microimage terminal. This terminal can locate a single image from a library of millions of stored frames in less than ten seconds.

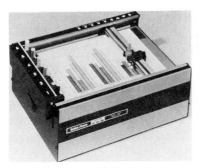

Figure 6-34.   A flatbed plotter.

To read the microfilm or microfiche that COM produces, people either select the reels or cards by hand, and mount them onto the appropriate reading device, or use an auxiliary retrieval system driven by a minicomputer that automatically locates and mounts the desired frames. Such a system is shown in Figure 6-33. Reading usually takes place offline.

Microfilmed characters can sometimes also be read directly by computer systems, a process known as CIM (*C*omputer *I*nput *M*icrofilm). CIM, unfortunately, is an extremely slow process and has not been very successful commercially.

Plotters and Digitizers

A **plotter** is an *output* machine that uses drawing pens to produce charts, drawings, maps, three-dimensional illustrations, and other forms of hard copy. A **flatbed plotter,** which looks like a drafting board with pens mounted on it, is shown in Figure 6-34. Watching this machine draw is a remarkable experience and always attracts a crowd at a product demonstration. The plotter looks like a mechanical artist working in fast motion. As the plotter switches colors and begins new patterns, the audience is hard put to guess what the machine will do next. **Drum plotters,** which draw on paper rolled onto a drumlike mechanism, are also available. A drum plotter is shown in Figure 6-35.

Figure 6-35.   A drum plotter.

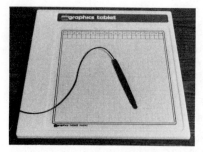

Figure 6-36.   Graphic digitizer.

An *input* device called a **digitizer** (see Figure 6-36) works in a manner almost the reverse of the plotter. A penlike stylus is used by the operator to "draw" on a flat *digitizing tablet.* You can think of the tablet as a matrix of thousands of tiny "dots." Each dot has a machine address. When you draw a line on the tablet, the stylus passes over dots, causing the status of these dots in machine memory to change from a 0-state to a 1-state. When the drawing is complete, it is stored in digital form as a large matrix of 0s and 1s and may be recalled at any time. As the number of dots per square inch in these digitizing tablets is increased, the computer-generated pictures produced become much sharper.

tomorrow

TALKING COMPUTERS STILL SCIENCE FICTION

In the now-classic *2001: A Space Odyssey,* author Arthur C. Clarke's vision of the future includes a computer that listens, understands and speaks. The machine—HAL 9000—not only acts in response to spoken commands, but responds verbally and eventually outthinks its masters.

Unfortunately, while conversing computers are integral to most visions of the future, they are as much a part of science fiction today as they were a decade ago. While researchers have developed impressive voice synthesis devices, many say there is no immediate solution to the difficulty of programming computers to listen.

There are two major problems facing voice recognition technology, according to Steve Levinson, a staff researcher with Bell Laboratories' Acoustic Research Department in Murray Hill, N.J. First, scientists just do not know enough about how humans speak to develop a machine that can understand speech. Second, voice recognition products developed to date have been far from conversational.

Most speech systems require their human users to speak deliberately and sometimes unnaturally. This, Levinson observed, has led to an acceptance problem and lack of demand for voice recognition products. Consequently, lack of demand has stifled widespread research and resulted in voice recognition systems that do not work well enough, Levinson said.

Critics of voice recognition technologies point to one of the first experiments in voice recognition, conducted about 30 years ago at Bell Labs. In that experiment, a machine was taught to recognize isolated spoken digits. Aside from the replacement by silicon chips of the tubes and transistors used in that early experiment, voice recognition technologies have not really progressed much in the past 30 years, according to critics.

Vendors of voice recognition hardware, however, disagree with these assessments. Jeff Gruza, manager of marketing development for Threshold Technology, Inc., a leading voice systems builder, admitted that voice recognition techniques are not yet perfect, but the main problem is that users sometimes overanticipate the advantages of a recognition system. He claimed that many firms have successfully implemented voice recognition systems, and most have boosted productivity or have overcome a tough problem by switching to a voice recognition system.

Typical voice recognition applications include data entry, particularly in unusual or harsh environments, quality control and merchandise sorting. Basically, any application that

Figure 6-37. Texas Instruments' Vocaid™. People unable to speak are helped to communicate by using touch-sensitive panels. Each panel activates a different spoken message.

Voice-Output Devices

For a number of years, computers have been able to communicate with users, after a fashion, by talking to them. How often have you dialed a phone number, only to hear, "We're sorry, the number you are trying to reach, 774-0202, is no longer in service" or "The time is 6:15 . . . the downtown temperature is 75 degrees." The machines responsible for such messages, **voice-output devices,** convert digital data in storage into messages made up of words that have been prerecorded.

A relatively recent application of a voice-output device is the speaking aid shown in Figure 6-37. Computerized voice

demands undivided use of a person's hands and eyes is ideal for voice recognition, Gruza said.

General Electric Co. has installed about six voice recognition systems over the past four years to perform quality-control functions in various manufacturing plants. Applications there range from testing printed-circuit boards to building major appliances, according to Jeff Erlich, manager of applied technology at GE's Bridgeport, Conn., Computer Management Group.

Unlike voice recognition critics and pundits, Erlich maintained that, despite lack of widespread acceptance, current voice technologies are fine. However, the stumbling block may be interfacing spoken input with standard data processing hardware. Instead of more research devoted to advancing speech recognition techniques, Erlich said he would prefer to see more packaged systems designed to mesh with traditional computer and other manufacturing hardware.

"In one case, I have a usable product; in the other case, I have nothing," he noted.

The keys to a successful voice recognition system, Erlich pointed out, are attention to detail and developing a system that is convenient for factory workers to use. That means incorporating commonly used jargon into the system so the worker talks to the recognition system in much the same way he talks to his associates, he explained.

Factory workers at GE reportedly like their computerized speech system because the workers "don't have to speak in an artificial way," Erlich said. The main reason for acceptance has been the use of systems that are tailored to the users, as opposed to simply replacing a terminal with a microphone, he claimed.

While voice systems are, for the most part, still in their infancy, the technology has made significant strides since Bell Labs' tube and transistor experiment about 30 years ago. For instance, while most voice recognition systems on the market today are user dependent (meaning the systems are geared to a singler user's voice pattern) and require the user to pause between inputs, advancing memory technology has increased system vocabulary.

In addition, advances in peripheral technology, such as improved microphones and filters, have reduced some earlier problems of background noise, which previously forced users to repeat inputs or virtually shout commands into the machines.

Source: Tom Henkel, *Computerworld*, January 17, 1983, pp. 10–12. © 1983 by CW Communications, Inc., Framingham, MA 01701. Reprinted from COMPUTERWORLD.

output is also used extensively at airline terminals to broadcast information about flight departures and arrivals and in the securities business to quote the prices of stocks and bonds.

One of the main limitations of this technology as it stands now is that the number of potential messages is quite small if the system must create them extemporaneously. Most voice-output devices have a vocabulary on the order of a few hundred words and a limited ability to combine words dynamically to form grammatical sentences. As a result, these devices are most useful when their messages are short—a telephone number, a bank balance, a stock price, and so on.

Summary and Key Terms

Input and output devices make it possible for people and computers to communicate. **Input devices** convert data and programs into a form that is comprehensible to the CPU. **Output devices** convert computer-processed information into a form that is comprehensible to people.

Display terminals, commonly called **Cathode-Ray Tubes (CRTs),** contain a televisionlike screen for output and, often, a keyboard for input.

One major way in which display terminals differ from one another is in degree of intelligence. *Intelligence* refers to the level of ability the machine has to do certain types of work. **Dumb terminals** have few operator conveniences to make work easy. **Smart terminals** often have flexible **cursor** movement and programmed **softkeys (function keys). User-programmable terminals** are essentially computers that the operator can program to do a wide variety of tasks automatically.

Display terminals also differ in display screen characteristics, including the availability of color, screen highlighting capabilities, paging and scrolling facilities, split-screening, touch sensitivity, and windowing.

Display devices can also be classified as alphanumeric display terminals or graphic display terminals. **Alphanumeric display terminals** are designed to output mostly character data. **Graphic display terminals** are designed to output graphic images. Display devices are also either general-purpose or special-purpose, respectively, depending on whether they can serve a wide range of possible applications or only one.

Printers, unlike display terminals, produce **hard-copy** output that you can take home with you.

All printers use either an impact or a nonimpact technology. In **impact printing,** the paper or ribbon is struck by a hammer to form characters. In **nonimpact printing,** a variety of techniques are used to form characters. A **solid-font mechanism,** produces a fully formed character like those made on a typewriter. A **dot-matrix mechanism** constructs printed characters out of closely packed dots.

Low-speed or **serial printers** output a character at a time. Because of their relatively low cost, they are popular units for small computer systems. Most serial printers are for output only. The exception is the **teleprinter,** which contains a keyboard for operator input.

High-speed printers are generally output-only devices. They are classified as either **line printers,** which produce a line of output at a time, or **page printers,** which produce a page of output at a time. Line printers must often be used with auxiliary devices such as **decollators,** which peel away carbon interleaves, and **bursters,** which separate pages along perforations.

Punched-card equipment is still used in data-processing work, although it is fading in significance. Some important punched-card devices are the **keypunch machine, card reader,** and **verifier.**

Source-data automation refers to technologies for collecting data in machine-readable form at the point at which the data originate. Some of these technologies include Optical Character Recognition (OCR), Magnetic Ink Character Recognition (MICR), and voice input.

Optical Character Recognition (OCR) refers to a wide range of optical-scanning procedures and equipment designed for machine recognition of marks, characters, and codes. *Optical marks* are most frequently seen in test-taking situations, where students pencil in responses on special forms. Probably the best known use of *optical characters* is the **Point-of-Sale (POS) systems** used widely at check-out stations in stores. In many of these systems, the characters on the price tag are coded in a special font that is both machine- and human-readable. Some

POS systems use *optical codes,* such as **bar codes**. A famous example of a bar code is the **Universal Product Code (UPC),** which is used on the labels of most packaged supermarket goods.

Magnetic Ink Character Recognition (MICR) is a technology confined almost exclusively to the banking industry. MICR characters, preprinted on bank checks, enable the checks to be rapidly sorted, processed, and routed to the proper banks.

Voice-input devices enable computer systems to understand the spoken word. Voice-input technologies have tremendous work-saving potential but, unfortunately, have been slow to mature because of their relative complexity.

Computer Output Microfilm (COM) is a way of placing computer output on microfilm media such as *microfilm reels* or *microfiche cards.* COM can result in tremendous savings in paper cost, storage space, and handling. The production of microfilm can be either an online or offline operation, depending on the equipment used and the needs of the organization.

A **plotter** is an output device that uses drawing pens to produce graphic output such as charts, maps, engineering designs, and so forth. A **flatbed plotter** uses a drawing surface that resembles a drafting table. A **drum plotter** draws on a cylindrically backed surface.

A **digitizer** is an input device that enables an operator to create a drawing on a flat surface and to have the drawing saved in computer memory.

Voice-output devices enable computer systems to compose intelligible spoken messages from digitally stored words and phrases.

Review Questions

1. List several types of input and output devices. State whether each device is used for input, output, or both.
2. Identify the ways in which display terminals differ.
3. Describe the differences between impact and nonimpact printing.
4. Identify several characteristics of low-speed printers and high-speed printers.

5. Explain how punched cards are processed.
6. Why are punched cards fading in importance?
7. What is source-data automation and why is it significant?
8. Provide some examples of real applications that use each of these OCR technologies: marks, characters, and codes.
9. How does MICR differ from OCR?
10. What are the limitations of voice-input and voice-output devices?
11. What is the principal difference between a plotter and a digitizer?
12. What are the major advantages afforded by COM?

Chapter 7

Teleprocessing

Chapter Outline

OVERVIEW

TELEPROCESSING IN ACTION

TELEPROCESSING MEDIA: PROVIDING THE CONNECTION

Types of Media
Media Speed
Media Mode
Media Signal

ACQUIRING FACILITIES

Common Carriers
Value-Added Networks
Local Networks

TELEPROCESSING HARDWARE

The CPU and Teleprocessing
Terminals: How Do They "Talk" to the Computer?
Hardware for Managing Communications Traffic

OVERVIEW

Despite the thousands of labor-saving inventions that we have come to take for granted, modern life remains remarkably "inconvenient" in many ways.

Take shopping, for instance. If you want to know what's on sale at the supermarket, you must lay your hands on a copy of the store's ad or go to the store in person to pick up a flyer or look at the shelves. The inconvenience of grocery and other kinds of shopping increases rapidly with the number of stores whose prices and goods you want to investigate. No wonder shopping can consume whole days.

Or suppose that you're a baseball fan and you want detailed information, not just the score, about an away game that your favorite team has just played. You must wait for the write-up in tomorrow's paper, whether you want to or not.

Today, we take such minor irritations for granted, but the day is fast approaching when we'll be able to acquire information about sales items and other merchandise in stores and order it, and read about the latest game *when* we want to—all without leaving our own living rooms. Advances in *teleprocessing* will make all this possible.

Teleprocessing is a marriage of two terms, *telecommunications* (communication over a distance) and *data processing*. When two or more machines in a computer system are transmitting data over a long distance, and data are being processed somewhere in the system, teleprocessing is taking place. Teleprocessing technologies have long been available to businesses and large organizations. With teleprocessing, a manager at company headquarters can instantly receive information on inventory from a warehouse in another part of town, say, and then transmit that information to a division office across the country or on the other side of the world.

With the increasing availability and plummeting costs of microcomputers, the advantages of teleprocessing are coming into the home. Already home computer users can tie into information services for anything from stock prices to airline schedules. And the kinds of information these services offer are rapidly expanding.

In this chapter, we'll talk about how data are sent over distances. We will begin by describing the media, such as phone wires or microwaves, that carry the data, as well as the nature of the signals in which the data are encoded.

Next, we'll discuss the various ways in which people or organizations can get the facilities required for long-distance transmission of data.

Finally, we'll touch on some of the devices that have been invented to solve a key problem in teleprocessing—how to coordinate the incoming and outgoing streams of data flowing between the CPU and remote peripheral devices such as terminals. If fifty terminals are transmitting data to the same CPU at the same time, some means of efficiently coordinating fifty sets of input and fifty sets of output must be present.

TELEPROCESSING IN ACTION

Back in the early days of computing, the computer and its support equipment were located, more or less, in the same room. As long as this arrangement was necessary, use of a computer was not very flexible, since people had to come to the computer to take advantage of it. Certain applications, such as computerized reservation systems for air and train travel, were impossible. However, as computer teleprocessing matured, convenient access to the computer through remote terminals became possible.

Take the case of a mail-order catalog firm. Figure 7-1 shows a teleprocessing network that links both floors of the firm's North Chicago headquarters and its South Chicago warehouse to a CPU. Such a configuration can be called a teleprocessing system because data processing is taking place *and* all the terminals, both at headquarters and at the warehouse, are in a location "distant" from the CPU. This distance may be as small as a couple of hundred feet, as in the headquarters, or as great as several thousand miles.

Each day the firm processes nearly 1000 phone and mail orders from its customers. At North Chicago headquarters, eight terminals (six CRTs and two printers) are configured to the CPU. The computer's storage device contains, among other things, data about up-to-date product prices, the quantity of items in stock, and the firm's customers. Authorized clerks and warehouse personnel may draw on any of these data in the course of processing the order.

When an order is received at headquarters, it is keyed on a CRT by a clerk and routed to the warehouse. Two printers are

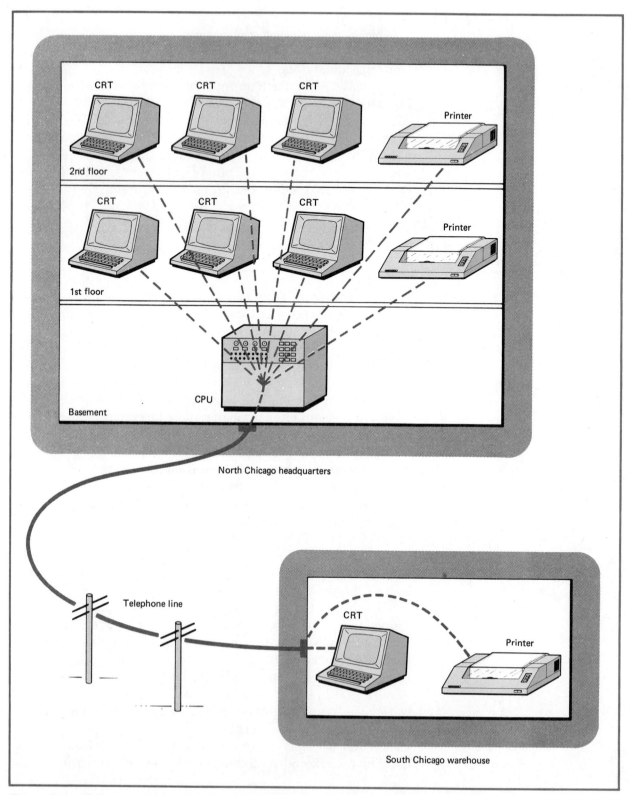

Figure 7-1.   *Teleprocessing system for a mail-order catalog firm.*

available at the headquarters site for billing, preparing out-of-stock notices to customers, and various other purposes.

At the warehouse, a single CRT is used by personnel to update stock counts as soon as products are either received from vendors or shipped out to customers. All data sent to or received from this CRT are transmitted over ordinary phone lines and processed at the headquarters computer. A printer is also available at the warehouse to obtain customers' orders in hard-copy form.

A teleprocessing configuration, such as the one shown in Figure 7-1, often consists of the following elements:

1. A *computer* handles processing.

2. *Terminals* send and receive data from the CPU over distances of various lengths.

3. The data are sent over *communications media*. In this case, ordinary phone lines carry the data between the remote warehouse terminal and the CPU, and special cables link the peripheral devices at headquarters to the CPU.

4. Devices called *modems* convert computer signals into a form compatible with the phone lines, and vice versa.

5. *Communications management devices* optimize the flow of messages to and from the CPU.

The role that these elements play in a teleprocessing network will be explained throughout the chapter.

Teleprocessing systems are often much more complicated than the one just described, and even that one is not as simple as it might appear. Difficult problems related to the management of remote devices can arise. For example, if several terminals on the system are competing for service, how will the system handle the requests? This problem can be especially knotty if the CPU and terminals have been manufactured by a number of different vendors, utilizing a variety of communication codes and data-transmission techniques. Also, if some of the terminals are used very sparingly, how can the teleprocessing system be set up to minimize line costs? These are a few of the problems that this chapter will address. Solutions to teleprocessing problems are particularly important because communications costs often constitute a major data-processing expense.

TELEPROCESSING MEDIA: PROVIDING THE CONNECTION

A simple teleprocessing system is shown in Figure 7-2. Two hardware units, distant from each other, transfer messages over some type of **communications medium.** The hardware units may be a terminal and a computer, two computers, or some other combination of two devices. The medium might be privately operated or public phone lines, microwave, or some other alternative. When a message is transmitted, one of the hardware units is designated the *sender;* the other, the *receiver.* There are several ways in which the message can be sent over the medium, as this section will demonstrate.

Types of Media

Communications media fall into one of two classes: physical lines and microwave signals.

Physical Lines. Three types of physical lines are used in teleprocessing systems today: twisted wire, coaxial cable, and fiber optic cable. **Twisted wire** is the technology that has been in use the longest. The telephone system, which carries most of the data transmitted in teleprocessing systems, consists predominantly of twisted wire. Strands of wire are twisted in pairs and combined to form cables. In some cases, several thousand pairs may be placed into single cables, which might connect major switching stations in a large city. By contrast, only a few pairs are needed to connect your home phone to the closest telephone pole. Generally, each twisted pair in a cable can accommodate a single phone call between two people or two machines. Since most of the phone system was set up many years ago to accommodate voice transmission, it is not the ideal medium for computer teleprocessing. However, the phone network does have three big advantages:

1. It is a vast communications network, linking virtually any two points in the United States.

2. Because it is shared by a large number of users, and most of its capital investment has been recovered, it's cheap.

3. Despite its relatively slow speed, it transmits data fast enough for many computer applications.

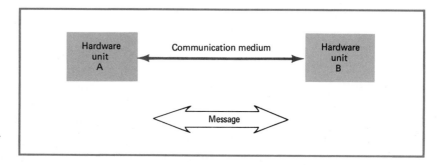

Figure 7-2. A simple teleprocessing system.

Coaxial cable, the medium employed by cable television, was developed primarily because a phenomenon called *crosstalk* exists in twisted wire when transmission occurs at high speeds. Crosstalk occurs when a conversation taking place in one twisted pair interferes with a conversation taking place in another twisted pair. For example, on many phone lines you can sometimes hear background conversations. With voice communication this problem isn't serious. However, crosstalk can inhibit the high-speed transmission required for television reception and some other types of sophisticated communication. Thus, coaxial cable was developed to fill the need for a fast, relatively interference-free transmission medium. Coaxial cable is also used extensively by the phone companies, typically as a replacement for twisted wire.

One of the most promising developments in cable technology is **fiber optics,** shown in Figure 7-3. An innovation whose

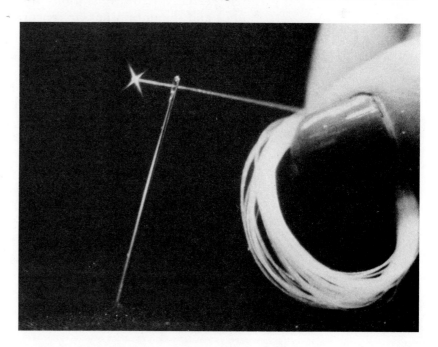

Figure 7-3. Fiber optic
cable strand.

potential is just beginning to be explored, fiber optic cable consists of thousands of clear glass fibers, each approximately the thickness of a human hair. The fibers are so transparent that if someone were to make a half-mile thick "window" from such material, you could see through it as clearly as through a normal window. Transmission is made possible by the transformation of data into light beams, which are sent through the cable by a laser device at incredibly fast speeds—on the order of billions of bits per second. Every hairlike fiber has the capacity to carry a few television stations or, alternatively, a few thousand two-way voice conversations.

The principal advantages of fiber optics over wire media include speed, size, weight, resistance to tapping, and longevity. For example, it is not unusual for a fiber optic cable to have ten times the data-carrying capacity and one-twentieth the weight of a standard coaxial cable.

Microwave. **Microwaves** are high-frequency radio signals. Sounds, letters, numbers, and video all can be converted to microwave impulses. Microwave transmission works by what is known as a *line-of-sight* principle. The transmission stations do not have to be within actual sight of each other, but rather, they should have a relatively obstruction-free path. When one microwave station receives a message from another, it amplifies it and passes it on. Because of mountains and the curvature of the earth, microwave stations are normally placed on tall buildings and mountaintops to ensure an obstacle-free transmission path.

Microwave signals can be sent in two ways: via terrestrial stations or by way of satellite. Both of these technologies can transmit data in large quantities at much higher rates of speed than twisted wire or coaxial cable.

Terrestrial microwave stations, illustrated in Figure 7-4, must be no greater than 25 to 30 miles apart if they are to communicate with each other directly. This limitation arises because the moisture at the surface of the earth causes "noise," which impedes communication between stations. As you can imagine, it is quite expensive to build all the repeater stations needed to connect distant locations.

Communications satellites were developed to reduce the cost of long-distance transmission via terrestrial repeater stations, as well as to provide a cheaper and better overseas communications medium than undersea cable.

Communications satellites, such as the ones shown in Figure 7-5, are usually placed into an orbit about 22,300 miles

TELEPROCESSING

The marriage of computer data processing and telecommunications

Start with telephone, radio, and television, add sophisticated communications technologies such as satellites, microwave transmission, and high-speed digital cable, then combine with modern computer data processing systems, and you have today's world of teleprocessing. This Window gives you a glimpse into this world.

1.   A terrestrial microwave station on the East Coast aims at a satellite to collect and transmit data.

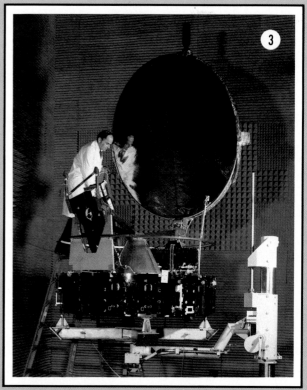

2.   A Hughes Aircraft Company HS 376 satellite with its reflective solar panel (inside the lid). The panel converts sunlight to the energy that powers the satellite, enabling it to operate anywhere from 7 to 12 years.

3.   A closeup of the reflective solar mirror.

COMMUNICATIONS SATELLITES.   How they are built, launched, and used.

4.   A space shuttle blasts off from Cape Kennedy. The launch in November 1982 marked the first use of an orbiting space vehicle to deploy a commercial communications satellite—the Satellite Business System's SBS-3.

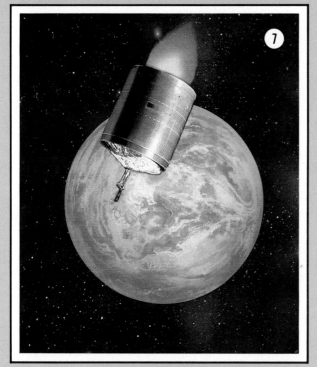

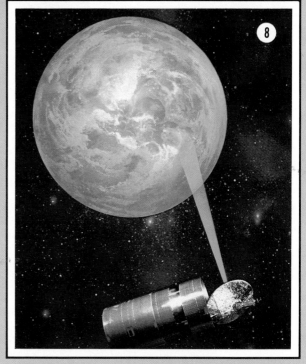

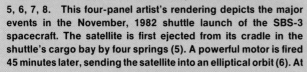

5, 6, 7, 8. This four-panel artist's rendering depicts the major events in the November, 1982 shuttle launch of the SBS-3 spacecraft. The satellite is first ejected from its cradle in the shuttle's cargo bay by four springs (5). A powerful motor is fired 45 minutes later, sending the satellite into an elliptical orbit (6). At the height of the orbit, about 22,300 miles above the earth's surface, another rocket fires to bring the satellite into a circular orbit over the equator (7). When the satellite is in position, the antenna and the outer solar panel extend (8).

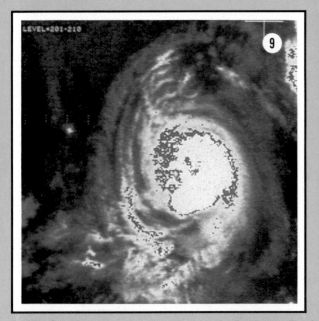

LEVEL=201-210

9

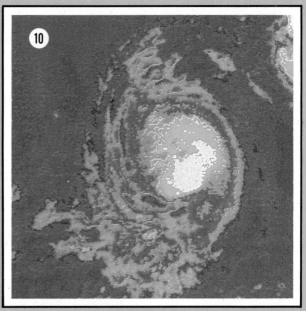

10

9, 10. Satellite views of a hurricane in the Carribean. The images are computer-enhanced with colors to indicate warmer and colder areas of the storm.

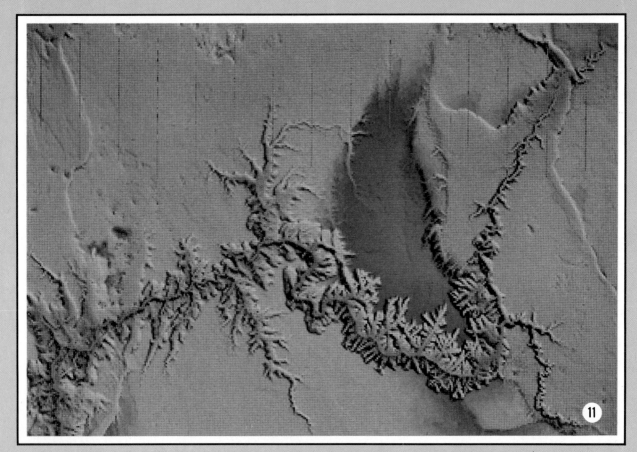

11

11. A computer-enhanced satellite view of Arizona's magnificent Grand Canyon.

FIBER OPTIC CABLE Fast, compact, long-lived, and secure, fiber optic cable is used increasingly to replace conventional twisted-wire and coaxial-cable networks.

12. Hair-thin loops of glass fiber are the transmission media for fiber optic systems. Light from a laser, not electricity, flows through the fibers. Typically, twelve fibers are embedded between two strips of plastic in a flat ribbon. As many as twelve ribbons may be stacked in a cable that can carry more than 40,000 voice channels.

13. The first underwater installation of optical cables for telephone service, at Lake Washington in Seattle, Washington, in 1982.

14. Optical cables for telephone transmission being installed in New York City.

VIDEOTEX Videotex is the generic name for commercial information systems that join television and computer technologies. These systems are still in their infancy. Some of those in existence today offer a variety of services, including up-to-date financial information, news, and the ability to bank, pay bills, and in some cases shop from a personal computer.

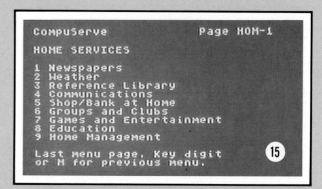

```
CompuServe                    Page HOM-1
HOME SERVICES
1 Newspapers
2 Weather
3 Reference Library
4 Communications
5 Shop/Bank at Home
6 Groups and Clubs
7 Games and Entertainment
8 Education
9 Home Management

Last menu page. Key digit
or M for previous menu.
```

15

15. A menu-driven software package that permits subscribers to use their home computers to gain access to large, commercially operated data banks.

16

16. Using Videotex to access transportation information. The experimental system in the photograph shows keyboard terminals developed at Bell Laboratories that are attached to modified color television sets. The system is being tested in 160 Florida homes. Participating families obtain a variety of consumer-oriented information from a centralized database. The system can also be used to pay bills, shop, and buy tickets.

17. In some Videotex systems subscribers can obtain information about exciting travel opportunities.

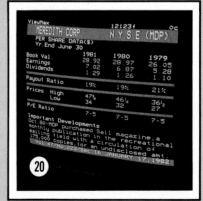

18. Perusing tonight's dining possibilities. As Videotex information banks continue to become more sophisticated, you may soon be able to key commands such as "lobster thermidor" into a home system to find instantly all the participating restaurants in your area offering this dish at a price you can afford.

19. A screen menu prompting subscribers to make bank transactions by computer.

20. In many Videotex systems subscribers can access financial data banks to find the latest trading information on stocks, bonds, and other securities. Some systems also enable subscribers to buy and sell securities.

COMMERCIAL TIMESHARING SERVICES: USING SOMEONE ELSE'S COMPUTER

Many organizations and individuals meet their computing needs by dialing up a remote computer system over the telephone network. Firms owning these computer systems are known as timesharing firms. One of the largest of these outfits is McDonnell Douglas Automation Company (McAUTO), which accommodates remote clients through a vast network of teleprocessing facilities in its St. Louis center. The site contains a seven-building complex housing approximately $150 million worth of hardware and some 2500 employees. McAUTO services thousands of terminals operated by commercial clients throughout the country.

21. McAUTO's St. Louis facility. Longer than a football field, the three-story computer center contains about a dozen mainframes, several assorted minicomputers, and two full floors of peripheral equipment.

22. Monitoring online operations in McAUTO's control center is a 24-hour-a-day job. Using CRT terminals, the operators can determine the progress of jobs in process and inform clients of the status of their programs.

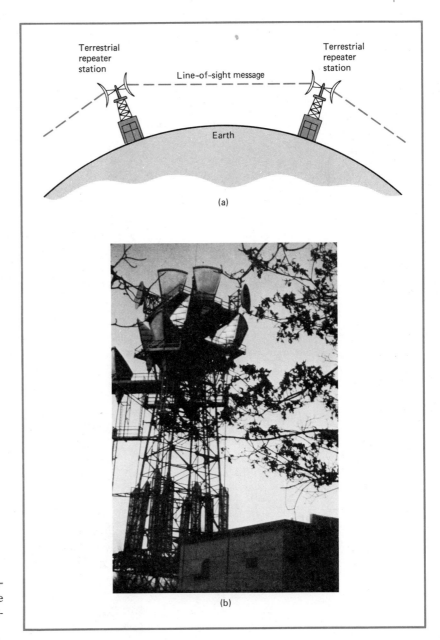

Figure 7-4.   Terrestrial micro-wave. (a) Terrestrial microwave transmission. (b) A microwave station.

above the earth. Because they travel at the same speed as the earth rotates, they appear to remain stationary over a particular spot. Satellites suffer one disadvantage compared to land-based media. Since they are so far from the surface of the earth, it takes about a half second for a signal to leave the earth, reach the satellite, and return to earth. In some teleprocessing applications this delay is critical, making land-based media more desirable. In other cases, the delay is not a problem.

Media Speed

The speed of a communications medium, generally measured in terms of the number of bits that can be transmitted per second (bits per second, or bps), partly determines the uses to which it can be put. Media can be grouped by speed into three grades, or *bandwidths*. The speed of transmission is proportional to the width of the frequency band.

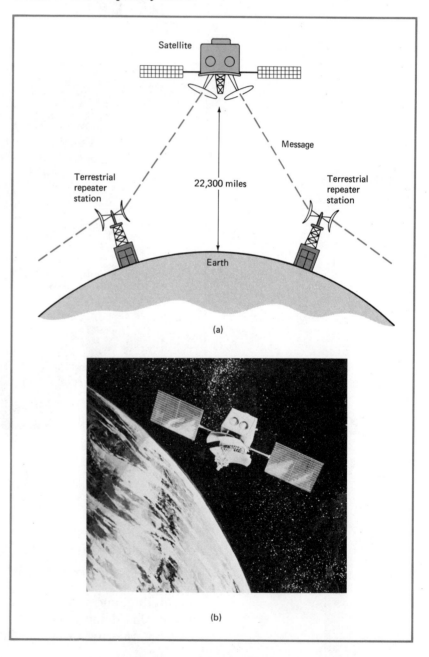

(a)

(b)

Figure 7-5. Communications satellites. (a) Satellite transmission. (b) A commercial satellite.

The Satellite Business

Ever since the launching of Sputnik I by the U.S.S.R. in 1957, the public has had a curious fascination with satellites. However, although most people know that these machines can hover above alien countries to spy on others or that there are friendly ones to beam back live coverage of international sporting events, people commonly know very little else about satellites. Who makes them? What services do they offer? How are these services of benefit to the general public?

It is important to note that there are two types of satellite operators in the United States: the federal government and commercial operators. The commercial operators launch satellites to make a profit. As of early 1983, there were fourteen commercial satellites in orbit, all owned and operated by four companies: RCA, Western Union, Comsat, and Satellite Business Systems. All these satellites were manufactured either by RCA or Hughes Aircraft Company and launched under the supervision of NASA. The spacecraft of these two firms are remarkably dissimilar in appearance. The RCA satellites resemble windmills, whereas the Hughes versions look like large oil drums.

The operators generally do not provide services directly to the public. Instead, they sell "slots" on their satellites to qualifying, interested parties. The buyers of these slots are called *transponders*. The transponder generally signs a lease with the operator for a specified amount of transmission capability. The satellites now in use carry an average of about twenty transponders apiece.

The transponder, in turn, transmits a product over the satellite to yet another party. For example, Ted Turner's Cable News Network,

Home Box Office, and Showtime are transponders who disseminate television programs to organizations such as local cable television companies. The cable television companies, in turn, transmit these programs to local viewers.

Satellites can carry digital, voice, or video information. Thus, they need not limit their transmissions to material for the television industry, although television does account for a very large share of commercial satellite traffic. An organization that needs to transmit large amounts of digital information by satellite can become a transponder itself, or possibly try to buy a slice of the capacity of an existing transponder. Cable television programmers who have excess capacity at certain times of the day often try to find corporations that want to transmit data during these hours. Becoming a transponder is expensive. An open slot on a satellite can cost tens to hundreds of thousands of dollars per month, depending on factors such as the age of the satellite and its orbital location.

Cable television: Still the backbone of the commercial satellite business.

Narrowband transmission refers to a medium with a data-carrying capacity in the range of 45 to 150 bps. These rates are suitable only for very low-speed operations such as telegraph and teletype communication.

Voice-grade transmission (1800 to 9600 bps) represents a medium level of speed. This kind of transmission derives its name from the fact that spoken messages can be transmitted in this speed range. On regular telephone lines, the most common voice-grade line, speeds of 1800 bps are possible. To realize higher speeds (up to 9600 bps), a private line must be obtained from the phone company and *conditioned*. To condition a line, technicians place amplifiers at given intervals along the line to clean up the interference that accompanies the higher speeds.

Wideband transmission rates (19,200 to 500,000 or more bps) are possible only with coaxial and fiber optic cable, and microwave media.

Media Mode

Communications media can also be classified in terms of whether or not messages can be sent in two directions. In the vernacular of communications, transmission mode is said to be simplex, half-duplex, or full-duplex.

In **simplex transmission** data can be transmitted in a single, prespecified direction only. An example from everyday life is a doorbell—the signal can go only from the button to the chime. Although simplex lines are cheap, they are not very common for business teleprocessing. Teleprocessing with most peripheral equipment involves two-way communication. Even receive-only (RO) devices, such as high-speed printers, communicate an acknowledgment back to the sender device.

In **half-duplex transmission** messages can be carried in either direction, but only one way at a time. The press-to-talk radio phones used in police cars employ this mode of transmission. Only one person can talk at a time. Often, the line between a CRT or teleprinter and the CPU is half-duplex. If the computer is transmitting to the terminal or if it's working on a program, the operator cannot send new messages until the computer is finished.

Full-duplex transmission is like traffic on a busy two-way street. The flow moves in two directions at the *same* time. Full-duplexing is ideal for hardware units that need to pass large amounts of data between each other, as in computer-to-computer communication. Full-duplex channels are generally not needed for terminal-to-computer links, because the response of the operator is often dependent on the results sent back from the computer. Word-processing environments are an exception to this rule because typists should not be held up waiting for the computer system to respond to each line of input.

Media Signal

There are two possible ways to classify the signal sent on a line: analog and digital.

The phone system, established many years ago to handle voice traffic, carries signals in an **analog** fashion, that is, by a *continuous* sine wave over a certain frequency range. The continuous wave reflects the myriad variations in the pitch of the human voice. Unfortunately, data-processing machines are **digital** devices. They are built to handle data coded into two *discrete* states—that is, as 0- and 1-bits. This difference between analog and digital states is illustrated in Figure 7-6.

Because digital impulses can't be sent over analog phone lines, some means of translating each kind of signal into the other had to be developed. Conversion of signals from digital to continuous-wave form is called *modulation,* and translation from continuous waves back to digital impulses is termed *demodulation.* A single device called a **modem** (coined from the words "*mo*dulation" and "*dem*odulation") takes care of both operations. As Figure 7-7 shows, when a terminal sends a remote CPU a message that must be carried over an analog line, a modem is needed at both the sending end (to convert from

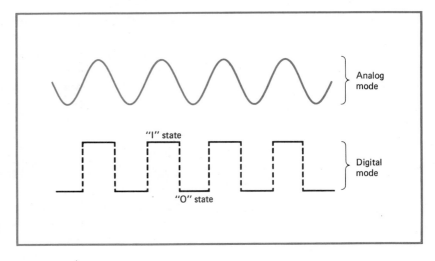

Figure 7-6.   Analog and digital transmission.

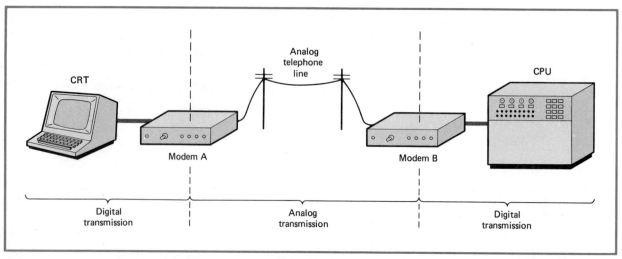

Figure 7-7. How modems work. An operator at a CRT terminal types in data that are encoded digitally and sent to modem A. Modem A converts the data to analog form and sends them over the phone lines to modem B. Modem B reconverts the data back to digital form and delivers them to the CPU. When the CPU transmits back to the terminal, these steps are reversed.

Figure 7-8. Modem for permanent contact between two points. This modem can be hard-wired to both the terminal and to the phone line connecting the remote computer. Hard-wired means that a dedicated line is established between the terminal and computer system. As soon as the operator turns on the terminal, contact is automatically established with the computer.

digital to analog) and the receiving end (to convert from analog to digital). A variety of modems are commercially available.

In many cases modems are "hard-wired" to the terminal and the phone wires, forming a permanent link between the two (see Figure 7-8). This is not always the case, however. In many situations, it is necessary to be able to move the terminal or to use one modem to service alternatively two or more terminals. For example, engineers, sales personnel, and others may want to take a terminal home or travel with it in order to have constant access to data and computing capacity. To allow this flexibility, a special kind of modem called an **acoustic coupler** was developed. These modems (shown in Figure 7-9) have a cradle which holds the headset of the phone. Users dial the telephone number of the computer system, and when they hear a high-pitched sound, they place the headset into the cradle to establish a connection between the remote terminal and the CPU. The coupler converts the digital signals of the terminal into audible tones, which the receiver of the phone picks up and sends in analog form to a modem at the other end of the line. There, the analog signals are reconverted to digital form for processing by the computer.

Although physical lines have traditionally been analog, digital lines have recently become available. These lines can

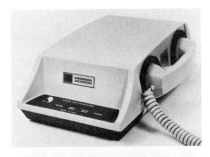

Figure 7-9.   *Acoustic couplers.* These special modems, such as the one at the upper left, have an acoustic cradle to receive the headset part of the phone. Because the terminal isn't hard-wired to a specific computer system, the operator could conceivably establish a connection to any computer system that has a phone number. The hand-held terminal (lower left) can be used with a small acoustic device to make remote computer inquiries (right).

transmit data faster and more accurately than their analog counterparts. And, of course, no modem is necessary. The public phone network does not yet contain many digital lines. Generally, they must be acquired from the phone company or from a private vendor specializing in such equipment.

ACQUIRING FACILITIES

An organization needing to teleprocess data has several options for network facilities. The most significant of these are the common carriers, value-added network (VAN) services, and local network vendors. Some organizations may be able to build their own communications networks; however, this option is prohibitively expensive, except in rare instances.

Common Carriers

Common carriers are companies licensed by the government to provide communications services to the public. The most prominent of these, of course, are the phone companies. Among the less noticeable common carriers are the *specialized carrier companies,* such as those which provide satellite transmission facilities.

Most telecommunications are regulated by the state and federal governments. To get an operating license, a potential carrier must submit a list of proposed services and prices to the appropriate regulatory body. Such a list is called a **tariff.** If the proposed communications service does not cross state lines, a license need be obtained only from that state's public utilities commission. If the proposed service does involve transmission of messages across state lines, a federal agency, the Federal Communications Commission (FCC), must grant a license after it has examined the carrier's tariff.

An organization can obtain two types of communications lines from a carrier such as the phone company: switched lines or leased lines. A **switched line** permits users to "dial up" the computer from their terminals, using the public telephone network. The user dials the computer system's number, and the call is routed, or switched, through some path in the public phone network to the proper destination. All acoustic-coupler modems, such as those shown in Figure 7-9, are designed to accommodate switching.

Switched lines are attractive because a person can dial any computer that has a phone number and gain access to it. Also, using the public phone network is often inexpensive because, like your phone at home, charges are based directly on the number and length of calls. Unfortunately, switched lines can transmit data only at slow rates. As a result, switched lines are not practical for devices such as graphics display terminals, which require fast transmission speeds to communicate pictures. It is also possible to get annoying busy signals on switched lines, just as it is on your home phone.

Leased (private) lines cost more than switched lines, but they circumvent many of the problems inherent in switching. A leased line provides a dedicated connection between two points. Thus, you are placed into immediate contact with a *given* computer system every time you flip the "on" switch at the terminal.

Private lines are normally leased from a common carrier at a fixed cost. Because only the leasing party uses the line, it can be specially conditioned to transmit data at higher rates of speed. It is also possible to lease a private line capable of digital rather than analog transmission, thus eliminating the need for modems and permitting even faster transmission rates. In sum,

Type of Line	Advantages	Disadvantages
Switched	• Operator can choose calling destination • Inexpensive for low volume of work	• Slower speed • Possible to get busy signal • Expensive for high volume of work
Leased (private)	• No busy signals • Higher speed supports more applications • Inexpensive for high volume of work	• No choice of calling destination • Expensive for low volume of work

Figure 7-10. Comparison of switched and leased lines.

users of a private line get to transmit data quickly and in volume, at a fixed cost, with no threat of busy signals. However, they don't have the flexibility to dial up other computer systems. Figure 7-10 compares the advantages and disadvantages of switched and leased lines.

Value-Added Networks

Value-added networks (VANs) are provided by companies that lease the facilities of a common carrier in order to offer additional services using those facilities. Services—which might include data processing and information storage—are, in turn, sold to others.

One type of VAN company is the computer time-sharing firm. These organizations, which include firms such as McAuto, Boeing Computer Services, National CSS, and Tymshare, provide computer processing and data storage to the general public over the common carrier phone network. A subscriber to one of these services can call up the VAN company's computer system and use whatever facilities are needed and available. The subscriber is then billed.

Local Networks

Local networks are privately owned networks that connect terminals and computers in close proximity to each other—for example, in the same building, on the same college campus, and so forth. Network components are purchased or leased from vendors who specialize in this type of product.

Local networks generally use either a "baseband" or "broadband" coaxial cable technology, combined with sophisticated message-routing techniques. These networks permit faster and cheaper communication than equivalent networks set up with leased lines provided by a carrier. The baseband

tomorrow

VIDEOTEX: A CORNERSTONE OF THE ELECTRONIC HOUSEHOLD

Electronic technology has the power to alter our society in radical and unexpected ways. The business world has already felt an abundance of such changes. For example, firms that once hired clerks to hand-record financial events in gigantic logbooks now use computing equipment both to enter and to keep track of transactions. Also, information that was once available only informally, through interpersonal contact, is now computerized and accessible at the nearest display screens.

In the home, computerization is perhaps less evident. A communications technology called videotex, however, may begin a new era of highly visible home computing. *Videotex* (alternatively known as *Viewdata*) is the generic name for computer-based information systems that combine the technologies of television, computers, and telecommunications to make possible the storage and manipulation of large banks of online data containing both pictures and words.

Using a videotex system, people can access the banks of pictures and text in their own living rooms through their television sets or personal computer display screens. The only additional items needed are an authorized billing code and, in most cases, a special adapter similar to the small hardware box frequently seen on home cable television systems. Current experimental systems of videotex offer a variety of information about news events, weather, sports, shopping, and travel. With such systems, viewers might be able to learn the supermarket specials of the week, the box scores of selected sporting events around the country, transportation schedules for winter cruises to the West Indies, current news from the pages of periodicals such as *The Wall Street Journal* or *The New York Times*, the most up-to-date stock and bond prices, and so on. In some videotex systems, people can even buy goods and services electronically from their homes. To get access to information, the viewer simply presses buttons on a keyboard, or on a device that looks like an electronic calculator, to tell the remote host computer what to do.

Videotex systems are still experimental in the United States. Great Britain, however, pioneered the implementation of the technology, and the British have had a videotex system since 1979. The system was developed and is now operated by British Telecom, the country's government-owned carrier. Many other countries have followed Britain's lead, most notably Canada, Finland, France, West Germany, Japan, and Sweden. In the United States, the development of videotex has been far less centralized, and a number of independent commercial enter-

products, such as Xerox's Ethernet, support only data and voice communications but not some of the newer computer-based applications such as high-speed graphics and teleconferencing. The more expensive but faster broadband products, such as Wang's Wangnet, however, can support video transmission as well.

Local networks are only feasible where a large number of devices must share the same network at a single site. "Local nets" are expected to play a major role in the "automated office," which is discussed in Chapter 14.

You'll find a summary of the characteristics of communications media in Figure 7-11.

prises rather than the government have assumed the burden of invention.

The potential of videotex is enormous. Some promising areas of application are listed here.

- **Information retrieval** Users will be able to select information from the various databases offered by the videotex service to which they subscribe.

- **Transaction processing** Users will be able to pay bills, shop, and transfer funds without leaving their homes. Unlike information retrieval, transaction processing

requires the videotex network to have two-way message-handling capabilities.

- **Electronic mail** A network subscriber will be able to create and store messages and then route them to anyone else in the network. An electronic mail service can also include a digitized "community bulletin board," which would allow subscribers to post messages for all subscribers to read.

- **Computing** Users will be able to play interactive games with other subscribers, take part in electronically conducted polling, and perform a number of other computational tasks involving other network users. For example, The Warner Brothers Qube cable system in Columbus, Ohio, lets football fans watching television answer such questions as "If you were the coach, would you pass deep, pass shallow, or hand off to a back?" The computer quickly summarizes the responses and reports the results to the fans before the next play is shown.

- **Telemonitoring** Monitoring devices could be used with Videotex to keep track of certain conditions in the home and to send messages concerning any abnormal states to a central computer. Such a feature could detect break-ins, accidents, and natural disasters at a much more sophisticated level than is now possible.

Videotex: The marriage of television, communication, and computer technologies.

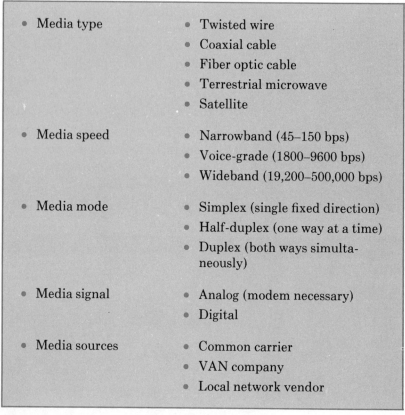

• Media type	• Twisted wire
	• Coaxial cable
	• Fiber optic cable
	• Terrestrial microwave
	• Satellite
• Media speed	• Narrowband (45–150 bps)
	• Voice-grade (1800–9600 bps)
	• Wideband (19,200–500,000 bps)
• Media mode	• Simplex (single fixed direction)
	• Half-duplex (one way at a time)
	• Duplex (both ways simultaneously)
• Media signal	• Analog (modem necessary)
	• Digital
• Media sources	• Common carrier
	• VAN company
	• Local network vendor

Figure 7-11. Communications media at a glance.

TELEPROCESSING HARDWARE

In the last section we covered the various types of communications media and the devices that support their operation. In this section we will discuss teleprocessing-oriented computers, communications properties of terminals, and special "communications management hardware" that is designed to optimize the flow of communications traffic.

The CPU and Teleprocessing

Almost all larger computers made today can carry on some form of teleprocessing. The crucial question, of course, is how well a particular computer can fill an organization's teleprocessing needs. For example, different computers are built with different numbers of *ports,* which resemble in principle the wall sockets around your home. Each port can service a remote peripheral device. Some computers come with a large number of ports, demonstrating a strong capacity to support peripherals, whereas other computers have few. Although "port-sharing devices" can theoretically increase the number of ports, there are usually practical limits on how many of each type of device a computer system can support before its capacity is exceeded. You can only do so much on a single machine. Also, not every computer can support the variety of specialized communications management hardware that may be necessary for building an effective teleprocessing system. We'll discuss this hardware later in this section.

In addition to special hardware, communications software must also be acquired if the system is to operate in a teleprocessing environment. For example, a software package called a *telecommunications monitor* must be available to handle the communications traffic which the computer encounters from its attached peripherals. The monitor specializes in communications tasks and interfaces with the regular operating system available with the computer.

Terminals: How Do They "Talk" to the Computer?

As you learned in Chapter 6, terminals vary widely in a number of performance factors, including degree of intelligence, speed, output, and so on. Terminals may also differ in a number of communications-oriented factors.

Codes. You'll recall from Chapter 4 that two codes are especially popular for representing data as strings of binary bits in computer systems: *Extended Binary Coded Decimal Interchange Code* (EBCDIC) and *American Standard Code for Information Interchange* (ASCII). EBCDIC uses 8 bits to represent a character, whereas ASCII employs a 7-bit byte. Another version of ASCII, called ASCII-8, has an 8-bit byte. Both EBCDIC and ASCII codes have an extra bit, called the parity bit, that makes it possible for computers to detect transmission errors.

Although ASCII has evolved as the most popular of the two codes for *sending* data between distant devices, many computers (most notably those manufactured by IBM) use EBCDIC to *process* data. If terminals and the CPU differ in the codes they employ, some provision must be made in the teleprocessing system to translate from one code to another. It's actually quite common to find computers using an EBCDIC code supporting ASCII terminals.

Parallel and Serial Transmission. Terminals differ in the number of channels, or tracks, they use to transmit data. The bits used to represent characters may be transmitted in parallel or in serial. If, for example, all the 8 bits needed to convey the letter *H* are sent out at once in eight separate channels, **parallel transmission** is being used. On the other hand, if the bits representing *H* are sent out one at a time over a single channel, **serial transmission** is occurring. Figure 7-12 illustrates the difference between the two.

As you might guess from looking at Figure 7-12, parallel transmission is much faster than serial transmission. However, because it requires many more channels, parallel transmission is also more expensive. Computers and terminals generally communicate with each other in serial. Computers, of course, need to communicate at high speeds with other peripherals such as disk and tape units. Therefore, telecommunications links between disk and tape units and the CPU must be capable of parallel transmission.

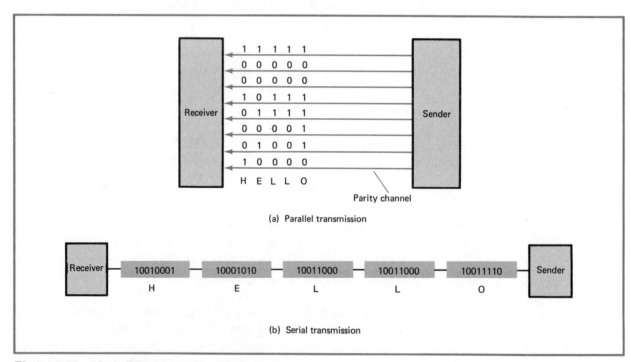

Figure 7-12. *Parallel and serial transmission.*

Asynchronous Versus Synchronous Transmission. Serial transmission can be classified further in terms of whether it's asynchronous or synchronous. In **asynchronous transmission**, one character at a time is transmitted over a line. When the operator strikes a key on the terminal, the byte representation of the character is sent up the line to the computer. Striking a second key sends a second character, and so forth. Since the amount of data that even the fastest typist can generate is very small compared to the quantity the line could accept, there is a lot of "idle time" on the line.

Synchronous transmission corrects for this deficiency by dispatching data in blocks of characters rather than one at a time. Each block might consist of thousands of characters. Because there is no idle time between the individual characters in the block, the utilization of the line is much more efficient. Synchronous transmission is made possible by a "buffer" in the terminal, a storage area large enough to hold a block of characters. As soon as the buffer is filled, all the characters in the buffer are sent up the line to the computer.

The differences between asynchronous and synchronous transmission are illustrated in Figure 7-13. As the figure indicates, in asynchronous transmission, a start bit precedes each byte representation of a character, and a stop bit follow each character. When the sending machine has no character to send, it transmits a steady stream of stop bits. The machine at the receiving end "listens" to the line for the start bit. When it senses this bit, it counts off the regular bits used to represent the character. When it encounters the stop bit it reverts to a "listen-to-the-line" state, waiting for the next start bit.

In synchronous transmission, each block of characters is preceded by one or more "sync" (synchronous) bytes. The machine at the receiving end listens to the line for this byte. When it's sure it has sensed it (some systems use more than one sync byte to ensure this step), the receiving machine starts reading the characters in the block. Since it knows the speed of transmission and number of characters per block, it can interpret the message. After the block is finished, the receiving mechanism continues to "listen" to the line for the next sync byte. Synchronous transmission is commonly used for data speeds of 2000 bps and higher.

Many CRT terminals are designed for synchronous transmission, especially those that transfer data at high speeds. Teleprinters, on the other hand, are limited by the slow speed of the typing operation on input and by having a slow mechanical

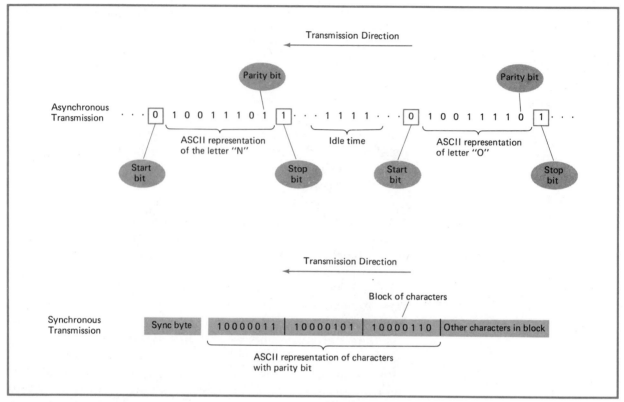

Figure 7-13. *Asynchronous and synchronous transmission.* Each byte is preceded by a start bit and followed by a stop bit in asynchronous transmission, whereas in synchronous transmission, large blocks of bytes are preceded by a sync byte.

printing head for output. As a result, they are usually asynchronous. Synchronous equipment is more expensive and requires a special modem. The greater initial cost, however, may be offset by greater speed and the lower costs resulting from more efficient use of transmission channels.

Protocols. Because manufacturers have long produced terminals that use a variety of transmission techniques, standards for the industry have been a major problem. Everyone recognizes the need for standardizing transmission, but the form that such standards (called **protocols**) should take is still widely debated. Both national and international groups have tried to develop protocols. Nevertheless, a number of incompatible guidelines are now in effect. Adding to the problem is the fact that many of the protocols are still subject to change because major subsections of them have not yet been implemented. Today, and well into the future, you can expect to see many pieces of equipment that simply can't "talk to" one another directly.

Hardware for Managing Communications Traffic

Now that we've covered some of the basic elements of teleprocessing systems, let's explore some of the ways in which these systems have been made more efficient. There are a number of machines available to enhance the efficiency of telecommunications networks. The most notable of these *communications management devices* are controllers, multiplexers, concentrators, and front-end processors.

Controllers. **Controllers,** which are often specialized minicomputers, are devices that supervise communications traffic in a teleprocessing environment. Hence, they relieve the CPU of a considerable processing burden. In large data-processing systems, most peripheral devices communicate directly with controllers, which manage the messages and communicate them to the CPU. When the CPU finishes processing the work, it sends it back to the controller, leaving it to the controller to route the outputs to the proper peripheral devices.

One type of controller, the *terminal controller,* specializes in coordinating the activities of a number of terminals. As shown in Figure 7-14, terminals, controllers, and the CPU may be connected in either a point-to-point configuration or in a multidrop line. In a **point-to-point configuration,** each terminal is connected directly to the computer (Figure 7-14*a*) or its controller (Figure 7-14*b*). In a **multidrop line,** a number of terminals are attached to the same line, which connects with a controller (Figure 7-14*c*).

Controllers collect messages from the terminals hooked up to them and pass the messages on to the CPU when appropriate. The CPU processes the messages and sends them back to the controllers for delivery to the terminals. Thus, controllers free the CPU from the need to deal with, in some cases, as many as several hundred terminals.

Two major terminal management techniques used by controllers are polling and contention. Both can be illustrated with the terminal configuration shown in Figure 7-14*c*. There, termi-

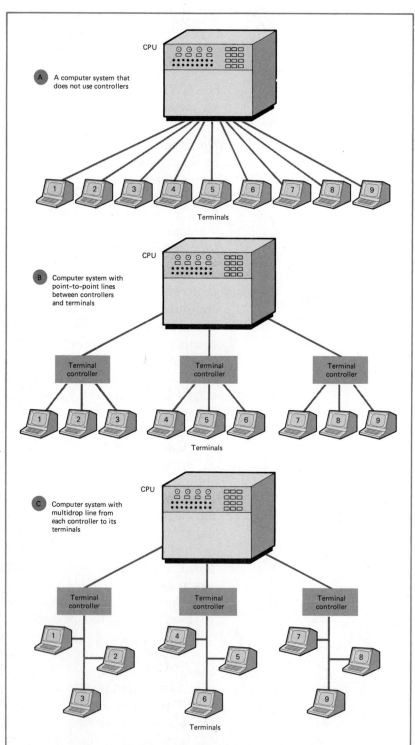

Figure 7-14. Terminal controllers. The computer in A has no controllers and must manage nine different terminals. Disadvantages of this configuration include diversion of the resources of the CPU to the management of terminals and the high cost of nine separate lines. In B and C, controllers coordinate clusters of three terminals. The controllers manage input and output from the terminals and communicate with the computer. Because messages can be collected before they are sent, the CPU is relieved of the burden of communicating directly with the terminals. The line costs are lowest in configuration C because the terminals are "dropped" off a single shared line leading to the controller.

nals are multidropped off a single line from each controller. When **contention** is used, each terminal "contends" for use of the line. If a terminal is unsuccessful at seizing the line, it gets a busy signal and must try again. The line might have enough capacity for one or two terminals, but with contention, there is never enough line capacity to service all the dropped terminals at once.

With **polling,** the controller polls the terminals in a round-robin fashion, asking each if there is a message to send. If there is, it's sent; if not, the next terminal on the controller's polling list is queried. In Figure 7-14c the terminals attached to the controller at the left may be polled in the order 1, 2, 3, 1, 2, 3, and so on. If one terminal is sending more often than the others, it can be polled more regularly. So if terminal 3 normally accounts for 50 percent of the activity, the polling sequence might be 3, 1, 3, 2, 3, 1, 3, 2, etc. When messages are transmitted from the CPU they are *addressed* back to the proper terminal. Like a bus in a city, the message stops at each of the terminals on the line dropped from the controller until it encounters the one with the designated address.

The choice between contention and polling is often based on how busy the terminals are. If the terminals are active most of the time, contention produces many busy signals and is therefore somewhat undesirable. Polling works much better in such an environment, since the controller encounters eager-to-send terminals each time it calls from the polling list. If, on the other hand, the terminals aren't very active, the polling device would waste a lot of time. In this case, contention management would be more suitable.

Multiplexers. Communication lines almost always have far greater capacity than a single terminal can use. Many terminals can work adequately at speeds of 300 bps, and voice-grade lines can transmit between 1800 and 9600 bps. Since communications lines are expensive, it is desirable for several low-speed devices to share the same line. A device called a **multiplexer** makes such line sharing possible. Figure 7-15 illustrates the use of two multiplexers servicing several terminals and a CPU. The first *multiplexes,* or combines, the data from low-speed lines into a high-speed line. The second unit *demultiplexes* the incoming character stream, so that the CPU appears to get the messages from the terminals individually. The device shown in the figure, known as a *time-division multiplexer,* provides a time slice on the high-speed line for each terminal, whether the terminal is active or not. A more sophisticated class of devices, called *statistical multiplexers,* allocates more time slices to busy terminals than to less active ones.

Concentrators. A **concentrator** is a machine that combines control and multiplexing functions, as well as other things.

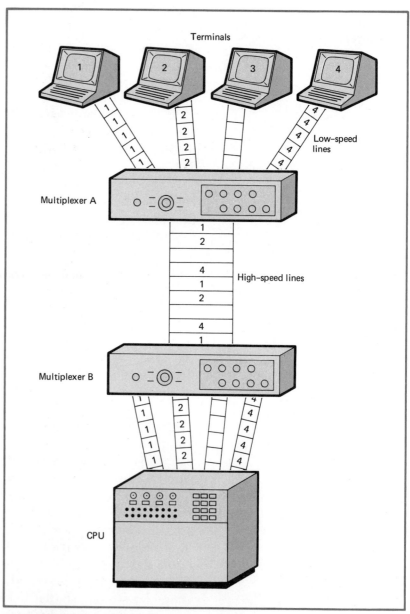

Figure 7-15. A system with two multiplexers. Assume that terminals 1, 2, and 4 are sending a continuous stream of characters, whereas terminal 3 is sending nothing. The messages are intertwined (multiplexed) at multiplexer A, sent over the high-speed line, and then separated (demultiplexed) at B. When the CPU transmits to the terminals, these steps are reversed.

Intelligent Phones

The marriage of computing and communications technologies has produced some useful off-spring, including the intelligent phone. This device enables time-pressed people to avoid the annoyance of getting busy signals, being put on hold for long periods of time, having to redial numbers, misdialing, and so forth.

What is an intelligent phone? It is a microprocessor-controlled device that gives a telephone capabilities well beyond those of a regular phone. In some cases, the microprocessor device is built into the phone; in others, it is placed into a separate unit. Although today's intelligent phones have a variety of features, most of them offer repeat dialing, repertory dialing, on-hook dialing, and elapsed timing.

Repeat Dialing. Virtually all intelligent phones are capable of repeat dialing. This feature enables the last number dialed to be stored in the memory of the microprocessor, so you don't have to dial again if you get a busy signal. You simply press a button, and the call is automatically redialed for you. Many phones, in fact, will automatically redial this number several times, until the call is placed successfully. In some phones, the redialing will stop after five or ten minutes if the number you are trying to reach is still busy.

Repertory Dialing. Repertory dialing is a feature that lets you store frequently called numbers in the phone's memory. For example, suppose you want to dial the 65th phone number on your list. You need only key in the number 65 to reach the party corresponding to this list position. The microprocessor unit in the phone automatically fetches the correct phone number and dials the call for you. Some systems permit you to store 100 or more phone numbers.

On-Hook Dialing. With on-hook dialing, you can avoid the frustration of being put on hold. Instead of having to put up with, "Sorry, Ms. Jones is on another line . . . will you hold please?" followed by a lengthy musical score

that you've probably heard before in the supermarket, you can pursue other work at your desk, the receiver still on the hook. You don't need to pick up the receiver until you hear, through the small speaker built into the phone, that Ms. Jones is answering.

Elapsed Timing. This feature consists of a display device that shows the length of the call. Some units even include an alarm unit, so you won't miss an important meeting if your attention is diverted by the party you are speaking to.

Many intelligent phone systems incorporate several other features beyond those discussed so far. Some phones are integrated with tape units that "speak" voice-synthesized messages to people whose number has just been dialed. The responses of those answering any message can then be recorded in digital form on a second tape. A computer analysis of the responses (if they are simple enough) can be made quickly by processing the second tape on a computer system. Repeat and repertory dialing used in such a system permit many more calls per unit of time than could be made by a person.

An intelligent phone having only a few standard features can be inexpensive. For as little as about $100 more than the cost of the dumb unit you presently have in your office or home, you may be able to enjoy some of the benefits of intelligent phoning.

Intelligent phones: Another case of putting "smarts" into a dumb product.

Commonly, it is a minicomputer with a memory that provides a store-and-forward capability. Thus, messages from slow devices like asynchronous teleprinters can be stored at the concentrator until enough characters are collected to make forwarding to another device worthwhile. In addition to this store-and-forward capability, a concentrator also handles the following tasks:

- It checks characters to see if they are the right size, in the right sequence, and error-free.

- It compresses data before sending them along the high-speed line. By eliminating trailing blanks on fixed-length messages and converting numbers to represent them with the minimum number of bits, a concentrator can reduce the length of a message by 50 percent or more.

- It performs code conversions, for instance, from ASCII to EBCDIC, *and* speed conversions, by compensating for transmission-rate differences among devices.

- It handles statistical multiplexing.

- It performs polling and contention.

In airline reservations systems, concentrators placed at key sites, such as Boston, New York, Los Angeles, and other transportation centers, allow many agents to share communications lines. Messages initiated by agents are sent to the concentrator, stored, multiplexed with messages from other agents, and transmitted at very high speed over long-distance lines to a central processing site. Using the long-distance line in such a fashion minimizes communications costs.

Front-End Processors.   A **front-end processor** is the most sophisticated type of communications management device. Generally, it is a programmable minicomputer located at the site of the main CPU. It can perform all the communications functions of a concentrator, as well as relieve the CPU of routine computational burdens. For example, a front-end processor can check for valid user account numbers and validate or change the format of incoming data.

A network using several of the devices described in this section is shown in Figure 7-16. A panel of photographs further illustrating communications in computing is provided in Window 5.

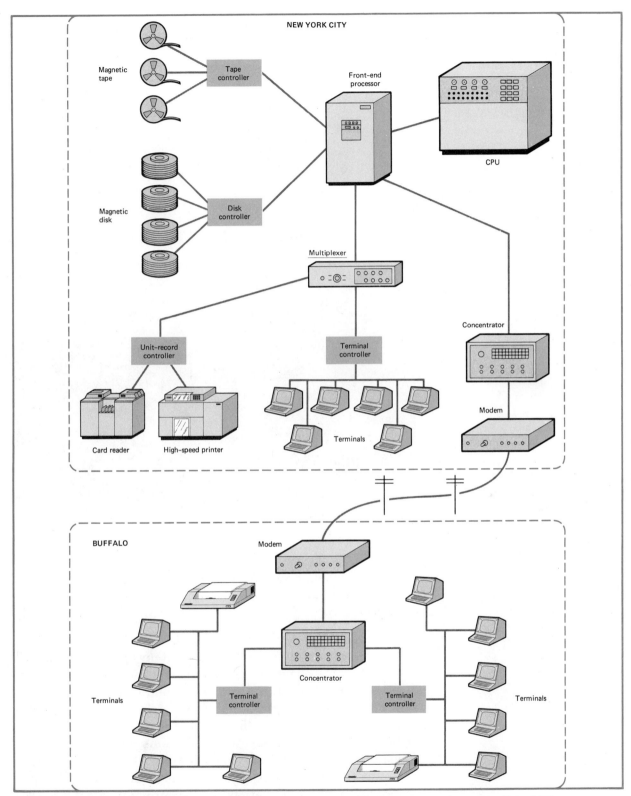

Figure 7-16.   A teleprocessing system distributed over two cities, New York City and Buffalo, N.Y.

Figure 7-17.   Teleprocessing at work. Indiana Bell's "Dimension 2000" provides powerful communications facilities at the construction site of the Marble Hill nuclear generating station near Madison, Indiana.

Summary and Key Terms

A **teleprocessing** system is one in which data processing is taking place *and* the data are being transmitted over a distance.

Messages sent in a teleprocessing system are communicated over some type of **communications medium.** Physical lines, such as **twisted wire, coaxial cable,** and **fiber optics** constitute one major class of media. Commercial messages are also commonly sent through the air, in the form of **microwave** signals. **Terrestrial microwave stations** are used to accommodate land-based microwaves. **Communications satellites** are used to reduce the cost of long-distance transmission via terrestrial microwave stations and to provide better overseas communications.

The *speed* of a data-communications medium is measured in bits per second (bps). The slowest rates of speed are referred to as **narrowband transmission.** Medium-speed lines, which are the type commonly found in the public phone network, are capable of **voice-grade transmission.** The highest rates of speed, referred to as **wideband transmission,** are possible only with coaxial cable, fiber optic cable, and microwaves.

Communications media can either be in the simplex, half-duplex, or full-duplex *mode.* In **simplex transmission,** messages can only be sent in a single direction (for example, a doorbell). In **half-duplex transmission,** messages can be sent both ways but not simultaneously (for example, press-to-talk phones). **Full-duplex transmission** permits transmission in two directions simultaneously (for example, a busy two-way street).

Signals sent along a phone line travel in an **analog** fashion, as continuous waves. Computers and their support equipment, however, are **digital** devices that handle data coded into two discrete states—0s and 1s. For two or more digital devices to communicate with each other over the analog phone lines, a device called a **modem** must be placed between each piece of equipment and the phone lines. Modems perform digital-to-analog and analog-to-digital conversion. Modems that are not hard-wired to specific equipment and that have an acoustic cradle to accept a phone headset are called **acoustic couplers.**

Common carriers are companies licensed by the government to provide communications services to the public. Common carriers are regulated by the Federal Communications Commission (FCC) or by a state regulatory agency. To get an operating license each carrier has to submit a **tariff,** covering proposed services and prices, to the appropriate regulatory agency. Carriers generally offer **switched lines** and **leased (private) lines** to the public.

Value-added networks (VANs) are provided by companies offering data-processing services to the public over the facilities of a common carrier. A **local network** is a fast-access private network consisting of machines at a single location that share programs and data.

Almost all larger computers made today can carry on some form of teleprocessing. Terminals communicate with such computers in a variety of ways. To exchange data, the terminal and computer must use the same communications codes. Transmission between compatible machines is either in **parallel** or in **serial, synchronous** or **asynchronous.** Factors that determine which of these types of transmission are used include the speed at which data must be transferred between the machines and the capabilities of both the machines and the communications media. Because there are so many ways to transmit data, many industry groups have tried to develop sets of standards (called **protocols**). Nonetheless, a number of incompatible guidelines are now in effect.

Communications management devices enhance the efficiency of teleprocessing traffic. Common devices are controllers, multiplexers, concentrators, and front-end processors.

Controllers are machines that supervise communications traffic between the CPU and peripheral devices such as terminals. Terminals can be hooked up to a controller in either a **point-to-point configuration** (one line from each terminal to the controller) or on a **multidrop line** (a single line sent out from the controller to service a cluster of terminals). Either terminals must compete with each other for service, a process called **contention,** or they are polled in an orderly (noncompeting) fashion, a process called **polling.**

Multiplexers are devices that enable several low-speed devices to share a high-speed line. **Concentrators** are machines that perform the functions of both the controller and the multiplexer, among other things. A **front-end processor** is the most sophisticated communications management device—it can perform the concentrator's function as well as some of the tasks normally done by the computer.

Review Questions

1. What is teleprocessing?
2. Name some types of communications media and explain how they differ.
3. What are the differences among simplex, half-duplex, and full-duplex transmission?
4. Identify some alternatives for acquiring network facilities.

5. Compare switched and leased lines.
6. How do parallel and serial communications differ?
7. Explain the distinction between asynchronous and synchronous transmission.
8. Identify the different strategies used by terminal controllers to manage terminals.
9. What is the purpose of multiplexing?
10. Identify some of the tasks that communications management devices perform to relieve the CPU of communications burdens.

Suggested Readings

Fitzgerald, Jerry, and Tom S. Eason. *Fundamentals of Data Communications.* New York: Wiley, 1978.

Housley, Trevor. *Data Communications and Teleprocessing Systems.* Englewood Cliffs, N.J.: Prentice-Hall, 1979.

Sherman, Kenneth. *Data Communications: A Users Guide.* Reston, Va.: Reston, 1981.

Module C

SOFTWARE

So far, you've read a great deal about the *hardware* parts of a computer system—the CPU, storage devices, peripheral and auxiliary devices, and so on. But hardware by itself cannot process data any more than the various instruments of an orchestra can play a symphony without musicians, a conductor, and a musical score. Without *software,* a computer system would be interesting to look at perhaps, but essentially useless.

As mentioned earlier, the term *software* often includes programs, manuals, and processing procedures. Alternatively, software may be thought of as the collection of all instructions that enable data to be processed on computer systems. Programs are the kind of software of most interest to us here. Without programs, the computer is just a useless hunk of metal. Because programs are so important, the terms *software* and *programs* are often used interchangeably in practice.

Computer programs fall into two general categories—systems programs and applications programs. The former are programs that assist the running of other programs. These include the operating system, language translators, and utility programs. Applications software, in contrast, consists of programs that perform processing tasks for users. These include programs for payroll, order entry, billing, accounting, inventory control, management report generation, and transaction processing (such as that performed by travel agents and airline personnel to book passengers).

Systems software is discussed in Chapter 8. Applications software, the main subject of this module, is discussed in Chapters 9, 10, 11, and 12.

STANDARD COBOL COMPILE LINK AND GO PROCEDURE
LEVEL 004 060178
PLEASE REPORT ABENDS TO
AUDITOR'S FINE POINT

Chapter 8

Systems Software

Chapter Outline

OVERVIEW

Systems software consists of programs that coordinate the various parts of the computer system to make it run rapidly and efficiently. The activities carried on by system programs are quite diverse. These programs often decide where data entering the system is to be stored; they schedule the many jobs awaiting processing on almost all large computers; they keep track of who's trying to log onto the computer and how much time is spent on each job; and they also translate the application program that you are using into the binary code that the computer can understand.

In this chapter we'll first look at the role of systems software. Then we'll consider the operating system, which controls computer system operations by assigning and scheduling system resources as well as keeping track of activity in the computer system. We'll also look at some of the processing techniques that allow modern operating systems to balance the demands of a number of users competing for the computer's time. We will conclude the chapter with a discussion of language translators and utility programs, which perform vital services for users and programmers.

THE ROLE OF SYSTEMS SOFTWARE

The role of **systems software** is basically to act as a mediator between applications programs and the hardware of the computer system. Systems software interprets the requirements of every incoming program and makes available whatever hardware, software, and data resources are needed to produce the desired results

Most users aren't aware of what systems software is doing for them. When you log on to a computer system, for example, you may not realize that a system program is put to work checking the validity of your ID number. And although it may seem to you, sitting and typing at your terminal, that the computer is responding to your commands only, in fact it may actually be dealing with dozens of other users at almost the same time. It is systems software that makes this illusion possible.

THE OPERATING SYSTEM

Before the 1960s, human operators ran computers manually to a large extent. For each incoming data-processing job, the operator had to reset by hand a number of circuits on the computer. In fact, every role of the computer system—input, output, processing, and storage—required substantial operator supervision and intervention.

On these early computers, jobs could be processed only in a serial fashion—one program at a time. Because they could only handle programs serially, these computers sat idle for long periods of time while the operators took care of manual procedures between jobs.

The development of operating systems greatly improved the efficiency of computers. An **operating system** is a collection of programs that manage the activities of the computer system. Operating systems do away with much of the manual work formerly required to process programs. Today's operating systems enable the processing of several jobs concurrently and, in many cases, permit the computer to be left completely unattended by the operator while users and programmers run programs.

The primary responsibility of the operating system is control. It makes sure each valid, incoming program is scheduled for processing in an orderly fashion and that the system's resources are made available to run the programs optimally. To help you understand the role of the operating system, we can compare its activities to those of a receptionist working in the lobby of a large office.

The main duties of the receptionist are to screen visitors and direct them to the right people. After visitors have identified themselves satisfactorily, the receptionist finds out what they want. If, for example, a visitor wishes to chat with someone in the organization to get information for a magazine story, the receptionist might direct the visitor to a public relations person on the fifth floor. If a quick call reveals that the person is available, the visitor is routed upstairs. All visitors must sign a logbook at the reception desk before they enter the offices and as they leave.

Operating systems do some of the same kinds of things. First, they generally check to see that people trying to gain access to the computer system are authorized users. When a user's identification number is found to be valid, he or she is signed in (or "logged on"). Then, the operating system determines which resources of the computer system will be needed to do the user's job. It then automatically assigns these resources to the work request if and when they are available.

Generally, the user will need to tap a number of the system's resources. A typical job might employ the number-crunching power of the CPU, a language translator that understands how to interpret the programming language commands that the user types in, primary memory to store intermediate results, data and programs stored in secondary memory, and a printer for output. It is the operating system that makes available all these facilities. Often, the user doesn't even know how the operating system is activating resources to get the work done. Finally, when the user leaves the computer system, he or she is automatically logged off. In effect, the operating system is the go-between, meshing the user's application program with the resources of the system.

Although all operating systems perform the tasks just described, they differ in terms of how effectively they do so. A good operating system, for example, increases the productivity of the computer more than an inferior system. If the operating system schedules facilities well, given the diverse and sometimes unpredictable needs of users, it makes efficient processing possible.

Operating systems should be tailored specifically to meet the needs of certain classes of users. A system that provides acceptable performance in one type of environment may do poorly in another. Thus, an operating system that makes the computer system *easy to use* might mesh perfectly with the needs of teachers and students at a university but fail miserably at a scientific laboratory where *security* and a *fast execution time* are likely to be of more concern.

Functions of the Operating System

Now that you have a general idea of what operating systems do, we can discuss their functions in greater detail. Most of these functions, as we noted earlier, can be seen as aspects of a single general mission: to control the operations of the computer system.

Assignment of System Resources. When the computer is first activated, a program called the **supervisor** (or **monitor**), a major component of the operating system, is also activated. The supervisor will always be in primary memory when the computer is on. On most large, general-purpose computers, other programs in the operating system are brought into primary memory from secondary storage only as they are needed. The supervisor has the ability to mobilize other programs in the operating system to perform system tasks for applications programs.

Once the supervisor activates any other program in the operating system, the supervisor cedes control to that program until its role is complete. On completion, control returns to the supervisor, which may call up other system programs required by the job. The supervisor operates somewhat like a master of ceremonies, repeatedly introducing the next speaker on the program after the previous one has finished his or her talk.

In addition to the supervisor, a number of other programs in the operating system have a hand in determining what parts of the computer system will be mobilized for any given job. One of these is the **job-control program.** This program reads *job-control statements,* which encode instructions to the operating system written by the programmer. These instructions, written in a **job-control language (JCL),** permit users and programmers to specify what I/O devices are to be used, which language the user or programmer is employing, any customized requests for output format, and any other special processing needs of the program. JCL, in effect, gives the user a channel for communicating directly with the operating system.

In the absence of special JCL instructions from the user, the job control program makes some standard assumptions about how things are to be done. On any given job, the assumptions made by the job-control program are called the **default** options. Often, you can override the defaults by typing in your own JCL commands. Thus, if the default on output is 24-line screen images delivered to the CRT, and you want hard-copy output from the high-speed printer—say, five copies at fifty lines per page—you may be able to override the default by entering a JCL command such as

```
PRINTER, LINES = 50, COPIES = 5
```

Although some of the content of job-control statements is standard information, such as the name of the job to be processed, the name of the user, and the user's account number, much of the information helps to orient the computer to the job at hand. For example, when a user enters a program and wants the computer to execute it, the operating system has no idea what language the program is written in. The system does not know whether to treat the program as a BASIC program, a

Some Functions of JCL

- Identify the name of the job to be processed, the name of the user, and the user's account number.

- Declare any unusual requirements that exceed the standard allowances of the computer center—for example, any extraordinarily large storage, CPU time, or printed output needs.

- Identify the language in which the program is written.

- Specify special instructions for output—for example, the input/output device used, the number of copies of output desired, any special printing fonts needed (such as those printing both upper- and lowercase characters), and so forth.

- Identify the nature of the input or output files—for example, do they have sequential, indexed sequential, or relative organizations?

- Assign secret passwords to data files or programs.

- State directions to operate a terminal in a certain way. For example, should a display terminal operate in the page or scroll mode? How many characters should the teleprinter output per line?

- Specify whether or not the system should produce a dump of main memory when a program stops because of an error.

Figure 8-1.   Some functions of JCL.

FORTRAN program or something else. Thus, the user must include a JCL statement telling the control program what language is being used. This command permits the operating system to mobilize the proper translator needed to convert the user's program into machine language. Some functions of JCL are given in Figure 8-1.

The operating system assigns other kinds of resources as well. At any time, large computers are likely to be processing a number of programs concurrently, each with its own needs for tape or disk devices, storage requirements, and so on. It is the operating system that keeps track of which facilities in the system are being used and which are therefore free for assignment to new programs. Also, because space in main memory is at a premium, the operating system must allocate shares of it to the various programs, some of which may be very large.

Scheduling of Resources and Jobs.   Closely related to the process of assigning system resources to a job is that of scheduling resources and jobs. The operating system helps decide not only *what* resources to use (assignment) but also *when* to use them (scheduling). This task can become extremely complicated when the system must handle a number of jobs at once.

Scheduling programs in the operating system determine the order in which jobs are processed. A job's place in line is not necessarily on a first-come, first-served basis. Some users may have higher priority than others, the devices needed to process the next job in line may not be free, or other factors may affect the order of processing.

The operating system also schedules the operation of parts of the computer system so that they work on different portions of different jobs at the same time. Because input and output devices work much more slowly than the CPU itself, millions of calculations may be performed for several programs while the contents of a single program are printed or displayed. Using a number of techniques, the operating system juggles the various jobs to be done so as to employ system devices as efficiently as possible. Later in the chapter, we'll discuss some of these methods of processing a number of jobs at, more or less, the same time. These procedures are known collectively as *interleaved processing techniques.*

Monitoring Activities. A third general function of operating systems is monitoring—keeping track of activities in the computer system while processing is under way. The operating system terminates programs that contain errors or exceed either their maximum running time or storage allocations. It also sends an appropriate message to the user or operator. Similarly, if any abnormalities arise in I/O devices or elsewhere in the system, the operating system sends a message to the user's or operator's terminal.

Bookkeeping and security are also among the monitoring tasks of the operating system. Records may be kept of log-on and log-off times, the running time of programs, a list of programs that each user has run, as well as other information. In some environments, these records enable the organization to bill users. The operating system also can protect the system against unauthorized access by checking the validity of users' ID numbers and reporting attempts to breach the security of the system.

In the following section, we will examine some of the assignment and scheduling techniques that computers employ to handle a large number of jobs at the same time.

Interleaved Processing Techniques

Larger computers, specifically minicomputers and mainframes, often take advantage of sophisticated processing techniques, such as multiprogramming, time-sharing, spooling, virtual storage, and multiprocessing, to operate more efficiently. These operating system features enable computers to process many programs at almost the same time and, consequently, to increase the number of jobs that the system can handle in any period of time.

The Operating System on Your Personal Computer

To a great extent, operating systems on personal computers are similar to those on larger machines. In both cases they allocate the resources of the computer system to users' application programs. However, the operating systems on the smaller computers differ from those in larger computers in that many of them don't permit several users to work with the system at once. Multiprogramming, time-sharing, and spooling are not available on most micros.

On personal computers, the operating system is often loaded into main memory with the assistance of "bootstrap programs," which reside in ROM chips. As the accompanying diagram suggests, the bootstrap program brings the operating system from disk into main memory as soon as the machine is turned on (step A in the figure). Of course, the disk containing the operating system must be on the disk drive for this step to occur. In turn, the operating system automatically loads the file directory (also on the same disk), which contains the names, disk locations, creation dates, and other statistics pertaining to all the programs and data files on the system. The operator is then informed that the computer can accept commands from the keyboard.

In step B, the operator requests the operating system to make the BASIC package translator available. This piece of systems software lets the operator create, modify, and run BASIC programs on the computer system. The translator changes each statement written in BASIC into the machine language of the computer. Before the operating system brings the BASIC translator into primary memory, it checks to see if enough storage is available there to load it. Once the translator has been loaded, the operator is again notified on the display device that the computer system is ready for more commands.

In step C, the operator commands the computer system to load applications program 12. As usual, the operating system consults the file directory to determine the size of the program, and checks main memory to see if enough space is available. If storage is adequate, the applications program is brought into main memory, and the operator is notified of this fact.

Once the applications program has been loaded, the operating system places the operator in contact with the BASIC language translator. The translator contains all the facilities that the operator needs to create, modify, and run programs. As the operator modifies program 12, say by adding more statements, the changes are entered into main memory. When the operator is finished typing in the additional statements, the modified version of program 12 can be run or transferred to disk for later use.

Multiprogramming. **Multiprogramming** is somewhat similar to the operation of a busy dentist's office. The dentist *concurrently* attends to several patients in different rooms within a given period of time. The dentist may pull a tooth in room 1, move to room 2 to prepare a cavity for filling, move back to room 1 to treat the hole created by the pulled tooth, and so forth. Assistants do minor tasks as the dentist moves from patient to patient.

In a computer system with a multiprogrammed operating system, several applications programs may be stored in main

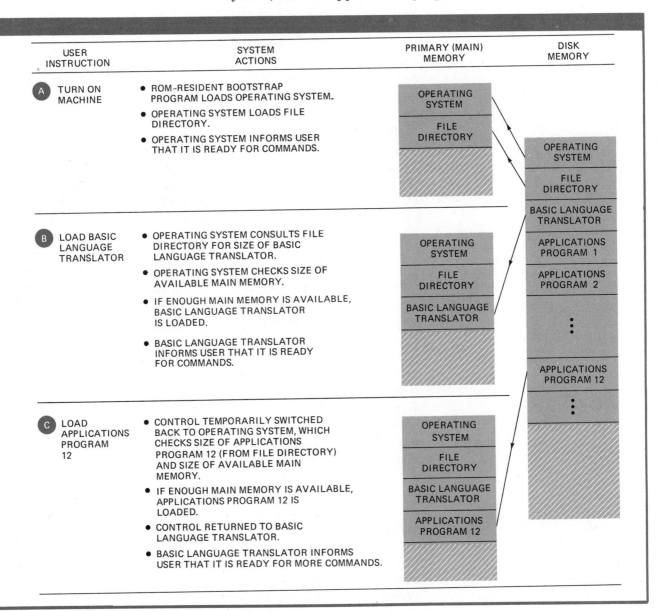

USER INSTRUCTION	SYSTEM ACTIONS	PRIMARY (MAIN) MEMORY	DISK MEMORY
A TURN ON MACHINE	• ROM-RESIDENT BOOTSTRAP PROGRAM LOADS OPERATING SYSTEM. • OPERATING SYSTEM LOADS FILE DIRECTORY. • OPERATING SYSTEM INFORMS USER THAT IT IS READY FOR COMMANDS.	OPERATING SYSTEM / FILE DIRECTORY	OPERATING SYSTEM / FILE DIRECTORY / BASIC LANGUAGE TRANSLATOR / APPLICATIONS PROGRAM 1 / APPLICATIONS PROGRAM 2 ... APPLICATIONS PROGRAM 12 ...
B LOAD BASIC LANGUAGE TRANSLATOR	• OPERATING SYSTEM CONSULTS FILE DIRECTORY FOR SIZE OF BASIC LANGUAGE TRANSLATOR. • OPERATING SYSTEM CHECKS SIZE OF AVAILABLE MAIN MEMORY. • IF ENOUGH MAIN MEMORY IS AVAILABLE, BASIC LANGUAGE TRANSLATOR IS LOADED. • BASIC LANGUAGE TRANSLATOR INFORMS USER THAT IT IS READY FOR COMMANDS.	OPERATING SYSTEM / FILE DIRECTORY / BASIC LANGUAGE TRANSLATOR	
C LOAD APPLICATIONS PROGRAM 12	• CONTROL TEMPORARILY SWITCHED BACK TO OPERATING SYSTEM, WHICH CHECKS SIZE OF APPLICATIONS PROGRAM 12 (FROM FILE DIRECTORY) AND SIZE OF AVAILABLE MAIN MEMORY. • IF ENOUGH MAIN MEMORY IS AVAILABLE, APPLICATIONS PROGRAM 12 IS LOADED. • CONTROL RETURNED TO BASIC LANGUAGE TRANSLATOR. • BASIC LANGUAGE TRANSLATOR INFORMS USER THAT IT IS READY FOR MORE COMMANDS.	OPERATING SYSTEM / FILE DIRECTORY / BASIC LANGUAGE TRANSLATOR / APPLICATIONS PROGRAM 12	

memory at the same time. The CPU, like the dentist, works on only one program at a time. When it reaches a point in a program at which peripheral devices or other elements of the computer system must take over some of the work, the CPU moves on to another program, returning to the first program when it is ready to be processed again. While the computer is waiting for data for one program to be accessed on disk, for example, it can perform calculations for another. The systems software for the disk unit works like the dental assistants—it does background work, in this case, retrieving the data stored on disk.

Multiprogramming is feasible because computers can perform thousands of computations in the time it takes to ask for and receive a single piece of data from disk. Such disk I/O operations are much slower than computation because the computer has to interact with and receive communications from another device to obtain the data it needs. It must also contend with the slower access speeds of secondary memory.

Time-Sharing.   **Time-sharing** is a very popular technique for computer systems that support numerous terminals. The operating system cycles through all the active programs in the system that need processing, giving each one a small time slice on each cycle.

For example, say there are twenty programs on the system and each program is to be allocated a time slice of one second (the time slice is usually much smaller than this, and all slices aren't necessarily equal). The computer will work on program 1 for one second, then on program 2 for one second, and so forth. When it finishes working on program 20 for one second, it will go back to program 1 for another second, program 2 for another second, and so on. Thus, if there are an average of twenty programs on the system, each program will get a total of three seconds of processing during each minute of actual clock time, or one second in every twenty-second period. As you can see, in a time-sharing system, it is difficult for a single program to dominate the CPU's attention, thereby holding up the processing of shorter programs.

Both time-sharing and multiprogramming are techniques for working on many programs concurrently, by alloting short periods of uninterrupted time to each. They differ, however, in the way they allot time. In time-sharing, the computer spends a fixed amount of time on each program and then goes on to another. In multiprogramming, the computer works on a program until it encounters a logical stopping point, as when more data must be read in, before going on to another. Many computers today combine time-sharing and multiprogramming techniques to expedite processing.

Spooling. Some input and output devices are extremely slow. Card readers and printers, for example, work at a snail's pace compared to the CPU. If the CPU had to wait for these slower devices to finish their work, the computer system would be faced with a horrendous bottleneck. For example, suppose the computer has just completed a five-second job that has generated 100 pages of hard-copy for the printer. On a printer that prints 600 lines per minute, this job would take about ten minutes to print. If the CPU communicated directly with the printer, primary memory would be tied up for ten minutes waiting for the printer to complete the job. As a result, other programs could not be processed while this output was being transferred from main memory to paper.

To avoid such a delay, disk devices on almost all large systems contain **spooling** areas to store output destined for the printer (Figure 8-2). As the computer processes a program, the operating system rapidly transfers, or "spools," the output from main memory to the disk spooling area. The computer is then free to process another program, leaving it to another system program to transfer the output of the first program from disk to printer. At any one time, the spooling area may contain over 100 completed jobs, waiting to be delivered to output devices. As long as space remains in the *output spooling area,* the CPU can continue to operate without delay.

As Figure 8-2 shows, spooling is also used extensively to hold, or stage, input on its way to the computer. As programs enter the computer system, they are stored in an *input spooling area,* or *queue.* When the operating system is ready to deliver the next program to the CPU, it checks the queue to see which one to process next. On many computer systems, some users can assign a high priority to their programs. In this case, the computer attends to their jobs before those that may have been in the queue longer but have a lower priority.

Virtual Storage. In the early days of computing, users who had large programs faced numerous problems loading them into main memory. Often, the programmer had to split such programs into pieces manually, so that only small portions of them resided in the limited main memory space at any one time. In the early 1970s, a virtual storage feature became available on some operating systems. It permitted users the luxury of writing

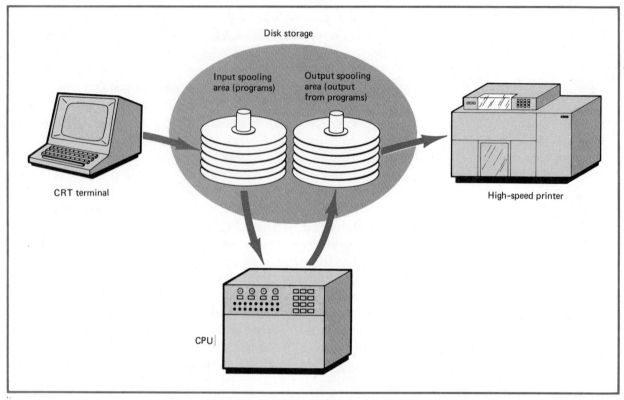

Disk storage

Input spooling area (programs)

Output spooling area (output from programs)

CRT terminal

High-speed printer

CPU

Figure 8-2. Spooling. Input is spooled while waiting to be processed, and output is spooled before it is sent to the printer.

extremely long programs which would automatically be split up and managed by the operating system. **Virtual storage** refers to a special, fast-access area on disk, which can be viewed as a large extension of main memory. The operating system delivers programs to be processed to the virtual storage area. Here, they are subdivided into either fixed-length "pages" or variable-length "segments." Whether the programs are subdivided into pages or segments depends on the capabilities of the operating system.

A virtual storage system using **paging** breaks a program into pages. If a program is 40K bytes long, and the paging system divides programs into 4K-byte lengths, the program will be divided into ten pages. As the computer works on the program, it stores only a few pages at a time in main memory. As other pages are required during program execution, they are selected from virtual storage and written over the pages in main memory that are no longer needed. All the original pages, or modified ones, remain intact in virtual storage as the computer processes the program. So if a page that has been written over in main memory is needed again, it can readily be fetched. This process, illustrated in Figure 8-3, continues until the program is finished.

The operating system may use a variety of rules to determine which pages to keep in primary memory. One rule might require a new page to be written over the page that has been used least recently. On the other hand, a page with a high overall frequency of use (even though it may be the least recently used at any time) is a logical candidate for remaining in primary memory.

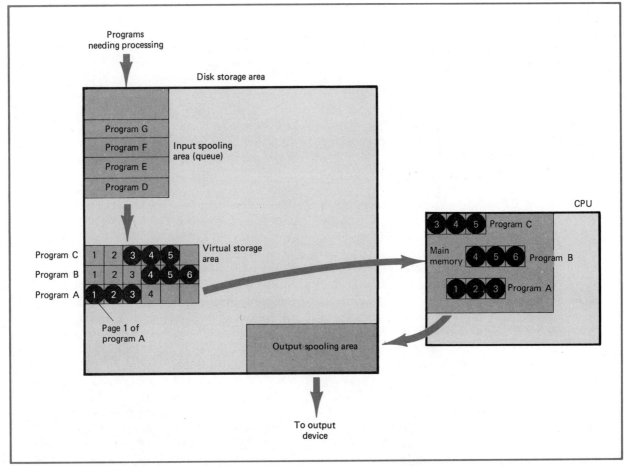

Figure 8-3. *Virtual storage based on a paging system.* In this system, programs awaiting processing are transferred from the input spooling area to the virtual storage area. In virtual storage, programs are divided into pages of fixed length, perhaps 4000 bytes each. When the computer is ready to process a program, the operating system transfers a certain number of pages (three, in the example here) into main memory. The computer then processes the program until it needs a new page, whereupon the required page is delivered to main memory, writing over the one that is no longer needed. The computer system continues in this fashion, selecting desired pages of a program from virtual storage, until the program is completed. At that point, the program output is delivered to the output spooling area and a new program is read into its area of virtual storage.

Segmentation works somewhat like paging, except that the segments are variable in length. Each segment normally consists of a contiguous block of logically interrelated material from the program. As in paging, a segment that is needed in main memory is written over one that isn't. Many systems that use segmentation employ a combination of segmentation and

tomorrow

PARALLEL PROCESSING: A KEY TO TOMORROW'S COMPUTING NEEDS

A general principle of work is that two or more workers, doing a job together, can complete it faster than one of them working alone. Curiously, however, until recently few attempts have been made to apply this principle to computers. Despite the fact that computer systems have evolved at an astounding rate over the past fifty years, most of them are still driven by a single processor. A single processor can only perform instructions in *serial,* or one step at a time, whether it be working exclusively on one program or interleaving several.

In the worldwide race to develop ever faster computer systems for tomorrow, scientists are experimenting with ways to have two or more processors and memories perform tasks in *parallel.* Just as it is difficult to coordinate two or more workers who are simultaneously dedicated to completing a single job. So, too, it is difficult to coordinate the parallel efforts of several processors and memories that work at superhuman speeds. Nonetheless, many industry insiders see parallel processing, or multiprocessing, systems as the wave of the future. Several approaches to such systems are currently under study.

One approach, developed by James Browne at the University of Texas at Austin, involves a network consisting of four processors and nine memories. The Texas Reconfigurable Array Computer (TRAC), as it is named, works through a complex synchronization of the processors with the memories. When a processor needs a memory, it more or less "calls up" the memory as you would dial a number on your telephone. Because the processors are not all "bottlenecked" at a single central memory, and the processors simultaneously execute program instructions, machines such as TRAC are capable of faster overall processing speeds than conventional devices.

A second approach, proposed by Jack Dennis at MIT, is *data flow computers.* These devices, which are still at the drawing-board stage, work with a large number of processors and memories. Like TRAC, each processor can draw upon the resources of any of the memories. However, these machines are characterized by a radical departure from computers as we know them today. Today's computers perform instructions in the order programs tell them to, fetching data from memory on an as-needed basis. Data flow computers, on the other hand, are sent "data packets" from memory and perform whatever computations are called for in the packet.

Yet another approach is the *binary-tree computer,* which is being researched at the University of North Carolina at Chapel Hill. This machine involves several processors hooked up hierarchically in a tree-type network, with instructions and data passing to and from processors through the "branches" of the tree. It has led to the development of an entirely new type of programming language, in which program instructions and their data are interspersed.

Although scientists all over the world are busily at work constructing parallel processing machines, it will be several years before most become a practical reality. Nonetheless, because common sense would seem to tell us that one hundred heads are better than one, these machines would seem to be a sure bet for tomorrow.

paging. A program is first segmented into logically related blocks, which are further divided into pages of fixed length.

Not all operating systems on large computers use virtual storage. Although this technique permits processing of larger programs, it requires extra computer time to swap pages or segments in and out of main memory.

Multiprocessing. **Multiprocessing** refers to the use of two or more computers, linked together, to perform work on programs in parallel, i.e., at the same time. Whereas multiprogramming processes several programs *concurrently* on a *single* machine, multiprocessing may handle several jobs *simultaneously* (at precisely the same insant) on *several* machines.

Because of the availability of low-cost microprocessors, many computer manufacturers are designing systems to do multiprocessing. Since the machines can work as a team and can operate in parallel, jobs can be processed much more rapidly than they could on a single machine.

LANGUAGE TRANSLATORS

As mentioned earlier, computers can execute programs only after they've been translated into machine language. There are two reasons why people don't generally write programs in this language. First, machine-language instructions consist of complex-looking strings of 0s and 1s. For example,

```
010110000111000000000000100000010
```

Few people enjoy or are successful at writing long programs consisting of statements like this. Second, machine-language instructions have to be written at the most detailed level of exposition. For example, the computer can't directly add A and B, placing the result in C, with a single instruction such as

```
C = A + B
```

Even a simple task like this may require three or more machine-language instructions, such as

1. Load the value represented by A from main memory into a register.

2. Add the value represented by *B* from main memory into the same register.

3. Place the sum obtained into another storage area.

Such detailed statements are sometimes called *microinstructions*, since they cannot be subdivided further into smaller commands. An instruction such as *C = A + B*, on the other hand, is an example of a *macroinstruction*. Macroinstructions must be broken down into microinstructions by the computer system before they are processed. All high-level languages (such as BASIC, FORTRAN, and COBOL) use macroinstruction-type statements to spare the programmer the tedious task of explaining in fine detail to the computer how to do the work.

A **language translator** is simply a system program that converts an applications program written in a high-level language or in assembly language into machine language. In other words, it converts a program with macroinstructions into one with binary-based microinstructions. There are three common types of language translators—compilers, interpreters, and assemblers.

Compilers.   A **compiler** translates a high-level language program entirely into machine language at one time. Every compiler-oriented language requires its own special compiler. Thus, a COBOL program needs a COBOL compiler; it cannot run on a FORTRAN compiler. In addition, a compiler that works for machines of one manufacturer will not work on the machines of another. For example, you can't run a FORTRAN program on an IBM computer using a FORTRAN compiler that was created for a Honeywell computer.

The program that you write in a high-level language and enter in the computer is called a **source module** (or **source program**). The machine-language program that the compiler then produces from it is called an **object module** (or **object program**).

Before the object module is actually executed, it is normally bound together with other object modules that the CPU may need in order to process the program. For example, most computers can't compute square roots directly. To do so, they rely on small "subprograms," which are stored in secondary memory in object module form. So if your program calls for calculation of a square root, the operating system will bind the object module version of your program together with this square root routine to form an "executable package" for the computer.

The binding process is referred to as *linkage editing* (or the *link-edit stage*), and the executable package that is formed is called a **load module.** A special system program, called a **linkage editor,** is available on computer systems to do the binding automatically. In fact, most people who write their own programs don't even realize that link editing will take place. The operating system takes care of this operation automatically.

It is the load module that the computer actually executes, or runs. When your program is ready to run it has reached the *GO stage.* Figure 8-4 shows the complete process, from compil-

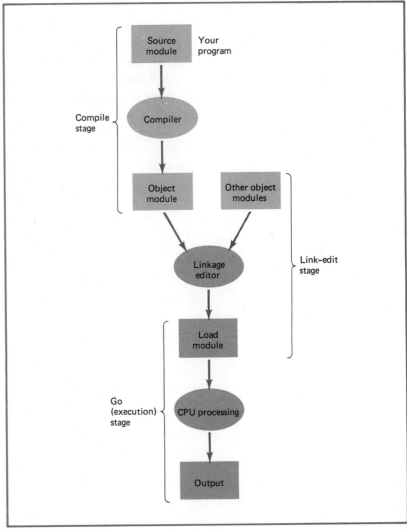

Figure 8-4. *Compile, link-edit, GO.* A compiler and a linkage editor convert a source module into a load module, which is processed by the CPU.

ing to link editing to execution. Both object and load modules can be saved on disk for later use, so that compilation and linkage editing need not be performed every time the program is executed.

Interpreters. An **interpreter,** unlike a compiler, does not create an object module. Interpreters read, translate, and execute source programs one line at a time. Thus, the translation into machine language is performed while the program is being run.

Interpreters have advantages and disadvantages relative to compilers. The major advantage is that an interpreter requires much less storage space. Also, the interpreter does not generate an object module that has to be stored. Many versions of BASIC use interpreters rather than compilers, and for this reason, require less storage than compiler-oriented languages such as COBOL and FORTRAN. This is a major reason why BASIC is so popular on microcomputers, which have limited storage capacity.

The major disadvantage of interpreters is that they are slower and less efficient than compilers. The object program produced by a compiler is entirely in machine language, so it can be executed very quickly. Interpreters, in contrast, translate each statement immediately before executing it, which takes more time because a statement must be reinterpreted *every time* it is executed. In addition, the object module of a compiled program can be saved on disk, so the source program doesn't have to be translated again every time the program is run. With an interpreter, the program must be translated anew every time it is run.

Assemblers. The third type of translator, the **assembler,** is used exclusively with assembly languages. It works like a compiler, producing a saveable object module. Each computer system typically has only one assembly language available to it; thus, only one assembler need be acquired.

UTILITY PROGRAMS

Some tasks are performed so often in the course of processing that it would be extremely inefficient if every user had to code them into programs over and over again. Sorting records and copying programs from tape to disk (or from disk to tape) are

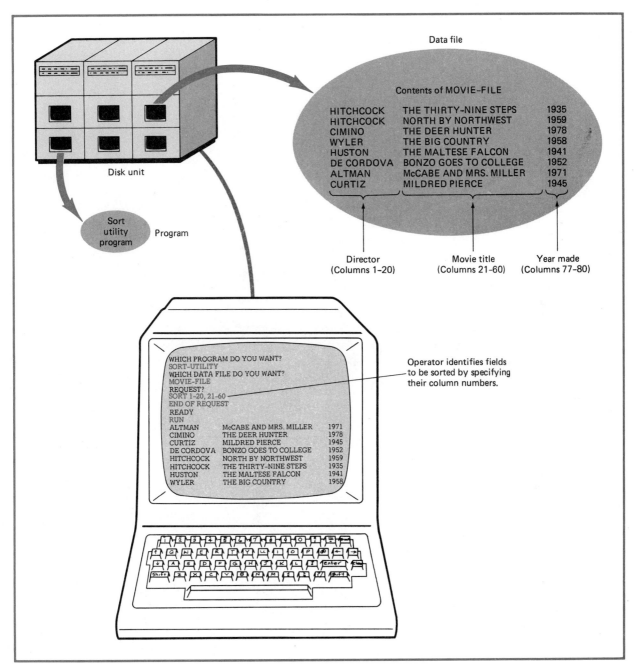

Figure 8-5. *A sort utility program in action.* The terminal operator requests that a movie file be sorted alphabetically, first by director (columns 1 to 20) and then by movie title (columns 21 to 60). Note that the second sort reverses the order of the two Alfred Hitchcock movies.

examples of such tasks. To eliminate the need for users and programmers to waste time writing such routines, computer systems normally have available several **utility programs**— kept in secondary storage—to perform these functions. An organization can often buy the utility programs it needs from a software vendor. Otherwise, it might have the programs written by its own programming staff.

To appreciate how a sort utility might work, see Figure 8-5. Sort utilities are normally very flexible. You can operate one independently, as illustrated in the figure, even changing the order of the original fields of the file or suppressing some of the fields on output. Also, some languages permit you to imbed a "call" to the sort utility in the computer programs you write.

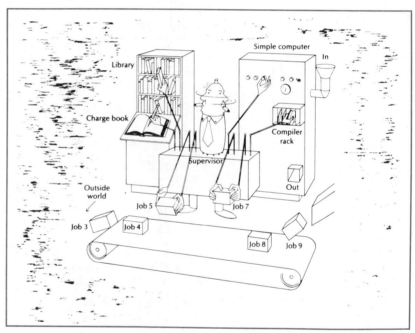

Systems software in action.

Summary and Key Terms

Systems software consists of programs that coordinate the various parts of the computer system to make it run rapidly and efficiently. The role of systems software is basically to act as a mediator between applications programs and the hardware of the computer system.

An **operating system** is a collection of programs that manage the activities of the computer. The functions of the operating system—which include assignment of system resources, scheduling of resources and jobs, and monitoring activities—can be seen as aspects of a single general mission: to control the operations of the computer system.

Two of the most prominent programs of the operating system are the supervisor program and the job-control program. The **supervisor** (or **monitor**) is a program that controls all the other parts of the operating system. The **job-control program** enables both users and programmers to communicate with the operating system with a **job-control language (JCL).** When interfacing with the operating system, one can use the standard system **defaults,** chosen by the operating system, or request customized service through JCL commands.

Larger computers, specifically minicomputers and mainframes, often take advantage of sophisticated processing techniques, such as multiprogramming, time-sharing, spooling, virtual storage, and multiprocessing, to operate more efficiently.

In a computer system with **multiprogramming,** the computer can work on several programs *concurrently*. For example, while the computer is waiting for data for one program to be accessed on disk, it can perform calculations for another.

Time-sharing is a technique in which the operating system cycles through all the active programs in the system that need processing, giving each one a small slice of time on each cycle.

Disk devices on almost all large systems contain input and output **spooling** areas to enable the CPU to process jobs in an efficient way. The *input spooling area* (or *queue*) contains jobs awaiting processing by the CPU, whereas the *output spooling area* contains printer-destined output.

Virtual storage refers to a special fast-access area on disk, which can be viewed as a large extension of main memory. The operating system delivers programs to be processed to the virtual storage area, where they are subdivided into either fixed-length *pages* (a process called **paging**) or variable-length *segments* (a process called **segmentation**).

Multiprocessing refers to the use of two or more computers, linked together, to perform work on programs in parallel—that is, at the *same* time.

A **language translator** is a system program that converts an applications program written in a high-level language or in assembly language into machine language. There are three common types of language translators—compilers, interpreters, and assemblers.

A **compiler** translates a high-level language program entirely into machine language at one time. The program written by the user or programmer, called a **source module (source program)**, is translated by the compiler into an **object module (object program)**. The object module version of the program is then input to a **linkage editor,** which combines it with supplementary object modules needed to run the program, to form a **load module.** It is the load module that is executed by the computer.

Interpreters read, translate, and execute source programs one line at a time. Thus, the translation into machine language is performed while the program is being run.

The third type of translator, the **assembler,** is used exclusively with assembly languages.

A **utility program** is a type of system program written to perform repetitive data-processing tasks—for example, sorting records and copying programs from tape to disk (or from disk to tape).

Review Questions

1. What is systems software?
2. What is an operating system and what are its major functions?
3. Describe multiprogramming, time-sharing, spooling, virtual storage, and multiprocessing.
4. What are the differences among a compiler, an interpreter, and an assembler?
5. Describe the differences among a source module, object module, and load module.
6. What is the purpose of a utility program?

Suggested Readings

Ashley, Ruth, and Judi N. Fernandez. *Job Control Language: A Self-Teaching Guide.* New York: Wiley, 1978.

Davis, William S. *Operating Systems: A Systematic View.* Reading, Mass.: Addison-Wesley, 1983.

Lorin, H., and H. M. Deitel. *Operating Systems.* Reading, Mass.: Addison-Wesley, 1981.

Chapter 9

Applications Software Development

OVERVIEW

If you wanted to build a house, you'd probably begin with some research and planning. You might speak to various people about home design, draw up some floor plans, estimate the cost of materials, and so forth. In other words, you wouldn't start digging a hole and pouring concrete on the very first day. Producing a successful applications program also requires planning and discipline. The process involved is called *program development*.

Years ago, the cost of hardware was the dominant concern in establishing a computer system, and developing good applications program software was often a secondary consideration. The cost of hardware has plunged in recent years, however, whereas the cost of labor has increased dramatically. Writing programs is a labor-intensive task. Thus, many organizations today are finding that they spend about 70 percent of their total computing costs on software.

What's more, many large organizations have discovered that up to 80 percent of their software costs are spent just on maintaining existing programs. For example, every time a tax rule changes, several programs must be altered to reflect the new rates and policies. In addition, these programs have to be subjected to a lengthy testing process to be sure they run correctly. If programs are poorly written to begin with, the maintenance cost can approach ridiculous proportions. In some cases, an old program will have to be scrapped and completely redone.

In this chapter and the next we will describe some useful practices for properly developing applications programs. In both these chapters our focus is on a set of techniques called *structured programming*. As you read these chapters, keep in mind that it is never enough just to write a program that works. Good programs must be easy to understand and easy to maintain. A well-planned program may take slightly longer to write initially, but the subsequent savings in maintenance costs will generally make the effort well worthwhile.

This chapter begins with a general discussion of the role of applications software and the way program development is conducted in organizations. It goes on to discuss the program development cycle and concludes with a discussion of the advantages and disadvantages of vendor-supplied software in relation to software developed in-house.

THE ROLE OF APPLICATIONS SOFTWARE

Applications software consists of programs that direct computer systems to produce outputs for computer users. Every computer application that interfaces with users, from video games to the tracking of a space shuttle, from printing mailing lists to compiling U.S. census returns, requires applications software.

Consider an example. It's a hot Saturday night and you want to cool off at a local movie theater, but you don't have enough cash. You go to the automatic teller machine at your bank, slip in a plastic card, respond to the questions that appear on the screen by pressing the appropriate keys, and presto—movie money. Without an applications program, however, the convenience of automatic tellers would be impossible. It's an applications program that, among other things, tells the system what messages to put on the screen, how to respond to the keys you press, what to do if your balance is too low or if you enter the wrong ID number, how much cash to deliver, and so on. In other words, the program specifies how the system should respond to any combination of circumstances to assure that you get efficient service and that both you and the bank are protected from theft.

Creating applications software is closely related to the process of systems development, which we discuss in detail in Chapters 15 and 16. Systems development involves the analysis, design, and implementation of complete computer systems, including hardware, systems software, applications software, data, people, and procedures. If a bank without automatic teller machines considered installing them, for example, it would probably go through the complete systems development process. Only part of that process would involve designing and creating the applications programs to make the machines do useful work.

Once a system is in place and running, however, there is still a need for new or modified applications software. The bank may decide, for example, to modify its automatic teller system to permit customers to make withdrawals with their credit cards as well as with their bank cards. Or a bank executive may ask to see a report on machine transactions daily instead of weekly. These kinds of applications involve applications software development, but they do not necessarily involve full-blown systems development.

THE DATA-PROCESSING DEPARTMENT

In most large organizations, systems development and the development of applications software are two of the jobs of the data-processing department. This department performs a service role—providing and coordinating computer resources—for other departments in the organization, such as accounting, finance, sales, and manufacturing. Figure 9-1 is an organization chart that shows a typical structure for a data-processing department. At the head of the department is the director of data processing, who is responsible for planning and creating computer systems and for overseeing their day-to-day operation.

Under the director of data processing are three areas:

- Systems analysis and design
- Programming
- Operations

Two of these areas—systems analysis and design and programming—are directly involved in creating applications software. The people who do the creating are *systems analysts* and *programmers*. **Systems analysts** (or *analysts*) are the people who actually define the requirements for applications software. They work with the people who will use the software to assess their needs and to translate those needs into a plan. They then determine the resources required to implement the plan. The analysts create a set of specifications for every program in the system that outlines

- What the program must do
- How the program should work
- What programming language to use
- How the program will be tested
- What documentation the program needs

Programmers then take these specifications and translate them into code—a series of statements in a programming language. **Maintenance programmers** monitor the software on an ongoing basis, correcting errors and altering software as applications change.

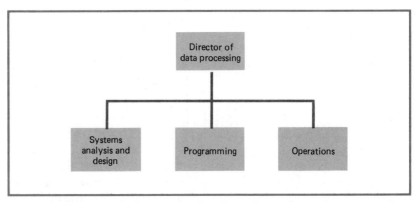

Figure 9-1.   A typical organizational structure for a data-processing department.

THE PROGRAM DEVELOPMENT CYCLE

There are two ways organizations acquire applications programs: writing them internally (sometimes called in-house development) and buying them from an outside source. Whichever method is chosen, certain steps should be followed to ensure that the software does its job at a reasonable cost.

Creating successful programs commonly involves five stages:

- **Analysis**   Identifying and defining the problem to be solved; deciding whether the solution involves software; and if it does, defining input, output, and processing requirements.
- **Design**   Planning the solution to the problem.
- **Coding**   Writing the program.
- **Debugging**   Finding and eliminating errors in the program.
- **Documentation**   Writing manuals for the people who will use the program and for maintenance programmers.

These five stages are often called the **program development cycle.** The first two stages are usually the job of systems analysts; the last three, of programmers. The exact division of jobs, however, varies from organization to organization.

When a program is purchased from an outside source, it will not be necessary to follow all these stages. Some of them, such as writing the program and documentation, will be done by the vendor. The special considerations that must be made when buying software are treated at the end of the chapter.

ANALYSIS

A problem for a systems analyst often begins as a request that the computer system produce specific information. The scope of the solution can range from revamping the entire system to simply providing a new piece of information on an existing printed report. **Analysis** of the problem involves two steps: (1) identifying the problem and deciding what kind of solution is called for, and (2) if the solution involves software, developing the requirements the software must meet.

Identifying the Problem

The first thing a systems analyst must do in studying a potential problem is to decide if any problems do, in fact, exist. This may be the single most difficult task for the analyst, since it involves a shrewd sense of perspective, a thorough knowledge of the user's job, and excellent communication skills. It requires a sagacity you can't generally learn from books.

Suppose, for example, the sales manager complains to the data-processing department that she is getting important information too late and that the reports she is getting are inadequate. The systems analyst must ascertain if there really are serious problems. Perhaps the information the manager needs is available in reports she already receives, but she doesn't know where to look for it. Also, does she really need the information she is asking for? Does she need it as promptly as she says she does? Getting answers to questions like these clearly requires sensitivity and tact.

In addition to determining whether or not these problems exist, the analyst must also decide if a computer solution is appropriate. A user has a real need for data-processing resources if their use will result in benefits to the organization as a whole. These benefits may be realized through reduced costs, better service, improved information for decision making, and so forth. Are the benefits of providing the sales manager with the information she needs likely to justify the costs of creating it?

Once the analyst has determined that any of these problems are serious and that the need for computer resources is legitimate, the next question is "What approaches will best solve the problems?" For the problems posed by the sales manager, some possible approaches are:

- Add the manager's name to the circulation list for an existing report that provides the information she needs when she needs it.
- Modify existing software and procedures to produce the report she needs.
- Develop new software and procedures to produce the report she needs.
- Acquire a new computer system to serve both the manager and other users who may have similar problems with the existing system.

And of course, there many other possibilities. Software solutions, as you can see, may be just some of many possible approaches. For now, however, we will deal only with software development and defer the more general issue of systems development until Chapters 15 and 16.

Developing Software Requirements

Once the analyst has settled on a software solution, the next job is to specify the constraints the software must meet. This step involves defining the output the software is to produce, the input needed to produce this output, and the processing tasks the system must perform. Output requirements are always developed first, because you can't know what to put into a system or what to ask it to do without knowing what you need to get out.

Defining Output. The analyst should define output in terms of content, format, timing, and flexibility.

- **Content** What type of information must the application provide and at what level of detail? A sales manager may want a report on sales by region for each product the company makes but may not need to know the specific date on which each sale was made. Too much detail can sometimes complicate a report and obscure important information.

- **Format** How should the information be presented? Will it appear as a printed report or on a CRT screen? If the latter, the analyst should consult the users to see which of a number of screen formats is preferable. Likewise, if the output is to be a printed report, the analyst and users will have to decide how it is to be organized—how many columns, how many rows, how columns and rows are to be labeled, what comments and explanations are needed, and so forth.

- **Timing** When do users need the information? Daily? Weekly? Monthly? On demand? Some users, for example airline clerks who interact directly with clients, need a fast response time. Hence the analyst might require the software to provide users with a response in five seconds or less at least 95 percent of the time.

- **Flexibility** Programs should not be so rigidly designed that they cannot be modified to meet changing conditions. In one well-known case, a bank installed a query system that analysts designed to provide information users told them they needed. However, the analysts neglected to anticipate that once the system was installed, the users—in this case trust officers—would begin to ask new types of questions and demand new types of reports. Since the system wasn't flexible enough to adapt to the new requests, it was regarded as a failure.

Defining Input. After specifying the output, analysts must determine what input is needed to produce it. This job involves four issues: data needed, data availability, procedures for new data, and data entry.

- **Data needed** What data does the application require? For example, if the application is to provide a monthly report on the sales of a particular product, the system must have data on each sale of that product and the date of sale.

- **Data availability** Are the data needed currently available? Sales invoices, for example, may contain all the data needed to generate monthly reports on product sales.

- **Procedures for new data**   If new data are needed, how are they to be gathered? Suppose, for example, a company was trying to decide how to market a product, and it wanted information in the sales report that showed how many purchases were for home use and how many were for business. The analyst might decide to redesign the sales invoice so that it provided this information.

- **Data entry**   How are the data to be entered into the system? The analyst, for example, may recommend new data-entry procedures or the hiring of new data-entry personnel.

Defining Processing.   Processing describes the actual work the system does. The analyst must define the processing tasks involved in the application and the constraints that people and equipment impose on the way those tasks are carried out.

- **Processing tasks**   What processing tasks must the software accomplish? Producing a sales report, for example, may require a program that can, among other things, sort a large file of sales data by date and product, classify each according to such criteria as product and region, and compute totals and percentages.

- **People constraints**   How sophisticated about computers are the users who will interact directly with the system? If they are not very sophisticated, the software will have to be easy to use. For example, the software may have to be designed so that the system gives clear prompts to users on what to do, when to do it, and how to backtrack to an earlier point if they make a mistake or get confused.

- **Equipment constraints**   The software must be designed to work on the computer, peripheral equipment, and systems software that are available or feasible to acquire. It doesn't make sense to design software that needs two disk drives, for example, if the system has only one and the expense of a second drive is prohibitive.

THE DESIGN STAGE: STRUCTURED TECHNIQUES

In the **design** stage of the program development cycle, analysts work from the software requirements developed in the analysis stage to spell out as precisely as possible the nature of the programming solution that will enable the system to meet those requirements. They determine all the tasks each program must do as well as how the tasks will be organized or sequenced when the program is coded. Only when the design is complete does the next stage begin—the actual coding of the programs.

In the early days of computing, design and coding were not clearly separated. Programmers were relatively free to solve problems their own way. They would often begin coding with an unsystematic idea of the requirements the programs must meet. Such a nondisciplined approach had many problems.

First, a programmer might be making substantial progress on a program only to find that a key function had been omitted. As a result, large pieces of the program might have to be reorganized. Second, the logic behind programs written in this freewheeling way was usually obscure. What's more, each programmer had a personalized coding style. What seemed systematic to one might seem incomprehensible to another. Programs written this way "worked"—in the sense that they did the job they were supposed to do—but they were very hard for anyone but the original programmers to understand. They were, especially, a nightmare for maintenance programmers—the people who had to keep them up to date whenever some aspect of the application changed. These unfortunates, faced with a tangle of confused code, would usually just patch a program up with their own bit of new code rather than write it over. The result was even more confusion. Organizations found themselves dependent for critical applications on software that no one understood very well. As computer systems came to be used for ever more applications, it became clear that some order was needed to prevent financial calamity.

One solution that evolved was to stress program planning (design) and to separate the planning process from the actual coding. *Planning* became the job of systems analysts; *coding,* the job of programmers.

At the same time, a group of techniques evolved that made program design more systematic and programs themselves easier to read and maintain. These techniques are usually grouped together under the term *structured program design,* or *structured programming.* Actually, **structured programming** originally referred only to the use of certain logical structures in programs themselves (we will discuss these structures in Chapter 10), but it has come to apply to a whole body of design and coding practices.

Writing Maintainable Programs

As you struggled with your first few program assignments in school, you probably didn't give much thought to program maintenance. If you're like most students in beginning programming courses, you probably work on one program assignment, solve it in one fashion or another, and then quickly move on to something new. Few students look back at an old program, reevaluate its logic, and modify it to do a few new things. Old programs are like movies one has seen before—they're generally not as interesting the second time around.

Unfortunately, maintaining old programs is crucial in most commercial data-processing settings. If you can't write programs that someone else can easily read, your effectiveness will be very limited. Programs are expensive to develop, and their continuity from year to year is often critical.

Programs that provide organizations with day-to-day accounting and operating information must be maintained constantly. Changes in hardware, for example, may force input and output statements to address different devices. Or a department may become unionized, forcing a modification in a payroll program for a union dues deduction. Or state and federal taxing agencies might change their policies, requiring revisions in a number of programs. Or a table may need to be expanded, new transaction codes may need to be defined, the format of an output report may need to be revised, and so forth. Thus, no matter how "perfectly" the initial program works when it is written, some change must be anticipated. Since a data-processing program may have a useful life of twenty years or more, and it is highly likely that several programmers will be maintaining it during this period, it is important to adopt a highly readable coding style.

What's a good style? Ideally, programs should be written in a structured fashion, using a set of standard rules that have been developed by the data-processing shop. These guidelines will make it easier for programmers to follow each other's code. Even if you're among the most talented of programmers, you should realize that the people who must understand your work may be far less gifted. Furthermore, if many people are involved in maintenance, the code may have to be written in a form that the least talented programmer can understand. It has been estimated that in a team of programmers, the best and worst programmers differ in performance by at least a factor of ten.

Thus, readability is generally the "bottom line" for commercial data-processing programs, not execution speed or length. For most commercial programming jobs, creative artists need not apply!

```
10    GO TO 30
20    GO TO 50
30    READ A RECORD
40    GO TO 20
50    PRINT A RECORD
60    END
```

Bad code: Headaches for the maintenance programmer.

Design Aids for Structured Programming

Program design aids are tools that help analysts plan structured programs. Many such tools have been developed, but four of the most important are

- Structured program flowcharts
- Pseudocode

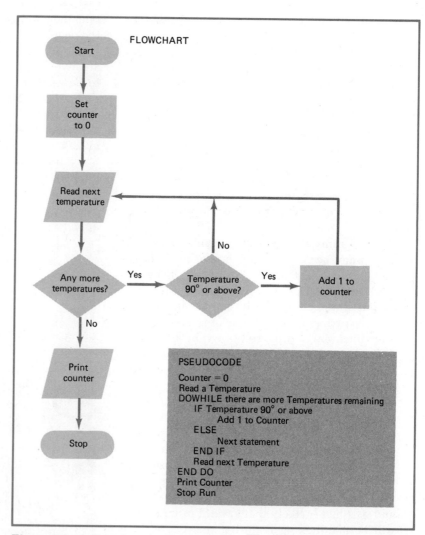

Figure 9-2. Flowchart and pseudocode. The flowchart and pseudocode shown here count the number of temperatures over 90° in a list. Flowcharts use graphical symbols and arrows to show the operations to be performed and the logical flow of the program. Pseudocode uses English-like statements to achieve the same objectives.

- Structure charts
- HIPO (Hierarchy plus Input-Process-Output) charts

These design aids, and structured programming in general, are the main subjects of Chapter 10. We will discuss them only briefly here to show their place in the program development cycle.

Program flowcharts and pseudocode are both tools for outlining in detail the steps a program will follow. Flowcharts, as you can see in Figure 9-2, display the steps and their relation to each other pictorially. Pseudocode, in contrast, outlines the steps of the program in a form that closely resembles actual programming code (hence *pseudo*code).

Structure charts and HIPO charts, unlike flowcharts and pseudocode, do not show the specific steps of a program. Rather, they show how the parts of a program—called *modules*—relate to each other. As Figure 9-3 shows, each module represents a specific programming task—calculating city tax, for example. The modules are arranged hierarchically in what is called a top-down fashion. *Top-down* implies that the top modules control the ones beneath them, and as the modules are developed, the topmost ones are designed and coded first.

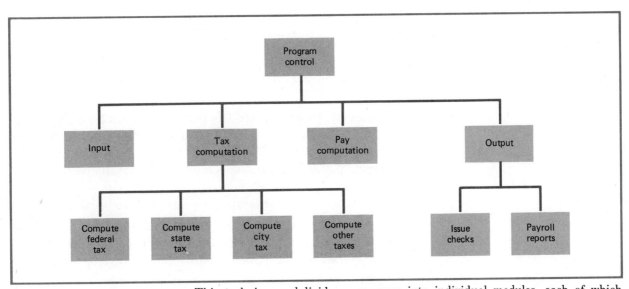

Figure 9-3. Structure charts. This technique subdivides a program into individual modules, each of which represents a well-defined processing task. The modules are then arranged hierarchically in a top-down fashion, as illustrated here for a payroll application. HIPO charts use a similar diagram for illustrating the hierarchy of modules in a program.

Modularity and top-down design are important aspects of structured program design, and we will discuss them in Chapter 10.

Choosing a Language

Another important decision the analyst must make during the design phase is the selection of a programming language. This decision is closely related to the nature of the application the program is for. A business-oriented language like COBOL, for example, is commonly used for business applications, whereas a scientifically oriented language like FORTRAN is more likely to be used for scientific or engineering applications. Because it reflects the nature of the application, the choice of language often also affects the choice of design aids. Some design aids are better suited to certain applications than others. An accounting problem to be coded in a structure-oriented language like COBOL is almost always better suited to structure charts and pseudocode than to flowcharts. On the other hand, scientific problems with a high degree of visual content are best planned with the aid of flowcharts.

The characteristics of some of the more popular programming languages are discussed in Chapter 11.

PROGRAM CODING

Once analysts have finished the program design for an application, the next stage is to code the program. **Coding,** which is the job of programmers, is the process of writing a program from a set of specifications. These specifications generally include

- The name of the programming language to be used
- Design aids such as HIPO or structure charts (that show the organization of the program) or flowcharts or pseudocode (that show the steps involved in processing)
- A timetable to complete the program

The program is often written on coding forms, such as those shown in Figure 9-4. These forms are designed for specific programming languages, and the column restrictions are identified to reflect the conventions of the language. Thus, coding

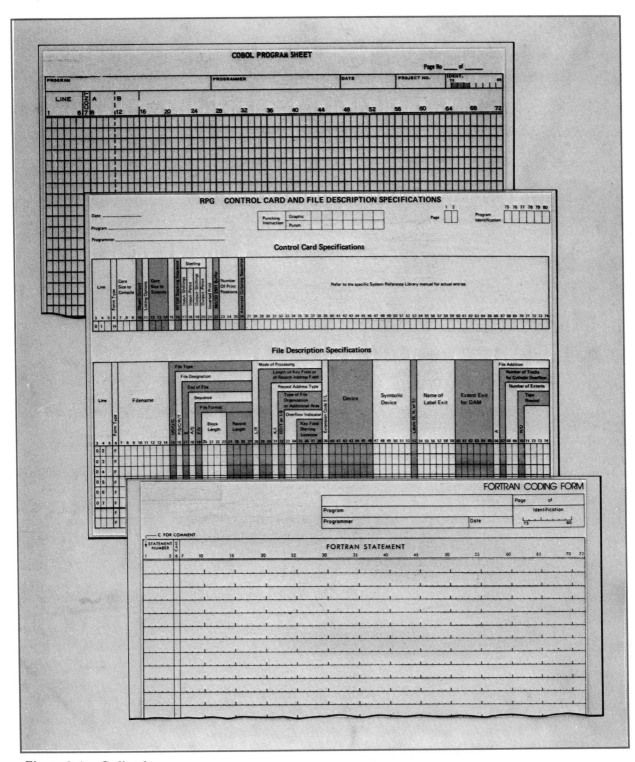

Figure 9-4. Coding forms.

programs on the forms helps programmers avoid errors. In many organizations, the programmer will code the program onto the form and hand it to a data-entry operator, who keys the program exactly as it appears.

Getting the Most for Your Money: Increasing Programmer Productivity

Many organizations have taken steps to prevent the kind of freewheeling programming style of earlier times. Programming is labor-intensive, and when poorly managed, it can be a severe drain on an organization's resources. Among the techniques that have been developed to increase programmers' productivity are shop standards, structured walkthroughs, and chief programmer teams. The purpose of all these techniques is to ensure that programmers produce good programs that are as free of errors as possible and that are easy to maintain.

Shop Standards.   Many data-processing departments enforce a set of "shop standards," which are essentially a list of rules designed to constrain freewheeling programming styles. These rules may cover items such as the following:

- **Acceptable program structures** Any programming problem has many solutions, but only some solutions conform to the rules of structured programming. Many shops require programmers to use only those programming structures—or conventions for grouping program statements—that are acceptable in structured programming. (We will discuss these structures in Chapter 10.)

- **Naming conventions** Naming conventions are uniform ways of naming variables in a program. For example, a shop might require that variables relating to input fields be labeled with the suffix "-IN," as in "EMPLOYEE-IN" or "ADDRESS-IN."

- **Comment conventions** Comments within a program help explain how the program works. They are especially useful in long and logically complex programs. Most shops have conventions that dictate when and how to add comments.

Rules like these help make programs readable and easy to maintain. If everyone in an organization writes programs by the same set of conventions, maintenance programmers always know what to expect. Unconstrained creativity is strictly discouraged in commercial programming.

Structured Walkthroughs. Some data-processing shops employ a technique called a structured walkthrough during the coding stage. A **structured walkthrough,** at the coding stage, is a peer evaluation of a programmer's work. The coding is evaluated by four or five other members of the staff, and a meeting is held to discuss good and bad features of the program. The process is intended to help programmers improve their coding skills and to ensure the success of important programs by subjecting them to close scrutiny. It is not intended as a formal appraisal of performance—in fact, it is recommended that the programmer's boss not participate. Walkthroughs are held early in the coding process, when errors are least costly to fix.

Some organizations also conduct a walkthrough during the design stage, to ensure that the systems analyst has properly planned the application. When a walkthrough is conducted at the design stage it is commonly called a *formal design review;* at the coding stage, a *formal code inspection.* Some organizations use informal procedures to accomplish walkthrough-type tasks.

Chief Programmer Team. When a program (or set of programs) is expected to be very large, with say 20,000 or more lines of code, several programmers may be assigned to the coding operation. A **chief programmer team** is simply a team of programmers coordinated by a highly experienced person called the *chief programmer.* The chief programmer will assign the program modules to the programmers on the team. He or she will ordinarily code the most critical modules and assign less important ones to subordinates. The modules are typically coded in a *top-down* fashion, in which the higher-level modules are coded and integrated before the ones below them.

The chief programmer is also responsible for fitting all the individual modules into a workable whole by some target date. He or she will normally have the assistance of a *backup programmer,* who helps with the coding and integration of modules, and a *librarian,* who performs many of the clerical tasks associated with the project. An organization chart for a chief programmer team is shown in Figure 9-5.

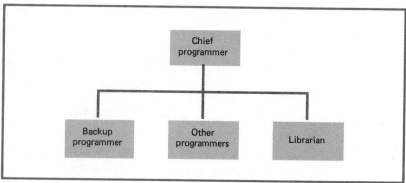

Figure 9-5.   Organization of a chief programmer team.

DEBUGGING PROGRAMS

Debugging is the process of making sure a program is free of errors, or "bugs." Debugging is usually a lengthy process, often amounting to over 50 percent of the total development time for an in-house program.

Preliminary Debugging

The debugging process often begins after the program has been typed. At this point, the programmer will visually inspect the program, before running it, for typing errors. This is called a *desk check*. When a desk check reveals no apparent errors, the program is then initially executed to see if it runs clean.

Rarely are any programs error-free at this point. It is not unusual for a very long program to have well over a hundred errors of one sort or another. The systems software of the computer will usually provide a list of informative "error messages" to the programmer, indicating the source of many of the bugs. At this point, the programmer again desk checks the code to see what's wrong and then makes the necessary corrections. This "run/desk check/correct" process may continue several times.

Sometimes, after the easy errors have been corrected, the programmer's desk checking may fail to weed out the remaining errors. Diagnostic ("dummy") statements may need to be inserted temporarily to show how the program is executing. Or more drastically, the programmer may request a "storage dump" of main memory (see Chapter 4) to find out what is

Dr. Grace Hopper and the First Computer Bug

Okay, computer trivia buffs, here's an easy one. Hands on the buzzers, please! Identify the first "computer bug."

If you guessed Vincent Price's unfortunate friend Andre, who in the 1958 movie *The Fly* was adorned with the head of an insect of the same name in a computer teleprocessing error ... you're wrong. The first computer "bug" was actually discovered by Captain Grace Hopper, a pioneer in the development of COBOL and assembly languages. In 1945, on a hot summer day, she was working on a pre-first-generation electromechanical computer when the machine suddenly went dead.

She and her colleagues opened the machine to investigate. According to Dr. Hopper, "...inside we found a moth that had been beaten to death [by one of the electromechanical relays]. We pulled it out with tweezers and taped it to a log book.... From then on, when the officer came in to ask if we were accomplishing anything, we told him we were 'debugging' the computer."

A relative of the first computer bug.

happening in the computer when the program aborts. If all else fails, the programmer can ask someone else for help. Sometimes a few minutes of consultation can save several days of wasted effort. In any case, the programmer will normally have to employ many strategies to get the program into working order.

Testing

At some point in the debugging process, the program will appear to be correct. At this point the original programmer, or preferably someone else, will run the program with extensive *test data*. Good test data will subject the program to all the conditions it might conceivably encounter when finally implemented. The test data should also check for likely sources of coding omissions; for example, will the program issue a check or a bill for a $0.00 amount? Does the program provide for leap years when dating reports? Many more program bugs are often found during the testing phase of the debugging process. Although rigorous testing does significantly decrease the chance of malfunctioning when a program is implemented, there is no foolproof guarantee that the completed program will be free of bugs.

Purchased software should also be tested before implementation. A firm buying a package from an outside vendor must keep in mind that the programs may have been developed for a different type of company or for another type of computer or operating system. If so, modifications may have to be made to enable the programs to work satisfactorily. In any case, few

How Costly Is a Program Bug When Discovered Late?

Ask the New York State Taxation and Finance Department. About 3.3 million 1981 state income tax forms were mailed out with incorrect peel-off address labels. The error was traced to a programming bug that added a zero at the beginning of the social-security-number field on the label and dropped the last digit in this field. The error was detected after nearly 40 percent of the 1981 forms were in the mail. The error was immediately corrected, and the remaining forms were sent out with correct social security numbers.

A problem created by the mistake was that when taxpayers completed and returned the forms, the department would have to differentiate between the correct and incorrect labels. To solve the problem, at least partially, the department printed crosshatched marks at the bottom of the correct labels. Unfortunately, many problems still needed to be solved. What if the operator failed to recognize the crosshatched marks and entered the wrong social security number? What if the taxpayer forgot to attach the accompanying tax slip provided by his or her employer? What about the public relations problem created by a public sensitive to government blunders, delays in receiving refunds, and

the cost to taxpayers of the many hours wasted coping with such errors?

packages are completely bug-free to begin with, which is another good reason to test them thoroughly.

Proper debugging is vitally important because an error that may cost a few dollars to fix at this stage in the development process may cost many thousands of dollars to fix after the program is implemented in the real world.

PROGRAM DOCUMENTATION

Program **documentation** includes manuals that enable users, maintenance programmers, and operators to interact successfully with a program. On the user level, documentation normally consists of a user's manual. This manual should provide instructions for running the program, a description of language commands, several examples of situations the user is likely to encounter, and a troubleshooting guide to help with difficulties. The user's manual is an extremely important piece of documentation. If it is poorly written, users may refuse to interact with the program altogether. There are a few notorious examples of commercial packages that are so poorly documented at the user level that many of their strongest features are seldom tried. In a few cases, adopting companies have had to rewrite the vendor's documentation completely to get their users involved.

Programmer documentation usually consists of any aids that simplify maintenance of the program. These might include a program narrative, design tools such as flowcharts and structure charts, an annotated listing of the program, a description of of inputs and outputs, and so forth. There should also be a set of procedures to help programmers test the program.

Operator documentation includes manuals that assist operators in mounting tapes, printed forms, and the like, which are needed to get programs "up and running." Since operator documentation is machine dependent, a company purchasing a package must often rewrite this part of the vendor-supplied documentation to suit its own equipment.

Although documentation is included here as the last step in the program development cycle, you should see it as an ongoing process. For example, as analysts develop display formats in the analysis stage of development, or flowcharts in the design stage, they should immediately write them out in a form suitable for the maintenance programmer's documentation package. If they

tomorrow

ACQUIRING PROGRAMS TODAY
THAT WORK TOMORROW:
A LESSON FROM THE TRENCHES

When either buying programs or writing them yourself, you must remember that conditions change over time. A program that works well today might not meet important needs in the future. Although it is impossible to foresee all the needs a program might have to meet tomorrow, or even make accommodations for them today if you could, it's still important to think about program flexibility. If it takes a team of highly paid analysts and programmers a year to design and implement a program, it had better be useful for a while.

Consider the example of Timothy King, a "programming wiz" who made the mistake of not planning for the future. Timothy received A's in all his college computer courses. After he graduated, he went to work as a programmer/analyst for a small manufacturing firm. The firm had little computer experience. One of his first tasks was to design a system that would provide timely product information to the company's production supervisor.

Timothy met with the supervisor, Elizabeth Frank, and the two immediately became good friends. They jointly planned a series of computer programs that Timothy would write to fill Elizabeth's needs. A CRT terminal was already available near her office, which would give her convenient access to the computer system when she needed information about a product.

When the programs were finished, Elizabeth loved them, and they clearly increased her effectiveness as a manager. To many observers, Timothy had succeeded. Then, when everything seemed to be going along well, another firm made Elizabeth a good offer. She was gone within a week. In the meantime, with his first project "completed," Timothy was given another assignment in an office across town.

When a new production supervisor, Art Thomas, was hired, problems with Timothy's programs began to surface. First, Art complained that the system delivered only summary information on individual products. He was new to the company, and he wanted to examine figures in depth. It soon became apparent that the programs had to be substantially rewritten to provide the kind of information he needed.

Second, Art found the program commands overly complicated. Elizabeth Frank, it turned out, had minored in computer science in college. Art Thomas, however, had no special interest in computers. In fact, he regarded them as a bit of a nuisance, although he fully understood the need to use them in his work.

To make matters worse, Timothy had provided very little documentation to show how the programs worked. Since Elizabeth Frank had interacted so well with the programs from the outset of the development, he hadn't really given much thought to what might happen if she left the company.

A maintenance programmer was assigned to the project and quickly discovered another serious problem: unstructured programming code. As it turned out, Timothy was such a "hot shot" programmer in college that he rarely attended classes. Thus he learned little about developing a structured and readable programming style. Moreover, he preferred writing elegant, tricky programs rather than the readable kind. He had a habit of carefully scanning the programming reference manuals for interesting types of little known commands, which he would then incorporate into his programs. This type of behavior won him applause from his programming friends at school. It won him no applause, however, from the maintenance programmer, who could not easily figure out how to revise many of Timothy's programs. Finally, out of frustration, he found himself throwing away large blocks of code and starting all over from stratch.

Timothy, needless to say, was soon looking for a new job.

leave this task until later, they will probably forget many important details.

If you've ever had the frustration of trying to put together a product from poorly written instructions, you should appreciate how valuable good documentation can be.

THE MAKE-OR-BUY DECISION

Once a set of requirements has been established for a software solution to a problem, a decision must be made about whether the programs should be created in-house or acquired externally from a vendor. This consideration, which often takes place after the analysis or design stage of the program development cycle, is frequently called the *make-or-buy decision.*

Before IBM "unbundled" its hardware and software pricing in the late 1960s, few software-only vendors existed. The company that sold you your hardware also supplied much of your software, all at one lump sum. What the computer manufacturer couldn't supply was developed in-house by each organization.

With unbundling came a wave of independent software houses. Packaged applications software became increasingly available for all the common business functions, including payroll, financial accounting, and so forth. These packages normally consist of one or several programs, documentation (usually of fairly high quality), and possibly, training. With the infusion of new firms into the software industry, the relative quality of vendor-supplied software has increased dramatically.

The Pros and Cons of Packaged Software

Advantages. Today, for routine business applications, a significant amount of the software used in practice is vendor-supplied. This makes a great deal of sense from the point of view of timing, uncertainty, and cost.

- Timing Vendor-supplied software can be implemented almost immediately. In-house software, in contrast, may take months, or even years, to design, code, and debug.

- **Uncertainty** With packaged software, the shrewd buying organization knows what it's getting—a product of stated quality at a stated price. If the buyer is lucky, the product may also have a proven track record and an active group of users to "trade notes" with. When software is developed in-house, it's difficult to predict how the final product will work and what its cost will be eventually. Even estimates of development time are, at best, educated guesses. During the project's duration, a key programmer may resign, technology might change the nature of the application, potential users may not like the way the system works when it is finally implemented, and so forth. What's more, since people tend to be overoptimistic when estimating costs, many projects developed in-house are completed over budget.

- **Cost** The economics of purchased software are relatively simple. The cost of the software is distributed over several organizations, so the price per user can be relatively low, even allowing the vendor a substantial profit. Costs for in-house software, on the other hand, are often completely absorbed by a single organization.

  Also, when vendor-supplied software already has a large base of users, newly hired programmers may already be familiar with it, saving the time and cost of training them. And programmers like to work with popular software packages because it increases their marketability.

Disadvantages. Purchased software, although it has many advantages, is not always appropriate. If a package was originally developed for a business that works differently from the one it's being sold to, and the vendor has made only superficial attempts to adapt it to the current buyer's needs, it may prove to be more trouble than it's worth. Also, for some applications, little or no appropriate packaged software exists. In such cases, in-house development is the only alternative.

Summary and Key Terms

Applications software consists of programs that direct computer systems to produce outputs for computer users. Creating, acquiring, and maintaining good applications software is one of the major data-processing expenses in any organization.

In most large organizations, the development of applications software is one of the jobs of the data-processing department. In this department, **systems analysts** are the people who work with users to assess needs, translate those needs into a list of technical requirements, and design the necessary software. The design specification is then handed to a **programmer,** who codes the program from it. **Maintenance programmers** monitor the software on an ongoing basis, correcting errors and altering the software as applications change.

Creating successful programs commonly involves five stages: analysis, design, coding, debugging, and documentation. These five stages are often called the **program development cycle.**

Analysis in the program development cycle is the process of identifying and defining the problem to be solved; deciding whether the solution involves software; and if so, defining input, output, and processing requirements.

In the **design** stage of the program development cycle, analysts work from the software requirements developed in the analysis stage to spell out as precisely as possible the nature of the programming solution that will enable the system to meet those requirements. A group of techniques has evolved that has made program design more systematic and programs themselves easier to read and maintain. These techniques are often grouped together under the term **structured programming.** Many tools are available to help the analyst plan structured programs, including structured program flowcharts, pseudocode, structure charts, and HIPO charts.

Once analysts have finished the program design for an application, the next stage is to code the program. **Coding,** which is the job of programmers, is the process of writing a program from a set of specifications. Programming is labor-intensive, and when poorly managed, it can be a severe drain on an organization's resources. Among the techniques that have been developed to increase programmers' productivity are shop standards, structured walkthroughs, and chief programmer teams.

Many data processing shops employ **structured walkthroughs** during the coding stage. A structured walkthrough is a peer evaluation of a programmer's work. The coding is evaluated by four or five other members of the staff, and a meeting is held to discuss good and bad features of the program. Some organizations also conduct a walkthrough during the design stage, to ensure that the systems analyst has properly planned the application.

A **chief programmer team** is simply a team of programmers coordinated by a highly experienced person called the *chief programmer*. The chief programmer will assign the program modules to the programmers on the team and coordinate the fitting of all the individual modules into a workable whole by some target date.

Debugging is the process of making sure a program is free of errors, or "bugs." Debugging is usually a lengthy process, often amounting to over 50 percent of the total development time for an in-house program.

At some point in the debugging process, the program will appear to be correct. Then the programmer, or preferably someone else, will run the original program with extensive *test data*. Good test data will subject the program to all the conditions it might conceivably encounter when finally implemented.

Program **documentation** includes manuals that enable users, maintenance programmers, and operators to interact success-fully with a program. Although noted as the final stage of the program development cycle, documentation is an ongoing pro-cess that should be addressed from the outset of a project.

Some organizations choose to buy their software rather than create it in-house. This consideration, which often takes place after the analysis or design stages of the program development cycle, is frequently called the *make-or-buy decision*.

Review Questions

1. What is applications software?
2. Name the stages in the program development cycle.
3. What types of decisions must be made in defining software requirements?
4. Why have structured techniques evolved as a major strategy in program design?
5. What design specifications must the systems analyst pro-vide for the programmer before program coding can begin?
6. Name three ways to increase programmer productivity.
7. Why is program documentation important?
8. Name some advantages and disadvantages of buying pack-aged software.

Suggested Readings

Hughes, Joan K., and Jay I. Micht[...] to Programming. Englewood C[...] 1977.

Kernighan, Brian, and P. J. Plauger. The E[...] ming Style. New York: McGraw-Hill, 19[...]

Parikh, Girish. Techniques of Program and S[...] nance. Cambridge, Mass.: Winthrop, 1982.

Stevens, Wayne P. Using Structured Design. New Yo[...] 1981.

Weinberg, Gerald M. The Psychology of Computer Progr[...] ming. New York: Van Nostrand Reinhold, 1971.

Yourdon, Edward. Structured Walkthroughs. Englewood Cliffs, N.J.: Prentice-Hall, 1979.

Yourdon, Edward, and Larry L. Constantine. Structured Design. Englewood Cliffs, N.J.: Prentice-Hall, 1979.

Chapter 10

Program Design Aids and Structured Programming

Chapter Outline

OVERVIEW

In Chapter 9, you learned how organizations develop applications software. In that chapter we focused on the program development cycle, which begins with problem analysis and ends with implementation. In this chapter we will focus on one stage of that cycle—design—specifically, on tools for designing structured programs.

We will begin with a discussion of one of the earliest and most widely used program design aids—program flowcharts. We will then describe structured programming and structured program design. Next, we will discuss design aids for structured programming—structured program flowcharts, pseudocode, structure charts, and HIPO charts. Finally, we will cover decision tables and other design aids.

WHAT ARE PROGRAM DESIGN AIDS?

It's extremely difficult just to sit down and write a good program if it is to be at all long or complex. Before you begin coding, you need a plan for the program. **Program design aids** are, essentially, program planning tools. They consist of various kinds of diagrams, charts, and tables that outline either the organization of program tasks or the steps the program will follow. Once a program is coded and implemented, program design aids also provide excellent documentation for maintenance programmers.

Many of the aids we will discuss in this chapter were developed as tools for structured programming. One of the oldest and still one of the most popular design aids, however, was in use long before structured programming became popular. This is the program flowchart.

Because it is hard to discuss structured programming without resorting to a design aid to help illustrate the concepts involved, we will introduce you to program flowcharts before we move on to structured programming and other design aids.

PROGRAM FLOWCHARTS

Program flowcharts use geometric symbols, such as those in Figure 10-1, and familiar mathematical symbols, such as those in Figure 10-2, to provide a graphic display of the sequence of

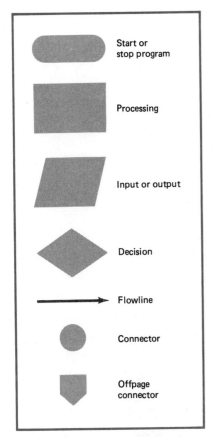

Figure 10-1. ANSI program flowchart symbols.

steps involved in a program. The steps in a flowchart follow each other in the same logical sequence as their corresponding program statements will follow in a program.

For many years, flowcharting symbols were nonstandardized, making it difficult for one programmer to follow the work of another. Today, there are a number of standards. Among the most popular are those developed by ANSI, the American National Standards Institute (see Figure 10-1). To help you understand what these symbols mean and show you how to use them, let's consider some examples.

Tuna, Turkey, or Nothing. The flowchart in Figure 10-3 illustrates the process involved in making a decision about lunch. The process is a simple one. You wish to make and eat a tuna sandwich for lunch. If you're out of tuna, however, you'll try turkey. If you're out of turkey, you're not interested in lunch.

This flowchart uses four symbols: start/stop, processing, decision, and connector. The lines with arrows that link the symbols are called **flowlines**—they indicate the flow of logic in the flowchart.

Every flowchart begins and ends with an oval-shaped **start/stop symbol.** The first of these symbols in the program contains the word *Start;* the last, the word *Stop.* The diamond-shaped **decision symbol** always indicates a question, which will generally have only two possible answers—yes or no, true or false. Decision symbols should always have one flowline entering and two flowlines (representing the two possible outcomes) exiting.

The rectangular-shaped **processing symbol** contains an action that needs to be taken—"Make tuna sandwich," "Eat

Symbol	Meaning
$<$	Less than
$\leq$	Less than or equal to
$>$	Greater than
$\geq$	Greater than or equal to
$=$	Equal to
$\neq$	Not equal to

Figure 10-2. Mathematical symbols used in flowcharts.

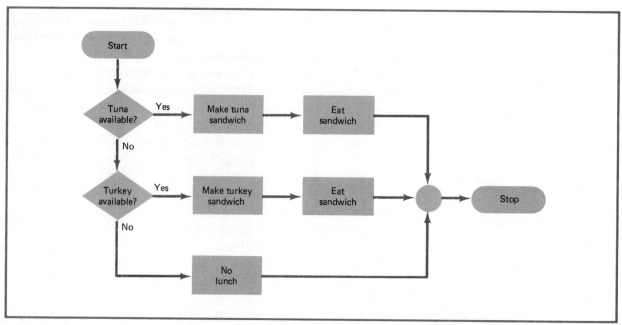

Figure 10-3. A simple program flowchart. The situation represented by the flowchart is the following: You would like to make (and eat) a tuna sandwich for lunch, but if you can't have tuna, you'll take turkey. If neither is available, you'll skip lunch.

sandwich," and so forth. The **connector symbol** provides a logical point on the flowchart for several flowlines to meet.

Scanning a File for Employees with Certain Characteristics.

Now let's consider a more complicated example. A common problem in data processing is scanning an employee file for people with certain characteristics. Suppose, for example, the personnel department of a company wanted a printed list of all employees with computer experience and at least five years of company service. A flowchart that shows how to accomplish this task, and also totals the number of employees meeting these conditions, is shown in Figure 10-4.

There are several interesting differences between this flowchart and the previous one. First, this flowchart involves a *looping* operation. We "read" a record, inspect it, and take an action; then read another record, inspect it, and take another action; and so on, until the file is exhausted. When the computer reads a record, as indicated by the **input/output symbol,** it brings it into main memory and stores its contents (or field values)—for example, employee's ID and name, address, phone, department, years of service, and previous experience.

After reading a record, we immediately check to see if it is the last one in the file. We assume here that the last record in the file is not really a true record at all, but a "dummy" record (for example, name field is "Bozo the Clown"). We put this dummy record at the end of the data file so the computer system will know, on reading and inspecting it, that it has encountered the end of the file. If we've reached the last record, we take steps to end the program. If we haven't, we check the two fields we're interested in—company service and computer experience—to

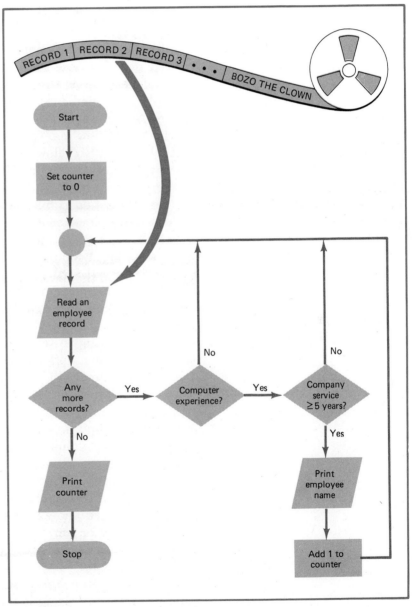

Figure 10-4. Scanning an employee file. The situation represented by the flowchart is the following: Print the names of all people in an employee file with computer experience and at least five years of company service. Also, count the number of such people and print out this count.

see if they meet the criteria we've established. Only if an employee has *both* computer experience and at least five years of service do we print his or her name (shown by the input/output symbol). Otherwise, we bypass the print operation and immediately read the next record.

The flowchart in Figure 10-4 is also different from the previous one in that it contains two types of branching mechanisms. A program *branches* whenever a statement in a block of code is capable of directing the program somewhere besides the next line of code.

In a **conditional branch,** represented by the diamond-shaped decision box, the program proceeds to either of two places depending on the condition encountered in the box. For example, if the name in the name field is not "Bozo the Clown" in the "Any more records" box, we branch to the box indicated by the "Yes" flowline. Otherwise, we branch to the box indicated by the "No" flowline. Thus, the condition involved is whether or not the "Bozo the Clown" record is currently in memory.

In an **unconditional branch** the program proceeds to a certain step *every time* it comes to a certain statement. Every time we come to the statement "Add 1 to counter" for example, we make an unconditional branch back to the "Read an employee record" step.

Another important observation to be made about the flowchart in Figure 10-4 concerns the totaling of employees who meet the selection criteria. To get this total, we "count" every employee meeting the criteria. To perform operations such as counting, we must define special areas in main memory to hold the values of the totals. We establish a name—"Counter" in the example—to represent the memory area that will hold the total. At the beginning of the program, "Counter" is set to zero. Whenever we find an employee meeting the selection criteria, we increase its value by one. After we've read the entire employee file, we output the value of "Counter" just before the program ends. It's good practice in any flowchart to set all counts or sums to zero at the beginning. Otherwise, when the program is coded and executed, you may get incorrect results. Setting a count or sum to a specific value at the beginning of a program or flowchart is called **initializing.**

Computing an Average. Another common problem encountered in data processing is computing the average of a set of numbers. Figure 10-5 is a flowchart for computing the average of a set of examination scores.

Computing an average involves three basic operations:

- Summing all scores ("Sum" in the flowchart)
- Counting the number of scores ("Counter" in the flow-chart)
- Dividing "Sum" by "Counter" (producing "Average" in the flowchart)

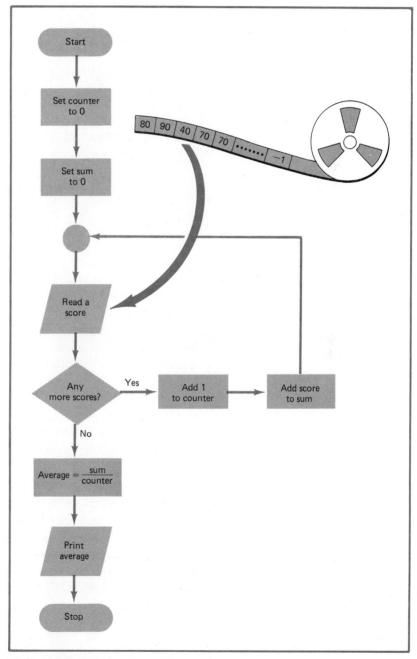

Figure 10-5.   A flowchart showing how to compute the average of a set of examination scores.

When the Value of "Score" Is	The Operation "Add Score to Sum" Does the Following
80	Adds 80 to 0, producing "Sum" = 80
90	Adds 90 to 80, producing "Sum" = 170
40	Adds 40 to 170, producing "Sum" = 210
. . .	. . .
−1	Not performed

Figure 10-6. *The effect of the "Add Score to Sum" operation in Figure 10-5.*

At the beginning of the flowchart in Figure 10-5, "Sum" and "Counter" are set to zero. A dummy data record with a score of −1 marks the end of the data file. Each time the processing operation

```
Add Score to Sum
```

is executed, the value of "Score" in the record being processed is added to the current value of "Sum." Figure 10-6 summarizes the results of this operation. The dummy data record of −1 on the last record alerts the computer system to end the counting and summing, to compute and print the average, and to end the program.

Further Uses of Connector-Type Symbols. As we've already seen, the connector symbol can be used to provide a logical point on the flowchart for flowlines to meet. The connector symbol can also be used to prevent clutter in the flowchart or to avoid the confusion created by the need to cross flowlines. Figure 10-7, a redrawn version of Figure 10-4, illustrates the use of a connector symbol to prevent flowchart clutter.

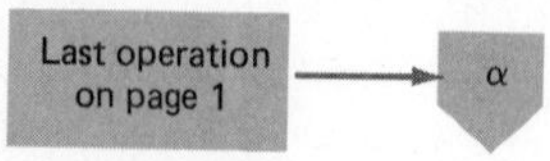

The **offpage connector symbol** is used instead of the connector symbol when we want to continue a flowchart from one page to another. For example, we can draw the offpage connector at the bottom of page 1 and, at the start of page 2, resume the flowchart with

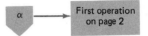

Flowchart symbols are often drawn with the aid of a plastic flowcharting template, such as the one shown in Figure 10-8. These templates are usually available in office supply and college book stores.

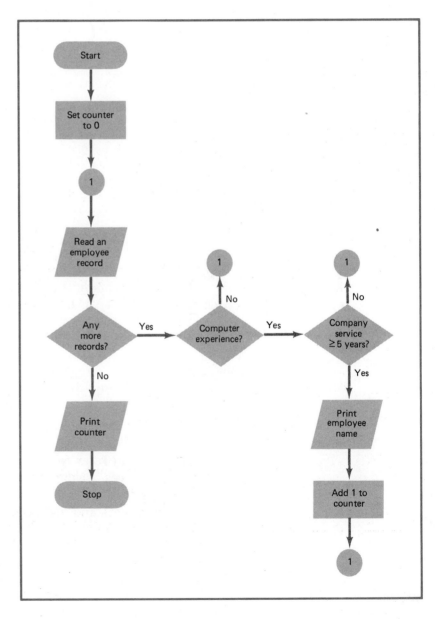

Figure 10-7. Alternate representation of the flowchart in Figure 10-4.

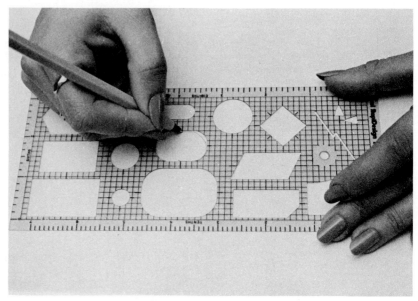

Figure 10-8.   Flowcharting template.

STRUCTURED PROGRAM DESIGN

Although the flowchart is a powerful tool for designing programs, it isn't always appropriate nor does it guarantee a good program. As we mentioned in Chapter 9, most programming problems have many solutions, but some solutions are better than others. Even if a program "works," in the sense that it executes the application it was written for, it is of little value if maintenance programmers can't understand and modify it.

Starting in the mid-1960s, a series of studies began to establish a body of practices for good program design. These practices have often been identified with the terms *structured programming* or *structured program design*. There is much debate today over exactly what specific practices fall under these terms. Depending on who you talk to, **structured programming** can refer to one or more of a variety of program design practices—using the specific control structures of sequence, selection, and looping; using pseudocode; following top-down design and development; using chief programmer teams for program development; and so forth. Although there is no precise, universally accepted definition of structured programming, most people will agree that its main thrust is to

- Increase programmer productivity
- Enhance program clarity by minimizing complexity
- Reduce program testing time
- Decrease program maintenance cost

This section discusses two design practices that are often included under definitions of structured programming—the use of three basic control structures and top-down design.

The Three Basic Control Structures

Advocates of structured programming have shown that any program can be constructed out of three fundamental **control structures:** sequence, selection, and looping. Figure 10-9 (next page) illustrates these structures by using flowchart symbols.

A **sequence control structure** is simply a series of procedures that follow one another. The **selection** (or **if-then-else**) **control structure** involves a choice: *if* a certain condition is true, *then* follow one procedure; *else,* if false, follow another. A loop is an operation that repeats until a certain condition is met. As the figure shows, a **looping** (or **iteration**) **control structure** can take two forms: DOWHILE and DOUNTIL. With **DOWHILE,** a loop is executed as long as a certain condition is true ("do while true"). With **DOUNTIL,** a loop continues as long as a certain condition is false ("do until true"). You should also note that a major difference between these two forms of the looping control structure is that with DOUNTIL the loop procedure will be executed at least once, because the procedure appears before any test is made about whether to exit the loop. With DOWHILE, the procedure may not be executed at all, because the loop-exit test appears before the procedure.

The three basic control structures are the major building blocks for structured program flowcharts and pseudocode, which are discussed later in the chapter.

Top-Down Design

A long book without chapters, sections, or paragraphs would be hard to read. In the same way, programs are easier to read if they are broken down into clearly labeled segments, or **modules,** each of which performs a well-defined task.

Program modules should be arranged hierarchically, in a top-down fashion, so that their relationship to each other is apparent. Such an arrangement is similar to the organization charts many companies use to show the relationship among job titles. **Top-down design** indicates that modules are refined first at the highest levels of the hierarchy and then at succes-

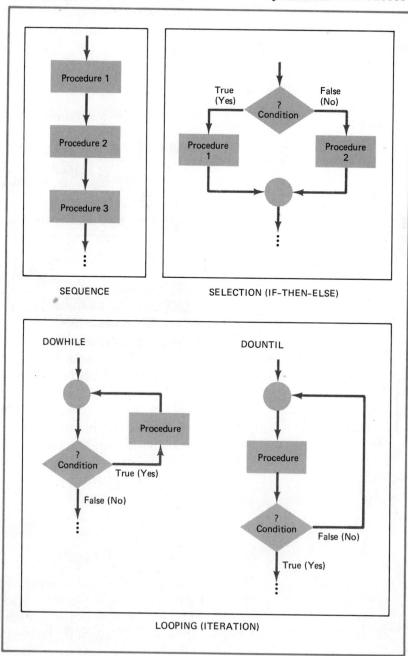

Figure 10-9. The three fundamental control stuctures of structured programming.

sively lower levels. Lower-level modules should do the actual work in the program, whereas higher level modules should perform control functions, switching from one lower-level module to another as appropriate.

The use of top-down modular constructions for designing programs is illustrated later in the chapter, in the sections on structure charts and HIPO charts.

AIDS FOR STRUCTURED PROGRAM DESIGN

An outgrowth of the trend toward structured programming has been the development of a number of tools for structured program design. In this section we will discuss some of these tools, including structured flowcharts, pseudocode, structure charts, and the HIPO method.

tomorrow

THE FUTURE OF APPLICATIONS PROGRAM DEVELOPMENT

A number of futurists in the world of computers predict that traditional applications program development will disappear by the turn of the century. What may emerge to take its place is an entirely new discipline: *information analysis.*

Historically, the way that applications programs have been developed is that user needs are carefully assessed, a program specification is prepared and, eventually, a program is coded. Unfortunately, this process is very time-consuming and expensive. In many cases, important user requests are relegated to a long waiting list because analysts and programmers are simply not available to develop these requests immediately.

A number of important changes are taking place in the world of computers that can alter this situation dramatically. First, packaged software is becoming both increasingly more "user-friendly" and available for a growing number of applications. Second, users are becoming less

intimidated by computers, and the user of tomorrow will soon be the child of today who is being introduced to computers before entering kindergarten. Third, computer power is becoming more visible in businesses, with the terminal or personal computer on every desk top a forseeable reality.

Now, enter the information analyst. Unlike the traditional analyst or programmer, the information analyst will be responsible for assembling off-the-shelf software packages and routing them to the appropriate users. Instead of using traditional analysis and design techniques, the analyst can get a rough idea of the user's needs, have the appropriate package "tele-shipped" to the user's site on a trial basis, and have the user experimenting with the package on the very same day. This process eliminates a lengthy needs analysis, program design tools such as flowcharts and structure charts, and also, the entire coding operation. Although it is not likely that all applications will be developed this easily, there is certainly a very large number that can.

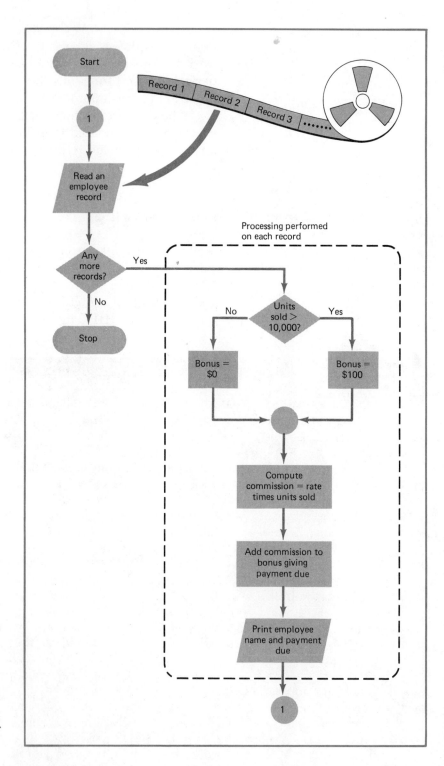

Figure 10-10. Computing payments due to salespeople.

Structured Program Flowcharts

Structured program flowcharts are, simply, program flowcharts that have been drawn by using the three control structures of structured programming. Figures 10-10 and 10-11 show how these structures can be combined into a single flowchart.

Figure 10-10 is a flowchart for computing payments owed to salespeople. Each record contains the name and number of

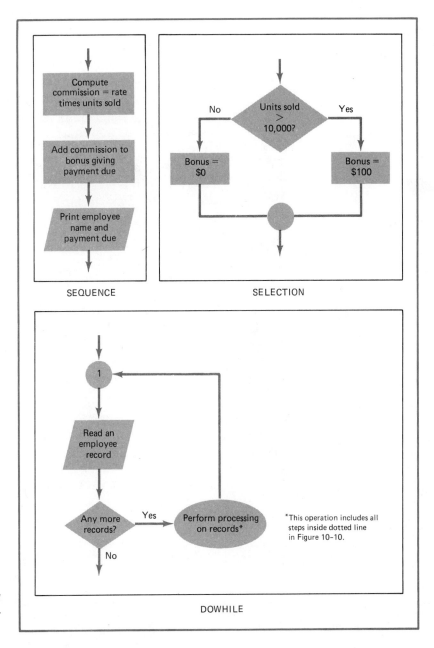

Figure 10-11.   The three control structures as they are used in Figure 10-10.

units sold for each salesperson. The salespeople are paid on commission, which is a percentage of the value of sales. In addition, if they sell over 10,000 units of the company's product, they get a $100 bonus. As records are read sequentially, the payment due is computed and the name of the salesperson is output with the amount due. The flowchart uses three control structures: SEQUENCE, SELECTION, and DOWHILE, as shown in Figure 10-11.

Pseudocode

An alternative to the flowchart that has become extremely popular in recent years is **pseudocode.** This structured technique uses Englishlike statements in place of the graphic symbols of the flowchart. An example of pseudocode is shown in Figure 10-12.

Pseudocode looks more like a program than a flowchart. In fact, it's often easier to code a program from pseudocode than from a flowchart because the former provides a codelike outline

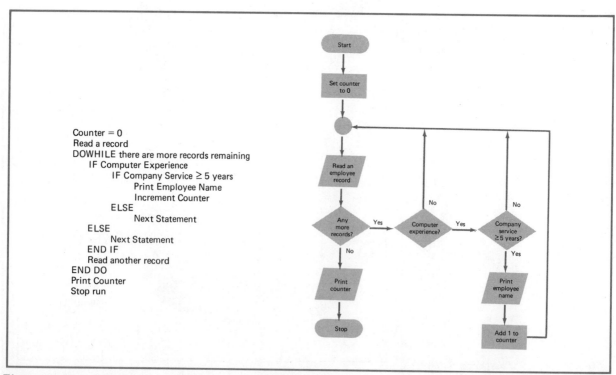

Figure 10-12. Pseudocode to solve the employee file problem of Figure 10-4. (The flowchart of Fig. 10-4 is at the right.) The problem requires printing the names of all people in an employee file with computer experience and at least five years of company service. A count of the number of such people is also required as output.

of the processing to take place. As a result, the program designer has more control over the end product—the program itself. Unlike a flowchart, pseudocode is also easy to modify and can be embedded into the program as comments. Flowcharts, however, because they are visual, are sometimes better than pseudocode for designing logically complex problems.

There are no standard rules for writing pseudocode, but Figure 10-13 describes one set of rules that has a wide following. Note that all words relating to the three control structures of structured programming are capitalized and form a "sandwich" around other processing steps, which are indented. As you can see in Figure 10-14 (next page), indentation is also used when one control structure is nested within another.

SEQUENCE CONTROL STRUCTURE

> BEGIN processing task
> Processing steps
> END processing task

The steps in the sequence structure are normally written in lowercase letters. If the steps make up a well-defined block of code, they should be preceded by the keywords BEGIN and END.

SELECTION CONTROL STRUCURE

> IF condition
>> Processing steps
> ELSE
>> Processing steps
> END IF

The key words IF, ELSE, and END IF are always capitalized and tiered. The condition and processing steps normally are written in lowercase letters. The processing steps are indented from the key words in the manner illustrated.

LOOP (DOWHILE AND DOUNTIL) CONTROL STRUCTURES

> DOWHILE condition   DOUNTIL condition
>> Processing steps   Processing steps
> END DO   END DO

The keywords DOWHILE (or DOUNTIL) and END DO, are always capitalized and tiered. The condition and processing steps follow the same lowercase convention and indentation rules as the selection control structure.

Figure 10-13.   Some rules for pseudocode.

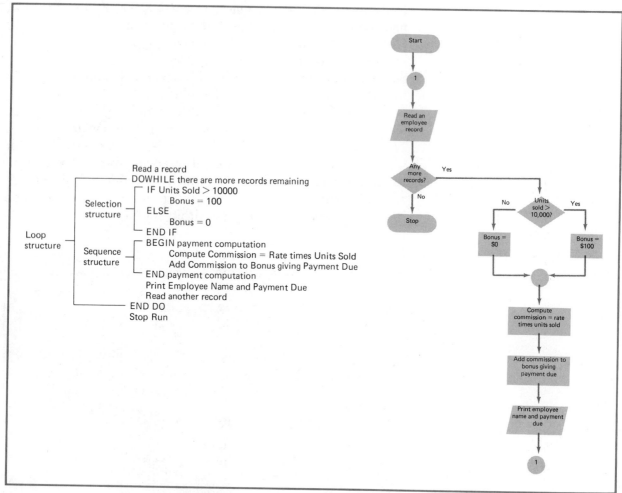

Figure 10-14. *Pseudocode to solve the problem of Figure 10-10.* (The flowchart of Fig. 10-10 is at the right.) Each employee record contains the name and number of units sold for each salesperson. As records are read sequentially, the payment is computed and the name of the salesperson is output with the amount due.

Structure Charts

Structure charts, unlike flowcharts and pseudocode, depict the overall organization of a program but not the specific processing logic involved in step-by-step execution. They show how the individual segments, or modules, of a program are defined and how they relate to each other.

A typical structure chart looks like a corporate organization chart. It consists of several rows of boxes connected by lines. Each box represents a program module. The modules in the upper rows serve *control* functions, directing the program to process modules under them as appropriate. Those modules in the lowest boxes serve specific processing functions. These are the modules that do all the program "work." The lines connect-

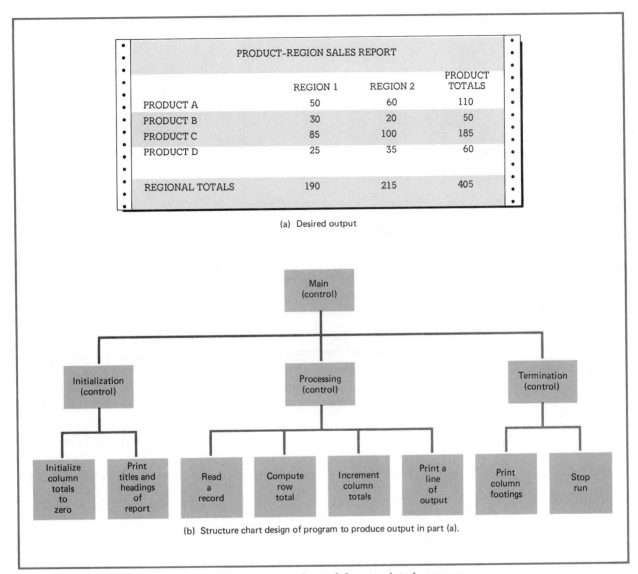

PRODUCT-REGION SALES REPORT

	REGION 1	REGION 2	PRODUCT TOTALS
PRODUCT A	50	60	110
PRODUCT B	30	20	50
PRODUCT C	85	100	185
PRODUCT D	25	35	60
REGIONAL TOTALS	190	215	405

(a) Desired output

(b) Structure chart design of program to produce output in part (a).

Figure 10-15.   *Program output and the structure chart of the associated program.*

ing the boxes indicate the relationship of higher-level to lower-level modules. Figure 10-15*b* is a structure chart for a program to produce the sales report shown in Figure 10-15*a*.

Structure charts can be written to reflect various levels of detail. The chart in Figure 10-15*b* shows a high level of detail; the one in Figure 10-16, which shows the processing of a CRT inquiry, a low level.

HIPO Charts

Another useful tool for structured design is the **HIPO (Hierarchy plus Input-Process-Output)** charts. The HIPO method

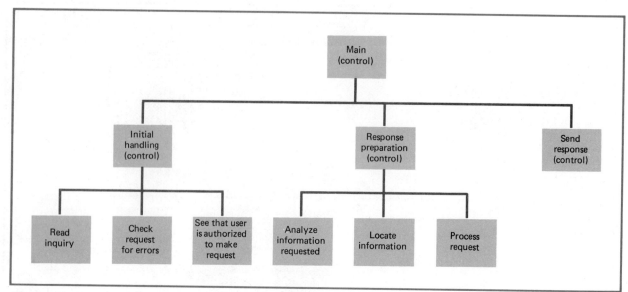

Figure 10-16.   A structure chart for processing a CRT inquiry.

involves the preparation of a set of three different types of diagrams, which vary in the level of detail they address.

The most general of the diagrams is the *Visual Table of Contents* (VTOC), shown in Figure 10-17. The VTOC is identical to a structure chart, except that it contains hierarchically sequenced reference numbers in the lower-right-hand corner of each module.

At the second level of detail in the HIPO method are

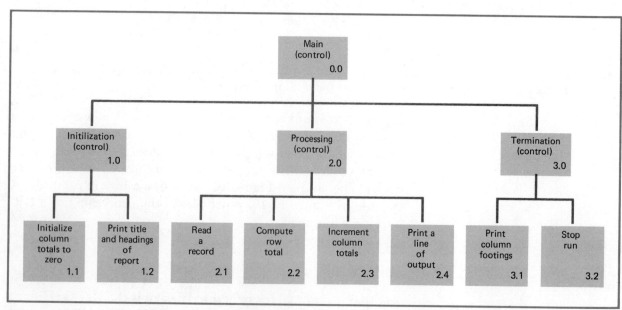

Figure 10-17.   VTOC of the problem depicted in Figure 10-15.

overview diagrams, which show the input, processing, and output involved in each module. Each overview diagram also has a module reference number that corresponds to a module in the VTOC diagram. Figure 10-18 shows overview diagrams for three of the modules in Figure 10-17.

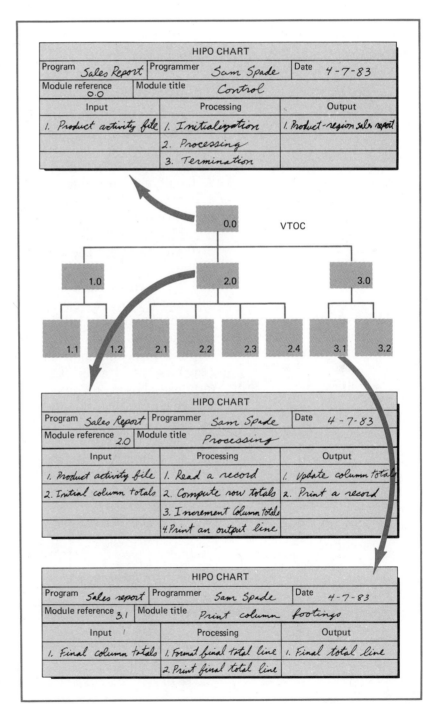

Figure 10-18. HIPO overview diagrams for VTOC shown in Figure 10-17.

The third level of detail in the HIPO method, the *detail diagram,* contains complete information about the data required and the processing to be performed in each module. The contents of a detail diagram often depend on the complexity of the module it represents, since its main purpose is to aid the programmer in coding.

DECISION TABLES

All the tools discussed in the preceding section can be used to design an entire program. **Decision tables,** in contrast, are generally used to design only a portion of a program. They are especially useful for clarifying a series of complicated conditional branches. Whenever a choice among actions depends on which of many possible combinations of criteria have been met, a decision table ensures that no possible combinations are overlooked.

Figure 10-19 shows the format for decision tables. The *heading* describes the problem to be solved. Under it, in the rows, are listed the important criteria (*conditions*) to be satisfied, followed by the possible *actions* to be taken. The vertical columns (*rules*) represent all the possible cases that may be encountered in practice.

Figure 10-20 shows a decision table for determining how to respond to people applying for a job. There are two possible responses: send a rejection letter or grant an interview. The response chosen for any applicant depends on three criteria: college education, previous experience, and other qualifications. An applicant who satisfies any two of these criteria will be granted an interview; others will get a rejection letter. In each vertical column of the table, a "Y" signifies a "yes," an "N" a

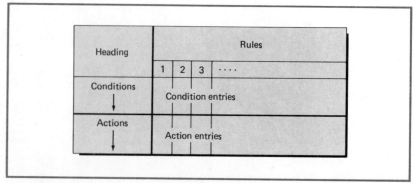

Figure 10-19.   The format of a decision table.

Hiring Applicants		Rules					
		1	2	3	4	5	6
Conditions	College education?	N	N		Y	Y	
	Experienced?	N		N	Y		Y
	Other qualifications?		N	N		Y	Y
Actions	Rejection letter	X	X	X			
	Interview				X	X	X

Figure 10-20.   A simple decision table. The table specifies the following: If a job applicant does not meet at least two important criteria (conditions), send a rejection letter (the first action); otherwise, grant an interview (the second action).

"no." A blank entry indicates that it doesn't matter if the answer is Y or N.

The problem in Figure 10-20 is a simple one. Decision tables, however, can represent extremely complex situations. They can have

- Any number of condition and action rows
- Several Y and N values in any single column
- Several X values in any single column (indicating that multiple actions are possible)

In fact, the more complicated the situation, the more useful is a decision table. Many people can keep track of the possible outcomes of a simple problem in their heads, but as the number of criteria and actions multiplies, a tool like a decision table becomes imperative.

OTHER DESIGN AIDS

The design aids covered in this chapter are only a sampling of those currently used by commercial organizations. Other methods of considerable importance include Warnier-Orr diagrams, Nassi-Schneiderman charts, Meta Stepwise Refinement, Chapin charts, and a number of others. Some shops have even created their own design aids. Many schools offer advanced computer courses that place these tools in their proper perspectives.

Help! Which Design Aid Do I Use?

A concern voiced by many students in computer-related courses is that because they learn about so many programming design aids in college, they aren't always sure which ones to apply to any given problem in real life. Unfortunately, there's often no easy solution to this problem. Asking your teacher "which design aid do I use?" can be like asking a tennis coach "when the ball is hit over the net to me, which shot do I use to hit it back?" The only possible response may be an unhelpful "it depends."

Fortunately, if you are a beginning programmer/analyst, the choice of a design aid is often made for you. In many data-processing shops, the tools used in program design are standardized. For example, a shop that does most of its applications programming in COBOL may require a structure chart and pseudocode to be created during the design stage. Once the program is completely coded and a copy of it saved for documentation, both the structure chart and pseudocode are placed in the docu-

mentation package, with the program listing, for further reference.

Occasionally, programming shops will experiment on new types of design aids. A shop may do this when it undertakes a special project independent of its main body of programs. Here again, the choice of the design aid is usually made by an experienced person such as the data processing manager or the project leader.

Just because a shop requires a certain type of design aid doesn't mean programmers and analysts can't use tools of their own choosing for personal reference. Some people have their own unique way of solving problems, and it would be foolish for an organization to attempt to prevent them from using methods that increase their productivity. Nonetheless, if several people are to work together on the same programming problem, they need a standard set of tools. These tools act, in effect, as a common language that enables programmers, analysts, and users to understand each other.

Summary and Key Terms

Program design aids are program planning tools. They consist of various kinds of diagrams, charts, and tables that outline either the organization of a program or the steps it will follow. Once a program is coded and implemented, program design aids also provide excellent documentation for maintenance programmers.

Program flowcharts use geometric symbols and familiar mathematical symbols to provide a graphic display of the sequence of steps involved in a program. The steps in a flowchart follow each other in the same logical sequence as their corresponding program statements will follow in a program.

The lines with arrows that link the symbols in a flowchart are called **flowlines.** They indicate the flow of logic in the flowchart. Every flowchart begins and ends with a **start/stop**

symbol. The diamond-shaped **decision symbol** always indicates a question, which will generally have only two possible answers, such as "yes" or "no." The rectangular-shaped **processing symbol** contains an action that needs to be taken. The **input/output symbol** can be used to indicate a read operation or the production of a report. The **connector symbol** provides a logical point on the flowchart for several flowlines to meet. The **offpage connector symbol** is used instead of the connector symbol to continue a flowchart from one page to another.

A program *branches* whenever a statement in a block of code is capable of directing the program somewhere besides the next line of code. In a **conditional branch,** represented by the diamond-shaped decision box, the program proceeds to either of two places depending on the condition encountered in the box. In an **unconditional branch,** the program proceeds to a certain step every time it comes to a certain statement.

It's good practice in any flowchart to set all counts or sums to zero at the beginning. Otherwise, when the program is coded and executed, you may get incorrect results. Setting a count or sum to a specific value at the beginning of a program or flowchart is called **initializing.**

Starting in the mid-1960s, a series of studies began to establish a body of practices for good program design. These practices have often been identified with the terms *structured programming* or *structured program design.* There is indeed much debate today over exactly what specific practices fall under these terms.

Although there is no precise, universally accepted definition of **structured programming,** most people will agree that its main thrust is to increase programmer productivity, enhance program clarity by minimizing complexity, reduce program testing time, and decrease program maintenance cost.

Advocates of structured programming have shown that any program can be constructed out of three fundamental **control structures**—sequence, selection, and looping.

A **sequence control structure** is simply a series of procedures that follow one another. The **selection** (or **if-then-else**) **control structure** involves a choice: *if* a certain condition is true, *then* follow one procedure; *else,* if false, follow another. A **looping (iteration) control structure** repeats until a certain condition is met. A loop can take two forms: **DOWHILE** and **DOUNTIL.**

Programs are easier to read if they are broken down into clearly labeled segments, or **modules,** each of which performs a well-defined task. Program modules should be organized hierarchically, in a top-down design, so that their relationship to each other is apparent. **Top-down design** indicates that modules are defined first at the highest levels of the hierarchy and then at successively lower levels.

An outgrowth of the trend toward structured programming has been the development of a number of tools for structured program design. Four examples of these tools are structured program flowcharts, pseudocode, structure charts, and HIPO charts.

Structured program flowcharts are, simply, program flowcharts that have been drawn by using the three control structures of structured programming. **Pseudocode** is a structured technique that uses Englishlike statements in place of the graphic symbols of the flowchart. **Structure charts,** unlike flowcharts and pseudocode, depict the overall organization of a program but not the specific processing logic involved in step-by-step execution. The **HIPO (Hierarchy plus Input-Process-Output) method** involves preparing a set of three different types of diagrams, which vary in the level of detail they address.

Decision tables are used to clarify a series of complicated conditional branches. Whenever a choice among actions depends on which of many possible combinations of criteria have been met, a decision table ensures that no possible combinations are overlooked.

Review Questions

1. Why are program design aids useful?
2. What is the purpose of each of the flowcharting symbols depicted in Figure 10-1?
3. Provide a flowchart to read a list of positive values and output the number of these values that are greater than 25. Assume the dummy value −1 appears at the end of the list.

4. What are the objectives of structured programming?
5. Name the three fundamental control structures of structured programming and provide an example of each.
6. What is the difference between the DOWHILE and DOUNTIL control structures?
7. What is the difference between a flowchart and a structure chart?
8. Provide a pseudocode solution to the flowchart in Figure 10-5.
9. Name the three design aids that comprise the HIPO method.
10. What is the purpose of a decision table?

Suggested Readings

Bohl, Marilyn. *Tools for Structured Design.* Palo Alto, Calif.: SRA, 1978.

Katzan, Harry. *Systems Design and Documentation: HIPO.* New York: Van Nostrand, 1976.

Richardson, Gary L., Charles W. Butler, and John D. Tomlinson. *A Primer on Structured Program Design.* New York: Petrocelli, 1980.

Stern, Nancy B. *Flowcharting: A Tool for Understanding Computer Logic.* New York: Wiley, 1975.

Yourdon, Edward. *Techniques of Program Structure and Design.* Englewood Cliffs, N.J.: Prentice-Hall, 1975.

```
    02    FILLER              PIC X(11)    VALUE SPACE.
    02    FILLER              PIC X(6)     VALUE 'ANNUAL'.
    02    FILLER              PIC X(4)     VALUE SPACE.
    02    FILLER              PIC X(4)     VALUE 'YEAR'.
    02    FILLER              PIC X(6)     VALUE SPACE.
    02    FILLER              PIC X(9)     VALUE 'EDUCATIO
    02    FILLER              PIC X(5)     VALUE SPACE.
    02    FILLER              PIC X(3)     VALUE 'SEX'.
    02    FILLER              PIC X(5)     VALUE SPACE.
    02    FILLER              PIC X(10)    VALUE 'GEOGRAPH
    02    FILLER              PIC X(5)     VALUE SPACE.
    02    FILLER              PIC X(8)     VALUE 'JOB CODE
    02    FILLER              PIC X(7)     VALUE SPACE.
    02    FILLER              PIC X(7)     VALUE 'MONTHLY'
    02    FILLER              PIC X(7)     VALUE SPACE.

01  HEADING-3.
    02    FILLER              PIC X(9)     VALUE SPACE.
    02    FILLER              PIC X(6)     VALUE 'NUMBER'.
    02    FILLER              PIC X(31)    VALUE SPACE.
    02    FILLER              PIC X(6)     VALUE 'SALARY'.
    02    FILLER              PIC X(4)     VALUE SPACE.
    02    FILLER              PIC X(5)     VALUE 'HIRED'.
    02    FILLER              PIC X(7)     VALUE SPACE.
    02    FILLER              PIC X(5)     VALUE 'LEVEL'.
    02    FILLER              PIC X(15)    VALUE SPACE.
    02    FILLRR              PIC X(10)    VALUE 'PREFEREN
    02    FILLER              PIC X(20)    VALUE SPACE.
    02    FILLER              PIC X(6)     VALUE 'SALARY'.
    02    FILLER              PIC X(8)     VALUE SPACE.

01  DETAIL-LINE.
    02    FILLER                          PIC X(9)    VALUE SP
    02    DL-EMPLOYEE-NO                   PIC X(6).
    02    FILLER                          PIC X(6)    VALUE S
    02    DL-DEPT                         PIC X(3).
    02    FILLER                          PIC X(3)    VALUE S
```

Chapter 11

Programming Languages

Chapter Outline ➡

OVERVIEW

A BRIEF HISTORY OF PROGRAMMING LANGUAGES

ASSEMBLY LANGUAGES

HIGH-LEVEL LANGUAGES

    BASIC
    COBOL
    FORTRAN
    Pascal

OTHER HIGH-LEVEL LANGUAGES

VERY-HIGH-LEVEL LANGUAGES

    Report Generators
    Word-Processing Software
    Electronic Worksheets (Spreadsheets)
    Graphics Packages

OVERVIEW

Until recently, many of the people who used computer output rarely interacted directly with the computer themselves. They depended on systems analysts and programmers to create, debug, and run programs that would produce the outputs they needed. There were two major reasons for this pattern. First, hardware that would permit many people to work inexpensively with computer systems simply wasn't available. CRTs, for example, were not always as widespread and sophisticated as they are today, and personal computers are largely a phenomenon of the last decade. Second, programming languages were hard for most people to master, so writing applications programs was a full-time job. Most users didn't have the time or ability to write their own.

Technological advances in hardware and software over the last several years have started to change this picture. Miniaturization paved the way for personal computers and inexpensive, highly intelligent CRTs. This development made it possible for users to interact easily with computer systems hardware. Also, a number of "user-friendly" programming languages have emerged that make it relatively straightforward for end users to do their own programming. Thus the two impediments that kept users alienated from computer systems for so many years are gradually disappearing. Today, many users can write and run their own programs.

Necessity has also played an important role in these developments. The demand for computer applications has expanded much faster than the supply of analysts and programmers needed to create them. There is now a shortage of qualified personnel in many areas, and many important program requests are relegated to a waiting list. A user might wait months, or even years, for a new program to be developed. The response of many organizations has been to get the users involved directly with the computer.

In this chapter we will cover many of the different kinds of programming languages now available. We will start with a brief history and then discuss assembly languages, high-level languages and finally, the very high-level languages. A number of languages in the latter category are called *user-friendly,* because they make programming tasks much easier for end users to learn and perform.

A BRIEF HISTORY OF PROGRAMMING LANGUAGES

The earliest programming languages—machine and assembly languages—are called **low-level languages** because programmers coding in these languages must write instructions at the finest level of detail. Each line of code corresponds to a single action of the computer system. Machine language, which consists of strings of 0 and 1 bits, is the "speaking tongue" of the computer. Few people actually write programs in machine language any more, but all programs written in high-level languages must eventually be translated into machine language to be executed. We discussed the software that does the translating—assemblers, compilers, and interpreters—in Chapter 8. Assembly languages, which represent machine instructions in a code that is easier to understand than strings of 0s and 1s, is still used frequently by some programmers but is beyond the grasp of most end users.

The next languages to appear were **high-level languages.** Included in this category are what have come to be known as the "traditional" types of programming languages—for example, BASIC, COBOL, FORTRAN, Pascal, PL/1, APL, and many others. There are well over 100 such languages currently in use, and many of these languages are available in several versions. High-level languages differ from their low-level ancestors in that they require less coding detail. For example, low-level languages require programmers to assign values to specific storage locations and registers in the CPU. The programmer isn't burdened with these tasks when coding in the high-level languages. The translators that convert high-level languages to machine language supply the detail. As a result, programs in high-level languages are shorter and easier to write than those in their low-level counterparts.

Some high-level languages, such as BASIC, are relatively easy even for users to learn. However, many users dislike programming in high-level languages. Some feel that there are too many rules to remember and that the step-by-step logic involved is too complex. Other users are just too busy to do the volume of programming required to meet their needs with these languages. Yet many of these people could benefit by writing their own programs, if this task was somehow made easier. **Very-high-level languages** which first began to appear in the 1960s, were developed to meet a number of *specialized* user needs.

We can compare a very-high-level language to a knowledgeable chauffeur. To get where we want to go, we need only give the chauffeur instructions at a general level, like "take me to City Hall," instead of a detailed one, like "from here you make a right; then three blocks later make a left...." In the same way, with very-high-level languages we need only prescribe *what* the computer is to do rather than *how* it is to do it. This type of facility makes programming much easier. Thus, low- and high-level languages are sometimes called **procedural languages,** because they require people to write detailed procedures telling the computer how to do individual tasks. Very-high-level languages, in contrast, are called **nonprocedural languages.**

Very-high-level languages, as well as advances in interactive display technology, are bringing more people into contact with the computer than ever before. These languages do have some serious disadvantages however. For one thing, they lack flexibility—generally, each is designed to do one specific kind of task. You can't, for example, process a payroll with a word-processing language. Because they are locked into specific applications, very-high-level languages are sometimes called *problem-dependent languages.* A second major disadvantage is that there are many important applications that are not serviced by these languages. Nonetheless, for the areas in which they are available, they offer obvious advantages to both programmers and users.

ASSEMBLY LANGUAGES

Assembly languages are like machine languages in that each line of code corresponds to a single action of the computer system. But assembly languages replace the 0s and 1s of machine language with symbols that are easier to understand and remember, such as "A" for "Add" and "L" for "Load." Because they are closely related to machine languages, which take special advantage of the way the computers they run on are built, assembly programs consume less storage and, in some cases, run much faster than their easier-to-use high-level language counterparts. This constitutes their primary advantage.

Unfortunately, assembly-language programs (one is shown in Figure 11-1) take longer to write and maintain than those written in high-level languages such as BASIC, COBOL, or FORTRAN. Also, they are very machine dependent. An assembly program that works on an IBM machine, for example,

Labels	Commands		Comments
AVERAGE	START	0	BEGINNING OF PROGRAM
	PRINT	NOGEN	SUPPRESS MACRO EXPANSIONS
	INITIAL		BEGIN EXECUTION
	RWD	9	READ NUMBER OF NUMBERS
	LR	8,9	KEEP A COPY IN REGISTER 8
	L	6,=F'1'	DECREMENT FOR COUNTING
	SR	5,5	INITIALIZE SUM TO ZERO
LOOP	RWD	2	READ A NUMBER
	AR	5,2	ADD THE NUMBER TO SUM
	SR	9,6	DECREMENT LOOP COUNTER
	BNM	LOOP	LOOP BACK IF MORE DATA
	MR	4,6	PREPARE FOR DIVISION BY NUMBER
	DR	4,8	OF NUMBERS TO COMPUTE AVERAGE
	WWD	5	QUOTIENT TO REGISTER 5
	WWD	4	REMAINDER TO REGISTER 4
	EOJ		PROCESSING COMPLETED
	END	AVERAGE	END OF PROGRAM

Figure 11-1.   An assembly-language program. This program computes the average of several numbers and outputs the result.

would need substantial modification to run on a Honeywell or DEC computer. With hardware costs decreasing and software development costs on the rise, assembly languages are gradually losing their competitive edge to higher-level languages in many applications. Nonetheless, they are still frequently used because of their efficiency and ability to meet special-purpose needs.

HIGH-LEVEL LANGUAGES

High-level languages are what come to the minds of most people when they think of programming languages. Included in this category are BASIC, COBOL, FORTRAN, Pascal, and many others. Because of their general design, these languages can be used to solve a wide range of computer problems. All of them require the programmer to write a set of procedures that inform the computer precisely, in a step-by-step fashion, *how* to do the work required. To do so, programmers need a reasonable understanding of how both the language and the computer work.

BASIC

In the early days of computing, before personal computers, CRTs, teleprinters, and online processing, writing and debugging programs was a painfully slow process. Would-be programmers submitted their punched-card programs to the operator of the computer system and then waited as much as several hours or a day or two for the results. Often, the program wouldn't work, and the programmer would receive instead a list of cryptic error messages. These had to be properly diagnosed, the bugs corrected, and the program resubmitted. Getting even a modest program written and debugged could take several days or weeks. It thus took a special kind of persistence to master programming, and many people just weren't interested.

Nonetheless, computer scholars realized that the computer was potentially a tool that could benefit noncomputer professionals in many ways, but only if they could be encouraged to learn programming. Clearly there was a need for an easy-to-learn beginner's language that could work in a "friendly," nonfrustrating programming environment.

BASIC (*B*eginner's *A*ll-purpose *S*ymbolic *I*nstruction *C*ode) was designed to meet these needs. It was developed at Dartmouth College in combination with the world's first time-sharing system. Students communicated with the computer through their own terminals, and turnaround time was usually a matter of seconds. A modest program could easily be conceived, coded, and debugged in a few hours. BASIC also proved to be extremely easy to learn, and many students found it possible to write programs after only a few hours of training.

Over the years, BASIC has evolved into one of the most popular and widely available programming languages. Because it is easy to use and the storage requirements for its language translator are small, it works well on almost all personal computers. There are many versions of BASIC available, from "stripped down" ones suitable for pocket computers to powerful mainframe versions that rival the processing power of COBOL.

Key Features.   Almost every key feature of BASIC is related to its ease of use for beginners. Among such features are simplified naming of variables, optional formatting, conversational programming mode, and good diagnostics.

Simplified naming of variables.   The rules for classifying and naming variables in BASIC are generally simple. Variables are classified as either numeric (for example, A = 6) or alphanumeric (for example, A$ = HELLO). Variable names can begin with any letter of the alphabet. This straightforward naming convention permits beginners to move on quickly to other features of the language.

Optional formatting. Languages such as COBOL have a detailed set of rules that one must always follow for specifying the format of inputs and outputs. Although such "data declaration" rules are useful for complex programs, they are predominately "housekeeping tasks" to the beginner. Mastering them can interfere with learning how computers solve problems. With most versions of BASIC, however, one can almost completely ignore formatting data at the outset and address it later.

Conversational programming mode. Because BASIC was specifically designed to work on terminals, almost all versions easily enable users and programmers to "converse" interactively with the computer. This characteristic makes it possible for beginners to use BASIC to write creative applications programs.

Good diagnostics. The quality of the error messages generated by a language is extremely important to a beginner. Error messages are supposed to indicate why a program has failed to work. But if a 200-line program doesn't work, and the error messages are confusing or inadequate, the result is often frustration. In BASIC, the error messages are better than in most other languages. Also, many versions of BASIC come with an online syntax checker that identifies certain kinds of errors in each line of code as it is keyed into the computer system.

Limitations. Despite its many advantages, a key weakness in many versions of BASIC is that they are not designed to facilitate structured programs. A long, unstructured BASIC program may be hard to follow. Also, since there are so many versions of BASIC available, a program developed on one computer may need substantial modifications to run on another.

A sample BASIC program, designed to operate in a conversational mode, is shown in Figure 11-2 (on the next page).

COBOL

COBOL (*CO*mmon *B*usiness-*O*riented *L*anguage), which was first introduced in the early 1960s, is the primary business data-processing language in use today. Until it appeared, there

```
10 REM THIS PROGRAM ACCEPTS NUMBERS AND OUTPUTS
20 REM THEIR SQUARES AND SQUARE ROOTS.
30 PRINT "ENTER A POSITIVE NUMBER AFTER THE QUESTION MARK   "
40 PRINT "TO RECEIVE THE SQUARE AND SQUARE ROOT OF THAT NUMBER.   "
50 PRINT "WHEN YOU HAVE NO MORE NUMBERS, ENTER A NEGATIVE NUMBER. "
60 INPUT X
70 IF X<0 THEN 130
80 PRINT "NUMBER","SQUARE","SQUARE ROOT"
90 PRINT X,X**2,SQR(X)
100 PRINT
110 PRINT
120 GOTO 30
130 PRINT "SO LONG - SEE YOU NEXT TIME."
140 END
```

(a) A BASIC program

```
RUN
ENTER A POSITIVE NUMBER AFTER THE QUESTION MARK
TO RECEIVE THE SQUARE AND SQUARE ROOT OF THAT NUMBER.
WHEN YOU HAVE NO MORE NUMBERS, ENTER A NEGATIVE NUMBER.
?8
NUMBER          SQUARE          SQUARE ROOT
 8               64              2.82843


ENTER A POSITIVE NUMBER AFTER THE QUESTION MARK
TO RECEIVE THE SQUARE AND SQUARE ROOT OF THAT NUMBER.
WHEN YOU HAVE NO MORE NUMBERS, ENTER A NEGATIVE NUMBER.
?-1
SO LONG - SEE YOU NEXT TIME.
```

(b) Output from the program

Figure 11-2.　An interactive BASIC program and its output. The program is designed to accept positive numbers as input and to output the squares and square roots of those numbers.

was no language particularly suitable for business applications, such as payroll, billing, payables and receivables, and so forth. After all, the early language pioneers were engineers and mathematicians, not business people. As more and more businesses purchased computer systems, however, the need for a business-oriented language became apparent. Representatives from the major computer manufacturers met in Washington with users from industry and government to discuss such a product. They subsequently formed a committee to draft a language, and the result was COBOL.

Key Features. Many features differentiate COBOL from other languages. Almost all of them relate to its business data-processing orientation, including machine independence, self-documentation, and input/output orientation.

Machine independence. Business data-processing programs generally have to last a long time. For example, a company may expect to use many of its payroll or accounts receivable programs for ten or even twenty years. During this span of time, an organization may buy new hardware or change completely from one computer system to another. Thus, programs written for one system should be able to run on another with little modification. In other words, the language in which the programs are written should be relatively *machine independent*. COBOL was specifically developed to meet this important requirement.

In 1968 the American National Standards Institute (**ANSI**) established a successful COBOL standard, which was revised in 1974. An updated standard is currently being developed. Over the years, vendors have supplied language translators that meet these standards, so that COBOL programs written in conformation with the standard will generally work on any type of computer system with little modification.

Self-documentation. Because business data-processing programs must last a long time, they need ongoing maintenance. As business conditions change, the programs often have to be modified. For example, a change in tax policy could require several changes in a payroll program. Since programmers tend to change jobs often, the person doing the maintenance is not likely to be the original author of the program. Thus, it's extremely important for program logic to be easy for others to follow. As we saw in Chapters 9 and 10, good design techniques promote logical, easily maintained programs. COBOL lends itself to good program design in three ways: readability, modularity, and proper use of the three control structures of structured programming.

Readability is important because business data-processing programs usually consist of thousands of lines of code. To promote readability, COBOL permits variable names of up to thirty characters. Thus, variable names (for example, TAXES, GROSS-PAY, NET-PAY) can be written out fully and not compressed into obscure abbreviations. COBOL also uses English-like verbs (such as SUBTRACT) and connectives (such

ANSI Standards and the COBOL-80 Controversy

One of the early problems in the development of programming languages was lack of standardization. For example, when COBOL was first created, each software manufacturer producing a COBOL compiler for sale was free to interpret how each command should work. Thus, one manufacturer might build a compiler that was quite different from that of another, and a COBOL applications program written for one wouldn't run on the other unless modified substantially. Since COBOL was created specifically for the development of applications programs with long useful lives, and these programs would presumably have to work on a number of different compilers and computer systems, something clearly had to be done.

To achieve compiler compatibility, ANSI (the American National Standards Institute) established a COBOL standard in 1968. The standard specified a list of rules that manufacturers of COBOL compilers had to comply with in order to have their products bear the label "1968 ANS COBOL." In effect, this was a "seal of approval." Organizations were eager to acquire compilers carrying this seal because it assured them that they could change compilers without having to rewrite their existing applications programs. ANSI has also developed standards for some of the other popular programming languages.

A software manufacturer was not prohibited from putting features into its compiler that went beyond the ANSI standard, as long as the product contained all the ANSI-prescribed features as well. Such extended features are often referred to as "enhancements." Some programming shops strictly avoid these enhancements, even though they do offer some compelling conveniences, because using them potentially locks an applications program into a particular compiler or software manufacturer.

In 1974, ANSI set up a revised COBOL standard. As before, software manufacturers complying with this standard could market their products with the label "1974 ANS COBOL." Some data-processing shops continued to use the 1968 compilers, but it became evident that software manufacturers would eventually stop

as FROM and GIVING) to enhance readability. As a result, statements in COBOL often tend to read like regular English sentences; for example,

```
SUBTRACT TAXES FROM GROSS-PAY GIVING NET-PAY.
```

Modularity is important because programs are easier to develop and maintain if they are divided into clearly defined segments, where each segment performs an independent task. COBOL is designed to encourage such modularity. It is easy to represent functional hierarchies in COBOL, and the language lends itself to structured design aids such as structure charts (see Chapter 10).

A good COBOL program looks like a well-organized outline. Every COBOL program is divided into four distinct divisions:

supporting these older programs. As in other fields, when products are made obsolete by newer ones, both expertise and interest in them fades. Thus, if a data-processing shop chose to continue with an outdated compiler for a long time, and an error in the compiler cropped up, the shop might have to correct it on its own without help from the manufacturer. Most shops simply do not have the in-house expertise to do this. Incidentally, virtually all commercially available compilers contain errors of one sort or another. In fact, some large system programs may have thousands of errors in them when they are first marketed. It's just a matter of time before these errors make themselves apparent.

In 1980, ANSI again proposed to change the COBOL standard. This change involved some modifications that were not compatible with the 1974 version of the language. For example, some COBOL language statements available under the 1974 standard were not available in the proposed 1980 version. Also, the meaning of many COBOL words was changed—which meant that many programs written for the 1974 standard would not run on compilers that met the newly proposed standard unless modified and tested substantially. But large organizations now have millions of dollars invested in working COBOL programs. Many of them objected to the proposed standards, claiming they would entail a substantial, perhaps unbearable, maintenance expense. One company even threatened to sue ANSI if the new standard was adopted. ANSI has since gone "back to the drawing boards," and COBOL-80 is still in development.

ANSI: A seal of approval.

1. An *Identification Division,* which identifies the name of the program, the author, and other details. This division exists mostly for documentation purposes.

2. An *Environment Division,* in which the file names created by the programmer are linked to specific input/output equipment. Here, for example, the programmer would specify that a particular input file, say DISKFILE, is located on disk, and that a particular output file, say PRINTFILE, is to be routed to a printer.

3. A *Data Division,* in which the programmer names and defines all the variables in the program and indicates their relationship to each other.

4. A *Procedure Division,* which specifies the actual procedures the computer system must follow to create the desired output.

The first three divisions ensure that all important specifications are stated explicitly in the program. In other languages, such as BASIC, many of these specifications are implied rather than stated, making long programs more difficult to maintain.

Divisions of COBOL programs may be subdivided into sections, and sections further subdivided into paragraphs. Each paragraph may contain one or more statements. For example, a payroll program may have a section named TAX-SECTION in its Procedure Division. Within that section, it may have paragraphs such as FEDERAL-TAX-PARA, STATE-TAX-PARA, and CITY-TAX-PARA. The individual statements in these paragraphs would do the "work" of the program, such as computing taxes.

Finally, because it supports the three major program control structures—sequence, selection, and looping—better than many other languages, COBOL lends itself to well-structured programs.

Input/output orientation. Business data processing, in contrast to scientific and engineering applications, involves the manipulation of large files with many business-type records. Thus, much of the work in business data-processing applications relates to reading and writing records, and COBOL has been designed to be particularly effective in this area. It contains provisions for defining explicitly and easily the format of input and output records. For example, it is a very straightforward process to edit dollar amounts on output with dollar signs, decimal points, and commas, and also to round off these amounts.

Limitations. Because COBOL programs use long, English-like names and specify formats in fine detail, they tend to be lengthy. Also, a large and sophisticated language translator is needed to convert programs to machine language, making COBOL difficult to implement on many smaller computers. And because of its business data-processing orientation, it is usually not suitable for scientific or engineering applications, which use a number of complicated formulas.

Despite its limitations, however, COBOL is likely to remain in the forefront of business data-processing applications for many years. Currently, some 70 to 80 percent of computerized business applications in large firms are coded in COBOL. With millions of dollars invested in COBOL programs, and thousands of programmers versed in its use, it seems likely that the language will endure for many more years.

A sample COBOL program is shown in Figure 11-3 (on pages 328 and 329).

FORTRAN

FORTRAN (*FOR*mula *TRAN*slator), which dates to 1954, is the oldest surviving commercial high-level language. It was designed by scientists and is oriented toward scientific and engineering problem solving.

Business data-processing applications involve sophisticated input/output operations and relatively simple computations. Scientific and engineering applications, in contrast, require complex computations and relatively simple input/output operations. Determining the trajectory of a rocket, for example—a classic engineering application—requires intricate and precise computations. Preparing a payroll, in contrast—a typical business data-processing application—involves reading employee records and writing both checks and reports, but the computations performed on each record are relatively simple.

Because of FORTRAN's ability to perform sophisticated computations, however, it has proved useful for certain kinds of business applications. These are applications with more of a problem-solving nature than a routine data-processing nature involving massive files of records. Some examples are sales forecasting, determining the least expensive way to manufacture a product, and simulating complex production processes.

Key Features. The key feature of FORTRAN is its ability to express sophisticated computations easily. Although BASIC is competitive in this area, FORTRAN is generally superior for many applications because it enables faster program execution and greater accuracy.

Fast program execution. FORTRAN generally uses a compiler as its language translator. Compilers run programs faster than the interpreters used by most versions of BASIC because compilers translate each statement only once, rather

```
        IDENTIFICATION DIVISION.
          PROGRAM-ID. SIMPLE.
          AUTHOR. PARKER.

        ENVIRONMENT DIVISION.
        CONFIGURATION SECTION.
          SOURCE-COMPUTER. UNIVAC-VS9.
          OBJECT-COMPUTER. UNIVAC-VS9.
        INPUT-OUTPUT SECTION.
          FILE-CONTROL.
            SELECT DISKFILE ASSIGN TO DISK-A1F2-V.
            SELECT PRINTFILE ASSIGN TO SYSLST.

        DATA DIVISION.
        FILE SECTION.
        FD   DISKFILE
             LABEL RECORDS ARE STANDARD.
        01   DISKREC.
             05 PART-DESCRIPTION-IN      PIC X(20).
             05 PRICE-IN                 PIC 999.
             05 UNITS-ON-HAND-IN         PIC 9(5).
        FD   PRINTFILE
             LABEL RECORDS ARE OMITTED.
        01   PRINTLINE                   PIC X(120).
        WORKING-STORAGE SECTION.
        77   WS-END-OF-FILE.             PIC X(3) VALUE 'NO'.
        01   HEADING-LINE.
             05 FILLER                   PIC X(9)  VALUE SPACES.
             05 FILLER                   PIC X(11) VALUE 'DESCRIPTION'.
             05 FILLER                   PIC X(10) VALUE SPACES.
             05 FILLER                   PIC X(5)  VALUE 'PRICE'.
             05 FILLER                   PIC X(7)  VALUE SPACES.
             05 FILLER                   PIC X(5)  VALUE 'UNITS'.
             05 FILLER                   PIC X(4)  VALUE SPACES.
             05 FILLER                   PIC X(11) VALUE 'TOTAL VALUE'.
        01   DETAIL-LINE.
             05 FILLER                   PIC X(5)  VALUE SPACES.
             05 PART-DESCRIPTION-OUT     PIC X(20).
             05 FILLER                   PIC X(4)  VALUE SPACES.
             05 PRICE-OUT                PIC $ZZ9.99.
             05 FILLER                   PIC X(5)  VALUE SPACES.
             05 UNITS-ON-HAND-OUT        PIC ZZ,ZZ9.
             05 FILLER                   PIC X(5)  VALUE SPACES.
             05 INVENTORY-VALUE          PIC $ZZZ,ZZ9.
```

Figure 11-3.   A sample COBOL program and its output. The program is designed to accept the name of a product, its unit price, and the number of units on hand as input, and to output this information along with the total dollar value of the stock on hand.

```
PROCEDURE DIVISION.
010-HOUSEKEEPING.
    OPEN INPUT DISKFILE
        OUTPUT PRINTFILE.
    READ DISKFILE
        AT END MOVE 'YES' TO WS-END-OF-FILE.
    PERFORM 020-HEADINGS.
    PERFORM 030-PROCESSIT
        UNTIL WS-END-OF-FILE = 'YES'.
    CLOSE DISKFILE
         PRINTFILE.
    STOP RUN.
020-HEADINGS.
    WRITE PRINTLINE FROM HEADING-LINE
        AFTER ADVANCING 1 LINE.
030-PROCESSIT.
    MULTIPLY    UNITS-ON-HAND-IN
        BY      PRICE-IN
        GIVING  INVENTORY-VALUE.
    MOVE PART-DESCRIPTION-IN TO PART-DESCRIPTION-OUT.
    MOVE PRICE-IN            TO PRICE-OUT.
    MOVE UNITS-ON-HAND-IN    TO UNITS-ON-HAND-OUT.
    WRITE PRINTLINE FROM DETAIL-LINE
        AFTER ADVANCING 1 LINE.
    READ DISKFILE
        AT END MOVE 'YES' TO WS-END-OF-FILE.
```

(a) A COBOL program

```
    DESCRIPTION            PRICE        UNITS      TOTAL VALUE
SMALL WIDGETS            $150.00          100      $ 15,000
LARGE SKY HOOKS         $200.00           50      $ 10,000
BLIVETS                 $100.00        3,000      $300,000
```

(b) Output from the program

Figure 11-3. *(Continued)*

than several times. Since scientific and engineering programs are characterized by many computations and frequent looping, execution speed is a primary concern.

Accuracy. Almost all versions of FORTRAN have a "double-precision" capability, which permits results to be calculated to several significant digits. This feature minimizes the rounding errors that are compounded when a lengthy series of related computations is performed.

Limitations. FORTRAN was developed well before structured programming began to be emphasized, so it is somewhat weak in this area when compared with some of the newer languages. The latest ANSI standard in FORTRAN, however, created in 1977, provided a number of structured facilities for the language to make it competitive with some of the structured languages.

Also, the logic of FORTRAN programs is more difficult to follow than the logic of some other languages, and it is clearly inferior to COBOL for business data-processing applications. However, FORTRAN will probably remain a popular scientific and engineering language for years to come. It has a large base of loyal users, its compilers are widely available, and there is a large bank of FORTRAN programs currently in use.

A sample FORTRAN program is shown in Figure 11-4.

```
C ECONOMIC ORDER QUANTITY COMPUTATION
C
      READ (1,100) ID,IUNITS,OC,UC,CC
  100 FORMAT (I5,1X,I5,1X,F5.2,1X,F5.2,1X,F4.2)
      EOQ = SQRT(2.0*IUNITS*OC/(UC*CC))
      WRITE (2,200) ID,EOQ
  200 FORMAT(1X,'THE EOQ FOR PRODUCT ',I5,' IS ',F10.2)
      STOP
      END
```

(a) A FORTRAN program

```
THE EOQ FOR PRODUCT 10563 IS     1000.00
```

(b) Output from the program

Figure 11-4.   A sample FORTRAN program and its output. The program is designed to compute the *economic order quantity* of a product in inventory. The economic order quantity of a product is determined by the formula

$$EOQ = \sqrt{\frac{2*IUNITS*OC}{UC*CC}}$$

where IUNITS is the number of units used annually, OC is the cost of placing an order, UC is the cost of one unit, and CC is the inventory carrying cost. This formula is widely used in business to determine the ideal quantity of goods to buy each time goods are bought. EOQ was calculated assuming ID = 10563, IUNITS = 8000, OC = 12.50, UC = 1.00, and CC = 0.20.

Pascal

Pascal, named after the mathematician Blaise Pascal, is a relatively new programming language. It was developed about 1970 by Professor Niklaus Wirth of Zurich, Switzerland.

Key Features. Pascal was created primarily to fill the need for a teaching vehicle that would encourage structured programming. Its key features are an easy-to-learn structured orientation and memory efficiency.

    Easy-to-learn structured orientation. Although BASIC still remains a strong favorite among beginners, Pascal is far superior to most versions of BASIC (and even COBOL) in its structured programming capability. This makes Pascal an easier language to work with for complicated programs. Pascal also has an explicit data-specification facility similar to COBOL's Data Division. As a result of these traits, Pascal has been enthusiastically received. Many universities have replaced courses in BASIC and FORTRAN with courses in Pascal.

    Memory efficiency. Pascal compilers are extremely small, given the processing power of the language. Thus, the language can be implemented easily on most personal computers. This feature also makes the language ideal for educational environments.

Limitations. Pascal's major weakness is that it has marginal input/output capabilities. Thus, it is not as suitable as COBOL for business data-processing applications. As a problem-solving language, however, it is expected to give FORTRAN and BASIC severe competition.

A sample Pascal program appears in Figure 11-5 (on the next page).

Other High-Level Languages

The high-level languages discussed so far are among the most popular of those used today. Three others that you should know something about are PL/1, APL, and Ada.

PL/1. PL/1 (*Programming Language 1*) was introduced in the mid-1960s by IBM as a general-purpose language. That is, it

```
PROGRAM SUMANDCOUNT (INPUT,OUTPUT);
(*SUM AND COUNT A SET OF VALUES*)
CONST   ENDOFDATA:=-1;
VAR     SUM,VALUE:REAL;
            COUNT:INTEGER;
BEGIN
SUM:=0;COUNT:=0;
READLN(VALUE)
WHILE VALUE<>ENDOFDATA DO
        BEGIN
        SUM:=SUM+VALUE;
        COUNT:=COUNT+1;
        READLN(VALUE)
        END;
WRITELN('THE NUMBER OF VALUES COUNTED IS',COUNT:3);
WRITELN('THE SUM OF THE VALUES IS',SUM:7:2);
END.
```

(a) A Pascal program

```
THE NUMBER OF VALUES COUNTED IS 43
THE SUM OF THE VALUES IS 456,23
```

(b) Output from the program

Figure 11-5. A sample Pascal program and its output. This program is designed to read a list of values, count the number of values in the list, and total the values.

was designed for *both* scientific and business data-processing applications. It's an extremely powerful language, with strong capabilities for structured programming. Variants of PL/1, such as PL/C, have been developed for teaching purposes.

Despite PL/1's high credentials, it has not been used as widely as one might expect. There are several reasons for this. First, the language was initially available only on IBM machines, and other computer manufacturers were slow to adopt it on their equipment. Since IBM mainframes are found less commonly in academic settings than in industry, few programmers learned to use PL/1 in school. Second, COBOL had a substantial head start in business data processing. Not only did companies have many thousands of dollars invested in working COBOL programs, but also COBOL programmers have always been more available in the marketplace. Third, BASIC and FORTRAN were already well entrenched for scientific,

USER-FRIENDLY COMPUTING

Making computing easier for the user

During the early days of computers, only scientists and engineers were able to take advantage of the awesome processing powers of these machines. Over the years, computer systems have become easier and easier to use, making them directly available to ever more people. Window 6 gives you a look at the nature of user-friendly computing.

1.   Understandable output. If you can't easily digest the information the computer system sends to you, it doesn't matter how lovable your system is in other ways. The display on this Dasher G300 terminal from Data General Corporation demonstrates the variety of formats in which some of the newer software packages can deliver information. On any program run, users can choose from numerous output formats those that are most meaningful to them.

FRIENDLY SYSTEMS
FOR CHILDREN

2. A child ruminates over the solution to a programming problem at an Atari computer camp.

3. A preschooler plays with Mattel's Teach and Learn Computer®. The child places an overlay on the unit, inserts the appropriate disk in the built-in slot provided, and reacts to verbal instructions produced by an audio device in the machine.

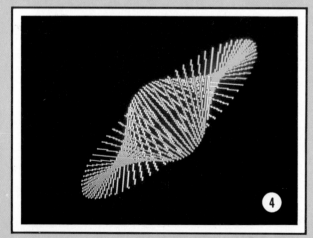

4. LOGO, an interactive programming language developed at MIT, enables children to create graphical output with simple commands. The image shown here was shot from a display screen on an Apple computer system.

5. In Atari's "States and Capitals" game, children can guess the name of the state that is highlighted on the map and, subsequently, the capital of that state. The software package keeps track of correct guesses and requires that you spell correctly when responding.

FRIENDLY SYSTEMS
FOR ADULTS

6. An executive uses a touch-sensitive menu to request graphs of data taken from a financial database. The system shown represents a joint effort by Computer Pictures Corporation and Cullinet Software to bring critical operating information to top management in a highly understandable and controllable form.

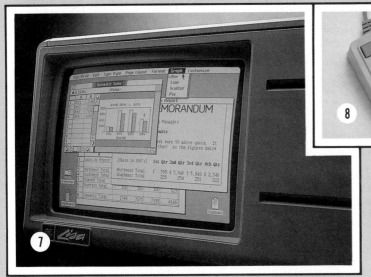

7. Apple's Lisa is a personal computer system specifically designed to let managers work the way they do at their desks. You control the system with a cursor-movement device called a mouse (8), which enables you to select options on the screen. To store a document, for example, use the mouse to move the document's identifying symbol onto a folder symbol. Or, to dispose of a document, move its identifier onto the wastebasket symbol.

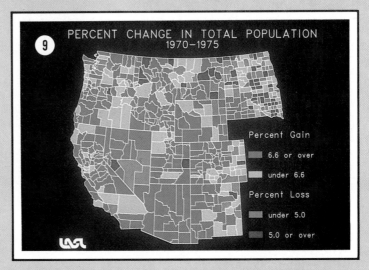

9. Friendly output. Some sophisticated software packages enable you to create informative, color-coded maps of computer-stored data easily. This example, illustrating population shifts by county, was produced at Los Alamos National Laboratory. A number of companies currently use such maps to pictorially display sales information by region, for marketing strategy purposes.

PERCENT CHANGE IN TOTAL POPULATION
1970-1975

Percent Gain
6.6 or over
under 6.6

Percent Loss
under 5.0
5.0 or over

COMPUTER-ASSISTED INSTRUCTION An important function of the computer is to teach people interactively—not only programming, but other subjects as well. This type of computing is called computer-assisted instruction (CAI). With CAI, a computer program poses a question to a user at a display device ... and the user responds. Then, based on the response, the computer selects another question, and so forth.

10. Children learning on an IBM Personal Computer.

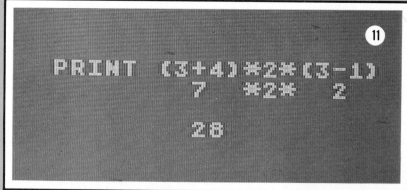

11. An Atari program that teaches how a computer system interprets a BASIC language PRINT statement. The program also poses multiple-choice questions about how BASIC works.

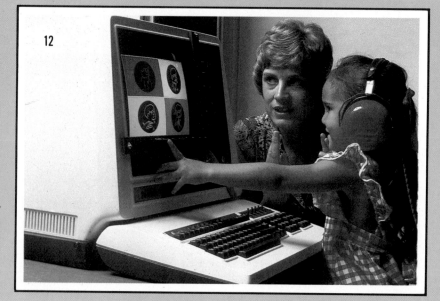

12. A program called "Computer Assisted Instruction on Language and Reading for the Deaf" is used with a Ramtek color terminal to display different parts of speech, helping deaf students learn about nouns, verbs, adjectives, and adverbs.

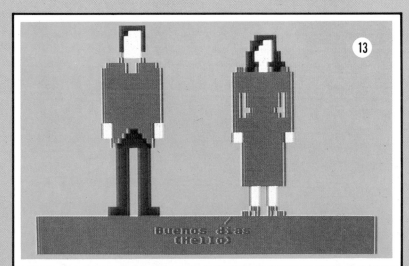

13. Atari's Conversational Spanish is one of the many software packages available that teach foreign-language constructs interactively.

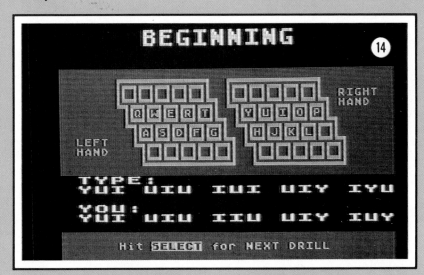

14. Learning typing by computer. This program poses touch-typing exercises and monitors your progress.

15. Atari's Music Composer™ lets you compose songs, re-create old tunes, or experiment. As you enter musical notes through the keyboard, you hear the melody from an audio unit as it is simultaneously displayed on the screen. You can change the tempo and pitch, or even ask the program to play different sections of your piece in any order you choose.

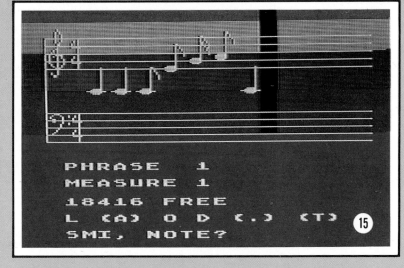

USERS These three pages show the diversity of computer system users who depend upon some form of system friendliness.

16. An agricultural association in Reims, France uses an IBM System/38 computer to help more than 4000 farmers and wine producers manage their businesses effectively.

17. A woman uses an automated teller station at the Hartford National Bank in Connecticut.

19. An operator at a power plant uses a computer system to monitor plant operations.

18. Ex-president Jimmy Carter prepares his memoirs on Lanier's No Problem™ word processor in his Plains, Georgia office.

20. A salesman at Fortunoff, a leading New York retailer specializing in fine goods, uses an NCR point-of-sale terminal to record sales, monitor inventories, and authorize credit purchases.

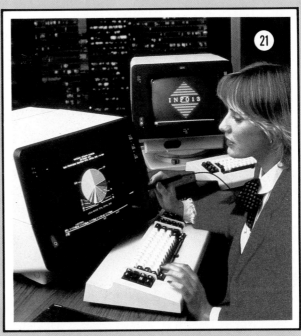

21. A marketing specialist in San Francisco uses a terminal for planning purposes and business correspondence.

22. Office workers frequently use computer systems to process documents, maintain mailing lists, and manage electronic schedules and messages.

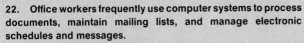

23. A researcher uses an IBM color display system in Italy.

24. A motel reservation clerk operates NCR's 2160 Lodging System.

25. A fire department employee in Kansas City uses a computer system to rapidly access information in a fire incident.

26. A wheat cooperative serving over 50,000 farmers in Alberta, Canada, operates a network of IBM computers installed at more than 120 grain elevators for daily inventory and sales accounting. Farmers also use the system to obtain the latest wheat prices.

engineering, and business problem-solving applications. They were generally perceived as easier to use than PL/1 and their language translators were more available. Nonetheless, PL/1 has a respectable following, and those that use the language swear by it.

APL.   APL (*A Programming Language*) was developed in 1967, under the auspices of IBM, to perform problem-solving work rapidly. It is a tremendously compact language, and it can only be used with a special keyboard. Like BASIC, it is a highly interactive language.

APL has two modes of operation: *calculator* and *program.* In the calculator mode, APL is like a powerful desk calculator. In other words, the user types in a single APL expression, and the computer instantly supplies a response. APL uses a special set of symbols to enable users to perform complex mathematical computations in a single step. The same special symbols can be used to write complete computer programs in the program mode.

Supporters claim that APL programs can be written in a small fraction of the time it takes to write comparable FOR- TRAN programs. Critics argue that APL is difficult to learn because it uses too many special symbols and employs certain programming conventions that are completely contrary to those of other languages. Most APL programs are extremely difficult for anyone but the original programmer to read. This trait is often acceptable in scientific and engineering environments, however, where programs often have short useful lives.

Ada.   For many years, much of the software written for the armed services was in machine or assembly language. In the 1970s, many branches of the services began to convert applications to high-level languages. There was no single standard for all the branches, however, and systems developed by one branch were not always compatible with those of the others. The U.S. Department of Defense soon declared a moratorium on these divergent efforts and directed the branches to cooperate in creating a single language standard. Existing languages were surveyed and, for one reason or another, rejected. The end result, in 1980, was the development of a new structured language, **Ada**, named after the Countess of Lovelace, a colleague of the nineteenth-century computer pioneer Charles Babbage. (See the box about the Countess of Lovelace in Chapter 3.)

It is still too early to tell what effect Ada will have both in and beyond the Department of Defense. Supporters predict that the language, which resembles Pascal, will be widely embraced by both the academic and business worlds. Critics point to PL/1 and history, scoffing, "who needs another programming language?"

VERY-HIGH-LEVEL LANGUAGES

Very-high-level languages offer the attractive advantage of being relatively easy to learn and to use. Some of these languages are called *user-friendly,* because they enable end users with little or no formal training in programming to work "painlessly" with the computer system on certain kinds of interactive applications after only a few hours of training. Compared to high-level languages, however, very high-level languages lack flexibility—each is designed to solve only a specific type of problem.

Many very-high-level languages are available in the marketplace, and generally there is more than one for each applications area. In this section we will discuss the distinctive features of some of the major types of very high-level languages, including

- Report generators
- Word-processing software
- Electronic worksheets
- Graphics packages

A number of other user-friendly software packages are shown in Window 6.

Report Generators

Most business reports have a number of characteristics in common. They usually contain a title, page and column headings, a main body, column totals and subtotals, page footings, and so forth. Report generating languages, or **report generators,** capitalize on these similarities of format.

They work as follows. Users or programmers provide facts about what the report should look like. These facts are often supplied on special forms, which are subsequently machine-

tomorrow

PROGRAMMERLESS SYSTEMS

The initial wave of general-purpose, "semiprogrammerless" systems, such as Apple's Lisa computer system, has led a number of industry futurists to speculate anew about the future of "conventional programming." Conventional programming involves the writing of applications software in procedural languages such as COBOL, FORTRAN, PL/1, BASIC, and Pascal. Most of these languages were originally designed in the 1950s and 1960s to work within the limits of the computer systems available at that time. Over the years, these languages have been modified to some extent to take advantage of advances in hardware and software technology. Colleges and universities continue to stress procedural language skills heavily, largely because these languages are still the backbone of applications programming in commercial settings. And of course, these skills give students insight into how computer systems process data. Unfortunately, many commercial end users find these languages either too difficult or too time-consuming to learn. Thus, these languages are generally employed only by programmers or the more sophisticated end users.

Lisa is representative of a new breed of computers. Although conventional procedural languages are available on this machine, users can do some types of work simply by pointing to choices displayed on a screen. For example, a user can make a file available for processing by simply pointing to the image of the file displayed on the screen. Or to temporarily clear the file from the machine's workspace, the user can point to an image of a waste can.

All this power-at-a-fingertip enables users to bypass the programmer for many applications. This new type of "programming," if you are bold enough to call it that, is absolutely necessary to meet the increasing demands of people for computer power. Many organizations already have such large backlogs of computing requests that users must wait for inordinate periods of time to get anything done. What's more, users have traditionally had difficulty in communicating their needs to analysts and programmers. Programmerless systems place people with ordinary skills into positions where they can easily create, store, retrieve, and manage their own information banks on computer systems.

coded. The language package then determines how the job will be done and creates (generates) a computer program to produce the report.

Used for the right kinds of tasks, report generators can save a considerable amount of coding and debugging time compared to the traditional types of programming languages such as COBOL. And because many of them are easy to learn, they permit users to do their own programming. Two well-known report generators are RPG and the so-called data management system (DMS) languages.

RPG.   IBM developed **RPG** (*R*eport *P*rogram *G*enerator) in the early 1960s to produce reports quickly on small computers. The RPG user or programmer need only fill out forms to describe the desired report to the RPG language translator. The information declared on the form includes answers to questions such as the following:

- What records in a file will be used to produce the report?
- What fields should be read from each record?
- What computations are to be done?
- What subtotals and totals should be taken?
- How will the report be formatted?

Several improvements have been made on RPG over the years. Updated versions of the language, such as RPGII and RPGIII, are currently very popular. Because RPG compilers are normally small, the language is widely used on small business systems. RPG is not standardized like many of the high-level languages, however, so there are different versions for different computer systems.

Data Management System (DMS) Languages.   These software systems, which include proprietary packages such as *Easytrieve* and *Mark V,* are large-computer counterparts to RPG. *Proprietary* means they are not in the public domain but are each owned by some software vendor who sells a license for use. They are generally more powerful and easier to use than RPG, but also more expensive.

Although these packages all work differently, they share a number of properties. Figure 11-6 illustrates how many of them function in principle. The user or programmer fills in a form on a CRT for a simple report request. The form asks for different facts about the report to be prepared. The figure shows, for example, that a user wants a deductions report for all employees in departments 212–214, sorted by department and totaled. When the user types a "/" symbol, indicating a field has been filled with data, the system responds by sending the cursor to the beginning of the next highlighted input field on the CRT. The user can also specify special output options, such as double-spacing. With many DMS languages, the report is automatically page-numbered, dated, and centered.

Word-Processing Software

Word processing refers to the application of computer technology to the preparation of typed documents. These documents include letters, legal contracts, books and manuscripts, and so forth. This textbook, for example, was created with the use of word-processing software.

Word processing can work in many ways. One method is to use a word-processing software package on a general-purpose computer system. These packages are widely available for most

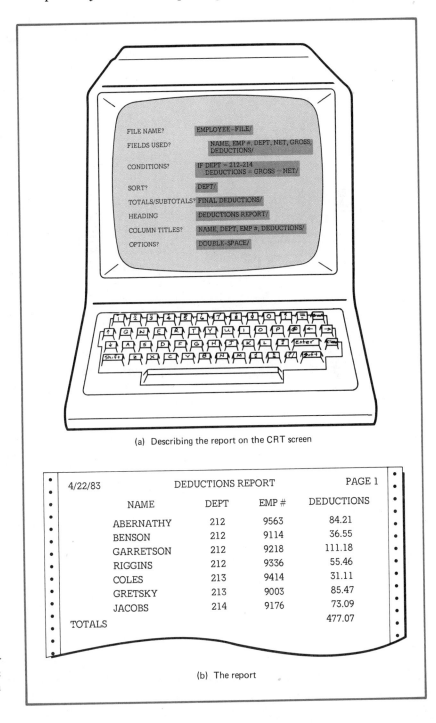

(a) Describing the report on the CRT screen

4/22/83	DEDUCTIONS REPORT			PAGE 1
	NAME	DEPT	EMP #	DEDUCTIONS
	ABERNATHY	212	9563	84.21
	BENSON	212	9114	36.55
	GARRETSON	212	9218	111.18
	RIGGINS	212	9336	55.46
	COLES	213	9414	31.11
	GRETSKY	213	9003	85.47
	JACOBS	214	9176	73.09
TOTALS				477.07

(b) The report

Figure 11-6.   Using a data management system to produce a report. (a) Describing the report on the CRT screen. (b) The report.

computers. Another is to buy a dedicated word-processing system—a computer system that specializes in word-processing applications.

Word processing has many benefits. If you misspell words, want to revise a document, or would like to reformat it, all you need to do is sign onto your computer system, take a few seconds to make the changes, and have the system retype the entire document automatically. Other benefits available on many word-processing packages include

- *An automatic spelling-checker,* which is made possible by a dictionary stored in the computer system. Many systems will enable you to add new entries to the dictionary when you wish to do so.
- *A word-wrap function,* which allows you to type continuously, without hitting the return key.
- *An edit facility,* which enables you to search automatically for all occurrences of a particular word or phrase and to change it to something else. For example, if you misspell *heaven* (as *heven*) 59 times in a document, only one edit command needs to be issued to make all the necessary changes; for example,

```
CHANGE "HEVEN" TO "HEAVEN"
```

The availability of better software combined with small, powerful microprocessors and memories should make word processing more commonplace every year. It seems likely that conventional typewriters, as we know them today, will disappear in the not-too-distant future because of the word-processing boom.

Electronic Worksheets (Spreadsheets)

Electronic worksheets first came to public notice in the late 1970s when a Harvard Business School student and a programmer friend produced a package called VisiCalc® (the *Visi*ble *Calc*ulator) for personal computers. To say it was a huge success is an understatement. It shattered sales records for software and, according to many people, revolutionized personal computing.

The principle behind VisiCalc and other similar packages is to view the CRT screen as a *window* looking in on a big worksheet. The worksheet, for example, may be composed of

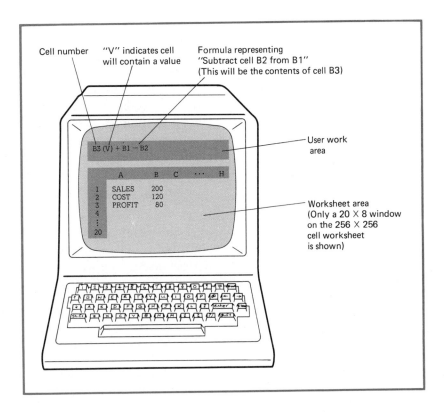

Figure 11-7. An electronic worksheet.

256 rows and 256 columns. Each of the 65,536 (256 × 256) "cells" formed at the intersection of the rows and columns may contain a word, number, or formula. The CRT screen is big enough to allow the user to see only a few rows and columns at any one time. However, users can press keys on the keyboard that will move the worksheet around so they can see other portions of it.

The use of an electronic worksheet is illustrated in Figure 11-7. In this example, the user wishes to compute a business income statement, where expenses are 60 percent of sales, and profit is the difference between sales and expenses. The user work area of the screen allows users to perform tasks like placing alphanumeric labels or numeric values into any of the cells of the worksheet. Columns are identified by numbers, and rows by letters, and each cell by a letter and number pair. A *label* (L) is an entry that cannot be manipulated mathematically. A *value* (V) is an entry that can. The user has entered the following six commands into the user work area:

1. A1 (L) SALES
2. A2 (L) COST
3. A3 (L) PROFIT
4. B1 (V) 200
5. B2 (V) .6*B1
6. B3 (V) +B1-B2

As a command is issued in the user work area, it is processed, and the results are transferred by the software package to the worksheet. In commands 1 through 4, a direct transfer is made. In commands 5 and 6, the computer first makes the computation indicated by the formulas and then transfers the result to the worksheet.

Electronic worksheets are particularly good for "what-if" types of queries. For example, suppose the user in Figure 11-7 wants to know what the profit would be if sales were $5000. The user simply types in the command

```
B1   (V)  5000
```

and the computer system will automatically rework all the figures according to the formulas. Thus, the computer responds

```
SALES   5000
COST    3000
PROFIT  2000
```

Most worksheets also have commands for automatically adjusting for inflation factors and computing rates of return, averages, and so forth. Electronic worksheets can perform computations in seconds that would require several hours to do manually or by writing a program in a high-level language. A particularly attractive feature of these packages is that users can learn to prepare budgets and financial schedules with them after only a few hours of training.

Graphics Packages

Graphics packages make it possible for users to "draw" graphs painlessly, either on a CRT screen or hard-copy plotter. The user normally needs to specify only what type of output is desired, how it will be labeled, and the absolute size of each attribute to be represented.

An example of a graphics package in operation is shown in Figure 11-8. The user is first presented with a menu, such as that shown in Figure 11-8a. After the user selects the pie-chart option, a "form" is presented on the screen for the user to fill out (Figure 11-8b). Generally, the screen is entirely preformatted, so that once the user has typed an entry into a field, the package automatically tabs to the next field. When the user is finished, a "Y" (signifying "yes") must be typed in the appropriate place. Then, the output shown in Figure 11-8c is produced on the

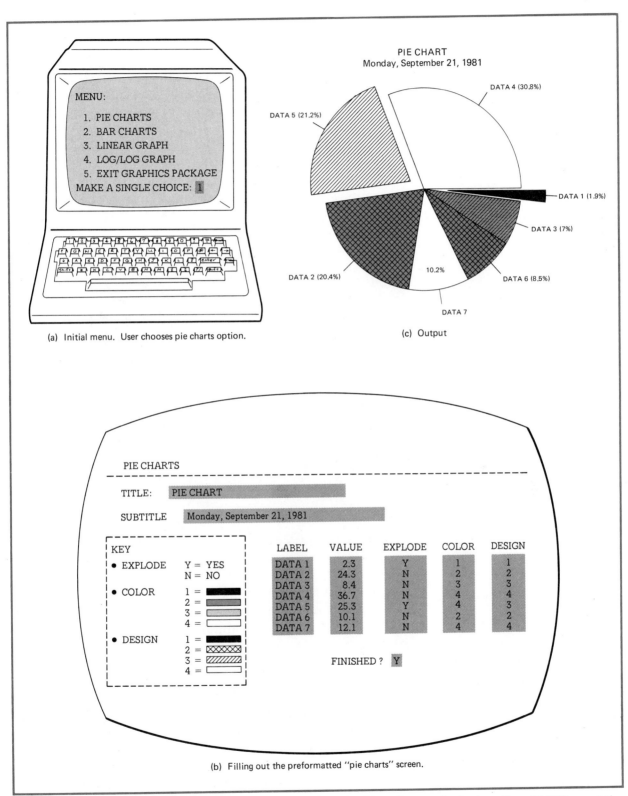

(a) Initial menu. User chooses pie charts option.

(c) Output

(b) Filling out the preformatted "pie charts" screen.

Figure 11-8. *How a graphics package works.* (a) Initial menu. User chooses pie charts option. (b) Filling out the preformatted pie charts screen. (c) The completed pie chart output.

attached plotter (or CRT, if desired). Note that the entries in the value column of Figure 11-8*b* are automatically calculated as percentages of the total when output on the pie chart.

Summary and Key Terms

The earliest programming languages—machine and assembly languages—are called **low-level languages** because programmers coding in these languages must write instructions at the finest level of detail.

The next languages to appear were the **high-level languages.** Included in this class are what have come to be known as the "traditional" types of programming languages—BASIC, COBOL, FORTRAN, Pascal, PL/1, APL, and many others. High-level languages differ from their low-level ancestors in that they require less coding detail and make programs easier to write.

Very-high-level languages are those in which users prescribe *what* the computer is to do rather than *how* it is to do it. This type of facility makes programming much easier. Low- and high-level languages are sometimes called **procedural languages,** because they require people to write detailed procedures telling the computer how to do individual tasks. Very-high-level languages, in contrast, are called **nonprocedural languages.**

Assembly languages are like machine languages in that each line of code corresponds to a single action of the computer system. But assembly languages replace the 0s and 1s of machine language with symbols that are easier to understand and remember. Unfortunately, assembly-language programs take longer to write and maintain than those written in high-level languages. They are also very machine dependent.

BASIC (*B*eginner's *A*ll-purpose *S*ymbolic *I*nstruction *C*ode) was designed to meet the need for an easy-to-learn beginner's language that could work in a "friendly," nonfrustrating programming environment. Over the years, BASIC has evolved into one of the most popular and widely available programming languages. Because it is easy to use and the storage requirements for its language translator are small, it works well on almost all personal computers. Nearly every advantage of

BASIC is related to its ease of use for beginners. Among these advantages are simplified naming of variables, optional formatting, conversational programming mode, and good diagnostics. A key weakness in many versions of BASIC is that they are not designed to facilitate structured programs.

COBOL (*CO*mmon *B*usiness-*O*riented *L*anguage) is the primary business data-processing language in use today. Almost all of its key features relate to its business data-processing orientation. These include machine independence, self-documentation, and input/output orientation. The primary disadvantages of COBOL are that programs tend to be lengthy, the language is difficult to implement on many smaller computers, and it is usually not suitable for scientific or engineering applications.

FORTRAN (*FOR*mula *TRAN*slator), which dates back to 1954, is the oldest surviving commercial high-level language. It was designed by scientists and is oriented toward scientific and engineering problem solving. The key feature of FORTRAN is its ability to express sophisticated computations easily. Although BASIC is competitive in this area, FORTRAN is generally superior for many applications because it permits faster program execution and greater accuracy. The disadvantages of FORTRAN include a weakness for business data-processing applications.

Pascal, named after the mathematician, Blaise Pascal, is a relatively new programming language. Pascal was created primarily to fill the need for a teaching vehicle that would encourage structured programming.

PL/1 (*P*rogramming *L*anguage *1*) was introduced in the mid-1960s by IBM as a general-purpose language. That is, it was designed for both scientific *and* business data-processing applications. It's an extremely powerful language with strong capabilities for structured programming.

APL (*A P*rogramming *L*anguage) was developed in 1967, under the auspices of IBM, to perform problem-solving work rapidly. It is a tremendously compact language, and it can only be used with a special keyboard.

Ada is a relatively new structured language initiated by the Department of Defense. It is still too early to guess what success the language will meet in the business and academic worlds.

Most business reports have a number of characteristics in common. They usually contain a title, page and column headings, a main body, column totals and subtotals, page footings, and so forth. **Report generators** capitalize on these similarities of format. Two well-known report generators are RPG and the so-called data management system (DMS) languages. IBM developed **RPG** (*R*eport *P*rogram *G*enerator) in the early 1960s to produce reports quickly on small computers. The DMS languages include a number of proprietary software packages that are often large-computer counterparts to RPG.

Word processing refers to the application of computer technology to the preparation of typed documents. These documents include letters, legal contracts, books and manuscripts, and so forth. Software packages are widely available to perform word processing on most computer systems.

Electronic worksheets first came to public notice in the late 1970s when a Harvard Business School student and a programmer friend produced a package called VisiCalc® (the *Visi*ble *Calc*ulator) for personal computers. Electronic worksheets enable users to prepare rapidly budgets and financial schedules on the computer after only a few hours of training.

Graphics packages make it possible for users to "draw" graphs painlessly, either on a CRT screen or hard-copy plotter. The user normally needs to specify only what type of output is desired, how it will be labeled, and the absolute size of each attribute to be represented.

Review Questions

1. Why is it easier today than in the past for users to write and run their own programs?
2. What are the primary differences between low-level, high-level, and very-high-level languages?
3. Why are assembly languages fading in importance?
4. What are the particular strengths of BASIC as a programming language?
5. What are the features of COBOL that make it attractive for business data-processing applications?
6. What accounts for the popularity of FORTRAN?
7. What need was Pascal created to fill?
8. Briefly describe PL/1, APL, and Ada.
9. What is the purpose of a report generator?
10. Why are electronic worksheets so popular?

Suggested Readings

Bent, Robert J., and George C. Sephares. *Business BASIC.* Monterey, Calif.: Brooks Cole, 1980.

Boillot, Michel, and Mona Boillot. *Understanding Structured COBOL.* St. Paul, Minn.: West, 1982.

Dock, V. Thomas. *Structured FORTRAN IV Programming.* St. Paul, Minn.: West, 1979.

Feingold, Carl. *Fundamentals of Structured COBOL Programming.* Dubuque, Iowa: Brown, 1983.

Gomez, Alfredo C. *The Basics of BASIC.* New York: Holt, 1983.

Kudlick, Michael D. *Assembly Language Programming for the IBM Systems 360 and 370.* Dubuque, Iowa: Brown, 1980.

LePage, Wilbur R. *Applied APL Programming.* Englewood Cliffs, N.J.: Prentice-Hall, 1978.

Mazlack, Lawrence. *Structured Problem Solving with Pascal.* New York: Holt, 1983.

Mullish, Henry, and Richard Kastenbaum. *RPG and RPGII Primer: A Modern Approach.* New York: Holt, 1982.

Olson, Jack L., and Wilson T. Price. *Elements of Structured COBOL,* 2nd ed. New York: Holt, 1982.

Pollack, Seymour, V., and Theodor D. Sterling. *A Guide to Structured Programming in PL/1,* 3rd ed. New York: Holt, 1980.

Price, Wilson T., *Using Business BASIC.* New York: Holt, 1983.

Wegner, Peter. *Programming with Ada: An Introduction by means of Graduated Examples.* Englewood Cliffs, N.J.: Prentice-Hall, 1980.

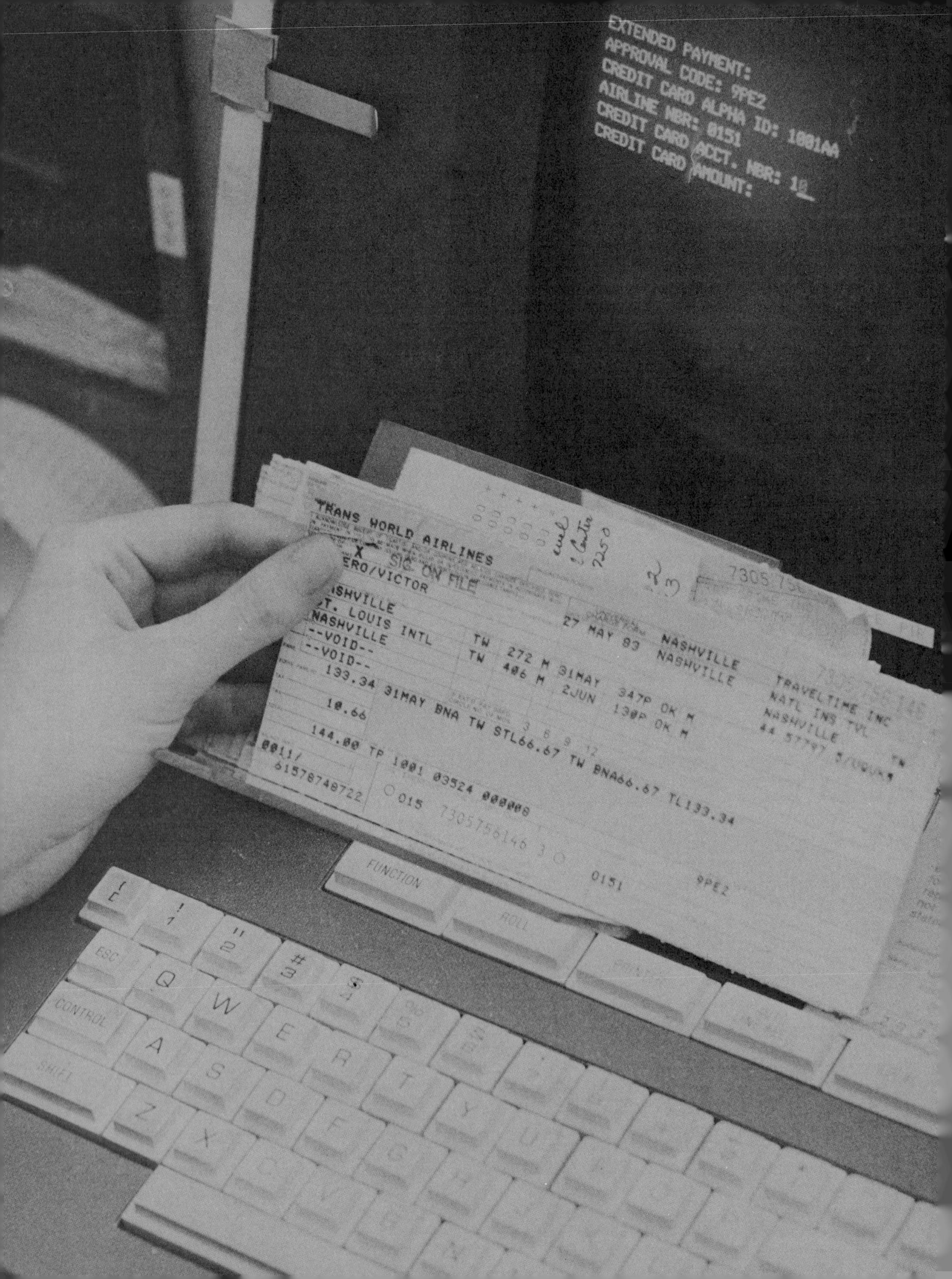
EXTENDED PAYMENT:
APPROVAL CODE: 9PE2
CREDIT CARD ALPHA ID: 1001AA
AIRLINE NBR: 0151
CREDIT CARD ACCT. NBR: 10
CREDIT CARD AMOUNT:
TRANS WORLD AIRLINES
SIG. ON FILE
NASHVILLE
ST. LOUIS INTL
NASHVILLE
--VOID--
--VOID--
27 MAY 83 NASHVILLE
NASHVILLE
TW 272 M 31MAY 347P OK M
TW 406 M 2JUN 130P OK M
133.34 31MAY BNA TW STL66.67 TW BNA66.67 TL133.34
10.66
144.00 TP 1001 03524 000008
TRAVELTIME INC
NATL INS TVL
NASHVILLE
015 7305756146 3 0
0151
9PE2
FUNCTION
ROLL
ESC
CONTROL
SHIFT

Chapter 12

Database Processing

Chapter Outline

OVERVIEW

You're a sales manager, and an order comes in for 10,000 units of one of your company's products. You need to find out quickly if the order can be filled from stock in inventory. If it can't, you need to know how long it will be before enough stock will be available. It would be convenient, you think, if you could sit down at a computer terminal and find the answer to both questions by using a single applications program. Unfortunately, access to two data files may be required: an inventory file and a vendor order file. If the files are structured in different ways, it may be difficult to answer both queries with a single program.

Until the development of database processing in the late 1960s, most data files and the applications programs that used them were created in an interdependent fashion. That is, the files were application-specific. When a FORTRAN program was written to satisfy a need, a FORTRAN-compatible data file was created to use with it. COBOL programs, written to satisfy other needs, used COBOL-compatible files; BASIC programs, BASIC-compatible files; and so forth. Each of these languages has its own rules for requiring how data are formatted into files. For example, COBOL requires each item of data to appear in specific programmer-defined columns of a record, whereas most versions of BASIC use commas rather than column positioning to separate each item of data.

Even if the same programming language were involved, however, the way a data file is organized might make it incompatible with a new applications program. If the file had been organized for sequential access, for example, it wouldn't work with a program that required direct access to data.

One way around these obstacles is to create a "duplicate" file—a restructured version of the original that is acceptable to a new applications program. But this solution can lead to waste and confusion as "duplicates" proliferate. Each version of a file, although it contains essentially the same data as the others, takes up storage space. And when one file is updated, all the others must be updated independently. If updates are made at different times or not done uniformly, computer reports can reflect conflicting information.

Database management systems offer a more efficient solution. In this chapter we will take a look at these powerful systems. We will start with a definition of the database approach. Then we'll discuss the ways in which database processing can be useful. We'll go on to explain how database management systems work, and we'll conclude with a discussion of approaches to database management.

THE DATABASE APPROACH

A **database management system (DBMS)** is a special software package for storing data and providing easy access to them. The data themselves are placed on disk in a **database,** which is simply an integrated collection of data. Data in the database are written compactly in a common format, in a manner allowing access in many ways. Users and programmers can gain access to the data they need by using a variety of programming languages. The DBMS serves as an interface between the applications programs and the data. The DBMS will locate the data and convert them from the common format into the format required by the applications program.

A DBMS is a large, complex, and expensive system with many software components. There are several different types commercially available, and systems are generally leased or purchased either from mainframe vendors or independent software houses. A database processing environment is illustrated in Figure 12-1.

WHY DATABASE PROCESSING?

A Simple Example

To appreciate why and when database processing can be useful, consider the following situation. A college has many computerized data files but does not use a DBMS. Whenever there is a need for developing a new application on the computer system, programs and data files are specially created for that application. Three files that are used frequently are the student master file, the faculty master file, and the class file. Characteristics of these files are given in Figure 12-2.

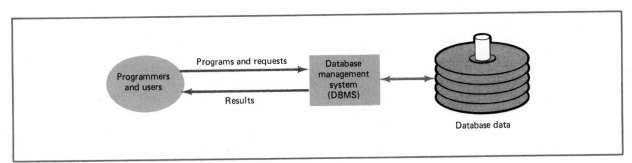

Figure 12-1.   The database environment.

As you can see, each of the files was established at a different time, by different people, to do different things. The files are all organized *sequentially* because the applications they were originally created for required only sequential access

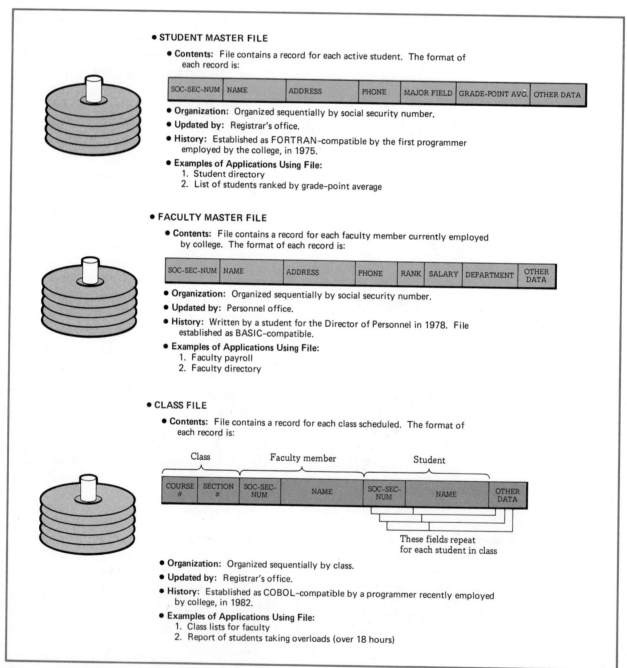

Figure 12-2.   Characteristics of three college files.

to records. The programming language originally chosen for each application reflects a variety of factors, including the skills of the programmer, the languages available on the computer system at the time of program development, and the preferences of data-processing management.

In their present form, the data in these three files can be used to perform many useful tasks. The student master file, for example, is the source for the annual student directory. To produce the directory, a FORTRAN program extracts the name, address, and phone number from each student record in the file, sorts the records alphabetically by name, and prints the results. The faculty master file and a BASIC program are used to prepare faculty payroll checks. And so forth. These applications are relatively straightforward—each involves sequential access to only one of the existing files.

Suppose, however, that a new application called for the use of two or more of these files. Perhaps the administration has a rule that only students with at least a 2.0 grade-point average can take advanced courses, and it wants to know whether the rule is being followed. To answer such a query requires checking *both* the student master file and the class file. But the student master file is FORTRAN-compatible, whereas the class file is COBOL-compatible. This produces a dilemma because the data-formatting requirements of the two languages are different. A common "quick" solution to this kind of problem is to have a programmer convert one of the data files into a format compatible with the other. This process would duplicate one of the files, however, wasting expensive programmer time and requiring extra storage space. A potentially more serious problem is that the answer to the query may be needed before a programmer can make the conversion and write a new applications program.

A look at Figure 12-2 should convince you that there are many important queries that would involve accessing more than one data file. For example:

- Are any students on academic probation taking overloads? (For example, is a student with a grade-point average of less than 1.5 taking more than five courses?)
- How many nonmajors are enrolled in each business class?
- What is the average number of credit hours taught by faculty in each department?

A second problem with the filing system in Figure 12-2 is that all the files permit only *sequential* access. Many important applications, however, require *direct* access. For example, if students frequently dropped by the registrar's office to find out whether they were enrolled in a specific class, the registrar would need to access the class file directly, by the name of the student. Developing an applications program to meet this need would require reorganizing the file to permit direct access.

A third major problem inherent in the filing system of Figure 12-2 is data redundancy. The social security numbers and names of each student and faculty member appear many times in storage. If, for example, John Smith took six courses, his name would appear seven times (once in the student master file and six times in the class file). This type of redundancy wastes a great deal of disk space. With a better management system, John Smith's name and social security number might need to appear only once.

In addition to wasted storage space, this kind of redundancy increases the chances of errors in the system. Suppose, for example, Professor Joan Lee leaves school before the beginning of the new semester. Joan teaches three computer science classes, all of which appear in the class file. She is also listed in the faculty master file. Upon her resignation, the personnel director purges Joan's record from the faculty master file and immediately notifies the registrar's office so it may update the class file. The registrar, however, misunderstands the name as "John Lee." As a result, John Lee, a philosophy professor, gets no class lists the first week of the semester, and the computer science department gets class lists for the departed Joan. Furthermore, a college financial administrator informally hears about this mixup at a dinner party and starts wondering how much faith to put in the computer reports the finance office receives weekly. The point here is that altering the same data item in several files increases both data-handling costs and the possibility of data-handling errors. Inaccurate information breeds distrust in computers, which may seriously impair organizational effectiveness.

A fourth major problem with the college's file management strategy is that the programs accessing the files are locked into a specific record structure. If a record structure changes for any reason—for example, with the addition of a new data field—the programs using that file generally must also be changed. A small modification in only one file might mean, for a large organization, changing dozens of programs and performing several lengthy tests on them to make sure they run correctly. Most organizations spend well over half of each programming dollar just maintaining old programs. It would be much better if

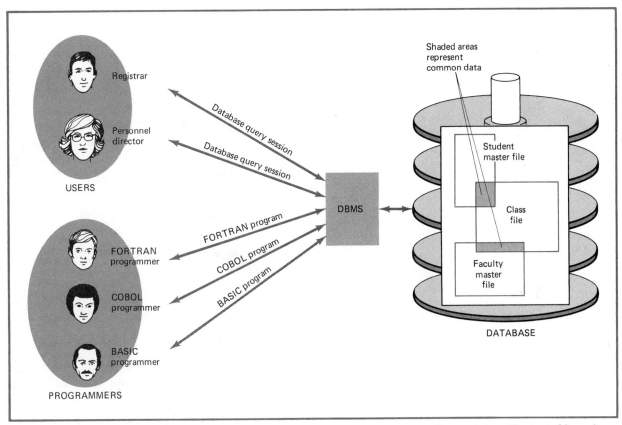

Figure 12-3. *Possible database scenario.* The three college data files shown in Figure 12-2 are illustrated here, in a database environment.

programs didn't need to change when a new field was added to records in a file—in other words, if the programs were somewhat independent of the structure of the data in the file.

Database processing can eliminate many of the disadvantages of the college's file strategy. A database solution for the college might look something like Figure 12-3. Programmers, communicating in different languages, interact with the database through the DBMS. The DBMS seeks the data required and makes them available for processing by the programs. Most database systems also provide a *query/update facility,* which permits both programmers and nonprogrammers easily to retrieve, add, delete, or modify data in the database by using simple, English-like commands. For example, if the personnel office wishes to find all faculty hired since January 1, 1980, it might issue a command as simple as

```
PRINT ALL FACULTY RECORDS
WHERE HIRING-DATE > 1/1/80
```

Advantages and Disadvantages of a DBMS

As suggested in the previous section, the major advantages of a DBMS are

- **Integrated data** Programs written in any language supported by the DBMS can theoretically make use of any data in the database. This use permits easy answering of queries or generation of reports involving many different data files.
- **Program-data independence** Programs often do not have to be changed when the structures of the data files they use change.
- **Nonredundant storage** Valuable disk space can be saved by eliminating redundant data.
- **Data integrity** Fewer errors are made because updates on data items shared by several files need be made only once.

These technical advantages translate into fewer personnel, fast response to problems, and the ability to adapt more rapidly to new and changing environments.

There are, however, several disadvantages to database processing that an organization should consider. The major disadvantage is cost. Significant expenses are normally incurred in the following areas:

- **Database software** A sophisticated DBMS is expensive. An organization may spend between $50,000 and $300,000 to obtain one for its mainframe. More affordable, but less powerful, database systems are also available for minicomputers and microcomputers.
- **New hardware** A DBMS requires a great deal of main memory when processing programs. Thus, an organization might find it necessary to upgrade to a bigger, more powerful computer system as a result of a DBMS acquisition.
- **Specialized personnel** Both database systems and the databases themselves are usually very complex. Highly specialized personnel are needed to develop and support them, and naturally, such people are expensive.
- **Conversion effort** Moving from a traditional file-oriented system to a database system often entails an expensive, large-scale conversion. Data must be reorga-

COSTAR: A Medical Database System

For the past decade, Massachusetts General Hospital has been involved with the development and implementation of COSTAR (*CO*mputer-*ST*ored *A*mbulatory *R*ecord), a computer-based medical information system. Programmed in, appropriately enough, MUMPS (*M*assachusetts General Hospital *U*tility *M*ulti-Programming *S*ystem), COSTAR manipulates an extensive patient history database.

A useful feature of the system is the Medical Query Language (MQL), a "friendly" query/update facility intended for doctors and other hospital personnel with little or no programming experience. With MQL, an authorized user can type in simple commands at a terminal and receive answers to complex requests within seconds. For example, a user who typed in commands like those at the right would get a list of all female patients over forty whom Dr. Miller had diagnosed as having hypertension in the past two years.

```
WHEN SEX=FEMALE
    AND AGE OVER 40
    AND CODE = HYPERTENSION
    AND PROVIDER = MILLER
    AND DATE AFTER (TODAY - 2 YEARS)
LIST NAME.
```

Doctors can also use the system to request medical records on specific patients before or during the patient's hospital visit.

COSTAR also ties the hospital's billing and receivables system into the patient database, making it an administrative tool as well as a medical one. When patients receive service, hospital personnel update their medical histories in the database. The system then prepares bills automatically. And administrators can tap the up-to-date financial data stored in the database for long-term planning as well as for daily operations.

nized and programs rewritten. Fortunately, this is a one-time expense.

Cost, however, is not the only problem. Database processing can increase a system's vulnerability to failure. Since the data are highly integrated in the database, a problem with one file might affect several others. At worst, the failure of a key element might render the whole system inactive.

Despite the disadvantages, however, thousands of organizations have installed DBMSs and many more are expected to follow suit. Database processing is not only here to stay but also rapidly spreading.

HOW A DBMS WORKS

There are two ways to approach how a DBMS works: from a practical perspective and from a technical one. Here we'll concentrate on practical considerations and address only those technical issues that are necessary for you to understand the practical matters involved.

The Database Administrator

The **database administrator (DBA)** is the person or group of people in charge of designing, implementing, and managing the ongoing operation of the database. The DBA sets up the database, assists applications programmers and users working with it, provides data security, and so forth. In other words, the DBA manages the overall operation of the database system. Although the DBA controls the design of the database, he or she does not have direct knowledge of any of the actual data values stored there. Authorized users and programmers manage these data values themselves.

Data Description: Setting Up the Database

One of the most important jobs of the DBA is **data description.** This job involves organizing the data in the database so that programmers and users have access to them, so that they are stored as efficiently as possible, and so that the security of the database is maintained. There are two levels of data description—logical and physical.

- The **logical (conceptual) data description** is a description of the data from the point of view of programmers and users.

- The **physical data description** is a description of the way the data are actually stored on disk. In other words, it is a description of where the data items are physically located.

These two levels of description are needed because the way programmers and users think of data may not correspond to the way they are stored. For example, a programmer might think of an address as consisting of a street address field, a city field, a state field, and a zip code field. Yet when data corresponding to these fields are stored on disk, they may be placed in four physically different locations that have no apparent logical relationship to each other as far as the programmer is concerned.

The way the data files are physically stored in secondary memory is much more machine-oriented than the user's or programmer's logical conception of them. The DBMS might store the files in a creative way to minimize the use of storage space and to provide rapid access.

The concepts of logical and physical descriptions have their counterparts in a public library. The card catalogue contains a logical description of the organization of the books in the library (by Library of Congress reference numbers). This logical description may be completely unrelated to the way the books are physically organized on the shelves. To find a book, you first determine its logical description from the card indexes, and then its physical location from a floor plan of the library.

The DBMS itself acts as the interface between these two types of descriptions. When a user, referring to the logical description, asks for specific data in terms of records and fields, the DBMS translates the request into the physical description, locates the appropriate data in storage, and makes them available.

The logical description of many databases also has two levels. At one level is a description of the organization of the *entire* database. This global data description is often called a **schema.** At another level are descriptions of specific *portions* of the database. These descriptions are often called **subschemas.** Every subschema is a subset of the schema. Each one describes all the data used in a specific program or set of programs.

Subschemas are particularly useful for control purposes. It is unwise, for security reasons, to allow users and programmers to see the entire schema. They should be allowed only enough knowledge of the database to do their jobs. The people responsible for writing or using a mailing list program, for example, should not have knowledge about sensitive information such as faculty salaries.

The DBA creates, stores, and modifies schemas and subschemas with the help of a **data definition language (DDL).** In other words, the DBA uses a special database language (or languages) to create the logical descriptions of the database. There are also languages that help automatically organize data onto disk. With such a facility, called a **device media control language (DMCL),** the DBA constructs the physical description of the database.

Data Manipulation: Using the Database

As we said, the DBA controls the design of the database but does not control the actual values of the data. The DBA, for example, specifies how large a data item is to be (for example, can it be 20 characters long or 30?); whether it consists of letters, numbers, or both; and so forth. Once such issues of data definition have been decided, it is up to authorized users or programmers to assign actual data values to the fields in each of the records. The use of these data to prepare reports, answer customers' requests, and the like, is known as **data manipulation.** Whereas data definition is the responsibility of the DBA, data manipulation is the job of users and programmers.

There are generally two ways to manipulate data in a DBMS—with a query/update facility and with a data manipulation language. The **query/update facility** is a program that is generally purchased as part of the DBMS. It enables users to extract information and update records easily. The **data manipulation language (DML)** allows an organization's programmers to create new applications programs which use the database.

The DML is simply a set of commands that enables the language the programmer normally works with to function in a database environment. For example, if the programmer writes programs in COBOL, a COBOL DML must be used. The DML may consist of thirty or so commands, which are used by the programmer to interact with data in the database (see Figure 12-4 for a sample of these commands). Thus, a COBOL program in a database environment consists of a mixture of standard COBOL statements and COBOL DML statements, such as the

DML Command	Purpose
CREATE	Creates a record
STORE	Stores data in the database
FETCH	Retrieves data from the database
INSERT	Inserts a record
MODIFY	Changes data in a record
FIND	Locates a record
DELETE	Deletes a record

Figure 12-4. *Some typical DML commands.*

small block of code that follows which deletes an employee's record from a database:

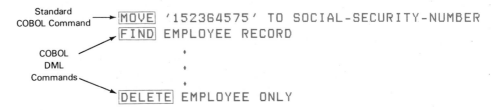

```
Standard
COBOL Command ────► MOVE '152364575' TO SOCIAL-SECURITY-NUMBER
                ┌─► FIND EMPLOYEE RECORD
 COBOL          │           •
  DML           │           •
Commands ───────┘           •
                ┌─► DELETE EMPLOYEE ONLY
```

The program containing this mixture of statements is then fed to the DBMS's COBOL *precompiler,* as shown in Figure 12-5. The precompiler translates this program into a standard COBOL program, which can then be executed with the regular COBOL compiler available on the system.

The high-level languages which are supported by a DML are called **host languages.** These are the languages that are used in a DBMS environment. Several of them may be available on any particular system. Languages that a DBMS commonly employs as hosts are COBOL, FORTRAN, PL/1, and BASIC.

Other Database Features

Database systems normally also include software to prevent unauthorized access, to circumvent conflicts that may arise when two users need the same data at the same time, to inform users or programmers about characteristics of data in the database, and to provide for backup and recovery if the system fails.

Preventing Unauthorized Access.   Database users (and programmers) can protect files, records, and fields with passwords. Also, the DBA can allow some users to make modifications to certain fields of files, whereas other users of those files are only

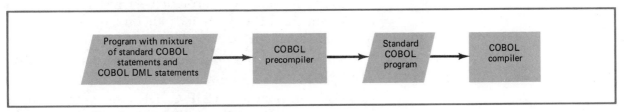

Figure 12-5.   Use of a COBOL precompiler.

permitted query capability. For example, in an airline database, a regular clerk or agent may not be allowed to rebook a special-rate passenger on an alternate flight, but a high-level supervisor (who knows the password) can.

Concurrent Access.   In many cases, users need access to the same data at more or less the same time. This can cause several problems. For example:

- Suppose a single seat remains available on a flight. Two agents seize it at the same moment and sell it to different customers.
- Suppose a program is tallying a series of customer balances in a database. When this program is halfway finished, another program transfers $5000 from account 001 (which has already been tallied by the first program) to account 999 (which hasn't). Thus, the first program will "double count" the $5000 and obtain erroneous results.

To prevent such problems, most database systems allow users to place a temporary "lock" on certain blocks of data, to ensure that there will be no other modifications to these data while they are being processed.

Data Dictionary Facility.   The **data dictionary** is similar in concept and organization to an ordinary dictionary in that it contains definitions for an alphabetical list of words. The words are those encountered in the company's data-processing environment. Among them would be, for example, names of fields, records, files, schemas, subschemas, programs, and so on. Thus, if we look up the field ZIP-CODE in the data dictionary for a typical DBMS we might find

- The definition of ZIP-CODE. This definition would probably include a short description of what ZIP-CODE means as well as supplementary information, such as the number of characters in ZIP-CODE and whether or not they are numeric, alphabetic, or something else.
- The names of all the programs and subschemas that use ZIP-CODE.
- Any alternate names that ZIP-CODE assumes in programs. For example, ZIP-CODE may be called ZCODE in program

T-6742 and ZIPPER in program B-606. These alternate names are known as *aliases*.

The data dictionary facility is particularly helpful if, say, a data field changes its properties. For example, if we need to change ZIP-CODE from a 5-digit to 9-digit field at some point in the future, we can use the dictionary facility to supply the names of all the programs which must be appropriately modified.

Backup and Recovery. Software is normally provided with the DBMS so that if the computer system "crashes" for any reason, vital data are not destroyed and processing can resume later at the approximate point of interruption. For example, suppose a customer in a banking database environment is in the process of transferring $10,000 from a savings to a checking account. Suddenly, the computer "crashes," after the savings account has been debited but before the checking account has been credited with the amount. When the computer has been brought up again, the partial transaction would probably be "rolled back" to put both accounts in their original states. Then the entire transaction would be started over.

APPROACHES TO DATABASE MANAGEMENT

Now that you know how a database environment operates, it's time to consider an issue that contributes to the overall performance of commercial database packages—the way in which they organize data.

Relationships among data can take many forms, which are often called **data structures.** Three types of data structures important in database processing are

- Hierarchical (or tree) structures
- Network structures
- Relational structures

An example of each of these appears in Figure 12-6.

In a **hierarchical data structure** relationships among types of data records always take the form of one-to-many. In

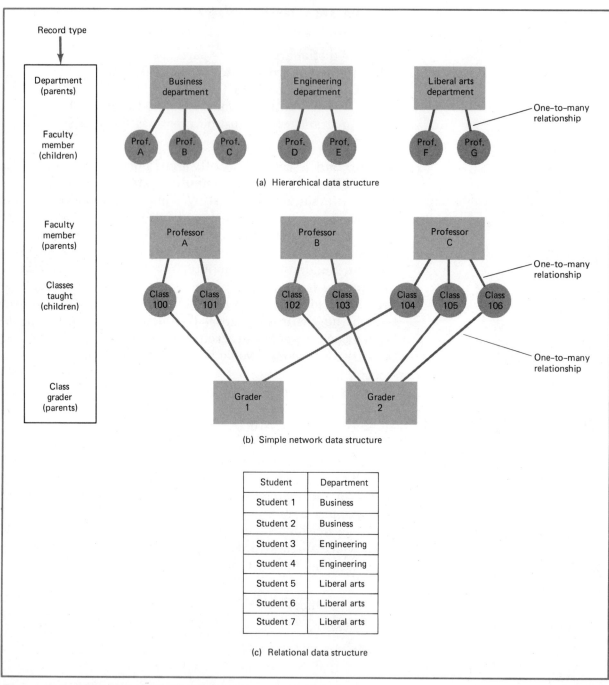

Figure 12-6. *Database data structures.*

the figure, note that each department can have many faculty members, whereas each faculty member may be affiliated with only one department. In studying data structures, we often use the terms *parents* and *children* to characterize relationships. For example, each department in Figure 12-6a is a parent and each professor is a child. In a hierarchical structure, a child can never have more than one parent, although a parent can have more than one child.

The **simple network data structure** in Figure 12-6b differs from the hierarchical one in that children can have more than one parent. For example, class 100 (a child) is affiliated with professor A and grader 1 (parents). As in a hierarchical structure, however, the relationship among record types remains one-to-many. Also, in a simple network structure, a child can't have two or more parents from the same record type. So class 100 couldn't be taught by two professors or graded by two graders.

The **relational data structure** is sometimes called a *flat* (or *two-way*) *table structure.* The table contains rows (records) and columns (fields of the records). You should note in Figure 12-6c that although we have organized the "student name/ department" relationship as a table, this particular relationship could also have been structured hierarchically, with departments as parents and students as children. This illustrates an interesting point: data can be structured in more than one way. How we choose to structure the data depends both on how easy they are to represent with any of the possible structures and on the particular capabilities of the database system available with regard to these data structures.

Commercial database systems differ in the ability and ease with which they can manipulate each of these structures. Traditionally, most database systems have relied on hierarchical and network structures. IMS (*I*nformation *M*anagement *S*ystem), a major database product offering of IBM, works best with hierarchical structuring and simple types of networks. IDMS (*I*ntegrated *D*atabase *M*anagement *S*ystem), ADABAS (*A*daptable *DA*ta *BA*se System), and System 2000, three other popular packages, employ network-type modeling. Relational database systems are becoming increasingly popular and are regarded by some as "the wave of the future." Relational database products permit the use of more powerful DBMS software, so that they are much simpler to use than their hierarchical or network database counterparts.

tomorrow

RELATIONAL DATABASES: THE WAY OF THE FUTURE

A major impediment to the widespread use of database systems has been ease of use. This deficiency historically has extended from the design of the database by the database administrator right down to the manipulation of the query language by the end user. Relational database systems have been developed largely to overcome this problem. The early relational systems, though simple, were unable to manipulate data quickly in large commercial-level applications. Recently, through improved hardware and software techniques, viable relational systems have started to appear more commonly in applications environments. The most popular relational query language is IBM's SQL (*S*tructured *Q*uery *L*anguage), designed for use with IBM's relational database system, System R.

Data in relational databases are stored in tables, such as those in the accompanying figure. Each table has a name, such as EMPLOYEE and OFFICE in the example. These tables are similar in concept to *files*. The rows of the tables are like

EMPLOYEE		
NAME	OFFICE-LOCATION	DEPARTMENT
Doney	Phoenix	Acctg.
Black	Denver	Sales
James	Cleveland	Sales
Giles	San Diego	Acctg.
Smith	Miami	Acctg.
Fink	San Diego	Sales
. . .	. . .	. . .

OFFICE	
LOCATION	MANAGER
San Diego	Hurt
Cleveland	Holmes
Miami	Jonas
Phoenix	Alexis
. . .	. . .

Two database relations.

Summary and Key Terms

A **database management system (DBMS)** is a special software package for storing data and providing easy access to them. There are several different types commercially available, and systems are generally leased or purchased either from mainframe vendors or independent software houses.

The data themselves are placed on disk in a database. A **database** is an integrated collection of data. Users and programmers in a database environment can gain access to the data they need by using a variety of programming languages.

The major advantages of a DBMS include integrated data, program/data independence, nonredundant storage, and data integrity. These technical advantages translate into fewer personnel, fast response to problems, and an ability to adapt more rapidly to new and changing environments. The major disad-

records, and the columns are like *fields*. Many of the tables have one or more columns in common with other tables. It is through these columns that the data in the tables are *related*. In our example, the EMPLOYEE and OFFICE tables are related through the "city" column in each (called OFFICE-LOCATION in one and LOCATION in the other).

If we wanted to retrieve the names of all employees in the San Diego office, we could use a SQL command such as

```
SELECT NAME
  FROM EMPLOYEE
WHERE OFFICE-LOCATION = 'SAN DIEGO'
```

The system would access the EMPLOYEE table to select the names of all employees who worked in San Diego. This query, as you can see, involves only one table.

The power of relational database systems, however, rests in their ability to link the data in more than one table. Suppose, for example, we wanted to know which employees worked under the office manager named Jonas. We would enter a command such as

```
SELECT NAME
  FROM EMPLOYEE
WHERE OFFICE IS IN
  (SELECT LOCATION FROM OFFICE
  WHERE MANAGER = 'JONAS')
```

The system would find Jonas in the OFFICE table, determine that he or she managed the office in Miami, and then use the EMPLOYEE table to find all employees who worked in Miami. In other words, the system would *relate* these tables to retrieve the needed information.

This principal, applied on a large scale to databases with many tables and many interrelations, makes possible the efficient retrieval of information. And the simple commands of a language like SQL make relational systems relatively easy to use. Commands similar to the ones shown here make it possible to modify, insert, or delete entries or tables in the database as well as retrieve information.

vantage of a DBMS is cost. Significant expenses are normally incurred in purchasing database software, upgrading hardware, acquiring specialized personnel, and converting to a database system. Despite the disadvantages, however, thousands of organizations have installed DBMSs and many more are expected to follow suit.

The **database administrator (DBA)** is the person or group of people in charge of designing, implementing, and managing the ongoing operation of the database. The DBA sets up the database, assists applications programmers and users working with it, provides for data security, and so forth.

One of the most important jobs of the DBA is **data description.** This job involves organizing the data in the database so that programmers and users have access to them, so that they are stored as efficiently as possible, and so that the security of the database is maintained. There are two types of data description: the logical (conceptual) description and the physical description.

The **logical (conceptual) data description** is a description of the data from the point of view of programmers and users. The logical description of many databases has two levels. At one level is a description of the organization of the *entire* database. This global data description is often called a **schema.** At the other level are descriptions of specific *portions* of the database. These descriptions are often called **subschemas.** Each subschema describes all the data used in a specific program or set of programs. The DBA creates, stores, and modifies schemas and subschemas with the help of a **data definition language (DDL).**

The **physical data description** is a description of the way the data are actually stored on disk. The way the data files are physically stored in secondary memory is much more machine-oriented than the user/programmer logical conception of them. A **device media control language (DMCL)** is used by the DBA to construct the physical description of the database.

The use of data to prepare reports, answer customers' requests, and the like is known as **data manipulation.** There are generally two ways to manipulate data in the DBMS—with a query/update facility and with a data manipulation language. The **query/update facility** is a program generally purchased as part of the DBMS. It allows users to extract information and update records easily. The **data manipulation language (DML)** allows an organization's programmers to create new applications programs which use the database. The high-level languages supported by a DML are called **host languages.** Languages that a DBMS commonly employs as hosts are COBOL, FORTRAN, PL/1, and BASIC.

Database systems normally also include software to prevent unauthorized access, to circumvent any conflicts that result from concurrent accesses, to inform users or programmers about characteristics of data in the database (called a **data dictionary** facility), and to provide for backup and recovery if the system fails.

Relationships among data can take many forms, often called **data structures.** Three types of data structures important in database processing are **hierarchical data structures, simple network data structures,** and **relational data structures.** Commercial database systems differ in the ability and ease with which they can manipulate each of these structures.

Review Questions

1. What is a database management system?
2. Identify the advantages and disadvantages of database management systems.
3. What is the role of the database administrator?
4. What is the difference between the logical (conceptual) description and physical description of the database?
5. Why are subschemas used in database processing?
6. What is the difference between data description and data manipulation?
7. How do database management systems solve the problem of concurrent access?
8. What is a data dictionary?
9. Differentiate between the three types of data structures cited in this chapter.

Suggested Readings

Bradley, James. *Introduction to Data Base Management in Business.* New York: Holt, 1983.

Kroenke, David. *Database Processing,* 2nd ed. Palo Alto, Calif.: SRA, 1983.

Martin, James. *An End User's Guide to Data Base.* Englewood Cliffs, N.J.: Prentice-Hall, 1981.

Martin, James. *Strategic Data Planning Methodologies.* Englewood Cliffs, N.J.: Prentice-Hall, 1982.

Ullman, Jeffrey D. *Principles of Database Systems.* Potomac, Md.: Computer Science Press, 1980.

Module D

COMPUTER SYSTEMS

This module integrates many of the concepts from earlier chapters, which introduced various parts of computer systems. A computer system consists of the computer itself, as well as any support equipment, programs, data, procedures, and people found in its environment. In other words, all the components that contribute to making the computer a useful tool can be said to be part of a computer system.

Chapters 13 and 14 discuss various types of computer systems and how they may be acquired. Chapter 13 focuses on personal uses of computer systems, and Chapter 14 on commercial uses. Chapters 15 and 16 discuss how these systems are developed, from preliminary investigation to implementation.

Chapter 13

Personal Computer Systems

OVERVIEW

Often affordably priced between a few hundred and a few thousand dollars, personal computer systems have been marketed for home use since the mid-1970s. People acquire such systems for a variety of purposes: to play video games, to manage personal finances such as bank accounts and taxes, to maintain mailing lists of friends and acquaintances, to prepare correspondence and manuscripts, and so on. In the last few years, these systems have been installed in businesses where they are used for such commercial purposes as managing records and preparing mailing lists.

Today, personal-computer-based processing is one of the fastest growing areas of the computer field, expanding about 40 to 60 percent annually. Some industry observers predict that by the mid-1980s there will be as many as 50 million systems in operation. As the processing capability of such systems increases, and their cost declines even more dramatically, they will become attractive and affordable to larger numbers of people. You will probably own a personal computer in your lifetime.

We begin the chapter by covering the common types of hardware and applications software found with personal computer systems. Next, we discuss the systems software available for these computers. We then talk about how you would shop for these components in order to acquire a configuration of hardware and software appropriate to your needs. We close with a discussion of the organizations and publications through which you can learn more about personal computer systems.

In Window 7, a panel of photographs further illustrates the nature and use of personal computers.

HARDWARE

Many personal computer systems contain at least five pieces of hardware: the processor itself, a secondary storage device, a video display unit, a keyboard, and a printer. In some systems, all or most of these devices are housed in a single hardware unit, whereas in others you can select each device separately. Figure 13-1 shows two different personal computer systems.

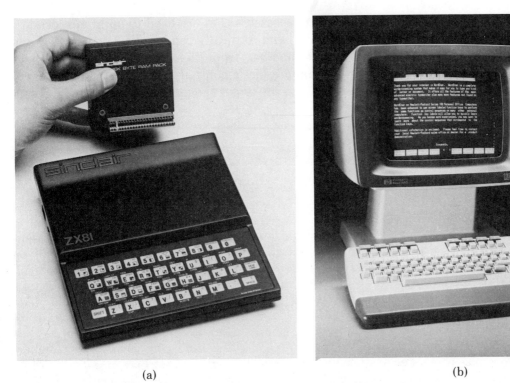

(a)   (b)

Figure 13-1.   Two microcomputer systems. (a) The Timex Sinclair ZX81. (b) The Hewlett Packard HP-125.

The Processor Unit

Microprocessors.   **Microcomputers,** as we mentioned in Chapter 1, are computers driven by microprocessors. A **microprocessor** is a CPU that is engraved on a silicon chip no larger than your fingernail. Microprocessors are the central processors in microcomputer systems as well as in such products as electronic scales, digital watches, children's learning toys, microwave ovens, and video games. **Personal computers** are, technically, microcomputers used by individuals to meet various *personal* needs, whether at work or at home. Because the terms *personal computer* and *microcomputer* are so often used synonymously in practice, we will use the two terms interchangeably in this chapter.

Microprocessors can be classified by the number of bits they can manipulate per operation. The microprocessors that power electronic gadgets such as watches, toys, and so forth typically manipulate a small number of bits at one time, often 2 or 4. The microprocessors that are used to build microcomputers, on the other hand, typically can handle 8 or 16 bits at once. As you may remember from the discussion of word size in Chapter 4, the more bits a computer can manipulate at a time, the faster it is, and the larger the main memory it can accommodate.

tomorrow

HOW MUCH POWER CAN THE MICRO PACK?

If the computing industry continues to evolve at the rate at which it has during the past fifty years, it is entirely possible that tomorrow's microcomputers will pack the power of today's mainframes. What this means is that within a scant ten to twenty years, you may have at your disposal the computing power of many of today's corporations. You'll also benefit from more sophisticated hardware and software.

Today's personal computer systems are burdened by two severe limitations, small memory and slow speed. Small memories limit the size of the programs microcomputers can handle. So-called "user-friendly" programs, which many say are the key to even greater acceptance of personal computers, are long, somewhat complex, programs. Consequently, they require large amounts of memory. Unfortunately, all that extra friendliness demands a lot of storage, which limits the ability of the personal computer system to do work requiring an abundance of user-helpful tasks.

The friendlier programs become, the faster they'll need to be in order to employ certain forms of "intelligent thinking." To simulate human thought, a program requires high computing speeds in order to execute instructions rapidly. According to one estimate, if machines are to mimic the human mind, they must be able to execute commands at the rate of trillions of instructions per second. The fastest computers today are only able to execute billions of instructions per second. Nonetheless, even the most conservative futurists predict tremendous increases in both the speed and memory of personal computers.

Personal computers of the future will also have powerful peripherals. As the economics and technology of peripherals improve, it will be even easier to run a business from your home than it is today. Writers, for example, may take over some of the functions of their publishers. They may be able to create and produce a book almost entirely at home. They may digitize photos and artwork and store them in the computer. Home printers might deliver output much like that of today's digital phototypesetters. Electronic mailboxes may permit almost instantaneous transmission of manuscripts to and from proofreaders. This and many other forms of enterprise once the province of business organizations may become possible for individuals.

A microchip of today (inset) *compared with a UNIVAC I system of the 1950s.*

Many types of microprocessor chips are available for small systems, including the Intel 8080 and 8088, the Zilog Z80, and the Motorola 6800. The Intel 8080 is an 8-bit chip, whereas the 8088 is 16 bits, making it four to six times faster than the 8080. The type of chip in your microprocessor can greatly affect the capability of the machine. Operating systems are written to serve a specific chip, and an applications program that works with one operating system generally does not function on another, unless modified. So if the chip that supports your computer is rare, you may have difficulty finding applications programs that run on it.

RAM. The primary memory of microcomputers is also etched onto silicon chips, and often is built into the microprocessor chip itself. As we mentioned in Chapter 4, this kind of primary memory is commonly called **Random Access Memory (RAM).**

Most personal computer systems in use today have between 16 and 64 kilobytes of RAM, although powerful systems with up to 512 kilobytes or more are available. In addition, most systems allow you to expand the capacity of main memory. Thus, if you buy a 16-kilobyte RAM computer and later want to expand it to 32 kilobytes, you can usually do so, although with some systems, you have to send the whole computer unit back to the manufacturer. In other cases, you need only buy another circuit board, remove the cover from the computer unit, and plug the board into the appropriate mount.

Most microcomputer RAM is *volatile,* which means that the contents of memory are lost when the computer is shut off.

ROM. As we discussed in Chapter 4, **ROM** stands for **read-only memory.** It consists of nonerasable hardware modules that contain program software. You can neither write over these programs (that's why they're called "read-only") nor can you destroy their contents when you shut off the computer's power (that is, they're *nonvolatile*).

Often, key systems software such as the operating system are stored in detachable ROM modules in the computer's hardware unit. This arrangement makes the operating system available to perform useful tasks at the moment that the computer's power is turned on. Some computer systems even enable you to purchase your favorite software packages, such as BASIC or electronic worksheets, in ROM form. If you buy packages in this form, you avoid having to load them from disk or tape every time you want to use them.

Many microprocessor chips also contain some ROM to perform various system functions. The 8-bit Motorola MC6805 microprocessor shown in Figure 13-2 contains 64 kilobytes of RAM as well as 2.5 kilobytes of on-chip ROM.

The Microcomputer Unit. The microprocessor chip, circuitry to the input/output devices, and any RAM and ROM modules supplementing the memory already on the chip are housed in the microcomputer hardware unit. A number of these microcomputer units are available for home use. In fact, there are currently *hundreds* of microcomputers commercially available, with dozens more being introduced each month. A diverse selection of microcomputers is featured in Window 7.

Secondary Storage

As with larger computers, the primary memory of microcomputers can hold only the data and programs the computer is currently processing. If you want to keep data and programs for repeated use, you must have a secondary storage unit.

Both tape and disk devices are available for use with personal computers. Digital cassette tapes can be mounted on a standard portable cassette recorder. However, despite this convenience, tape (especially cassette tape) is a much slower

Figure 13-2.   A microprocessor chip.

medium than disk, as you may recall from Chapter 5. Disk units are mechanically faster and they permit direct access. On the typical microcomputer system, disk storage is often provided by 5¼-inch floppy disks and one or two disk drives. Because floppy disk systems are so much more powerful and versatile than cassette systems, the better and more sophisticated software is generally available only on disk. However, at $300 to $500 apiece, floppy disk drives are far more expensive than cassette devices, which usually sell for well under $100.

In Chapter 5, we also mentioned the arrival on the market of Winchester disk drives for microcomputer systems. In this hard-disk device, the disk access arms and read/write heads are all sealed in the same container. Winchester systems are much faster and can store much more than floppy disk systems, but they are fairly expensive. Although most personal computer users don't need and can't afford Winchesters, they are becoming very popular for business applications.

The Keyboard

For most people, a personal computer system would be useless without a keyboard, since it is often the main vehicle for input. Potential buyers should carefully evaluate keyboards, considering several factors.

First, not all keyboards have the same key arrangement. Although the keys on most are in a format similar to that of a conventional typewriter, other formats are available. Second, the keyboards of most microcomputer systems have several function keys, which communicate specific software commands when they are pressed. A "delete" key, for example, deletes characters from the screen, and a "page forward" key flips through pages of a file one at a time. The number of such keys, as well as their functions and placement, vary widely among manufacturers. The use of function keys is shown in Figure 13-3. Third, keyboards differ with respect to touch. Some are sculpted to match the contour of the fingertips, whereas others, such as that on the Timex Sinclair (shown in Figure 13-1), have a flat membrane panel with touch-sensitive areas corresponding to keys. Additionally, manufacturers space keys differently, so that keys that feel just right to one person may feel too far apart to another. Finally, some keyboards are separate units that can be placed wherever convenient, even in the user's lap, whereas others are built into the display unit of the system.

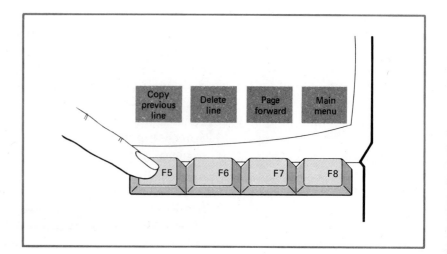

Figure 13-3. *The use of function keys.* Function keys enable you to input instructions to the computer by depressing a single key instead of by typing a complicated set of commands.

The Display Unit

Almost every personal computer system has a video display unit, or monitor. A **monitor** is simply a display terminal without a keyboard. It resembles a television set with only one channel. It allows you to see your input as you enter it and the computer's output as the computer responds. The features of monitors are essentially the same as those of keyboard-oriented display terminals, which we discussed in Chapter 6.

Many microcomputer systems allow you to use a television set as a monitor. A small device called an RF-modulator converts the computer's output to a form that can be received over a channel on your television set. Unfortunately, the standard television set does not provide as clear a picture as a monitor specially designed for a computer system. So although your home television might be adequate for video games, it is probably not suitable for applications such as word processing, where you must be able to examine small characters of text with care, perhaps for long periods of time.

Two-color monitors are available for as little as $100, whereas full-color monitors may cost several hundred dollars.

The Printer

If you are using your computer system for any purpose other than playing computer games, you'll probably need some form of printed output. You may want a copy of a computer program you've just debugged, a recipe to send to a friend, a paper you've written, and so on.

Most printers adapted for use with home computers are *serial printers,* which we discussed extensively in Chapter 6. Serial printers output a character at a time. Generally, these devices range in price from $300 to $2000, depending largely on whether a dot-matrix or solid-font (full character) printer is chosen. Solid-font printers are generally more expensive than dot-matrix printers.

Connecting Peripheral Devices to a Personal Computer

The number of peripheral devices that a microcomputer can support is limited by the storage capacity of its primary memory, as well as by the number and arrangement of the slots (or *ports*) into which peripherals can be plugged. In Figure 13-4, which shows a hypothetical configuration that closely resembles the IBM Personal Computer system, you can observe some of the principles involved in connecting peripherals to the computer.

In the system shown in Figure 13-4, there are built-in attachments for a cassette tape unit, a speaker, and a keyboard. The user plugs these peripherals into the ports allocated to them. Each port is designed to accommodate a specific peripheral device.

The computer shown also has five expansion slots, which can accept any of a variety of specific peripheral devices. Among the devices that can be added to personal computer systems are a game-control adapter, a modem (for teleprocessing), printers (for both draft-quality and letter-quality output), secondary storage devices, monitors (both color and black-and-white), and modules to expand primary memory. These devices must compete for the available expansion slots. Each slot can accommodate an adapter, and each adapter can support a limited number of specific devices. Ultimately, however, the number of peripherals is restricted by the capacity of primary memory.

Personal computer systems differ in the nature and number of built-in attachments and expansion slots. Also, systems vary in the number and types of peripherals that may be configured to adapters.

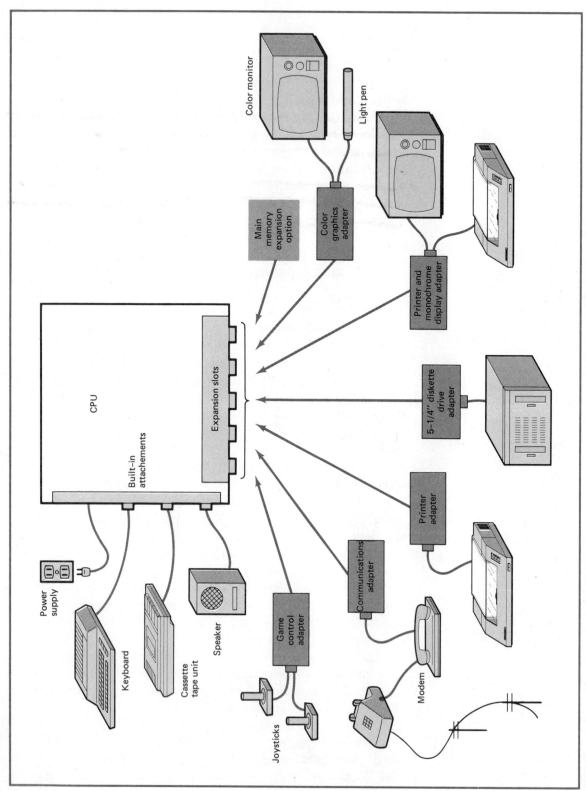

Figure 13-4. *Connecting peripheral devices to a microcomputer.* The system shown has three built-in attachments for a keyboard, a cassette tape unit, and a speaker. It also has five expansion slots that can accommodate a variety of other peripheral devices.

PERSONAL COMPUTER SYSTEMS

Here come the PCs!

Personal computers (or PCs) have taken the country by storm, with sales approaching the $10 billion mark. Used by young and old alike, personal computer systems can cost anywhere from a few hundred to several thousands of dollars. As you peer through Window 7, you'll see a variety of personal computing equipment and applications.

1. An enthusiastic user of an Apple computer system.

PORTABLE PERSONAL COMPUTERS Many personal computers are specifically designed so that you can easily carry them from place to place.

3. The Commodore 64 computer, shown here with an array of peripherals, combines a substantial internal memory with a low price.

2. The cigar-box-sized Epson HX-20 has 16K RAM, 32K ROM (both expandable), a built-in printer, a scrollable screen, and a micro cassette drive in its upper right corner.

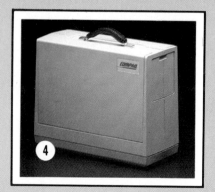

5. The COMPAQ Portable Computer and its carrying case (4). With 128K bytes of main memory, a 16-bit microprocessor, and two built-in disk drives, this system is specifically configured for business and professional applications.

DESK-TOP SYSTEMS Do you have a spare desk or table top in your home or office for some computing equipment? If so, perhaps one of the systems pictured below (which constitute a very small sample of the desk-top systems currently available) might be the answer to your computing needs.

6. Apple //e computer with Monitor III, two disk drives, and a printer. A wide range of peripherals and software has made Apple computers very popular.

7. The Televideo 970 computer features a tiltable screen with a 132-column display. Like almost all of the other personal computers in its class, it can be linked to a variety of support devices.

8. Apple's Lisa is one of the most powerful personal computers currently on the market. It features a number of advanced graphical techniques that simulate the way people handle office work at their desks.

9. The IBM Personal Computer is one of the best-selling computers of all time. Available for as little as $1500, it can be used at work, school, or home.

PERIPHERALS FOR PERSONAL COMPUTERS When personal computers first appeared, there was little by way of support equipment to go with them. Today, this is no longer the case, as the rich variety of peripherals shown here indicates.

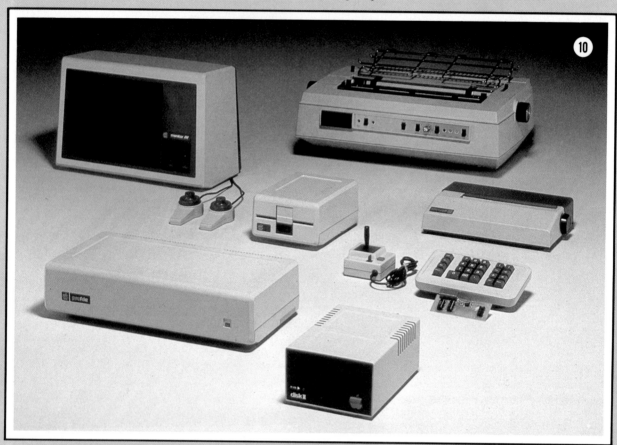

10. A small sample of the peripheral devices produced by Apple Computer, Inc.

11. A floppy disk drive. Many personal computer systems have expansion interfaces that allow you to increase the number of drives on your system as new processing needs develop.

12. A letter-quality "daisywheel" printer is the ideal output device for attractive business correspondence.

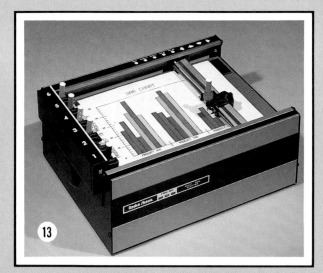

13. A color plotter produces multicolored hard copy.

14. A portable terminal. You can take this unit "on the road" with you, to communicate remotely with any computer at the end of a phone line.

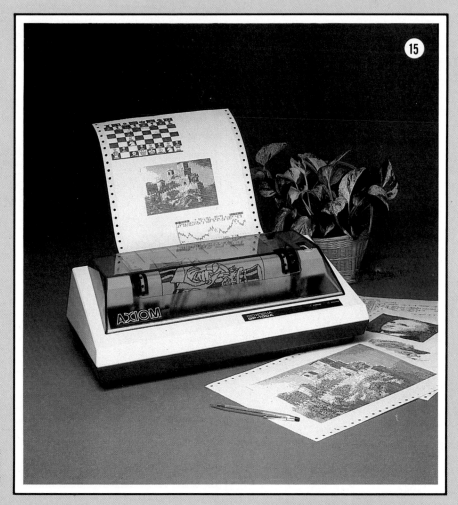

15. Axiom's GP-100 dot-matrix printer can be hooked up to a variety of personal computers to produce attractive graphic output.

16. In the classroom.

17. At home, for business and personal uses.

USING PERSONAL COM-
PUTERS Shown on this page
are some of the more common
uses. For a more exotic application, inspect the facing page.

18. At conferences.

19. As a desk-top office tool.

20, 21. The "House of the Future at Ahwatukee," in Phoenix, Arizona, features an advanced, computerized home management system designed by Motorola. The system can be used to reduce energy consumption, maximize the home's "comfortability," turn lights on or off as a person enters or leaves a room, provide extensive security, greet people by name as they enter the home, and provide all the usual types of personal computing services for the household. For example, if the system senses that a room in the home is too hot, it checks the outside temperature to see if the appropriate doors and windows should be opened (automatically, of course). If the outside air is too warm, and the humidity level in the room is suitable, the system may elect to turn on the evaporative cooler. If it is too humid, the central air conditioning will probably be activated.

COMPUTER STORES

22, 23. Firms such as Computerland and Radio Shack have hundreds of stores nationwide catering to personal computer users.

24. The interior of a Computerland store in Oakland, California. The store carries popular hardware and software products from a number of different vendors, as well as a variety of books and journals aimed at personal computer users. An advantage to shopping at a computer store is that you can generally try out the hardware and software before you buy.

APPLICATIONS SOFTWARE FOR PERSONAL COMPUTERS

The variety of tasks microcomputers can handle is quite extensive. As the need for personal computer programs developed, software firms and individual entrepreneurs quickly appeared to satisfy the demand. In fact, many fortunes were made virtually overnight by programmers working on their own who found themselves in the right place at the right time. Some of these applications and the software developed to accommodate them are discussed here.

Electronic Games

Electronic games now constitute the most popular use of home computers and represent an enormous market. In 1982 alone, the home video game market accounted for revenues of almost $2 billion, about 20 percent of the $7 billion electronic game market. In comparison, Hollywood sold slightly over $3 billion worth of movie tickets to U.S. audiences during the same period.

There are three different types of electronic games:

- The quarter-guzzling arcade games, each of which can provide only one game, that have sprouted in supermarkets, fast-food restaurants, and game parlors.
- Cartridge-type games designed for game controllers, such as those sold by Coleco Industries and Atari. Controllers are designed to be plugged into your home television set. Some game controllers can also access the resources of general-purpose personal computer systems, such as those highlighted in Window 7.
- Games stored on disk and cassette tape, which can be run on a general-purpose personal computer system.

Arcade games are generally of higher quality than similar home versions. Home systems intended for extensive game playing generally can be equipped with a game controller to load the prepackaged cartridges; a joystick, which looks like the stick shift in an automobile (and can move spaceships, Pac-people, and the like in different directions on the monitor screen); and an audio output unit, which makes sounds when important action is taking place on the screen.

Masters of Trivia in the Broadcast Booth

In recent years, microcomputers have greatly increased the sophistication of the facts and figures that baseball, football, basketball, and hockey announcers have been communicating to their audiences. Take the case of the Oakland A's professional baseball team. The A's recently acquired a portable Apple II Plus microcomputer system to assist announcers Lon Simmons and Bill King both at home and at road games. The computer gives the announcers access to a wealth of interesting statistical information at electronic speeds.

Here's how the system works. Before each game, information about the players on both the A's and the opposing team is transmitted to the micro from a minicomputer located in Philadelphia. This larger computer generates and stores a large, up-to-date bank of statistics on all players and teams in the American League. The current batting average, averages against opposing pitchers and teams, averages against left- and right-handed pitchers, average with runners in scoring position, slugging percentage, doubles, triples, home runs, stolen bases, attempts at steals—all these statistics and more are available on every player. An extensive software package on the Philadelphia system generates the statistics from large files that have been compiled pitch by pitch during every game played.

Once the information for the game at hand has been loaded on the microcomputer, Simmons and King can supplement their play-by-play commentary by requesting facts about each player. For example, if Dwayne Murphy is batting, with a runner at third base, the announcers can check out Murphy's batting average with runners in scoring position. Or if a lefthanded relief pitcher comes into the game with speedster Rickey Henderson on first base, the micro system can instantly retrieve the rate at which

Henderson has succeeded in stealing bases against left-handed pitchers, or even against that particular pitcher. Also, because the results of each pitch of the game being played are entered into the microcomputer system as the contest unfolds, Simmons and King can request the number of pitches that a pitcher has thrown (broken down by balls and strikes), the number of times the pitcher has fallen behind the batter in the ball-strike count, the number of times the ball has been hit out of the infield, and so on.

Says Simmons, "The computer gives us instant information. You don't have to thumb through 50 pounds of paper to get the information you need to know."

A number of cartridges are currently available for the most popular arcade games, such as PAC-MAN™, SPACE INVADERS™, and DONKEY KONG™, to name just a few. Cartridges vary in price, often costing between $20 and $50. Game cartridges that work on one system do not necessarily run on another, unless a special adapter is purchased.

Personal Finance and Planning

A number of prepackaged programs are available to do financial planning, prepare taxes, manage bank accounts, schedule appointments, maintain lists of friends and acquaintances, file recipes, and plan diets and menus. Of the many packages available, one of the most popular is VisiCorp's VisiCalc®. This is an electronic worksheet, designed for both professional and personal use. As we mentioned in Chapter 11, users of such packages can view the display screen as a worksheet composed of large numbers of columns and rows. Formulas, labels, and values entered in the cells at the intersection of the columns and rows can be manipulated easily. In 1979, when VisiCalc was first marketed, many hailed it as one of the most significant software innovations of all time. Apple Computer, Inc. was the first microcomputer manufacturer to make VisiCalc available, and according to one claim, the company sold 200,000 computers as a result. Today, VisiCalc and other electronic worksheets are available for most personal computer systems.

Word Processing

Word processing, the electronic preparation of documents, can be implemented on personal computer systems in a number of ways. One option is to acquire a general-purpose personal computer system and to buy a word-processing software package. A basic word-processing package may cost between $150 and $500, depending on how sophisticated it is. Special features such as spelling aids are often packaged and priced separately. Micropro International's Wordstar™, Radio Shack's Scripsit™, and VisiCorp's VisiWord™ are popular word-processing packages.

A second, and more expensive, option is to buy a computer system especially designed for word processing. In these systems, microcomputers are packaged with special software and hardware to simplify word-processing tasks. In Chapter 14 we'll discuss computer systems specifically built for commercial-level word-processing applications.

People who acquire a personal computer system for word processing should select a printer carefully. A letter-quality printer or high-quality dot-matrix printer are recommended.

Education

Education by computer can take many forms for people of all ages. You can learn arithmetic, spelling, music, foreign languages, chemistry, and even programming languages by interacting at your own pace with programs that you can buy from a number of software firms. Educational programs vary widely in difficulty. An elementary one might require you to compute the daily profit made in a front-yard lemonade stand, whereas a complex one might ask you to create three-dimensional surfaces with multivariate calculus.

Automatic Home Controls

You can also use your personal computer to manage your home environment automatically. Computers can help regulate temperature, manage fuel and electricity consumption, open and close drapes, control kitchen appliances, turn lights on and off, supervise security, and even monitor the watering of your garden. In addition to the software that drives these applications, you'll need to buy special hardware that receives instructions from the computer and translates them into the appropriate mechanical activity, such as switching on the furnace or sounding a burglar alarm.

Information Networks

As we mentioned in Chapter 7, one of the more interesting applications of home systems is in the area of communications. Using a phone and a personal computer system, you can dial data banks in order to obtain current prices on stocks and other securities, airline and hotel information, consumer product information, news, recipes, horoscopes, and many more types of information. Well over 1000 data banks are currently available in the United States. They are maintained by service firms such as Dow Jones, Micronet, Compuserve, and The Source.

To use such a service, you need a modem, which enables your computer system to exchange information with the service company over ordinary phone lines. Once you've made phone contact with the company, its software systems generally provide easy-to-use menus of available screens, which let you choose from among their information offerings. After you have made a request from your keyboard, the information is sent over the phone lines to your video monitor.

The potential of home information networks has scarcely begun to be realized. In Chapter 18, we will cover some of the future possibilities of such systems in more depth.

Since most people who use personal computer systems are not accomplished programmers, many applications software packages are exceptionally **user-friendly.** In other words, both the programs and their supporting documentation are designed to be easy for the average person to use. In addition, many programming languages are available for personal computer users who want to write their own applications programs.

When selecting software products, buyers should pay attention to the fact that many packages need a minimum amount of RAM, and possibly disk storage as well. Many word-processing packages, for example, require a disk unit and at least 32 kilobytes of RAM. Some accounting packages, on the other hand, may require two disk units and at least 64 kilobytes of RAM. So look carefully at the software you may need before buying any hardware.

SYSTEMS SOFTWARE

Language translators adapted to personal computers are widely available for high-level languages such as BASIC, Pascal, FOR-TRAN, and APL, to name just a few. Like the applications packages, language translators are constrained by hardware. For example, COBOL translators are less common on personal computers because they require large memories. Also, Pascal sometimes requires a system with two disk drives.

A number of operating systems, which allocate the hardware of a specific system to the demands of applications programs, have been written for microcomputers. Perhaps the most famous are Digital Research's CP/M™ (and, later, CP/M-86™), Bell Laboratories' UNIX™, and Radio Shack's TRSDOS™.

Operating systems are developed to conform to the physical limitations of specific microprocessor chips and are often written in the assembly language available with the chip. Chips differ in the number of registers available, RAM, ROM, and so forth. As a result, their assembly languages, which address specific storage locations, are not interchangeable. Since prepackaged applications programs are written to interface with a

Tips on Buying a Microcomputer for a Small Business

There are virtually hundreds of microcomputer-based systems available commercially in today's marketplace. Although this makes it a safe bet that there's a system out there that will meet the needs of almost any small business, it does raise the very serious issue of how to choose among the staggering array of options available. Here are a few helpful hints to help you make a wise selection.

- Don't be conned into thinking that a computer will solve all of your problems. When misapplied, the computer will only make things worse than they already are.

- Before buying anything, analyze the applications involved and define your needs. Only after you have a general idea of your software requirements should you make decisions on hardware.

- The software you consider should be easy to learn, easy to use, and be able to handle routine operator errors. If the user interface is bad, you'll be hard pressed to get the system to do anything but confuse people.

- If you are inexperienced, retain the services of an independent consultant to help you examine your needs. It also often helps to acquire a system from a local dealer or computer services company that can provide the required support and "hand holding" to bring the system into operation and to maintain it adequately. Normally, computer manufacturers will not provide this type of service.

- Before you buy, check out the experiences of companies similar to yours as well as the customers of the dealership or computer services company from which you are considering buying your system. Ask the customers if the systems performed as expected, what problems they have encountered, and so forth. It also helps to visit a customer site or two, because often questions you didn't anticipate will occur to you.

- Make sure the system you buy can be upgraded as processing needs expand. Sometimes a system that looks like a bargain is only a bargain in the short run if at all. It will likely cost you much more than

particular operating system, an applications program that works with one operating system usually does not work with another. Thus, the choice of an operating system is critical.

CP/M has been a popular operating system on 8-bit machines because so many applications programs are available to interface with it. It was initially written for the 8-bit Intel 8080 chip and subsequently modified to run on several other popular chips. CP/M-86, which uses Intel's newer 16-bit 8088 microprocessor, quickly became a major operating system when IBM announced that its Personal Computer would support it. As sales of this machine soared, many programs that were compatible with CP/M were modified at once so they could run under CP/M-86.

---

you expected as your processing environment changes.

- It's almost always important to have adequate backup or support available if the system you acquire should suddenly break down. Does the dealership offer an adequate warranty? Is a maintenance contract available? If the computer goes down, the consequences can be disastrous. Make sure that both your hardware and software contracts cover everything.

- Carefully investigate possible areas of hardware and software compatibility. Not every piece of hardware you may need can be plugged into the system you are thinking of buying. Likewise, not all applications software can be run on the operating system you may acquire.

- Make sure you can affud the personnel required to keep the system up and running if you can't do it yourself. A widespread myth is that "user-friendliness" means that anyone with two fingers can use the system. If you know little about computers, you will almost always need outside help.

- Manual data-handling procedures can easily be as important as the automated ones. Computers have a way of quickly producing volumes of information that, if not managed properly, can drown an organization in a sea of paperwork. Also, be sure to take steps to ensure the accuracy of the data going into the system and information coming out. Errors can seriously undermine the effectiveness of the computer.

SHOPPING FOR A SYSTEM

Selecting a microcomputer-based system for your home must begin with the all-important question: "What do I want the system to do?" Once you've decided what types of applications the system must service, you must then decide what applications software to buy or to write, given your budget and talents. Finally, you need to select the hardware and systems software that best meet the requirements imposed by your earlier choices.

Where should you shop for hardware and software? One possibility is the computer store. Chain stores such as Computerland and Byte carry the products of a number of vendors in their showrooms. Generally, the salespeople at these stores are knowledgeable about computers and will help you try out the equipment before you buy or lease. As is the case with a stereo system, you can buy a whole computer system at once or the individual components separately. A complete system generally includes the offerings of more than one vendor, because few companies manufacture a full line of products for personal computers. Even the giant IBM does not make the printer, the disk drives, and most of the software that are generally packaged with the IBM Personal Computer.

Some stores, such as those operated by Radio Shack, are run by vendors of computer products. Generally, these stores are oriented toward showcasing the wares of the vendor. Other stores specialize in specific types of products, perhaps selling only software or video game systems. These stores carry the merchandise of several vendors. Large department stores such as Sears, J. C. Penney, Macy's, and Montgomery Ward also sell home computer systems, as do a number of office equipment dealers.

Another possible source of computer products is mail-order firms. These companies publish price lists or catalogs and will ship products to you upon request. A disadvantage of shopping this way, however, is that you need to know exactly what you want, since most mail-order firms don't maintain showrooms. However, because these companies don't have to pay for a showroom, their prices are often lower than those of the computer stores.

You can also acquire computer resources by contacting manufacturers directly. Some manufacturers, however, only sell in quantity.

LEARNING MORE ABOUT PERSONAL COMPUTERS

A wealth of resources is available to those who want to learn more about personal computer systems and their uses. Organizations, computer shows, magazines, newspapers, newsletters, and catalogs are all sources of information about computers. Many of these sources specialize in serving microcomputer users.

Computer clubs are an especially effective vehicle for getting an informal education in computers. Clubs are generally organized by region, product line, or common interests. Apple computer enthusiasts join such clubs as Apple-Holics (Alaska), Apple Pie (Illinois), or Apple Core (California). There is even the CP/M Users Group, organized around the popular operating system. Clubs such as The Amateur Computer Group of New Jersey, on the other hand, serve the needs of a more diverse group of personal computer buffs. Some clubs function as exchange groups. For example, A.P.P.L.E. (Apple Puget Sound Program Library Exchange) gives thousands of Apple users access to software at reduced rates, for a nominal membership fee. Another type of organization is the professional association. The Personal Computing Society, for example, enables personal computer users from around the nation to mobilize in shaping the future of microcomputing.

Computer shows provide another opportunity to learn about personal computers. These shows typically feature a number of vendor exhibits as well as seminars on various aspects of computing. The West Coast Computer Faire, held in the San Francisco area, and the Business and Home Computer Show, are two events specifically oriented toward smaller computers. Even the nation's largest show, the National Computer Conference, gears several exhibits and seminars to the interests of the home user.

Periodicals are another major educational tool. Magazines such as *Byte, Creative Computing, On Computing, Interface Age, Mini-Micro Systems, Kilobaud Microcomputing,* and *Personal Computing* focus on personal computers. These magazines vary tremendously in reading level. You can probably find and browse through all of these publications and more at your local computer store. In addition to the monthly periodicals, the biweekly newspaper *Infoworld* is another useful resource. It is relatively easy to read and is addressed specifically to the personal computing community.

Personal computer owners are frequently sent newsletters by the vendors of their computers, often announcing new products or creative applications. For example, the *TRS-80 Microcomputer News* serves Radio Shack users, and Apple owners receive *Softalk*. Newsletters are even directed to owners of certain kinds of software. People interested in software that is compatible with CP/M, for example, may subscribe to *Lifelines*.

Another good source of information about personal computers is the catalogs put out by vendors. Some manufacturers, such as Radio Shack, periodically publish catalogs of their products. Other literature, such as *Ye Compleate Computer Catalog* and *The Sensational Software Catalog*, contains information about the products of a number of vendors. You can buy such publications at computer stores.

Finally, one of the best ways to learn about any aspect of personal computing is to read a book on the subject. A host of soft- and hard-covered books are available, ranging in difficulty from simple to highly sophisticated. These volumes include a large number of "how-to" books on such subjects as operating popular personal computers, programming in microcomputer-based languages, the fundamentals of personal computers, and so forth. You can find such books in your local library, computer stores, and, increasingly, bookstores. A brief list of current books on personal computing is provided in the Suggested Readings at the end of this chapter.

Summary and Key Terms

Many personal computer systems contain five major pieces of hardware: the processor itself, a secondary storage device, a video display unit, a keyboard, and a printer.

Microcomputers are computers driven by microprocessors. **Microprocessors** are the central processors in microcomputer systems, as well as in products such as electronic scales, digital watches, children's learning toys, microwave ovens, and video games. **Personal computers** are technically microcomputers that are used by individuals to meet various personal needs, whether at work or at home. The terms *personal computer* and *microcomputer* are often used synonymously in practice.

The primary memory of microcomputers is etched onto silicon chips and is often built into the microprocessor chip itself. This memory is called **RAM,** for **Random Access Memory.**

ROM stands for **read-only memory.** It consists of nonerasable hardware modules that contain program software. Many microprocessor chips also contain some ROM to perform various system functions.

As with larger computers, the primary memory of microcomputers can hold only the data and programs the computer is currently processing. If you want to keep data and programs for repeated use, you must have a secondary storage unit. Both tape and disk devices are available for personal computers.

For most people, a personal computer system would be useless without a keyboard, since it is often the main vehicle for input. Potential buyers should carefully evaluate keyboards before deciding on one.

Almost every personal computer system has a video display unit, or **monitor.** A monitor is simply a display terminal without a keyboard. Many microcomputer systems allow you to use a television set as a monitor.

If your are using your computer system for any purpose other than for playing computer games, you'll probably need some form of printed output. Most printers adapted for use with home computers are serial printers.

The number of peripheral devices that a microcomputer can support is limited by the storage capacity of its primary memory, as well as by the number and arrangement of the slots (or ports) into which peripherals can be plugged.

Applications software for personal computers is numerous and includes packages for electronic games, personal finance and planning, word processing, education, automatic home controls, and information networks. Since most people who use personal computer systems are not accomplished programmers, many applications software packages are exceptionally **user-friend-ly.** In other words, both the programs and their supporting documentation are designed to be easy for the average person to use.

Language translators adapted to personal computers are widely available for high-level languages such as BASIC, Pascal, FOR-TRAN, and APL, to name just a few.

A number of operating systems, which allocate the hardware of a specific system to the demands of applications programs, have been written for microcomputers. Among the more popular of these are CP/M, CP/M-86, UNIX, and TRSDOS.

There are numerous options available in shopping for personal computer systems, including computer stores, department stores, mail-order firms, and the hardware and software manufacturers.

A wealth of resources is available to those who want to learn more about personal computer systems and their uses. Organizations, computer shows, magazines, newspapers, newsletters, books, and catalogs are all sources of information about computers.

Review Questions

1. Identify the major pieces of hardware in a personal computer system.
2. Distinguish among a microprocessor, microcomputer, and personal computer.
3. What is the significance of the particular microprocessor chip used by a personal computer system?
4. Name several applications for a personal computer system.
5. Why is it important to choose a well-known operating system for your personal computer?
6. Name some places where you can acquire a personal computer system.
7. State some ways to learn more about personal computer systems.

Suggested Readings

Cortesi, David E. *Inside CP/M: A Guide for Users and Programmers*. New York: Holt, 1982.

Devoney, Chris, and Richard Summe. *IBM's Personal Computer*. Indianapolis: Que, 1982.

Perry, Robert L. *Owning Your Home Computer*. New York: Everest House, 1980.

Perry, William E. *So You Think You Need Your Own Business Computer: A Manager's Guide to Selecting, Installing, and Using the Right Small Computer System*. New York: Wiley, 1982.

Rinder, Robert M. *A Practical Guide to Small Computers for Business and Professional Use*. New York: Monarch Press, 1981.

Sawusch, Mark. *1001 Things to Do With Your Personal Computer*. Summit, Pa.: Tab Books, 1980.

Zaks, Rodnay. *Your First Computer*. Berkeley: Sybex, 1980.

Chapter 14

Commercial Systems

Chapter Outline

OVERVIEW

In earlier chapters, you read about some of the parts of computer systems—specifically the hardware and software—that permit computers in organizations to function. In this chapter, we take a look at computer systems as wholes rather than as collections of parts, showing some of the ways in which the parts combine to help fill the information needs of businesses and other organizations.

Every computer is manufactured to best accommodate only certain types of applications. For example, some computer systems are designed primarily to provide fast responses to a large number of users on terminals, whereas other systems are better suited to routine data-processing tasks such as payroll and billing. Still other machines are ideal for the "number-crunching" work required by scientists. Although some computers are manufactured to handle many functions, one function is often added at the expense of another. Therefore, it is extremely important to define accurately and in advance the tasks to be computerized. Only then can system design and acquisition proceed efficiently.

We begin this chapter by introducing you to some of the kinds of tasks for which computers are used in businesses and other organizations. Most of these types of work can be seen as primarily either batch or online processing applications, a distinction made at the beginning of the chapter.

Next, we look at the range of applications of computer systems in commercial settings—from routine clerical tasks to high-level decision making. We then go on to discuss ways in which large organizations with many divisions can "distribute" their computer systems over a wide geographical area.

We conclude with a brief description of the options facing the organization that has reached the stage of acquiring computer resources. This last section provides an overview of the computer industry and specifies where organizations can acquire systems and services.

BATCH AND ONLINE PROCESSING: WHAT'S THE DIFFERENCE?

From your reading so far in this book, you probably have some idea of the variety of tasks that computers in business and industry now perform. As you read the more systematic discussion of these applications in the following pages, you may find it helpful to keep in mind the distinction between batch and online processing. Some tasks, such as payroll, accounts receivable, and accounts payable lend themselves to batch processing. Inventory management and many types of decision support, as you will see, often tend to be handled in an online mode.

Let's immediately consider an example. There are two ways that you can update your checking account balance in your own checkbook register. You can do it after each check or deposit is made, or you can do it periodically, after several checks and deposits. This is essentially the difference between online and batch processing.

Batch Processing

In **batch processing,** transactions or requests are collected in batches, which are sent to the CPU for processing at periodic intervals. Issuing payroll checks is a classic example of a batch operation. Once every week or two weeks, all employees are paid at once in a batch—the most efficient way of doing the job.

Billing is another operation that is often done in the batch mode. Companies maintain a file of customer transactions, which include purchases and payments. At a certain time of the month, this transaction file is processed against a master file of all customer balances. The computer system updates the balance in each account and writes bills that are sent to the customers.

Online Processing

Online processing by computer is a more recent innovation than batch processing. It evolved out of the time-sharing systems that were developed in the mid-1960s. In online processing, the data are entered directly into the system as they are collected, and they are immediately processed. Generally, users enter data and commands from terminals connected to a central processor. There are two major types of online processing: time-sharing and real-time processing.

Time-Shared Processing. In **time-shared processing** (or **time-sharing**), which we covered from another perspective in Chapter 8, users generally work independently, solving their own problems. The problems being solved are not necessarily related to one another. Although computer response should be relatively fast, immediate response is not absolutely critical. Each job is processed as the computer encounters the predetermined time slices that have been allocated to the job.

Time-sharing is common among computer systems at colleges and universities. Students sit at terminals, each working independently on a class assignment. What one student does generally has no effect on the work of another. Time-shared systems usually provide very fast response time at the beginning of a semester, when nobody seems overly worried about deadlines. During the closing weeks of the semester, however, when everybody desperately needs to use the computer and lines form at terminals, response by the CPU can be slow. A BASIC program that took ten minutes to key and run early in the semester may now take a half hour or more.

Real-Time Processing. Systems that utilize **real-time processing** help to control real-life activities as these activities are actually happening. Thus, information must be supplied by the computer system when it is needed. Real-time responses must therefore be extremely and consistently fast. Another characteristic of real-time systems is that one transaction can alter the environment in which the next transaction takes place, making the second transaction dependent on the first.

Airline reservation systems are a good example of real-time systems. Suppose, for example, you want to fly to Fort Lauderdale over spring break to catch some sun on the infamous beaches there. When you call the airline, a reservations agent seated at a CRT terminal fields your inquiries about flights. Because you have had the foresight to call several weeks in advance, some seats are still available, but these are going fast, not only at the airline you have called, but at other airlines as well. The real-time system, however, allows the reservations agent to provide you immediately with up-to-date information on seat availability. As a result, you may decide to book a seat quickly with that airline rather than to wait.

The fact that your success at booking a flight might very well mean another person's failure later to get a seat on that plane illustrates a second feature of real-time environments. The outcome of one transaction can affect what happens in a later one. All the reservations agents are working interdependently on a common problem: booking passengers. Thus, the central file that lists seats filled and seats available must be completely up to date. With batch-processing systems, in contrast, records are not updated until a batch is submitted for processing.

Another real-time application is found in banking. You may know you're honest, but the bank teller must nevertheless check your account at the terminal before you can withdraw money. The ability to check accounts and update them on the spot protects the bank from overwithdrawals. Often, however, any deposits you make are not recorded until the end of the day, together with all the other deposits made that day. In other words, deposits are usually processed in the batch mode.

Both the airline and banking examples given here are called *transaction-processing systems,* because they process transactions. This class of real-time systems typically uses database technology, with powerful query facilities for users.

Many computer systems can perform both batch and online processing, but they often do not do both equally well. Thus, several of a company's decision-support systems may be run on a real-time-oriented computer system, whereas routine data-processing applications are performed on separate batch-oriented machines. Because they usually require a large number of lines, teleprocessing capability, many terminals, and sophisticated software, online systems are typically more expensive than batch-oriented ones.

COMMERCIAL APPLICATIONS

Many computer applications in business, nonprofit organizations, and government fall into one of four categories:

- **Routine data processing**   Included in this category are the record-keeping and accounting tasks that organizations must handle regularly.
- **Management information systems and decision-support systems**   These systems provide decision makers with access to needed information.
- **Office systems**   These systems cut down on the time-consuming paperwork normally generated by communication within and between offices.
- **Design and manufacturing**   This category includes computers used to guide robots in factories and to help with industrial design.

In the following pages we'll look at each of these types of applications.

Routine Data Processing

A typical company must process a number of routine jobs, most of which involve some form of record keeping. In some smaller organizations, the scale of these tasks may not warrant computerization. Clerks may be able to take care of payroll, sales orders, inventory control, accounts receivable and payable, and general ledger manually. However, these routine jobs were among the earliest commercial applications of computers, and are still among the most important. In fact, to many people in the computer industry, the term *data processing* still denotes the automated processing of such routine tasks.

Payroll. Payroll systems compute deductions for taxes, insurance, social security, and so forth, and write paychecks to employees for the remainder. A computer-written paycheck and an earnings statement are shown in Figure 14-1. These systems also prepare reports for managerial and taxing agencies of the federal, state, and local governments. Each program in a payroll system performs a single task, for example writing paychecks. This division of labor is consistent with the "modular approach" to program development, in which a system of programs work together on separate tasks to complete a larger job, and output from some programs serves as input to others. Also, the payroll system communicates with the general ledger system, which as you'll see, incorporates payroll data and other financial information into programs designed to summarize the financial status of the organization.

Sales Order Entry. All businesses that sell merchandise must have a system for processing customers' orders as they are received by mail, telephone, or some other means. This system, which is often computerized, is called a *sales order entry system*. It consists of all hardware, software, data, procedures, and people needed to process the orders. Each order contains the customer's name, as well as a description and the quantity of the items desired. A good system permits fast processing of orders and screens out bad credit risks. The sales order entry system must also interface with the inventory control system, because the stock levels of products are reduced by orders received from customers.

```
DATE: 8/25/83                                                                    90-1200
                                                                                   0414

                                  SMITH COMPANY

PAY *234 DOLLARS AND 50 CENTS                    $**234.50           CHECK NUMBER
                                                                         822
TO THE
ORDER OF      MARTHA JONES

VALLEY BANK                      _____

                        ⑆0223⑈0680⑆ 4066 02210⑈
```

Employee number	Employee name	Dept.	Pay period	Pay period ended	Check no.	Check date
4044	MARTHA JONES	A-2	16	8/25/83	822	8/25/83

Earnings and statutory deductions								
Hours	Rate	Regular pay	Overtime pay	Other pay	Gross pay	Fed. w/tax	F.I.C.A. tax	State tax
60	3.50	210.00	55.20	15.00	280.20	21.05	16.60	3.05

Voluntary deductions							
Medical ins.	Life ins.	Credit union	Union dues	Charity	Savings bonds	All others	Net pay
5.00							234.50

Social Security and W-2 information					
Social security no.	Exempt	Y.T.D. gross	Y.T.D. fed. w/tax	Y.T.D. F.I.C.A.	Y.T.D. state tax	Not negotiable
415-85-2136	X	7,301.66	694.21	487.66	81.07	

Figure 14-1. *A paycheck and earnings statement.*

Inventory Control. The units of merchandise that a company has in stock to sell at a given moment is called its *inventory*. An inventory control system keeps track of the number of units of each product in the inventory and ensures that the proper quantities of products are maintained.

As the sales order entry system processes a customer's order, the inventory control system checks if the desired goods are in stock. If they are, the goods are made available for shipment, the number of units ordered is automatically subtracted from inventory balances, and the accounts receivable system is alerted to bill the customer. If the goods are not in stock, they may be placed on back order, and the system notifies the order entry personnel to send the customer a notice to that effect.

A good inventory control system must maintain an economical inventory level. If too little stock is kept in inventory, customers may become frustrated when what they order is frequently out of stock. Eventually, they may decide to buy elsewhere because of the poor service. If the company maintains too much inventory, the money spent to maintain goods on the shelf cannot be used to earn interest in financial accounts or other investments. Most inventory control systems contain a variety of mathematical routines that help analysts calculate an economical inventory level for each product.

Besides monitoring stock levels automatically, almost all inventory control systems generate an assortment of reports for management. Among these documents are inventory stock status reports (shown in Figure 14-2) and summaries listing fast-moving and slow-moving items, back orders, and so forth.

Accounts Receivable. The term *accounts receivable* refers to the amounts owed by customers who have made purchases on credit. Because about 90 percent of the business transacted in the United States is done on a credit basis, the accounts receivable system is a critical computer application in most companies. It keeps track of customers' purchases, payments, and account balances. The system also calculates and prints customers' bills (a sample of which appears in Figure 14-3) and management reports. Other output includes sales analyses,

SMITH COMPANY   *** INVENTORY STOCK STATUS ***   9/29/83   PAGE 1

ITEM	ITEM DESCRIPTION	BEG QTY	QTY REC	QTY SOLD	ON HAND	ON ORDER	AVAIL	UNIT PRICE
1002	RESISTOR-TYPE B	0	600	200	400	100	500	.15
1003	RESISTOR-TYPE D	0	0	0	0	100	100	2.20
1006	RESISTOR-TYPE E	0	0	0	0	50	50	6.85
1008	SEALING TAPE-1 INCH	200	100	50	250	0	250	3.00
1010	SEALING TAPE-1.5 INCH	100	0	30	70	0	70	3.71
1012	LIGHT FIXTURE-TYPE 6	0	0	0	0	0	0	4.31
1014	LIGHT FIXTURE-TYPE 7	0	0	0	0	0	0	4.03
1015	HEX SCREW	300	250	50	500	200	700	.65
1016	BIT NUT	0	600	100	500	0	500	.21
1018	WRENCH	0	30	30	0	100	100	8.55
1020	SOCKET SET	250	40	80	210	0	210	30.35

Figure 14-2. Inventory stock status report.

Sold to:	Ship to:	SMITH COMPANY
P.J. JOHNSTON 498 CANYON BLVD. BOULDER, CO 80302	E.D. ADAMS 307 EARL PLACE FLAGSTAFF, AZ 86001	Customer no. 807214

Today's date	Order date	Order no.	Shipping instructions	Stated terms	Salesperson
09/21/83	09/21/83	61027	VIA EZ MOVERS	2% 30 DAYS NET 60	4617

Quantity ordered	Quantity shipped	Description	Unit price	Extended amount	Discount amount	Net amount
40	40	RESISTOR-TYPE B	.15	6.00		6.00
100	50	RESISTOR-TYPE E	6.85	342.50	63.25	279.25
100	100	SEALING TAPE-1 INCH	3.00	300.00	50.00	250.00
		FREIGHT CHARGE				37.55
		PACKING CHARGE				75.80

Tax	Additional charges	Invoice amount	Invoice number
19.46	53.04	721.10	12102

Figure 14-3. A customer's bill (invoice).

which describe changing patterns of products and sales, as well as detailed or summary reports of current and past-due accounts (shown in Figure 14-4).

When interest rates are high, the billing procedures of the accounts receivable system can be especially critical because the sooner the bill is mailed, the sooner it will be paid and the sooner the receipts can begin to earn interest for the company. Also, studies have shown that delays in billing increase the likelihood of nonpayment.

			SMITH COMPANY	AGED TRIAL BALANCE			8/28/83 PAGE 001
ACCOUNT	INVOICE NUMBER	TOTAL DUE	CURRENT	OVER 30	OVER 60	OVER 90
00711	11511	714.20	714.20			
01516	11536	85.33	85.33			
03244	10218	42.03			42.03	
10772	10715	185.22		185.22		
13211	11530	66.75	66.75			
14831	11682	1,930.47	1,930.47			

Figure 14-4.   An accounts receivable report, showing past-due accounts.

Accounts Payable.   The term *accounts payable* refers to the money a company owes to other companies for the goods and services it has received. In contrast to receivables, which reflect a portion of the money coming in, payables reflect part of the money being spent.

An accounts payable system keeps track of bills and often generates checks to pay those bills. It involves recording who gets paid and when, handling cash disbursements, and advising managers if they should accept discounts offered by vendors in return for early payment. The interest that could be earned by delaying payment may outweigh the value of discounts for early payment.

An accounts payable system might allow a company treasurer, for example, to sit at a CRT terminal and rapidly obtain information about the organization's bills. The treasurer can, among other things, call up a list of the bills due on a given date, as shown in Figure 14-5. If the system is good, the treasurer will be able to retrieve billing information quickly for any combina-

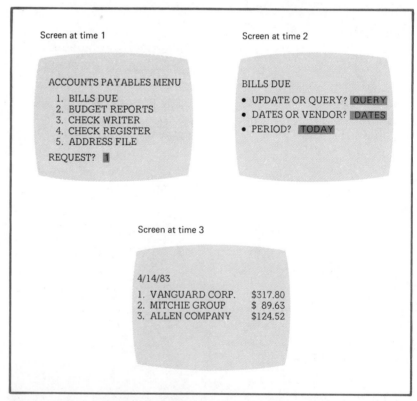

Figure 14-5.   A dialogue with a payables system. At time 1, the operator indicates a desire to see what bills must be paid by entering option 1 after the request prompt. At time 2, the operator requests all bills due today. The computer system locates these bills and presents them, as shown on the screen at time 3.

tion of dates and vendors. When the system writes checks, a check register report is prepared for the treasurer, showing to whom checks were issued; the invoice numbers involved; and the amount, date and number of each check.

General Ledger.   A general ledger (G/L) system keeps track of all financial summaries, including those originating from accounts receivable, accounts payable, and other sources. It determines whether the books balance. A typical G/L system can produce accounting reports, such as income statements, balance sheets, and general ledger balances (see Figure 14-6).

GENERAL LEDGER FOR: JONES COMPANY   DATE: 07/30/83
                                                     CLIENT: 7200

ACCT./REF. NO.	BEGIN. BAL.	TRANS.	ENDING BAL.
1001 CASH ON HAND			
1001 BEGIN BAL.	700.00		
1001 ENDING BAL.			700.00
1009 CASH-OPERATING ACCOUNT			
1009 BEGIN BAL.	23,300.07		
1009 103		10,752.41	
1009 302		−10,300.00	
1009 ENDING BAL.			23,752.48
1025 ACCOUNTS RECEIVABLE			
1025 BEGIN BAL.	105,633.82		
1025 103		156,121.33	
1025 103		−154,000.31	
1025 ENDING BAL.			107,754.84
5800 TELEPHONE & UTILITIES			
5800 BEGIN BAL.	602.14		
5800 705		88.32	
5800 ENDING BAL.			690.46
8700 FEDERAL INCOME TAXES			
8700 BEGIN BAL.	21,054.83		
8700 900		2,617.70	
8700 ENDING BAL.			23,672.53
8710 STATE INCOME TAXES			
8710 BEGIN BAL.	8,402.66		
8710 900		753.01	
8710 ENDING BAL.			9,155.67
		LEDGER TOTAL	0.00
		NET PROFIT IS	67,000.65

Figure 14-6.   Activity sheet produced from a general ledger system.

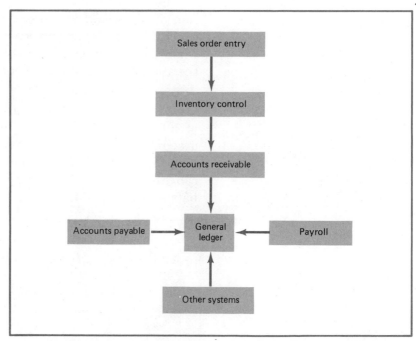

Figure 14-7.   Relationship among systems performing routine data processing.

Once a company has decided to computerize one or more of the routine activities we have just discussed, it must decide whether to develop the appropriate software itself or buy it from a vendor. If the company is new or in the process of overhauling the existing system, it may choose to buy from a vendor. These packages can cost several thousands of dollars or, in the case of microcomputers, only a few hundred. Payroll packages are the most popular because the payroll operation is similar in many companies, and the cost of keeping up with federal, state, and city tax legislation is almost too much for any one company to bear by itself. Inventory-control packages are the least popular, since inventory practices differ widely among companies. Naturally, any package that a company buys must work together with the other systems that it already operates. Figure 14-7 illustrates the relationship among the various systems described in this section.

Management Information Systems and Decision-Support Systems

During the early days of commercial computing, businesses purchased computers almost exclusively to perform routine data-processing tasks. Used in this way, the computer could cut clerical expenses considerably. However, as time passed, it became apparent that the computer could do much more than perform clerical routines. It could also provide information to assist management in its decision-making role. However, this function required new ways of organizing and distributing output to the various levels of management in business organizations.

Management Information Systems.   A system built to perform the dual role of providing routine data processing and generating information for use by decision makers is called a **management information system (MIS)**.

The function of a management information system is to provide managers at many levels of a company with the kind of information they need. Top-level managers, for example, spend much of their time plotting the company's future moves. To set goals and plan ways of achieving them, they need information about trends in data, not only for single departments but also for the whole company.

The information needs of middle management are slightly different. In order to carry out the strategies devised by their superiors, these managers need to know what is happening in their departments. Therefore, reports summarizing the flow of money and products under their jurisdiction are especially useful. Middle managers also need reports that describe any problems in the performance of production, for example, missed deadlines or quotas.

Lower-level management has still another set of priorities and information needs. Supervisors are charged with coordinating and controlling the activities of workers so that higher-level goals are met. These managers need reports that help them coordinate workers and materials—reports on inventory, shipping, purchases, payroll, and so on. Many of the clerical tasks mentioned earlier generate data most directly relevant to lower-level management.

As management information systems became popular, they were plagued by some serious problems. Some firms, misled by the exaggerated claims of computer vendors, expected far more from the systems than the systems could actually provide. When corporate users discovered that MIS could not provide information about all aspects of a business nor anticipate all its needs, many became disillusioned. In other cases, some businesses that had recently installed a MIS constantly had to alter key practices in order to adapt to rapid changes in computer technology, thus increasing the likelihood of the system failing.

Management information systems, however, have provided many benefits to the business world. These systems can inform management of trouble spots in the organization. For example, failure to meet production quotas, excessive spending, and so on can be reported. Management can incorporate much more information into decisions and spend less time gathering it. As a result, managers have more time to do things that computers cannot, such as thinking creatively and interacting with people.

As MIS has evolved, two key trends have developed: (1) people have generally become more "systems conscious," and (2) executives have come to recognize information as a critical resource. In fact, top management has often created a high-level executive position, such as vice president of MIS (whose position in organizational structure is shown in Figure 14-8), in recognition of the value of managing information resources. This person oversees the entire information network in the firm, ensuring that routine data-processing systems are working properly and that managers are getting useful information at the right time.

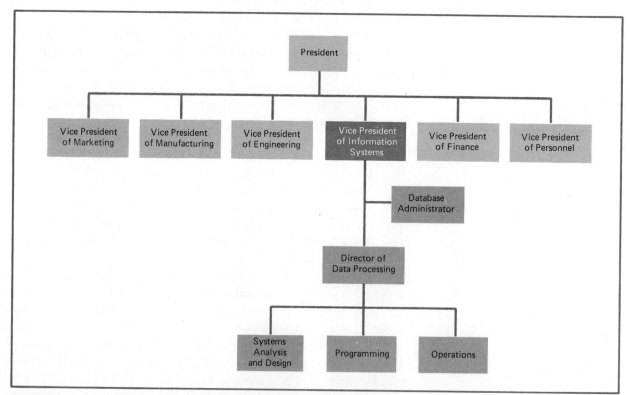

Figure 14-8. *An organization chart showing the information systems' function.* The vice president of information systems oversees all aspects of data processing and information distribution.

Decision-Support Systems. During the 1970s, commercial users began to call for systems that could field questions as they occur to managers. In response, the computer industry developed the **decision-support system (DSS).** Unlike the traditional MIS, DSS permits posing new questions at a terminal while the user is online. The DSS always employs interactive terminals. The traditional MIS, on the other hand, often provides fixed, preformatted information in a standardized way. A typical product of the MIS is a computer report that the data-processing department might circulate at regular intervals to various departments. By contrast, a DSS user (such as an inventory manager) might sit down at a terminal and request the price of an item. The manager might then decide to ask for the average price of several items, and then the inventory status of a different item. Managers can pose their own questions as the need evolves and receive answers at once.

A second difference between DSS and MIS has to do with scope. Most decision-support systems are less ambitious in scope than management information systems. Rather than developing large, interdependent systems to meet an organization's information needs, many DSS designers concentrate on smaller problems.

In practice, the distinction between MIS and DSS is not always as clear as in theory. Many people use the two terms interchangeably. Also, because the decision-making functions of MIS and DSS are sometimes incorporated into routine data-processing systems, people are justifiably confused about what to call the overall system.

Office Systems

In recent years, computer technology has been applied to the task of reducing paperwork in the office. The more fully computerized offices have been termed **automated offices** (or **offices of the future**). Automated office systems include a variety of technologies and processing techniques, some of which are illustrated in Window 8.

Probably the most widespread of the office systems technologies is **word processing.** IBM coined the term in 1964, when it first marketed the magnetic tape selectric typewriter (MT/ST). This machine enabled secretaries to store "canned" portions of documents on a tape unit connected to the typewriter. The typist could interweave fresh text with the preprepared materials. Today, word processing is accomplished in a number of ways.

One option is to buy a word-processing software package for use on a general-purpose computer. This option is especially popular with people who have their own personal computers and want to do modest amounts of word processing. Such software packages are available for computer systems of all sizes.

Another option is to acquire a "word-processing system"— a dedicated computer system that comes with software and hardware especially designed for word-processing applications. The software features may include continuous-typing capabilities (so you never have to hit the return key), powerful facilities for making corrections, and commands for merging documents automatically. Some software may even help you to write or to spell. Hardware features almost always include a special keyboard containing preprogrammed *function keys* (also called *softkeys*), which speed the preparation of documents. Some of these systems are *standalone,* in that they are single, self-contained units that can accommodate only one operator. Others are *shared-logic* systems, in that they consist of several

Technical Writers Get Help from Editing System

BALTIMORE—Technical editors lament the convoluted styles of some technical writers who turn simple sentences into verbal quagmires. But at Westinghouse Electric Corp.'s Integrated Logistics Support Division here, a mechanized editing system is being tested that not only identifies awkward word and sentence structure, but suggests alternatives as well.

The system is an enhancement of the Westinghouse Computer-Aided Readability System, which the division has used since 1976. That uses the well-known Flesch and Flesch-Kincaid formulas for military technical materials to check technical manuals for compliance with military specifications for readability.

The basic readability system is a software package designed in-house and stored on floppy disks that are indexed according to the grade level of writing that is desired. The system scans each document as it is entered into Westing-house's Xerox Corp. 860 word processor and notifies the editor of words and sentences that exceed the Flesch standard for readability.

The readability system is written in Microsoft, Inc.'s BASIC and is designed to run on any system with the Digital Research, Inc. CP/M operating system, according to Westinghouse software developer Edward Pierce.

The readability system not only flags unwieldy words, but includes a substitution dictionary of 900 to 1,000 difficult, nontechnical words with between one and five suggested substitutes, according to Douglas Kniffin, director of the editing project. "Each suggested substitute is shorter in terms of numbers of characters or words than the original phrase," said Kniffin. "It is also a more familiar word."

For example, the system will suggest "admit" or "note" instead of "acknowledge." Or it will offer "usual" instead of "conventional." The

terminals sharing the resources of a word-processing-oriented computer.

In addition to word processing, a number of other computer technologies contribute to office automation. Some technologies facilitate communication. *Electronic mail,* for example, makes it possible to send letters, memos, manuscripts, legal documents, and the like from one computer terminal to another. *Teleconferencing* makes it possible for a group of people to meet electronically, avoiding the time and expense they would incur if they were to get together physically in one spot. Teleconferencing systems permit participants to see each other on video screens as well as to hear each other.

Another element of the automated office makes it easier to schedule appointments for executives. *Office management systems* permit computerized arrangement of meeting times for executives, "electronic calendars," and a number of other functions.

Computer graphics technologies have been adapted to office use to help executives present information clearly and

---

dictionary will eventually be expanded to include about 2,000 words, Kniffin said.

Soon to be incorporated on the system will be a phrase substitute dictionary that performs the same function for 350 common and awkward phrases. "A tendency to" will become "tends," and "at the present time" will become "now."

The mechanization doesn't stop there. If the text still fails to fall within readability guidelines, the dictionary can zero in on abstract nouns and suggest more understandable alternatives.

The research for the mechanized editing system consumed nearly four years of work by Kniffin and Pierce, with editing information drawn from more than 250 books and studies on readability. Although Westinghouse at present has no plans to market the system commercially, Kniffin said the potential for other applications is almost endless.

"Our future plans include an identifier which will convert passive to active voice, a sexual bias check, a paragraph length monitor and controlled logistics vocabularies," Kniffin said. "The controlled vocabularies will contain literally thousands of words which have only one accepted meaning for our work. The system basically matches every word in the document against a computer dictionary."

Similar systems may eventually prove useful in computer-aided translation. "I've done a little work translating English into Spanish and, as a basic, literal translation, the system works quite well," Kniffin said.

Source: Paul Gillin, *Computerworld,* October 18, 1982. © 1982 by CW Communications, Inc. Framingham, MA 01701. Reprinted from COMPUTERWORLD.

effectively. They make it possible, for example, to prepare pictures and slides for presentation at meetings. *Computer reprographics* refers to the use of a number of technologies, including intelligent copiers, computer microfilm, computer-assisted typesetting and printing, automated collating, and so on, to help in the preparation of printed documents. Reprographics includes all stages of document preparation, from generation of the text at the word processor to delivery of the finished product at the point of distribution.

Factory Applications: CAD/CAM

Computers are widely used in industrial settings to improve productivity both at the design stage—through computer-aided design (CAD)— and at the manufacturing stage—through computer-aided manufacturing (CAM). You can see some examples of CAD/CAM in Window 1 and Window 4.

Computer-Aided Design. Using **computer-aided design (CAD),** designers can dramatically reduce the time they spend at the drafting board. Using light pens and specialized graphics terminals, engineers can sketch ideas directly into the computer system, which can then be instructed to analyze the proposed design in terms of a number of criteria. Taking into account the subsequent output of the computer, the designer can modify the drawings until a desirable design is achieved. Before the arrival of CAD, the designer had to produce by hand preliminary sketches and then advanced designs, representing refinements on the sketches. After models were built and tested, the designer had to prepare production drawings, which are used to build the equipment needed to manufacture the new product, whether it be a truck or a new toaster. Today, computer-aided preparation of sketches and advanced designs is fairly common, and computerization of production drawings will soon be available. CAD is especially helpful in the design of automobiles, aircraft, ships, and electrical circuits, including computer circuits.

Computer-Aided Manufacturing. Computer applications are not limited to the design phases of manufacturing. More and more of the actual process of production on the factory floor is becoming computerized. **Computer-aided manufacturing (CAM)** includes the use of computers to help manage manufacturing operations and to control machinery used in manufacturing processes. One example is a system that observes production

THE OFFICE OF THE FUTURE

A look at the movement to automate office functions

First there was the manual typewriter and hand-cranked adding machine. Later, a little electricity produced additional excitement around the office. Then followed the copier ... the remote copier ... the "intelligent" copier ... electronic typewriters with computer system interfaces ... typing-oriented computer systems ... and— egad!—office personnel enrolling in computer courses by the boatload to learn more about the technological revolution that is rapidly invading their work environments. A glance through this Window will enable you to see some of the many computer applications that are changing office work.

1. Modern office settings are characterized by a variety of workstations designed to facilitate computer-assisted tasks.

WORD PROCESSING   One of the most important computer applications at the office is word processing, the automated creation, storage, and retrieval of documents. Some word processors operate as independent (standalone) units; others as workstations to a central computer (resulting in a "shared-logic" system). Some have special keyboards, character fonts, and displays; others don't. The diversity of word processing options currently in the marketplace is indeed astounding.

2.   A rich variety of text and graphic information can be created on the two-page display screen of Xerox's 8010 Star Information System. This display shows English text and its Russian equivalent.

3. The Lanier No Problem™ word processor can operate both as a standalone unit or as a workstation in a shared-logic environment.

4. The Xerox 850 Display Typewriter has a 24-character window on its front panel that lets you inspect documents before they are typed. The floppy disk drives with the system can store almost 300 pages of text, which you can access by keyboarding the title of any stored document.

5. The Xerox 850 display station enables you to inspect a full page of text at a time. As you proof pages for suitability, you can depress a key or two on the keyboard to have them automatically typed by an attached printer. Like many computing devices designed specifically for word processing environments, the 850 enables you to type continuously without hitting a return key and to select special fonts, such as boldface, to make typed documents more attractive.

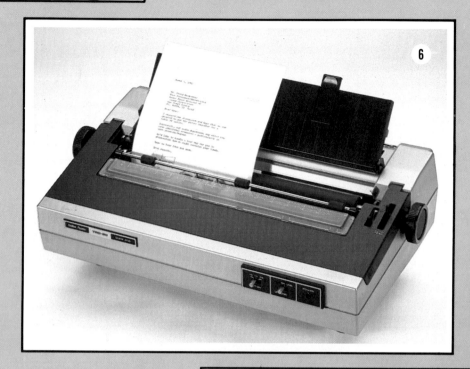

6. Even personal computer systems are capable of serious word processing, as exemplified by this letter-quality printer from Radio Shack.

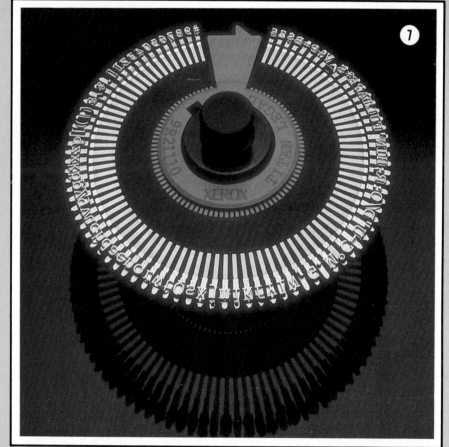

7. Most letter-quality printing is done with a daisywheel print element. You can get a variety of different character sizes or sets by simply changing printwheels, as you would a golf-ball element on a conventional electric typewriter.

TELECONFERENCING   An alternative to conventional meetings, teleconferencing has the potential to significantly reduce travel time and expenses. Although teleconferencing is by no means widespread today, many industry observers expect it to enter significantly into the office environment as the marriage between the computer, television, and communications continues to blossom.

8. The vertical "stick" in the photograph is a teleconferencing microphone/loudspeaker with an audio pick-up radius of twelve feet. It enables the meeting participants within its range to walk freely about the room and have their voices telecommunicated to a remote location.

9. Video teleconferencing.

BUSINESS GRAPHICS Computer systems are increasingly being used to assemble and graphically display business information for reports, presentations, and planning purposes. Many office networks installed today are designed to facilitate business graphics.

10. Using computer-generated graphics at a management presentation.

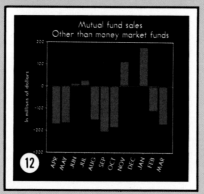
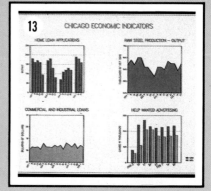

11, 12, 13. Most standard graphics software packages enable information to be presented in pie-chart, bar-chart, or line-chart form. The user can label the selected graph type and color it in a variety of ways.

14, 15, 16, 17. Sophisticated graphics software packages permit information to be presented in a variety of attractive ways.

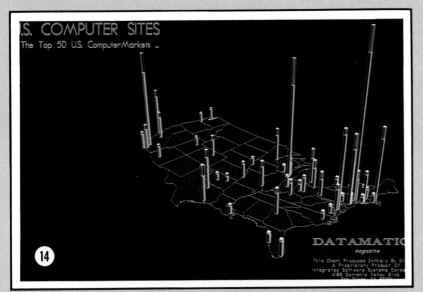

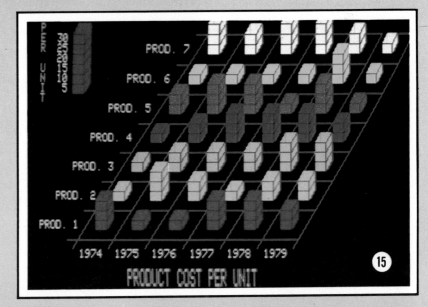

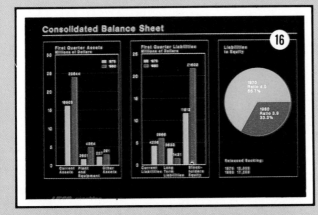

OTHER EQUIPMENT

18

18. Microprocessors are rapidly appearing in a variety of office products, such as this Micro General Corporation postal scale.

19

19. Facsimile. A facsimile machine is a copier that can digitize a document, drawing, or photograph at one location and send it to another. The machine shown here is the Xerox Telecopier 410.

in an oil refinery, performs calculations, and opens and shuts appropriate valves when necessary. Another system being used in the steel industry works from preprogrammed specifications to oversee the shaping and assembly of steel parts. CAM is also widely employed to build cars and ships, monitor power plants, manufacture food and chemicals, and perform a number of other functions.

One type of CAM that has caught the attention of the news media is **robotics,** the study of the design, building, and use of robots. *Robots* are machines that, with the help of a microprocessor, can mimic a number of human activities in order to perform jobs that are too monotonous or dangerous for their flesh-and-blood counterparts (see Figure 14-9). Some robots can even "see" by means of imbedded cameras and "feel" with sensors that permit them to assess the hardness, temperature, and other qualities of objects. Robots can represent a substantial savings to a corporation, since they don't go on strike, don't need vacations, and don't get sick.

In 1982, there were some 25,000 robots on the job around the world. Industry analysts predict that by 1985 robotics will become a $1 billion industry. The auto industry is now using robots to weld cars and paint them, and electronics firms employ robots to assemble calculators. Elsewhere, robots help to mine coal and even build other machines. In fact, a well-known sushi chef in Japan is not even a human at all, but a

Figure 14-9.   An industrial robot.

robot. Whether robots are like Captain Video's TOBOR or R2D2 of *Star Wars* fame, they will probably always capture the imagination of people everywhere.

Despite this fascination, the acceptance of robot technology has been particularly slow in the United States and Europe, where unions fear that workers will lose their jobs to machines. In Japan, where many companies virtually guarantee workers employment until age 60, robots have been embraced quickly. Japan is now the world's leading robot producer, representing 50 percent of the worldwide market.

DISTRIBUTED DATA PROCESSING

How does a large company with many departments and divisions meet its data-processing needs, especially if some divisions are located across the country or around the world from headquarters? In the early days of computing, the answer was simple. Usually a single computer center located at headquarters served the entire company. Any division that required computer support had to arrange for facilities and programmers at headquarters. This *centralized* organization was dictated by the expense and size of the computers then available and by limitations in telecommunications technology.

As demands for computer resources increased, centralized systems experienced a great deal of strain. As the number of remote users grew in many organizations, the central computer became overloaded, and turnaround time slowed to unacceptable levels. Moreover, the central computer was not set up to do all tasks equally efficiently. Users' needs varied, yet they were compelled to use the central computer.

With the advent of minicomputers, microcomputers, and advanced telecommunications hardware, alternatives to a centralized system became possible. Many of these alternative systems are collectively called **Distributed Data Processing (DDP)** systems. This is, unfortunately, one of those computer terms that is defined in different ways by different people. As used here, it refers to a system configuration in which a single application or related applications are accommodated on two or more geographically dispersed computers.

A DDP system is typically composed of a large- or medium-sized central computer and a number of decentralized minicomputers or microcomputers located in places that are geographically remote from the central computer. Jobs that involve the whole firm, or that are too large for the smaller

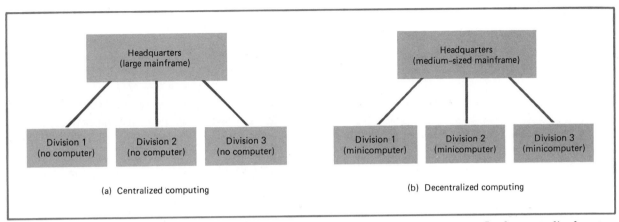

Figure 14-10. Centralized and decentralized computing in a hypothetical company. In the centralized system shown (a) all processing takes place on a single large mainframe computer, whereas in the decentralized system depicted (b) processing is shared by a smaller, centrally located mainframe and a number of local minicomputers.

computers, are done on the central computer, whereas smaller jobs that only a single remote department or branch needs can be done on the department's own mini or micro. Note that DDP differs from multiprocessing, in which more than one computer works on a job at the same time, but the computers are not necessarily distant from one another. In DDP, the job can be done at different times and always involves multiple locations. DDP is also slightly different from online processing, which involves decentralized terminals but a single, centralized computer which does the processing.

Figure 14-10 illustrates a shift from a centralized to a DDP system. A company with a single headquarters and three geographically dispersed divisions might originally have handled all data processing on a mainframe at headquarters. This arrangement is shown in Figure 14-10(a). The DDP arrangement shown in Figure 14-10(b), in which the size of the central computer facility is reduced and each division retains its own mini, provides each division with more control over its own operations. The activities taking place on each of the minis are integrated into the corporate-level data-processing system to facilitate top-down planning and control.

Types of DDP Networks

There are two basic types of distributed network designs: star and ring.

A **distributed star network** often consists of a central

computer, to which several remote minicomputers are connected. This configuration is illustrated in Figure 14-10(b). In a common variant of this pattern several user-programmable terminals are connected to a host CPU. This type of distributed star network can be seen in Figure 14-11(a). The distributed star network is especially well suited to an organization with several related plants or divisions, because each division may need access to common centralized files, yet also need to do its own local processing. It is important to remember that in such a system, the workload, whether it be processing or storage, is distributed among several locations. Thus, a system in which a number of dumb terminals are linked to a central computing site, where all processing and storage takes place, is not a *distributed* star network. Instead one might more accurately call it simply a *star network.*

A less common and more expensive alternative is the **distributed ring network,** in which a central computer is absent, and a number of computers are connected serially to one another. A major advantage of this configuration is that all

tomorrow

COMMUNITY MICROCOMPUTING SYSTEMS

With the influx of personal computers into business organizations, and improvements in telecommunications facilities, we are rapidly approaching the age of community microcomputing systems. In such a system, several microcomputers can communicate in a local network with one another and with a number of shared peripherals. Such a local network might consist of a single corporate building where managers, staff workers, line personnel, secretaries, and even company presidents have desk-top computer systems. These desk-top stations can exchange information through a communications network privately operated by the corporation. Users in such an environment also share programs and data residing on common storage. Some futurists see community microcomputing as an answer to a number of computing needs in the 1980s.

There are many interesting uses for such systems. For example, an electronic mail system can be established to transmit correspondence from one microcomputer station to another. Thus, a secretary can type a letter at a terminal and send it to the manager who dictated it. The manager, in turn, can proofread and edit the letter at his or her own private desk-top station and then route it to another station within the corporation.

A second interesting application of electronic mail is appointment scheduling. A person can electronically check the stored appointment calendars of colleagues in the network and, on finding a common open period, schedule a meeting. This is done by creating a computerized meeting announcement, which is subsequently routed and stored in the local electronic-mailbox memory of each station involved.

A third application of electronic mail is in the area of project management. Workers on a

points in the network are more likely to retain access to a computer in case of a failure. For example, if a communication path between two of the points breaks down, an alternative path is available.

Distributed ring networks are implemented in situations in which communication between machines is not needed on a regular basis but is sometimes necessary. Departments in a business firm may each need the data-processing facilities of a local computer and may also need to communicate with the computers of other departments to update records from time to time. A distributed ring network is shown in Figure 14-11(b). As you can see, a message sent from computer 1 to computer 3 must be routed through computer 2 or 4.

Often, computer networks are not a simple star or ring pattern but some combination of simple patterns. A **multistar network,** for example, consists of several remote computers hooked up to a central computer in a star pattern, with each remote computer also connected to a number of local terminals in another star configuration (see Figure 14-12).

common project can send status reports to the central storage area on the computer system. At any time, the most up-to-date status of the entire project can be retrieved and analyzed by management. Unlike an office memorandum typed on a piece of paper, an electronically recorded message cannot be easily lost or misplaced.

Another resource that users of community microcomputing systems might have at their disposal is one or more databases. For example, if there were a community system in a college, faculty members advising students could examine and update files authorized for their use. Also, students who have access to the system could tap the resources of the library (but certainly not the grade database). The possibility that students could interact with professors in course-related work introduces some interesting theories about how education may eventually evolve. A number of universities and colleges already require entering students to have their own microcomputers. Where this trend will lead, no one knows.

Community systems: A microcomputer on every desk top.

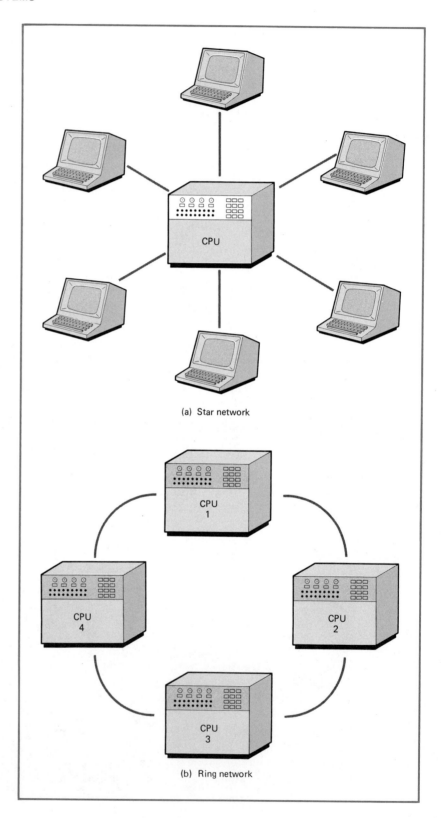

(a) Star network

(b) Ring network

Figure 14-11. Distributed star and ring networks. In the star network (a), user-programmable terminals are connected to a host CPU. The terminals perform some of the processing locally, and the remainder is done by the host CPU. Distributed ring networks, such as that shown in (b), typically feature computer-to-computer communication, without a central host computer.

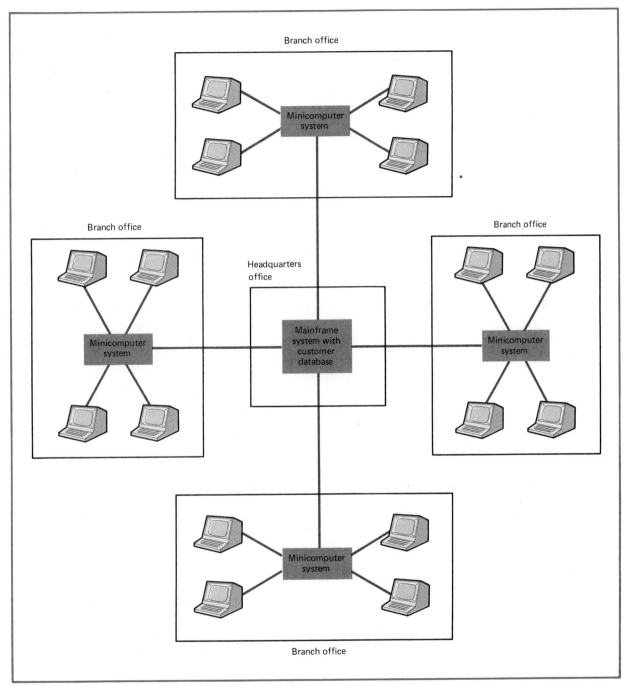

Figure 14-12.   A multistar network. An example of such a configuration is a branch banking system. Each bank has its own terminals and minicomputer, which is hooked up to a large central computer. The central computer might contain the customer database, which is used to prepare the monthly balance statements for all customers. If each of the branch banks were in a different city, the bank would probably distribute its customer database to the local sites to reduce communication costs.

To DDP or Not to DDP?

The decision to convert a centralized system to a DDP system is not always easy, since DDP systems, despite their many advantages, suffer from certain flaws. First, the advantages. DDP gives users much better access to computer facilities, since the facilities are local and users face competition only from others in their departments or divisions (enabling better control). Moreover, the applications software that is run on the system can be much better tailored to local needs than software that must serve a number of local units. Response time is also faster, since the user does not have to wait for input and output to be transmitted to and from the central computer. Also, because a number of smaller computers can assume much of the work formerly done by the central computer, the latter facility is relieved of much of its workload. If the central computer has been overburdened, DDP can improve the response time for jobs by balancing the work more effectively.

Among the disadvantages of DDP is the fact that, typically, less of the total capacity of the system is used than in a centralized system. Some branches of a company, for example, may not use their local computers very much, even though the computers are dedicated solely to the branches' needs. Another disadvantage is that the branches of an organization installing DDP must carefully coordinate purchases of software and hardware as well as data management practices. Different packages designed to do the same thing can create nettlesome interface problems, as can the purchase of equipment from different vendors that must be meshed into a coherent system that stretches across the branches. The many components of a DDP—the hardware, software, and services for all the locations at which processing will occur—make its construction quite a complex process. Finally, it costs more to staff many data-processing sites than it does to staff a single centralized site, where all processing occurs.

Although DDP networks can be expensive, the advantages of better service, control, and locally produced decision-making information often make them a wise choice.

THE COMPUTER INDUSTRY

So far, we have looked at the kinds of jobs that computers do in commercial settings and some of the basic configurations in which computer systems can be arranged once management has decided what tasks the system should perform. When the system has been designed, the next step is to acquire the necessary hardware, software, and computer services. This is no easy task in today's bountiful computer marketplace. Once a company is ready to buy, it has a variety of potential suppliers to investigate.

Given a set of applications and financial constraints, an organization can generally find the resources it needs by contacting one or more companies in the three major sectors of the computer industry. These sectors specialize in

- Hardware, including computers and peripherals
- Software
- Services

Many companies supply several of these resources, and some offer all of them.

Hardware Suppliers

This sector is made up of companies that manufacture and sell their own hardware as well as those that simply sell the hardware of other companies.

A number of firms manufacture computers. Some are particularly strong in mainframes, others in minis, and still others in microcomputers. Only a few large firms, such as IBM, can offer products on all three levels. Because the computer market is so big, virtually every manufacturing company has chosen to specialize in certain areas. For example, some firms concentrate on specific applications, such as Lanier in word processing, and NCR Corporation in point-of-sale (POS) and banking applications.

Computer hardware may be acquired directly from the manufacturer or indirectly from a third party. One type of third party is the leasing company. These companies buy computer equipment in quantity from manufacturers and lease it directly to other firms. The customer might not inherit the full range of services offered by the manufacturer; however, leasing companies can generally undercut the lease rates of manufacturers by 10 to 30 percent. Approximately 60 percent of computer hardware is leased rather than purchased outright, because leasing provides the flexibility to change systems as the need arises.

A second way to acquire a computer system indirectly is to

Silicon Valley

As the demand for new products emerges, often so do geographical centers that specialize in manufacturing them. This phenomenon occurred in the auto industry, which found a home in Detroit, whereas Rochester, New York, has become a major center for photography. Similarly, during the past fifteen years, California's "Silicon Valley" has burgeoned as a center for the manufacture of computing products. Firms in the valley make semiconductor memories, microprocessors, disk drives, microcomputers, and many other products. Although other regions, such as the Route 128 belt outside of Boston, have developed into important high-tech areas, probably none has had so rapid a transformation, replete with such an unusual assortment of rags-to-riches stories, as Silicon Valley.

Known properly as the Santa Clara Valley, the area is located just south of San Francisco Bay and stretches through the communities of San Jose, Palo Alto, Mountain View, Santa Clara, Cupertino, Saratoga, and Los Gatos. The valley acquired its nickname during the 1960s and 1970s, as numerous silicon-based semiconductor manufacturers flocked to the area. Not too many years ago, rich groves of pears and apricots abounded there. Since the price of real estate in the valley has soared to stratospheric levels, however, farming has diminished. It is currently the home base of companies such as Atari, Apple, Hewlett-Packard, Intel, National Semiconductor, Varian, Memorex, Ampex, Tandem, and Amdahl. In addition, IBM has a major research center there.

Why the rush to Silicon Valley? Some feel that the presence of nearby Stanford University has been a major influence, providing highly trained personnel to staff computer firms and to conduct related research. Others credit the favorable climate. Whatever the reason, the area has certainly drawn an abundance of talent, which in turn, has produced a wealth of success stories.

Tandem Computers, for example, is still less than ten years old and already enjoys annual sales in excess of $300 million. Every employee in the company is eligible for gift stock options, the value of which varies with the profits of the firm. Those who have been with the company since it went public in 1977 have received options approaching $100,000.

Then there's the case of Steven Jobs, the president and founder of Apple Computers. Apple now grosses almost $2 billion, even though it is less than ten years old. Although some claim that Jobs never designed any of the hardware or software for the original Apple computer, he did foresee the potential of the invention of his friend, Steve Wozniak. Jobs, who founded the company while only in his mid-twenties, claims that his company has made millionaires of close to 300 employees.

Already, land in Silicon Valley is scarce. In the next five years, nearly half the new workers moving into the valley will have to seek housing in another county, according to one prediction. Many valley-based companies have already been forced to build factories and research facilities in other western states. Nonetheless, the area has continued to grow in popularity. For those who live there, the good weather and high-powered computer expertise combine to create an environment that is hard to match.

Silicon Valley: High tech moves to rural surroundings.

go to a *turnkey vendor*. These companies buy hardware from a number of manufacturers and configure it into their own systems. The word *turnkey* connotes the fact that many of these systems are extremely user-friendly. Once you log on, or "turn the key," they're often as easy to manipulate as a car. Sometimes these turnkey companies are called *original equipment manufacturers (OEMs)* because they buy equipment made by other firms and "manufacture" their own systems out of it.

Commercial users who want to acquire microcomputer hardware have still a third indirect method: the computer store. Chains such as Computerland sell or lease the computers, peripherals, and software of a number of manufacturers. Increasingly, some of the larger department stores, such as Sears and Montgomery Ward, are also carrying computer products. Even the large discount drug stores now stock computer products, side by side with watches and cameras.

Many of the companies that manufacture computers, especially large computers, also make peripherals. Since almost all large computers must be closely coordinated with their disk units, there are few mainframe manufacturers that do not make their own disk units. Most independent companies that specialize in peripherals concentrate on certain types of equipment. For example, Shugart makes mostly small disk systems, and Eastman Kodak concentrates on microfilm applications. Many of these companies also produce I/O media that can be mounted on their equipment as well.

Software Suppliers

In recent years there has been a virtual stampede into the software business. Entrepreneurs have been attracted to the field because the amount of capital required to start a software firm is low. All you really need is time and some good ideas.

Third-party acquisition is less common in this sector than in hardware. In most cases, the firm selling software has also produced it. Like firms in other sectors of the computer industry, however, software firms usually specialize in a particular area, such as database systems, accounting packages, systems software, and so on. Packages may cost as little as $100 or as much as $500,000.

In addition to applications software, organizations must buy systems software. This software can often be bought from the computer manufacturers, as many of these firms also sell systems software for their machines. The decisions a firm makes about the hardware and systems software it buys dictate the range of applications software it can buy. Applications packages are written for specific computers and operating systems—so let the buyer beware.

Service Suppliers

Although advances in microcircuitry have made it easier than ever for a firm to buy its own computer, this is not always the best course of action. In some cases, it's better to use someone else's CPU and expertise. A small company may not have any computer experts on its staff, or a large company may run out of capacity on its own computer system and need to use a piece of someone else's system temporarily. Firms that are in business to sell expertise and computing services are called *computer-services companies.*

These companies work in a variety of ways. Some offer a mainframe or minicomputer system, a few software products, and a staff of experts. Their customers generally buy a CRT and teleprinter from the service company or their own sources and connect them to the service company's system over ordinary phone lines. The service company's staff advises the customer on how to set up applications. The staff also provides any necessary training in the operation of terminals. The fee schedule is often based on a monthly fixed cost, CPU connect time, secondary storage needs, and any special equipment or services that an application requires. Fees can vary dramatically from company to company, so it's always best to shop around.

Some computer-services companies make it even easier for their customers. For example, if a client firm is willing to collect data in machine-readable form, the service company can send a "bagman" over to the firm at the day's end. This person picks up the data, delivers it to the service company for overnight processing, and returns computer output to the client firm at the beginning of the next day.

The advantages of computer-services companies are that they provide needed expertise and equipment, and charges are based on usage. The major disadvantage is loss of control. Important reports may be delivered late, the user might get busy signals when access to the computer is critical, valuable programs or data may be stolen and used to the disadvantage of the firm, and so on.

Summary and Key Terms

Many types of data processing fall into two categories: batch processing and online processing. In **batch processing,** transactions or requests are collected in batches, which are sent to the CPU at periodic intervals for processing. In **online processing,** the data are entered directly into the system as they are collected, and they are immediately processed.

There are two major types of online processing: time-shared and real-time processing. In **time-shared processing** (or **time-sharing**) users generally work independently, solving their own problems, as in educational environments. Systems which utilize **real-time processing** help to control real-life activities, as these activities are actually happening.

Many computer applications in business, industry, and government fall into one of four categories: routine data processing, management information systems and decision-support systems, office systems, and design and manufacturing systems (CAD/CAM).

Routine data processing covers tasks such as record keeping and accounting that organizations must handle regularly. Among the specific tasks included in routine data processing are payroll, sales order entry, inventory control, accounts receivable, accounts payable, and general ledger.

Management information systems and decision-support systems provide decision makers with access to needed information. A system built to perform the dual role of providing routine data processing and generating information for use by decision makers is called a **management information system (MIS).** Unlike the traditional MIS, a **decision-support system (DSS)** permits the definition of new questions at an interactive terminal while the user is online.

In recent years, computer technology has been applied to the task of reducing paperwork in the office. The more fully computerized offices have been termed **automated offices** (or **offices of the future**).

Probably the most heralded of the office system technologies is **word processing,** which enables a typist to prepare documents by interweaving fresh text with "canned" text. Office systems also include hardware and software for electronic mail, teleconferencing, office management, computer graphics, and computer reprographics.

Computers are widely used in industry to improve productivity both at the design stage—through **computer-aided design (CAD)**—and at the manufacturing stage—through **computer-aided manufacturing (CAM)**. One type of CAM that has caught the attention of the news media is **robotics,** the study of the design, building, and use of robots.

A **Distributed Data Processing (DDP)** system is a system configuration in which a single application or related applications are accommodated on two or more geographically dispersed computers. A **distributed star network** often consists of a central computer, to which several remote minicomputers are connected. A less common and more expensive alternative is the **distributed ring network,** in which a central computer is absent, and a number of computers are connected serially to one another. Often, computer networks are not a simple star or ring pattern but some combination of simple patterns. A **multistar network,** for example, consists of several remote computers hooked up to a central computer in a star pattern, with each remote computer also connected to a number of local terminals in another star configuration.

DDP networks have their advantages and disadvantages. Although they can be expensive, the advantages of better service, control, and locally produced decision-making information often make them a wise choice.

Given a set of applications and financial constraints, an organization can generally find the resources it needs by contacting one or more companies in the three major sectors of the computer industry. These sectors specialize in (1) hardware, including computers and peripherals; (2) software; and (3) services. Many companies supply several of these resources, and some offer all of them.

Review Questions

1. What is the difference between batch and online processing?
2. Provide some examples of routine data-processing tasks.
3. What is the difference between a management information system and a decision-support system?

4. Provide some examples of automated office systems.
5. What is the difference between computer-aided design and computer-aided manufacturing? Provide some examples of each.
6. Define Distributed Data Processing (DDP).
7. Identify some of the advantages and disadvantages of DDP.
8. What are the three main sectors of the computer industry?
9. What is a turnkey vendor?
10. What type of role is served by the computer-services company?

Suggested Readings

Burch, John G., Felix R. Strater, and Gary Grudnitski. *Information Systems: Theory and Practice,* 2nd ed. New York: Wiley, 1983.

Chorfas, Dimitris N. *Office Automation: The Productivity Challenge.* Englewood Cliffs, N.J.: Prentice-Hall, 1982.

Katzan, Harry, Jr. *An Introduction to Distributed Data Processing.* Princeton, N.J.: Petrocelli, 1978.

McLeod, Raymond, Jr. *Management Information Systems,* 2nd ed. Palo Alto: SRA, 1983.

McWilliams, Peter A. *The Word Processing Book: A Short Course in Computer Literacy.* Los Angeles: Prelude Press, 1982.

Senn, James A. *Information Systems in Management.* Belmont, Calif.: Wadsworth, 1982.

Waite, Mitchell, and Julia Arca. *Word Processing Primer.* New York: McGraw-Hill, 1982.

Chapter 15

Systems Development I

OVERVIEW

All organizations must have systems for handling routine data processing and for getting information to people who need it. These systems don't just happen, especially when computers are involved. They require considerable planning. The process of planning, designing, and implementing data-processing and information systems, whether computerized or not, is called systems development. Unfortunately, since no two organizations are exactly alike, there is no sure-fire formula for successful systems development. A procedure that works well in one situation may fail miserably in another.

In this chapter and the next, we focus on the systems analyst, whom we first discussed in some detail in Chapter 9. There, we talked about the role of the analyst in designing applications software, which is only one part of the development of a system. Here in Chapter 15, we broaden our coverage of the analyst's role to discuss the development of whole systems. Specifically, we address some of the techniques that systems analysts employ to maximize the success of the systems they create.

Systems development is often subdivided into five steps, or phases:

- Phase 1: Preliminary investigation
- Phase 2: Systems analysis
- Phase 3: System design
- Phase 4: Acquisition of resources
- Phase 5: Systems implementation

This chapter covers the first two of these phases. Both the preliminary investigation and the systems analysis phases are used to determine if there is a need for creating a new system or modifying an existing one. Chapter 16 covers the last three phases, which deal with designing specifications for the system, acquiring computer resources to fit these specifications, and implementing the system.

We begin this chapter with an explanation of what it is that the analyst designs—the system itself. Then, after a discussion of the role of the systems analyst, we move to phase I of systems development, the preliminary investigation, during which the analyst must gain some idea of the nature and scope of the problem and propose some possible solutions. If management decides to continue with the project, development proceeds to phase II, systems analysis. In this phase, the analyst gathers data about the existing system and employs a number of analytical tools to arrive at formal proposals for management to consider. Chapter 15 ends at this point, and Chapter 16 resumes with coverage of the later phases of development.

WHAT IS A SYSTEM?

A **system** is a collection of elements and procedures that interact to accomplish a goal. A football game, for example, is played according to a system. It consists of a collection of elements—two teams, a playing field, referees—and procedures—the rules of the game—that interact to determine which team is the winner. A transit system is a collection of people, machines, work rules, fares, and schedules that get people from one place to another. And a computer system is a collection of people, hardware, software, data, and procedures that interact to accomplish data-processing tasks.

In this chapter we're interested in a particular set of systems—those that organizations establish to accomplish routine data processing and to direct information to the people who need it. These kinds of systems are not always computerized. After all, organizations had systems for handling routine paperwork and for getting information to managers before electronic computers ever existed.

Take Bellwood Garage, for example, which started out as a small business in the town of Bellwood. The garage specializes in automotive maintenance and repair work. A customer arriving at the garage is routed to the owner, or when the owner is absent, to the head mechanic. The customer describes the problems with the vehicle and specifies the repairs to be made or the routine maintenance required. The owner or mechanic then gives the customer a cost estimate of the work and the probable time of completion. Later, when the customer arrives to claim the vehicle, he or she is told the actual total amount due, and if desired, the charges are explained. Upon payment, a receipt is issued to the customer. A copy of the receipt is also filed at the garage. These procedures, which coordinate the activities at the garage so that customers are serviced and the garage gets paid, constitute part of a *manual system* for routine data processing. When systems are computerized, the computer system does part of the work that humans otherwise would have to do, from preparing customers' receipts to assembling information about business trends for management.

The function of a system, whether manual or computerized, is to keep an organization well managed and running smoothly. Systems are created and altered in response to changing needs within an organization and shifting conditions in the environment around it. When problems arise in an existing system or a new system is needed, systems development comes into play. **Systems development** is a process that consists of analyzing a system, designing a new system or making modifications to an old one, acquiring needed hardware and software, and getting the new or modified system to work.

Systems development may be required for any of a number of reasons. New laws may call for the collection of data never before assembled. The government may require new data on personnel, for example. Or the introduction of new technology, especially new computer technology, may prompt wholesale revision of a system. For example, an organization may wish to switch from a batch-oriented to an online-oriented system (as many banks have done) or to convert applications into a database environment. Or rapid growth may create strains in a system that had previously worked well. Or stiff competition from other organizations that produce the same goods or provide the same services may force management to streamline operations to save money or offer better services to the consumer. These kinds of pressure can often bring about major changes in the systems by which work is done in a business organization.

As you read on in this chapter, there are some facts you should consider about the nature of systems development. First, it is impossible to foresee every possible condition a system will encounter in the future. Because the conditions in which a system must operate are subject to change, some modifications must usually be made in any system at some point. Second, even if perfection were attainable, it is normally economically infeasible to try to solve every conceivable problem. A system that attempts to do everything might be so complicated that it would be impossible to administer efficiently, if at all. Third, there is often considerable uncertainty as to which system will work best in a given situation. Systems development is not an exact science like mathematics, in which a solution can be proved correct. Like most decisions in life, you're never sure that the alternatives you choose are the best ones.

tomorrow

DEVELOPING FLEXIBLE SYSTEMS

In developing systems today that work tomorrow, it is important to recognize the need to incorporate flexibility. Systems often take several months or years to develop, and the conditions that may be necessary for a system to work effectively change over time. The elements of change that can affect the performance of a system are present almost everywhere. The organization itself may change as may the technology and the environment in which the organization must operate.

As organizations evolve people change jobs, new jobs are created and old ones eliminated, attitudes and priorities change, and so forth. This can affect systems in many ways. For example, a manager who requires only summary information to make decisions may leave the organization and be replaced by a manager who requires an entirely different, highly detailed set of facts for the same types of decisions. Or, funds that supported a massive data collection and maintenance system in good times may suddenly dry up as the organization encounters lean times or as priorities change. Systems that don't account for such changes fall by the wayside.

Innovations in technology can also often result in sweeping reforms. For example, the migration to database technology in the 1970s caught many organizations unprepared, and many existing systems had to be revamped dramatically to fit into a database environment. Currently, the proliferation of personal computers into organizations is making many analysts wonder what the net effect will be on present systems and on future systems development efforts.

There are many environmental factors that may call for system changes. The government may require new data to be collected about an organization's employees, or it may ask that specific new safeguards be practiced to ensure the privacy of individuals on whom data is collected. New customer demands for better services—which are being provided by competitors—may also require changes to be made in current systems.

Although it is difficult to predict how changes taking place now and in the future will affect the systems of today, one fact is totally clear. An inflexible system stands very little chance of meeting with success in our world of constant change.

THE DATA-PROCESSING DEPARTMENT AND THE ROLE OF THE SYSTEMS ANALYST

In the typical business organization a number of people share responsibility for the development of systems. The director of information systems, or someone with a similar title, holds primary responsibility for systems development. Often, this position is at the level of vice president, part of top management. One of the director's duties is to oversee the formulation of a five-year plan that maps out what systems are to be studied and possibly revamped during that period. Because data and information processing affects not only the accounting functions in most firms but also most other departments, including sales, manufacturing, and personnel, a *steering committee* composed of executives in charge of these departments and other members of top management, such as the chief accountant and the financial vice president, normally approves the plan. This committee also sets broad guidelines on how computer activities are to be performed. It does not become highly involved with technical details or the administration of particular projects, however.

The technical details are the responsibility of the data-

The Fuzzy World of Systems Analysis and Design

When you take beginning courses in school, you are often shielded from the ambiguous nature of real problems. For example, a typical problem in mathematics might be to graph the equation $x^2 + y^2 = 1$. In elementary accounting, a problem might require you to prepare financial schedules based on a series of stated transactions. In computer programming, you may be asked to write a program that reads numbers, squares them, and outputs the result.

The solution to each of these problems is usually relatively clearcut. The tools that you need to solve such problems are generally clearly described in some easily identified section of a textbook. All the data you need to solve the problem are supplied for you. Also, once you reach a solution, it is usually either right or wrong; there are often no partly good, partly bad answers. Perhaps it's best that most courses in school function in this way. Sometimes it is best to learn the tools you need to solve real problems in unambiguous settings, such as textbooks and classrooms.

The world of systems analysis and design constitutes an environment altogether different from academia. True, systems analysts must also learn conceptual tools, but the emphasis is on bringing into play not only conceptual tools but also a number of reasoning abilities and experiences in order to find an acceptable solution to a real problem.

In systems analysis there are many sources of ambiguity. Often the problem itself is difficult to articulate. Even if it is well defined, the solution may not be obvious. One thing is certain, however: the best strategy for solving the problem does not usually appear in a specific chapter of a textbook on your shelf. To find a workable approach, systems analysts must draw not only on the books they have studied but also on every bit of experience that they have had from the crib to the present. Even when they have found a solution and implemented it, they'll probably never know whether they have chosen the "best" alternative. Hardly like school. But then that's the nature of systems analysis and design.

Sometimes, the process of defining the problem can be especially thorny. Take the case of John, a recent graduate of a college biology program, who has just begun a job with a state wildlife agency. John took a couple of computer and management courses in school, and since his background is stronger in these areas than that of other people in the agency, he is sent immediately to the site director to solve a computer-related problem.

After meeting with the director three times, John is frustrated. From his viewpoint, the director can't even clearly articulate the nature of the problem, if indeed there is one. All John can determine is that management of wildlife

processing department, the organization of which we described briefly in Chapter 9. This department varies widely in structure from one company to another. In one form the department is divided into three parts, as shown in Figure 15-1. Here the systems analysis and design group examines existing organizational systems which interface with the computer. Additionally, this group designs and implements new systems. The programming group codes computer programs from specifications cre-

properties is concerned, and somehow the computer should probably be used to generate a solution because of the masses of data involved.

To try to get a better feel for what the director may want, John brings home a stack of background material that is 2 feet high. John feels that he doesn't know enough about the director's job or the way in which the agency operates. The director apparently doesn't know enough about management and computers. Since the director is too busy to help solve his own problems, John must close the communication gap largely by himself.

Since John is new to the agency, a third, more experienced person, Lynn, is called in to help resolve the stalemate. Lynn isn't quite sure what the director wants either, but both she and

John decide to prepare a modest written proposal for the director and see how he reacts. They reason that it's probably best to immediately give the director something tangible to consider rather than to work independently in the dark on something ambitious. After a long period of independent development, an ambitious idea might get shot down, wasting considerable time. Better to start modestly and build the system gradually from positive feedback.

Following this strategy, John writes a small computer program in three days and runs some test data with it. When he presents the results, the director responds enthusiastically: "This is just what I need. Your approach seems so clear now that I see it in front of my eyes...." Suddenly John feels he has hit a responsive chord with the director, and the two seem to be communicating better than ever before. After three weeks of complete frustration, the two can now relax when talking to each other.

Not all definitions of problems are as difficult as this one. Sometimes, in fact, there is wide agreement on the problem and even on the methodology for the solution. But the success of almost all organizational systems development depends on the interaction of people. And when people and their imperfect ways of communicating are involved, almost any strange thing can happen at any stage of the development process.

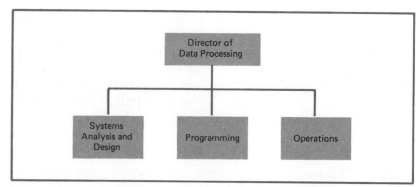

Figure 15-1. A possible organizational structure for a data-processing department.

ated by the **systems analyst.** The operations group manages day-to-day data processing once a system has become operational.

Generally speaking, the job of the systems analyst is to plan and implement systems that make use of computers that the company has or will acquire. Within the systems analysis and design group, systems analysts develop systems to meet the needs of various corporate users. When a system needs to be developed, the systems analyst interacts with the users to produce a solution. The analyst is generally involved in all stages of the development process, from the preliminary investigation to implementation.

Many organizations, of course, are not big enough to warrant a data-processing department. A small business like Bellwood Garage, for example, would have no reason to maintain such a department, especially since it doesn't yet have a computerized system. When a company like Bellwood needs the services of a systems analyst, it must turn to outside consultants.

We can more easily understand the varied activities of the analyst if we divide the process of systems development into phases. As we mentioned in the Overview, systems development typically has five phases (see Figure 15-2):

1. *Preliminary investigation.* During this phase the analyst studies the problem briefly and suggests a few possible solutions so that management can decide whether the project should be pursued further.

2. *Systems analysis.* If management decides after the preliminary investigation that further systems devel-

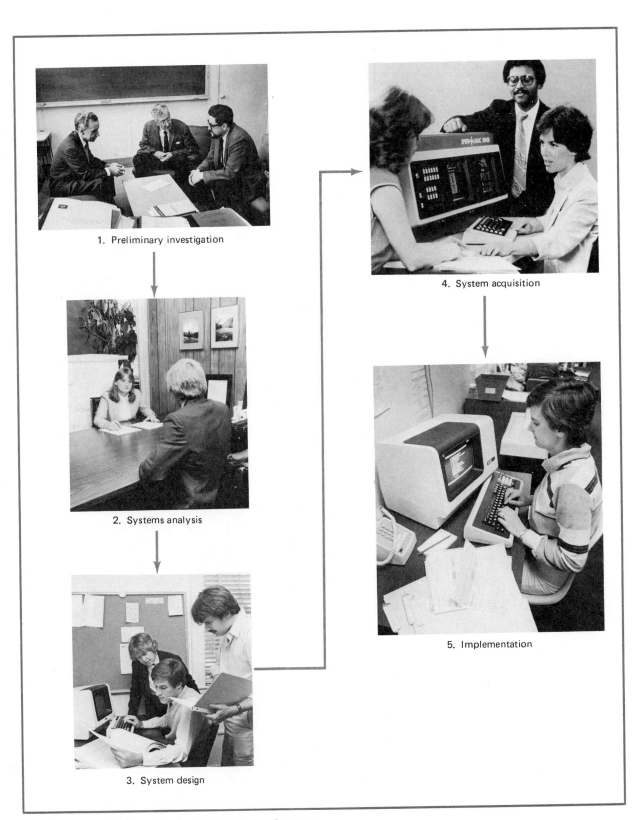

1. Preliminary investigation

2. Systems analysis

3. System design

4. System acquisition

5. Implementation

Figure 15-2. *The five phases of systems development.*

opment is warranted, the analyst must study the existing system in depth and make specific recommendations for change.

3. *System design.* During this phase, the analyst develops a model of the new system and prepares a detailed list of benefits and costs. Both the model and the list are incorporated into a report to management.

4. *System acquisition.* Upon management approval of the design model, the analyst must decide what software and hardware to obtain.

5. *Implementation.* After the components of the system have been acquired, the analyst supervises the lengthy process of adapting old programs and files to the new system, prepares specifications for programmers, and so forth.

In the remainder of this chapter we'll discuss the first two phases: the preliminary investigation and systems analysis.

PHASE I: THE PRELIMINARY INVESTIGATION

The first thing the systems analyst does when confronted with a new systems assignment is to conduct a **preliminary investigation.** One purpose of this investigation is to define the problem at hand and to suggest some possible courses of action. Another goal is to provide management with an initial estimate of the costs and benefits involved in changing the current system. Accordingly, the investigation should address the following questions:

*   What is the nature of the problem?
*   What is the scope of the project created by the problem?
*   What are some possible solutions, and which appears to be the best one?
*   What are the approximate costs and benefits of the solutions?

Let's consider each of these questions in greater detail.

The Nature of the Problem

Determining the true nature of the problems presented by the assignment is one of the key steps in the preliminary investigation. The analyst must take care at the outset to distinguish symptoms from problems.

Suppose, for example, you have been hired by the Bellwood Garage to look at the flow of work and information through the shop. The garage was set up by Charlie Higgins, the owner, in 1973. Over the years, change both within and outside the business has generated some serious problems. Although Higgins has resisted change in the past, he has come to realize that he needs professional advice. After all, he is a mechanic, not a systems expert. In desperation, he calls you in to help.

First, you hear some of the history of the business. Since 1973, a number of changes in the town of Bellwood have dramatically affected the garage. The expansion of Bellwood Junior College in 1974 and 1975 changed the personality of the town from a stable, family-oriented populace to a younger, more transient population. A couple of years later, the state decided to route a new highway past the edge of town, bringing new business to the garage. As a result, Bellwood Garage has grown steadily. In fact, in the decade during which the garage has been in business, it has tripled in size. This rapid growth, however, has not been without new problems. Systems that worked well ten years ago are straining under the increased load. Customers are complaining, and the profitability of the garage is suffering.

In conversations with a few people, including Charlie and the secretary who handles billing, you hear about some of the problems of the business in greater detail.

- Last week, a car spent nearly a week in the shop, and the customer complained. She, like some ex-customers, also pointed out that service is much faster in a competing garage just down the highway.

- A customer recently claimed that she had requested only an oil change but was given both an oil change and a tune-up. She refused to pay for the tune-up.

- A customer balked at paying a bill when the amount due was twice the amount of the estimate.

- A college student returned a car that he had brought in for service a week earlier. He claimed that the tune-up he had paid for was never performed. Higgins agreed that the car did need a tune-up, but it was difficult to tell how far the student had driven during the previous week. A mechanic remembered performing the service, but the student became angry and threatened to take the matter to small claims court.

A systems analyst must sift through a set of problems like these to ascertain that they really do exist and, subsequently, to figure out their true causes. The slow service, for example, may not be the fault of the mechanics. Instead, the problem may lie in the system for ordering parts. Investigation of the case of the week-long delay might reveal that it took Bellwood Garage almost a week to get the needed part. Furthermore, the estimate of the repair bill may have been understated, not out of intent to cheat the customer or incompetence on the part of the mechanic who made the estimate, but because unforeseen problems cropped up—and there was no formal procedure for notifying customers when this occurs.

Another aspect of determining the true nature of problems is to gauge their relative importance. The analyst must bring some perspective to this task. Some problems may be trivial; others, important. For Bellwood Garage the importance depends on how much money it is losing because of the problem. You can only determine this fact by gathering data and observing operations around the garage. Consistently slow service compared to that of competing garages may indeed be cause for serious concern, whereas the occasional irate fast talker who manages to con the garage out of additional service is not.

The Scope of the Project

In the preliminary investigation the analyst also has to determine the scope of the project created by the problem. Scope is a function of the nature of the problem and of what management is willing to spend. An organization may be ready to spend $100,000 or only $1000. Scope is also a function of what management is willing to change. Understandably, people in organizations often hesitate to switch from one procedure to another. Even though the current system may be somewhat inadequate, many people have a nagging, perhaps irrational, fear that a new one may prove to be disastrous. "After all," they argue, "isn't it better to operate inefficiently than not at all?" This apprehension is heightened when the introduction of

Research on Cyberphiliacs/Cyberphobiacs Reveals 30 percent of Workers Fear Computers

PHILADELPHIA—Computers can have strange effects on some people—they either love them so much that they cannot stop programming or they hate working with them enough to quit their jobs.

At least this is what Prof. Sanford Weinberg, a professor and administrator at St. Joseph's University here, is finding. Weinberg has been conducting research regarding cyberphiliacs (compulsive computer programmers) and cyberphobiacs (people who fear computers) since 1979.

At least 30% of the business community that deals with computers on a daily basis experiences some degree of cyberphobia, Weinberg said. Very often these are people who opted for nontechnical jobs, such as secretarial work or teaching, and who find themselves unwittingly thrust into an automated environment.

Fear of computers is a phobia, according to Weinberg, when it keeps people from functioning normally. The sufferers experience the same symptoms as those suffering from other phobias—nausea, sweaty palms and high blood pressure.

Weinberg has described an incident in which a policeman developed such a complex about the computer console in his police car that he shot it. Another sufferer attempted to thwart his enemy, the computer, by dumping pencil shavings and coffee into the console.

Treating the Phobia

"One of the major causes of the phobia is the feeling that you have lost control," Weinberg explained. Part of the treatment, therefore, is information about how the system works and what it can do.

It would seem that the proliferation of computers, particularly microcomputers, would lead to an increased level of computer literacy and, therefore, a reduction in cyberphobia. Weinberg said this is not the case. "Most people probably aren't getting educated about the problem," he said, adding that the computer education in high schools and colleges simply is inadequate. This also is reflected in the fact that young people, as well as older people, are suffering from this problem. He predicted that the numbers of people experiencing this fear of computers will increase as society becomes more and more computerized.

Weinberg pointed to the release of hardware and software products before they really are ready as a probable cause of the frustrations and "bad experiences" that create cyberphobiacs. He said that the way the marketplace works in the computer industry almost forces this release of products before they are perfect.

The other condition, the semiaddiction to computers, does not force people to switch jobs to try to avoid exposure to technology. As Weinberg described cyberphilia, it has the opposite effect of drawing people into programming to the exclusion of almost all other interpersonal relationships. "People I have talked to generally have no friends and are not married."

Whereas he has conducted workshops on cyberphobia for some large companies, the problem of cyberphilia has not attracted the same interest in a "cure." Weinberg explains this by noting that these compulsive programmers are not causing any problems in their firms. These "superprogrammers" are popular employees from a performance standpoint.

Source: Lois Paul, *Computerworld*, April 5, 1982. © 1982 by CW Communications, Inc. Framingham, MA 01701. Reprinted from COMPUTERWORLD.

computers is involved, because large dollar outlays are generally required, and many managers feel that they don't understand computers well enough to know if the costs are justified.

Because most systems in a business organization are inter-related, the analyst must draw some clear boundaries around the systems or subsystems to be studied. Inexperienced analysts frequently err on this count, developing overambitious solutions. Say, for example, a government agency that manages a number of city parks has hired an analyst to assess the potential recreational value of each park to decide which ones to improve most heavily. Let's also assume that the agency is willing to spend $100,000 annually on park improvement, or 5 percent of its budget. While the analyst looks over the potential of each park, she may discover that the organizational structure of the agency hinders effective park management. Suddenly, she's tempted to restructure the entire agency. Although to do so may indeed help the agency determine the recreational value of its parks, such a solution is probably much larger in scope than management had in mind.

Although systems analysts almost always find scores of problems that require attention in any system, they learn to accept some things as given and to find the best solution possible under the constraining circumstances. Completely new systems aren't always the answer. Sometimes a patchwork solution or minor alteration of an old system is all that is necessary.

Possible Solutions

Once the nature and scope of the problem have been defined, a number of solutions may be apparent. The important question at this point is: Does the problem have a simple, inexpensive solution that requires no further study, or is a new system or substantial alteration called for?

A mistake that many people make is to assume that all problems can be solved by computers. As the systems analyst for Bellwood Garage, for example, you might decide that a simple change in procedure—requiring customers to sign a work form upon arrival that indicates the services to be performed and the mileage on the vehicles—would cut down on customer deception and protect the garage from charges that it performed unwanted services. Given Bellwood's limited resources, this might well be the best immediate solution. Additionally, you might decide that Bellwood would be able to use a microcomputer system and terminal to an online auto parts database to considerable advantage for billing, payroll, and inventory.

To some problems there may not be a completely satisfactory solution. For example, no company, including Bellwood Garage, can completely avoid customers who don't pay their bills. It is more useful to think of minimizing some problems than eliminating them entirely.

Costs and Benefits

During the preliminary investigation the analyst should also provide a rough estimate of the costs and benefits of each recommended solution. How much should Bellwood Garage expect to spend on hardware and software, for example, if it acquired a microcomputer system or online terminal? How would company profitability benefit from installing a computer system?

Report to Management

At the end of the preliminary investigation the analyst writes a report to management with a brief description of the problems and some recommendations. If the problems have a simple solution that requires no further study, the analyst should state this clearly. If the recommendations involve extensive changes that require further study and expense, the analyst must outline the reasons for the proposed changes and summarize their costs and benefits. Once management has a preliminary "ballpark" estimate of the benefits and financial commitment involved, it can decide whether to abandon the project, implement an inexpensive or temporary solution immediately, or press forward to the next phase of development.

PHASE II: SYSTEMS ANALYSIS

Let's assume that based on the report evolving out of the preliminary investigation, management has decided to pursue systems development further. At this point, the **systems analysis** phase begins. During this phase, the main objectives are often to study the current system in depth to find out how it works and what it does, to compare these findings with some conception of what the system should be doing, and to present a detailed report to management. Stated simply, the three objectives of systems analysis are

- Fact collection
- Analysis
- A report to management

Fact Collection

The goal of fact collection is to gather evidence about what the current system does and to ascertain what information users need. Later in this phase these collected facts should enable the analyst to determine what's wrong with the current system and to generate some insights into possible solutions. These insights will become the basis for recommendations to management regarding the directions the project should take next.

Deciding which facts to collect depends largely on the problem being studied. Four sources of information about how the current system works are

- Written documents
- Questionnaires
- Interviews
- Personal observation

Written Documents. Special forms, manuals, diagrams, letters, and other written materials can provide helpful information about how the current system functions. An organization chart such as the one in Figure 15-3, covering the company functions that you're studying, is an especially useful document. These charts can provide an overview of company operations and demonstrate the relationship among people, levels of responsibilty, and the types of work that the various parts of the firm do.

At the outset of a project, the analyst may not be sure which documents will be most helpful. Naturally, you can't gather everything in sight, or you'll drown in a sea of paperwork. You should concentrate on collecting documents that tell you

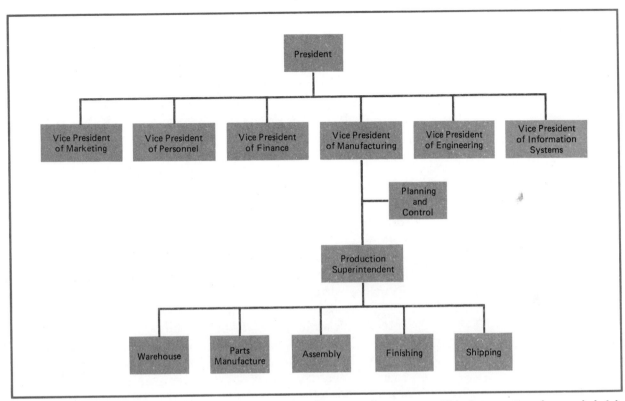

Figure 15-3. **An organization chart of the manufacturing area of a company.** This document can be very helpful to a systems analyst who must develop a system that involves the interaction of several manufacturing subunits.

the most about how the system works, as well as those that have a bearing on the key problems.

In the case of Bellwood Garage, you might want to collect samples of the work request form, the billing form, and the customer receipt to see if the lack of key data on these documents might be the cause of persistent problems. A simple change—such as providing more space to record in greater detail the repairs to be completed—might reduce some problems; for example, misunderstandings about repairs made and charges assessed.

Questionnaires. Questionnaires sent to system users are helpful for many reasons. They enable the analyst to obtain information rapidly and inexpensively from a large number of people. Also, they permit anonymous responses. If system users are geographically dispersed, questionnaires may be the only feasible means of getting information from them.

Questionnaires do, however, have a number of limitations. If many users do not respond, your results may be biased. Also, it is quite easy to create questions that are misleading, confusing, and produce biased answers in unpredictable ways. Constructing questions is a skill that is not to be taken lightly. You should study questionnaire design carefully if you think this source of information might be valuable.

Interviews. Interviews and questionnaires generally serve the same purpose: to gather information from system users. Questionnaires are helpful for amassing a great deal of information rapidly, whereas interviews allow you the flexibility to follow up interesting lines of questioning that you could not have anticipated in a questionnaire. Also, not all questions on the questionnaire are equally relevant to all subjects, but you can closely tailor an interview to the respondent.

Like writing questions, interviewing is a skill. A good interviewer almost always has a goal for the interview, such as, "This discussion should show me how customers are billed." The interviewer should prepare important questions in advance to ensure that the goal of the interview is met. In fact, it is often a good idea to send the interviewee, before the interview takes place, a letter containing some of the questions you will be asking. This is especially helpful if you have to travel for the interview and if it takes time for the interviewee to gather some of the documents you want to discuss. A preinterview letter also gives people the impression that you're organized and well prepared.

During the interview, you must also know how to be a good listener. It's often best to keep your mind open and mouth shut. To avoid communication problems, it's also important to keep the conversation at a level the user can understand. If you sense a possible misunderstanding, recite the facts as you see them; for example: "Now, as I understand the situation, this system has four parts. . . ." Before closing the interview, it's wise to ask a capstone question, such as "Do you think there is anything else I should be looking at?"

The interviewees should always include key executives. After all, they eventually authorize payment if big changes must be implemented. If they lack interest in either the problem or your approach, you'll have to do some serious rethinking.

If you're just a beginner, one further caution: Don't believe everything the interviewee says. Although most people don't lie deliberately, they often distort truths, misinterpret questions, and provide opinions rather than facts. When you present your findings to management, you want to be sure that you can back up every fact that's important to your analysis.

Observation. Suppose you've determined how a system works by employing some combination of documents, interviews, and questionnaires. The next step is to observe the system yourself. Observation can help you interpret people's responses to your earlier questions and to understand their points of view. Observation can also answer such questions as: Does the system actually work the way the people involved think it does? Is anything happening that I didn't expect?

Observation requires you to go to the workplace to watch the flow of work directly. Sometimes, by listening to what people say to each other and by watching what they do, you can detect interesting discrepancies between what they've told you in interviews and what they do in fact. Although people are aware of your presence and your purpose, they usually get used to you and relax some of their defenses after several visits, if you use the right interpersonal approach.

Analysis

After you've gathered information about the current system, it's time to analyze it to reach some conclusions. These conclusions will serve as the basis of your report to management at the end of the systems analysis phase.

Diagrams. A resource that can be particularly helpful in your analysis is diagrams of both the existing system and any new ones that you may propose. One especially useful tool is the **data flow diagram.** Figure 15-4 shows a data flow diagram for the order entry operation of a mail-order firm. Data flow diagrams provide a visual representation of data movement in an organization. They do not refer to any hardware devices, such as CRTs, disk units, tape drives, and so on. In many systems development applications it is important not to specify types of hardware too soon. Early commitments to certain types of equipment may limit the way in which you think about the system, and you can easily overlook some promising possibilities. Because they represent only the *logic* of the relationships among data, sources, destinations, flows, and data stores, data flow diagrams are referred to as *logical tools.*

System flowcharts, on the other hand, are *physical tools.* With this type of diagram, the analyst does select specific kinds of hardware devices. Figure 15-5 illustrates how such a flowchart could be created for a portion of the system depicted in Figure 15-4. You should note that the symbol for online storage in Figure 15-4 indicates the need for a disk unit, and the symbol for a document indicates the need for a printer. System flowcharts are not the same as *program flowcharts* (discussed in Chapter 10), which outline the steps that a program follows in processing data.

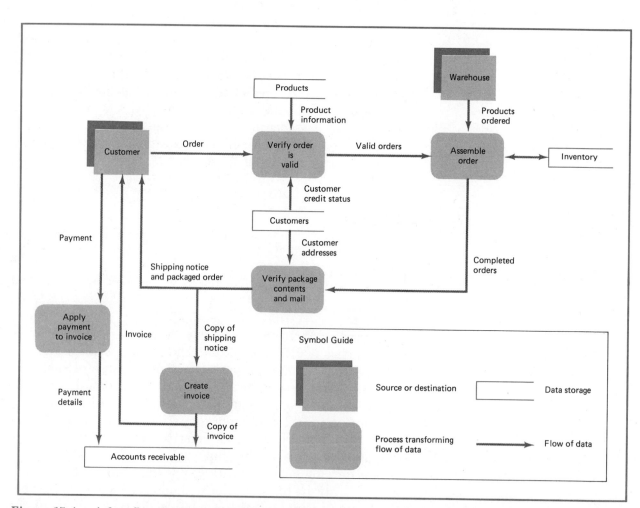

Figure 15-4.   A data flow diagram of a mail-order firm. An order triggers the process of verification and assembly of the goods ordered, and payment is recorded by accounts receivable.

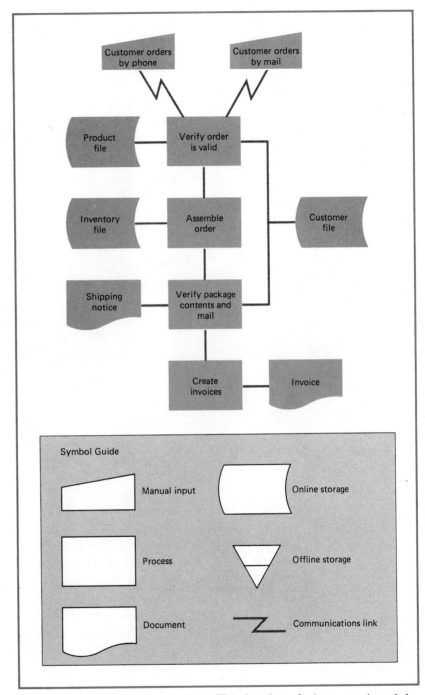

Figure 15-5.   A system flowchart. This flowchart depicts a portion of the mail-order firm's system shown in Figure 15-4.

Checklists. A second resource that can prove particularly helpful in analysis is a checklist. You might develop separate checklists for

- **System goals** For example, an accounts receivable system should get bills out quickly, identify good and bad credit risks for management, and inform customers rapidly about late payments.
- **The kinds of information needed to meet these goals** For example, what information is needed by management to identify good and bad credit risks? How will this information be collected and made available? What timing is required to get information to managers when they need it?
- **Strengths and weaknesses of the current system** For example, how does the present system measure up against these goals and information needs?

As you've probably already guessed, these lists should be developed in a top-down fashion. That is, first you decide the goals; then, management's information needs; and finally, the strengths and weaknesses of the existing system. There are several other types of checklists you might employ, depending on the requirements of the problem. Common sense must eventually dictate which type of checklist is most appropriate for the situation at hand.

Synthesis. At some point, the moment of truth will arrive: You'll need to provide some recommendations and be able to back them up. This is clearly the part of the analysis that is the most unstructured and therefore the most difficult. You must be able to *synthesize,* or combine, a number of seemingly unrelated facts into a coherent whole to reach a decision. Because almost every system is different in some respect, you can't depend on a textbook or formula approach to help you here. The ability to synthesize is characterized by a high level of common sense.

Report to Management

After collecting and analyzing the data, the systems analyst must report findings to management. This report covers many of the same subjects as the report at the end of the preliminary investigation, but it is much more thorough. In it the analyst presents all the important facts and conclusions that have come to light. The report should include

- A restatement of the goals, objectives, and scope of the project.
- A description of the current system and the problems it has generated.
- A brief review of alternatives.
- A recommendation that includes a preferred alternative.
- An estimate of the costs and benefits of the preferred alternative and a timetable indicating how long it will take to design and implement.

The report should be prefaced by a one- or two-page cover letter that summarizes the major findings. The length and detail of the report should be sufficient to convince management whether it should or should not proceed to the next stage of development, system design.

Summary and Key Terms

A **system** is a collection of elements and procedures that interact to accomplish a goal. Many organizational systems that perform routine data-processing tasks and provide information to managers are computerized. The function of a system, whether manual or computerized, is to keep an organization well managed and running smoothly.

Systems development is a process that consists of analyzing a system, designing a new system or making modifications to the old one, acquiring the needed hardware and software, and getting the new or modified system to work. Systems development may be required for any number of reasons; for example, changes in government regulations, new computer technology, rapid organizational growth, and so forth.

The director of information systems, or someone with a similar title, holds primary responsibility for the overall direction of systems development. The technical details are the responsibility of the data-processing department. The **systems analyst** is the person in the data-processing department who is involved most closely with the development of systems from beginning to end.

Systems development is often divided into five phases: preliminary investigation, systems analysis, system design, system acquisition, and implementation.

The first thing the systems analyst does in a new assignment is to conduct a **preliminary investigation.** This investigation addresses the nature of the problem under study, the potential scope of the systems development project, the possible solutions, and the costs and benefits of these solutions. At the end of the preliminary investigation the analyst writes a report to management with a brief description of the problem and some recommendations.

If, based on the report evolving out of the preliminary investigation, management decides to pursue systems development further, the **systems analysis** phase begins. During this phase, the main objectives are to study the current system in depth to find out how it works and what it does, to compare these findings with some conception of what the system should be doing, and to present a detailed report to management. Stated simply, the three objectives of systems analysis are fact collection, analysis, and a report to management.

The goal of fact collection is to gather evidence about what the current system does and what its users need. Four useful sources are written documents, questionnaires, interviews, and personal observation.

Facts, once gathered, must be analyzed. A number of tools are useful for this task, including **data flow diagrams, system flowcharts,** and checklists. The object of the analysis is to synthesize facts to reach concrete conclusions and recommendations.

After collecting and analyzing the data, the systems analyst must report findings to management. This report covers many of the same subjects as the report at the end of the preliminary investigation, but it is much more thorough.

Review Questions

1. Provide some examples of systems, both in business and in society.
2. What is systems development?
3. What are the main duties of the systems analyst?
4. Identify the five phases of systems development.
5. What is the purpose of the preliminary investigation?

6. What types of activities characterize the systems analysis phase of development?
7. Why are reports sent to management at the end of both the preliminary investigation and systems analysis phases of development?

Suggested Readings

Brooks, Frederick P. *The Mythical Man-Month: Essays in Software Engineering.* Reading, Mass.: Addison-Wesley, 1974.

Gane, Chris, and Trish Sarson. *Structured Systems Analysis: Tools and Techniques.* Englewood Cliffs, N.J.: Prentice-Hall, 1979.

Leeson, Marjorie. *Systems Analysis and Design.* Palo Alto: SRA, 1981.

Semprevivo, Philip C. *Systems Analysis: Definition, Process, and Design.* Palo Alto: SRA, 1982.

Weinberg, Gerald M. *Rethinking Systems Analysis and Design.* Boston: Little, Brown, 1982.

Wetherbe, James C. *Systems Analysis for Computer-Based Information Systems.* St. Paul: West, 1979.

Chapter 16

Systems Development II

OVERVIEW

So far, the analyst has completed the first two phases of systems development: the preliminary investigation and systems analysis. Both of these phases are often oriented toward learning whether an existing system should be altered or replaced. Suppose management has read the report evolving out of the systems analysis phase and decides to proceed with the project. What then?

At this point the analyst focuses on designing a new system, and subsequently, on acquiring it and making it operational. After managerial approval of the analysis-stage report, the ball is again in the court of the systems analyst, who must solve perhaps the hardest problem of development: what system will meet the needs of the organization better than the system now in place? The answers to this question are incorporated in still another report, delivered to management at the end of phase III, system design. This report spells out the requirements and components of the new system and provides a detailed estimate of its benefits and costs.

If management still endorses the project, the organization will proceed to the fourth phase of development, acquisition of the software and hardware needed in the new system. The analyst must select computer resources that can best meet the specifications established in the system design phase.

Finally, the system must be put into working order. Just having the components together does not mean that they will work together smoothly or that users will adapt to the new way of doing things immediately. Developing new programs, converting old facilities to new ones, and training personnel to use the new system are all part of the final phase of development, implementation.

PHASE III: SYSTEM DESIGN

The **system design** phase normally consists of four steps:

1. Review the goals and scope of the project.
2. Develop a model of the new system.
3. Perform a detailed analysis of benefits and costs.
4. Prepare a system design report.

Review the Goals and Scope of the Project

The design of the new system must conform to the goals and scope approved by management in the analysis phase. Thus, it is always wise to review these matters carefully before proceeding with the design. They define both the direction and limits of the development of the project.

This kind of review is common in types of design other than systems design. For example, an automobile designer must keep in mind the kind of product management wants when designing a car. If management wants a fuel-efficient automobile that will appeal to young people and sell for about $7000, the designer would be foolish to ignore these guidelines when creating a new car.

In fact, the systems analyst should review the project specifications not only at the beginning of the design phase but also throughout it. As the new system takes shape, the analyst must continually ask questions such as "Will this alternative meet the needs of users?" Or "Will the new system satisfy the budget requirements?" To answer these questions, the analyst should actively communicate with users and managerial personnel.

Develop a Model of the New System

Once the analyst understands the nature of the design problem, it is usually helpful to draw a number of diagrams of the new system. Diagrams can show how data will logically flow through the new system as well as how the various physical components of the systems will fit together.

Two diagrammatic tools frequently used for this purpose are data flow diagrams and system flowcharts. (We discussed these tools in Chapter 15 in the discussion of systems analysis.) These diagrams are helpful in both analysis and design. *Data flow diagrams* portray the movement of data and also the relationships among data, their sources, and their destinations. *System flowcharts* depict the relationships between the work to be done and the hardware in a system. Another option, of course, is to invent your own diagrams. The best tool is one that depicts the applications environment in a way that is most meaningful for the designer and others who might use the diagrams. The choice of a tool depends largely on the nature of the system and the design standards adopted by the organization.

When designing a system, the analyst must take into account the following considerations:

- Output requirements
- Input requirements
- Data access, organization, and storage
- Processing
- System controls
- Personnel and procedures

Output Requirements. Before designing any other part of the system, the analyst must go directly to the "bottom line": the outputs the system must produce. The outputs directly satisfy the needs of the users and dictate what inputs are required, what processing must be done, how data are to be organized and stored, and so forth.

In designing outputs, the analyst must take into account a number of factors. At the **logical design level,** general output requirements must be defined. Three decisions must be made at this level. First and most essentially, the analyst must answer the question, "What types of information do users need?" The analyst should have collected enough facts during the systems analysis phase to have a good idea of users' needs. Now the problem is to set up a system that meets them. Second, the analyst must consult with users to find out how detailed the outputs should be. Too much detail would waste computer resources and make it hard for users to find what they need. Too little implies that some critical needs for information are left unmet. Third, the analyst must determine when outputs are needed. Some outputs may be needed daily, others weekly or monthly, some at the end of a quarter, and some only once a year. Other types of information may be needed immediately. These general output requirements define the software needed for the system.

After these decisions at the logical design level have been made, the analyst must address considerations related to hardware. This is called the **physical design level.** First, the analyst must decide which output media to use. The options include display screen, plain or special-form paper, and microfilm, among others. Given one or more output media, the analyst can then select the appropriate output hardware—CRT terminals, printers, and so forth. Additionally, the analyst must

The Human Factor in System Design

Unless it takes into account the human beings who must use it, even the most rationally designed system will probably fail. No matter how well a system should work in theory, the acid test of success is how effectively it operates when actually implemented. Only at this time is it subjected to the trials and tribulations of interacting with the human race.

During the design stage, one of the most important factors to consider is the native ability of the user. When the airline reservations systems were first computerized in the 1950s and 1960s, for example, analysts had to ask several important questions about users' abilities: How sophisticated a dialogue with the computer could the typical airline agent handle? Could agents work with a programming language on a daily basis? How simple could such a specialized programming language be and still retain its effectiveness? Could the agent work with the language in distracting environments such as an airport or a busy travel agency, where demanding people and ringing phones are constant interruptions? The designers of the airline reservations system succeeded in handling the human parameters, but not all systems designers have been so fortunate.

Another important human element is the user's role in the organization. High-level managers who have few computer skills, for example, often balk at working at a display terminal in a busy area where they may be observed by lower-level workers in the firm, because they don't want to seem incompetent in front of their subordinates. Therefore, senior managers with successful images to protect often set higher standards for the friendliness of a system than do junior personnel without track records. Computer systems might threaten the position of people in an organization in other ways as well. Several behavioral researchers have found that data-processing personnel tend to resist acquisition of personal computers by their firms, because the employees who use the personal computers become independent of the data-processing department, diminishing the need for its services.

Equipment and workplaces must also take into account human frailties. The glare and flicker of CRT screens must be minimized: furniture should be adjustable and must be chosen carefully to prevent strain on the muscles and bones of the user. Equipment designers also must eliminate any bothersome noises that emanate from computing equipment. By designing systems in which it is comfortable and safe to work, analysts not only meet a social responsibility to users but also serve employers. Poorly treated workers tend to perform less effectively than those who are treated well.

Like any other people, those who interact with computer systems have their limitations. The systems analyst must plan around these limitations rather than expect people to rise to new levels of intellect or to change their predispositions in order to meet any extraordinary demands made by a new system.

define the format of the output on each medium and device. For example, the analyst must decide how to arrange the headings, spacing, columns, and all other elements on any printed reports. A valuable aid in planning the format of reports is the **printer spacing chart,** shown in Figure 16-1. The chart is a grid containing a cell for every print position on the page. The analyst blocks the elements of the report onto the grid in various proposed positions. Ultimately, the analyst and users choose one of these alternatives. If CRT output is desired, it too must be formatted in a similar way, taking into account the dimensions and capabilities of the screen.

Input Requirements.   Once the output considerations have been settled, the analyst must determine what inputs are needed to produce the necessary outputs and how these inputs should enter the system. Many of the considerations that influence the design of outputs also affect the inputs.

The first problem to be tackled is what data to gather. Certain information must be extracted from these data if the system is to generate the reports and other outputs users want. The system can't create detailed monthly sales reports, for example, without data on each individual sale during the month—the item sold, the salesperson, the item's price, and so forth. Thus, the analyst must ensure that these data are collected.

Once the analyst has identified the data required, he or she can define its format. When defining inputs for processing of printed sales reports, for example, the analyst specifies the length and contents of each of the data records as well as any codes that will be a part of them. The **record layout form**

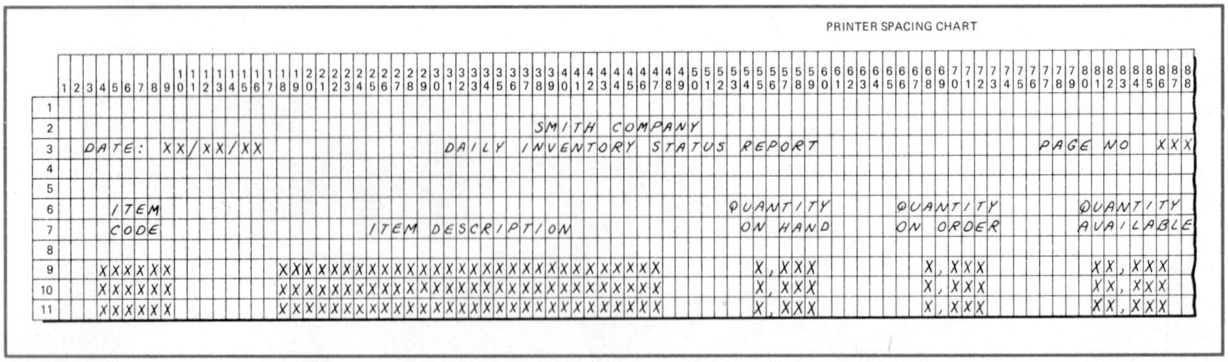

Figure 16-1.   A printer spacing chart. This chart is a formatting tool enabling the systems analyst to plan the format of a printed report.

shown in Figure 16-2 facilitates the process of formatting records. If the system is transaction-oriented, the form in which data are entered on the CRT screen is established.

Since output must be produced according to a schedule, input too must enter the system at the right time. If, for example, warehouse personnel want an inventory update by the first Monday of every week, and this information is now being supplied on Wednesday, the analyst must determine if the change is both suitable and possible.

Other input considerations include the choice of media and devices on which to enter the data. The input medium may be floppy disk, punched card, or OCR documents, to name a few alternatives. Devices include equipment on which these media may be mounted.

Data Access, Organization, and Storage. The analyst has to decide what kind of access is needed to the data—random or sequential—and, subsequently, the way the data should be organized. You'll recall from Chapter 5 that data can be organized in sequential, indexed-sequential, or relative files. Some applications such as billing may require only sequential files, whereas others such as inventory status reporting for decision support may call for relative files capable of rapid random access.

Another option in data organization is a database management system, which consists of a group of programs that coordinate access to a database. A database integrates a number of data elements so that many different applications

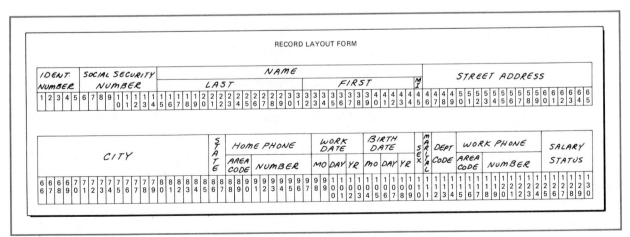

Figure 16-2. *A record layout form for describing the format of records in data files.*

programs can draw on them. In Chapter 12, we discussed the conditions under which this type of organization is appropriate.

Finally, the analyst must choose secondary storage media and devices. Depending on the type of access and file organization specified earlier, floppy disk, hard disk, tape, or perhaps some combination of these media is most appropriate. The choice of media, in turn, narrows the range of appropriate secondary storage hardware. If hard disk is the medium of choice, for example, the analyst must select an appropriate hard-disk storage unit.

Processing. Processing involves all points in the system where any work takes place. One of the most important of these sites is the CPU. To establish processing requirements, the analyst must decide what types of computations and input/output tasks are required and whether any specialized processing environments are necessary. For example, if the computer will be doing almost exclusively business-oriented computations, a computer system that excels in this type of processing should be selected. Or if many remote sites are involved in interrelated processing tasks, perhaps a distributed data-processing system should be considered. Other needs of the organization may necessitate real-time and/or database processing.

System Controls. *System controls* include provisions to ensure the security, accuracy, and privacy of information. These controls are also designed to protect the hardware and software resources of the firm.

Security controls protect data, programs, and equipment from destruction, unauthorized modifications, disclosure to unauthorized personnel, and other threats. Locks on doors, alarms, passwords to confidential programs and data, and disguises (called encryption) for programs and data are all methods of enhancing security. Other tactics include dividing job responsibilities in such a way that it is difficult for a single person to commit a criminal act. As insurance against destruction or theft, the system should allow for backup and recovery. That is, copies of important files and programs should be maintained at a remote site in case the originals are destroyed.

Accurate data are vital not only to routine data-processing operations but also to decision making. *Accuracy controls* ensure that data are correct and complete. For example, before a payroll check is written by a computer system, the system should test to see whether the amount of the check is reasonable. Also, it should count the number of checks issued, and that tally should be compared to a manual count.

Auditing is the practice of certifying that procedures in an organization are being followed as described, and that facts used internally by the organization or facts disseminated to outside parties are correct. Auditing not only ensures that businesses keep close track of their financial operations but also enables independent accounting firms to certify the legitimacy of the annual reports sent to stockholders. An accounting firm can find out how much money a company has made and spent only if it can trace business transactions from source documents to final recording. *Audit controls* ensure that this tracing can be done. The auditing system must provide an **audit trail,** so that specific outputs can be traced back to specific inputs. If you want to deduct medical expenses, you must establish the same types of trails when you prepare your taxes. If you claim $2000 in expenses, for example, you should set up a system of receipts to make your claim believable to the government, in case you are the object of a tax audit.

Privacy refers to the rights of people and organizations to determine when, how, and in what way information about them is to be disseminated to others. *Privacy controls,* many of which are the result of government regulation, ensure that these rights are protected.

The types of controls employed depend largely on whether the system is batch or online. For example, in batch processing, many of the accuracy controls test the correctness of the batch as a whole. In online processing, however, special controls must be built into each online applications program to verify the integrity of each piece of incoming data. For example, if a customer makes a $1000 purchase on a credit card, the control system should immediately check the validity of the account number and the customer's credit limit.

Personnel and Procedures.   The design of a system is incomplete unless the analyst spells out what personnel are needed to run the system and what procedures they should follow on the job.

Personnel specifications list the types of personnel who are needed to make the system operative. Because personnel usually constitute a major system cost, these specifications must be made with care.

Procedures indicate how the system works. For example, a procedure might state, "After clerks in the order entry department have received an order and investigated the legitimacy and credit status of the customer, they should send the associated order form directly to the warehouse to be filled." Many procedures are outlined in writing, so that the responsibilities of each person in the system are made clear. Visual aids, such as data flow diagrams and flowcharts, are helpful for documenting procedures.

Analysis of Benefits and Costs

As you probably already know, most organizations are acutely sensitive to costs, including computer system costs. Senior management understandably requires a detailed analysis of the costs and benefits of a system before it will give its approval.

Costs include both the initial investment in hardware and software and ongoing costs such as personnel and maintenance. Some benefits can be computed easily by calculating the amount of labor saved, the reduction in paperwork, and so on. These are sometimes called *tangible benefits,* because they are easy to quantify in dollars. Other benefits, such as better service to customers or improved information for decision makers, are more difficult to convert into dollar amounts. These are often called *intangible benefits.* Clearly, the existence of intangible benefits makes it more difficult for management to reach firm decisions. On projects with a high proportion of such benefits, management must ask questions such as "Are the new services that we can offer to customers worth the $100,000 it will cost us?"

In comparing alternative ways to spend its money, management must also take into account taxes and interest rates. A project that requires a million-dollar expenditure today is not quite as attractive as one that spreads the million dollars evenly over a ten-year period. Thus, the timing of costs and benefits is another important factor.

System Design Report

Once the design has been completed, and benefits and costs assessed, the analyst prepares a report for management. This report should provide all the facts that must be weighed before final approval can be given to the system. The analyst might preface such a report with a three to five-page cover letter summarizing the primary recommendations, the reasoning used to draw conclusions, and other important information. The report itself contains all the details on the system design as well as the associated costs and benefits. The important items to be covered in either the report or cover letter are

- The nature of the current system and its problems
- Design considerations imposed by the application
- All major recommendations
- A detailed statement of the costs and benefits of the new system
- A timetable showing how long it will take to acquire and implement the new system

When writing such a report, the designer should keep the explanation at the level of the reader. It is entirely possible that some of the senior managers who must grant final approval are unfamiliar with the project. Some of the executives who participated in earlier phases of development may have changed jobs, gone on vacation, or forgotten the details of the project. Therefore, the report should include all essential facts and should present them clearly in nontechnical language. It should also review the history of the project, stating why it was begun in the first place and repeating the conclusions of the preliminary investigation and the systems analysis phases.

PHASE IV: SYSTEM ACQUISITION

Once a system has been designed and the required types of software and hardware have been specified, the analyst must decide from which vendors to buy the necessary components. This decision lies at the heart of the **system acquisition** phase.

The Request for Quotation (RFQ)

Many organizations, especially governmental ones, formulate their buying or leasing needs by preparing a document called a **Request for Quotation (RFQ).** This document contains a list of technical specifications for equipment and software, determined during the system design phase. A sample RFQ for a microcomputer purchase is shown in Figure 16-3. A RFQ may range in length from a few pages to hundreds, depending on the magnitude and complexity of the acquisition. The RFQ is sent

REQUEST FOR QUOTATION

1. <u>General Information</u>. The Information Systems Group of the Ames Corporation wishes to acquire forty (40) microcomputer systems. These systems will be used for a variety of administrative and staff functions. Compatibility with existing systems is a major concern.

2. <u>System Requirements</u>. The following are the minimum requirements of the systems to be acquired:

    *   128K bytes of main memory
    *   Cassette tape interface
    *   Two 5¼-inch floppy disk drives
    *   RS232C asynchronous communications interface
    *   Tractor feed printer (minimum 60 characters per second, with up to 132 characters per line)
    *   Programmable audio output
    *   Monochrome display (minimum 24 lines by 80 characters, green phosphor preferred)
    *   Color graphics capability
    *   BASIC language in ROM module
    *   Operating system software to support communications to OS/MVS operating system on Ames Corporation mainframes
    *   Detatched typewriter-style keyboard with 10-key numeric pad
    *   All cables to connect aforementioned components

    The equipment must be new and in current production.

3. <u>Additional Needs</u>. The quote should include the cost of each of the following, where available:

    *   Electronic worksheet software
    *   Word processing software
    *   Operating system software
    *   Diagnostic software

4. <u>Required Quote Specifications</u>. All quotes must be received by the Purchasing Director at Ames (P.O. Box 8402) by January 15, 1984. Quotes must include:

    *   Technical specifications of each item
    *   Purchase price of each item, showing both quantity one and quantity forty cost
    *   Maintenance cost of each item
    *   Cost of manuals
    *   Installation and shipping charges
    *   Warranty period and specifications
    *   Delivery schedule (It is desired to have all units installed by June 15, 1984.)

5. <u>Questions</u>.
    Questions concerning bids should be sent to:

    John Long
    Director of Information Systems
    Ames Corporation
    P.O. Box 8415
    Colorado Springs, CO 80903

Figure 16-3. A Request for Quotation (RFQ) for a microcomputer purchase.

to all vendors who might satisfy the organization's needs. As you may recall from Chapter 14, there are many types of vendors in the marketplace and many types of sales arrangements. To acquire microcomputers like the ones specified in Figure 16-3, the buyer would probably contact retail computer stores and microcomputer manufacturers. Vendors should almost always

Contracts with Vendors: Think Before You Sign

An extremely important part of acquiring a computer system or computer-related service is the legal contract. Many vendors make promises about the performance of their merchandise that can be seductive. Therefore, it is always a sound idea to put all promises in writing in the event that something goes wrong. In addition, even though most vendors attempt to deal honestly with their customers, it is easy to misinterpret words and misstate facts. A properly written contract makes clear to everyone the terms of the arrangement.

Moreover, if you are making a major acquisition, you should seek the advice of an attorney with computer expertise before signing a contract. Contracts are almost always written in legal terms, and your understanding of an expression might be quite different from that of a court of law. A good computer lawyer can translate the requirements for your system into the appropriate legal wording.

When you have expressed a desire to acquire products or services, the vendor will ask you to sign the contract, or "standard purchase agreement." This document includes such items as important performance specifications, product warranties, delivery dates, maintenance provisions on equipment or software, payments, trade-in arrangements, and so forth. Since the contracts are provided by the vendor, they are almost always written in its favor. Naive buyers sometimes have the impression that they must accept all the terms in the vendor's standard contract in order to complete the purchase. To the contrary, portions of the contract can be

changed or deleted without rewriting the entire document. You just cross out the sections you don't like and either insert the reworded clauses or write them on the back of the contract.

While examining a proposed purchasing agreement, you must be sensitive to the many things that might go wrong. The timing of service, for example, is a seemingly minor detail that if overlooked can temporarily cripple an organization. The contract should ensure that emergency service calls will be made within a set period of time after proper notification. Otherwise, equipment in need of repair may stay that way for weeks. Also, to cover the possibility that a vendor will have difficulty in correcting a problem, the contract should have a penalty clause.

Whether you are buying a large or a small system, you should take the contract seriously. All important considerations should be written in terms that either you or your lawyer can understand.

be encouraged in the RFQ to visit or phone the organization where the system is to be installed, to obtain additional information.

Evaluating Bids

Once vendors have submitted their bids—or quotes—in response to the RFQ, the organization acquiring the resources must decide which bid to accept. Two useful tools for making this choice are a vendor rating system and a benchmark test.

Vendor Rating System. One system for rating vendors is illustrated in Figure 16-4. In many **vendor rating systems** such as the one in the figure, important criteria for selecting computer system resources are identified and each is given a weight. For example, in Figure 16-4, the "60" for hardware and "30" for documentation may be loosely interpreted to mean that hardware is twice as important as documentation to this organization. Each vendor submitting an acceptable bid is rated on each criterion, with the associated weight representing the maximum possible score. The buyer then totals the scores and—possibly—chooses the vendor with the highest total.

Although such a rating tool does not guarantee that the best vendor will always have the highest point total, because many important factors may be difficult to quantify, it does

Criterion	Weight (Maximum Score)	Vendor 1 Score	Vendor 2 Score
Hardware	60	60	40
Software	80	70	70
Cost	70	50	65
Ease of use	80	70	50
Modularity	50	30	30
Vendor support	50	50	50
Documentation	30	30	20
		360	325

Vendor 1 has
highest total score

Figure 16-4. A point-scoring approach for evaluating vendors' bids.

have the advantage of being simple to apply and somewhat more objective than other techniques. If several people are involved in the selection decision, each one may be asked to rate vendors independently. Then the scores are averaged. Because each criterion must be considered separately and is limited by its weight, this procedure minimizes bias. Bias can arise because people tend to select vendors whose equipment they are familiar with, simply because they are afraid to learn new systems.

Benchmark Tests. Some organizations, after tentatively selecting a vendor, make their choice conditional on the successful completion of a **benchmark test.** Such a test normally consists of running a *pilot* version of the new system on the hardware and software of the vendor under consideration. To do this, the acquiring organization generally visits the benchmark testing center of the vendor and attempts to determine how well the hardware/software configuration will work if installed.

Benchmark tests are expensive and far from foolproof. It's very possible that the pilot system will perform admirably at the benchmark site but the real system, when eventually installed at the site of the acquiring organization, will not. Benchmark testing is just another means of minimizing the uncertainty in choosing among vendors.

PHASE V: IMPLEMENTATION

Once arrangements have been made with one or more vendors for delivery of computer resources, the **implementation** phase begins. This phase includes all the remaining tasks that are necessary to make the system operational and successful.

To ensure that the system will be working by a certain date, the analyst must prepare a timetable. One tool for helping with this task is a **Gannt chart,** illustrated in Figure 16-5. The chart shows when certain activities related to implementation must start and finish. In order to prepare such a chart, the analyst responsible for scheduling must know how many data-processing personnel will be assigned to each activity as well as the work requirements of the activity. Some of the implementation schedule is actually prepared during earlier phases of systems development. For example, the cost and availability of personnel must be known in order to obtain managerial approval at the end of the system design phase, and a vendor delivery schedule must be agreed upon as part of the system acquisition phase.

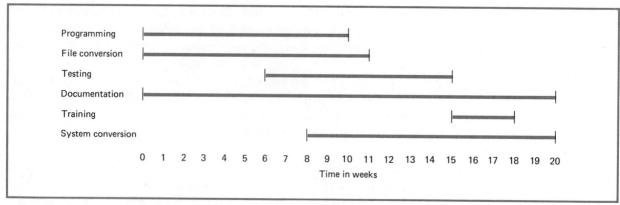

Figure 16-5. A Gannt chart.

Implementation consists of many activities, including

- Programming/file conversion
- Debugging
- Documentation
- Training
- System conversion
- Feedback and evaluation
- Maintenance

Programming/File Conversion. Often, a new system requires creation and modification of programs and data files. The analyst tells programmers the specifications that all programs and data must meet if they are to operate successfully on the new system. The programmers then code the programs and data according to these specifications. As we mentioned in Chapter 9, program specifications describe what the program must do, how it should be designed, the language in which it will be written, and they way in which it will be tested and documented.

Debugging. Before any programs in the new system are made operational, they must be free of errors, or "bugs." Debugging means much more than developing programs that seem to work. One of the most important steps in debugging is subjecting programs to a set of rigorous tests. Thorough testing can prevent costly mistakes later on. A small bug that could have been fixed for a few dollars during the testing stage may cause thousands of dollars of damages if incorrect data are generated when the program is operational. We also talked about debugging in some depth in Chapter 9.

Documentation.   The preparation of the written documents that describe how a system and its various components work is called *documentation.* Typical documents are system and program flowcharts, data flow diagrams, user manuals, system manuals, and sample input and output forms. Documentation should be prepared during all phases of development as the system is taking shape.

Unfortunately, some organizations wait until almost the entire system is finished to begin documentation. As a result, the preparation of the documents is often rushed, and the analyst can easily forget how certain parts of the system work. If poor documentation is the result, it will usually take longer for people to understand how to work effectively on the system.

Training.   Training is often provided for a fee by the vendors supplying certain elements of the system. Training enables users, programmers, and key support personnel to learn what they need to know about the vendor's product. Training often occurs in classes that are paced by training workbooks. There may even be homework. Some of the classes are general enough so that almost everyone who will use the system can attend. Some are conducted in "computerese," making a highly technical background a prerequisite. Often, training involves actually using the new hardware and/or software.

System Conversion.   The process of changing from the old system to the new one is called *system conversion.* There are many different approaches to system conversion.

The new system is sometimes phased in slowly, piece by piece. When one part of the system is working well, the next piece is made operational. This approach avoids the problems associated with introducing too many changes too soon.

In other cases, the new system and old system are run in *parallel* for a period of time. If the new one fails, the old one is available for backup. This is not possible in all cases, because the old and new systems may be entirely dissimilar.

Feedback and Evaluation.   Once the new system is operational, its performance must be appraised by comparing the

System Documentation

In many fields, documentation—written descriptions of how something works— is a way of life. For example, a durable-goods manufacturer would never even attempt to begin to produce an item before a detailed blueprint was available. Additionally, if it had to test the suitability of a product, such a firm would keep a written journal of the results for later reference.

By contrast, managers often follow a different, more informal set of procedures. With the exception of many of those in financial institutions and a handful of other organizations, systems and procedures are generally not well documented. People often follow word-of-mouth instructions as they do their jobs. In some cases, not only can this cause people to perform their jobs incorrectly but also, if the system needs to be modified at some point, it may be very difficult for the systems analyst to determine what the current system is supposed to be doing.

There are five types of documentation associated with a system. As a rule, each type should be prepared as the system is being developed. Unless the details of a project are recorded immediately, they may very well be forgotten. A number of psychologists have reported that after a week, we can recall only about 10 percent of what we have learned today. After three weeks, this percentage drops off to nearly zero! If someone with essential knowledge about a system leaves, the practice of document-as-you-go may save the organization from potential disaster.

The five types of documentation are

- **Documentation of the life-cycle of the project** This part of the documentation package is a journal of the effort to develop the system, from start to finish. Its importance cannot be overemphasized. To take just one instance in which this kind of documentation is helpful, suppose a manager wants to find out whether the project team has thoroughly investigated some specific system alternative. The systems analyst should be able to find a convincing answer to such a question, with numbers to back it up, in this part of the documentation. Documents of this type include narratives telling how subsystems work, memos, and backup documents on such subjects as the initiation of the project, identification of problems and potential solutions, needs assessment, approvals, computation of costs and benefits, progress reports, minutes from meetings, and so forth.

- **System documentation** Included here are the design aids and other materials that

actual performance of the system with the performance expected of it. The analyst should address the following questions:

- Is the system actually delivering the benefits that it was expected to provide?
- Are all the outputs from the new system useful?
- Are operating costs running at expected levels?

In addition to the system itself, the whole systems development process should be evaluated at this time. Was everything com-the systems analyst has prepared from a set of user requirements. Generally, this part of the documentation package consists of the system specifications, notes on the system design, one or more diagrams of the system, and special instructions for program coding. When completed, portions of the system documentation package are turned over to the programming staff.

- **Program documentation** In this category are annotated programs and a number of supporting documents describing how the programs work. When completed, the documentation package for a program is typically stored in a "program vault," which

contains the documentation packages for other programs as well. If the documentation of programs is centrally located, it can easily be consulted when maintenance or auditing of programs is necessary.

- **Operations documentation** This form of documentation is available for the benefit of the operations staff. It generally includes instructions to computer-room operators, data-entry personnel, tape librarians, and other staff members. Thus, if a problem occurs at 3 A.M., when a program is being run, the operator can consult the documentation package. If such a package does not exist, the operator has no alternative but to awaken the programmer from a sound sleep in order to solve the problem.

- **User manuals** These documentation aids assist the users of the system. A good user manual for an applications program describes how to run the program and handle errors. It also provides instructive examples of various routines in the program. User documentation is often one of the most critical elements of the entire documentation effort. If the user manuals are poor, many people who could benefit from the system may elect not to use it.

pleted on schedule? Was the system implemented within budget, or were there serious cost overruns?

Maintenance.   Ongoing maintenance is important to any system. If the system has been designed well, it should be flexible enough to accommodate changes over a reasonable period of time with minimal disruption. If at some point, however, a major change becomes necessary, another system will be needed to replace the current one. At this point, the systems development cycle, from the preliminary investigation to implementation, begins all over again.

tomorrow

THE CHANGING FACE OF SYSTEMS DEVELOPMENT

There are many problems with the way information systems have traditionally been developed in organizations. First, systems often take too long to analyze, design, and implement. By the time a system is finally put into operation, important new needs surface which were not part of the original plan. Also, sometimes users lose interest and independently develop information channels of their own, which they are reluctant to abandon when the organization's system is finally in place. Second, the system being developed is often not the right one. Managers almost always have difficulty expressing their information needs, and it is not until they begin to use a system that they discover what it is they really need.

To plan systems today that are usable tomorrow, researchers are experimenting with a number of new development tools. Two tools that are gaining popularity are *heuristic development* and *prototyping.*

A heuristic can be defined loosely as a "rule of thumb," such as "never change a winning game," a rule followed by competitors in many sports. The fact that users almost always request changes once a system is operational suggests that systems development should be a heuristic or evolutionary development process. With heuristic development, users are given the opportunity to work with outputs of the system and to provide some useful feedback to the analyst before a massive development effort is undertaken. In this way, strategies that don't seem to work can be abandoned and the promising ones can be explored further until the best solution is reached. When this trial-and-error process firmly establishes a desirable and stable output system, an input system is then developed. Designing an input system after developing an output system is a logical sequence.

Prototyping, like heuristic development, is an iterative process. In heuristic development the focus is on refining an *output* system first; the focus in prototyping is on developing a small model—or prototype—of the *overall* system. As users work with the prototype and suggest modifications, the prototype may be "scrapped" in order to undertake a conventional, large-scale development effort, or perhaps a second prototype is developed to gain new insights into user needs.

Both heuristic development and prototyping proceed through roughly the same logical sequence of phases as traditional systems development. The difference, is that both of these newer methodologies develop systems by going through several, less-ambitious iterations of the traditional process, refining the system at each iteration through interactive user feedback.

Summary and Key Terms

The **system design** phase of systems development consists of four steps: (1) reviewing the goals and scope of the project, (2) developing a model of the new system, (3) performing a detailed analysis of benefits and costs, and (4) preparing a system design report.

Reviewing the goals and scope that were approved by management in the analysis phase is important because the goals and scope respectively define the direction and limits of the development of the project.

When designing a system, the analyst must take into account the following considerations: output requirements; input requirements; data access, organization, and storage; processing; system controls; and personnel and procedures.

Output considerations include determining the information users need, the level of detail required, when the outputs are needed, media, devices, and output format. The first three of these constitute the **logical design level** for output; the last three, the **physical design level**. A valuable aid in planning the format of outputted reports is the **printer spacing chart.**

Input considerations are similar to those for output. A valuable aid in planning the format of input records is the **record layout form.**

Data access, organization, and storage considerations include determining the types of access users need to data, organizing data elements to permit these sorts of accesses, and choosing the appropriate storage media and devices.

Processing involves all points in the system where work takes place, especially the site of the main CPU. To establish processing requirements the analyst must decide what types of computational and input/output tasks are required and whether any specialized processing environments are necessary.

System controls include provisions to ensure the security, accuracy, and privacy of information. These controls are also designed to protect the hardware and software resources of the firm. The systems established to ensure accuracy must provide an **audit trail,** so that specific inputs can be traced back to specific outputs.

The design of a system is incomplete unless the analyst spells out what personnel are needed to run the system and what procedures they should follow on the job. Personnel specifications list the types of personnel that are needed to make the system operative. Procedures indicate how the system works.

Once the design has been completed, and benefits and costs assessed, the analyst once again prepares a report for management. This report should provide all the facts that must be weighed before final approval can be given to the system.

Once a system has been designed, and the required types of software and hardware have been specified, the analyst must decide from which vendors to buy the necessary components. This decision lies at the heart of the **system acquisition** phase.

Many organizations, especially governmental ones, formulate their buying or leasing needs by preparing a document called a **Request for Quotation (RFQ).** This document contains a list of technical specifications for equipment and software, determined during the system design phase.

Once vendors have submitted their bids in response to the RFQ, the organization acquiring the resources must decide which bid to accept. Two useful tools for making such a choice are a vendor rating system and a benchmark test. In most **vendor rating systems,** important criteria for selecting computer system resources are identified and weighted. Data-processing personnel then rate each vendor on each criterion. A **benchmark test** normally consists of running a pilot version of the new system on the hardware and software of the vendor that is under consideration. To do this, the acquiring organization generally visits the benchmark testing center of the vendor and attempts to determine how well the hardware/software configuration will work if installed.

Once arrangements have been made with one or more vendors for delivery of computer resources, the **implementation** phase begins. This phase includes all the remaining tasks that are necessary to make the system operational and successful, including programming and file conversion, debugging, documentation, training, system conversion, feedback and evaluation, and maintenance. A **Gannt chart,** showing when activities related to implementation must start and finish, is normally prepared at the beginning of the implementation phase.

Review Questions

1. Identify the four steps of the system design phase of systems development.
2. What considerations must the systems analyst take into account when developing a model of the new system?
3. Why must output requirements be addressed before all other considerations when one is developing a model of a new system?

4. Identify several types of system controls.
5. What is the difference between tangible and intangible benefits?
6. What types of items should be incorporated in the report to management at the end of the system design phase?
7. What is the purpose of a RFQ?
8. Identify the activities of the implementation phase of systems development.

Suggested Readings

Ferrari, Domenico. *Computer Systems Performance Evaluation.* Englewood Cliffs, N.J.: Prentice-Hall, 1978.

Squire, Enid. *Introducing Systems Design.* Reading, Mass.: Addison-Wesley, 1980.

Wetherbe, James C. *Cases in Systems Design.* St. Paul, Minn.: West, 1979.

Module E

COMPUTERS IN SOCIETY

No study of computers is complete without a look at the impact these machines have had on the very fabric of the society in which we live. In the workplace computers have created many jobs and careers but have also made others obsolete. Likewise, in society as a whole, they have created both problems and opportunities. Many people praise them as a major source of progress. Others wonder if we are indeed any better off today than we were before ENIAC.

Chapter 17 covers the important subject of computer-related jobs and careers. Chapter 18 discusses many of the problems and opportunities created by the computer revolution.

There isn't another
software company in the
able to offer anythi
as advanced as Millenn

For six good reaso

The Millennium
environment is borderless.

6. High quality pe

2. Millennium has common
functions across all
applications.

TECHNICAL CLIENT SUPPORT

TECHNICAL CLIENT SUPPORT

3. All Millennium syste
are real-time, on

TECHNICAL CLIENT SUPPORT

DATA BASE SPECIALIST

4. All
are

Chapter 17

Career
Opportunities

Chapter Outline ➤

OVERVIEW

If you're interested in obtaining computer-related employment, welcome to a relatively "hot" job market. The demand for computer professionals in government and industry has been booming over the past decade, a trend expected to continue into the 1990s. With computer technology making inroads into almost every phase of life, the U.S. Department of Labor has predicted that computer jobs will expand at more than four times the average national occupational growth rate over the next several years.

The explosive demand for computer professionals has been accompanied by an unusually acute shortage of qualified people, a trend also expected to persist for some time. A major cause of this lack is the short supply of teachers in the field. Because graduates of computer fields can earn almost as much as their professors as soon as they graduate, many would-be instructors are lured away by high-paying jobs in government and industry. Without teachers, colleges and universities are hard-pressed to expand their academic programs to meet the growing demand. Also, schools find computer curricula particularly expensive to maintain. Not only must top salaries be paid for good teachers, but also costly hardware and software must be continually acquired. When academic budgets are being cut, as is often the case today, this need is difficult to fulfill.

Thus, a degree in a computer field (if you get into a program) will probably land you several job offers and a good starting salary if your grades are high enough. You will also find that computer people are generally capable of more mobility than those in other occupations. For example, a skilled COBOL programmer potentially can work for any of the thousands of organizations that use this language. A production supervisor in the automobile industry, on the other hand, may be limited by specialized experience strictly to manufacturing plants in that particular industry. Because of such flexibility and the favorable supply-and-demand situation, computer people have been notoriously prone to job hopping—which has heightened the pressure on salaries even further in their favor.

But beware. Jobs for people with training in computers are plentiful right now and may stay that way for a while, but not necessarily forever. Because of the enormous attention computers have received in the press lately, students are signing up for computer courses by the hundreds of thousands. This trend, if it continues, may flood the marketplace with people looking for computer-related jobs, making employers more selective. In any case, just taking a few computer courses is usually not enough to guarantee you a good position. As in any field, success depends on hard work, skill, and dedication.

This chapter begins by introducing you to some of the jobs and careers possible in the computer field. Next, it covers the various educational paths to follow to prepare for entry-level jobs. Finally, it discusses finding a job and ways of maintaining professional skills and developing new ones.

JOBS AND CAREERS

There are so many computer-related jobs that it's impossible to cover them all adequately in a single chapter. To set some limit, we'll consider only those that involve supplying users with computer-generated information. These are the jobs that require substantial training in some computer field. Included among them are equipment operators, programmers, systems analysts, and computer managers. Excluded are computer salespeople, personnel engaged in manufacturing computer hardware, service engineers, and users.

We'll look first at some specific jobs. Then we'll consider ways to combine jobs into various career paths. Window 9, which follows page 492, is a picture essay on computer-related jobs and careers. Figure 17-1 (next page) shows how computer jobs are organized in a typical organization.

Computer Jobs

Computer Operations Personnel. These include data-entry operators, computer equipment operators, system librarians, and managers who supervise the day-to-day running of a computing center. All these people perform a service for others working with the computer system. Their responsibility lies in making the data processing and information systems operating environment as efficient as possible.

Data-entry operators transcribe data files, programs, and other documents into machine-readable form. In the past, this process usually involved keypunching onto cards. With the recent decline in punched cards, however, data entry on key-to-tape or key-to-disk units has become increasingly important. Also, the word-processing boom has created another data-entry job: the word-processing operator.

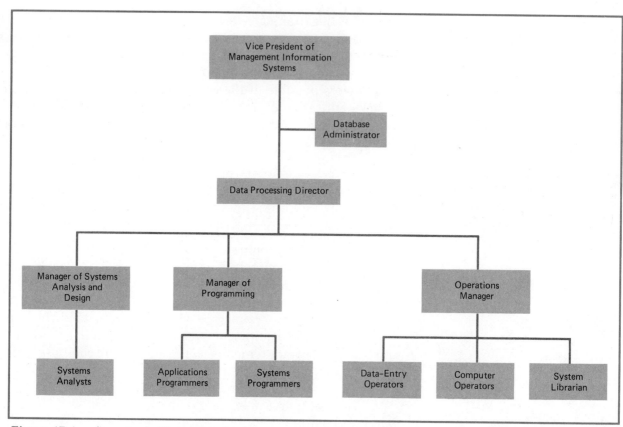

Figure 17-1.   *An organization chart showing common computer jobs and their relation to one another.*

A high-school diploma and good typing skills are the major requirements for entry-level data-entry jobs. At some point in the future, however, voice input technology may completely revolutionize the data-entry function, making typing skills superfluous.

Computer operators are responsible for setting up equipment for various jobs, mounting and dismounting tapes and disks, and monitoring computer operations. If a program is in an "endless loop," a terminal breaks down, a user is performing an unauthorized activity, or the computer "crashes," the operator is the one who initiates a solution to the problem. Since many commercial computers run nearly twenty four hours a day, an operator's responsibilities extend over a single eight-hour shift.

Entry-level personnel in this area should have at least an associate's degree from a junior college or a certificate from a technical institute. Some companies train operators on the job, whereas others require experience with a particular system.

System librarians are responsible for managing data files and programs stored offline on cards, tapes, disks, microfilm, and all other types of storage media. These media may contain backup copies of important programs and data files, items that are stored offline because they are not needed on a day-to-day basis, and archival data kept for legal purposes. The librarian catalogues all the library items, purges materials no longer needed, and prevents unauthorized access to restricted material. A high-school education and some knowledge of data-processing concepts are generally enough for an entry-level position as a system librarian.

Computer operations managers oversee the entire operation of the computer system. Their duties include scheduling jobs to be run, hiring and assigning operations personnel, supervising machine maintenance, and monitoring operations to make sure the system runs efficiently. This is not an entry-level position. Computer operations managers often must have at least three to five years of experience in the operations field.

Programmers. Programmers generally fall into two categories: systems programmers and applications programmers.

Systems programmers write and maintain systems software. Since this class of programs is very technical, systems programmers must have a good technical knowledge of computers. They often have had rigorous training in subjects such as assembly language, compiler design, operating systems, and the architecture of computer systems. An entry-level job usually requires a college degree in a technically oriented field such as computer science.

Applications programmers write and maintain the programs that serve end users. Because there's still a shortage of people in this area in many parts of the country, entry-level requirements vary widely. Many applications programmers have computer-related degrees from four-year or community colleges. Others are certified by technical institutes. In some cases, companies hungry for applications programmers have hired people with degrees in other areas virtually "off the street," trained them, and pressed them into service. In general, however, a person seeking an entry-level job as an applications programmer should have a college degree in a computer-related field. Other useful assets are a strong knowledge of COBOL and skill with a problem-solving language such as BASIC, FORTRAN, or Pascal.

Some people make programming a career, advancing from trainee to senior-level or chief programmer. In some cases, advancement involves specializing in a certain area, such as banking or database applications. It is also possible in many organizations to move from programming to a position in systems analysis. This is not always the best career path, however. Programmers have to spend a lot of time working alone on technical problems, and many have chosen their profession because they enjoy independence. Systems analysts, in contrast, spend most of their time dealing with other people and must have excellent communications skills.

Systems Analysts. **Systems analysts** plan and implement computer systems. They form the critical interface between management and users and then between users and programmers. Management dictates the priority of the problems to be solved. Handed a problem, the analyst must work with users to

tomorrow

PROGRAMMER EXTINCTION?

"Futurist sees Programmers Out in Cold by '90s"... "Programmer Extinction Predicted"... So read a number of recent headlines that have addressed predictions of how the computing world may turn out at some point beyond tomorrow ... and just when you decided to enroll in your first computer programming course. What about all those other headlines that read "Programmer Shortage Expected to Continue"? What in the world is going on?

Yes, you can expect the shortage of good programmers to continue. Not all programmers, mind you, just the good ones. In fact, if you excel at programming, you can expect to be well-employed for many years. Until the world develops machines that can think for themselves, programmers will be in high demand.

What the futurists are addressing in their predictions, which are not likely to come true in the short run, is the continuing development of user-friendly computing products. Computers at some point will presumably be so friendly that all users will need to do is point to what they want done on a screen menu—or better yet, speak to the machine—to do highly sophisticated forms of work. Although the time frame for these changes is debatable (futurists predict

anywhere from ten years to a lifetime or more), it is clear that computer systems are moving relentlessly in this direction. Given the current backlog of computer work in organizations and the growing desire of people to do their own computing, it is obvious to any business entrepreneur that a strong demand exists for friendlier machines. As such friendliness continues to be supplied in the marketplace, who will need the programmer?

The obvious reply, of course, is that someone needs to program all this friendliness into the machines. Unless computer systems can think entirely on their own, this will clearly be the job of the programmer. Also, although the nature of programming may change, it seems that the demand for people with computer skills will remain high. A sea of friendly products can easily create a hostile environment that will confuse the unwary buyer. People will still need plenty of advice to find the system that best fits their needs.

The moral to this story? If you've committed yourself to a career in computers, expect the demand for computer-related skills to remain high. Nonetheless, you are living in a world of rapid change. Don't let your bank of skills develop in a narrow way. Look out for what appear to be the fading and coming technologies.

find the best solutions. The analyst then translates these solutions into a system design and sets the technical specifications for applications programs to be written by programmers. The general duties of the analyst are covered in detail in Chapters 9, 15, and 16.

Good systems analysts must be literally jacks of all trades. They must have a high level of technical knowledge about computers, computer systems, and the computer industry in order to design state-of-the-art systems. They also have to be personable and possess excellent communications skills, since they have to interact with many different kinds of people, including managers, users, and programmers. They must be as comfortable speaking "computerese" with experts as they are speaking plain English with people who have no technical knowledge. Systems analysts should also have some background in business, since most data-processing systems are business oriented. Analysts should certainly be familiar with business terms like *accounts receivable, pro-forma cash flow, direct costs,* and so on. Some knowledge of accounting is a particularly helpful asset.

Many systems analysts have college degrees in computer-related fields. Some positions, such as the programmer/analyst slot in small companies (which combines the programmer and systems analyst functions), are entry level. Most companies require systems analysts to have a few years of computer-related experience.

Data Processing and MIS Management.   At the highest level of computer management are positions such as data processing director and vice president of information systems. The exact titles of these jobs vary from company to company.

The **data processing director** oversees all data-processing personnel, including programmers, systems analysts, and operations personnel (see Figure 17-1). He or she is given a budget and a long-range plan by the vice president of information systems. In turn, the director sets up budgets and plans for the areas under his or her control. Generally, this position requires several years of computer-related experience in a variety of jobs.

The **vice president of information systems** oversees routine data-processing and information systems activities as well as planning in the newer computer-related areas such as teleprocessing and database processing. He or she also works with key company executives to establish the overall direction of computer activities for the company. The job usually requires a master's degree in business or computers and extensive computer-related and managerial work experience. A recent survey indicated that the average work experience for a vice president of information systems is almost fifteen years.

Career Options

There are many ways to build computer-based careers. One possibility is to begin with an entry-level job and then move up the organizational ladder into positions of greater and greater responsibility. Suppose, for example, you joined a company with an organization like the one shown in Figure 17-1. You might start as a programmer trainee; later become a full-fledged applications programmer; and then, after many years' experience, become a manager. A managerial position requires a broad exposure to a number of computer functions as well as an ability to plan and direct other people. If you supplemented your work experience with additional education or an advanced degree, you might continue up the ladder to a high executive position.

A second possibility is to specialize in a highly marketable area of data processing where the demand for your services is likely to remain strong. There are several ways to do this. Some people specialize by focusing on a certain *industry*. For example, you might choose to become an expert in the analysis and design of computer systems for banks or insurance companies. Or perhaps it's the airline industry that fascinates you. In any case, if you have detailed knowledge of the kinds of computer-related problems faced by a specific industry, and if you know how to solve those problems, you will have a competitive advantage when seeking jobs in that industry. Another way to specialize is by choosing a specific *technology*—for example, database processing, teleprocessing, word processing, or small business systems. A database expert, for instance, would be in demand by any company using a database system. Still another option is to specialize in some data-processing *function*. People who can write clear, concise documentation that users can easily understand, for example, are a great asset to any organization.

A third possibility is to mold a career around a certain life-style. Some people, for example, for one reason or another, prefer to work only part time or during unusual hours. Programming is ideally suited for these people, because it allows a great deal of independence. Programmers are pretty much on their own once they understand the specifications of a project. Some programmers, in fact, telecommute—they do their jobs at home on a terminal or personal computer. This not only saves them gas and commuting time but also can spare them from unproductive office politics. And if they get their jobs done on schedule, no one cares if they take the kids to the playground in the afternoon or work from 1 A.M. to 5 A.M. Of course, working at home is not for everyone. Some people need the social stimulu. of an office to work well.

FORMAL EDUCATION FOR ENTRY-LEVEL JOBS

Going to school is one of the best ways to train for an entry-level position in computers. Although you can learn a great deal on your own or through on-the-job training, a degree or certificate is often a requirement for obtaining a job. It convinces potential employers that you've had formal training in certain areas and that you've met the standards of a particular institution. In other words, it legitimizes your claim that you know something and can work hard.

There are many types of schools that offer some type of education in computers. These include four-year colleges and universities, two-year community colleges, and technical institutes. Course offerings vary widely among such schools. It's wrong to assume that four-year colleges and universities offer better computer education than the community colleges or technical institutes. In many cases, the reverse is actually true. And it doesn't necessarily follow that the so-called prestige schools have computer curricula superior to those of lesser-known institutions. Computer education is a relatively new phenomenon. Schools that have worked aggressively to make it a top priority are generally the ones that have the best resources and provide the best training.

Computer Curricula

If you're interested in pursuing studies in computers there are many curricula available to you, the most common of which follow. The specific names given to such programs vary widely from school to school.

Unrealistic Expectations Haunt DP Collegians

The vast disparity between what many new users of data processing systems expect in terms of computer services and what they actually receive is well known. In recent discussions with college students, several other areas of DP in which expectations are often unfulfilled were uncovered.

Bob Stewart, a philosophy major at a private college, talked about students who want to have computer savvy in a hurry.

"A surprisingly large number of muddle-headed students choose computer-related courses, blindly thinking that a few Basic programs under their belts will qualify them for high-paying computer jobs after graduation," he said. "I think they are influenced by success stories of recent graduates who use computers daily in their work. Basic courses are open to anyone, so everyone is taking them."

Unrealistic Expectations

"But many students, particularly the younger ones, are unrealistic about how well they will do in the course," Stewart said. "These individuals expect to expand their minds instantly merely by plugging in a machine.

"You know, there are no courses quite like those dealing with computers. Computer education requires a entirely new approach to study because it involves unfamiliar terminology, unique logical expressions and powerful equipment. The students have no idea of the work that is required to complete homework assignments and lab exercises on time. So what happens? They wind up failing their courses or dropping them, and these students suffer as a result.

"Do you want to know how bad it can get? Ten people out of 35 dropped the Introduction to Computers class that I was in!"

Family Expectations

Tony Charles, a business major at a large state university, described the situation of many students who take computer courses because of unrealistic expectations on the part of their families.

"Bob talked about students who made their own decisions about a computer-oriented curric-

Data Processing/Information Systems. The **data processing/information systems** curriculum is often coordinated by a college or department of business. The primary emphasis is on directly providing services for end users, and many of the computer courses have a "business applications" flavor. These courses often include introductory data processing, BASIC or FORTRAN, COBOL, systems analysis and design, and management information systems. Some schools also offer training in RPG, database processing, office systems, and computerized auditing as well. Because the degree program is coordinated by the business school, students must also take several business courses. These courses can be particularly helpful to anyone aspiring to be a systems analyst or manager. Most of the graduates of these programs assume entry-level work as applications programmers or programmer/analysts.

ulum and found the going very rough. But there's another group that has even more of a problem, namely, the group of students who are goaded, or even coerced, into the DP field by well-intentioned parents with high, but often unjustified, hopes for prosperous careers for their college kids.

"These people don't understand that they're being victimized by a modern-day myth surrounding computers and perpetuated by all the publicity about the machines. This is the notion that 'everything' will be computerized and that unless students are 'into' computers, job prospects will be bleak and they will walk off the graduation platform with their diplomas in hand and head straight for the local bread line.

"As if parental forces aren't enough, students are also on the receiving end of intense pushing and shoving from other family members. I suppose that college students have always been subjected to such pressures, but today's parents are a lot wiser. They no longer have to foot the bill for seven years to make their chil-

dren physicians or lawyers; they've learned that four years worth of college in a computer-related science is enough to get the kid a decent job."

The Message Is Heard

"The message is being heard. Many students start their computer education by signing up for seemingly elementary courses," Charles said. "Then they have to send the tragic word home about dropping the computer courses, claiming that the work load was just too much to handle.

"I would think that much of this anguish could be avoided if all concerned took a cold hard look at a student's scholastic record and study habits and made some realistic assessments about his success before tossing him into the computer arena.

"But asking families to exercise reason on this subject may be akin to barking at the moon, particularly when millions of parents see a computer on the cover of *Time* magazine's 'Man of the Year' issue for 1982."

Source: Jack Stone, *Computerworld*, Feb. 14, 1983, page 59. Reprinted by permission of the author.

Computer Science. The **computer science** curriculum is often coordinated by a college or department of computer science or engineering. The training provided is much more technical than that in a data processing/information systems program, since the primary emphasis is on the design of software. Graduates of these programs often find jobs as systems programmers, with responsibility for designing compilers, operating systems, and utility programs. They are also sought for the design of complex applications software packages such as database management systems. A surprising number of graduates of these programs, however, take positions as applications programmers. These students have usually prepared themselves by cross-registering for business-oriented courses such as COBOL and systems analysis and design. Some even take an accounting course or two, since accounting is generally regarded as the language of business. Of course, cross-registration works both ways. Data processing/information systems majors often enroll in computer science courses, such as assembly-language programming and operating systems, which enable them to sharpen their technical skills.

Computer Engineering. Some schools also support a **computer engineering** curriculum. This degree program is designed primarily to prepare students to design computer hardware systems. Graduates of such programs are usually sought by hardware manufacturers.

Computer Operations. In addition to their other computer offerings, community colleges and technical institutes typically provide practical training in **computer operations.** Students enrolled in these courses often plan to become computer or data-entry operators. Courses involve a great deal of hands-on, practical training, enabling students to move on quickly to entry-level positions in government and industry.

FINDING A JOB

No matter what type of school or program you choose, the day will come when you must seek a job. Often, the placement office at the institution you attend will help you set up interviews with potential employers. Finally, after all that work and money, your degree or certificate is almost in hand and payday seems to be around the corner. But don't relax too soon. Unless you prepare for your interview, you may be badly disappointed.

Interviewing for Jobs. There's one approach to job interviews that if practiced diligently, will dramatically increase your chances of success: empathize with the interviewer. In other words, put yourself in the "shoes" of the interviewer. In particular, try to imagine what qualities are likely to attract his or her attention. Suppose, for example, you are an interviewer who has just met two candidates with similar qualifications. One was silent through most of the interview, responding only "yes" or "no" to your questions and never volunteering anything. The other expressed a lively interest in you, your company, and the job in question. This candidate had many ideas and asked lots of

CAREER OPPORTUNITIES

A look at life beyond college

In a way, this Window permits you to glimpse the future ... your own possible future. It gives you a look at the professional life you may find beyond school.

1. "High tech" companies often have attractive facilities in desirable locations. This photograph shows Hewlett-Packard offices in Grenoble, France. Headquartered in California's famed "Silicon Valley," Hewlett-Packard has plants in a number of locations, many in the western half of the United States.

OPERATIONS PERSONNEL Operations personnel perform the important task of keeping the central computer facilities running smoothly. They mount tapes and disks, ensure the availability of system resources to authorized programmers and users, call maintenance personnel when "emergencies" occur, and so forth.

2. Computer operators, like people in other types of work, often collaborate on computer problems.

3. The so-called "computer room" is the place where the operations personnel usually work. These rooms contain the main pieces of hardware, such as the computer and its secondary storage devices. As a general rule, such rooms are restricted exclusively to authorized operations staff.

4. A computer operator manipulates some switches at a computer system console to check the status of the system.

5. The task of entering large amounts of data into the computer system is performed by data-entry personnel.

6. Operators in the computer room are typically charged with mounting and dismounting tapes for various jobs.

7. The operations manager is in charge of the day-to-day operation of the central computing facilities. Since many centers function 24 hours a day, the manager must schedule shifts, hire and discharge personnel, and ... most importantly ... keep the systems humming at the pace needed to get the work done.

8. The tape librarian is responsible for managing tapes. Some libraries consist of tens of thousands of tape volumes.

PROGRAMMERS AND ANALYSTS A user describes a problem to a systems analyst. Subsequently, the analyst decides how the application will be fitted into the organization's computing environment, and translates the solution to the programmer in technical terms.

9. A systems analyst oversees the programming process, ensuring that the programmer codes the application with respect to specific guidelines.

10. Often, beginning programmers work at partitioned workstations. They have their own desks and display stations, and usually share other facilities.

11. It is not unusual for programmers to collaborate on common problems, just as students help each other with complex course assignments or joint projects.

13. Programmers in scientific environments often work with a wide variety of sophisticated input and output devices. This programmer is producing special video effects for Mid-Ocean Pictures of Hollywood, California.

12. Maintenance programmers are, among other things, responsible for keeping applications programs current, altering them to reflect modifications in the system.

14. Programmer/analysts developing a billing and order support system at Bell Laboratories in Piscataway, New Jersey. The system provides service representatives with access to customer billing orders and also generates customer service orders.

COMPUTER MANAGEMENT   Life at the top

15.   The MIS manager controls the entire network of computing throughout an organization. This includes specifying a "game plan" for the director of data processing, determining the permissible extent of activities such as personal computing, developing communications strategies, and tailoring computing to meet corporate goals.

16.   On important projects, key computer managers often assist the systems analyst in seeing that the needs of the user are met.

TRAINING

17. Most firms offer special training sessions to new computer employees, to smooth transition into the organization's operations. Sometimes, training may extend for several months or more.

18. Vendors of software and hardware often provide special training classes for their customers. Here, at an IBM education center in Tampa, Florida, customers learn to use software and color graphics to solve business problems.

pertinent questions about career opportunities in the company. Which of the two candidates would you be likely to recommend for hiring?

Many people are understandably nervous for their first few interviews and, as a result, are unusually silent. The ability to present yourself well, however, is one of the most important skills both for landing a job and for keeping it. Sometimes taking a course in speech or just practicing with friends will help you get over the jitters. In any case, grades notwithstanding, the best jobs often go to people who can project competence, confidence, and a sincere interest during the interview.

Resumé Preparation.   It also helps to prepare a one- or two-page written overview of your employment interests and qualifications before your interview. This document is called a *resumé,* or *vita* (see Figure 17-2 on the next page). You should give the resumé to the interviewer before your scheduled appointment. This practice helps to give the impression that you're prepared. Interviewers, being only human, are often tremendously influenced by a first impression. Writing an effective resumé is an art in itself. Many schools keep samples of model resumés on file for interested students to inspect.

MAINTAINING SKILLS AND DEVELOPING NEW ONES

One of the things that people find exciting about the computer field is its rapid rate of change. Someone with "computer fever" trying out new equipment or software is like an excitable five-year-old opening birthday presents. But rapid change also has a less pleasant side to it—constant retraining. When the computer system you've known and loved for the past five years is unplugged and wheeled away for a newer one, you and your co-workers will have to retrain. If the new system involves many recent technologies that you aren't familiar with, the retraining may take a long time.

Retraining is a fact of life in the computer field. If you want to keep yourself current and marketable, you must have some knowledge of the latest technologies. There are a variety of ways that you can effectively "retool" yourself or develop new skills. Among them are attending classes, seminars, and exhibitions; reading; and participating in professional associations.

```
                              ALEX P. GOMEZ

PERSONAL DATA

  • Mailing Address:     1615 Weatherford Road
                         Flagstaff, Arizona 86001
  • Home Phone:          (602) 774-8654
  • Birthdate:           April 10, 1964
  • Marital Status:      Single


EDUCATIONAL BACKGROUND

  Northern Arizona University, B.S. 1983
  • Major:  Business
  • Area of Concentration:  Data Processing/Information Systems
  • Grade Point Average:  3.82

JOB OBJECTIVE

  I am presently seeking an entry-level position as an applications
  programmer or a systems analyst in the Southwest.


ACADEMIC TRAINING

  During my four years in college I have taken courses in the following
  areas of computers:

  • Introduction to Data Processing
  • COBOL (two courses)
  • Systems Analysis (two courses)
  • Database Programming
  • Advanced Programming Seminar
  • Advanced BASIC
  • Assembly Language
  • Operating Systems


EXTRACURRICULAR ACTIVITIES

  • Track Team - 4 years (Co-captain, 1983)
  • Class Secretary, 1983
  • Mountaineering Club
  • Data Processing Club (President, 1983)
  • Data Processing Award (1982 and 1983)
  • Business Honor Society (1981-1983)


REFERENCES

  Available on request
```

Figure 17-2. A resumé prepared by a graduate of a data processing/information systems program. This graduate is seeking a position as a programmer or systems analyst.

Attending Classes.   Many universities, junior colleges, and computer institutes offer courses on a nondegree or continuing-education basis. These courses are particularly visible in large cities, where there's a large market for such services. Many of the courses are taught at night to accommodate people who work during the day. Some companies also hold regular classes, and even have schools, for training employees in the latest computer technologies.

A more ambitious possibility is to enroll in a graduate school. Many universities have master's and doctoral degree programs in areas such as information systems, computer science, and computer engineering.

Attending Seminars. Many individuals and companies offer seminars around the country on a variety of computer topics. An expert on teleprocessing, for example, may travel the lecture circuit with an intensive, three-day seminar on the subject, charging, say, $350 per person. The speaker may present the seminar on January 11, 12, and 13 in Phoenix; on January 15, 16, and 17 in Los Angeles; then on to San Francisco; and so on. Some seminars, especially those conducted by hardware and software vendors, are offered free. The computer trade publications maintain a list of seminars and details about them.

Attending Exhibitions. Vendors of computer products frequently sponsor joint trade shows to demonstrate new hardware and software to the public. The largest of these is the annual National Computer Conference (NCC). In 1982, the NCC enabled approximately 100,000 people to inspect the offerings of some 700 vendors, displaying their wares on over 320,000 square feet of floor space.

Reading. This is one of the most inexpensive ways to learn about new technologies. Fortunately, computer literature is abundant, and several sources carry up-to-date information.

The most current information is found in the so-called computer newspapers. *Computerworld,* which many professionals regard as the *Wall Street Journal* of the computer establishment," contains news items and special features of general interest to a wide audience of professionals. *Infoworld* specializes in developments concerning small computers.

A second source of written information is the computer journals (see Figure 17-3), many of which are published monthly. Each is generally targeted to a specific audience—small-computer users, the banking industry, and so on. Each journal prints articles of potential interest to its readership.

A third source is books. If there's a specific topic you want to learn about in some depth, there are generally several books available to meet this need. Some of these are written at very technical levels, whereas others are aimed at audiences who are relatively unsophisticated about computers. One way to learn

Figure 17-3. A selection of computer journals.

Professional Computer Organizations

There are many professional associations serving the computing community. A sample of the more important of these is listed here with a brief description of each.

AFIPS. The American Federation of Information Processing Societies is a national consortium of professional organizations. Its main function is to represent the interests of its member organizations and to distribute information among them. Some of the constituent associations of AFIPS include the American Institute of Certified Public Accountants (AICPA), the Institute of Electrical and Electronics Engineers (IEEE), the American Statistical Association (ASA), as well as several of the organizations listed below.

ACM. The Association for Computing Machinery is the largest professional association devoted specifically to computers. The ACM helps to advance the study of an extremely wide range of computer-related areas, including information processing, small systems development, programming languages, and computer education. High levels organization

ASM. The Association for Systems Management is an international organization dedicated to the advancement and continuing education of systems analysts and systems managers in business, industry, and government.

BDPA. The Black Data Processing Associates, open to people of all races, is dedicated to the professional advancement of minority groups in the data-processing community.

DPMA. The Data Processing Management Association consists of approximately 300 chapters. Its membership includes managers and supervisors of data-processing installations, educators and executives with a special interest in data processing, and representatives of vendor organizations. Its activities include many of those supported by ACM, with a particular emphasis on data-processing management.

ICCP. The Institute for Certification of Computer Professionals is a nonprofit organization established to test and certify computer personnel. A major activity is the administration of the Certificate in Data Processing (CDP) examination. The examination consists of five sections—data-processing equipment, computer programming and software, principles of management, quantitative methods, and systems analysis and design. All people sitting for the exam must have at least five years of related work experience. Recently, the ICCP established the Certificate in Computer Programming (CCP), which gives formal recognition for competence and experience in programming. These certificates, like degrees from colleges and universities, help establish one's claim to knowledge in certain areas of computing. Independent companies have prepared guides and mini-courses to help candidates pass these examinations.

WDP. Women in Data Processing, open to both males and females, is dedicated to promoting the entry and advancement of women in data processing.

more about computers is to go to your local library or bookstore and browse through the shelves devoted to computer books, looking for ones that seem interesting.

A fourth source of materials is the topical reports that are issued periodically by research companies such as Auerbach and Datapro (see Figure 17-4). These reports, which are each usually fewer than thirty pages, are assembled into looseleaf binders. Each binder contains current information on related topics that

Figure 17-4. Some commercially available research reports.

is not easy to find in other places. Even though some of the information may also be available in textbooks, these topical reports are far more current. Also, these reports often contain useful comparisons of specific computer products.

A fifth source is the computer product vendor. Although such literature is often biased toward the vendor's products, some of it is extremely well presented and informative. And much of this information is available without charge.

Joining Professional Associations. Computer people often join professional associations to keep up to date. Members of these associations stay current through meetings, workshops, and informal contact with other people having similar interests. Many associations have local chapters in major cities. Organizations such as the ACM (Association for Computing Machinery) and DPMA (Data Processing Management Association) also have student chapters. The box on the opposite page lists some major associations.

Summary and Key Terms

The demand for computer professionals in government and industry has been booming over the past decade, a trend expected to continue into the 1990s.

Computer professionals include operations personnel, systems analysts, and managers.

Computer operations personnel include data-entry operators, computer equipment operators, system librarians, and operations managers. **Data-entry operators** transcribe data files, programs, and other documents into machine-readable form. **Computer operators** are responsible for setting up equipment for various jobs, mounting and dismounting tapes and disks, and monitoring computer operations. **System librarians** are responsible for managing data files and programs stored offline on cards, tapes, disks, microfilm, and all other types of storage media. **Computer operations managers** oversee the entire operation of the computer system. Their duties include scheduling jobs to be run, hiring and assigning operations personnel, supervising machine maintenance, and monitoring operations to make sure the system runs efficiently.

Programmers generally fall into one of two categories: systems programmers and applications programmers. **Systems programmers** write and maintain systems software. **Applications**

programmers write and maintain the programs that serve end users.

Systems analysts plan and implement computer systems. They form the critical interface between management and users and, subsequently, between users and programmers.

At the highest level of computer management are positions such as data processing director and vice president of information systems. The **data processing director** oversees all data-processing personnel, including programmers, systems analysts, and operations personnel. The **vice president of information systems** oversees routine data processing and information systems activities as well as planning in the newer computer-related areas such as teleprocessing and database processing.

There are many ways to build computer-based careers. One possibility is to begin with an entry-level job and then move up the organizational ladder into positions of greater and greater responsibility. A second possibility is to specialize in a highly marketable area of data processing where the demand for your services is likely to remain strong. For example, many people specialize by concentrating on a specific industry, technology, or function. A third possibility is to mold a career around a certain life-style, such as working for yourself.

Going to school is one of the best ways to train for an entry-level position in computers. Many types of schools offer some kind of education in computers. These include four-year colleges and universities, two-year community colleges, and technical institutes.

If you're interested in pursuing studies in computers there are many curricula available to you. The **data processing/information systems** curriculum is often coordinated by a college or department of business. The primary emphasis is on directly providing services for end users, and many of the computer courses have a "business applications" flavor. The **computer science** curriculum is often coordinated by a college or department of computer science or engineering. The training provided is geared toward the design of software. Some schools also support a **computer engineering** curriculum. This degree program is designed primarily to prepare students to design computer hardware systems. In addition to their other computer offerings, community colleges and technical institutes typically provide practical training in **computer operations.** Students enrolled in these courses often plan to become computer or data-entry operators.

No matter what type of school or program you choose, the day will come when you must seek a job. Often, the placement office at the institution you attend will help you set up interviews with potential employers. Before your job interview, you should prepare a one- or two-page resumé of your employment interests and qualifications.

Retraining is a fact of life in the computer field. There are a variety of ways to maintain your skills and develop new ones. Among them are attending classes, seminars, and exhibitions; reading; and participating in professional associations.

Review Questions

1. Why is there such a big difference today between the demand for computer professionals and the supply of qualified ones?
2. Name the responsibilities associated with the following jobs: data-entry operator, computer operator, system librarian, computer operations manager, systems programmer, applications programmer, systems analyst, data-processing director, vice president of information systems.
3. Discuss some ways to build computer-based careers.
4. What are the differences between the data processing/information systems curriculum and computer science curriculum?
5. What is the importance of a resumé in seeking a job?
6. Identify several ways you can effectively maintain your computer skills or develop new ones.

Suggested Readings

Editors of Consumer Guide. *Computer Careers: Where the Jobs Are and How to Get Them.* New York: Fawcett, 1981.

McDaniel, Herman. *Careers in Computers and Data Processing.* Princeton, N.J.: Petrocelli, 1978.

Gundfast, Sandra (Ed.). *Peterson's Annual Guide to Careers and Employment for Engineering, Computer Scientists and Physical Scientists.* Princeton, N.J.: Peterson's Guides.

Stanat, Kirby W., and Patrick Reardon. *Job Hunting Secrets and Tactics.* Chicago: Follett, 1977.

SEPH B. TREASTER

gents raided the homes of a dozen young computer en- round the country Wednes- nvestigation of unauthorized nto scores of large commer- efense Department comput- al authorities said yester-

in damage to computers and computer systems.

A complete list of the computers broken into was not available, but the mother of one of the youths whose computer was seized said agents had told her they were investigating intrusions into computers at the Massachusetts

puters, computer and telephone equipment and files from youths in Los Angeles, Detroit, Tucson, Ariz., Norman, Okla., and several other cities, the au thorities said

"In most cases," said one agent, "the searches were quite routine. There were no incidents and the only seized were things listed in the ints."

e were no arrests. According to

Concern for Guarding Software Mu

By Jeffry Beeler
CW West Coast Bureau

Among users and vendors alike, concern for safeguarding and controlling proprietary programs has reached unprecedented proportions. Their concern stems from a growing

ers can copy NCR-developed software. The NCR spokesman characterized the statement as more of a reaffirmation of the firm's existing software policy than a formulation of a new one.

Change in Users' Practice

Users, too, are increasingly making efforts to guard against breaches of sensitive program data. One such user is ITT, which reportedly has dropped its policy of requiring vendors to make available source code with all the programs that ITT acquires. That change in ITT's practice was reportedly adopted to minimize the company's legal exposure in the event that the confidentiality of its purchased software is someday compromised. Repeated attempts were

COMPUTER SERVICE FOCUS OF INQUIRY

l Outsiders Said sed a Message Owned by GTE

l B. TREASTER

tigators who seized oment from youths y last week say their g on computer enthu- ized use of an elec- service that has 130 nts. ervice, which operates

FAA Technical Research Center

ven Dismissed for Alleged System Misuse

By Peter Bartolik
CW Staff

NTIC CITY, N.J. — Seven es were dismissed from deral Aviation Administra- A) jobs at a technical re- enter here in June and July edly misusing government rs to duplicate nongovern- rograms, it was recently

atement issued April 30, the

formation made available since then points more to a scheme of duplicating video games or home computer programs on a nonprofit basis.

The technical center is a research and development facility for the FAA's aviation safety systems, employing about 1,200 people and sprawling over 5,000 acres in Atlantic City and three adjacent townships.

FAA and FBI officials have re-

cal Center and seized "numerous software and hardware equipment items."

Mark Baylen, legal counsel for the FAA Technical Center, told *Computerworld* recently that government officials "have removed seven individuals for misuse of government property."

The FBI confirmed in April that it had been in computer mis that it conduc search at the was alleged t puter systems plicate and d ware progr

products for use by outside commercial and/or industrial firms," according to a prepared statement issued then by James Cagnassola Jr., special agent in charge of the FBI's Newark division.

FBI officials contacted since the dismissals began in late June have declined to comment beyond the statement issued in April, claiming

Crime Prevention Bill ns Momentum in House

By Jake Kirchner
W Washington Bureau

NGTON, D.C. — A recent- uced bill to help small busi- eter computer crime has onsiderable momentum in weeks since it was intro- arnering support from in- aw enforcement and com- ne experts.

on Wyden (D-Ore.), spon- Small Business Computer revention Act, has been

period now contained i shorter time is necessa cause of the seriousne lem and because com ogy is changing so rap

Computer crime Parker of SRI Interna Menlo Park, Calif., sup month amendment. P supports the bill becau to be some way "to ale ness] management to potential solutions; n

German DPer Charged With Stealing

By Patricia Keefe
CW Staff

ATLANTA — A West German systems analyst was arrested at Harts- after ervice estiga- found s con- y val- e U.S. GmbH, f Josef inter- roper- creates dustry ently,

operations shortly after Reiter's arrest.

Reiter's attorney denied the charges, contending that Reiter was the victim of a squabble between the German company and its subsidiary. The 32-year-old Reiter, who had just completed a six-month stint as a contract employee with the subsidiary, was on his way home to Munich with his wife and 22-month-old baby when he was arrested. His family was allowed to continue on to West Germany, but Reiter was taken into custody, according to the lawyer, Andrew Economou.

After spending 11 days in jail on $25,000 bond, Reiter was freed on $10,000 personal recognizance, despite the fact that he is a foreign na-

tional. "This shows to me that the government doesn't think a great deal of their case," Economou said.

The government has until Aug. 11 to indict Reiter or drop the charges, which include larceny under the North Carolina statute.

Although the president of the U.S. subsidiary, Hans Hellmig, had originally filed the charges, alerting police that Reiter was on his way out of the country, Economou claims his client did not steal the tapes. The attorney also disputes the value placed on the tapes — $420,000 — which are said to contain programs for Spartan Foods, a South Carolina chain of restaurants.

Rather than stealing the tapes, Reiter maintains that he was re-

spon by of to br ny. " shou Econ twee ent c know midc As omou were joine certa Gern E succ U.S. wou

Congress Unit Cites Need To Shield Info. Sys. Content

By LLOYD SCHWARTZ

WASHINGTON (FNS) — The Congressional Office of Technology Assessment reports the challenge for intellectual-property legislation will be in protecting the content of information systems.

"By many measures," OTA advised a House Judiciary Committee overview session on copyright and nological change, "it seems onable to expect that software be much more important in our e pi se n ftware.

It noted some estimates place the ratio at $4 of investment in software for $1 invested in hardware. One market research group expects computer software sales to triple from $4.5 billion to $13.5 billion by 1986.

SA's Computer Mail as Read by Intruders

By JOSEPH B. TREASTER

ne young computer enthusi- nvestigation by the Federal say they were able to rum- gh the electronic mail of the eronautics and Space Ad-

at the space agency in acknowledged yesterday had been intruders in the he electronic mail service scribes to from a Virginia hich has 129 other clients.

als said they could not im- etermine how extensive the d been, but they said they the intruders had not ss to any information that mful to national security. s deny any maliciousness, they heard from computer someone had destroyed tities" of information.

ficant Loss Doubted

NASA officials said they nediately know how much d been done, William spokesman for the agen- did not believe that NASA ny significant amounts of

other computer friends that had destroyed "large amour terial" in the NASA section of and that intruders had f agency "to shut down its a Telemail."

Mr. Lushina said that as knew, NASA's section of Tel never been forced out of servi

Some of the youths whose c were seized acknowledged had used the Telemail servic paying, but they all denied d information in the system.

One whose home was raide Green, a 17-year-old senior a Hills High School in Beve Calif., would not say if he ha the Telemail system, but he s lieved that two dozen compu siasts had gained access to section. He said he believed t five of them had learned how through the section. The o said, left and received mes their friends in subsections been created for their exclusi the more advance intruders.

Issues for DP Chiefs: Legal Liability, Protectio

Commercial Sites Seen More Open To Invasion

By Jeffry Beeler
CW West Coast Bureau

WOODBRIDGE, Va. — Commercial systems are much more vulnerable to invasion by telephone than government processors like the one recently penetrated by a group of youthful "hackers" in Milwaukee, a computer security expert said here last week.

In the public sector, most systems operating under the same roof are physically isolated from each other to minimize the potential damage from breaches of data

computers ar such major p in software, t proach it over

In 1982, t Statistics esti persons were mers and sys than those e computers

Mr. Weinga vance of tech dustry struct value of info about prot property.

"Given the terests involv issues need t gress when co fecting intelle

Rep. Robe Wis.), presidin ing, said the H mitte the a evalu These prote mask

By Jeffry Beeler
CW West Coast Bureau

SAN FRANCISCO — Information systems chiefs are suffering a new set of management headaches as a result of the industry's growing recognition of software as an asset, according to lawyer Susan Nycum.

One headache is the increased risk of legal liability that systems managers now face if a proprietary program in their companies' possession is intentionally or accidentally disclosed, Nycum said during a recent interview.

Software's coming of age as an asset is also confronting information systems managers with at least one other challenge by helping to transform the face of their jobs, she added.

Once concerned primarily with managing just computers, DP executives are now increasingly being called upon to oversee information.

As software's potential as a money-making commodity has steadily grown, so too has the realization by information systems managers that proprietary programs need to be carefully protected. "If a piece of [confidential] software belongs to your own company, you have to worry about what happens if it falls into another firm's hands," the attorney with Gaston Snow & Ely Bartlett said.

"If you're licensing a program from someone else, you have to make sure your organization is adequately protected from the potential legal fallout" that could result if the confiden-

tiality of the work is comprom

Either way, proprietary co ries serious risks for the s managers who are entrusted safeguarding it.

The industry's emerging ness of software's commercia is also forcing management i tion systems executives to r radically the nature of thei tions. Systems managers tod involved in a "whole differen pational] ball game" from t they were playing just a sho ago, Nycum explained. Until ly, they thought of themselv marily as running a "closed But now, their companies a creasingly calling on them t the role of a corporate infor

Laws to Bar Computer Misuse Remain Scarce

By DAVID BURNHAM
he New York Times

N, Sept. 7 — A third of omputers began their ment as the central en- an government, busi- inications, the rules to use of computers are ncomplete.

, for example, the As- omputing Machinery sion under which any

worded code of ethics could be censured or expelled. So far, not a single case has been brought against any of the 60,000 computer specialists who belong to the association.

Three weeks ago the New York Legislature approved a bill giving all New Yorkers the right to see and correct the information held about them in the generally computerized files of state agencies, and the bill has been signed by Governor Cuomo. But 40 states have no such "fair information

shared computerized patient information with other institutions. The proposal was defeated in the House and never considered by the Senate.

With the disclosure several weeks ago of the casual penetration of government and industry data bases by a small group of computer enthusiasts from Milwaukee, a new wave of debate has arisen over questions of right and wrong involving computers.

The current concern about the ethics of computer use has been fed by the

time, informati are being requ eds of "the peo ill who are ope ple Compute er personal c d. "They have ms, and they h a whole bu ges they didn before." Nycu inuing shift i hardware m

ncern Mounting Over Data Controls For Credit Reporting Agencies

you saw the back-page se that told of a low-grade ar Games — the indictment for allegedly tapping into r data base via a remote stealing credit card num- ging a ton of fancy elec- dware to the accounts of ng card holders and ship- ooty to his personal drop handful of the purloined belonged to well-known res.

hardly the first time such t has been recorded; that very is commonplace ex- y the event was down- the press.

st be optimistic that credit agencies spend the time y necessary both to pro- files and to protect their ut from this latest spate of r the years on such opera- cerns about their effective- egitimate. Having had one y wrenching experience , I, for one, am very skepti- redit agency performance.

ply for the "executive credit" service with my bank, a fancy name the bank uses for its system that automatically credits funds to a zero-bala count through the device of th draft check. Naturally, I subn personal financial statement of the credit review, which I really mind because I was in g nancial shape at the time, my ly income more than covering penses and credit card payme

Well, you can imagine the

ter an interminable drive and long stay in an entry queue, I obtained a look at what purported to be a record

NBS Unit Urges Use of Passwords to Combat Computer Cr

WASHINGTON (FNS) — Passwords remain the most cost-effective method of personal identification when requesting services from a computer system, the National Bureau of Standards has advised a House subcommittee considering the growing problem of computer crime and security.

The NBS Institute for Computer Sciences & Technology recently completed a proposed standard

microcomputers for performing the security functions for other systems or as components of microcomputer-based systems.

Dr. Katzke said once an individual has been identified and his identity authenticated, the EDP system should limit the individual's access to only those resources he is authorized to use. A guideline on user cross-authorization is being readied. It will help

puter crime and security, reported securi tants find it hard to sell their services businesses.

While many firms are offering computer packages to provide protection of data, he these forces alone are not enough to solve th and to reach the potential for crime reducti panying increasing use of computers. M that would set up a T r to keep track of compu trol techniques.

en (D., O.), heading the considering legislative the scope of such cri gh losses could run as h zed small firms lack t s to respond to comput roup president, Comsh Association of Data ms (ADAPSO), noted crime goes well beyon ing with payroll lists checks to a criminal's a changing the comp record of the invento

Congress Urged to Address Federal DP Security

By Jake Kirchner
CW Washington Bureau

WASHINGTON, D.C. — A congressional mandate for a coherent, governmentwide computer security effort may be needed to correct the current lack of adequate security arrangements in many federal programs, a recent study by a Capitol Hill research group has concluded.

"Protecting computer and information resources continues to re-

federal agencies indicates a need for more direction from policymakers."

The study, prepared by CRS information science and technology specialist Louise G. Becker, comes on the heels of a federal agency report showing that the government does not have complete information or the means to gather it on the full extent of computer crime and abuse in agency programs.

The CRS study similarly reported

computer security issues from the single perspective associated with a specific set of problems. The omnibus approach to computer security has rarely been taken, partially due to the myriad of problems encountered and the fragmented responsibilities."

The 250-page CRS study, described as "a cursory introduction to this multifaceted subject," examined computer security from the perspec-

discrepancies in policies, misinterpretations of requirements and lack of prioritization have left the federal agencies with a 'patch quilt' and 'Band-Aid' approach to providing for the security of federal information resources."

At present, the report said, some federal DP security experts tend to view the problems "from a narrow technical orientation." The report suggested a need to balance technical

Chapter 18

Problems and Opportunities

OVERVIEW

Since the early 1950s, when the era of commercial computing began, computers have rapidly woven their way into the very fabric of modern society. In the process, they have created both problems and opportunities.

This book has so far focused on the opportunities. In the text and in the Windows, you've seen how these machines design many of the clothes you wear, process the purchases you make, control much of the information you receive, run the transportation systems you travel on, and so forth. Without computers, many of the conveniences you take for granted today would simply be impossible. Yet, hard though it may be to believe, the impact of computers on our lives is really just beginning. As you'll see in this chapter, new developments are fast approaching that may change our living habits still further.

Although the "computer revolution" has brought undeniable benefits to society, it has also brought some troubling side effects. Like any revolution, it has been disruptive in many ways. Some jobs have been created, others lost, and still others threatened. Additionally, an increasing number of once pleasant jobs have become monotonous. Computers have also increased access to information immensely, creating new possibilities for crime and threatening personal privacy. Clearly, some controls will always be needed to limit the dangers these awesome machines pose.

This chapter highlights three important problems: computers and health in the workplace, computers and crime, and computers and privacy. It concludes with a look at some of the emerging technologies that will soon be changing our lives even more.

COMPUTERS, WORK, AND HEALTH

One of the first criticisms leveled at the entry of computers into the workplace was that their very presence resulted in job-related stress. When computers came in, people were often laid off and had to find new jobs, a situation that typically causes stress. Clerical workers especially worried about job security. They were often bewildered about the full potential of computers in the office and never knew when a machine might

CRTs: Are they hazardous to your health?

replace them. But even a number of people who were not laid off found that their jobs had changed significantly and that they had no choice but to retrain. Airline agents, for example, had to learn how to manipulate a database language and to work with CRT terminals. Many were never able to make the transition successfully.

Another complaint, often voiced by CRT users, is that computers dehumanize work. People whose jobs once involved pleasant interaction with co-workers found themselves staring at a blinking screen several hours a day.

In a 1981 study, the National Institute for Occupational Safety and Health (NIOSH) found that CRT data-entry operators showed the highest level of stress ever observed in any employee group. As many as 80 to 90 percent of the operators interviewed in this study and previous ones complained about some form of health problem. The complaints centered primarily on visual, muscular, and emotional disorders. These included blurred eyesight, eye strain, acute fatigue, headaches, and backaches. Workload, workspace, boredom, job control, and career development concerns were also voiced. The study also found a link between job pressure and CRT use, so one can only conclude from the research that CRT abuse, rather than use, affects people in harmful ways.

There is no question, of course, that computers have altered the structure of work in many industries, just as mechanized farm machinery altered the nature of agriculture, and airplanes and automobiles altered the nature of travel. Many people have had to accept these disruptions as the price of "progress" or "keeping up."

COMPUTER CRIME

Computer crime is loosely defined as the use of computers to commit unauthorized acts. Some states have laws that address computer crime directly; others do not. In practice, however, even in states that do have such laws, computer crime is hard to pin down.

One reason is that it is often difficult to decide when an unauthorized act is really a crime. No one would doubt that a bank employee using a computer system to embezzle funds from customers' accounts is committing a crime. But what about a state board of education employee who uses the office computer to trace the lineage of racehorses? A case like this actually occurred in a state with a law that defined computer crime as the unauthorized use of a computer "for commercial or industrial gain." When the employee was brought to trial, the court ruled in his favor, arguing that he wasn't using the computer for gain. This decision alarmed many people in the data-processing community because it seemed to imply that unauthorized personal use of someone else's computer is not a crime.

Another problem in pinning down computer crime is that judges and juries are often bewildered by the technical issues involved in such cases. Also, companies that discover computer criminals among their employees are often reluctant to press charges because they fear adverse publicity.

Some Case Studies

To get some idea of the variety of forms that computer crime can take and some of the problems involved in dealing with it, let's look at some case studies. All these cases are either true or are closely modeled on actual situations.

Case 1. A computer operations employee at a university, who is also a student there, tampers with the student database, changing grades he's received and giving himself credit for courses he hasn't taken. His deceit is discovered by accident and he is pressed to resign. No formal charges are filed against him, however, for two reasons. First, the case would be hard to prosecute because the evidence is circumstantial. It appears as if someone had gained access to the database involved by creating a temporary false user account, but poor systems controls made it impossible to determine for sure who it was. Several people were privileged to authorize such accounts, so the employee could easily argue in court that he had been framed. Second, administrators feared it would cause great embarrassment to the university if the case were made public.

Case 2. A programmer working for a bank alters a program so that withdrawals against his own account are never recorded. To keep the books balanced, he taps what appear to be dormant accounts for the funds he withdraws. The employee is discovered when one account he taps turns out to be not so dormant. The depositor is persistent enough to persuade the bank to produce an original withdrawal slip for a questionable transaction. It turns out to be missing. Suspicious, the bank investigates further, finally comparing the computer program involved to its backup version. They differ by several lines of code.

The bank has a fairly strong case for embezzlement. The programmer cannot adequately explain why the deposits in his account over a certain period of time are in excess of his income. But fearing that publicity from the case would make depositors think their accounts were in jeopardy, the bank discharges the employee without pressing charges.

Case 3. A programmer working for a bank alters a program so that the interest computed in randomly selected, interest-earning accounts is "shaved off" by a few cents and the sums immediately posted to her account. This method of embezzlement is commonly called the *salami technique*. The theory behind it is that since customers have trouble computing interest anyway, and usually quit if they are within a few cents of an expected total, they are not likely to notice the missing funds. A few cents taken from many accounts, however, can amount to a considerable sum over many years when posted to a single account. And since no money is diverted out of the bank's system of accounts, the books of the bank balance.

The programmer's act is discovered during a routine audit, when an accountant with computer expertise tests the program involved with some dummy transactions. Independent tallies differ significantly from the program-generated ones. Again, fearing negative publicity, the bank releases the programmer but does not press charges.

Case 4. A part-time college student regularly walks by a telephone company warehouse on his way to school. He occasionally scavenges through trash cans for discarded equipment and technical manuals. From the manuals he learns about the telephone company's computer system. He eventually obtains some users' identification numbers and account codes, which enable him to tap into the system illegally. He alters some computer programs and has telephone equipment delivered to him without charge. He forms a corporation to sell the equipment to unwitting third parties.

Over time, the scam nets over a million dollars in stolen equipment. The deception is finally discovered when a disgruntled associate of the thief alerts the authorities. The thief is convicted but serves only forty days at a prison farm and pays the telephone company a mere $8500 settlement.

Case 5.   A computer services company programmer resigns her job and forms a competing firm. Many of the programs the new company offers are remarkably similar to those offered by the older one, and are priced at better rates. The older company accuses the programmer of duplicating its programs. Expert testimony convinces the jury that the programmer could not have created programs so similar to those of the older company in so short a time without copying them. The programmer is convicted and fined $50,000.

As these cases show, computer crime has many forms. Some cases involve the use of the computer for theft of financial assets, such as money or equipment. Others involve the copying of data-processing resources such as programs or data to the

Were You Superzapped or Salami-Sliced?

As in many fields, a specialized jargon has evolved in the area of computer-related crime. Here is a sampling—with definitions—of some of the more colorful terms.

Data Diddling.   This is one of the most popular ways to perform a computer crime. It involves altering valid data on the computer system in some unauthorized way. Data diddlers are often found changing grades in university files, falsifying input records on bank transactions, and so forth.

The Trojan Horse.   This is a procedure for adding instructions to a computer program so that it will still work, but will also perform unauthorized duties. For example, a bank worker can subtly alter a large program, containing thousands of lines of code, by adding a small "patch" that instructs the program not to withdraw money from a certain account.

Salami Methods.   These involve altering programs so that many small dollar amounts are shaved from a large number of selected transactions or accounts and deposited in another account. The victims of a salami operation generally are unaware that their funds have been tapped, because the amount taken from any individual is trivial. The recipient of the salami slicing, however, benefits from the aggregation of these small shavings. Often, these can add up to a substantial amount.

Superzapping.   This is a technique made possible by a special program available on most computer systems that bypasses all system controls when the computer "crashes" and cannot be restarted with normal recovery procedures. This program, in effect, is a "master key" that can provide access to any part of the system. The superzap program is a highly privileged "disaster aid," which very few people working with a computer system are authorized to use. In the wrong hands it can be used to do almost any unauthorized task. In one reported case, a computer operator who was allowed to use the superzap program to make certain specific changes fraudently directed substantial funds to accounts of friends.

Trapdoors.   These are diagnostic aids, used in the development of systems programs, that enable programmers to gain access to various

disadvantage of the owner. In still other cases such data as grades are manipulated for personal advantage. Computer crime is estimated to cost individuals and organizations billions of dollars annually. No one knows for sure what the exact figure is, because so many incidents are either undetected or left unreported.

Preventing Computer Crime

There are many ways organizations can combat computer crime. Some of them are discussed in the rest of this section.

Hire Trustworthy People. Employers should carefully investigate the background of anyone being considered for

parts of the computer system. Before the programs are marketed, these aids are supposed to be removed. Occasionally, however, some blocks of diagnostic code are overlooked, so that a person using the associated systems program may get unauthorized views of other parts of the computer system. In one publicized case, a trap-door was discovered by some users of a time-sharing service, and they were able to examine, criminally, a number of supposedly protected passwords. They later used the passwords to gain unauthorized access to confidential programs.

Logic Bombs. These are programs designed to be executed at random or at specific times to perform unauthorized acts. In one celebrated case, a programmer inserted a logic bomb in a system that would cause a company's entire personnel file to be destroyed if his name were removed from it.

Scavenging. As the name implies, this technique involves searching through trash cans, offices, and the like for information that will permit unauthorized access to a computer system. Students, for example, will often look

through discarded listings at a computer center for an identification number that will open to them the resources of others' accounts.

Data Leakage. Many pieces of data generated by organizations are highly confidential and not intended for the eyes of outsiders. Generally, these organizations will carefully control any computer outputs leaving their premises. In data leakage, however, confidential data are coded in sophisticated ways so that they can be removed undetected. For example, sensitive data could be transformed through a coding process to make them look like useless nonsense. Then, after they leave the organization virtually unnoticed, they can be decoded and the original output used for unauthorized purposes.

Wiretapping. Remember Watergate? Well, there are many documented cases of people who have wiretapped computer systems to obtain information illegally. Some transmission facilities, such as satellites, are highly susceptible to wiretapping (as evidenced by all those "illegal" rooftop devices that intercept cable TV without pay). Others, such as fiber optic cable, are extremely difficult to penetrate.

sensitive computer work. Some people falsify resumés to get jobs. Others may have criminal records.

Separate Employee Functions. An employee with many related responsibilities can more easily commit a crime than one

Terrorism Vexing International DP Crime Experts

LOS ANGELES—Smuggling, terrorism and sabotage by computer are a few of the potential crimes currently worrying experts in international computer crime, according to Jay Bloombecker, director of the National Center for Computer Crime Data.

If a computer criminal accessed a French computer from the UK and instructed the company to transport inventory to Brazil where he could claim it, which country would prosecute him if he was caught?

The answer is that there would be considerable confusion because of the state of international extradition laws, Bloombecker said in a recent interview, but the UK would most likely be able to prosecute. So the criminal could conceivably select the nation with the most lenient computer crime laws from which to access another country's computer.

Terrorists with data communications expertise could pose another problem. "It strikes me as unlikely that bombs will be the way to sabotage computers," Bloombecker said. "The motivation to use computer knowledge against the establishment is there. Terrorists will find the computer an attractive target. We haven't handled terrorism very well in the past and this won't get any better with the introduction of the computer."

As the number of people with computer knowledge increases, so will the incidence of international computer crime, especially crimes using remote-access terminals. High-technology theft and data piracy are other problems that could become commonplace as the users of remote terminals "capitalize on national boundaries," Bloombecker said.

100,000 Sites

"There are more than 100,000 computer sites in the U.S. and Western Europe alone that are constantly talking to one another—transferring funds, transmitting critical data and sensitive personal and diplomatic information," according to Barry Schrager, president of SKK, Inc., a systems software and consulting firm. SKK co-sponsored with Racal-Milgo, Inc. a conference on international crime titled "Operation Safeguard."

"In addition to main computer sites, there are several million computer terminals with the ability to access mainframe computers," Schrager said. "The opportunity for computer crime is, therefore, enormous."

The first step in eliminating this opportunity is to look at the kinds of crimes that are being committed now, Bloombecker said. The next step is to create a model law that can be applied internationally.

The National Center for Computer Crime Data has worked with the international police agency, Interpol, and local police forces to encourage the creation of a model law. Unless extradition laws are improved through an agreement made among nations, computer crime will rise as quickly on an international basis as it has in the U.S., Bloombecker said.

Source: Jim Bartimo, *Computerworld*, July 12, 1982, p. 11. © 1982 by CW Communications, Inc., Framingham, MA 01701. Reprinted from COMPUTERWORLD.

with a single responsibility. For example, the person who authorizes adding new vendors to a file should not be the same person who authorizes payments to those vendors.

Restrict System Use. People using a computer system should have access only to the things they need to use to do their jobs. An operator, for example, should be told only how to execute a program and not what the program does. Also, an airline agent should not be allowed to delete a passenger's reservation initiated at another agency or to book a passenger at a special rate if the duration period assigned to the rate has expired.

Protect Sensitive Programs and Data with Passwords. On many systems, users can protect programs and data with passwords. For example, a user might specify that anyone wanting access to a program named AR-148 must first enter the password "FRED." Users can protect particularly sensitive files with several passwords. It is also a good idea to change passwords frequently. Unfortunately, this practice is seldom followed.

Encrypt Sensitive Programs and Data. *Encryption* is the process of disguising data and programs by using some coding method (see Figure 18-1). The encrypting procedure must provide for both the coding and decoding. As with passwords, the encryption method should be changed regularly if it is protecting particularly sensitive materials.

Devise Staff Controls. Overtime work should be carefully scrutinized, because computer crimes often occur when the criminal is not likely to be interrupted. Sensitive documents that are no longer needed should be shredded. Access to the computer room or program/data library should be strictly limited.

Record and Manage Important System Transactions. The systems software should include a program for maintaining a log of every person gaining or attempting access to the system. The log should contain information on the terminal used, the data files and programs used, and the time at which the work began and ended. Such a log makes it possible for management to isolate unauthorized use of the system.

Conduct Regular Audits. Unfortunately, many crimes are discovered by accident. System controls (see Chapter 16) should be inspected and tested on a regular basis to ensure that no foul play is taking place.

Original Character	Substituted Character	Original Character	Substituted Character
A	I	Ø	R
B	blank space (Ƅ)	1	Z
C	Ø	2	7
D	U	3	:
E	C	4	A
F	.	5	T
G	J	6	4
H	B	7	K
I	@	8	−
J	H	9	+
K	O	−	L
L	>	+	#
M	$	.	W
N	5	,	9
O	&	$	?
P	<	(	N
Q	1	)	E
R	)	&	=
S	V	@	M
T	6	#	S
U	D	?	8
V	,	<	(
W	2	>	X
X	Y	=	3
Y	G	:	F
Z	Q	blank space (Ƅ)	P

Figure 18-1. A simple data encryption scheme. In this scheme, each character is replaced by its code equivalent. For example, the word **HELP** is encrypted as **BC>** < by using the character substitutions shown. This is an extremely simple method of encryption that could be easily "cracked" by a novice code breaker. More sophisticated techniques use the computer to make character substitutions randomly.

COMPUTERS AND PRIVACY

Almost all of us have some aspects of our lives we would rather keep private. These may include a sorry incident from the past, sensitive medical or financial facts, or certain tastes or opinions. Yet we can appreciate that at times selected people or organizations have a legitimate need for some of this information. A doctor needs an accurate medical history of patients. Financial information must be disclosed to credit card companies and

IRS computer in West Virginia. How safe is sensitive personal information once it's filed in a computer databank?

college scholarship committees. A company or the government may need to probe into the lives of people applying for unusually sensitive jobs.

Once personal information has been made available to others, however, no matter how legitimate the need, there is always the danger that it will be misused. Some of the stored facts may be wrong. Facts may get to the wrong people. Facts may be taken out of context and used to draw distorted conclusions. Facts may be collected without one's knowledge or consent. **Privacy,** with respect to information processing, refers to how information about individuals is used and by whom.

The problem of how to protect privacy and ensure that personal information is not misused was with us long before electronic computers existed. But modern computer systems, with their ability to store and manipulate unprecedented quantities of data and to make those data available to many locations, have added a new dimension to the privacy issue. The greater the ability to collect, store, and disseminate information, the greater the potential for abuse of that information.

Most of us, understandably, want some control over the kinds of facts that are collected about us, the way they are collected, their accuracy, who uses them, and how they are used. In this section we will look at some of the problems created by the widespread use of computers to provide information about individuals. Then we'll discuss the types of government legislation that have emerged for our protection.

Some Problem Areas

Involuntary Collection. A big fear many people have is that sensitive information about them will be gathered without their knowledge and will then fall into the hands of the wrong people. Let's look at a simple example that shows how computer technology has actually made this type of abuse easier.

Say you enjoy reading and keeping up on a wide variety of topics. One day you order several books from a mail-order catalog on a controversial subject. Unknowingly, you have probably placed yourself on a computerized mailing list. What's more, your order will probably be analyzed by computer to reveal (correctly or incorrectly) your "purchasing tastes." The company that you originally dealt with may also sell its mailing list to other companies interested in people with specific purchasing tastes. Thus, a piece of data about you that you may not want widely known has been collected, stored, and distributed.

For many months, you're flooded with junk mail from various companies you'd rather not deal with. In fact, you have to think twice now before asking someone to pick up your mail.

It is, of course, possible to write companies, requesting them to drop your name from their mailing lists. But even if you do, it may be months before the flood begins to ebb. And unfortunately, with so many transactions linked to credit card and banking identification numbers today, almost anytime we make a purchase data can be collected on us and filed in computer data banks without our ever knowing about it.

Disclosure.   Most people would agree that credit card companies should have the right to check the credit history of an applicant, and that employers should be able to check into the backgrounds of people seeking jobs. But when an honest, hardworking person with an impeccable credit history is denied credit, or a perfectly qualified applicant is denied a job, a number of questions come to mind. Decisions like these are often based on data stored in computer files. What types of data are in the files? Where did they come from? Are they accurate? Are the people making the decisions accidentally confusing two people with the same name? What procedures do they use to make their decisions?

As the many horror stories about people who have suffered because the wrong facts slipped into a data file suggest, these are serious questions. They have led many people to argue for the right of disclosure—the right of a person denied credit or a job to examine the data on which the decision was based and to correct any errors.

Unauthorized Use.   The federal government, local governments, and private organizations maintain various data banks with enormous amounts of information about millions of people. The Internal Revenue Service alone collects detailed information about every taxpayer every year. Figure 18-2 shows the size and scope of some of the most important federal data banks. Many people fear the information in these data banks could easily be abused—to monitor people's lives without their consent, for example, or to harass people who object to government policies. Considering that many data banks maintained by the federal government can be interrelated by social security number, the degree of control that a person or organization with access to just one of them could exercise is indeed frightening. On the other hand, of course, these data banks do serve legitimate needs.

Department of Health, Education and Welfare

Content: Marital, health, and financial data on people receiving government aid.

Size: Approximately 700 data systems with over a billion records.

Treasury Department

Content: Data on taxpayers; foreign travelers; dealers in alcohol, firearms, and explosives; and persons believed by the Secret Service to be a threat to the President.

Size: Approximately 1000 data systems and 1 billion records.

Justice Department

Content: Data on criminals, criminal suspects, aliens, persons linked to organized crime, securities-laws violators, and people under FBI investigation.

Size: Approximately 200 data systems and 200 million records.

Defense Department

Content: Data on service personnel and persons investigated for matters such as employment, security, or criminal activity.

Size: Over 2000 data systems and 300 million records.

Department of Transportation

Content: Data on pilots, aircraft and boat owners, and motorists with suspended or revoked licenses.

Size: Over 200 data systems with approximately 25 million records.

Department of Commerce

Content: Primarily census bureau data.

Size: Approximately 100 data systems and 500 million records.

Department of Housing and Urban Development

Content: Data on applicants for housing assistance and federal loans.

Size: Approximately 60 data systems and 30 million records.

Veterans Administration

Content: Primarily data on veterans and dependents who have received government benefits.

Size: Approximately 50 data systems and 150 million records.

Department of Labor

Content: Data on people in federally financed work and job training programs.

Size: Approximately 100 data systems and 20 million records.

Civil Service

Content: Data on government employees or applicants for government jobs.

Size: Approximately 15 data systems and 100 million records.

Based on data from *U.S. News & World Report*, April 10, 1978.

Figure 18-2.   Some personal data banks maintained by the federal government.

As a result of the fear of unauthorized use, virtually every time a new data bank is proposed, people voice concern about its potential for abuse. For example, a proposal was made recently to create an upgraded national computer network to identify problem drivers when they apply for license registration. The intended use of the network is certainly legitimate, but the proposal raised fears that the data might be used improperly to deny people employment.

Legislation

Since the early 1970s, the federal government has sought to protect the rights of citizens by passing legislation to limit the abuse of computer data banks. Some important laws that have been enacted for this purpose are the Fair Credit Reporting Act, the Freedom of Information Act, the Education Privacy Act, and the Privacy Act.

The **Fair Credit Reporting Act** (1970) is designed to prevent private organizations from unfairly denying credit to individuals. It stipulates that people denied credit must have the right to inspect their credit records, and this service is to be provided free of charge. Individuals not denied credit can also look at their records for a nominal fee. If a serious objection is raised about the integrity of the data, the credit agency is required by law to investigate the matter.

The **Freedom of Information Act** (1970) gives individuals the right to inspect data concerning them that are stored by the federal government. The law also makes certain data about the operation of federal agencies available for public scrutiny.

The **Education Privacy Act** (1974) protects an individual's right to privacy in both private and public schools receiving any federal funding. It stipulates that an individual has the right to keep matters such as course grades and evaluations of behavior private. Also, individuals must have the opportunity to inspect and challenge their own records.

The **Privacy Act** (1974) primarily protects the public against abuses by the federal government. It stipulates that any data federal agencies collect must have a legitimate purpose. It also states that individuals must be allowed to learn what information is being stored about them and how it's being used and have the opportunity to correct or remove erroneous or trivial data. This act augments considerably the provisions of the Freedom of Information Act. It outlaws abuses such as the preparation of covert "enemies lists" that were made public during the Watergate investigation.

Most privacy legislation, as you can see, relates to the conduct of the federal government and the organizations to which it supplies aid. Similar legislation has been enacted by some state governments to protect individuals from abuses by state agencies. The Privacy Act of 1974 also requires the federal government to establish a commission to oversee the activities of private enterprise. The Privacy Protection Study Commission, formed through this mandate, has presented several bills to Congress to limit abuses by the private sector. These bills have been aimed at specific segments of industry and have tried to establish the following principles:

- Individuals should know the policies and practices by which organizations gather data about them. Specifically, individuals should be told if data are being gathered about them and how they are being used.
- Individuals should have the right to inspect data being gathered about them.
- There should be limits on the types of data collected.
- There should be constraints on how the data are used.
- Record-keeping organizations bear the responsibility for their information practices.

NEW OPPORTUNITIES

Despite the dangers highlighted in earlier sections of this chapter, the use of computers in society will undoubtedly become ever more widespread. If you think about the enormous changes in computer technology that have taken place in just the past few years, it's natural to wonder what's coming next.

We can expect some important trends to continue: computers and computer systems will become cheaper, more powerful, and "friendlier." These trends will result primarily from further microminiaturization, improved teleprocessing facilities, and better software. As advances in these areas fuse, they are likely to bring about sweeping changes in the way we live and do business.

Invisible Money

Let's look at banking, for example. It's been possible for many years to transfer money from one account to another completely electronically, without the use of checks. This process is called *electronic funds transfer (EFT)*. One place you can see EFT in action today is at the automatic teller machines of your local bank (see Figure 18-3). As you withdraw money, there's an electronic transfer of funds out of your account. The potential uses of EFT extend well beyond teller machines, however.

One EFT scenario is as follows. You buy a number of items at a supermarket and it's time to pay. You pull out a bank card,

Figure 18-3. An automatic teller machine.

which a store cashier inserts into a terminal. Your balance is electronically checked, and if satisfactory, the amount of your purchase is automatically subtracted from your local bank account and added to the account of the supermarket (which may use a different bank). No check is ever written. The transaction is processed entirely electronically.

Also in the future, credit cards are likely to have their own built-in memories (such cards are already technologically possible, but they currently cost about $10 apiece to produce). When the card is used, the transaction is automatically recorded and stored in the card's memory. The card owner can then insert the card into a personal computer to get a record of transactions. This record can be checked against the bank statement.

In addition to the convenience that EFT can bring to credit card customers, it also promises to bring enormous savings to the banking industry. Today banks process 35 billion checks annually. This task constitutes one of their largest expenses. By 1990, however, EFT is expected to eliminate about 10 to 15 percent of the check market. It is also expected that EFT will save banks a sizeable portion of the work connected with credit card processing.

But EFT also has many disadvantages. You could be robbed electronically in a microinstant by a stealthy thief. Worse yet, if the system controls are poor, you might never be able to get your money back from the bank. And with so many of your purchases recorded in a computer databank, the potential exists for someone to analyze your purchasing habits and to use the information against you.

It's commonly assumed by industry experts that EFT will be slow to penetrate the checking system. Consumer resistance is still too strong, and any major changes in the banking system will have to meet stringent federal standards.

Communications

One place where the impact of the computer will eventually be felt strongly is in electronic mail. It's already possible, using a *facsimile machine,* to reproduce electronically both text and pictures and send them from one location to another. When facsimile, color picture digitization, and computers are combined in the future, sending a friend a letter might work something as follows. You prepare a handwritten letter on paper, in the traditional way. You then mount the letter and photographs you wish to send onto a digitizing device, attached to your personal computer, which copies them electronically. After you type in a few simple commands, images of the documents are routed to a friend's personal computer. The friend has an "electronic mailbox" facility on this computer that stores any incoming materials and catalogues them. The mailing costs are charged to your account through EFT.

Another promising area in which computer technology could improve communications is rural medicine. According to the 1980 census, almost 60 million people live in rural areas. On a per capita basis, rural areas have nearly 60 percent fewer doctors than metropolitan areas. With *teleconferencing,* however, patients in remote areas could avail themselves of good medical facilities. For example, a person in need of care in a remote area of the Pacific Northwest might go to a small, regional medical facility. There, a teleconference is arranged with a specialist in Seattle. The doctor and patient can see each other on television screens. The nurse at the regional facility takes blood and urine samples, which are placed under a microscope device attached to a television camera and computer. Digital images of the samples are transmitted to Seattle,

tomorrow

TELECOMMUTING TO WORK

Here you are. You just had breakfast and are ready to begin your work day. You sit down at the personal computer workstation in your home and turn the system on. You're a tax accountant and you bring up on the monitor screen the requests that have been sent to your system since you left it at 3 P.M. yesterday, when you went to play tennis. Clients can call your home at any time of the day or night. If you aren't available, the computer system takes the request and files it in an electronic in-basket for you to inspect at your convenience. When the client speaks, the voice is digitized and stored. If data need to be sent, they can be transmitted at high speeds from the client's computer system to yours. All these processes reverse themselves when you call the client back.

You prepare a few tax returns from requests in your in-basket by using an automatic tax preparation program. If you have a thorny problem, you can contact a tax consultation service through the small satellite dish antenna on your roof. The consultation service provides information through a query program with an enormous base of tax information. The service supplements the program with a human tax expert, whom you can communicate with through your monitor screen and audio unit.

After a few hours' work you decide to read the financial section of the "newspaper" to check your stock portfolio. You place a call, and the appropriate text is sent to you, also by way of satellite. You notice that a company you are particularly interested in has hired a new president. You key in some code on the keyboard, indicating you want more information on that company. It is immediately transmitted to you and, on your request, routed to the printer attached to your system so you can read it later.

The alarm on your system indicates that it's time for a meeting. You press several more keys and the images of people across town are transmitted to your home.

Sound futuristic? Maybe. But some forms of *telecommuting* (working at home at a computer station rather than traveling to an office) are already a reality. Many typists and computer programmers, for example, work at home on terminals or computers. Several banks in the Chicago area are, in fact, already supplying part-time secretaries with their own word processors so they can work at home. And companies such as Citibank in New York have built videoconferencing facilities to save travel costs and to enable quick financial decisions to be made face-to-face when multiple sites are involved.

How much will telecommuting take hold in the next twenty years? It's anyone guess. On the positive side, telecommuting can save workers both the time and expense involved in traveling to work. It can also save business the expense of maintaining office space. On the negative side, telecommuting limits the interpersonal contact that often makes working in an office lively and productive. And telecommuting will require a major cultural adjustment for those organizations used to on-site supervision of employees.

where they are immediately computer-analyzed. After inspecting the results of the analysis and questioning the patient, the doctor prepares a prescription. The prescription is transmitted to the regional facility, where it is printed and formally authorized with a local signature.

Entertainment

Imagine receiving personalized newspapers or magazines at home through your microcomputer (see Figure 18-4). To enjoy this convenience, you first dial a news or magazine service on your home computer system. The system includes a video storage unit, your television set, and a high-quality color graphics printer. You select from an extensive menu of available items the news you want to read. The master menu may be manipu-

Figure 18-4.   Electronic publishing.

tomorrow

ONLINE U.

Joe Smith was preparing to go to bed. Four lectures and one exam made tomorrow appear to be a very long day. When you added in the books he would have to look through at the library and the fact that he had to register for three courses for next term, a good night's sleep seemed a must. You'd think that when you had a skiing accident and were confined to a bed for a week, they'd make life a little easier on you.

Come again? How can Joe do all these things from a bed? Why, by being a student at Online University, the distributed institution of higher learning.

As you may have guessed, the preceding story is fictitious. There is no Online University, although at schools such as Britain's Open University students can attend lectures at home through radio and television. Nonetheless, scenarios such as the one described may be commonplace in the not-too-distant future. Most of the technology needed for such an institution exists today. One of the few major stumbling blocks is cost. As communications and equipment costs continue to drop relative to the cost of labor, however, electronic schools may someday seriously challenge the traditional structure of education.

Already television is used fairly successfully to distribute educational fare. Today, through well-prepared television programs, some of the best teachers can reach students in even the remotest areas.

Imagine the possibilities. As facilities improve for personalizing video-voice packages, students will be able to order programs and have them immediately transmitted to their homes. A professor might store lectures in a central electronic memory and transmit both the voice and video segments to students on request. Even exams might be transmitted, taken, and sent back through a computer system. Students would simply write their responses to the exam, page by page, on a digitizing tablet. The answers would be stored electronically in the local memory of the system and then be sent back to the professor for grading. The professor could also place a time limit on the exam and command the computer system to reject exams if they're submitted late. The instructors who teach these courses might live anywhere in the country, packaging and sending video-voice educational packets electronically from their homes. They would then submit students' grades to subscribing universities.

Although all this is technologically possible, many practical and ethical problems remain. For example, if lectures of only the "best" professors are packaged for transmission, what will happen to all the remaining teachers? Is it really possible to provide quality education in such a depersonalized fashion?

But even if the world is not yet ready to address all these issues, electronic libraries and online registration are very much a reality in some places. For example, some research materials in medicine and other fields are already being stored in electronic form. And several colleges and universities have converted to online systems for course registration. Many of these registration systems operate in *real-time,* much the way airlines' reservations systems do. A terminal operator can check the most up-to-date enrollment of a class to make sure it's not full before registering a student for it.

The computer has made giant strides into the academic world, where it first saw the light of day. Whether or not it will completely alter that world in some of the ways described here is anyone's guess.

lated with a friendly query language, so that a command such as

```
DISPLAY "BASEBALL"
```

will give you a specialized directory of all baseball materials available. You could obtain a New York *Daily News* account on a New York Mets game played that day, or a *Sports Illustrated* article on the Celtics' chances for the upcoming NBA season—all while at your home in Bonners Ferry, Idaho. The materials are transmitted directly to your home for storage. You can then inspect them over your television screen or have them printed on your high-resolution graphics printer to take on your weekend camping trip. Again, EFT systems will bill you for the materials you order.

There are many other possibilities for such do-it-yourself newspapers and magazines. Consider an electronic library, capable of storing many books and periodicals in machine-readable form. Library users call in from home computers and inspect materials on the display screens connected to their systems. Some materials can even be printed on request.

Musical pieces and movies could also be digitized and sent to the home. This would enable people to enjoy these works at their own convenience. Phone conversations might be supplemented with a video image of the person you're talking to. In fact, you might even be able to video-select dates on your computer system. All these possibilities are really very close to widespread availability.

Summary and Key Terms

Since the early 1950s, when the era of commercial computing began, computers have rapidly woven their way into the very fabric of modern society. In the process, they have created both problems and opportunities. Three important problem areas are computers and health in the workplace, computers and crime, and computers and privacy.

One of the first criticisms leveled at the entry of computers into the workplace was that their very presence resulted in job-related stress. In many cases, people were laid off, job security was threatened, and workers complained that computers dehumanized their jobs.

Computer crime is loosely defined as the use of computers to commit unauthorized acts. Some states have laws that address computer crime directly; others do not. In practice, however, even in states that do have such laws, computer crime is hard to pin down. It is often hard to decide when an unauthorized act is really a crime, judges and juries are often bewildered by the technical issues involved, and companies are reluctant to press charges.

There are many ways organizations can combat computer crimes: hiring trustworthy people, separating employee functions, restricting system use, protecting sensitive programs and data with passwords, encrypting sensitive programs and data, devising staff controls, recording and managing important system transactions, and conducting regular audits.

Most of us, understandably, want some control over the kinds of facts that are collected about us, the way they are collected, their accuracy, who uses them, and how they are used. The problem of how to protect **privacy** and ensure that personal information is not misused was with us long before electronic computers existed. But modern computer systems, with their ability to store and manipulate unprecedented quantities of data and make those data available to many locations, have added a new dimension to the privacy issue. The greater the ability to collect, store, and disseminate information, the greater the potential for abuse of that information.

Since the early 1970s, the federal government has sought to protect the rights of citizens by passing legislation to limit the abuse of computer data banks. Some important laws enacted for this purpose are the Fair Credit Reporting Act, the Freedom of Information Act, the Education Privacy Act, and the Privacy Act.

The **Fair Credit Reporting Act** is designed to prevent private organizations from unfairly denying credit to individuals. The **Freedom of Information Act** gives individuals the right to inspect data about them stored by the federal government. The **Education Privacy Act** protects an individual's right to privacy in both private and public schools receiving any federal funding. The **Privacy Act** primarily protects the public against abuses by the federal government.

Despite the dangers posed by computers, the use of them in society will undoubtedly become ever more widespread. We can expect some important trends to continue: computers and computer systems will become cheaper, more powerful, and "friendlier." These trends will result primarily from further microminiaturization, improved teleprocessing facilities, and better software. As advances in these areas fuse, they are likely to bring about sweeping changes in the way we live and do business.

Review Questions

1. Identify some specific problems caused by the rapid spread of computer use in society.
2. Why is computer crime so difficult to pin down?
3. Name some of the forms computer crime can take.
4. Name some ways in which organizations can prevent computer crime.
5. Name some rights of individuals that computer privacy laws have tried to protect.
6. Name some ways in which computers may change the way we live in the future.

Suggested Readings

Graham, Neill. *The Mind Tool: Computers and Their Impact on Society,* 2nd ed. St. Paul, Minn.: West, 1980.

Hoffman, Lance J. (Ed.). *Computers and Privacy in the Next Decade.* New York: Academic Press, 1980.

Martin, James. *Security, Accuracy, and Privacy in Computer Systems.* Englewood Cliffs, N.J.: Prentice-Hall, 1973.

Martin, James. *Telematic Society: A Challenge for Tomorrow.* Englewood Cliffs, N.J.: Prentice-Hall, 1981.

Parker, Donn B. *Crime by Computer.* New York: Scribner, 1976.

Toffler, Alvin. *The Third Wave.* New York: Morrow, 1980.

Whiteside, Thomas. *Computer Capers: Tales of Electronic Thievery, Embezzlement, and Fraud.* New York: Thomas Y. Crowell, 1978.

Appendix

A BEGINNER'S GUIDE TO BASIC

BASIC (Beginner's All-purpose Symbolic Instruction Code) is one of many programming languages widely in use today. A **programming language** is a set of rules used to create a computer program. The **computer program** is what you enter into the computer system to produce results.

A BASIC computer program is very similar to a recipe. It consists of a list of **instructions** which the computer must carry out in a specified sequence to produce the desired result. Each of the instructions in a BASIC program must be written in strict accordance with the rules of the BASIC language. These rules are referred to as **syntax.** If you make a seemingly trivial syntax error in writing the program, such as misspelling a word or omitting a comma, the computer system will reject your program or give unexpected, incorrect results.

The purpose of this appendix is to teach you how to write useful, simple BASIC programs. BASIC is one of the easiest to learn of all the major programming languages. You should be able to create programs for business use, game playing, and performing difficult, repetitive computations after reading this appendix and practicing on a computer available to you.

There are many versions of the BASIC language available today. This appendix has been written to conform to the most common BASIC usage, the guidelines for minimal BASIC proposed by the American National Standards Institute (ANSI). Thus the programs that follow will work on most machines. A two-color format is used in this appendix to distinguish programs and their inputs from the outputs they produce.

The need to practice BASIC on a computer can't be emphasized enough. Programming, like driving a car or playing a sport, is a skill which is mastered mostly by practice. Since it is easy for a beginner in any endeavor to make mistakes at the beginning, practicing can initially be very frustrating (can you remember your first day with a musical instrument?). However, if you really want to learn BASIC and if you start off by writing simple programs rather than complicated ones, you will find BASIC relatively easy. So, be patient . . . and start playing with your computer as soon as possible.

Here's what's on the following pages.

Section 1

A BASIC Primer

A SIMPLE EXAMPLE

Let's get into BASIC immediately by looking at a relatively simple problem and developing a BASIC program to solve it. The example given in Figure A1-1 will show you both some of the rules of BASIC and the manner in which computers carry out instructions in a logical, step-by-step fashion.

The problem is to write a BASIC program that adds the numbers 8 and 16. We want the computer to print the answer like this:

```
THE ANSWER IS   24
```

There are many ways to solve this problem, including the one shown in Figure A1-1 on the next page.

The six numbered instructions in the figure make up a **BASIC program.** In most cases, you will be typing in instructions such as these at a keyboard hooked up to a computer. When you have finished typing the instructions, you normally then type the word RUN, to command the system to execute (that is, to carry out) your program. You should study this program carefully before proceeding further. Sometimes the purpose of an instruction will be obvious. The comments which follow should clarify the other instructions.

Before we go into detail about precisely how the program works, you should observe the following important points about the program in Figure A1-1:

1. Each of the six numbered instructions is a **BASIC program statement.** The computer completes the operation described in each statement. It then automatically moves on to another statement.

    Each BASIC program statement begins with a key word, telling the computer what type of operation is involved: for example, REM, READ, LET, PRINT, DATA, and END. These key words may be thought of as the vocabulary of the computer system when you are writing BASIC programs. You must always stay strictly within this vocabulary. If, for example, you substitute DATUM or DATTA for DATA in line 50, the computer system will not know what you want to do!

```
10 REM THIS PROGRAM ADDS TWO NUMBERS
20 READ A,B
30 LET C=A+B
40 PRINT "THE ANSWER IS ";C
50 DATA 8,16
60 END

RUN
THE ANSWER IS  24
```

BASIC program

Command instructing computer to "execute" program

Program output

Figure A1-1.   A simple BASIC program.

2. Each program statement is identified by a **line number;** for example, 10, 20, 30, and so on. Line numbers are normally written in increments of 10 rather than 1, which allows you to easily insert new statements in the program later. All line numbers must be integers (whole numbers), and all lines must have different line numbers.

    The computer will always execute statements in the sequence specified by the line numbers unless instructed to do otherwise. Ways to do this are discussed later in this section. Because the line numbers are what specify the order of program statements, you can type in the lines in any order, such as 30, 60, 10, 50, 20, and 40. Before the computer system runs your program, it will automatically put all the statements in proper order (by line number).

3. In this program, three **variables** (A, B, and C) were used. When the computer system begins to execute the program, it will set up separate storage locations for A, B, and C. A storage location can be thought of as a "bucket" which can hold only one item (for example, a number) at a time.

    The storage locations represent the memory of the computer with respect to the program being run. For example, when we ask the computer in line 40 to print the value of C, the computer consults its memory to find the value.

    It is possible, as we will see in later programs, to change the values of variables such as A, B, and C several times during the execution of a program. It is because their values are allowed to change that they are known as variables. When A, B, and C are given new values, their old values are lost.

    Now let's see, statement by statement, how the program works.

```
10 REM THIS PROGRAM ADDS TWO NUMBERS
```
The REM (remark) statement is actually ignored by the computer. However, even though the computer doesn't use it, the REM statement is very helpful to the programmer. It allows you to place informative comments (such as the program title or description) within the body of the program.

```
20 READ A,B    and    50 DATA 8,16
```

The READ and DATA statements are always used together in BASIC. The READ statement instructs the computer to assign data to the specified variables. The DATA statement provides these data. Note that the computer assigns values one at a time and in the order they are typed in the READ and DATA statements. Thus when the READ statement is executed, the computer sets A equal to 8 and B equal to 16.

```
30 LET C=A+B
```

The computer system always reacts to a LET statement by computing the value indicated by the expression on the right side of the "=" sign and assigning it to the variable named on the left side. Thus statement 30 will cause the following actions to be taken:

1. The computer system looks up the values of A and B in memory (finding 8 and 16, respectively).
2. The values of A and B are added (producing 24).
3. The value of the right side of the expression (24) is assigned to C.

```
40 PRINT "THE ANSWER IS ";C
```

The PRINT statement is used when we want the computer system to output something; for example, the results of a computation. The PRINT statement above consists of three elements:

1. A phrase appearing inside quotes (THE ANSWER IS). The computer system will print this phrase exactly as it appears. These **literal** phrases are handy in PRINT statements to label output.
2. A formatting character (;). The semicolon instructs the computer system to leave only one space between the literal phrase and the value of C.
3. A variable (C). The computer system will look up the value of C in memory and print its value.

If you are using a display device (television-type screen), PRINT instructs the computer to display the information on the screen.

```
60 END
```

On many computer systems, the END statement must physically be the last statement in the program. It instructs the computer system that the program is finished.

At this point you can start to see how BASIC works. Now is a good time to test your knowledge of some of the fundamental concepts just introduced by practicing on your computer system. You might try some of the following suggestions:

1. Type and run the BASIC program in Figure A1-1. Did you get the same result as this appendix?

2. Try altering the PRINT statement so it produces nicer output. For example, to get the computer system to output

    ```
    THE SUM OF  8 AND  16 IS  24
    ```

    your PRINT statement should look like

    ```
    PRINT "THE SUM OF ";A;"AND ";B;"IS ";C
    ```

3. Try making the expression in statement 30 more complicated to see what the effects are. For example, A and B could be multiplied by specifying A*B instead of A+B in statement 30. Note that in BASIC, an asterisk is used to tell the computer to multiply. Multiplication is explained in more detail later.

    As another example, can you guess what the program below produces?

    ```
    10 READ X,Y,Z
    20 LET W=X+Y-Z+100
    30 PRINT X;Y;Z;"ANSWER =";W
    40 DATA 10,20,30
    50 END
    ```

4. Tinker with the DATA statement by changing the data values (try some negative numbers or numbers with decimal points). Also, experiment to see if it matters where the DATA statement appears. Try placing it as the first, second, or third statement of your program. Finally, try splitting a single DATA statement into several DATA statements. For example, split line 40 of the program in suggestion 3 above into

    ```
    40 DATA 10
    41 DATA 20,30
    ```

Running BASIC programs is a relatively simple task, and is described in some detail later in this section. All you need to concentrate on at this point are the RUN and LIST commands, as well as the instructions relating to correcting or changing lines. The RUN command executes your program and produces output. The LIST command will display the lines of your program in proper order upon your computer terminal. So—get started now! If you can write simple programs today, the complicated ones you encounter later will seem much easier.

A TOUGHER EXAMPLE

The program we just looked at was rather simple. The values of the variables didn't change, and the computer wasn't asked to execute a statement out of numerical order. In most programs, however, the values of the variables do change, and the computer is asked to **branch** to a statement other than the one which immediately follows.

Let's now consider a program which reflects these two added complications. We will write a program to compute and output the squares of 8, 16, and 12.

Before **coding** (that is, writing out) this problem in BASIC, let's consider what tasks are involved in solving this problem. Additionally, let's think about the order in which these tasks must be presented to the computer. This process is called the **design phase** of developing a computer program. It's not that different from building a house. You don't start putting the roof together before you've fully designed the whole structure and decided when the roof will be made relative to other sections.

In designing this program, it seems that the following approach is attractive:

1.   Read a number.
2.   Square the number.
3.   Print out the result of step 2.
4.   Go back to step 1.

The fundamental structure involved here is called a **loop.** Thus the computer system is to read 8, square it (producing 64), output the result (64), loop back to step 1, read 16, square it . . . and so on. There is only one problem with the four-step solution just described—once the computer system fully processes the last number (12) and goes back to step 1, there are no more numbers to read. This problem is frequently solved by putting a **trailer value** (such as -1) at the end of the data list and directing the computer to leave the loop immediately after this trailer value is read. Thus we could refine our loop as follows:

1.   Read a number.
1.5   If the number $= -1$ go to step 5; otherwise process step 2.
2.   Square the number.
3.   Print out the result of step 2.
4.   Go back to step 1.
5.   End the program.

Once the design of the program is established, the coding in BASIC becomes relatively straightforward, as you will see by observing the program which appears in Figure A1-2 (page A-8).

It will take the computer 18 steps to fully execute this program, as shown in Figure A1-3 (page A-8).

The design phase of computer programming is extremely critical. Programs used to help run businesses are usually in operation for several years, and they need to be constantly modified to meet changing business conditions. Thus a program that is designed in a hasty fashion will often cause numerous maintenance problems over the years for programmers who have to keep it up to date. Simply stated, poorly designed programs are almost always expensive head-

```
10 REM THIS PROGRAM SQUARES NUMBERS
20 READ A
30 IF A=-1 THEN 80
40 LET B=A**2
50 PRINT "THE SQUARE OF ";A;" IS";B
60 GOTO 20
70 DATA 8,16,12,-1
80 END
RUN
THE SQUARE OF  8 IS 64
THE SQUARE OF  16 IS 256
THE SQUARE OF  12 IS 144
```

Figure A1-2.   Program to compute and output the squares of several numbers.

aches. A few extra dollars spent on initial design may save hundreds of dollars or more later.

There are numerous guidelines for good program design. Many of these are covered in Chapters 9 and 10 of the textbook. For example, professional programmers usually write programs that include only

Step	Statement Executed	Value of A in Storage	Value of B in Storage	Action Taken
1	20	8		8 taken from data list and assigned to A
2	30	8		8 ≠ −1; therefore go to next statement
3	40	8	64	B computed
4	50	8	64	Computer system prints THE SQUARE OF 8 IS 64
5	60	8	64	Computer directed to line 20
6	20	16	64	16 taken from data list and assigned to A
7	30	16	64	16 ≠ −1; therefore go to next statement
8	40	16	256	B computed
9	50	16	256	Computer system prints THE SQUARE OF 16 IS 256
10	60	16	256	Computer directed to line 20
11	20	12	256	12 taken from data list and assigned to A
12	30	12	256	12 ≠ −1; therefore go to next statement
13	40	12	144	B computed
14	50	12	144	Computer system prints THE SQUARE OF 12 IS 144
15	60	12	144	Computer directed to line 20
16	20	−1	144	−1 taken from data list and assigned to A
17	30	−1	144	−1 = −1; therefore go to line 80
18	80	−1	144	The program ends

Figure A1-3.   Steps the computer system must take to fully execute the problem in Figure A1-2.

certain forms of the three fundamental **control structures: sequence, selection,** and **looping.** Also, good programmers code many comments in their programs as a **documentation** aid, so that other programmers can easily understand how the programs work. Additionally, it is also a good practice to choose variable names carefully and systematically, both so that other programmers can quickly grasp the underlying logic involved and so that you will remember easily what they mean if you have to alter the program months after you wrote it! Most companies will have a set of written guidelines, or *shop rules,* for their programmers to ensure that programs are written in a very consistent and readable fashion. So it is very important that from the outset of your programming experience you think very carefully about the design of your programs.

WRITING ACCEPTABLE BASIC EXPRESSIONS

Now that we've covered some broad fundamentals concerning how BASIC works, let's consider more closely rules for writing BASIC instructions. This subsection addresses allowable characters, formation of variables and constants, and writing mathematical expressions.

BASIC Character Set

When you are typing in a program you must use only those characters which are understood by the version of BASIC available to your computer system. Such characters are known as the BASIC character set. These characters fall into three groups:

Alphabetic: ABCDEFGHIJKLMNOPQRSTUVWXYZ
Numeric: 0123456789
Special: . , + & ! < > / @ ( ) - * =   (and so on)

Variables

Variables are of two fundamental types: numeric and string. **Numeric variables** can be assigned only numbers, whereas **string variables** can be assigned any character strings. Let us look at numerical variables first.

Numeric Variables.   The program below contains six numeric variables:

```
10 LET A=6.5
20 LET B=8.04
30 READ C1,C2,C3
40 D=A+B-(C1+C2+C3)
50 PRINT D
60 DATA 3,2,0.04
70 END
RUN
9.5
```

Each of the variables (A, B, C1, C2, C3, and D) is allocated a storage location by the computer at execution time. Each location may store a number while your program is executing.

BASIC varies in the way numeric variable names may be created by the programmer. The most universal convention is to allow the name to be composed of either

1.   A single alphabetic character (for example, A, B, and D), or

2.   A single alphabetic character followed by a single digit (for example, C1, C2, and C3).

Thus, for example, the following numeric variable names are allowable under this convention:

```
C8, F1, X, I, I8, T
```

while the following are not:

C12	Too many characters
8C	First character not alphabetic
F&	Second character must be numeric

If your computer was purchased within the past few years, it probably allows longer numeric variable names in BASIC—up to 30 characters long in many systems. This allows variable names to be chosen as better reminders of what the variables stand for. The first character must still be alphabetic; other characters can be letters or digits.

In this Appendix we will stick with the older convention, since it will work on any computer system using BASIC.

String Variables.   A string is a collection of related characters; for example,

```
JOHN Q. DOE
1600 PENNSYLVANIA AVENUE
THX-1138
```

Strings may be assigned to variable names and manipulated by computer systems. For example, the program below contains only string variables

```
10 LET A$="AT THIS EXAMPLE"
20 LET B$="LOOK CAREFULLY "
30 PRINT B$;A$
40 END
RUN
LOOK CAREFULLY AT THIS EXAMPLE
```

There are two string variables in this short program: A$ and B$. The computer allocates storage space to string variables in essentially the same way it allocates storage to numeric variables. In other words, the storage location set up for A$ contains the string

```
AT THIS EXAMPLE
```

and the location set up for B$ contains the string

```
LOOK CAREFULLYb
```
  (b̷ represents a blank space)

Since A$ and B$ are variables, they can contain different strings throughout the course of the program, but only one string at any given time. An important difference between numeric and string variables is that we can perform conventional arithmetic with numeric variables but generally not with string ones.

BASIC varies in the way string variable names may be created by the programmer. The original and most universal rule is to use a single alphabetic character followed by a dollar sign ($). Thus with this convention the following string variable names are allowable:

```
A$, B$, C$, T$, Z$
```

while the following are not:

F1   Dollar sign is not second character

P2$ Too many characters

T   Dollar sign missing

$ Leading alphabetic character missing

Again, many newer systems allow longer names.

Some computer systems require that the string assigned to a string variable be enclosed in quotes; for example,

```
10 A$="EVERY GOOD "
20 C$=" DOES FINE"
30 READ B$
40 PRINT A$;B$;C$
50 READ B$
60 PRINT A$;B$;C$
70 DATA "BOY","GIRL"
80 END
RUN
EVERY GOOD BOY DOES FINE
EVERY GOOD GIRL DOES FINE
```

Constants

Like their variable counterparts, **constants** may be either numeric or string. Unlike variables, however, the value of a constant doesn't change (although constants can be assigned to variables, which can change).

Numeric Constants. A **numeric constant** is simply a number; for example, 81, −54, .001. When creating arithmetic expressions in BASIC it is often useful to assign numbers to or to use numbers in combination with numeric variables. Some examples are

```
LET A=5.0        5.0 is a numeric constant
LET B=A+2        2 is a numeric constant
LET C=.01*A+B    .01 is a numeric constant
```

While the numeric constant chosen can be an integer number or a number with a decimal point, the use of commas or dollar signs is not allowed as part of the constant itself. The following are invalid representations of numeric constants in a BASIC program:

```
LET A=2,000      Comma invalid. LET A=2000 is valid
DATA $6,$3.52    $ invalid. DATA 6,3.52 is valid
```

In many cases we would like to precede a number by a $ sign. This can be done very simply, as the following short example suggests:

```
10 LET A=5.21
20 PRINT "$";A
30 END
RUN
$ 5.21
```

String Constants. A **string constant** is simply any collection of allowable BASIC characters enclosed in quotes; for example,

```
"HELLO 12?"
"GOODBYE MY LOVELY"
"145-86-7777"
```

String constants can be assigned to string variables, such as

```
10 LET A$="EVERY GOOD "
```

or be declared independently of any variables, as in the PRINT statement below

```
10 PRINT "THE VALUE OF INVENTORY IS $";X
```

A string constant is often referred to as a literal.

Mathematical Expressions

BASIC allows the programmer to create complex mathematical expressions involving numeric variables and numeric constants. The following operations are permitted:

Operation	BASIC Symbol Used
Addition	+
Subtraction	−
Multiplication	*
Division	/
Exponentiation	** or ^

For example, suppose A = 1, B = 3, and C = 2. The following statements would produce the results indicated:

`LET D=A+B-C`	(D is assigned a value of 2. The previous value of D is lost.)
`IF B=A+C THEN 70`	(A+C is computed as 3. Since that is the value of B, the computer branches to statement 70.)
`LET C=B/2`	(The right-hand side equals 1.5, which is assigned to C. The previous value of C is lost.)
`PRINT A*B`	(A and B are multiplied, and the product, 3, is printed.)

Now, consider a more complicated expression, such as the one below:

```
LET C=C-A+B/(C+4)**2
```

The question arises here as to which operation the computer will perform first. BASIC recognizes the following order of operations (commonly known as the **hierarchy of operations**):

1. All operations within parentheses are performed first, starting with the innermost set of parentheses.

2. Exponentiation is performed next.

3. Multiplication and division are performed next, and the computer executes these from left to right in the expression.

4. Addition and subtraction are performed last, also left to right.

Thus the expression just given would be evaluated as follows under this set of rules:

Step	Operation Performed
1	(C+4) evaluated. Result is 6
2	6**2 evaluated. Result is 36
3	B/36 evaluated. Result is .083333
4	C−A evaluated. Result is 1
5	1 is added to .083333. Result is 1.083333
6	C is assigned the value 1.083333. The previous value of C is lost

To be fully sure that you understand the hierarchy of operations, you should study the following examples. Assume in the examples that $W = 1$, $X = 2$, $Y = 3$, $Z = 4$.

Example 1   LET A=Y/W*Z
(A would be assigned a value of 12, since division and multiplication, being on the same level of hierarchy, are performed left to right.)

Example 2   LET B=(X+Y)*(W+1)**2
(B would be assigned a value of 20. Parenthetical expressions are evaluated first, then exponentiation, and finally multiplication.)

Example 3   LET C=((Z−W)*X)**2/2
(C would be assigned a value of 18. The computation in the innermost parentheses are performed first, yielding $Z-W=3$. Then contents of the outermost parentheses are evaluated, yielding $3*2=6$. After all of the parenthetical expressions are evaluated, the 6 is squared. Finally, the result of all the previous operations, 36, is halved to produce 18.)

Most major programming languages have a hierarchy of operations identical to that of BASIC.

MORE ON ELEMENTARY BASIC STATEMENTS

So far, we've informally shown the use of the REM, READ, DATA, IF, LET, PRINT, GOTO, and END statements. Let's now consider further the permissible usage of these statements.

READ and DATA Statements

As mentioned earlier, the READ and DATA statements are always used together. When a READ is executed, the computer will assign values appearing in the DATA statements to the respective variables named in the READ. The format of each of these statements is shown below:

> READ list of variables (separated by commas)
> DATA list of data items (separated by commas)

The DATA statements actually are never executed by the computer. Between the time the RUN command is issued and the program is executed, the computer system extracts all of the values from the DATA statements and prepares a "data list." It is this list that is referenced each time a READ is encountered. The DATA statement itself is ignored during program execution.

It is useful to think of a "pointer" attached to the data list. The pointer initially points to the first value in the data list. When this value is assigned, it then points to the second item, and so on. For example, consider the READ and DATA statements for the program in Figure A1-2 (page A-8):

```
20 READ A
70 DATA 8,16,12,-1
```

The pointer initially points to the 8. When statement 20 is first executed, the 8 is assigned to A and the pointer moves to the 16. When statement 20 is executed again, 16 is assigned to A (the previous value, 8, being erased) and the pointer moves to the 12 . . . and so on. When the −1 is finally assigned to A there are no more data to point to; thus if we tried to execute this (or another) READ statement again, the computer would inform us that it is out of data.

Because they are not executed, DATA statements may be placed anywhere in a program. In most implementations they must appear before the END statement. Also, several DATA statements can be used to hold the data. The program below, which is a rewritten version of the program in Figure A1-2, illustrates these points:

```
5 DATA 8
6 DATA 16,12
7 DATA -1
10 REM THIS PROGRAM SQUARES NUMBERS
20 READ A
30 IF A=-1 THEN 80
40 LET B=A**2
50 PRINT "THE SQUARE OF ";A;"IS";B
60 GOTO 20
80 END
```

You should note, however, that we could *not* have rewritten the data statements as

```
5 DATA -1
6 DATA 8,16
7 DATA 12
```

because the data list formed $(-1,8,16,12)$ would not produce the same results as the original program.

IF Statement

The IF statement typically follows the format below:

$$\text{IF relational-expression} \begin{Bmatrix} \text{THEN} \\ \text{GOTO} \end{Bmatrix} \text{line number}$$

A relational expression is one which contains one of the relational operators below:

Operator	Meaning
<	Less than
<=	Less than or equal to
>	Greater than
>=	Greater than or equal to
=	Equal to
<>	Not equal to

For example, the following are allowable IF statements:

```
IF A>B THEN 170
```
   (A>B is the relational expression.)

```
IF A-B<=C-D THEN 180
```
   (A−B<=C−D is the relational expression.)

```
IF A<>C*(D-E)**F THEN 220
```
   (A<>C*(D−E)**F is the relational expression.)

The computer executes an IF statement as follows:

1. The expression on each side of the relational operator is computed, resulting in a single value on each side.

2. If the statement is true (for example, A>B, where A=3 and B=1), the computer branches to the statement number appearing after the THEN (or GOTO); otherwise, the computer goes to the statement which appears immediately after the IF. The IF statement is an example of a **conditional branch**.

An IF statement can contain a relational expression involving string variables; for example,

```
IF S$="BOZO" THEN 220
```

Thus if the string BOZO is stored in S$, this statement would be true.

LET Statement

The LET statement typically follows the format below:

> LET variable-name = expression

An extremely important requirement of this format is that only a single variable name is allowed to appear on the left-hand side of the = sign. Thus

```
LET A=6*B-C**(N-1)
LET D=0
```

are allowable, whereas

```
LET A+B=C
```

is not. A single variable must appear on the left-hand side because—once the right-hand side expression is computed down to a single value—a storage location (as represented by a single variable) must be declared to store this value. Remember, A, B, C, and so on are acceptable names for storage locations, whereas A+B is not.

The = sign of the LET statement is more properly referred to as an **assignment** (or **replacement**) **symbol** than an "is equal to." To understand the basis of this nomenclature, consider the perfectly acceptable BASIC statement

```
LET I=I+1
```

This statement makes absolutely no sense if we interpret the = sign as meaning "is equal to." However, if we interpret this statement as instructing the computer to determine the value of I+1 and to assign the number obtained back to I, it does make sense. Thus if the value 6 were initially stored in I, this statement would add 6 to 1 and assign the result, 7, back to I (erasing the 6 that was there previously).

In many versions of BASIC the appearance of the word LET is optional in a LET statement. Thus

```
I=I+1
```

is equivalent to

```
LET I=I+1
```

PRINT Statement

The PRINT statement, being the main vehicle for obtaining BASIC output, is so pivotal that a separate section in this appendix is devoted exclusively to its use (see Section 4). So far, we have seen that one acceptable form of the PRINT statement is

$$\text{PRINT} \left\{ \begin{array}{l} \text{literal,} \\ \text{variable, or} \\ \text{expression} \end{array} \right\} ; \left\{ \begin{array}{l} \text{literal,} \\ \text{variable, or} \\ \text{expression} \end{array} \right\} ; \dots$$

Thus the following are allowable:

```
PRINT "A=";A
```
> If 6 is stored in A, the output is
```
A=6
```

```
PRINT A;B;C*Z;M$
```
> If 6 is stored in A, 72 in B, 16 in C, 2 in Z, and " ARE THE ANSWERS" in M$, the output is
```
6 72 32 ARE THE ANSWERS
```

```
PRINT A$;B$
```
> If "HIGH " is stored in A$ and "SCHOOL" in B$, the output is
```
HIGH SCHOOL
```

Other versions of the PRINT statement are covered in Section 4.

GOTO Statement

The simple format of the GOTO statement,

GOTO line-number

makes it one of the easiest BASIC statements to use. For example,

```
GOTO 810
```

will direct the computer to statement 810. The GOTO statement is an example of an **unconditional branch.**

Perhaps because of its simplicity, the GOTO statement is frequently overused, leading to programs difficult or impossible for a human to easily follow or "debug." Under no circumstances should you ever GOTO another GOTO statement. In any case, GOTO should be used as little as possible.

```
10 REM    THIS PROGRAM READS NUMBERS,
20 REM    SQUARES THEM, AND OUTPUTS THE
30 REM    RESULTS,
40 REM       AUTHOR - C,S, PARKER
50 REM       DATE - 8/22/83
60 REM ***********VARIABLES**********
70 REM    A = THE NUMBER TO BE SQUARED
80 REM    B = THE SQUARE OF THE NUMBER
90 REM ****************************
100 READ A
110 IF A=-1 THEN 160
120 LET B=A**2
130 PRINT "THE SQUARE OF ";A;"IS";B
140 GOTO 100
150 DATA 8,16,12,-1
160 END
```

Figure A1-4.   Program of Figure A1-2 rewritten with REM statements.

REM Statement

The REM (remark) statement is a very important tool in BASIC—
even though it is completely ignored by the computer when the
program is executed! Its purpose is to allow you to put useful
comments, or blank lines, in the program listing. The format of the
REM statement is

REM any remark

An example of the use of the REM statement is shown in Figure
A1-4. The output for the program in Figure A1-4 is exactly the same as
the output for the program in Figure A1-2 because the computer
system ignores the REM statements. REMs can appear anywhere in a
program. In some implementations they must appear before the END
statement.

END Statement

Generally, the END statement is physically the last statement in the
program; that is, it is the statement with the highest line number.
When the computer encounters this statement, it terminates execution of your program. The format of the END statement is

END

Some versions of BASIC do not require an END statement; however, its use is highly recommended because it leaves no doubt in anyone's mind where the program ends. The END statement is frequently used in combination with the STOP statement, which is discussed in Section 3.

DEVELOPING AND RUNNING BASIC PROGRAMS ON YOUR COMPUTER SYSTEM

Now that we've covered how to write simple BASIC programs, it's time to consider how to develop and run them on your computer system. Systems vary tremendously with regard to the specific *forms* of the system commands used. Fortunately, most of them have the same *types* of commands. These systems often differ only in the specific ways in which the commands must be typed.

System Commands

There are two major types of commands that you will use to write and run BASIC programs on your computer: **BASIC statement commands** (which are the BASIC program statements in the lines of your program), and **BASIC system commands** (which are outside of your program). We have already covered several statement commands (READ, PRINT, GOTO, and so on). These commands instruct the computer system what to do while it is executing your program.

System commands, on the other hand, are often used by the programmer to tell the computer to do something before or after it executes the program. Two examples are RUN and LIST. Some examples of common system actions, and how they are implemented on several Apple computer systems, the IBM Personal Computer, and several Radio Shack TRS-80 systems, are given in Figure A1-5. The form of these commands on larger computer systems is similar. You should check the system commands for your particular computer.

Interacting with Your System

Let's say that you want to "try out" your computer system by typing in the squares program of Figure A1-4. You would type in all 16 lines, pressing the RETURN (or ENTER) key after each line, as usual. Many versions of BASIC will check each statement for correct form (or *syntax*) when you press RETURN. Thus suppose you fumble at the keyboard while typing in the tenth line of your program, producing

100 READD A

Action Desired	Applesoft BASIC	IBM Personal Computer BASIC	TRS-80 Level II BASIC
To clear the computer's memory for a new program	NEW	NEW	NEW
To run a program	RUN	RUN	RUN
To list an entire program	LIST	LIST	LIST
To list lines 10–30 of a program	LIST 10, 30	LIST 10–30	LIST 10–30
To halt a program while it is executing	Depress "Control" and "C" keys	Depress "Control" and "Break" keys	Depress "Break" key
To retrieve a program (named FRED) from diskette	LOAD FRED	LOAD "FRED"	LOAD "FRED"
To retrieve a program (named FRED) from cassette tape	LOAD	LOAD "FRED"	CLOAD "FRED"
To store a program (named FRED) on diskette	SAVE FRED	SAVE "FRED"	SAVE "FRED"
To store a program (named FRED) on cassette tape	SAVE	SAVE "FRED"	CSAVE "FRED"

Figure A1-5. *BASIC system commands on some popular microcomputer systems.*

Your terminal probably has a backspace key which will let you fix the error if you have not hit the return key. If you have already hit the return key to enter the faulty line into the computer system, the following error message might be sent to the screen

```
INVALID COMMAND
```

At this point you may have to retype the entire line, including the line number. The computer system will then replace the old line 100 with the corrected version.

When you have finished typing your program, you will most likely be anxious for the computer to execute it immediately. Most systems require the user to type in the command

```
RUN
```

After you issue this command, one of the following will happen:

1. The program will run successfully, producing the correct answers

2. The program will run, but produce incorrect answers. This might happen if, for example, you typed in line 120 of the squares program as

```
120 LET B=A**3
```

The program would then produce cubes of numbers instead of squares! *Thus it is important that you look at your output carefully before you decide that your program works.*

3. The program stops unexpectedly in the middle of a run. This would happen in the squares program if line 150 were typed in as follows:

```
150 DATA 8,16,"HELLO",12,-1
```

The program would compute the squares of 8 and 16 successfully, but would stop (or abort) when it tried to assign the string "HELLO" to the numeric variable A. When BASIC runs into this situation while running the program it would likely display a message such as

```
ATTEMPT TO READ INVALID DATA ON LINE 100
```

and halt. At this point you must correct the error, or **bug,** in the program and try again. Learning how to correct, or **debug,** faulty programs is one of the most important skills you must develop to program well. As unusual as it may seem, even a good programmer can easily spend 50 percent of the time it takes to develop a program getting rid of bugs in it. This subject will be addressed in more detail later on.

SOLVED REVIEW PROBLEMS

Example 1

Company X has anywhere from 5 to 20 students employed on a part-time basis during the summer. This past week, five students were on the payroll. The students each worked different hours at different rates of pay, as shown below:

Student Name	Hours Worked	Rate of Pay
John Smith	20	$5.40
Nancy Jones	15	5.60
Bo Weeks	25	5.00
Millicent Smythe	40	4.80
Joe Johnson	20	5.10

The company would like you to write a BASIC program to compute and print the total pay due each student.

Solution

The program must read a number of records. This number varies from week to week. Each record contains a name, hours worked, and a rate of pay.

As usual, to stop the program it is convenient to employ a trailer record. The following steps show how the program might be designed:

1. Read a record (name, hours worked, rate of pay)

2. If Name=Bozo (the name on the trailer record), go to step 6; otherwise, continue with step 3

3. Compute pay due

4. Print student name and pay due

5. Go back to step 1

6. End program

This structure leads to the program in Figure A1-6.

Before we leave this example, let's consider some of the problems we might have run into if there were errors in the program. Also, we'll explore how we might correct such errors.

First, suppose we had typed in line 110 as follows:

110 D=H*R

When the computer encounters this statement it has a value for S\$, H, and P. However, it doesn't have the foggiest clue as to what R is, since we never assigned a value to it. In most versions of BASIC, when the computer is requested to use the value of a variable which it hasn't yet

```
10 REM THIS PROGRAM COMPUTES EMPLOYEE PAY
20 REM    AUTHOR: C.S. PARKER
30 REM ***********VARIABLES*************
40 REM    S$ = EMPLOYEE NAME
50 REM    H  = HOURS WORKED
60 REM    P  = HOURLY PAY RATE
70 REM    D  = PAY DUE
80 REM ********************************
90 READ S$,H,P
100 IF S$="BOZO" THEN 220
110 D=H*R
120 PRINT S$;" HAS EARNED   $";D
130 GOTO 90
140 REM *********DATA STATEMENTS*********
150 DATA "JOHN SMITH",20,5.40
160 DATA "NANCY JONES",15,5.60
170 DATA "BO WEEKS",25,5.00
180 DATA "MILLICENT SMYTHE",40,4.80
190 DATA "JOE JOHNSON",20,5.10
200 DATA "BOZO",0,0
210 REM *******************************
220 END
RUN
JOHN SMITH HAS EARNED   $ 108
NANCY JONES HAS EARNED   $ 84
BO WEEKS HAS EARNED   $ 125
MILLICENT SMYTHE HAS EARNED   $ 192
JOE JOHNSON HAS EARNED   $ 102
```

Figure A1-6.   A program to compute the pay due employees.

encountered during execution, it assumes the value is zero. Naturally, this can lead to some very surprising results in your programs! In the current problem, your program would show that everyone has earned $0.

You should quickly be able to find an error like the one just described by making a few simple deductions. For example, since all the values of D are printing as 0 and D is computed by H∗R, either H or R (or both of these variables) are equal to zero.

As a second example, suppose we had mistakenly typed in line 180 as follows:

```
180 DATA 40,40,4,80
```

The computer would execute our program successfully until it had printed out

```
BO WEEKS HAS EARNED $125
```

Then we might receive a message such as the following:

```
ATTEMPT TO READ INVALID DATA ON LINE 90
```

These two lines of output give us a clue to the error. The computer successfully completed the processing of Bo Weeks's record but subsequently "bombed" on line 90. Thus something must be amiss with the data in the next record. Now we would notice that the number 40 appears where "MILLICENT SMYTHE" should be, and BASIC cannot assign a numeric constant to a string variable!

Debugging programs is a skill which involves a lot of practice. You must learn to make deductions from the information given by the computer system (i.e., partial output, incorrect output, and error messages) to determine the source of the error.

Another technique that's recommended for particularly hard-to-find errors is the so-called dummy (diagnostic) PRINT statement. Suppose again that for line 110 you had typed

```
110 D=H∗R
```

You have deduced that either H, R, or both of these variables is zero, but you still can't put your finger on the error. However, you could now type

```
115 PRINT "H =";H;"  R =";R
```

The computer system would then respond with the following outputs after you type RUN

```
H = 20  R = 0
JOHN SMITH HAS EARNED   $ 0
H = 15  R = 0
NANCY JONES HAS EARNED   $ 0
```

and so on. Now the source of the error is obvious: R is zero for every record.

Once the dummy PRINT statement has served its purpose of uncovering the error, and the error has been corrected, statement 115 should be deleted so that it won't interfere with the normal output of the program. The form for doing this may be DELETE 115 on your system, or you may be able to simply type 115 and press RETURN (replacing the old statement 115 with a blank statement).

Example 2

ABC Company has a file which keeps the following information on employees:

- Name
- Sex (M or F)
- Age
- Department

The file has approximately 1000 employees, although the exact number is usually unknown. Write a BASIC program which will print out the names of all females over 40 who work in the accounting department.

Solution

This program involves a series of three IF statements which pose the three conditions we wish to check in each record: in other words, female?, over 40?, and accounting?. If a record passes all three checks we print the associated name; otherwise, we read the next record.

Since the data file is not given, we'll make up five "program test records" (including a trailer record) to illustrate how the program works. The program is shown in Figure A1-7.

```
10 REM THIS PROGRAM SELECTS FROM A FILE ALL
20 REM FEMALE EMPLOYEES OVER 40 WHO WORK IN
30 REM THE ACCOUNTING DEPARTMENT
40 REM    AUTHOR - C.S. PARKER
50 REM *******VARIABLES********
60 REM    N$ = EMPLOYEE NAME
70 REM    S$ = SEX
80 REM    A  = AGE
90 REM    D$ = DEPARTMENT
100 REM ********************
110 REM READ N$,S$,A,D$
120 IF N$="BOZO THE CLOWN" THEN 250
130 IF S$="M" THEN 110
140 IF A<=40 THEN 110
150 IF D$<>"ACCOUNTING" THEN 110
160 PRINT N$
170 GOTO 110
180 REM *********DATA STATEMENTS**********
190 DATA "JANE CRIBBS","F",25,"ACCOUNTING"
200 DATA "PHIL JONES","M",45,"ACCOUNTING"
210 DATA "ANNE WELLES","F",42,"ACCOUNTING"
220 DATA "MARY SMITH","F",41,"FINANCE"
230 DATA "BOZO THE CLOWN","M",99,"NONE"
240 REM ********************************
250 END
RUN
ANNE WELLES
```

Figure A1-7.   A selection program.

Program Exercises

Instructions: Write a BASIC program to do each of the following tasks:

1. Find the sum of each of the pairs of numbers below:

    6 and 8
    13 and 25
    14 and 33
    19 and 41

    Use trailer values at the end of your data list so that your program can sense when there are no more data.

2. Below are three sets of data. Each set of data has four variables: A, B, C, and D:

	Variables			
Set	A	B	C	D
1	8	15	10	4
2	6	5	3	2
3	4	0	5	2

    Plug the variables in each set of data into the formula below, and print out the results:

    $$X = A - B * C + A / D$$

3. Team A and Team B, crosstown rivals, played each other in baseball a total of five times over the course of a season. The results were as follows:

Game	Team A Score	Team B Score
1	8	5
2	6	7
3	2	0
4	0	1
5	5	4

    Write a program which will output, for each game, the team winning the game.

4. Salespeople at XYZ Company are paid a base salary of $10,000. This salary may be augmented by commissions, which are equal to 10 percent of gross sales, and by a bonus of $500. The bonus is awarded only to salespeople with over $80,000 in gross sales.

Compute and output the amounts earned by each of the sales-people below:

Salesperson	Gross Sales
Carlos Ortiz	$90,000
Jill Johnson	$70,000
Don Williams	$20,000
Dee Jones	$95,000
Al Ennis	$40,000

Your output should include the name of each salesperson and his or her earnings. Use trailer values at the end of your data list so that your program can sense when there are no more data.

5. Solve problem 4 assuming that the commission is computed as follows:

If Gross Sales Are in the Range	The Commission Rate Is
$ 1 – $30,000	6%
$30,001 – $60,000	8%
$60,001 – $80,000	10%
$80,001 and above	12%

Assume that the bonus is still in effect.

6. Grades in a course are awarded as follows: 90 and above = A, 80–89 = B, 70–79 = C, 60–69 = D, below 60 = F. Write a BASIC program which reads the data below and assigns letter grades:

Social Security Number	Score
182-66-1919	63
321-76-4344	81
821-66-0045	90
376-38-3202	54
802-11-1481	79
346-49-8911	75

Your output should include the social security number of each student and that student's letter grade. Use trailer values at the end of your data list so that your program can sense when there are no more items to be read.

7. A company running a copying service charges the following rates:

    The first 500 copies are billed at 5 cents per copy
    The next 500 copies are billed at 4 cents per copy
    Any additional copies are billed at 3 cents per copy

    Compute and output the amount each of the following customers is to be billed:

Customer	Copies
XYZ Amalgamated	1200
ABC Industries	200
TR Systems Limited	800

    Your output should include the name of each customer as well as the billing amount. Use trailer values at the end of your data list so that your program can sense when there are no more data.

8. Students at a university are billed as follows:

    Tuition = $100 per credit hour
    Activity fee = $30 for 6 hours or less
    $60 for 7–12 hours
    $75 for more than 12 hours

    The total amount a student will be billed each semester is computed by the formula below:

    Tuition fee + Activity fee − Scholarship

    Compute the amount due from the following students:

Student Name	Credit Hours This Semester	Scholarship Amount
Ed Begay	15	$700
Bill Mendoza	8	0
John Williams	3	0
Nancy Jones	12	500
Dennis Hall	6	0

    Your output should include the name of each student as well as the billing amount. Use trailer values at the end of your data list so that your program can sense when there are no more data.

Flowcharting Techniques

INTRODUCTION

A **program flowchart** is a diagram showing the flow of logic behind a computer program. For example, the flowchart in Figure A2-1 outlines the logic of the program shown in Figure A1-1.

As you can see from the example, a program flowchart consists of geometric symbols and arrows. Each symbol contains an operation which the computer must perform, while the arrows show the flow of the program logic (in other words, which operation is to be performed next).

As you have probably already noticed, not all of the symbols have the same shape. The shape of the symbol used depends on the type of operation being performed. The symbols used in this appendix, along with their program statement types, are shown in Figure A2-2.

You should note in Figure A2-1 that not every BASIC program statement will necessarily correspond to a flowchart symbol; conversely, not every flowchart symbol corresponds to a BASIC program

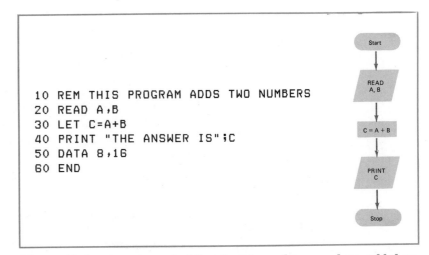

```
10 REM THIS PROGRAM ADDS TWO NUMBERS
20 READ A,B
30 LET C=A+B
40 PRINT "THE ANSWER IS";C
50 DATA 8,16
60 END
```

Figure A2-1.   A program and flowchart to read two numbers, add them, and output the result (previously presented in Figure A1-1).

Symbol	Name	Description
	Start/Stop	Used to begin and end every flowchart
	Input/Output	Used to represent the READ or INPUT statements on input, PRINT on output
	Assignment	Used to represent the LET statement
	Decision	Used to represent the IF statement
	Connector	Used to represent the NEXT statement or used to continue the flowchart when running out of room
	Loop	Used to represent the FOR statement

Figure A2-2.   Flowcharting symbols

statement. For example, there is no BASIC program statement counterpart to the flowcharting "START" symbol. The BASIC program shown actually begins with a REM statement. Also, there is no flowchart symbol for the DATA statement. The flowchart is intended to represent only the flow of program logic. This can be done without specifying actual values for the variables.

You should also note in Figure A2-1 that the flowchart need not contain every detail which will be specified in the program, but only those which are important for understanding the logical flow. Thus the flowchart indicates the output as PRINT C, whereas statement 40 of the corresponding program specifies in more detail:

```
PRINT "THE ANSWER IS ";C.
```

Flowcharts are useful both as design tools for developing the program and, later, as a program documentation aid. As a design tool, the flowchart lets the programmer "think through" the logical design of the program prior to writing it. This can be particularly helpful for the same reason a builder of a house consults a floor plan before constructing any individual room. Once the program is written, the

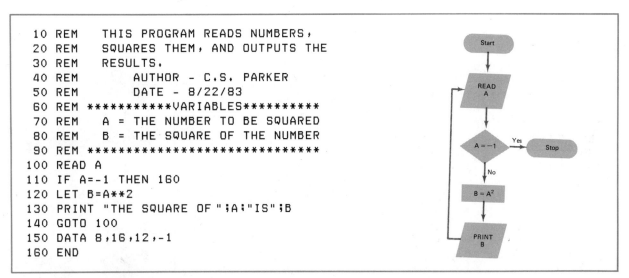

```
10 REM    THIS PROGRAM READS NUMBERS,
20 REM    SQUARES THEM, AND OUTPUTS THE
30 REM    RESULTS.
40 REM        AUTHOR - C.S. PARKER
50 REM        DATE - 8/22/83
60 REM ***********VARIABLES**********
70 REM    A = THE NUMBER TO BE SQUARED
80 REM    B = THE SQUARE OF THE NUMBER
90 REM ****************************
100 READ A
110 IF A=-1 THEN 160
120 LET B=A**2
130 PRINT "THE SQUARE OF ";A;"IS";B
140 GOTO 100
150 DATA 8,16,12,-1
160 END
```

Figure A2-3. Program and flowchart to compute and print the squares of several numbers (previously presented in Figure A1-4).

flowchart becomes a documentation aid: it generally is easier for others to understand how the program works by studying the flowchart rather than the program itself. Also, because of their simplicity, flowcharts can often be understood by nonprogrammers.

SOME FLOWCHART EXAMPLES

Now that we've covered some of the fundamentals of flowcharting, we'll look at two further examples.

First, let's reconsider the problem of Figure A1-4 (page A-19), which required a procedure to compute and print the squares of several numbers. The flowchart for this problem is given in Figure A2-3.

This flowchart introduces the use of the decision symbol. In BASIC, the diamond-shaped, decision symbol always has one arrow leading into it and two arrows leading out. The "Yes" (or "True") branch indicates the THEN condition (in other words, IF $A=-1$ THEN 160), while the "No" (or "False") branch directs the computer to execute the next statement.

Note that the GOTO statement of BASIC has no associated geometric symbol. It is represented by an arrow leading to the appropriate instruction.

Let's also take another look at the problem solved in Figure A1-7 (page A-25). There we were required to find all employees in a

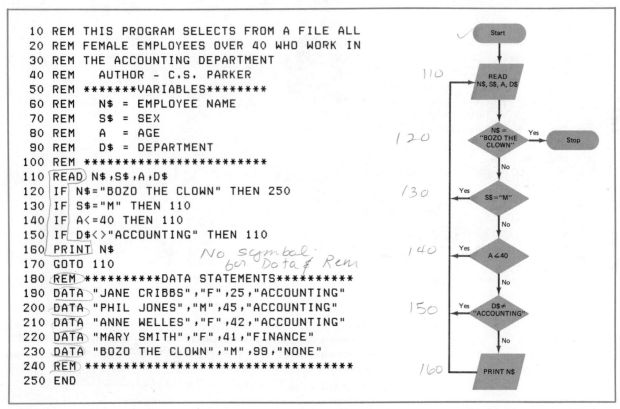

```
 10 REM THIS PROGRAM SELECTS FROM A FILE ALL
 20 REM FEMALE EMPLOYEES OVER 40 WHO WORK IN
 30 REM THE ACCOUNTING DEPARTMENT
 40 REM    AUTHOR - C.S. PARKER
 50 REM *******VARIABLES********
 60 REM    N$ = EMPLOYEE NAME
 70 REM    S$ = SEX
 80 REM    A  = AGE
 90 REM    D$ = DEPARTMENT
100 REM *********************
110 READ N$,S$,A,D$
120 IF N$="BOZO THE CLOWN" THEN 250
130 IF S$="M" THEN 110
140 IF A<=40 THEN 110
150 IF D$<>"ACCOUNTING" THEN 110
160 PRINT N$
170 GOTO 110
180 REM **********DATA STATEMENTS**********
190 DATA "JANE CRIBBS","F",25,"ACCOUNTING"
200 DATA "PHIL JONES","M",45,"ACCOUNTING"
210 DATA "ANNE WELLES","F",42,"ACCOUNTING"
220 DATA "MARY SMITH","F",41,"FINANCE"
230 DATA "BOZO THE CLOWN","M",99,"NONE"
240 REM **********************************
250 END
```

No symbol for Data & Rem (handwritten annotation)

Handwritten annotations next to flowchart: 110, 120, 130, 140, 150, 160

Figure A2-4. *Program and flowchart to solve an employee selection problem (previously presented in Figure A1-7).*

company who are female, over 40, and work in the accounting department. The associated flowchart is shown in Figure A2-4.

Numerous other examples of flowcharts will be presented in later sections of this appendix. Flowcharting is also covered in some detail in Chapter 10 of the text.

Expanding on the Basics of BASIC

COUNTING AND SUMMING

Now that we've covered a few fundamentals of how BASIC works, let's tackle a slightly more complicated problem. The example in Figure A3-1 (next page), a program to compute and print the average of a group of positive numbers, introduces two of the most fundamental operations in data processing: counting and summing. You should observe the "mechanics" of both of these operations very carefully, since they occur in almost every large-scale programming problem.

Three important observations should be made about the program in Figure A3-1:

1. Statements 100 (LET I=0) and 110 (LET S=0) establish *explicitly* the beginning values of I and S. Establishing beginning values for variables is called **initialization.** Most versions of BASIC will *implicitly* initialize all variables to zero before the program is executed; thus statements 100 and 110 are usually unnecessary. It is good practice, however, to explicitly initialize certain variables to zero whether it is necessary or not on your computer system. There are two reasons for this practice:

    a. Many programming languages will not automatically initialize variables to zero. This can lead to surprising results if you didn't explicitly initialize, since numbers from someone else's program may be lurking in the storage locations assigned to your variables. Thus your variables will assume these arbitrary values.

    b. When you initialize explicitly, the intent of your program becomes more evident. In other words, initialization is good documentation.

    Only the variables I and S require initialization to zero in this program. These are the variables that the computer needs to "look up" the values for on the right-hand side of the assignment symbol (=) in lines 140 and 150, respectively. The variables X and A don't have to be initialized, since they never appear on the right-hand side of an assignment symbol before the computer has explicitly assigned them a value.

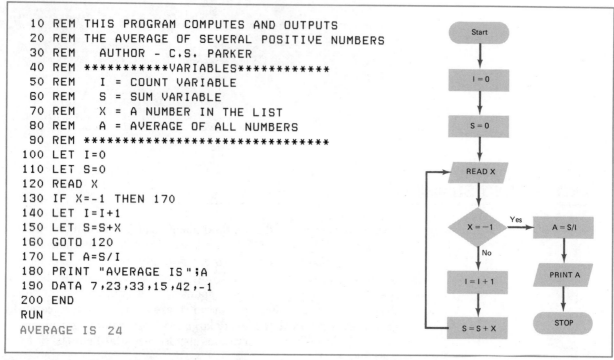

```
10 REM THIS PROGRAM COMPUTES AND OUTPUTS
20 REM THE AVERAGE OF SEVERAL POSITIVE NUMBERS
30 REM    AUTHOR - C.S. PARKER
40 REM ***********VARIABLES************
50 REM    I = COUNT VARIABLE
60 REM    S = SUM VARIABLE
70 REM    X = A NUMBER IN THE LIST
80 REM    A = AVERAGE OF ALL NUMBERS
90 REM ******************************
100 LET I=0
110 LET S=0
120 READ X
130 IF X=-1 THEN 170
140 LET I=I+1
150 LET S=S+X
160 GOTO 120
170 LET A=S/I
180 PRINT "AVERAGE IS ";A
190 DATA 7,23,33,15,42,-1
200 END
RUN
AVERAGE IS 24
```

Figure A3-1. *Program and flowchart to compute the average of several numbers.*

2. Statement 140 (LET I = I + 1) *counts* the number of numbers in the list. I is initially assigned a value of zero. Each time a positive number is read into storage for X (so that the "X = −1 test" is failed), 1 is added to the current value of I. Since only one number can be assigned to I at any time, the previous value of I is lost.

3. Statement 150 (LET S = S + X) *sums* the numbers in the list. As with I, S is initially zero. Each time statement 150 is executed, the current value of X is added to the current value of S. Thus S can be seen as a "running total," as follows:

When the Value of X Is	Statement 150 Does the Following
7	Adds 7 to the initial sum, 0, producing S = 7
23	Adds 23 to 7, producing S = 30
33	Adds 33 to 30, producing S = 63
15	Adds 15 to 63, producing S = 78
42	Adds 42 to 78, producing S = 120
−1	Statement 150 is not executed when X = −1

You should note that both the counting (I = I + 1) and summing (S = S + X) statements appear after the check for the last record (statement 130, IF X = −1 THEN 170). This is crucial. If these

statements appear before the last-record check, the values of I
and S will both be in error.

THE INPUT STATEMENT

The INPUT statement is one of the most useful statements in the
BASIC language. It permits the program *user* to operate in a **conversational (interactive) mode** with the computer system. In other
words, during the course of executing a program, the computer system
asks the user for a response, the user answers, and then, based on the
response given, the computer system asks the user for a response to
another question, and so forth. The format of the INPUT statement is
shown below:

> INPUT list of variables (separated by commas)

    Figure A3-2 (next page) shows the program in Figure A3-1
rewritten with the INPUT statement.
    You should carefully note the following:

1. The READ statement in Figure A3-1 has been changed to an
INPUT statement in Figure A3-2. With the READ statement, all
data to be assigned to X are placed in an associated DATA
statement; remember, READ and DATA statements are always
used together. When we use INPUT X, no corresponding DATA
statement is employed. Instead, we supply data to the computer
system as the program is running.

2. Data are supplied to the computer system as follows: Whenever
an INPUT statement is encountered, a "?" is output by the
system, and processing temporarily halts. At this point we must
enter as many data values as there are variables appearing after
the word INPUT in the program. These values must be separated
by commas. After we depress the RETURN key, the system will
assign the values to their corresponding variables and resume
processing. If the same or another INPUT statement is encountered, the system will again respond with a question mark and
await more input from the user.

3. In line 120, just before the INPUT statement, is a PRINT
statement which provides instructions for the user of the program. When writing programs which include INPUT statements,
it is always a good idea to include such a **prompting** PRINT
statement before each INPUT, so that the user will know both
how to enter data into the computer and how to stop the
program.

    The major advantage of the INPUT statement over READ is that
the user and computer system are involved in a dynamic dialogue. In

```
10 REM THIS PROGRAM COMPUTES AND OUTPUTS
20 REM THE AVERAGE OF SEVERAL POSITIVE NUMBERS
30 REM    AUTHOR - C.S. PARKER
40 REM ***********VARIABLES************
50 REM    I = COUNT VARIABLE
60 REM    S = SUM VARIABLE
70 REM    X = A NUMBER IN THE LIST
80 REM    A = AVERAGE OF ALL NUMBERS
90 REM *****************************
100 LET I=0
110 LET S=0
120 PRINT "ENTER A POSITIVE NUMBER (OR -1 TO STOP)"
130 INPUT X ◄─────────────────────┐
140 IF X=-1 THEN 180               ├─ INPUT statement
150 LET I=I+1
160 LET S=S+X
170 GOTO 120
180 LET A=S/I
190 PRINT "AVERAGE IS ";A
200 END
RUN
ENTER A POSITIVE NUMBER (OR -1 TO STOP)
?7
ENTER A POSITIVE NUMBER (OR -1 TO STOP)
?23
ENTER A POSITIVE NUMBER (OR -1 TO STOP)
?33
ENTER A POSITIVE NUMBER (OR -1 TO STOP)
?15
ENTER A POSITIVE NUMBER (OR -1 TO STOP)
?42
ENTER A POSITIVE NUMBER (OR -1 TO STOP)
?-1
AVERAGE IS 24
```

Figure A3-2.   Program of Figure A3-1 rewritten with the INPUT statement.

many cases the user may not know the inputs in advance, since they depend upon actions taken by the computer. An example of such a dialogue is shown in Figure A3-3.

Assume that the program in the figure was run by a user named John Q. Doe. In his first session with the computer system Mr. Doe failed in two attempts to guess the capital of Arizona. After consulting an atlas, he ran the program again, successfully.

The program in Figure A3-3 is an example of **computer-assisted instruction (CAI),** a procedure used by many schools as a supplementary educational aid to lectures.

Before we leave the program in Figure A3-3, observe the semicolon at the end of line 90. A semicolon appearing as the last character in a PRINT statement will cause the next item output by the

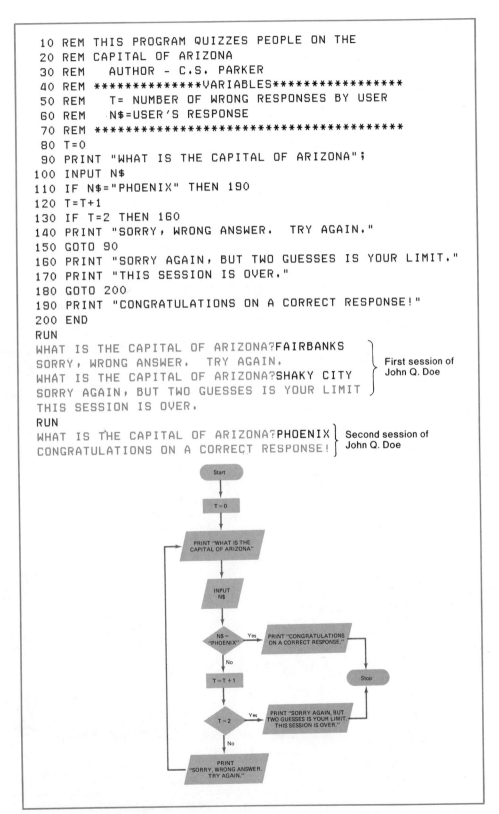

```
10 REM THIS PROGRAM QUIZZES PEOPLE ON THE
20 REM CAPITAL OF ARIZONA
30 REM    AUTHOR - C.S. PARKER
40 REM ***************VARIABLES****************
50 REM   T= NUMBER OF WRONG RESPONSES BY USER
60 REM   N$=USER'S RESPONSE
70 REM ****************************************
80 T=0
90 PRINT "WHAT IS THE CAPITAL OF ARIZONA";
100 INPUT N$
110 IF N$="PHOENIX" THEN 190
120 T=T+1
130 IF T=2 THEN 160
140 PRINT "SORRY, WRONG ANSWER.  TRY AGAIN."
150 GOTO 90
160 PRINT "SORRY AGAIN, BUT TWO GUESSES IS YOUR LIMIT."
170 PRINT "THIS SESSION IS OVER."
180 GOTO 200
190 PRINT "CONGRATULATIONS ON A CORRECT RESPONSE!"
200 END
RUN
WHAT IS THE CAPITAL OF ARIZONA?FAIRBANKS
SORRY, WRONG ANSWER.  TRY AGAIN.
WHAT IS THE CAPITAL OF ARIZONA?SHAKY CITY
SORRY AGAIN, BUT TWO GUESSES IS YOUR LIMIT
THIS SESSION IS OVER.
RUN
WHAT IS THE CAPITAL OF ARIZONA?PHOENIX
CONGRATULATIONS ON A CORRECT RESPONSE!
```

First session of John Q. Doe

Second session of John Q. Doe

Figure A3-3. *Use of INPUT statement for interdependent user–computer dialog.*

```
10 REM THIS PROGRAM PRODUCES A CANNED LETTER
20 REM    AUTHOR - C.S. PARKER
30 REM *************VARIABLES***************
40 REM   A$=NAME OF RECIPIENT
50 REM   B$=STATE OF RECIPIENT
60 REM *********PROGRAM INPUTS*************
70 PRINT "RECIPIENT(S)";
80 INPUT A$
90 PRINT "STATE";
100 INPUT B$
110 REM ********THE LETTER FOLLOWS***********
120 PRINT
130 PRINT
140 PRINT "DEAR ";A$;","
150 PRINT
160 PRINT "      I HAVE BEEN HAVING A GRAND TIME"
170 PRINT "IN COLLEGE, ALTHOUGH SCHOOL IS A"
180 PRINT "LOT OF WORK.  HOPE THINGS ARE GOING"
190 PRINT "WELL FOR YOU BACK IN ";B$;","
200 PRINT "SEE YOU LATER."
210 PRINT
220 PRINT "                        JOHN"
230 PRINT
240 PRINT
250 REM ************END OF LETTER***********
260 END
RUN
RECIPIENT(S)?MOM AND DAD
STATE?NEBRASKA

DEAR MOM AND DAD,

      I HAVE BEEN HAVING A GRAND TIME
IN COLLEGE, ALTHOUGH SCHOOL IS A
LOT OF WORK.  HOPE THINGS ARE GOING
WELL FOR YOU BACK IN NEBRASKA.
SEE YOU LATER.

                        JOHN


RUN
RECIPIENT(S)?DAISY MAE
STATE?CALIFORNIA

DEAR DAISY MAE,

      I HAVE BEEN HAVING A GRAND TIME
IN COLLEGE, ALTHOUGH SCHOOL IS A
LOT OF WORK.  HOPE THINGS ARE GOING
WELL FOR YOU BACK IN CALIFORNIA.
SEE YOU LATER.

                        JOHN
```

Figure A3-4. *Use of INPUT statement to write a "canned letter."*

computer system to appear on the same line. In other words, the carriage return is suppressed.

As a third example of the INPUT statement, consider an industrious college student who wishes to send "canned," computerized letters to family and friends. An example of such ingenuity is shown in Figure A3-4.

Such a program is one example of **word processing,** which loosely refers to computerized organization and generation of documents. You should carefully observe the "blank" PRINT statements in lines 120, 130, 150, 210, 230, and 240. When the word PRINT appears on a line with nothing specified to its right, a line is skipped on the output.

THE STOP STATEMENT

Execution of a STOP statement in a program causes the program to halt execution, often by immediate transfer to the END statement. Figure A3-5 illustrates the use of the STOP statement, which has the format below:

$$\boxed{\text{STOP}}$$

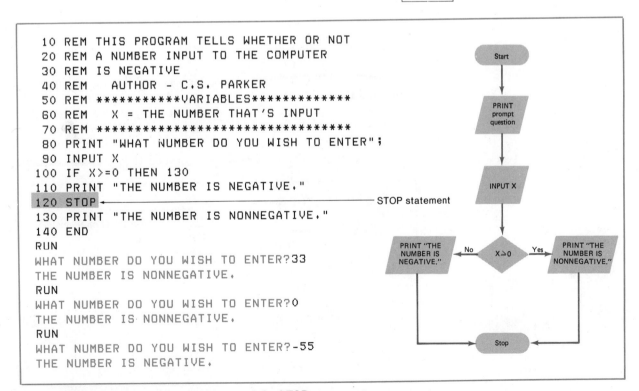

```
10 REM THIS PROGRAM TELLS WHETHER OR NOT
20 REM A NUMBER INPUT TO THE COMPUTER
30 REM IS NEGATIVE
40 REM    AUTHOR - C.S. PARKER
50 REM ***********VARIABLES*************
60 REM    X = THE NUMBER THAT'S INPUT
70 REM *******************************
80 PRINT "WHAT NUMBER DO YOU WISH TO ENTER";
90 INPUT X
100 IF X>=0 THEN 130
110 PRINT "THE NUMBER IS NEGATIVE."
120 STOP                                  ──── STOP statement
130 PRINT "THE NUMBER IS NONNEGATIVE."
140 END
RUN
WHAT NUMBER DO YOU WISH TO ENTER?33
THE NUMBER IS NONNEGATIVE.
RUN
WHAT NUMBER DO YOU WISH TO ENTER?0
THE NUMBER IS NONNEGATIVE.
RUN
WHAT NUMBER DO YOU WISH TO ENTER?-55
THE NUMBER IS NEGATIVE.
```

Figure A3-5.   Program illustrating use of the STOP statement.

THE FOR AND NEXT STATEMENTS

The FOR and NEXT statements, which allow the programmer to loop (repeat a program section) automatically, are among the most important statements in BASIC. For example, consider the short program given in Figure A3-6.

The FOR and NEXT statements form a "sandwich," or loop. All statements inside the loop are executed the number of times determined in the FOR statement. (Note that these statements are indented, making the program easier to read.) In Figure A3-6, I is first set equal to 1. Then everything inside the loop (that is, statement 20) is executed; I is then set equal to 2 and statement 20 is executed again, and so forth. After I is set equal to 5, and the loop is executed for the fifth time, control passes to the statement which immediately follows the NEXT statement (in other words, statement 40).

FOR and NEXT statements are always used together. They physically establish the beginning and end of the loop. Like READ and DATA, one statement makes absolutely no sense unless the other is present. The format of these statements is given below:

$$\text{FOR loop variable} = \begin{Bmatrix} \text{Beginning} \\ \text{value} \end{Bmatrix} \text{TO} \begin{Bmatrix} \text{Ending} \\ \text{value} \end{Bmatrix} \text{STEP increment}$$

$$\text{NEXT loop variable}$$

The use of the loop variable, beginning value, ending value, and increment will now be explained.

The variable I in the program of Figure A3-6 is an example of a **loop variable.** Note carefully that the chosen loop variable (which can be any acceptable BASIC numeric variable) must be included in both the FOR statement and its associated NEXT statement, as indicated in the figure.

In Figure A3-6 it was implicitly assumed that the loop variable

```
10 FOR I=1 TO 5                    ┐ FOR and
20     PRINT "HELLO, NUMBER";I      ┘ NEXT statements
30 NEXT I
40 PRINT "FINISHED."
50 END
RUN
HELLO, NUMBER 1
HELLO, NUMBER 2
HELLO, NUMBER 3
HELLO, NUMBER 4
HELLO, NUMBER 5
FINISHED.
```

Figure A3-6.   Simple usage of FOR and NEXT statements.

was to be incremented by 1 each time the loop was executed. The increment could also have been explicitly declared in a STEP clause, as shown below:

```
10 FOR I=1 TO 5 STEP 1
```

The results produced would be the same. If, on the other hand, we rewrite line 10 as

```
10 FOR I=1 TO 5 STEP 3
```

and run the program, the computer system would respond

```
HELLO, NUMBER 1
HELLO, NUMBER 4
FINISHED.
```

Since the next possible incremented value, 7, exceeds the terminal value of 5, the computer doesn't execute the loop for a third time, but passes control to statement 40.

It is also possible to let the loop variable work "backwards." For example, if we changed line 10 of Figure A3-6 to read

```
10 FOR I=5 TO 1 STEP -1
```

we would obtain

```
HELLO, NUMBER 5
HELLO, NUMBER 4
HELLO, NUMBER 3
HELLO, NUMBER 2
HELLO, NUMBER 1
FINISHED.
```

BASIC also allows programmers to use variables in FOR and NEXT statements. For example, the following sequence is also acceptable:

```
FOR Z=J TO K STEP L
                .
                .
                .
NEXT Z
```

If $J = 2$, $K = 10$, and $L = 3$, the loop will be performed 3 times, with Z taking on values of 2, 5, and 8 as the loop is executed.

Let's consider now a more comprehensive example to further explore the concept of looping. Consider again the "averages" problem solved in Figure A3-1 (page A-34). How can we solve this problem using FOR-NEXT loops? The flowchart and program solution appear in Figure A3-7 (next page).

You should note the following features in comparing the programs in Figures A3-1 and A3-7:

1. The logic of the program in Figure A3-7 is less complicated than that of Figure A3-1, even though the programs are the same length. A major reason for the gained simplicity is that the automatic initialization, incrementing, and testing done in a FOR-NEXT loop allows us to eliminate the statements:

```
10 REM THIS PROGRAM COMPUTES AND OUTPUTS
20 REM THE AVERAGE OF SEVERAL POSITIVE NUMBERS
30 REM     AUTHOR - C.S. PARKER
40 REM **********VARIABLES***********
50 REM     I = LOOP VARIABLE
60 REM     S = SUM VARIABLE
70 REM     X = A NUMBER IN THE LIST
80 REM     A = AVERAGE OF ALL NUMBERS
90 REM     N = THE NUMBER OF NUMBERS
100 REM ****************************
110 LET S=0
120 READ N
130 FOR I=1 TO N
140     READ X
150     LET S=S+X
160 NEXT I
170 LET A=S/N
180 PRINT "AVERAGE IS";A
190 DATA 5
200 DATA 7,23,33,15,42
210 END
RUN
AVERAGE IS 24
```

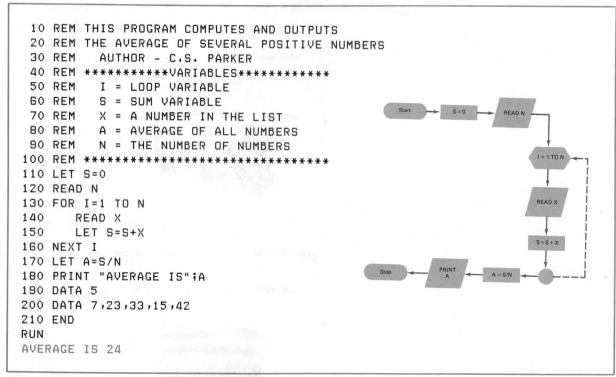

Figure A3-7.   Flowchart and program solution to the problem of Figure A3-1, using loops.

```
100 LET I=0
130 IF X=-1 THEN 170
140 LET I=I+1
```

Note also that -1 is eliminated in the DATA statement.

2. There are major differences in the flowcharts. Note especially the flowchart symbols used for FOR and NEXT, as well as the dotted line indicating automatic control back to the FOR statement.

You may be wondering at this point why a programming structure like the one shown in Figure A3-1 would ever be used, considering how complicated it is. The major advantage of this structure is that it doesn't require the programmer to know in advance the number of data items processed. In many data processing applications the number of records processed is unknown. In these situations it is useful to append a trailer record at the end of the data file and use an IF statement to detect it. Thus both of these structures—the FOR-NEXT loop and $I = I + 1$/IF—are frequently used in programs.

Let us now consider branching within a FOR-NEXT loop. For example, suppose that we wanted to read a list of ten numbers, summing only the positive ones. This problem is solved in the short program of Figure A3-8, using the variable-naming convention (lines 40 to 100) of Figure A3-7.

Note that if the number is negative $(X < 0)$, we wish to bypass the summation operation $(S = S + X)$ and read in the next number.

```
10 S=0
20 FOR I=1 TO 10
30    READ X
40    IF X<0 THEN 60
50    S=S+X
60 NEXT I
70 PRINT "THE SUM IS";S
80 DATA 5,-1,3,6,-14,20,4,2,40,10
90 END
RUN
THE SUM IS 90
```

Figure A3-8.   Branching within a FOR-NEXT loop.

However, instead of going directly to the FOR statement, we pass control to the NEXT statement (which will automatically bring us back up to the top of the loop). This raises a key point. If statement 40 was instead

$$IF \ X<0 \ THEN \ 20$$

the value of I would be erroneously reset to 1 when the THEN clause is invoked. Note that only through execution of the NEXT statement is the loop variable named in the FOR automatically incremented. If control is passed to a FOR by any statement other than its corresponding NEXT, the loop variable will be set (or reset) to its initial value.

Finally loops within loops (called *nested loops*) are allowed. Observe the program below:

```
          ┌───10 FOR I=1 TO 3
          │ ┌─20     FOR J=1 TO 2
I-Loop  J-Loop│ 30        PRINT I;J
          │ └─40     NEXT J
          └───50 NEXT I
              60 END
              RUN
               1   1
               1   2
               2   1
               2   2
               3   1
               3   2
               ↑   ↑
               Ⓘ   Ⓙ
```

The program executes the PRINT statement a total of 3 * 2 = 6 times. The outer loop variable (I) varies the slowest; the inner loop variable (J), the fastest.

In writing nested-loop programs, it is always important to enclose the inner loop entirely within the outer loop. Thus a program segment such as the one on the next page

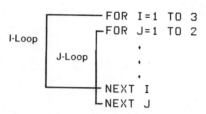

would not work because the loops cross instead of nest.

SOLVED REVIEW PROBLEMS

Example 1

Write a flowchart and BASIC program which will read in the ten values

$$-6, 8, 65, 4, 8, -21, 2, 46, -12, 42$$

and identify the highest number, lowest number, and average.

Solution

The solution shown in Figure A3-9 starts by declaring the first number in the list as both the highest and lowest value in the list.

Then the remaining nine numbers each "get a shot" at competing for highest or lowest value. They are individually read and checked against the current high and low values. As each number is being read and checked it is accumulated in a sum, so that the average may subsequently be computed. Note in line 190 how the loop variable can be used to "keep tabs" on what the program is doing. Note also in line 330 that a PRINT statement can output a value not calculated until the statement itself is executed.

Example 2

An auto rental company rents three types of cars at the rates below:

Car Type	Fixed Cost per Day	Cost per Mile
Compact	$10	$.15
Intermediate	$20	$.18
Large	$30	$.22

Thus, for example, a person renting a compact car for 3 days and driving 100 miles would be charged $10 * 3 + .15 * 100 = \$45$.

Write a flowchart and an interactive BASIC program which will accept

- Customer name
- Car type
- Number of days car held
- Miles traveled

as input. It should output the charge for each customer. Also, have the computer add up the total charges attributable to each type of car. Use the sample data in the table on the next page to test your program.

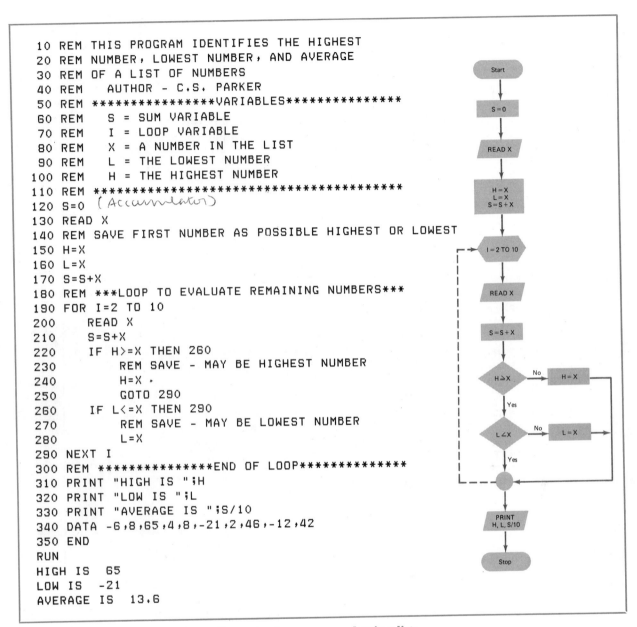

```
10 REM THIS PROGRAM IDENTIFIES THE HIGHEST
20 REM NUMBER, LOWEST NUMBER, AND AVERAGE
30 REM OF A LIST OF NUMBERS
40 REM    AUTHOR - C.S. PARKER
50 REM ****************VARIABLES***************
60 REM    S = SUM VARIABLE
70 REM    I = LOOP VARIABLE
80 REM    X = A NUMBER IN THE LIST
90 REM    L = THE LOWEST NUMBER
100 REM   H = THE HIGHEST NUMBER
110 REM ******************************************
120 S=0       (Accumulator)
130 READ X
140 REM SAVE FIRST NUMBER AS POSSIBLE HIGHEST OR LOWEST
150 H=X
160 L=X
170 S=S+X
180 REM ***LOOP TO EVALUATE REMAINING NUMBERS***
190 FOR I=2 TO 10
200     READ X
210     S=S+X
220     IF H>=X THEN 260
230         REM SAVE - MAY BE HIGHEST NUMBER
240         H=X .
250         GOTO 290
260     IF L<=X THEN 290
270         REM SAVE - MAY BE LOWEST NUMBER
280         L=X
290 NEXT I
300 REM **************END OF LOOP*************
310 PRINT "HIGH IS ";H
320 PRINT "LOW IS ";L
330 PRINT "AVERAGE IS ";S/10
340 DATA -6,8,65,4,8,-21,2,46,-12,42
350 END
RUN
HIGH IS   65
LOW IS   -21
AVERAGE IS   13.6
```

Figure A3-9. *Finding the highest, lowest, and average number in a list.*

Sample data:

Customer Name	Car Type	Days Held	Miles Traveled
Jones	Large	6	500
Smith	Compact	17	3000
Baker	Intermediate	8	250
Williams	Intermediate	8	1000
Winston	Large	3	500

The solution to this problem is provided in Figure A3-10. You should note that the program will terminate if the user types in "GOODBYE" when asked to supply a customer name. Also, the program will inform the user of incorrect input if the car type is not equal to 1, 2, or 3.

```
10 REM THIS PROGRAM COMPUTES THE CHARGES DUE ON
20 REM RENTED AUTOMOBILES
30 REM      AUTHOR - C.S. PARKER
40 REM **************VARIABLES*****************
50 REM      T=CAR TYPE (1=COMPACT)
60 REM                 (2=INTERMEDIATE)
70 REM                 (3=LARGE)
80 REM      N$=CUSTOMER NAME
90 REM      D=DAYS CAR HELD
100 REM      M=MILES TRAVELED
110 REM      C=CHARGE FOR CUSTOMER
120 REM      C1,C2,C3=TOTAL BILLINGS ON CAR
130 REM          TYPES 1,2, AND 3, RESPECTIVELY
140 REM ****************************************
150 C1=C2=C3=0
160 PRINT "ENTER CUSTOMER NAME"
170 PRINT "     NOTE: ENTER GOODBYE TO STOP PROGRAM"
180 INPUT N$
190 IF N$="GOODBYE" THEN 420
200 PRINT "ENTER DAYS CAR HELD, MILES TRAVELED, AND CAR TYPE"
210 PRINT "     NOTE: 1=COMPACT  2=INTERMEDIATE  3=LARGE"
220 INPUT D,M,T
230 IF T=1 THEN 290
240 IF T=2 THEN 330
250 IF T=3 THEN 370
260 PRINT "CAR TYPE";T;" DOES NOT EXIST"
270 GOTO 200
280 REM COMPACT CAR CALCULATIONS
290      C=.15*M+10*D
300      C1=C1+C
310      GOTO 390
320 REM INTERMEDIATE CAR CALCULATIONS
330      C=.18*M+20*D
340      C2=C2+C
350      GOTO 390
360 REM LARGE CAR CALCULATIONS
370      C=.22*M+30*D
380      C3=C3+C
390 PRINT N$;"     $";C
400 PRINT
410 GOTO 160
420 PRINT "TOTAL CHARGES ON CAR TYPE 1 ARE   $";C1
430 PRINT "TOTAL CHARGES ON CAR TYPE 2 ARE   $";C2
440 PRINT "TOTAL CHARGES ON CAR TYPE 3 ARE   $";C3
450 END
```

Figure A3-10. *An interactive program to determine auto rental charges.*

```
RUN
ENTER CUSTOMER NAME
     NOTE: ENTER GOODBYE TO STOP PROGRAM
?JONES
ENTER DAYS CAR HELD, MILES TRAVELED, AND CAR TYPE
     NOTE: 1=COMPACT  2=INTERMEDIATE  3=LARGE
?6,500,3
JONES     $ 290

ENTER CUSTOMER NAME
     NOTE: ENTER GOODBYE TO STOP PROGRAM
?SMITH
ENTER DAYS CAR HELD, MILES TRAVELED, AND CAR TYPE
     NOTE: 1=COMPACT  2=INTERMEDIATE  3=LARGE
?17,3000,1
SMITH     $ 620

ENTER CUSTOMER NAME
     NOTE: ENTER GOODBYE TO STOP PROGRAM
?BAKER
ENTER DAYS CAR HELD, MILES TRAVELED, AND CAR TYPE
     NOTE: 1=COMPACT  2=INTERMEDIATE  3=LARGE
?8,250,6
CAR TYPE 6 DOES NOT EXIST
ENTER DAYS CAR HELD, MILES TRAVELED, AND CAR TYPE
     NOTE: 1=COMPACT  2=INTERMEDIATE  3=LARGE
?8,250,2
BAKER     $ 205

ENTER CUSTOMER NAME
     NOTE: ENTER GOODBYE TO STOP PROGRAM
?WILLIAMS
ENTER DAYS CAR HELD, MILES TRAVELED, AND CAR TYPE
     NOTE: 1=COMPACT  2=INTERMEDIATE  3=LARGE
?4,1000,2
WILLIAMS     $ 260

ENTER CUSTOMER NAME
     NOTE: ENTER GOODBYE TO STOP PROGRAM
?WINSTON
ENTER DAYS CAR HELD, MILES TRAVELED, AND CAR TYPE
     NOTE: 1=COMPACT  2=INTERMEDIATE  3=LARGE
?3,500,3
WINSTON     $ 200

ENTER CUSTOMER NAME
     NOTE: ENTER GOODBYE TO STOP PROGRAM
?GOODBYE
TOTAL CHARGES ON CAR TYPE 1 ARE   $ 620
TOTAL CHARGES ON CAR TYPE 2 ARE   $ 465
TOTAL CHARGES ON CAR TYPE 3 ARE   $ 490
```

Figure A3-10.   (Continued)

Program Exercises

Instructions: Write a BASIC program to do each of the following tasks:

1. Read a list of positive numbers, sum all of the numbers greater than 10 in the list, and output that sum.

2. Sum all even numbers from 1 to 100 and output the square root of that sum. [*Hint:* the square root of any number X is $X^{1/2}$.]

3. Read a list of positive numbers, find the average of all numbers between 10 and 20 (inclusive) in the list, and output the average.

4. The following data show the weather in a city on ten successive days: Sunny, Cloudy, Rainy, Sunny, Sunny, Cloudy, Sunny, Sunny, Rainy, Cloudy.

   Write a program to read these ten weather observations and then count and output the number of sunny days.

5. Use FOR-NEXT loops to compute the sums S below:

$$S = 1 + 2 + 3 + 4 + \cdots + 10$$
$$S = 3 + 6 + 9 + 12 + \cdots + 30$$
$$S = 1 + 1/2 + 1/3 + 1/4 + \cdots + 1/1000$$

6. Write a program to convert several temperatures from Fahrenheit (F) to centigrade (C). Use the INPUT statement to supply each Fahrenheit temperature to the computer system for conversion. The formula below can be used to make the conversion:

```
C=(5/9)*(F-32)
```

   Use a trailer value, such as 9999 degrees, to stop your program.

7. The cost of sending a telegram is $2.80 for the first 20 (or fewer) words and 10 cents for each additional word. Write a program which will find the cost of a telegram after you have entered the number of words as input at a terminal.

8. A program is needed which will help students compute the squares of numbers. The student should be asked in turn to compute 10^2, 11^2, 12^2, 13^2, 14^2, and 15^2. When a question is answered correctly, the next question should be asked. If a question is answered incorrectly, it should be asked again. If a question is answered incorrectly twice, ask the next question on the list. Also, have the computer output the number of correct responses at the end of the session.

9. The population growth rate in a city has been projected at 5 percent per year for the next 10 years. The current population in the city is 31,840 residents. Write a program to find the population 10 years from now.

Section 4

Formatted Printing

SPACING OUTPUT

Producing neatly formatted output is one of the prized skills of computer programming. A sloppy looking report, even though it contains accurate information, is often not read. Readers of reports are generally favorably inclined toward well presented output.

So far we have learned two formatting vehicles to use with the PRINT statement:

1. The semicolon. This generally leaves a space or two between printed items.* When it is the last character in the PRINT statement, it forces the next output from the computer system to begin on the same line.
2. The "blank" PRINT statement. This is used to produce blank output lines.

There are three other techniques discussed in this section which will aid in formatting output:

1. The comma (,).
2. The TAB function.
3. The PRINT USING and IMAGE (:) statements.

COMMA PRINT CONTROL

The comma works in a manner somewhat similar to the semicolon, except that

1. It produces more space between the output data items.
2. The items are printed at fixed tab stops.

*The exception is that no spaces are provided between two strings separated by a semicolon (unless, of course, spaces appear within the string).

The fixed tab stops define so-called **print zones.** If you are on a terminal which can output 72 characters per line, the zones might be fixed as follows:

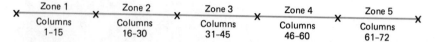

In any case, you should check your output device to find out where the zones begin and end. With the zones given above, the use of commas in a PRINT statement would have the effect shown in Figure A4-1. Positive numbers printed in a zone are preceded by a blank space, negative numbers by a minus sign.

If we wanted to total gross pay in this program and print it neatly on output we could add the following statements to this program:

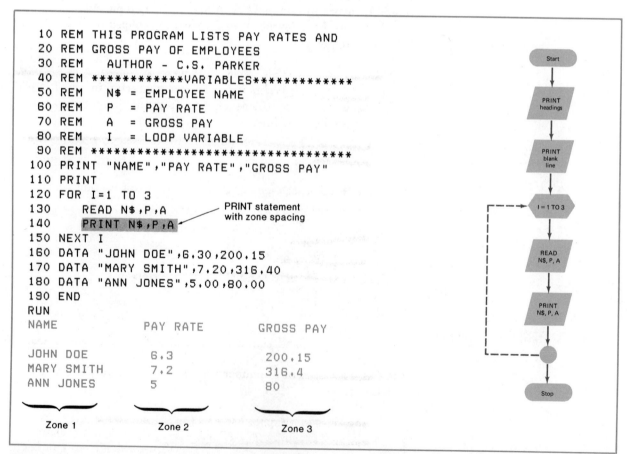

Figure A4-1. *Use of comma in PRINT for spacing.* **This simple program reads in names of people, along with associated pay rates and gross pay. This information is then output into print zones.**

```
115 S=0
145 S=S+A
155 PRINT
156 PRINT,,S
```

When the program is run, the output produced would look like this:

```
NAME              PAY RATE        GROSS PAY

JOHN DOE            6.3            200.15
MARY SMITH          7.2            316.4
ANN JONES           5              80

                                   596.55
```

There are two other interesting features to note about the use of the comma for spacing in a PRINT statement:

1. If the number of items to be output in a PRINT statement is too large to fit on one line of the output device used, a "wraparound" effect will occur; for example:

```
10 FOR I=1 TO 12
20 PRINT I,
30 NEXT I
40 END
RUN
 1         2         3         4         5
 6         7         8         9         10
 11        12
```

Only five data items are printed per line because only five print zones are available on the output device used. If we tried running this program on a different output device, say one with 6 zones, we would get six numbers per line.

2. If a particular data item is too large to occupy a single print zone, it will "overflow" into subsequent zones; for example:

```
10 PRINT "TODAY IS MAY 16, 1982","HELLO"
20 END
RUN
TODAY IS MAY 16, 1982        HELLO
↑                            ↑
└Begins in zone 1            └Begins in zone 3
                              (because the
                              first literal overflowed
                              into zone 2)
```

THE TAB FUNCTION

The TAB function of BASIC permits us to "tab" over to any column to start printing. Thus with the TAB function we don't have to begin printing at a zone boundary. The self-explanatory example on the next page will clarify its use.

Print Using "/   /"; A$

to move

1
2
3
(10) *instea*   1
                 2
                 3
                 10

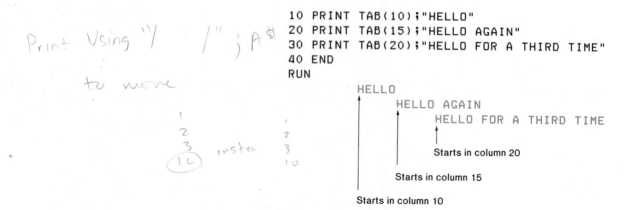

```
10 PRINT TAB(10);"HELLO"
20 PRINT TAB(15);"HELLO AGAIN"
30 PRINT TAB(20);"HELLO FOR A THIRD TIME"
40 END
RUN
        HELLO
                HELLO AGAIN
                        HELLO FOR A THIRD TIME

                        Starts in column 20

                Starts in column 15

        Starts in column 10
```

Note that there must be no space between the word TAB in a statement and the opening parenthesis.

It is possible to use several TAB functions on one line. You can also specify tabbing for a single, long output line which spans two PRINT statements. For example:

```
10 PRINT "PART NUMBER";TAB(20);"NAME";TAB(30);
20 PRINT "AMOUNT IN STOCK";TAB(50);"UNIT PRICE"
30 END
RUN
PART NUMBER          NAME    AMOUNT IN STOCK      UNIT PRICE
  Column 1             Column 20  Column 30          Column 50
```

Remember, the semicolon at the end of a PRINT statement (see line 10) will keep the output device on the same line.

You can also use variable names as tab stops; for example:

```
10 F=25
20 PRINT TAB(F);"GOODBYE"
30 END
RUN
                                        GOODBYE
                                          Column 25
```

Change
40 - 80
with   *80*
          or
          #
let column

THE PRINT USING AND IMAGE (:) STATEMENTS

The PRINT USING and IMAGE (:) statements are the most powerful instructions in BASIC for formatted printing. These two statements are always used together. Like the READ and DATA or the FOR and NEXT, one makes no sense without the other. The format of these statements varies from system to system;* however, the syntax presented in the examples to follow is used widely.

*Note that in some systems there is no explicit IMAGE statement; rather, the image directly follows PRINT USING, generally without the colon (:).

A program employing the PRINT USING and IMAGE statements appears in Figure A4-2. This program reads in names (N$), pay rates (P), and hours worked (H). It then computes and sums the amounts earned (A = P * H). You should examine this example carefully before reading further.

The program uses three PRINT USING and three IMAGE (:) statements. Each PRINT USING statement refers to the line number of an associated IMAGE statement. That IMAGE statement instructs the computer system how to format the output when the PRINT USING statement is executed.

Like the DATA statement, IMAGE is referenced but not executed, and it may appear anywhere in the program (before END).

If the PRINT USING statement doesn't have a variable list associated with it (such as line 150, which references line 120), every

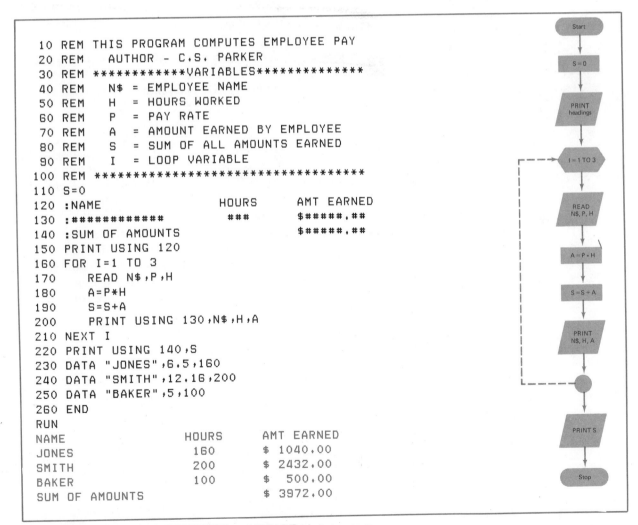

```
10 REM THIS PROGRAM COMPUTES EMPLOYEE PAY
20 REM    AUTHOR - C.S. PARKER
30 REM ***********VARIABLES**************
40 REM    N$ = EMPLOYEE NAME
50 REM    H  = HOURS WORKED
60 REM    P  = PAY RATE
70 REM    A  = AMOUNT EARNED BY EMPLOYEE
80 REM    S  = SUM OF ALL AMOUNTS EARNED
90 REM    I  = LOOP VARIABLE
100 REM ********************************
110 S=0
120 :NAME               HOURS        AMT EARNED
130 :#############      ###          $#####.##
140 :SUM OF AMOUNTS                  $#####.##
150 PRINT USING 120
160 FOR I=1 TO 3
170    READ N$,P,H
180    A=P*H
190    S=S+A
200    PRINT USING 130,N$,H,A
210 NEXT I
220 PRINT USING 140,S
230 DATA "JONES",6.5,160
240 DATA "SMITH",12.16,200
250 DATA "BAKER",5,100
260 END
RUN
NAME               HOURS        AMT EARNED
JONES               160         $ 1040.00
SMITH               200         $ 2432.00
BAKER               100         $  500.00
SUM OF AMOUNTS                  $ 3972.00
```

Figure A4-2.   *Use of PRINT USING and IMAGE (:) statements.*

character declared in the corresponding IMAGE statement is printed out exactly as it appears. On the other hand, if PRINT USING does possess a variable list (such as lines 200 and 220, which reference lines 130 and 140, respectively), then

1. All variable values are placed in the areas occupied by the pound (number) signs (#) of the associated IMAGE statement, in the order that the variable names appear in the PRINT USING. If the variable value contains a decimal point, you can specify where it must appear and the number of digits to the left and right of it. For example, a declaration such as

   ###.##

   would specify that 5.06 be printed as

   ⠀⠀⠀⠀⠀⠀⠀ꞵꞵ5.06

   You should note that the # is a special symbol when used with an IMAGE statement. On most systems no other character can be substituted to produce the same effect.

2. Any characters other than # in an IMAGE statement will be printed as they appear. Thus the dollar sign in lines 130 and 140 and the phrase SUM OF AMOUNTS in line 140 appear exactly on output as they do in the IMAGE.

As you can see by inspecting this program, a major advantage to PRINT USING and IMAGE is that they allow neat decimal-point alignment in columns. This is a "must" for reports used in business. The use of comma spacing or the TAB function does not provide this luxury, since variable values start printing in the zone boundary or tab stop indicated, leaving the decimal point to fall where it may. This can be seen in Figure A4-1; note that the gross pay for Ann Jones is not neatly lined up under the gross pay of the other individuals.

The values of string variables automatically begin at the far left (left-justified) within the #-sign fields. The values of numeric variables are aligned with respect to the decimal point. The example below should make this clear:

```
10 N$="BETSY JONES"
20 A=10
30 B=3.06
40 :###############   ###   ###.##
50 PRINT USING 40,N$,A,B
60 END
RUN
BETSY JONES              10    3.06
```

First # field (15 characters)

Second # field (3 characters)

Third # field (3 characters to left of decimal point, 2 characters to right)

If the values of any of the variables are too large to fit within the specified #-sign fields, either truncation, rounding, or output suppression (that is, spaces or nonnumeric symbols) will occur. Referring to the last example, if

```
N$="SHERIDAN P. WHITESIDE"
A=10.6
B=8321.46
```

the following output will be produced:

SOLVED REVIEW PROBLEMS

Example 1
Compute the square root ($I^{1/2}$), cube root ($I^{1/3}$), and fourth root ($I^{1/4}$) of all integers I in the range 1–10. The output should be neatly labeled and formatted.

Solution
The program and associated output are shown in Figure A4-3. You should note the use of the comma in lines 140 and 180, which keeps the output device printing on the same line. The blank PRINT statement in line 180 is extremely important; it negates the effect of the comma on line 160 when the fourth roots are printed and sends the output device to the next output line.

Example 2
Straight-line depreciation expenses are computed by the formula below:

$$\text{Annual depreciation charge} = \frac{\text{Original cost} - \text{Salvage value}}{\text{Useful life}}$$

Provide a depreciation schedule for a car which originally cost $7328 and will be worth approximately $600 at the end of its 10-year useful life. The depreciation schedule should show (for each year) the depreciation charge, total depreciation so far, and the (undepreciated) balance.

Solution
The program and associated output are shown in Figure A4-4.

Example 3
The TAB function is extremely helpful for printing various types of geometrical designs. The program in Figure A4-5 uses the TAB function to print a triangle.

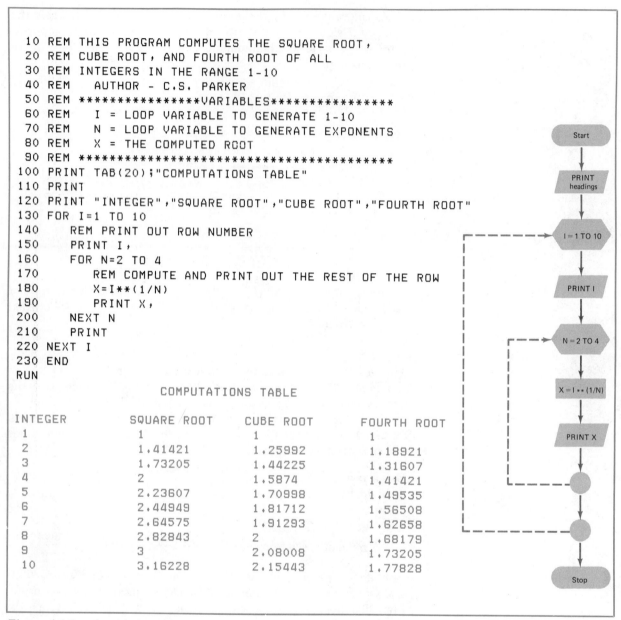

```
 10 REM THIS PROGRAM COMPUTES THE SQUARE ROOT,
 20 REM CUBE ROOT, AND FOURTH ROOT OF ALL
 30 REM INTEGERS IN THE RANGE 1-10
 40 REM    AUTHOR - C.S. PARKER
 50 REM ******************VARIABLES****************
 60 REM   I = LOOP VARIABLE TO GENERATE 1-10
 70 REM   N = LOOP VARIABLE TO GENERATE EXPONENTS
 80 REM   X = THE COMPUTED ROOT
 90 REM ****************************************
100 PRINT TAB(20);"COMPUTATIONS TABLE"
110 PRINT
120 PRINT "INTEGER","SQUARE ROOT","CUBE ROOT","FOURTH ROOT"
130 FOR I=1 TO 10
140     REM PRINT OUT ROW NUMBER
150     PRINT I,
160     FOR N=2 TO 4
170       REM COMPUTE AND PRINT OUT THE REST OF THE ROW
180       X=I**(1/N)
190       PRINT X,
200     NEXT N
210     PRINT
220 NEXT I
230 END
RUN
                  COMPUTATIONS TABLE

INTEGER        SQUARE ROOT    CUBE ROOT      FOURTH ROOT
1              1              1              1
2              1.41421        1.25992        1.18921
3              1.73205        1.44225        1.31607
4              2              1.5874         1.41421
5              2.23607        1.70998        1.49535
6              2.44949        1.81712        1.56508
7              2.64575        1.91293        1.62658
8              2.82843        2              1.68179
9              3              2.08008        1.73205
10             3.16228        2.15443        1.77828
```

Figure A4-3.   A program to compute roots.

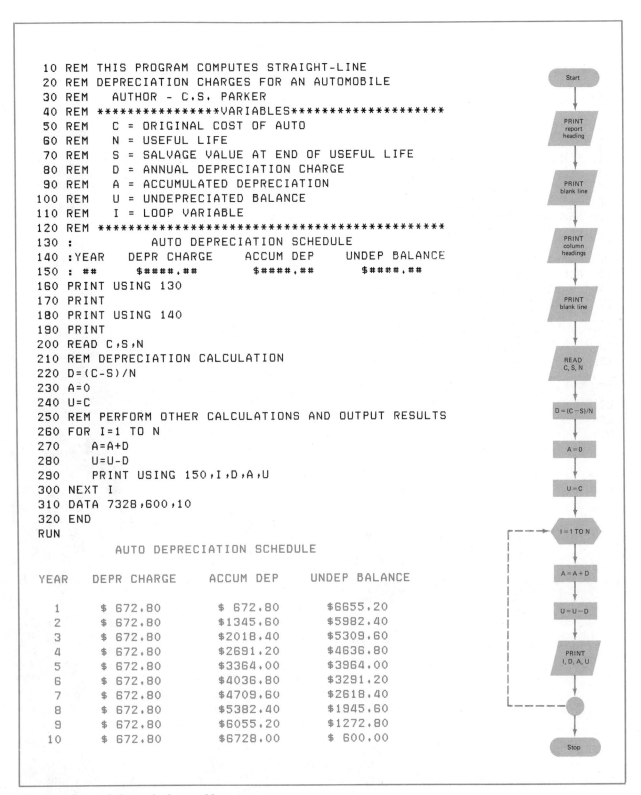

```
 10 REM THIS PROGRAM COMPUTES STRAIGHT-LINE
 20 REM DEPRECIATION CHARGES FOR AN AUTOMOBILE
 30 REM    AUTHOR - C.S. PARKER
 40 REM ****************VARIABLES********************
 50 REM    C = ORIGINAL COST OF AUTO
 60 REM    N = USEFUL LIFE
 70 REM    S = SALVAGE VALUE AT END OF USEFUL LIFE
 80 REM    D = ANNUAL DEPRECIATION CHARGE
 90 REM    A = ACCUMULATED DEPRECIATION
100 REM    U = UNDEPRECIATED BALANCE
110 REM    I = LOOP VARIABLE
120 REM **********************************************
130 :          AUTO DEPRECIATION SCHEDULE
140 :YEAR   DEPR CHARGE    ACCUM DEP    UNDEP BALANCE
150 : ##      $####.##      $####.##       $####.##
160 PRINT USING 130
170 PRINT
180 PRINT USING 140
190 PRINT
200 READ C,S,N
210 REM DEPRECIATION CALCULATION
220 D=(C-S)/N
230 A=0
240 U=C
250 REM PERFORM OTHER CALCULATIONS AND OUTPUT RESULTS
260 FOR I=1 TO N
270    A=A+D
280    U=U-D
290    PRINT USING 150,I,D,A,U
300 NEXT I
310 DATA 7328,600,10
320 END
RUN
          AUTO DEPRECIATION SCHEDULE

YEAR   DEPR CHARGE    ACCUM DEP    UNDEP BALANCE

  1     $ 672.80     $ 672.80      $6655.20
  2     $ 672.80     $1345.60      $5982.40
  3     $ 672.80     $2018.40      $5309.60
  4     $ 672.80     $2691.20      $4636.80
  5     $ 672.80     $3364.00      $3964.00
  6     $ 672.80     $4036.80      $3291.20
  7     $ 672.80     $4709.60      $2618.40
  8     $ 672.80     $5382.40      $1945.60
  9     $ 672.80     $6055.20      $1272.80
 10     $ 672.80     $6728.00      $ 600.00
```

Figure A4-4.   A depreciation problem.

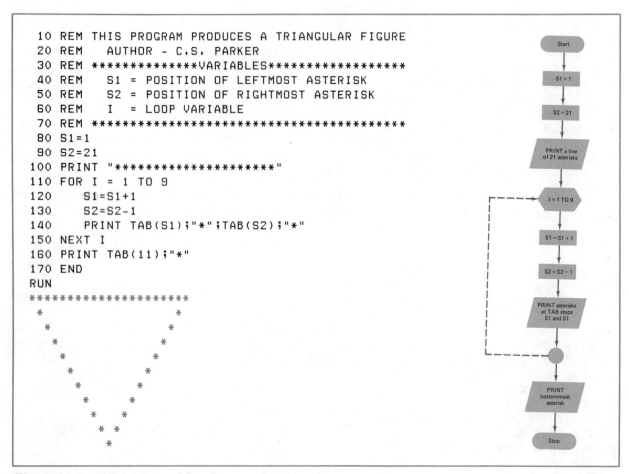

```
10 REM THIS PROGRAM PRODUCES A TRIANGULAR FIGURE
20 REM    AUTHOR - C.S. PARKER
30 REM **************VARIABLES******************
40 REM    S1 = POSITION OF LEFTMOST ASTERISK
50 REM    S2 = POSITION OF RIGHTMOST ASTERISK
60 REM    I  = LOOP VARIABLE
70 REM ****************************************
80 S1=1
90 S2=21
100 PRINT "********************"
110 FOR I = 1 TO 9
120     S1=S1+1
130     S2=S2-1
140     PRINT TAB(S1);"*";TAB(S2);"*"
150 NEXT I
160 PRINT TAB(11);"*"
170 END
RUN
********************
  *                 *
   *               *
    *             *
     *           *
      *         *
       *       *
        *     *
         *   *
          * *
           *
```

Figure A4-5. *A program and flowchart to produce a triangle.*

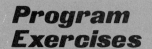

Program Exercises

Instructions: Write a BASIC program to do each of the following tasks:

1. Students in a class are required to take three exams. The class performed as follows on the exams last semester:

Student Name	Scores		
	Exam 1	Exam 2	Exam 3
Jo Smith	70	80	90
Ed Lynn	40	65	59
Richard Johnson	86	93	72
Linda Harris	95	75	86
Wendy Williams	77	83	78
David Rudolph	55	83	78

Compute the average on each of the 3 exams, the average of each of the 6 students, and the overall average of the 18 scores. Print the table above with these computed averages shown in their appropriate row and column positions. Use trailer values at the end of your data list so that your program can sense when there are no more records to be read.

2. Solve Problem 1 by printing letter grades in place of the average score of each of the six students. Use the following formula to assign grades to numbers: 90 and above = A, 80–89 = B, 70–79 = C, 60–69 = D, below 60 = F.

3. Redo the table below so that all of the decimal points line up and each column of data is centered below its column title:

```
Name                   Gross Pay

- - - -                - - - - - - - - -

Zelda Smith            $ 1000
Zeb Tsosie             $ 83.25
Zenon Jones            $    .50
```

4. If P dollars are invested in an account today at a compounded interest rate of $R\%$ per period, the amount in the account at the end of N periods is given by

$$S = P\,(1 + R/100)^N$$

For example, $100 will be worth $129.15 on 12/31/85 if it was invested on 12/31/80 at an interest rate of 5.25% compounded annually; that is,

$$S = 100\,(1 + 5.25/100)^5$$
$$= 100\,(1.0525)^5 = 129.15$$

Produce a table showing the value of 1 dollar at the end of 1, 2, 3, . . ., 10 years at interest rates of 10%, 10.5%, 11%, 11.5%, and 12%. The years should appear as rows of the table, the interest rates as columns. Make sure that your decimal points are lined up so that your output looks neat and professional.

5. Redo the depreciation schedule given in Figure A4-4 using the sum-of-the-years-digits depreciation method.

   The sum-of-the-years-digits method works as follows: Assume that an asset originally costs $4000, has a salvage value of $1000, and a useful life of 3 years. The asset will be depreciated $3000 (= $4000 minus $1000) over the 3-year period. The "sum-of-the-years-digits," based on a useful life (n) of 3 years, is computed as $1 + 2 + 3 = 6$. The procedure to compute the depreciation charge for each of the 3 years is given on the following page.

$$\begin{array}{lll}
\text{Year 1:} & (3/6) \times \$3000 = \$1500 \\
\text{Year 2:} & (2/6) \times \$3000 = \$1000 \\
\text{Year 3:} & (1/6) \times \$3000 = \underline{\$\ 500} \\
& & \$3000
\end{array}$$

Note that a fraction that is decreasing repeatedly multiplies a constant amount (cost minus salvage value). The fraction's denominator is always the "sum-of-the-years-digits," and the fraction's numerator is, for year i, equal to $n - i + 1$. A simple formula for computing the denominator is $n(n + 1)/2$. [Note that in a program this must appear as $N*(N + 1)/2$.] Note also, in the sample computation, that the full \$3000 is depreciated over the 3 years, so that the undepreciated balance at the end of the 3-year period is \$1000, the salvage value.

6. Figure A4-5 shows how to use the TAB function to produce a triangle. Use the TAB function to produce a square having ten asterisks on each side.

7. The program given in Figure A4-5 showns how to produce a hollow triangle. Revise this program so that the triangle is completely filled with asterisks.

Single Subscripting

INTRODUCTION

Subscripting is one of the most useful tools in BASIC, enabling the programmer to build and store lists of numbers or strings. Such lists are commonly called **arrays**. A **subscript** is simply a number which refers to a position in the list or array. For example, suppose that we wanted to place the data in the "averages" program of Figure A3-1 (page A-34) in a list. If we decided to call the list X, it might look as follows:

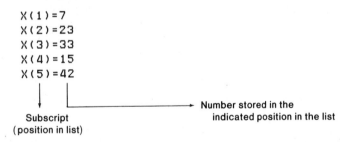

You should make certain you fully grasp the difference between a position in the list and the number stored in that position before reading further. If, for example, you were asked if $X(3) < X(4)$, how would you respond? (Note: 33 is not less than 15, so the answer is no.)

A SIMPLE SUBSCRIPTING PROBLEM

Let's again find the average of a set of numbers, expanding the problem to twelve values. Also, let's assume that we wish to output the difference of each of the numbers in the list from the average. A program to solve this problem is shown in Figure A5-1. As usual, study the problem carefully before reading the commentary which follows.

    The first thing that you may have noticed is the DIM (dimension) statement in line 120. This statement instructs the computer to reserve 12* storage positions for array X. This is necessary because

---

*Many versions of BASIC will also reserve a 13th storage location, for $X(0)$. Many skilled programmers, however, choose to ignore this storage position, since other programming languages often prohibit a zero subscript.

```
 10 REM THIS PROGRAM COMPUTES THE DIFFERENCES BETWEEN
 20 REM NUMBERS IN A LIST FROM THE AVERAGE OF THE LIST
 30 REM    AUTHOR - C.S. PARKER
 40 REM ****************VARIABLES************************
 50 REM    I  = THE LOOP VARIABLE
 60 REM    X  = THE ARRAY OF NUMBERS
 70 REM    N  = THE NUMBER OF NUMBERS IN THE LIST
 80 REM    S  = THE SUM OF THE NUMBERS IN THE LIST
 90 REM    A  = THE AVERAGE OF THE NUMBERS
100 REM    D  = THE DEVIATION OF A NUMBER FROM THE AVERAGE
110 REM ************************************************
120 DIM X(12)
130 LET S=0
140 READ N
150 REM READ AND SUM NUMBERS
160 FOR I=1 TO N
170    READ X(I)
180    LET S=S+X(I)
190 NEXT I
200 LET A=S/N
210 PRINT "NUMBER","AVERAGE","DIFFERENCE"
220 PRINT
230 REM RECALL THE X(I) VALUES, COMPUTE DEVIATIONS, AND OUTPUT RESULTS
240 FOR I=1 TO N
250    LET D=X(I)-A
260    PRINT X(I),A,D
270 NEXT I
280 DATA 12
290 DATA 5,10,11,13,4,6,8,14,2,15,1,7
300 END
RUN
```

(handwritten annotations: "subscript" pointing to X(I) on line 170; "Accumulating" underlining LET S=S+X(I) on line 180; "Average" next to LET A=S/N on line 200)

NUMBER	AVERAGE	DIFFERENCE
5	8	-3
10	8	2
11	8	3
13	8	5
4	8	-4
6	8	-2
8	8	0
14	8	6
2	8	-6
15	8	7
1	8	-7
7	8	-1

Figure A5-1. (a) *Program to compute differences of numbers in a list from the average of the list.*

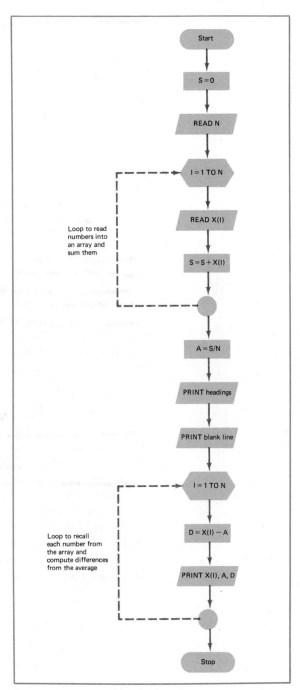

Figure A5-1.   (b) Flowchart for program in Figure A5-1(a).

each number in the array is assigned to a different variable—that is, $X(1)$, $X(2)$, ..., $X(12)$—and, as is the usual practice, each variable corresponds to a single storage location. Thus a total of 17 storage positions will be allocated to the variables in this program, as shown below:

$$X(1), X(2), X(3), \ldots, X(12), \quad S, N, I, A, D$$

Specified by the DIM
statement

Nonsubscripted
variables
in program

Many versions of BASIC will allow you to omit the DIM statement if the length of the array stored is 10 positions or less. In other words, the computer will react as if you had specified

```
120 DIM X(10)
```

in your program, even though this statement is absent. This is called *implicit* dimensioning. Most skilled programmers, however, prefer *explicit* dimensioning, where all arrays are declared in one or more DIM statements. The reasons for this are similar to the ones for explicitly initializing count and sum variables to zero: the intent is made clear, the opportunity for mistakes is minimized, and the practice is a good one to adopt if you program in other languages (BASIC is among a minority of languages permitting implicit dimensioning).

Since the array in our program has 12 positions, X must be dimensioned explicitly. If the DIM statement is absent, the computer will not automatically reserve space for $X(11)$ and $X(12)$. Thus the program will "bomb" when the computer attempts to manipulate one of these variables. It is, however, acceptable to reserve more storage positions in a DIM statement than you actually use.

The DIM statement, like a DATA statement, is not executed by the computer. Although there are several acceptable places to position it, it is good practice to put it at the beginning of the program to avoid potential problems.

If several arrays need to be dimensioned, it is possible to use one DIM statement or several. For example, both

```
10 DIM A(250),X(15),Y(20),Z(200),T3(6)
```

and the combination

```
10 DIM A(250),X(15)
20 DIM Y(20),Z(200),T3(6)
```

are acceptable to dimension the five arrays shown.

Another interesting feature of the program in Figure A5-1 concerns statements 170 and 180, which are contained in the first loop. Each time I is incremented, a single number is taken from statement 290 and assigned to the Ith variable in the X array. Thus when $I = 1$, $X(1)$ is assigned 5; when $I = 2$, $X(2)$ is assigned 10; and so on. When the computer exits the first loop and makes the computation in line 200, storage looks as follows:*

X(1) 5	X(2) 10	X(3) 11	X(4) 13
X(5) 4	X(6) 6	X(7) 8	X(8) 14
X(9) 2	X(10) 15	X(11) 1	X(12) 7
S 96	I 12	N 12	A 8
D 0			

When the second loop is encountered (line 240), the computer has all the information it needs in storage to compute the twelve differences (D = X (I) − A). Thus all that needs to be done in this loop is to successively recall from storage X(1), X(2), . . . , X(12), subtract A from these values, and compute the difference, D.

You should note that it would be extremely inconvenient to solve a problem like the one in Figure A5-1 without the use of subscripts. This is because we need to consider the values in the array twice—once to compute the average, and again to compute the differences.

A TOUGHER EXAMPLE

A common application is that of generating a frequency distribution from raw data. For example, suppose that all ten automobiles in a used-car lot possess a sales price under $5000. We would like to determine the number (or frequency) of cars for sale in each of the brackets below:

Bracket 1	$0.00 − $999.99
Bracket 2	$1,000.00 − 1,999.99
Bracket 3	$2,000.00 − 2,999.99
Bracket 4	$3,000.00 − 3,999.99
Bracket 5	$4,000.00 − 4,999.99

Before creating a BASIC program to solve this problem, let's examine a useful "trick" we'll exploit to convert the car prices into the proper brackets. Assume that the brackets are numbered 1 through 5.

---

*In some versions of BASIC I would be set to 13, even though the loop was only executed 12 times. This is because the first time NEXT is encountered, I is set to 2; the twelfth and last time NEXT is encountered, I is set to 13. Some computer systems will "roll back" this value to 12 upon leaving the loop.

If a car is priced at $2350, for example, it should fall into bracket 3. We can convert this price into the number "3" by performing the steps below:

1. Divide the price by 1000. (2350/1000 = 2.35)
2. Truncate the fraction from step 1. (2.35, when truncated, produces 2.)
3. Add 1 to the result of step 2. (2 + 1 = 3)

This "trick" will work for any of the prices encountered in this problem. Also, BASIC has a built-in function (INT) to enable you to rapidly do the truncation required in step 2. Thus if P = 2.35,*

$$INT(P)=INT(2.35)=2$$

A program to solve the frequency distribution problem is given in Figure A5-2.

Observe especially the following features in the program:

1. The "three steps" just presented are accomplished in one statement:

    $$170 \quad LET \quad K=INT(P/1000)+1$$

    Thus, when P = 1400, K = INT(1.4) + 1 = 2, identifying this price as belonging in bracket 2. When K = 2, the next statement,

    $$180 \quad LET \quad C(K)=C(K)+1$$

    is processed as C(2) = C(2) + 1. Thus the computer is instructed to increment the count in bracket 2 by 1. At the end of the program C(1) will represent the number of cars falling into bracket 1, C(2), the number of cars falling into bracket 2, and so on.

2. The C list is referenced by three different subscripts: I, K, and J: note C(I) in line 120, C(K) in line 180, and C(J) in line 260. Remember, the argument (in other words, the quantity within the parentheses) only represents a position in the list; any acceptable BASIC expression will suffice to identify this position.

STRING LISTS

The examples provided in the previous subsections illustrated lists of *numbers*. BASIC also allows the programmer to form lists of *strings*.

---

*You should note further that if A = 3.68, B = 4.30, and C = .01,

$$INT(A+B+C)=INT(3.68+4.30+.01)=INT(7.99)=7$$

suggesting that the argument in the INT function can be any valid BASIC arithmetic expression.

For example, suppose we wish to create a list of fruits (say, APPLES, ORANGES, BANANAS, PEACHES, and CHERRIES) and then output the list in reverse order. The program in Figure A5-3 does just this. Note that subscripted string variables are named in the same way as unsubscripted (**scalar**) ones—a single letter followed by the dollar sign.

```
 10 REM THIS PROGRAM GENERATES A FREQUENCY DISTRIBUTION
 20 REM    AUTHOR - C.S. PARKER
 30 REM *****************VARIABLES********************
 40 REM    I,J  = LOOP VARIABLES
 50 REM    C    = THE ARRAY OF BRACKET COUNTS
 60 REM    P    = THE PRICE OF A CAR
 70 REM    K    = THE CLASS A CAR FALLS IN TO
 80 REM ********************************************
 90 DIM C(5)
100 REM INTIALIZE BRACKET COUNTS TO ZERO
110 FOR I=1 TO 5
120    LET C(I)=0
130 NEXT I
140 REM DETERMINE A CAR'S BRACKET AND INCREMENT BRACKET COUNT
150 FOR I=1 TO 10
160    READ P
170    LET K=INT(P/1000)+1
180    LET C(K)=C(K)+1
190 NEXT I
200 PRINT TAB(15);"***CAR DISTRIBUTION***"
210 PRINT
220 PRINT "AT LEAST","BUT LESS THAN",,"COUNT"
230 PRINT
240 REM OUTPUT RESULTS
250 FOR J=1 TO 5
260    PRINT (J-1)*1000,J*1000,,C(J)
270 NEXT J
280 DATA 1400,2170,682,3340,4100
290 DATA 810,1258,750,3800,2801
300 END
RUN

              ***CAR DISTRIBUTION***

AT LEAST       BUT LESS THAN                COUNT

  0             1000                          3
  1000          2000                          2
  2000          3000                          2
  3000          4000                          2
  4000          5000                          1
```

Figure A5-2.   (a) Program to generate a car price distribution.

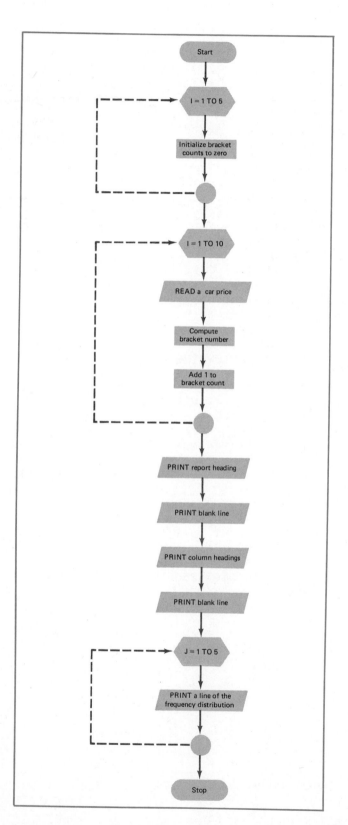

Figure A5-2. (b) Flowchart for program in Figure A5-2 (a).

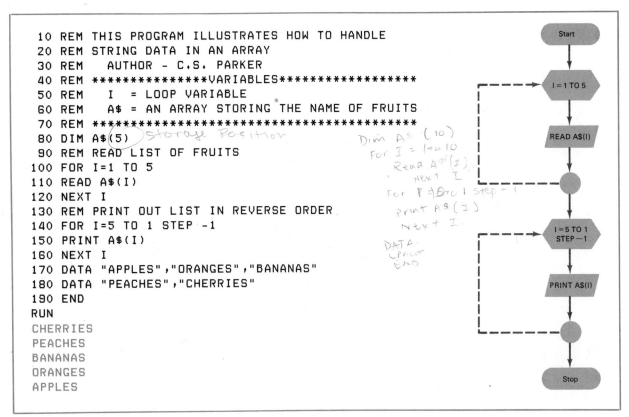

```
10 REM THIS PROGRAM ILLUSTRATES HOW TO HANDLE
20 REM STRING DATA IN AN ARRAY
30 REM    AUTHOR - C.S. PARKER
40 REM ****************VARIABLES*****************
50 REM    I = LOOP VARIABLE
60 REM    A$ = AN ARRAY STORING THE NAME OF FRUITS
70 REM *******************************************
80 DIM A$(5)
90 REM READ LIST OF FRUITS
100 FOR I=1 TO 5
110 READ A$(I)
120 NEXT I
130 REM PRINT OUT LIST IN REVERSE ORDER
140 FOR I=5 TO 1 STEP -1
150 PRINT A$(I)
160 NEXT I
170 DATA "APPLES","ORANGES","BANANAS"
180 DATA "PEACHES","CHERRIES"
190 END
RUN
CHERRIES
PEACHES
BANANAS
ORANGES
APPLES
```

Figure A5-3.   A program that manipulates a string list.

SOLVED REVIEW PROBLEMS

Example 1

A company which produces three products currently has eight sales-people. The sales of each product by each salesperson is given by the table below:

	Units Sold		
Salesperson	**Product 1**	**Product 2**	**Product 3**
William Ing	100	50	65
Ed Wilson	500	0	0
Ann Johnson	200	25	600
Edna Farber	150	30	500
Norris Ames	600	80	150
Elma Jace	100	410	800
Vilmos Zisk	300	30	60
Ellen Venn	400	0	0

The unit prices on products 1–3 are $1, 1.25, and .85, respectively.

Use the data above to produce the table below. Use subscripted variables to represent the totals associated with the three products and eight salespeople.

NAME	PRODUCT1	PRODUCT2	PRODUCT3	TOTAL
WILLIAM ING	100.00	62.50	55.25	217.75
ED WILSON	500.00	0.00	0.00	500.00
ANN JOHNSON	200.00	31.25	510.00	741.25
EDNA FARBER	150.00	37.50	425.00	612.50
NORRIS AMES	600.00	100.00	127.50	827.50
ELMA JACE	100.00	512.50	680.00	1292.50
VILMOS ZISK	300.00	37.50	51.00	388.50
ELLEN VENN	400.00	0.00	0.00	400.00
TOTALS	2350.00	781.25	1848.75	4980.00

Solution

A program and flowchart to solve this problem appear in Figure A5-4.

Example 2

Produce a flowchart and program to sort the following numbers from low to high: 7, 4, 1, 3, 2.

Solution

Although the task at hand seems relatively simple, the computer must perform several operations to complete it. There are many ways to sort numbers. One of the simplest of these is the **bubble sort,** which is illustrated in Figure A5-5 (page A-73).

The sorting begins by first comparing the first and second numbers in the list (line 190). If they are in the correct order, we leave them alone; otherwise, we exchange them. In the example, $X(1) = 7$ and $X(2) = 4$. Since $X(1) > X(2)$, we must exchange them, making $X(1) = 4$ and $X(2) = 7$. The exchange operation is accomplished in statements 210–230.

We proceed by comparing the second and third numbers in the list, again exchanging them if they are in the wrong order. Since $X(2) = 7$ and $X(3) = 1$, an exchange is again made, producing $X(2) = 1$ and $X(3) = 7$. Then we compare the third and fourth numbers, and, subsequently, the fourth and fifth. Again, exchanges are made if appropriate. After we have made these four comparisons of pairs and any appropriate exchanges, the list will be in this order: 4, 1, 3, 2, 7.

The set of operations we just performed constitutes our "first pass" through the list. As you can see, the list is not completely sorted; however, the largest number has dropped to the bottom. At this point, we must make another pass through the list, comparing $X(1)$ with $X(2)$, $X(2)$ with $X(3)$, and finally $X(3)$ with $X(4)$. Note that we have one less comparison to make on the second pass. Since the purpose of the first pass is to drop the largest number to the bottom of the list,

```
10 REM THIS PROGRAM CALCULATES PRODUCT SALES ATTRIBUTABLE
20 REM TO VARIOUS SALESPEOPLE IN A COMPANY
30 REM     AUTHOR - C.S. PARKER
40 REM ********************VARIABLES*********************
50 REM     A$   = THE SALESPERSON NAME
60 REM     M    = THE NUMBER OF SALESPEOPLE
70 REM     P    = THE ARRAY OF PRODUCT PRICES
80 REM     Q    = THE UNITS OF A PRODUCT SOLD BY A SALESPERSON
90 REM     S    = THE ARRAY SAVING PRODUCT SALES
100 REM              IN EACH ROW BEFORE THEY ARE OUTPUT
110 REM     T    = THE ROW TOTALS
120 REM     C    = THE ARRAY SAVING THE COLUMN TOTALS
130 REM     G    = THE GRAND TOTAL OF ALL SALES
140 REM     I,J  = LOOP VARIABLES
150 REM ****************************************************
160 DIM C(3),P(3),S(3)
170 PRINT USING 180
180 :   NAME        PRODUCT1    PRODUCT2    PRODUCT3    TOTAL
190 PRINT
200 READ M
210 REM INITIALIZE COLUMN TOTAL AND PRICE ARRAYS
220 FOR I=1 TO 3
230    C(I)=0
240    READ P(I)
250 NEXT I
260 G=0
270 REM MAIN COMPUTATIONS
280 FOR I=1 TO M
290    T=0
300    READ A$
310    FOR J=1 TO 3
320       READ Q
330       S(J)=Q*P(J)
340       C(J)=C(J)+S(J)
350       T=T+S(J)
360       G=G+S(J)
370    NEXT J
380    PRINT USING 390,A$,S(1),S(2),S(3),T
390    :###########   #####.##    #####.##    #####.##    #####.##
400 NEXT I
410 PRINT
420 PRINT USING 430,C(1),C(2),C(3),G
430 :TOTALS          #####.##    #####.##    #####.##    #####.##
440 DATA 8
450 DATA 1,1.25,.85
460 DATA "WILLIAM ING",100,50,65
470 DATA "ED WILSON",500,0,0
480 DATA "ANN JOHNSON",200,25,600
490 DATA "EDNA FARBER",150,30,500
500 DATA "NORRIS AMES",600,80,150
510 DATA "ELMA JACE",100,410,800
520 DATA "VILMOS ZISK",300,30,60
530 DATA "ELLEN VENN",400,0,0
540 END
```

Figure A5-4.   (a) A program to cross-classify sales data.

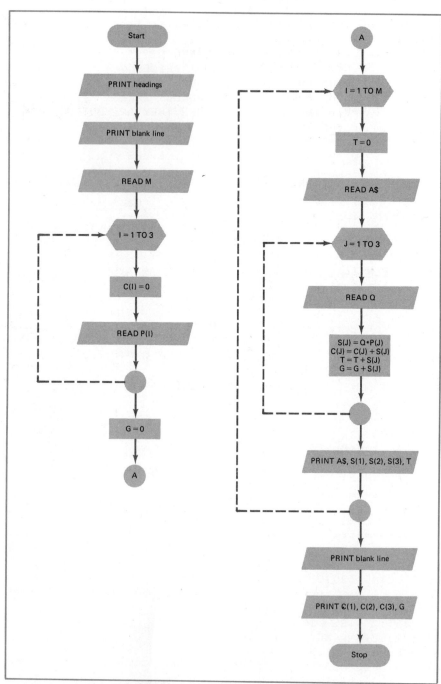

Figure A5-4. *(b) Flowchart for program in Figure A5-4 (a).*

```
 10 REM THIS PROGRAM SORTS A LIST OF NUMBERS
 20 REM     AUTHOR   - C.S. PARKER
 30 REM ****************VARIABLES***************
 40 REM    X   = THE ARRAY OF NUMBERS
 50 REM    I,J = LOOP VARIABLES
 60 REM    N   = THE NUMBER OF NUMBERS IN THE LIST
 70 REM    T   = A VARIABLE TO TEMPORARILY STORE
 80 REM                A VALUE
 90 REM ********************************************
100 DIM X(100)
110 READ N
120 REM READ NUMBERS INTO ARRAY
130 FOR I=1 TO N
140     READ X(I)
150 NEXT I
160 REM BUBBLE SORT ROUTINE
170 FOR I=1 TO N-1
180     FOR J=1 TO N-I
190         IF X(J)<=X(J+1) THEN 240
200             REM EXCHANGE OPERATION
210             T=X(J)
220             X(J)=X(J+1)
230             X(J+1)=T
240     NEXT J
250 NEXT I
260 REM OUTPUT ROUTINE
270 FOR I=1 TO N
280     PRINT X(I);
290 NEXT I
300 DATA 5
310 DATA 7,4,1,3,2
320 END
RUN
  1  2  3  4  7
```

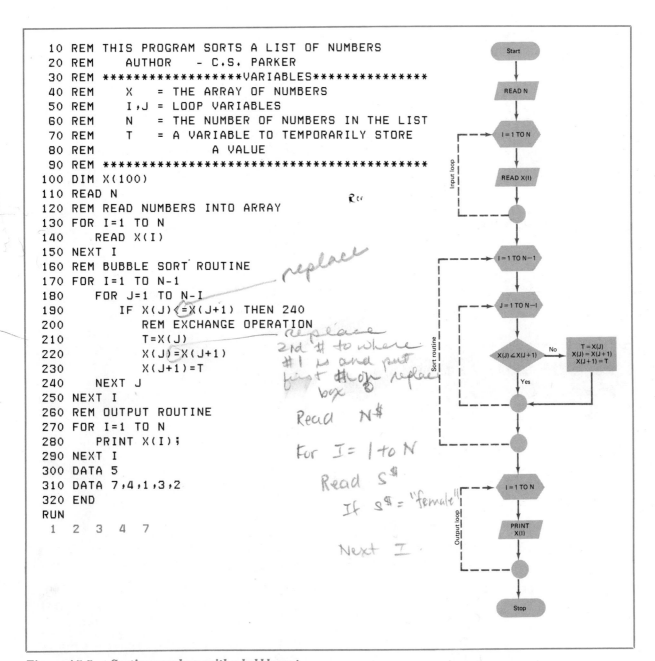

Figure A5-5.   Sorting numbers with a bubble sort.

(handwritten annotations:) replace; replace 2nd # to where #1 is and put first # on replace box; Read N#; For I = 1 to N; Read S#; If S# = "female"; Next I; X = A; whatever in X is now substitute to A

assigning it to X(5), it is unnecessary to check X(4) against X(5). Again, during the second pass (and any subsequent ones), exchanges are made if they are appropriate.

You should note that the list at the end of the second pass will be in the order 1, 3, 2, 4, 7. The list is not completely sorted; however, the second-largest number has fallen to the next-to-bottom position. Thus at the end of the second pass, two values, X(4) and X(5), are in their correct positions in the list. At this point a third pass is made, comparing X(1) with X(2), and X(2) with X(3). A fourth pass will also be necessary, comparing X(1) with X(2). At the end of the fourth pass, the list will be in sorted order.

Note that a list of N numbers will require $N - 1$ passes in a bubble sort. Also, each pass will involve the comparison of one fewer pairs of numbers than the pass before it. To make sure you fully understand how a bubble sort works, get out a pencil and paper and jot down what the computer is doing and what it has in storage at each step in the program execution.

Program Exercises

Instructions: Write a BASIC program to do each of the following tasks:

1. The following is a list of salaries of the six employees in a certain company:

Name	Salary
T. Jones	$43,000
F. Smith	$31,000
K. Johnston	$22,000
P. Miner	$18,000
C. Altman	$27,000
A. Barth	$19,000

Calculate and output the average salary for the company, as well as the names of all people whose salaries exceed the average.

2. Read the ten numbers in the list shown below and then output the list in reverse order (that is, 12, 43, 6, etc.):

    31, 15, 85, 36, 22, 81, 70, 6, 43, 12

3. The following list contains names and sexes of people at XYZ company: Janice Jones (female), Bill Smith (male), Debra Parks (female), Elaine Johnson (female), William Anderson (male), Art James (male), Bill Finley (male), and Ellen Ott (female).

Read the list into the computer in the order given; then prepare and output two separate lists—one composed of all of the males, the other of all of the females.

4. Twenty-five people took an exam, the scores being distributed as follows:

91, 83, 69, 35, 99, 64, 78, 71, 52, 89, 72, 100, 56, 63,
72, 77, 82, 95, 85, 71, 66, 54, 63, 82, 94

Prepare a frequency distribution of scores such as:

RANGE	NUMBER OF SCORES IN RANGE
90–100	?
80–89	?
. . . and so on	

5. An eight-student class in data processing has taken four tests in a semester, with the following results:

Student	Exam 1	Exam 2	Exam 3	Exam 4
Joan Blow	83	64	75	91
Cleon Jones	78	71	60	80
Jane Jackson	65	98	98	69
Bob Smith	81	45	72	55
Leon Russell	68	42	81	76
Sue James	80	70	60	96
John Doe	54	88	92	65
Linda Johnson	88	86	65	74

Write a BASIC program to produce a listing of students in descending order of total points scored on the examinations. List student name and total points scored on your output. (*Hint:* each time you exchange the total points for two students in the list, you must also exchange their names.)

Advanced Topics

DOUBLE SUBSCRIPTING

Data to be processed by the computer system are sometimes better represented in two-dimensional (table) form than in one-dimensional (list) form. For example, consider the data below, which show the vote distribution on a certain issue in different divisions of a university:

	Voted Yes	Voted No	Didn't Vote
Business	205	152	38
Liberal Arts	670	381	115
Engineering	306	251	47
Forestry	112	33	14

The above data, which include four rows and three columns of numbers, exist naturally in the form of a table. It would be most convenient if we could give the table a name (V, for example), and store any number in the table with reference to its row and column position. For example, 115, which is in row 2 and column 3, would be stored as V(2, 3).

Fortunately, BASIC permits us to represent two-dimensional tables in the simple manner just described. Thus we could store the table numbers in the 12 variables below:

$$V(1,1) = 205 \quad V(1,2) = 152 \quad V(1,3) = 38$$
$$V(2,1) = 670 \quad V(2,2) = 381 \quad V(2,3) = 115$$
$$V(3,1) = 306 \quad V(3,2) = 251 \quad V(3,3) = 47$$
$$V(4,1) = 112 \quad V(4,2) = 33 \quad V(4,3) = 14$$

It is relatively easy to create such a table in BASIC and, later, to access each of the numbers and process it as needed. To see how this might be done, refer to the program in Figure A6-1, which totals all of the numbers in the table and subsequently divides each number by this total.

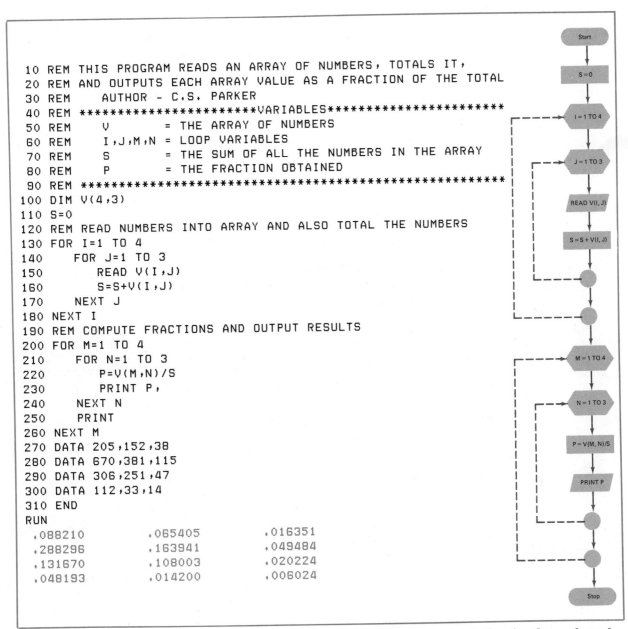

```
 10 REM THIS PROGRAM READS AN ARRAY OF NUMBERS, TOTALS IT,
 20 REM AND OUTPUTS EACH ARRAY VALUE AS A FRACTION OF THE TOTAL
 30 REM     AUTHOR - C.S. PARKER
 40 REM ********************VARIABLES*********************
 50 REM    V      = THE ARRAY OF NUMBERS
 60 REM    I,J,M,N = LOOP VARIABLES
 70 REM    S      = THE SUM OF ALL THE NUMBERS IN THE ARRAY
 80 REM    P      = THE FRACTION OBTAINED
 90 REM ***************************************************
100 DIM V(4,3)
110 S=0
120 REM READ NUMBERS INTO ARRAY AND ALSO TOTAL THE NUMBERS
130 FOR I=1 TO 4
140    FOR J=1 TO 3
150       READ V(I,J)
160       S=S+V(I,J)
170    NEXT J
180 NEXT I
190 REM COMPUTE FRACTIONS AND OUTPUT RESULTS
200 FOR M=1 TO 4
210    FOR N=1 TO 3
220       P=V(M,N)/S
230       PRINT P,
240    NEXT N
250    PRINT
260 NEXT M
270 DATA 205,152,38
280 DATA 670,381,115
290 DATA 306,251,47
300 DATA 112,33,14
310 END
RUN
 .088210         .065405         .016351
 .288296         .163941         .049484
 .131670         .108003         .020224
 .048193         .014200         .006024
```

Figure A6-1.   Program to read a table, total all the numbers in the table, and print the fraction that each number is with regard to the sum.

You should observe that in this program, as is the usual practice with subscripts, a DIM statement is immediately employed to declare the size of the table. Then nested loops are established in statements 130–180 to automatically generate the row (I = 1, 2, 3, 4) and column (J = 1, 2, 3) subscripts. Thus the first time these nested loops are executed,

I = 1, J = 1, V(1, 1) is assigned 205, and S = 0 + 205 = 205

The second time,

$I = 1, J = 2$, V(1, 2) is assigned 152, and $S = 205 + 152 = 357$

The third time,

$I = 1, J = 3$, V(1, 3) is assigned 38, and $S = 357 + 38 = 395$

The fourth time,

$I = 2, J = 1$, V(2, 1) is assigned 670, and $S = 395 + 670 = 1065$

The fifth time,

$I = 2, J = 2$, V(2, 2) is assigned 381, and $S = 1065 + 381 = 1446$

and so on.

The twelfth time,

$I = 4, J = 3$, V(4, 3) is assigned 14, and $S = 2310 + 14 = 2324$

In the nested loops in statements 200–260, we simply recall V(1, 1), V(1, 2), . . . , V(4, 3) successively from storage and, as we do so, divide each by the table sum and print out the fraction obtained. Note that the variables (M, N) used to represent the subscripts in the second set of nested loops are different than those (I, J) used in the first set. Although we could have used I and J again, the example illustrates that any choice of a subscript variable will do as long as the proper numbers are substituted by the computer to represent the row and column involved.

Two final points on the program in Figure A6-1 deserve comment. First, note that the PRINT statement in line 230 contains a comma. This keeps output belonging in the same row printing on the same line. Second, note the blank PRINT statement on line 250. This statement forces the output device onto a new line, where a new row of numbers is printed.

When working with tables, it is often helpful to be able to sum the values in rows and columns. For example,

205	152	38	395	
670	381	115	1166	←Row totals
306	251	47	604	
112	33	14	159	
1293	817	214	2324	

Column totals   Grand total

This can be done in BASIC by using a scheme such

1. Use singly subscripted variables, such as C(1),
    represent the totals of columns 1, 2, and 3, resp

2. Use singly subscripted variables, such as R(1), R(2), R(3), and
    R(4), to represent the totals of rows 1, 2, 3, and 4, respectively.

3. Use an unsubscripted variable, such as S, to represent the grand
    total.

A program to compute such sums is shown in Figure A6-2

```
 10 REM THIS PROGRAM SUMS UP THE ROWS AND COLUMNS
 20 REM OF AN ARRAY
 30 REM    AUTHOR - C.S. PARKER
 40 REM ****************VARIABLES*****************
 50 REM    V  = THE ARRAY OF NUMBERS
 60 REM    I,J = LOOP VARIABLES
 70 REM    C  = THE ARRAY SAVING COLUMN TOTALS
 80 REM    R  = THE ARRAY SAVING ROW TOTALS
 90 REM    S  = THE GRAND TOTAL OF THE NUMBERS
100 REM ****************************************
110 DIM V(4,3),C(3),R(4)
120 LET C(1)=C(2)=C(3)=R(1)=R(2)=R(3)=R(4)=0
130 REM READ NUMBERS INTO ARRAY AND SUM INTO ROWS AND COLUMNS
140 FOR I=1 TO 4
150    FOR J=1 TO 3
160       READ V(I,J)
170       R(I)=R(I)+V(I,J)
180       C(J)=C(J)+V(I,J)
190    NEXT J
200    PRINT V(I,1),V(I,2),V(I,3),R(I)
210 NEXT I
220 S=C(1)+C(2)+C(3)
230 PRINT C(1),C(2),C(3),S
240 DATA 205,152,38
250 DATA 670,381,115
260 DATA 306,251,47
270 DATA 112,33,14
280 END
RUN
 205          152          38          395
 670          381          115         1166
 306          251          47          604
 112          33           14          159
 1293         817          214         2324
```

Figure A6-2.   (a) Program for rows and columns using double subscripts.

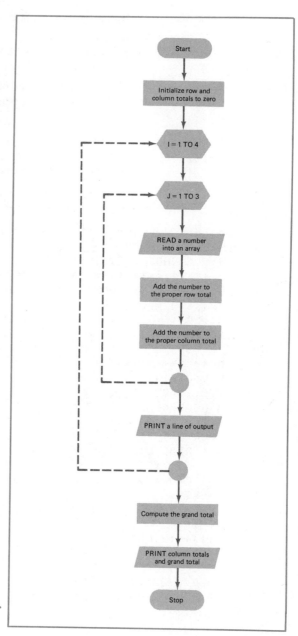

Figure A6-2.   (b) Flowchart for program in Figure A6-2 (a).

RANDOM NUMBERS

Many computer languages provide a means to automatically generate random numbers, and BASIC is no exception. **Random numbers** introduce the element of chance into a program, enabling the computer system, for example, to pick different cards from an imaginary deck, provide fictional athletic teams with unpredictable successes or failures with selected game strategies, and so forth.

A random number is a number which is formed through laws of probability. One easy way to generate random numbers is to use a ten-position "roulette wheel," such as the one shown here:

If we wanted to generate, say, a three-digit random number, we could spin the wheel three times. Perhaps we might obtain "4" on the first try, "0" on the second, and "8" on the third, thereby producing the random number 408. If we tried this repeatedly, we could form a list of several random numbers, such as 408, 616, 832, 009, and so on.

Random numbers are normally generated to **simulate** some real-world, physical process. For example, we could use the three-digit numbers just introduced to play a game of baseball. Thus, we might arbitrarily choose the following:

Any number generated between 000–699 represents an out.

Any number generated between 700–849 represents a single.

Any number generated between 850–929 represents a double.

Any number generated between 930–949 represents a triple.

Any number generated between 950–999 represents a home run.

For example, if a batter came to the plate and the number 408 was selected, the batter would be out. The selection of the number 962, on the other hand, would correspond to the batter hitting a home run, and so on. It's not too difficult to write a program to keep track of outs, innings, batters on base, and the score. If different random numbers are generated each time a game is played, we will get different results for each game.

BASIC provides a built-in function, RND, to allow us to automatically generate random numbers on computer systems. For example, the statement

```
LET X=RND
```

will request the computer system to generate a random number and place it in the storage location assigned to X. If we wanted to generate three random numbers and output them, we simply sandwich this statement, with a PRINT, in a FOR-NEXT loop, as in Figure A6-3.

People normally have different requirements for the selection of random numbers: some want three-digit fractions, others want two-digit integers, and still others want integers only in a certain range (say 1–52, representing the 52 cards in a deck). To accommodate these different needs, BASIC always supplies the random number in the same form—usually as a fraction between .000000 and .999999—and

```
10 FOR I=1 TO 3
20    X=RND
30       PRINT X,
40 NEXT I
50 END
RUN
 .186255           .413305          .987024
```

Figure A6-3.   A program that generates three random numbers.

leaves it to each programmer to transform this fraction into a form that meets the particular needs of the application. Observe that the program in Figure A6-3 has generated fractions in the range .000000–.999999.

When we want the random numbers in integer rather than fractional form, we can use the INT function to make the necessary transformation. In the program of Figure A6-3, all we need to do is modify the statement in line 20. For example, consider the following two transformations:

1. Suppose that we want only random integers between 0 and 999 (inclusive). If we change line 20 to read

        20 X=INT(RND*1000)

    we will get the desired results. For example, when RND is supplied as .186255, multiplying this number by 1000 yields 186.255. Then, INT(186.255) = 186.

2. Suppose that we want only two-digit random integers in the range 10–30. There are 21 integers in this range: 10, 11, 12, . . . , 30. We must change line 20 to read

        20 X=INT(21*RND+10)

    Note that since RND can only be in the range .000000–.999999, it is impossible for X to be any integer outside the range 10–30. At one extreme, when RND = .000000, the formula will yield X = 10; at the other, when RND = .999999, X = INT(20.999979 + 10) = INT(30.999979) = 30.

It is important to realize that most computerized random number generators will produce the same sequence of fractions every time a RUN command is issued. Thus, if we ran the program in Figure A6-3 50 times, we would generate the same sequence (.186255, .413305, and .987024) 50 times. To generate a different sequence of random numbers every time the program is run you should insert the command

                5 RANDOMIZE

in the program. This will place the random number generator at a different "starting point," so that the values of RND produced will be somewhat unpredictable.

Now that we've covered the fundamentals of generating random numbers, let's see how we can use RND in a BASIC program. Consider a bakery which can sell between 15 and 20 wedding cakes per day.

Cakes must be baked at the beginning of the day, when it is not known how many cakes will be sold. Cakes cost $11 to make, and they sell for $20. A cake baked but not sold can be sold the next day for $5 at a day-old bake sale. We wish to know

1. The expected average daily profit if 17 cakes are baked every day.
2. If baking 17 cakes daily is the best strategy for the bakery.

The bakery is faced with a classic supply–demand problem. If few cakes are baked, say 15, and 20 are demanded, the opportunity for $9 profit on each of the five extra cakes is lost. On the other hand, if several are baked, say 19, and only 16 are demanded, the bakery loses $6 ($11–$5) on each of the three extra cakes baked. With a strategy of producing 17 cakes daily, the bakery will either underbake, overbake, or bake the right amount on any given day.

We will solve this problem by simulating daily bakery operations over a long period of time (1000 days). To solve part (1) of the problem, we'll assume that each day the baker will bake (supply) 17 cakes. We'll have the computer system select a random integer in the range 15–20 each day. This number will represent the number of cakes demanded that day. Then, knowing supply (S = 17) and demand (D = some integer between 15 and 20) for the day, we can compute the profit for the day. If we average the profit for 1000 days, then we'll know how well the strategy "bake 17 cakes" is working. The program to solve part 1 of the problem is given in Figure A6-4 (next page). It is annotated to make it easier to follow.

To solve part 2 of the problem, all we need to do is compare the average daily profits for all possible strategies—that is, bake 15, 16, 17, 18, 19, or 20 cakes. The solution is given in Figure A6-5 (page A-85).

Note that the program in Figure A6-5 is created very easily from the one in Figure A6-4. All we needed to do was place an extra loop around the program (to vary S automatically from 15 to 20) and modify the PRINT statement in line 200 slightly.

A computerized simulation, such as the one just shown, enables the management of a company to easily answer "what-if" types of questions which might have a significant impact on operations. For example:

1. What will be the effect if the cost of making a cake rises to $12? Note that the only changes which need to be made in the program of Figure A6-5 are in the profit margin statements:

    ```
    150 P=P+(D*7-6*(S-D)
    170 P=P+(S*8)
    ```

2. What if the only other bakery in town closes, so that potential demand is now somewhere in the range of 18–25 cakes? Note that the only changes required in Figure A6-5 are the supply–demand statements:

    ```
    100 FOR S=18 TO 25
    130 D=INT(8*RND+18)
    ```

6.9
$\times .4$
$\overline{}$

$(6 * RND + 15)$

$0. - 6 \overset{+15}{-} 15$

$.9 - 5.9 - 20$
$\quad\quad +15$

$23 * RND + 15.$

$0 = 0$

$.9 -$

```
10 REM THIS PROGRAM SIMULATES A BAKERY OPERATION
20 REM      AUTHOR - C.S. PARKER
30 REM ***************VARIABLES****************
40 REM      S  = NUMBER OF CAKES BAKED DAILY
50 REM      D  = NUMBER OF CAKES DEMANDED DAILY
60 REM      P1 = AVERAGE DAILY PROFIT
70 REM      P  = TOTAL PROFIT OVER 1000 DAYS
80 REM      I  = LOOP VARIABLE
90 REM ***************************************
100 S=17
110 P=0
120 FOR I=1 TO 1000
130      D=INT(6*RND+15)
140      IF S<=D THEN 170
150      P=P+(D*9-6*(S-D))
160      GOTO 180
170      P=P+(S*9)
180 NEXT I
190 P1=P/1000
200 PRINT "AVERAGE DAILY PROFIT IS $";P1
210 END
RUN
AVERAGE DAILY PROFIT IS $ 145.935
```

This formula generates random integers in the range 15–20

D*9 − 6*(S − D) is the profit when supply > demand

S*9 is the profit when supply ≤ demand

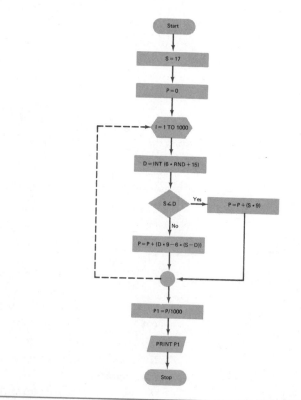

Figure A6-4. Simulating average daily profit for the strategy "bake 17 cakes."

```
10 REM THIS PROGRAM SIMULATES A BAKERY OPERATION
20 REM     AUTHOR - C.S. PARKER
30 REM ****************VARIABLES****************
40 REM     S  = NUMBER OF CAKES BAKED DAILY
50 REM     D  = NUMBER OF CAKES DEMANDED DAILY
60 REM     P1 = AVERAGE DAILY PROFIT
70 REM     P  = TOTAL PROFIT OVER 1000 DAYS
80 REM     I  = LOOP VARIABLE
90 REM ****************************************
100 FOR S=15 TO 20
110     P=0
120     FOR I=1 TO 1000
130         D=INT(6*RND+15)
140         IF S<=D THEN 170
150         P=P+(D*9-6*(S-D))
160         GOTO 180
170         P=P+(S*9)
180     NEXT I
190     P1=P/1000
200     PRINT "PROFIT FOR";S;"CAKES IS $";P1
210 NEXT S
220 END
RUN
PROFIT FOR 15 CAKES IS $ 135
PROFIT FOR 16 CAKES IS $ 141.51
PROFIT FOR 17 CAKES IS $ 145.53
PROFIT FOR 18 CAKES IS $ 146.82
PROFIT FOR 19 CAKES IS $ 145.77
PROFIT FOR 20 CAKES IS $ 142.86
```

These three statements are the only changes made from Figure A6-4

Figure A6-5. Simulating average daily profit for all baking strategies between 15 and 20 cakes.

With a computerized simulation, it is relatively easy to answer such "what if" questions within minutes. Often, such questions may take days or even weeks for an analyst to solve by hand.

You may be wondering, after looking at the bakery problem, "Why 1000 simulations? Why not 100, or 2000?" Choosing the best number of trials is somewhat of an art. One way the matter can be approached is as follows:

1. Try an arbitrary number of trials, say 1000. Then run the problem again with different random numbers, using the RAN-DOMIZE statement.

2. If the results you get by running the program the second time are within about 5 percent of the results the first time, the number of trials you are using is probably enough.

3. If the results are not within 5 percent, try 1500 trials and repeat the experiment. If the pairs of results are still not within 5 percent, try 2000 trials, and so on.

When the results you get from running the program seem to be relatively independent of the set of random numbers you use, you're probably running enough trials. The optimum number of trials depends largely on how complex the simulation is. In solving larger problems, you may need to start at 10,000 or even 100,000 trials, and increment the number of trials in larger steps if results are not within the suggested 5 percent.

FUNCTIONS AND SUBROUTINES

Name of function

$$DEF\ FNX\ (Y) = Y^3 + 3Y^2 + Y + 1$$

$$FNX\ (0) = 1$$

Functions

BASIC permits two types of functions: **library (built-in) functions** and **user-defined functions.** We have already covered two library functions: INT and RND. Since these functions are built into the BASIC language, the computer system knows exactly what type of action to take when it runs into one of them. There are many other library functions which are probably available with the version of BASIC used by your computer system. Below is a partial list of some of the more common ones:

Function	Purpose
ABS(X)	Returns the absolute value of X
SQR(X)	Calculates the square root of X (X must be $>=0$)
RND	Returns a random number between .000000 – .999999
SIN(X)	Computes the sine of X (X must be in radians)
COS(X)	Computes the cosine of X (X must be in radians)
TAN(X)	Computes the tangent of X (X must be in radians)
LOG(X)	Calculates the natural logarithm of X (X must be positive)
EXP(X)	Calculates the term e^x, where e is approximately 2.718
INT(X)	Returns the greatest integer $<=X$

Programmers also have the ability to define their own functions. This can be useful when there is a formula you need to use repeatedly which is not a library function. User-defined functions are specified with the DEF statement. For example, suppose we wanted to compute the commission due a salesperson as

15 percent of gross sales of "brand-name" items

10 percent of gross sales of "nonbrand" items

Thus if S1 represents gross sales of brand-name items and S2 gross sales of nonbrand items, the commission C may be calculated as

$$C=.15*S1+.10*S2$$

A program which computes this commission for three salespeople is given in Figure A6-6. You should inspect this program carefully before proceeding further.

Note in the program that the formula for computing the commissions is defined in line 90. The formula must be defined (with a DEF statement) before it can be used (as in statement 120).

The format of the DEF statement is

DEF FNx (y) = z

where x is a single alphabetic letter chosen by the programmer, y is a list of arguments (which may be as large as 5 variables, depending on the computer system used), and z is a valid BASIC expression. It is also permissible to use several DEF statements in a single program. Note that the word DEF must be followed by a space and then FN. You must remember, however, to define the functions early in your program, before you reference them.

You should also note that the formula, or function, in the figure also contains two *dummy arguments*, S1 and S2. The only significance of dummy arguments is that they demonstrate how the function will be computed. After reading in the salesperson information in line 110,

```
10 REM THIS PROGRAM COMPUTES SALES COMMISSIONS
20 REM     AUTHOR - C.S. PARKER
30 REM ****************VARIABLES**************
40 REM     S1,S2 = DUMMY ARGUMENTS
50 REM     A,B   = REAL ARGUMENTS
60 REM     N$    = SALESPERSON NAME
70 REM     I     = LOOP VARIABLE
80 REM ********************************************
90 DEF FNC(S1,S2)=.15*S1+.10*S2          ——— The function is defined here
100 FOR I=1 TO 3                  dummy argument
110     READ N$,A,B
120     PRINT N$,FNC(A,B)          ——— The function is executed here
130 NEXT I                        real argument
140 DATA "JOE SMITH",700.00,1000.00
150 DATA "ZELDA GREY",600.00,1200.00
160 DATA "SUE JOHNSON",1000.00,500.00
170 END
RUN
JOE SMITH        205
ZELDA GREY       210
SUE JOHNSON      200
```

Figure A6-6. *Use of user-defined function to compute commissions.*

the computer system prints out in line 120 the salesperson's name and total commission due. Before the computer calculates and prints the commission, it "refers" to line 90 and substitutes A for S1 and B for S2.

A and B are called *real arguments*. Real arguments are always substituted for corresponding dummy arguments, according to their respective positioning within the parentheses, whenever the function is used in the programs.

The program could have also been written by using the same variable names as both dummy and real arguments. All that you would need to change are lines 110 and 120:

```
110 READ N$,S1,S2
120 PRINT N$,FNC(S1,S2)
```

This ability to define a function is one of the most useful and most powerful features of BASIC. It is also the capability most overlooked, even by many skilled programmers.

Subroutines

BASIC **subroutines** are partial programs, or subprograms, which are contained within a BASIC program (called the "main program"). They are particularly effective when a series of statements in a program is to be performed numerous times or, perhaps, at many different places in the overall program.

Subroutines introduce two new statements, GOSUB and RETURN, which have the formats below:

```
GOSUB line number
RETURN
```

The GOSUB statement causes immediate branching to the first statement in the subroutine. The RETURN statement causes branching back to the main program, to the statement which immediately follows the invoking GOSUB (that is, the GOSUB that caused the branching). An example of a program which uses subroutines is given in Figure A6-7.

The program reads three pairs of numbers, adds each pair, and computes and outputs the square of each sum. Every time statement 120 (GOSUB 150) is executed, the computer goes to statement 150. It proceeds from this point until it encounters a RETURN statement. When the computer reaches the RETURN, it goes back to the main part of the program and continues with the statement following the invoking GOSUB: in other words, statement 130. The STOP statement is used in line 140 to prevent the subroutine from being executed a fourth time; in other words, the program should end as soon as the FOR-NEXT loop is finished.

Subroutines are useful because the programmer can assign complicated tasks or calculations to several subroutines and avoid clutter-

```
10 REM THIS PROGRAM READS PAIRS OF NUMBERS, SUMS EACH
20 REM PAIR, AND COMPUTES AND OUTPUTS THE SQUARE OF
30 REM    AUTHOR - C.S. PARKER
40 REM *********************VARIABLES*********************
50 REM    A,B = A PAIR OF NUMBERS
60 REM    S   = THE SUM OF THE PAIR
70 REM    X   = THE SQUARE OF THE SUM
80 REM    I   = LOOP VARIABLE
90 REM ****************************************************
100 FOR I=1 TO 3
110 READ A,B
120 GOSUB 150          GOSUB causes computer
                       to branch to indicated
                       statement (150)
130 NEXT I
140 STOP
150 REM ****THIS SUBROUTINE SQUARES NUMBERS****
160 S=A+B
170 X=S**2                              The subroutine
180 PRINT X
190 RETURN
200 DATA 2,6
210 DATA 8,12
220 DATA 10,5
230 END
RUN
 64
 400
 225
```

Figure A6-7.   A program containing a subroutine.

ing up the main part of the program. Each independent task should be done in a separate subroutine, making the main program logic much easier to follow. Such a *modular programming style* allows new programmers hired by a company to more quickly understand how existing programs work. It also makes debugging easier, since each subroutine can be tested independently with dummy variables. Finally, it is not uncommon for a programmer to have to revise his or her own program months after it was first written. You will be amazed at how hard it is to figure out what a badly organized program is doing—even if you yourself wrote the original program!

Program Exercises

Instructions: Write a BASIC program to do each of the following tasks

1. Write a program which reads the matrix

$$\begin{bmatrix} 8 & 7 & 3 \\ 2 & 4 & 1 \\ 6 & 5 & 8 \end{bmatrix}$$

adds the number 5 to each element (number) of the matrix, and prints the resulting matrix.

2. Write a general program which allows one to input a matrix of any size and output the *transpose** of the matrix. Assume, for simplicity, that the matrix will not exceed 20 rows and 20 columns.

3. Generate 1000 random integers in the range 1–100 (inclusive) and determine the number that are between 10–30 (inclusive).

4. Write a program to simulate the flipping of a coin. For example, generate 1000 random numbers between .000000 and .999999. If a random number is less than .5, it counts as a "head;" otherwise, it counts as a "tail." Output the number of heads and tails found in the 1000 "flips."

5. A line is 7 inches long. Simulate the probability that two points chosen at random will be within 1 inch of each other.

6. ABC Company has the following "accounts receivables" data:

Customer Name	Previous Balance	Payments	New Purchases
Clara Bronson	$700	$500	$300
Lon Brooks	100	100	0
Louise Chaplin	0	0	100
Jack Davies	50	0	0
Emil Murray	600	600	200
Tom Swanson	300	100	50
Lucy Allen	500	500	80

Write a subroutine which computes the new balance for each customer. Assume that unpaid portions of previous balances are assessed a 2 percent finance charge each month. The main part of your program should perform all the input/output functions necessary to support and supplement the subroutine.

*The transpose is another matrix that has the rows and columns of the original matrix switched. For example, the transpose of

$$\begin{bmatrix} 1 & 2 & 3 \\ 4 & 5 & 6 \end{bmatrix} \text{ is } \begin{bmatrix} 1 & 4 \\ 2 & 5 \\ 3 & 6 \end{bmatrix}$$

7. Problems in economic "time-series" often involve using the sine
    function SIN(X) to fit a curve to given data. Plot a sine curve from
    0–360 degrees. Your output should look roughly like the sample
    output below:

BASIC STATEMENT COMMANDS

Statement	Description	Example
DEF	Sets up a user-defined function (A-86)	`90 DEF FNC(S1,S2)=.15*S1+.10*S2`
DIM	Dimensions an array (A-61)	`120 DIM X(12)`
END	The last statement in a program (A-5, A-19)	`250 END`

FOR/NEXT	The beginning and ending statements in a loop (A-40)	`160 FOR I=1 TO N`
		`.`
		`.`
		`.`
		`190 NEXT I`

GOSUB/RETURN	Branch to a subroutine; Return to main program from subroutine (A-88)	`120 GOSUB 150`
		`.`
		`.`
		`.`
		`190 RETURN`

GOTO	An unconditional branch (A-18)	`140 GOTO 100`
IF	A conditional branch (A-16)	`110 IF A=-1 THEN 160`
INPUT	Enables data to be entered interactively (A-35)	`80 INPUT X`
LET	An assignment (replacement) statement (A-5, A-17)	`30 LET C=A+B`
PRINT	Displays or prints program output (A-5, A-17)	`160 PRINT N$`

PRINT USING/IMAGE (:)	Enable formatted output (A-52)	`100 PRINT USING 200,X`
		`.`
		`.`
		`.`
		`200:    ###.##`

READ/DATA	Assigns values to variables from a list of data (A-5, A-14)	`20 READ A,B`
		`.`
		`.`
		`.`
		`50 DATA 8,16`

REM	A program remark (A-4, A-19)	`100 REM DEPRECIATION CALCULATION`
STOP	Stops a program (A-39)	`80 STOP`

Numbers in parentheses in the second column are the pages on which the statement is described.

BASIC Glossary/Index

The number in parentheses at the end of each definition is the page of the appendix on which the term is boldfaced.

Array. A one- or two-dimensional subscripted variable list. (A-61)

Assignment (replacement) symbol. The "=" symbol used in a LET statement, which assigns the value implied on the right-hand side of the symbol to the variable declared on the left-hand side. (A-17)

BASIC (Beginner's All-purpose Symbolic Instruction Code). An easy-to-learn programming language developed at Dartmouth College in the 1960s. BASIC is widely used for instructional purposes and is the most popular language implemented on personal computers. (A-1)

BASIC program. A set of BASIC program statements that can be executed by the computer to produce useful output. (A-3)

BASIC program statement. See BASIC statement command. (A-3)

BASIC statement command. An instruction written in the BASIC programming language—for example, READ, LET, PRINT, and so forth. (A-20)

BASIC system command. An instruction that performs an action on a BASIC program—for example, RUN, LIST, DELETE, and so forth. (A-20)

Branch. The process of transferring control from one statement in a program to any statement out of the normal sequence. (A-6)

Bubble sort. A sorting method that works by successive comparisons and exchanges of values in a list, "bubbling" the largest (or smallest) value on each pass up (or down) the list. (A-70)

Bug. An error in a program or system. (A-22)

Coding. The writing of instructions that will cause the computer system to perform a specific set of actions. (A-7)

Computer program. A set of instructions that causes the computer system to perform a specific set of actions. (A-1)

Computer-assisted instruction (CAI). The use of computers to supplement personalized teaching instruction by providing the student with sequences of questions under program control. The progression through the questions in such a system enables students to learn at their own rate. (A-36)

Conditional branch. An instruction that may cause the computer to execute an instruction, other than the one that immediately follows, depending on the results of an operation, the contents of a storage location, and so forth. (A-16)

Constant. A value that doesn't change. (A-12)

Control structure. A pattern for controlling the flow of logic in a computer program. (A-9)

Conversational (interactive) mode. The use of the INPUT statement to enable a program user to interact with a program as it is running. (A-35)

Debug. The process of detecting and correcting errors in computer programs or in the computer system itself. (A-22)

Design phase. In program development, the process of planning a program prior to coding it. (A-7)

Documentation. Any nonexecutable written description of a program, procedure, or system (A-9, A-30)

Hierarchy of operations. The order of operations followed by a programming language when evaluating an expression. (A-13)

Initializing. Presetting a variable to a prespecified value before using it in a computation. (A-33)

Instruction. A program or system command that will cause the computer to take some action. (A-1)

Library (built-in) function. A mathematical function that is built into the BASIC language—for example, RND, INT, SIN, and so forth. (A-86)

Line number. An integer number which begins and identifies every BASIC program statement. (A-4)

Literal. Another name for a string constant. (A-5)

Loop. A series of program statements that are executed repeatedly until one or more conditions are satisfied. (A-7)

Looping. The control structure used to represent a loop operation. (A-9)

Loop variable. A variable used to control the number of times a loop is executed. (A-40)

Numeric constant. A constant that has a numeric value. (A-12)

Numeric variable. A variable that can assume only numeric values. (A-9, A-10)

Print zone. An output field where the output device may be directed when a comma is encountered in a PRINT statement. (A-50)

Program flowchart. A visual program design aid showing, step-by-step, how a computer program processes data. (A-29)

Programming language. A language used to write computer programs. (A-1)

Prompt. A message output by an interactive program explaining to the program user what input data are to be entered. (A-35)

Random number. An unpredictable number produced by chance. (A-80)

Scalar variable. A nonsubscripted variable. (A-67)

Selection. The control structure used to represent the decision operation. (A-9)

Sequence. The control structure used to represent operations that take place one after another. (A-9)

Simulation. The representation of a real-world process by a computer program. (A-81)

String constant. A constant that may be composed of any mix of characters from the BASIC character set. (A-12)

String variable. A variable that may assume any mix of characters from the BASIC character set as its values. (A-9, A-10)

Subroutine. A partial program, internal or external to a main program, that is invoked by some statement in the main program. (A-88)

Subscript. A quantity used to identify a position in an array. (A-61)

Syntax. The grammatical and structural rules of a programming language. (A-1, A-20)

Trailer value. A "dummy" value placed at the end of a data list to denote an end-of-data condition. (A-7)

Unconditional branch. An instruction that causes the computer to execute a specific statement other than the one that immediately follows in the normal sequence. (A-18)

User-defined function. A function created by a programmer with the DEF statement. (A-86)

Variable. A quantity that can assume any of a given set of data values. (A-4)

Word processing. The use of computer technology to create, manipulate, and print text material such as letters, documents, and manuscripts. (A-39)

Glossary

The terms shown in color were presented in the text as key terms. The boldfaced number in parentheses at the end of the definition of each of these terms indicates the page (or pages) on which it is boldfaced in the text. The terms shown in black are other commonly used and important words you will encounter in computer and data-processing discussions. The number in parentheses after the definition of each of these terms indicates the page on which it is first mentioned.

ABC. See Atanasoff-Berry Computer. (63)

Access mechanism. A mechanical device in the disk storage unit that positions the read/write heads on the proper tracks. (128)

Access motion time. The time taken by the access mechanism on a disk unit to move from one track position, or cylinder, to another when reading or writing data. (130)

Accumulator. A register that stores the result of an arithmetic or logical operation. (93)

Acoustic coupler. A special modem that converts electric signals to or from audible tones that can be transmitted over ordinary telephone wires. The device contains an acoustic cradle to receive a conventional telephone headset. (210)

Ada. A structured programming language developed by the Department of Defense and named after Ada Augusta Byron, the world's first programmer. (334)

An identifiable location in memory where data may be stored. Primary memory and devices such as the disk unit are addressable. (91)

Address register. A register containing the memory location of an instruction to be executed. (92)

Alphanumeric display terminal. A visual display device, containing a keyboard for input, that is designed primarily to display *text* material. Contrast with graphic display terminal. (162)

ALU. See Arithmetic/logic unit. (92)

American National Standards Institute (ANSI). An organization that acts as a national clearinghouse for standards in the United States. (72)

Analog computer. A computer that measures continuous phenomena—such as speed and height—and converts them into numbers. (91)

Analog transmission. The transmission of data as continuous wave patterns. (209)

Analysis. In program and systems development, the process of studying a problem area to determine what should be done. (264)

Analytical engine. A device conceived by Charles Babbage in the 1800s to perform computations. This machine is considered the forerunner to today's modern electronic computer. (60)

ANSI. See American National Standards Institute. (72)

APL. See A Programming Language. (317)

Applications programmer. A programmer who codes programs that do the useful work—such as payroll, inventory control, and accounting tasks—for end users of a computer system. Contrast with systems programmer. (485)

Applications software. Programs that do the useful work—such as payroll, inventory control, and accounting tasks—for end users of a computer system. Contrast with systems programs. (40, 261)

A Programming Language (APL). A highly compact programming language that is popular for problem-solving applications. (317)

Arithmetic/logic unit (ALU). The part of the computer that contains the circuitry to perform addition, subtraction, multiplication, division, and comparing operations. (92)

Artificial intelligence. The ability of a machine to perform actions that are characteristic of human intelligence, such as reasoning and learning. (110)

ASCII. An acronym for *American Standard Code for Information Interchange*. ASCII is a 7-bit code widely used to represent data for processing and communications. (102)

Assembler. A computer program that takes assembly-language instructions and converts them to machine language. **(252)**

Assembly language. A low-level programming language that uses mnemonic codes in place of the 0s and 1s of machine language. **(69, 318)**

Asynchronous transmission. The transmission of data over a line one character at a time. Each character is preceded by a "start bit" and followed by a "stop bit." Contrast with synchronous transmission. **(219)**

Atanasoff-Berry Computer (ABC). The world's first electronic digital computer, built in the early 1940s by Dr. John V. Atanasoff and his assistant, Clifford Berry. **(63)**

Audit trail. A means by which outputs can be traced back to the inputs that produced them. **(463)**

Automated office. An office that takes advantage of computer technology such as word processing, electronic mail, teleconferencing, and so forth. **(409)**

Auxiliary equipment. Equipment that works in a "standalone" mode, independent of CPU control. Some examples are keypunch machines, bursters, decollators, key-to-disk units, and key-to-tape units. **(31)**

Bar code. A machine-readable code consisting of sets of bars of varying widths. The codes are prominently displayed on the packaging of many retail goods and are commonly read with wand readers. **(183)**

BASIC. See Beginner's All-Purpose Symbolic Instruction Code. **(320)**

Batch processing. Processing transactions or other data in groups, at periodic times. **(397)**

Beginner's All-Purpose Symbolic Instruction Code (BASIC). An easy-to-learn high-level programming language developed at Dartmouth College in the 1960s. BASIC is widely used for instructional purposes and is the most popular language used on personal computers. **(320)**

Benchmark test. A test to measure computer system performance, under typical use conditions, prior to purchase. The test is analogous to the rigorous "test drive" you might make with a car prior to purchase. **(469)**

Binary. A number system with two possible states. The binary system is fundamental to computers because electronic devices often function in two possible states—for example, "on" or "off," "current present" or "current not present," "clockwise" or "counterclockwise," and so forth. **(97)**

Bit. A binary digit, such as 0 or 1. The 0 or 1 states are used by computer systems to take advantage of the binary nature of electronics. Bits are often assembled into bytes and words when manipulated or stored. **(97)**

Blocking. The combining of two or more records (into a "block") to conserve storage space and to increase processing efficiency. **(121)**

Blocking factor. The number of logical records per physical record on tape or disk. **(121)**

Buffer. A temporary storage area used to balance the speeds of two devices. For example, buffers are used within the computer unit to store physical records so that the logical records that comprise them may be processed faster. Buffers are also used in many terminals and data communications devices to store characters in large blocks before they are sent to another device. **(121)**

Bug. An error in a program or system. (276)

Burster. A device used to separate perforated, fan-fold paper into single sheets. **(176)**

Byte. A configuration of, say, 7 or 8 bits used to represent a single character of information. **(102)**

CAD. See Computer-aided design. **(412)**

CAD/CAM. An acronym for computer-aided design/computer-aided manufacturing. CAD/CAM is a general term applied to the use of computer technology to automate design and manufacturing operations in industry. **(412)**

CAI. See Computer-assisted instruction. (Window 6)

CAM. See Computer-aided manufacturing. **(412)**

Card reader. An input device that reads punched cards. **(178)**

Cassette tape. Magnetic tape, approximately ⅛-inch wide, that is housed in a small plastic cartridge. Cassette tape is read on a cassette tape unit. **(118)**

Cathode-ray tube (CRT). A peripheral device containing a televisionlike display screen and a keyboard. A CRT is commonly referred to as a display terminal. (157)

Central Processing Unit (CPU). The piece of hardware, also known as the "computer," that interprets and executes program instructions and communicates with input, output, and storage devices. (6)

Chief programmer team. A team of programmers, generally assigned to a large programming project, that is coordinated by a highly experienced person called the chief programmer. (275)

Coaxial cable. A transmission line developed for sending data and video images at high speeds. (203)

COBOL. See Common Business-Oriented Language. (317)

Coding. The writing of instructions in a programming language that will cause the computer system to perform a specific set of operations. (272)

COM. See Computer Output Microfilm. (188)

Common Business-Oriented Language (COBOL). A high-level programming language developed for business data-processing applications. (317)

Common carrier. A government-regulated private organization that provides communications services to the public. (211)

Communications medium. The intervening substance, such as a telephone wire or cable, that connects two physically distant hardware devices. (202)

Communications satellite. An earth-orbiting device that relays communications signals over long distances. (204)

Compiler. A computer program that translates a source program written by a user or programmer in a high-level programming language into machine language. The translation takes place all at once, before the translated program is executed. Contrast with interpreter. (250)

Computation. The act of calculating, that is, performing additions, multiplications, and so forth. (42)

Computer. See Central Processing Unit. (6, 26)

Computer-aided A general term applied to the use of computer technology to automate design functions in industry. (412)

Computer-aided manufacturing (CAM). A general term applied to the use of computer technology to automate manufacturing functions in industry. (412)

Computer-assisted instruction (CAI). The use of computers to supplement personalized teaching instruction by providing the student with sequences of instruction under program control. The progression through the instructional materials in such a system enables students to learn at their own rate. (Window 6)

Computer crime. The use of computers to commit unauthorized acts. (503)

Computer engineering. The field of knowledge that includes the design of computer hardware systems. Computer engineering is offered as a degree program in several colleges and universities. (492)

Computer operations. (1) The functions related to the physical operation of the computer system. (2) A curriculum offered in many schools that is oriented toward training students to enter the computer operations field. Computer operations curricula primarily train students to become computer or data-entry operators. (492)

Computer operations manager. The person who oversees the computer operations area in an organization. The computer operations manager is responsible for tasks such as hiring operations personnel and scheduling work that the system is to perform. (485)

Computer operator. A person skilled in the operation of the computer and its support devices. The operator is responsible for tasks such as mounting and dismounting tapes and disks, removing printouts from the line printer, and so forth. (484)

Computer Output Microfilm (COM). A term that refers to equipment and media that reduce computer output to microscopic form and put it on photosensitive film. (188)

Computer science. The field of knowledge that includes all technical aspects of the design and use of computers. Computer science is offered as a degree program in many institutions of higher learning. **(491)**

Computer-services company. A company that provides computer services to other organizations and individuals. These firms are often called *service bureaus.* (424)

Computer system. When you are buying a "computer system" in a store, the term generally refers to the equipment and programs you are being sold. When applied to a computer-based operation in an organization, it is commonly defined as all the equipment, programs, data, procedures, and personnel supporting that operation. **(5)**

Concentrator. A communications device that combines the features of controllers and multiplexers. Concentrators also have a store-and-forward capability enabling them to store messages from several low-speed devices before forwarding them—at high speeds—to another device. **(224)**

Conditional branch. An instruction that may cause the computer to execute an instruction other than the one that immediately follows in the program sequence, depending on the results of an operation, the contents of a storage location, and so forth. **(292)**

Connector symbol. A flowcharting symbol used to represent a junction to connect broken paths in a line of flow. **(290)**

Contention. A condition in a multipoint communications system in which two or more devices compete for use of a line. **(223)**

Controller. A device that supervises communications traffic in a teleprocessing environment, relieving the computer of a heavy processing burden. **(221)**

Control structure. A pattern for controlling the flow of logic in a computer program. The three basic control structures are sequence, selection (IF-THEN-ELSE), and looping (iteration). **(297)**

Control unit. The part of the CPU that coordinates the execution of program instructions. **(92)**

CPU. See Central Processing Unit. **(6)**

CRT. See Cathode-ray tube. **(157)**

Cursor. A highlighting symbol that appears on a video screen to indicate the position where the next character typed in will appear. **(158)**

Daisywheel printer. A serial printer with a solid-font printing mechanism consisting of a spoked wheel of embossed characters. Daisywheel printers are capable of producing letter-quality output. (167)

Data. A collection of unorganized facts that are not yet processed into information. **(8)**

Data access. Reading data from or writing data onto a device, either sequentially or directly. **(136)**

Database. An integrated collection of data stored on a direct-access storage device. **(349)**

Database administrator (DBA). The person or group of people in charge of designing, implementing, and managing the ongoing operation of a database. **(356)**

Database management system (DBMS). A software package designed to store an integrated collection of data and provide easy access to it. **(349)**

Data definition language (DDL). A language used by a database administrator to create, store, and manage data in a database environment. **(357)**

Data description. The process of defining data in a file or database so that users and programmers have easy access to them. **(356)**

Data dictionary. A facility which informs users and programmers about characteristics of data in a database or computer system. **(360)**

Data-entry operator. A member of a computer operations staff who is responsible for keying data into the computer system. **(483)**

Data flow diagram. A graphic systems analysis and design tool that enables a systems analyst to represent the flow of data through a system. **(447)**

Data management system (DMS). A software system that features a number of programs to automatically generate reports. (337)

Data manipulation. The process of using language commands to add, delete, modify, or retrieve data in a file or database. **(358)**

Data manipulation language (DML). A language used by programmers to supplement some high-level language supported in a database environment. **(358)**

Data movement time. The time taken to transfer data to or from disk once the read/write head is properly positioned on a disk track. **(130)**

Data organization. The process of establishing a data file so that it may subsequently be accessed in some desired way. Three common methods of organizing data are sequential organization, indexed-sequential organization, and relative organization. **(136)**

Data preparation device. An auxiliary device used to prepare data in machine-readable form. Some examples of data-preparation devices are keypunch machines, key-to-tape units, and key-to-disk units. **(33)**

Data processing. Operations performed on data to provide useful information to users. **(8)**

Data processing director. The person in charge of developing and/or implementing the overall plan for data processing in an organization and for overseeing the activities of programmers, systems analysts, and operations personnel. **(487)**

Data processing/information systems curriculum. A course of study, normally offered by a business school, that prepares students for entry-level jobs as applications programmers or systems analysts. **(490)**

Data structure. The relationship between data items. **(361)**

DBA. See Database administrator. **(356)**

DBMS. See Database management system. **(349)**

DDL. See Data definition language. **(357)**

DDP. See Distributed Data Processing. **(414)**

Debugging. The process of detecting and correcting errors in computer programs or in the computer system itself. **(276)**

Decision-support system (DSS). A system designed to provide information to managers to enable them to make decisions. Many decision-support systems use interactive terminals and enable managers to creatively define their own information needs when using the system. **(409)**

Decision symbol. A diamond-shaped flowcharting symbol that is used to represent a choice in the processing path. **(289)**

Decision table. A table showing all the circumstances to be considered in a problem as well as the outcomes from any given set of circumstances. **(308)**

Decollator. A device that automatically removes carbon interleaves from continuous, fan-fold paper. **(176)**

Default. The assumption made by a computer program when no specific choice is indicated by the user or programmer. **(239)**

Design. The process of planning a program or system. Design is normally undertaken after a problem has been thoroughly analyzed and a set of specifications for the solution has been established. **(267)**

Desk check. A manual checking process whereby a programmer or user scans a program listing for possible errors before submitting a machine-readable version of the program to the computer for execution. (276)

Device media control language (DMCL). A language used by the database administrator to create the physical description of a database on a direct-access storage device. **(357)**

Diagnostic. A message sent to the user by the computer system pinpointing errors in syntax or logic. Diagnostics are often referred to as *error messages.* (276)

Difference engine. A mechanical machine devised by Charles Babbage in the 1800s to automatically perform computations and print their results. A large version of the machine was never built because the manufacturing technology of the day was not advanced enough to produce the parts he needed. **(58)**

Digital computer. A computer that counts discrete phenomena, such as people and dollars. Virtually all computers that are used in businesses or in the home for personal computing are digital computers. (91)

Digital transmission. The transmission of data as discrete impulses. **(209)**

Digitizer. An input device that normally consists of a flat tablet that the operator traces over with a pen-like stylus or another cursor device. The patterns traced by the operator are automatically entered into the computer system's memory for subsequent processing. **(190)**

Direct access. Reading or writing data in storage in such a way that the access time involved is relatively independent of the location of the data. **(137)**

Disk access time. The time taken to locate and read (or position and write) data on a disk device. **(130)**

Disk address. An identifiable location on disk where data may be stored. **(130)**

Disk cylinder. All tracks on a disk pack that are accessible with a single movement of the access mechanism. **(129)**

Disk drive. A mechanism within the disk storage unit on which disk packs or diskettes are placed to be accessed. (133)

Diskette. See Floppy disk. (132)

Disk pack. A group of tiered hard disks that are mounted on a shaft and treated as a unit. A disk pack must be placed on a disk storage unit to be accessed. **(126)**

Disk storage unit. A direct-access secondary memory device on which disk packs, sealed disk modules, or floppy disks are mounted. Also called a *disk unit*. **(126)**

Display terminal. A peripheral device, commonly referred to as a CRT, containing a televisionlike screen and a keyboard. Also see alphanumeric display terminal, graphic display terminal, dumb terminal, smart terminal, and user-programmable terminal. **(157)**

Distributed Data Processing (DDP). A system configuration in which a single application or related applications are accommodated on two or more geographically dispersed computers. **(414)**

Distributed ring network. A DDP configuration consisting of physically distant machines that are hooked up serially to one another. **(416)**

Distributed star network. A DDP configuration consisting of physically distant machines that are directly connected to a single, common machine. **(415)**

DMCL. See Device media control language. **(357)**

DML. See Data manipulation language. **(358)**

Documentation. A detailed written description of a program, procedure, or system. **(279)**

Dot-matrix mechanism. The printing element of a dot-matrix printer, which outputs characters as a series of closely packed dots. Contrast with solid-font mechanism. **(170)**

DOUNTIL control structure. A looping control structure in which the looping continues as long as a certain condition is false ("do until true"). **(297)**

DOWHILE control structure. A looping control structure in which the looping continues as long as a certain condition is true ("do while true"). **(297)**

Drum plotter. An output device that draws on paper that is rolled along a cylindrically shaped drum. **(189)**

DSS. See Decision-support system. **(409)**

Dumb terminal. A terminal that is capable of only the simplest types of input and output operations. Such terminals, although inexpensive, contain few operator conveniences. **(158)**

A printout of the entire or partial contents of the main memory. **(108)**

E-cycle. The part of the machine cycle in which data are located, an instruction is executed, and the results stored. **(94)**

EBCDIC. An acronym for *Extended Binary-Coded Decimal Interchange Code*. EBCDIC uses an 8-bit byte and can be used to represent up to 256 characters. **(102)**

EDSAC. An acronym for *Electronic Delay Storage Automatic Calculator*. EDSAC was the world's first stored-program computer and was completed in England in 1949. **(66)**

Education Privacy Act. A federal law that protects an individual's right to privacy in both private and public schools receiving any federal funding. **(514)**

EDVAC. An acronym for *Electronic Discrete Variable Automatic Calculator*. Completed in 1950, EDVAC was the first stored-program computer built in the United States. **(66)**

EEPROM. See Electrically erasable programmable read-only memory. (112)

EFT. See Electronic funds transfer. (515)

Electrically erasable programmable read-only memory (EEPROM). An EPROM module capable of having its contents altered while plugged into a peripheral device. (112)

Electromechanical machine. A device that has both electrical and mechanical features. **(61)**

Electronic funds transfer (EFT). Pertaining to systems that transfer funds "by computer" from one account to another, without the use of written checks. (515)

Electronic machine. A device that functions according to electronic principles. (**63**)

Electronic mail. A software facility that enables users to send letters, memos, documents, and the like from one computer terminal to another. (411)

Electronic worksheet. A user-friendly software package enabling operators to quickly create tables and financial schedules by entering numbers, values, or formulas into cells on a display-screen grid. (**338**)

Encryption. The process of encoding data or programs to disguise them from unauthorized personnel. (462)

ENIAC. An acronym for *Electronic Numerical Integrator and Calculator*. Unveiled in 1946, ENIAC was the world's first large-scale, general-purpose computer. (**64**)

EPROM. See Erasable programmable read-only memory. (**112**)

Erasable programmable read-only memory (EPROM). A software-in-hardware module that can be programmed and reprogrammed under certain limited conditions, yet cannot be casually erased by users or programmers. (**112**)

External memory. See Secondary memory. (**10**)

Facsimile machine. A device that can transmit the images of pictures, maps, diagrams, and so forth. (517)

Fair Credit Reporting Act. A federal law (1970) designed to prevent private organizations from unfairly denying credit to individuals. (**514**)

Fiber optics. Fiber optic transmission technology employs cables composed of thousands of hair-thin transparent fibers along which data is passed from lasers as light waves. (**203**)

Field. A collection of related characters. (**38**)

File. A collection of related records. (**38**)

File-protection ring. A plastic ring that must be mounted at the center of a tape reel for data to be written onto the tape. (**124**)

Firmware. Software instructions that are written onto a hardware module. (**112**)

First generation. The first era of commercial computers, from 1951 to 1958, which was characterized by vacuum tubes as the main logic element. (**67**)

Fixed-length word approach. A storage approach in which more than a single character of data can occupy a single address. Each address holds a word of a fixed number of characters. Contrast with variable-length word. (**106**)

Flatbed plotter. An output device that draws on paper which is mounted on a flat drafting table. (**189**)

Floppy disk. A small disk made of a tough, flexible plastic and coated with a substance that can be magnetized. Floppy disks are popular in small computer systems and are most commonly found in two sizes (diameters): 5¼ inches and 8 inches. (**124**)

Flowline. A flowcharting symbol used to represent the connecting path between flowchart symbols. (**289**)

FORmula TRANslator (FORTRAN). A high-level programming language used for mathematical, scientific, and engineering applications. (**327**)

FORTRAN. See FORmula TRANslator. (**327**)

Fourth generation. The fourth era of commercial computing, from 1971 to the present, which is characterized by microminiaturization and the rise of the personal computer. (**78**)

Freedom of Information Act. The federal law (1970) providing individuals with the right to inspect data about them stored by the federal government. (**514**)

Front-end processor. A computer located at the front end of the main computer that relieves the main computer of certain computational chores. Such a device is often found in communications environments where it receives inputs from remote devices and processes some inputs itself and sends others (possibly partially processed) on to the main computer. (**226**)

Full-duplex transmission. Any type of transmission in which messages may be sent in two directions, simultaneously, along a communications path. (**208**)

Function key. A key on a display terminal that

executes a preprogrammed routine when depressed. **(159)**

Gantt chart. A bar chart used to represent scheduled deadlines, project milestones, and the duration of project activities. **(469)**

General-purpose computer. A computer capable of being programmed to solve a wide range of problems. (63)

Graphic display terminal. A visual display device, containing a keyboard, which is designed primarily to display *graphic* material. Contrast with alphanumeric display terminal. **(162)**

Half-duplex transmission. Any type of transmission in which messages may be sent in two directions—but only one way at a time—along a communications path. **(208)**

Hard copy. A printed copy of machine output—for example, reports and program listings. **(167)**

Hard disk. A rigid metal platter commonly 14 inches in diameter and coated on both sides with a magnetizable substance such as ferrous oxide. **(124)**

Hardware. Physical equipment in a computing environment, such as the computer and its support devices. **(11)**

Hashing. A key-to-disk mathematical transformation where the key field on each record determines where the record is stored. **(145)**

Heuristic. An intuitively appealing "rule of thumb" that is often used as part of a trial-and-error process to find a workable solution to a problem. (110)

Hexadecimal. Pertaining to the number system with sixteen possible states: 0, 1, 2, 3, 4, 5, 6, 7, 8, 9, A, B, C, D, E, and F. **(108)**

Hierarchical data structure. A data structure in which the relationship among data records is always one-to-many and in which "children" can have only one "parent." **(361)**

Hierarchy plus Input-Process-Output (HIPO) method. A set of diagrams and procedures used to describe program functions from a general to a detailed level. **(305)**

High-level language. See High-level programming language. **(72)**

High-level programming language. The class of programming languages used by most professional programmers to solve a wide range of problems. Some examples are BASIC, COBOL, FORTRAN, and Pascal. **(72)**

High-speed printer. A line or page printer that produces printed output at a rate of 300 lines or more per minute. **(175)**

HIPO method. See Hierarchy plus Input-Process-Output method. **(305)**

Host language. A programming language available for use on a specific computer system or subsystem. **(359)**

I-cycle. The part of the machine cycle in which the control unit fetches an instruction from main memory and prepares it for subsequent processing. **(94)**

IC. See Integrated circuit. **(74)**

IF-THEN-ELSE (selection) control structure. See Selection control structure. **(292)**

Impact printing. The formation of characters by causing a metal hammer to strike a ribbon into paper or paper into a ribbon. Contrast with nonimpact printing. **(167)**

Implementation. The phase of systems development that encompasses activities related to making the computer system operational and successful once it is delivered by the vendor. **(469)**

Indexed-sequential organization. A method of organizing data on a direct-access medium in such a way that it can be accessed directly (through an index) or sequentially. **(142)**

Information. Data that have been processed. **(8)**

Initialize. To preset a variable to a prespecified value before using it in computations. **(292)**

Input. Anything supplied to a process or involved with the beginning of a process. For example, data must be input to a computer system. Or, data must be keyed in to the system on an input device. Contrast with output. **(5)**

Input device. A machine used to supply data to the computer. Contrast with output device. **(5, 27, 156)**

Input/output (I/O) media. Objects used to hold data or information being input or output. Examples include punched cards, magnetic disk and tape, and paper. **(5, 31)**

Input/output symbol. A parallelogram-shaped flowcharting symbol used to represent an input or output operation. **(290)**

Instruction register. The register that holds the part of the instruction indicating what the computer is to do next. **(92)**

Integrated circuit (IC). A series of complex circuits that are etched on a small silicon chip. **(74)**

Interblock gap. The distance on magnetic tape or disk between the end of one physical record and the start of another. **(121)**

Internal header label. An identifying label appearing at the beginning of a tape reel. **(124)**

Internal memory. See Primary memory. **(10)**

Internal storage. See Primary memory. **(90)**

Interpreter. A computer program that translates a source program written by a user or programmer in a high-level language into machine language. The translation takes place on a line-by-line basis as each statement is executed. Contrast with compiler. **(252)**

Interrecord gap. See Interblock gap. **(121)**

I/O media. See Input/output media. **(5, 31)**

Iteration control structure. See Looping control structure. **(297)**

JCL. See Job-control language. **(239)**

Job-control language (JCL). A programming language used to invoke operating system routines. **(239)**

Job-control program. The systems program that decodes job-control language statements. **(239)**

KB. See Kilobyte. **(105)**

Key field. A field that is used to identify a record. **(120)**

Keypunch machine. An auxiliary device that uses a keyboard unit to place data directly on punched cards. **(177)**

Key-to-disk unit. An auxiliary device that uses a keyboard unit to place data directly on magnetic disk. **(131)**

Key-to-tape unit. An auxiliary device that uses a keyboard unit to place data directly on magnetic tape. **(123)**

Kilobyte (KB). Approximately 1000 (1024 to be exact) bytes. Primary memory on smaller computer systems is often measured in kilobytes. **(105)**

Language translator. A system program that converts an applications program into machine language. **(250)**

The process of placing a large number of integrated circuits (usually over 100) on a single silicon chip. (79)

Leased line. See Private line. **(212)**

Light pen. An electrical device, resembling an ordinary pen, that can be used to enter input on a display screen. (162)

Line printer. A high-speed printer that produces output a line at a time. **(175)**

Linkage editor. A system program that binds together related object module program segments so that they may be run as a unit. **(251)**

Load module. A complete machine-language program that is ready to be executed by the computer. **(251)**

Local network. A privately run communications network of several machines located within a mile or so of each other. **(214)**

Logical (conceptual) data description. The description of data from the point of view of users or programmers. Contrast with physical data description. **(356)**

Logical design level. The level of systems design that addresses fundamental design considerations, without any reference to hardware. Contrast with physical design level. **(458)**

Logical record. A data record from the point of view of a user or programmer. **(121)**

Logic element. The electronic component used to facilitate circuit functions within the computer. (66)

Looping (iteration) control structure. The control structure used to represent a looping operation. Also see DOUNTIL control structure and DOWHILE control structure. **(297)**

Low-level language. A highly detailed, machine-dependent programming language. Included in the class of low-level languages are machine language and assembly language. **(317)**

Low-speed printer. A small printer designed to output characters serially, at speeds from about 10 to 300 characters per second. **(172)**

LSI. See Large-scale integration. (79)

Machine cycle. The series of operations involved in the execution of a single machine-language instruction. **(94)**

Machine language. A binary-based programming language that can be executed directly by the computer. **(69, 106)**

Machine-readable. Any form in which data are encoded so that they can be read by a machine. **(5)**

Magnetic bubble storage. A memory that uses magnetic bubbles to indicate the "0" and "1" bit states. **(148)**

Magnetic core. A tiny, ring-shaped piece of magnetizable material capable of storing a single binary digit. Magnetic cores were popular as internal memories in second- and third-generation computers, but they have given way to semiconductor storage devices in the fourth generation. **(71)**

Magnetic disk. A secondary storage medium consisting of platters made of rigid metal (hard disk) or flexible plastic (floppy disk). **(124)**

Magnetic Ink Character Recognition (MICR). A technology confined almost exclusively to the banking industry, MICR involves the processing of checks inscribed with special characters set in a special magnetic ink. **(184)**

Magnetic tape. A plastic tape with a magnetic surface for storing data as a series of magnetic spots. **(118)**

Mainframe. A large computer capable of supporting powerful peripheral devices. **(20)**

Main memory. See Primary memory. **(90)**

Maintenance programmer. A programmer involved with keeping an organization's existing programs in proper working order. **(262)**

Management information system (MIS). A system designed to provide information to managers to enable them to make decisions. **(407)**

Mark I. Completed in 1944 by Howard Aiken of Harvard University, the Mark I was the first large-scale electromechanical computer. **(62)**

Mass storage unit. A storage device capable of storing billions of bytes of data online. **(147)**

Master file. A file containing relatively permanent information, such as customer names and addresses. The file is usually updated periodically. (142)

MB. See Megabyte. **(105)**

Mechanical calculating machine. A computer that works by means of gears and levers rather than by means of electric power. **(56)**

Megabyte (MB). Approximately one million bytes. The secondary storage capacity of many computers is measured in megabytes. **(105)**

Menu. A set of options provided at the terminal from which the operator is to make a selection. (163)

MICR. See Magnetic Ink Character Recognition. **(184)**

Microcomputer. The smallest and least expensive type of computer. **(20, 373)**

Microfiche. A sheet of film, often 4 by 6 inches, on which the images of computer output are stored. (188)

Microminiaturization. A term implying a very small size. **(79)**

Microprocessor. A CPU on a silicon chip. **(373)**

Microsecond. One millionth of a second. **(96)**

Microwave. An electromagnetic wave in the high-frequency range. **(204)**

Millisecond. One thousandth of a second. **(96)**

Minicomputer. An intermediate-sized and medium-priced type of computer. **(20)**

MIS. See Management information system. **(407)**

Modem. A contraction of the words *Mo*dulation and *dem*odulation. A communications device enabling computers and their support devices to communicate over ordinary telephone lines. **(209)**

Module. A related group of entities that may be treated effectively as a unit. **(297)**

Monitor. (1) A video display. **(378)** (2) The supervisor program of an operating system. **(238)**

Mouse. A device used to rapidly move a cursor around a CRT screen. (165)

Multidrop line. A communications configuration that uses a single line to service several terminals. **(221)**

Multiplexer. A communications device that interleaves the messages of several low-speed devices and sends them along a single, high-speed transmission path. **(223)**

Multiprocessing. The *simultaneous* execution of two or more program sequences by multiple computers operating under common control. **(249)**

Multiprogramming. The execution of two or more programs *concurrently* on the same computer. **(243)**

Multistar network. A communications network consisting of multiple distributed-star configurations. **(417)**

Nanosecond. One billionth of a second. **(96)**

Narrowband transmission. Low-speed transmission, characterized by telegraph transmission. **(208)**

Network. A system of machines that communicate with one another. (197)

Nonimpact printing. The formation of characters on a surface by means of heat, lasers, photography, or ink jets. Contrast with impact printing. **(170)**

Nonprocedural language. A very-high-level, problem-dependent programming language that informs the computer system *what* work is to be done rather than *how* to do the work. Contrast with procedural language. **(318)**

Nonvolatile storage. Storage that retains its contents when the power is shut off. (375)

Object module. The machine-language program that is the output from a language translator. Also called *object program.* **(250)**

OCR. See Optical character recognition. **(180)**

OEM. See Original Equipment Manufacturer. (423)

Office of the future. See Automated office. **(409)**

Offline. Anything not under direct control of the CPU. **(34)**

Offpage connector symbol. A flowchart symbol used to logically connect flowchart symbols from page to page. **(294)**

Online. Anything under direct control of the CPU. **(34)**

Online processing. Processing data interactively on a computer system. **(397)**

Operating system. A collection of systems software that enables the computer system to manage the resources under its control. **(76, 237)**

Optical character recognition (OCR). An information processing technology that takes machine-readable marks, characters, or codes and converts them into a form suitable for computer processing. **(180)**

Optical disk. A disk that is read by optical rather than magnetic means. **(149)**

A company that buys hardware from manufacturers and integrates it into its own systems. **(423)**

Output. Anything resulting from a process or involved with the end result of a process. For example, processed data is output as information. Or, information may be printed using an output device. Contrast with input. **(5)**

Output device. A machine used to output computer-processed data, or information. **(5, 27, 157)**

Page printer. A high-speed printer that delivers output one page at a time. **(176)**

Paging. A technique for dividing programs into fixed-length blocks or pages. **(246)**

Parallel transmission. Data transmission in which each bit in a byte has its own path. All of the bits in a byte are transmitted simultaneously. Contrast with serial transmission. **(218)**

Parity bit. An extra bit added to the byte representation of a character to ensure that there is always either an odd or even number of "1" bits transmitted with every character. **(103)**

Pascal. A structured high-level programming language that is increasingly being used for scientific, engineering, and even business applications. **(331)**

Pascaline. A mechanical calculating machine developed by Blaise Pascal in the 1600s. **(56)**

Peripheral equipment. The input and output devices and secondary storage units in a computer system. **(31)**

Personal computer. A microcomputer used for personal tasks. **(20, 373)**

Physical data description. The description of the way data are stored on a secondary storage device. Contrast with logical data description. **(356)**

Physical design level. The level of systems design that addresses fundamental design considerations, with specific reference to hardware. Contrast with logical design level. **(458)**

Physical record. A block of logical records. **(121)**

Plotter. An output device used for drawing graphs and diagrams. **(189)**

PL/1. See Programming Language/1. **(317)**

Point-of-Sale (POS) System. A computer system, commonly found in department stores and supermarkets, that uses electronic cash register terminals to monitor and record sales transactions, to check the validity of credit cards, and to perform other data-handling functions. **(182)**

Point-to-point configuration. A communications configuration in which there is a direct line from each machine to every machine that is served by it. **(221)**

Polling. In data communications, a line control method in which a computer or controller asks one terminal after another if it has any data to send. **(223)**

Port. A location on the computer through which a peripheral device may communicate. (216)

POS System. See Point-of-Sale System. **(182)**

Precompiler. A computer program that translates an extended set of commands available with a programming language to standard commands of the language. (359)

Preliminary investigation. In systems development, a brief study of a problem area to assess whether or not a full-scale systems project should be undertaken. **(438)**

Primary memory. Also known as main memory, internal storage, and primary storage, this section of the CPU temporarily holds data and program instructions awaiting processing, intermediate results, and output produced from processing. **(10, 90)**

Printer. A device that delivers computer output to paper. **(167)**

Printer spacing chart. A program and system design aid consisting of a grid representing all print positions on a page. The systems analyst places characters in the grid corresponding to the page positions at which these characters will appear on output. **(460)**

Privacy. In a data-processing context, a term referring to how information about individuals is used and by whom. **(511)**

Privacy Act. A federal law (1974) designed to protect the public against abuses by the federal government. **(514)**

Private line. A line that provides a dedicated connection between two points in a communications network. **(212)**

Procedural language. A high-level programming language designed to solve a wide class of problems. Procedural languages work by having the programmer code a set of procedures which tell the computer, step by step, how to solve a problem. Contrast with nonprocedural language. **(318)**

Processing. See Data processing. **(5)**

Processing symbol. A rectangular-shaped flowcharting symbol used to indicate a processing operation such as a computation. **(289)**

Program. A set of instructions that causes the computer system to perform specific actions. **(8)**

Program design aid. A tool—such as a flowchart, pseudocode, or structure chart—that helps the systems analyst plan how a program is to work. **(288)**

Program development cycle. All the steps an organization must go through to bring a computer program into operation. The steps of the program development cycle include analysis, design, coding, debugging, and documentation. **(263)**

Program flowchart. A visual design aid showing, step by step, how a computer program will process data. Contrast with system flowchart. **(288)**

Programmable read-only memory (PROM). A software-in-hardware module that can be programmed under certain restricted conditions and, once programmed, cannot be altered or erased. **(112)**

Programmer. A person whose job it is to write, maintain, and test computer programs. **(12, 263)**

Programming language. A language used to write computer programs. **(10)**

Programming Language/1 (PL/1). A structured, general-purpose, high-level language that can be used for scientific, engineering, and business applications. **(331)**

PROM. See Programmable read-only memory. **(112)**

Protocol. A set of conventions used by machines to establish communication with each other in a teleprocessing environment. **(220)**

Pseudocode. A technique for structured program design that uses English-like statements to outline the logic of a program. Pseudocode statements closely resemble actual programming code. **(302)**

Punched card. A cardboard card used with computer systems in which small punched holes are used to represent letters, digits, or special characters. **(177)**

Query processing. Processing that involves

requesting information through an online terminal. **(48)**

Query/update facility. A user-friendly language that enables users to add, delete, modify, or retrieve data from computer files or databases. **(358)**

Queue. A group of items awaiting computer processing. (245)

RAM. See Random Access Memory. **(110, 375)**

Random access. See Direct access. **(137)**

Random Access Memory (RAM). Any memory capable of being accessed directly. In the world of personal computers, the acronym RAM generally applies only to primary memory. **(110, 375)**

Read-only memory (ROM). A software-in-hardware module that can be read but not written upon. **(112, 375)**

Read/write head. A magnetic head on a disk access mechanism or tape unit that reads or writes data. **(119)**

Real-time processing. A type of online processing in which the computer system can receive and process data quickly enough to produce outputs that can affect the outcome of an ongoing physical process or activity. **(398)**

Record. A collection of related fields. **(38)**

Record layout form. A form used in program or system design that shows the arrangement and structure of data in a record. **(460)**

Register. A high-speed staging area within the computer that temporarily stores data during processing. **(92)**

Relational data structure. A data structure in which the relationships among data are represented in interrelated tables. **(363)**

Relative organization. A method of organizing data on a direct-access medium that uses a key-to-address (hashing) transformation procedure. **(145)**

Report generator. A very-high-level programming language used specifically to produce business reports. **(334)**

Report Program Generator (RPG). A report-generator language popular with small businesses. **(335)**

Request for Quotation (RFQ). A document containing a list of technical specifications for hardware, software, and services that an organization wishes to acquire. The RFQ is submitted to vendors, who subsequently prepare a bid

based on the resources they are able to supply. **(465)**

Response time. The time it takes the computer system to respond to a specific input. (266)

RFQ. See Request for Quotation. **(465)**

Robotics. The field devoted to the study of robot technology. **(413)**

ROM. See Read-only memory. **(112, 375)**

Rotational delay. In disk processing, the time it takes for the read/write heads to be aligned over the proper position on a track once the access mechanism has reached the track. **(130)**

RPG. See Report Program Generator. **(335)**

Schema. In many database systems a logical description of the entire database is called a schema. **(357)**

Secondary memory. Memory provided by technologies such as tape, disk, or mass storage, that supplements primary memory. **(10)**

Secondary storage device. A machine—such as a tape unit, disk unit, or mass storage device—capable of providing storage to supplement primary memory. **(27)**

Second generation. The second era of commercial computers, from 1959 to 1964, which was characterized by transistor circuitry. **(69)**

Segmentation. A technique for dividing programs into logical, variable-length blocks. **(248)**

Selection. The process of going through a set of data and picking out only those data elements that meet certain criteria. (42)

Selection (IF-THEN-ELSE) control structure. The control structure used to represent a decision operation. **(297)**

Semiconductor memory. A memory whose components are etched onto small silicon chips. **(80)**

Sequence control structure. The control structure used to represent operations that take place one after another. **(297)**

Sequential access. Reading or writing data in storage in a serial fashion. **(137)**

Sequential organization. A method of organizing data on a medium in such a way that access can only be achieved in a serial fashion. **(140)**

Serial access. See Sequential access. (110)

Serial printer. A low-speed printer that outputs one character at a time. **(172)**

Serial transmission. Data transmission in

which every bit in a byte must travel down the same path, one after the other. Contrast with parallel transmission. **(218)**

Simple network data structure. A data structure in which the relationship among data records is one-to-many and "children" can have more than one "parent." **(363)**

Simplex transmission. Any type of transmission in which a message can be sent along a path in only a single prespecified direction. **(208)**

Smart terminal. A display terminal containing sophisticated editing and formatting features designed to expedite input and output. **(158)**

Softkey. See Function key. **(159)**

Software. Although generally synonymous with computer programs, the term software also includes the manuals that assist people in working with computer systems. **(12)**

Solid-font mechanism. The printing element on a printer which produces solid characters, such as a daisywheel printer. Contrast with dot-matrix mechanism. **(167)**

Sorting. The process of arranging data in a specified order. **(46)**

Source-data automation. A term that refers to making data available in machine-readable form at the time they are collected. **(180)**

Source module. The original form in which a program is entered into an input device by a user or programmer, prior to being translated into machine language. Also called *source program*. **(250)**

Spooling. The process of temporarily staging input or output in secondary memory to expedite processing. **(245)**

Start/stop symbol. A flowcharting symbol used to begin and terminate a flowchart. **(289)**

Storage register. A register that temporarily stores data that have been retrieved from primary memory prior to processing. **(93)**

Stored-program computer. Any computer that contains a storage area for programs and data. **(66)**

Structure chart. A program design aid that shows the hierarchical relationship between program modules. It looks very similar to the common organization chart. **(304)**

Structured program design. See Structured programming. **(268, 296)**

Structured program flowchart. A flowchart embodying many of the principles of structured programming. **(301)**

Structured programming. An approach to program design that uses a restricted set of program control structures, the principles of top-down design, and numerous other design methodologies. **(268, 296)**

Structured walkthrough. A formal program development practice in which the work of a systems analyst or programmer is constructively reviewed by peers. **(275)**

Subschema. In many database systems, a logical description of a portion of the database is called a subschema. **(357)**

Summarizing. The process of reducing a mass of data to a manageable form. **(42)**

Supercomputer. The fastest type of mainframe computer. Typically, supercomputers are found in engineering or scientific research environments rather than in business data-processing shops. **(21)**

Supervisor. The central program in an operating system. The supervisor has the ability to invoke other operating system programs to perform various system tasks. **(238)**

Support equipment. All the machines that make it possible to get data and programs into the CPU, get processed information out, and store data and programs for ready access to the CPU. **(5, 26)**

Switched line. A communications line that feeds into a switching center, enabling it to reach virtually any destination in the network by means of a telephone number. **(212)**

Synchronous transmission. The transmission of data over a line a block of characters at a time. Contrast with asynchronous transmission. **(219)**

System. A collection of elements and procedures that interact to accomplish a goal. **(431)**

System acquisition. The phase of the systems development process in which equipment, software, or services are acquired from vendors. **(465)**

System design. The phase of the systems development process that formally establishes the parts of a new system and the relationship between these parts. **(456)**

System flowchart. A systems development aid

that shows how the physical parts of a system relate to one another. Contrast with program flowchart. **(448)**

System librarian. The person in the computer operations area who is responsible for managing data files and programs stored offline on cards, tapes, disks, microfilm, and other types of storage media. **(484)**

Systems analysis. The phase of the systems development process in which a problem area is thoroughly examined to determine what should be done. **(443)**

Systems analyst. A person who studies systems in an organization in order to determine what actions need to be taken and how these actions may best be achieved with computer resources. **(262, 436, 486)**

Systems development. The process of studying a problem area in an existing system, designing a solution, acquiring the resources necessary to support the solution, and implementing the solution. **(432)**

Systems programmer. A programmer who codes systems software. Contrast with applications programmer. **(485)**

Systems software. Computer programs—such as the operating system, language translators, and utility programs—that do background tasks for users and programmers. Contrast with applications software. **(40, 236)**

Tape unit. A secondary storage device on which magnetic tapes are mounted. **(119)**

Tariff. A list of proposed services and rates that a common carrier must file with the appropriate regulatory agency in order to be granted a license to service the public. **(212)**

Telecommuting. The substitution of teleprocessing at home for the commute to work. (518)

Teleconference. A conference that is held by people at different sites who, often, can see each other on video terminals. (411)

Teleprinter. A low-speed printer containing a keyboard. **(174)**

Teleprocessing. When two or more machines in a computer system are transmitting data over a long distance *and* data are being processed somewhere in the system, teleprocessing is taking place. **(198)**

Terrestrial microwave station. A ground station that receives microwave signals, amplifies them, and passes them on. **(204)**

Third generation. The third era of commercial computers, from 1965 to 1970, which was characterized by integrated circuit technology. **(76)**

Time-shared processing. A type of online processing in which the computer facility is shared by several users for different purposes at, more or less, the same time. The computer system interleaves the processing of the programs so it appears to each user that he or she has exclusive use of the computer. **(244, 397)**

Time-sharing. See Time-shared processing. **(244)**

Top-down design. A structured design tool that subdivides a program or system into well-defined modules, organized in a hierarchy, which are developed from the top of the hierarchy down to the lowest level. **(297)**

Track. A path on an input/output medium on which data is recorded. **(119)**

Transaction file. A file of occurrences—such as customer payments and purchases—that have taken place over a period of time. (142)

Transistor. A circuit device that dominated second-generation computers. **(69)**

True binary representation. A method for representing numerical values as a string of binary bits. **(101)**

Turnkey vendor. A company that sells "fully tested," complete computer systems to other firms. Typically the systems feature the hardware offerings of several vendors and are so easy to use that the acquiring firms presumably need only to "turn the key" to make the systems operational. (423)

Twisted wire. A communications medium that consists of pairs of wires, twisted together, and bound into a cable. The telephone system consists mainly of twisted-wire cabling. **(202)**

Unconditional branch. An instruction that causes the computer to execute a specific statement other than the one that immediately follows in the normal sequence. **(292)**

UNIVAC I. The first commercial electronic digital computer. **(67)**

Universal Product Code (UPC). The bar code that is prominently displayed on the packaging of almost all supermarket goods, identifying the product and manufacturer. A variety of optical scanning devices may be used to read the codes. **(183)**

UPC. See Universal Product Code. **(183)**

Updating. The process of bringing something up to date by making corrections, adding new data, and so forth. **(46)**

Upward compatible. A computer system that can do everything that a smaller model in the line or the previous model can do, plus some additional tasks. (73)

User. A person needing the services of a computer system. **(12)**

User-friendly. A computer program or system that is easy for noncomputer people to learn and/or use. **(385)**

User-programmable terminal. A display terminal containing sophisticated editing and formatting features as well as processing capabilities and (possibly) its own support devices. **(160)**

Utility program. A program used to perform some frequently encountered operation in a computer system. **(254)**

Vacuum tube. A circuit device that dominated first-generation computers. **(67)**

Value-added network (VAN). A network operated by a company that leases the facilities of a common carrier in order to offer additional services using those facilities. **(213)**

VAN. See Value-added network. **(213)**

Variable-length word approach. A storage approach in which a single character of data occupies a single address. Contrast with fixed-length word. **(106)**

Vendor rating system. An objective point-scoring procedure for evaluating competing vendors of computer products or services. **(468)**

Verifier. A device used to detect keypunching errors by rekeying data. **(179)**

Very-high-level language. A problem-specific language that is generally much easier to learn and use than conventional high-level languages such as BASIC, FORTRAN, COBOL, and Pascal. **(318)**

The process of placing a very large number of integrated circuits (usually over 1000) on a single silicon chip. **(79)**

Vice president of information systems. The person in an organization who oversees routine data processing and information systems activities as well as other computer-related areas. **(487)**

Virtual storage. A special fast-access area on disk where programs are "cut up" into manageable pieces and staged as they are processed. While the computer is processing a program, it fetches the pieces of it that are needed from virtual storage and places them into main memory. **(246)**

See Very-large-scale integration. **(79)**

Voice-grade transmission. Medium-speed transmission characterized by the rates of speed available over ordinary telephone lines. **(208)**

Voice-input device. A device capable of recognizing the human voice. **(187)**

Voice-output device. A device enabling the computer system to deliver output by the spoken word. **(191)**

Volatile storage. Storage that loses its contents when the power is shut off. (80)

Wideband transmission. High-speed transmission characterized by the rates of speed available over coaxial cable, fiber optic cable, and microwave. **(208)**

Winchester disk. A sealed data module that contains a disk, access arms, and read/write heads. **(135)**

Windowing. The process enabling a user to view portions of a large grid at a terminal screen. The user can move the grid around the screen so that the screen acts as a "window" to portions of the grid. (162)

Word. A group of bits or characters that are treated by the computer system as an entity and are capable of being stored in a single memory location. **(105)**

Word processing. The use of computer technology to create, manipulate, and print text material such as letters, documents, and manuscripts. **(51, 409)**

Credits

TEXT PHOTOGRAPHS

Fig. 6-10 (a) Lexicon Corporation of Miami, (b) Digital Equipment Corporation, (c) Qume Corporation, (d) Radio Shack Division of Tandy Corporation

Fig. 6-11 From David E. Cortesi, *Inside CP/M: A Guide for Users and Programmers;* copyright 1982 by Holt, Rinehart and Winston. Used by permission.

Fig. 6-12 International Business Machines Corporation

Fig. 6-15 Storage Technology Corporation

Figs. 6-16 and 6-17 Uarco Incorporated

Fig. 6-18 International Business Machines Corporation

Fig. 6-20 © Laimute E. Druskis, Art Resource

Fig. 6-21 International Business Machines Corporation

Fig. 6-24 NCR Corporation

Fig. 6-28 International Business Machines Corporation

Fig. 6-29 MSI Data Corporation

Figs. 6-32 and 6-33 Eastman Kodak Company

Fig. 6-34 Radio Shack Division of Tandy Corporation

Fig. 6-35 Auto-Trol Technology Corporation

Fig. 6-36 Apple Computer, Inc.

Fig. 6-37 Texas Instruments Incorporated

box on p. 164 (business graphics and man on shore) Image Resource Corporation; (bulldozer) Auto-Trol Technology Corporation

box on p. 165 (cross-hair cursor) Altek Corporation

box on p. 168 Information International, Inc.

Chapter 7, p. 196 National Aeronautics and Space Administration

Fig. 7-3 Western Electric

Fig. 7-4(b) Bell Laboratories

Fig. 7-5(b) National Aeronautics and Space Administration

Fig. 7-8 Anderson-Jacobson Corporation

Fig. 7-9 (a) Anderson-Jacobson Corporation; (b) and (c) Lexicon Corporation of Miami

Fig. 7-17 © Dave Repp, Design Photographers International, Inc.

box on p. 207 Cable News Network, Inc.

box on p. 215 Modular Computer Systems, Inc. (MODCOMP)

box on p. 223 Bell Laboratories

Module C, p. 232 © Arthur Tress, Photo Researchers, Inc.

Chapter 8, p. 234 © Freda Leinwand

page 254 From J. K. Rice and J. R. Rice, *Introduction to Computer Science;* copyright 1969 by Holt, Rinehart and Winston. Used by permission.

Chapter 9, p. 258 Hewlett-Packard Company

box on p. 269 © Joel Gordon, Design Photographers International, Inc.

box on p. 277 © Hans Pfletschinger, Peter Arnold, Inc.

box on p. 278 Courtesy Alida Chanler

Chapter 10, p. 286 © Mimi Forsyth, Monkmeyer Press Photo Service

Fig. 10-8 © Freda Leinwand

Chapter 11, p. 314 © Susan Berkowitz, Taurus Photos

box on p. 325 Courtesy Alida Chanler

Chapter 12, p. 346 © Michael Hayman, Photo Researchers, Inc.

Module D, p. 368 International Business Machines Corporation

Chapter 13, p. 370 © Jim Balog, Black Star

Fig. 13-1 (a) Timex Corporation, (b) Hewlett-Packard Company

Fig. 13-2 Motorola, Inc.

box on p. 374 Lawrence Livermore National Laboratory/James E. Stoots, Jr.

box on p. 382 United Press International, Inc.

box on p. 387 Epson America, Inc.

Chapter 14, p. 394 Sperry-Univac, a Division of Sperry Corporation

Fig. 14-9 Unimation, Inc.

box on p. 417 International Business Machines Corporation

box on p. 422 Hewlett-Packard Company

Chapter 15, p. 428 © Freda Leinwand

Fig. 15-2 (1) New York University, Art Resource, (2) and (3) © Freda Leinwand, (4) Sperry-Univac, a Division of Sperry Corporation, (5) © Ellis Herwig, Stock, Boston

box on p. 435 © Peter Southwick, Stock, Boston

Chapter 16, p. 454 © Freda Leinwand

boxes on pp. 459, 467 © Freda Leinwand

box on p. 474 Wang Laboratories

Module E, p. 478 © David Burnett, Contact Stock

Chapter 17, p. 480 © Freda Leinwand

Fig. 17-3 © Freda Leinwand

Fig. 17-4 Datapro Research Corporation

photo on p. 483 Sperry-Univac, a Division of Sperry Corporation photo on p. 491 © Mimi Forsyth, Monkmeyer Press Photo Service

photo on p. 492 © Freda Leinwand

Chapter 18, p. 500 Courtesy of *Computerworld, Electronic News,* and *The New York Times*

Fig. 18-3 International Business Machines Corporation

Fig. 18-4 Bell Laboratories

photo on p. 503 © Joel Gordon, Design Photographers International, Inc.

photo on p. 511 © Dennis Brack, Black Star

box on p. 518 Lanier Business Products, Inc.

Appendix, p. 524 © Robert A. Isaacs, Photo Researchers, Inc.

OTHER TEXT CREDITS

CP/M and CP/M-86 are registered trademarks of Digital Research, Inc.

Scripsit and TRSDOS are registered trademarks of Radio Shack Division of Tandy Corporation.

UNIX is a trademark of Bell Laboratories.

VisiCalc is a registered trademark of VisiCorp.

VisiWord is a trademark of VisiCorp.

WordStar is a registered trademark of MicroPro International.

THE WINDOWS

Window 1

1 Harris Corporation

2, 5, 15, 21, 48 Sperry-Univac, a Division of Sperry Corporation

3 Apple Computer, Inc.

4, 51 Mohawk Data Sciences Corporation

6 International Business Machines Corporation

7 Quotron Systems, Inc.

8–10 Digital Effects, Inc./Marsteller. Director: George Parker; Animators: Don Leich, Stan Cohen, Gene Miller, Judson Rosebush

11 Digital Effects, Inc./Cucumber Studios. Director: Jeffrey Kleiser; Animators: Don Leich, C. Robert Hoffman III, Stan Cohen

12, 13 Digital Effects, Inc./NBC. Director: Judson Rosebush; Animators: Alan Green, Don Leich, Gene Miller, and C. Robert Hoffman III

14 Digital Effects, Inc./McKinney, Silver, and Rockett. Director: Chris Woods; Animator: Don Leich

16 Modular Computer Systems, Inc. (MODCOMP)

17 The Foxboro Company

18, 35–38 Los Alamos National Laboratory

19, 20 McDonnell Douglas Automation Company (McAUTO)

22 Digital Effects, Inc./Harold Freidman Consortium. Director: George Parker; Animators: Don Leich, David Cox, D. L. Deas, Stan Cohen

23, 25–28 Evans & Sutherland

24 Megatek Corporation

29–31 Melvin Prueitt/Los Alamos National Laboratory

32–34 Matrix Instruments Inc./Loren Carpenter/Boeing Computer Services Co.

39 National Semiconductor Corporation

40, 47 NCR Corporation

41 Recognition Equipment Incorporated

42–45 Coleco Industries Inc.

46 Coleco Industries Inc./Peyo

49 3M

50 Image Resource Corporation/UCLA School of Medicine

52 Nelson Max/Lawrence Livermore National Laboratory

Window 2

1, 3, 8 McDonnell Douglas Automation Company (McAUTO)

2, 9, 10 Sperry Univac, a Division of Sperry Corporation

4, 11 Los Alamos National Laboratory

5, 13, 17 International Business Machines Corporation

6, 14 Digital Equipment Corporation

7 BASF Systems Corporation

12 Storage Technology Corporation

15 DatagraphiX, Inc.

16 Hewlett-Packard Company

18 Commodore International, Ltd./Uarco Incorporated

Window 3

1, 3, 6, 8, 10, 11, 18, 19, 23 Intel Corporation

2 Storage Technology Corporation

4, 5 Bell Laboratories

7, 9, 15, 20, 22   National Semiconductor Corporation

12–14, 17   Digital Equipment Corporation

16, 21   Sperry-Univac, a Division of Sperry Corporation

Window 4

1   Computer Graphics Laboratory, New York Institute of Technology/Dick Lundin

2, 3, 17   Image Resource Corporation

4   Ramtek Corporation

5   Lexidata Corporation

6, 18   Nicolet Zeta Corporation

7   Los Alamos National Laboratory

8–10   Integrated Software Systems Corporation (ISSCO)

11–14   Cullinet Software/Computer Pictures Corporation

15   CALCOMP

16   Chromatics, Inc.

19   Los Alamos National Laboratory/Melvin Prueitt

20   Digital Effects Inc./N. W. Ayer. Director: George Parker; Animators: Don Leich, C. Robert Hoffman III

21, 22   Lawrence Livermore National Laboratory/ Nelson Max

Window 5

1   Sperry-Univac, a Division of Sperry Corporation

2–8   Hughes Aircraft Company

9, 10   Matrix Instruments, Inc.

11   Lawrence Livermore National Laboratory

12, 16   Bell Laboratories

13, 14   Corning Glass Works

15   Atari, Inc.

17   Ramtek Corporation

18–20   Modular Computer Systems, Inc. (MOD-COMP)

21, 22   McDonnell Douglas Automation Company (McAUTO)

Window 6

1   Data General Corporation

2, 5, 11, 13–15   Atari, Inc.

3   Mattel, Inc.

4, 7, 8   Apple Computer, Inc.

6   Cullinet Software/Computer Pictures Corporation

9   Los Alamos National Laboratory

10, 16, 21, 23, 25, 26   International Business Machines Corporation

12   Ramtek Corporation

17   NCR Corporation/Connecticut National Bank

18   Lanier Business Products, Inc.

19   The Foxboro Company

20   NCR Corporation/Fortunoff

22   Quotron Systems, Inc.

24   NCR Corporation

Window 7

1, 6, 8, 10–12, 18, 19   Apple Computer, Inc.

2   Epson America, Inc.

3, 17   Commodore International, Ltd.

4, 5   Compaq Computer Corporation

7   Televideo Systems, Inc.

9   International Business Machines Corporation

13, 14, 16, 23   Radio Shack Division of Tandy Corporation

15   Axiom Corporation

20, 21   Presley Development Company of Arizona/ Motorola, Inc.

22, 24   Computerland

Window 8

1   Mohawk Data Sciences Corporation

2, 4, 5, 7, 19   Xerox Corporation

3   Lanier Business products, Inc.

6   Radio Shack Division of Tandy Corporation

8, 9   Bell Laboratories

10   Hewlett-Packard Company

11–13   SPSS, Inc.

14, 16, 17   Integrated Software Systems Corporation (ISSCO)

15   Image Resource Corporation

18   Micro General Corporation

Window 9

1, 12, 15   Hewlett-Packard Company

2, 13   CALCOMP

3   NCR Corporation

4, 6, 7, 9–11   Sperry-Univac, A Division of Sperry Corporation

5, 18   International Business Machines Corporation

8   McDonnell Douglas Automation Company (McAUTO)

14   Bell Laboratories

16   Chromatics, Inc.

17   Data General Corporation

Index